Memoirs of
A MAN
IN PAJAMAS

TRANSLATOR: ANDREA ROSENBERG

DESIGNER: KAYLA E.

EDITOR: CONRAD GROTH

PRODUCTION: C HWANG

PROMOTION: JACQ COHEN

VP / ASSOCIATE PUBLISHER: ERIC REYNOLDS

PRESIDENT / PUBLISHER: GARY GROTH

FANTAGRAPHICS BOOKS, INC.
7563 LAKE CITY WAY NE
SEATTLE, WA 98115

WWW.FANTAGRAPHICS.COM
@FANTAGRAPHICS

ISBN: 978-1-68396-757-6

LIBRARY OF CONGRESS CONTROL NUMBER: 2022951218

FIRST FANTAGRAPHICS BOOKS EDITION: SUMMER 2023

PRINTED IN CHINA

Memoirs of
A MAN IN PAJAMAS

Paco Roca

Translated by
Andrea Rosenberg

I

THE SELFISH GENE

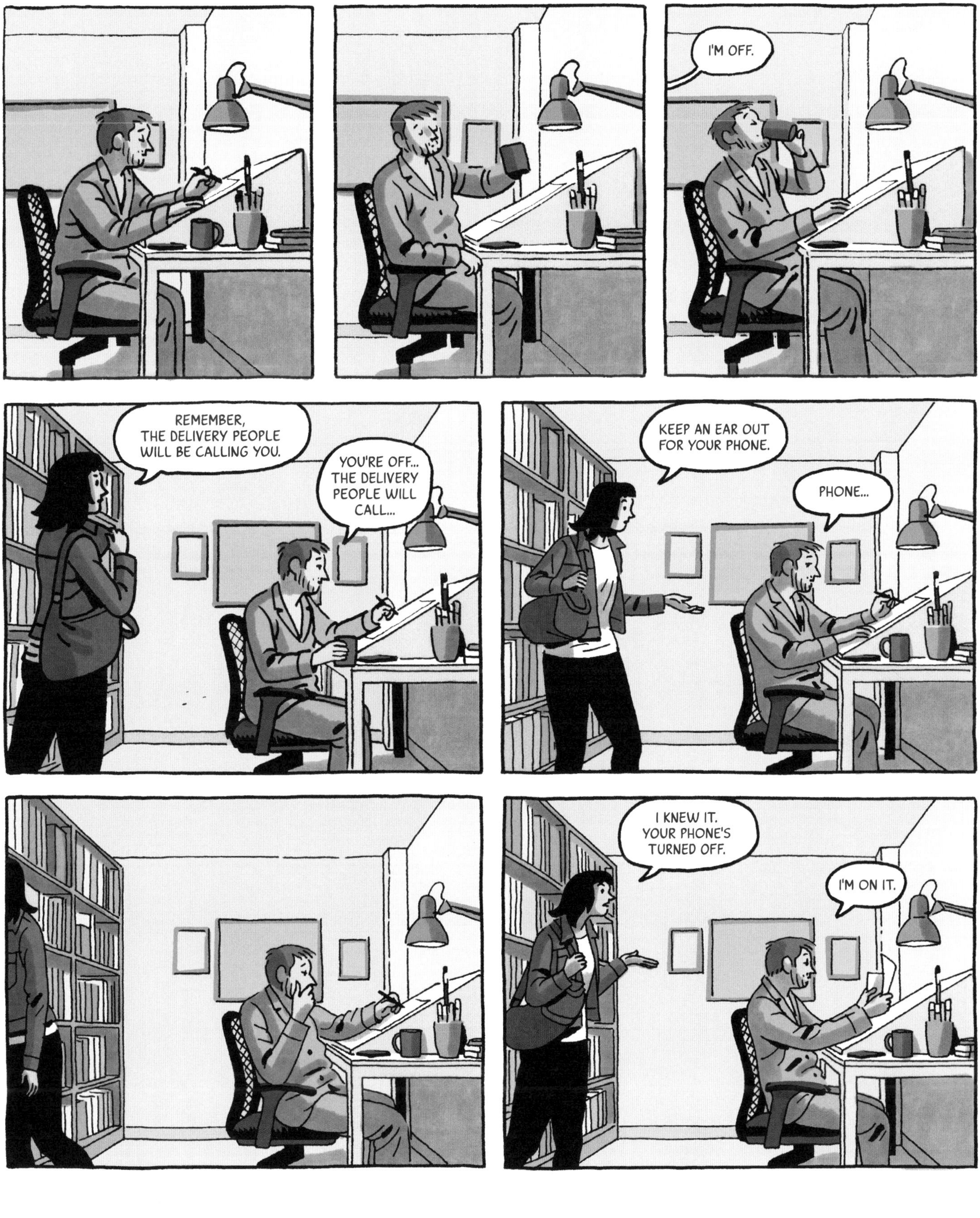
I'M OFF.
REMEMBER, THE DELIVERY PEOPLE WILL BE CALLING YOU.
YOU'RE OFF... THE DELIVERY PEOPLE WILL CALL...
KEEP AN EAR OUT FOR YOUR PHONE.
PHONE...
I KNEW IT. YOUR PHONE'S TURNED OFF.
I'M ON IT.

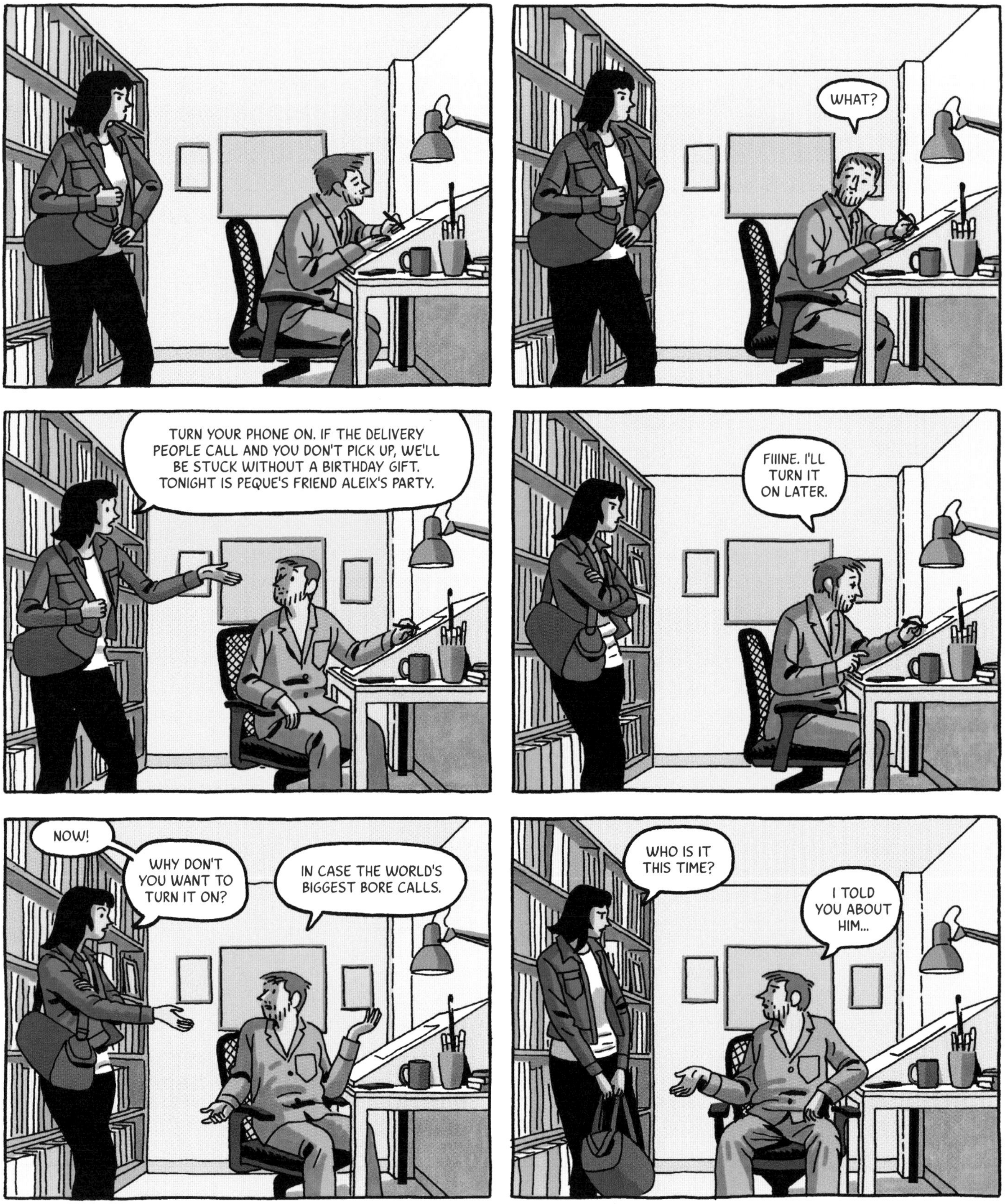
WHAT?
TURN YOUR PHONE ON. IF THE DELIVERY PEOPLE CALL AND YOU DON'T PICK UP, WE'LL BE STUCK WITHOUT A BIRTHDAY GIFT. TONIGHT IS PEQUE'S FRIEND ALEIX'S PARTY.
FIIINE. I'LL TURN IT ON LATER.
NOW!
WHY DON'T YOU WANT TO TURN IT ON?
IN CASE THE WORLD'S BIGGEST BORE CALLS.
WHO IS IT THIS TIME?
I TOLD YOU ABOUT HIM...

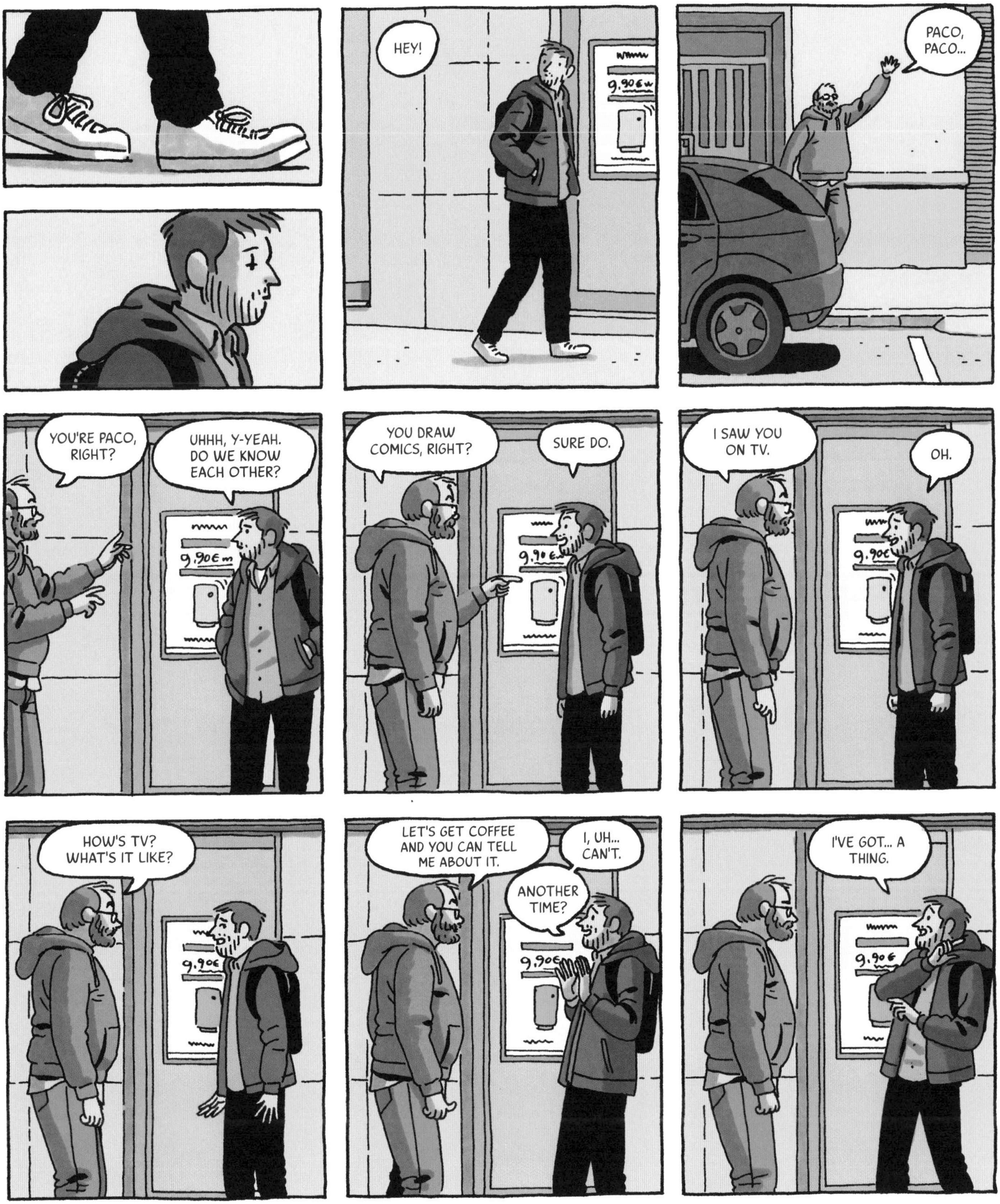
HEY!
PACO, PACO...
YOU'RE PACO, RIGHT?
UHHH, Y-YEAH. DO WE KNOW EACH OTHER?
YOU DRAW COMICS, RIGHT?
SURE DO.
I SAW YOU ON TV.
OH.
HOW'S TV? WHAT'S IT LIKE?
LET'S GET COFFEE AND YOU CAN TELL ME ABOUT IT.
I, UH... CAN'T.
ANOTHER TIME?
I'VE GOT... A THING.

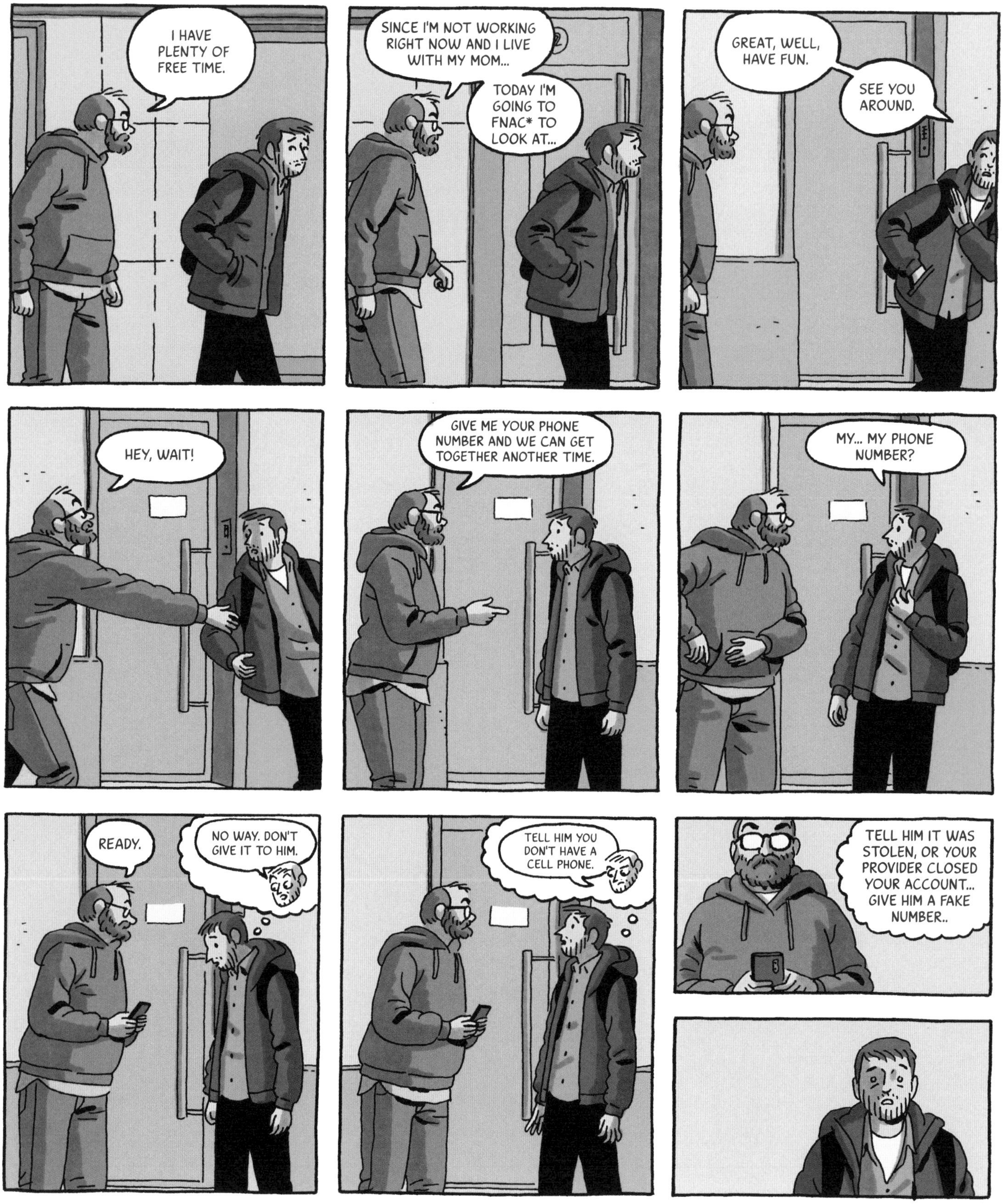
I HAVE PLENTY OF FREE TIME.
SINCE I'M NOT WORKING RIGHT NOW AND I LIVE WITH MY MOM...
TODAY I'M GOING TO FNAC* TO LOOK AT...
GREAT, WELL, HAVE FUN.
SEE YOU AROUND.
HEY, WAIT!
GIVE ME YOUR PHONE NUMBER AND WE CAN GET TOGETHER ANOTHER TIME.
MY... MY PHONE NUMBER?
READY.
NO WAY. DON'T GIVE IT TO HIM.
TELL HIM YOU DON'T HAVE A CELL PHONE.
TELL HIM IT WAS STOLEN, OR YOUR PROVIDER CLOSED YOUR ACCOUNT... GIVE HIM A FAKE NUMBER..

*FNAC IS A FRENCH MULTINATIONAL CHAIN THAT SELLS ELECTRONICS AND MUSIC/BOOKS/MOVIES.

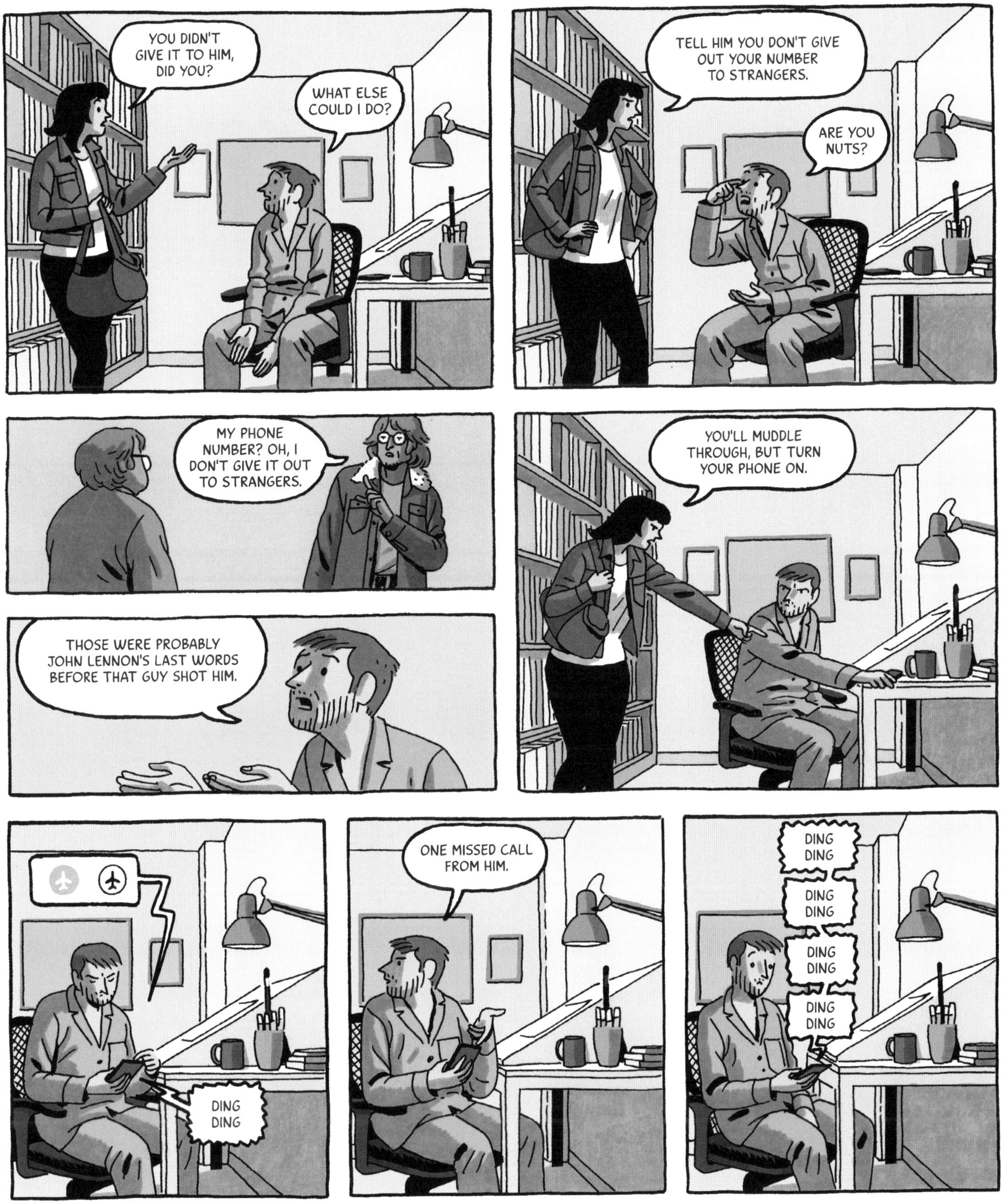
YOU DIDN'T GIVE IT TO HIM, DID YOU?
WHAT ELSE COULD I DO?
TELL HIM YOU DON'T GIVE OUT YOUR NUMBER TO STRANGERS.
ARE YOU NUTS?
MY PHONE NUMBER? OH, I DON'T GIVE IT OUT TO STRANGERS.
THOSE WERE PROBABLY JOHN LENNON'S LAST WORDS BEFORE THAT GUY SHOT HIM.
YOU'LL MUDDLE THROUGH, BUT TURN YOUR PHONE ON.
DING DING
ONE MISSED CALL FROM HIM.
DING DING
DING DING
DING DING
DING DING

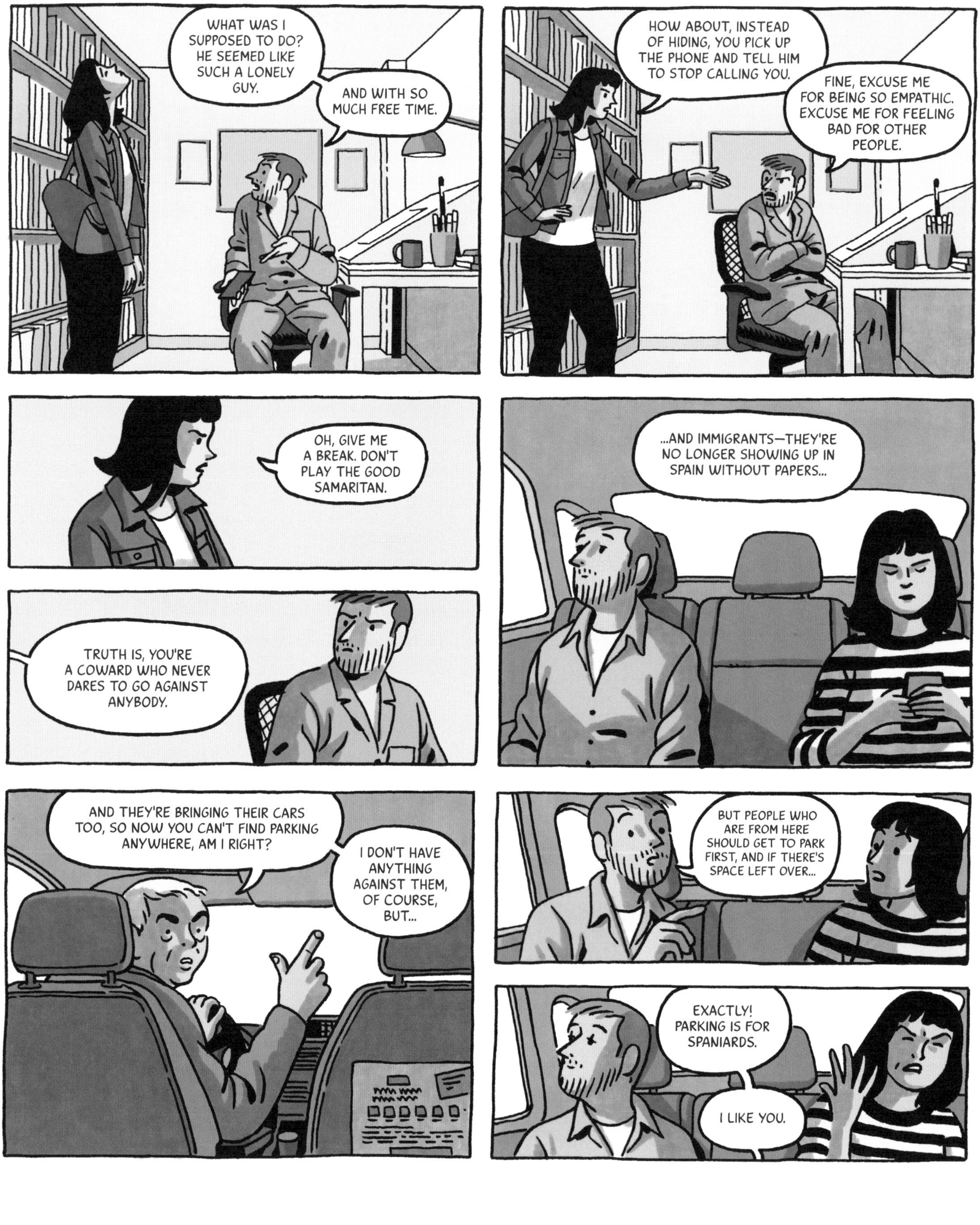
WHAT WAS I SUPPOSED TO DO? HE SEEMED LIKE SUCH A LONELY GUY.
AND WITH SO MUCH FREE TIME.
HOW ABOUT, INSTEAD OF HIDING, YOU PICK UP THE PHONE AND TELL HIM TO STOP CALLING YOU.
FINE, EXCUSE ME FOR BEING SO EMPATHIC. EXCUSE ME FOR FEELING BAD FOR OTHER PEOPLE.
OH, GIVE ME A BREAK. DON'T PLAY THE GOOD SAMARITAN.
TRUTH IS, YOU'RE A COWARD WHO NEVER DARES TO GO AGAINST ANYBODY.
...AND IMMIGRANTS—THEY'RE NO LONGER SHOWING UP IN SPAIN WITHOUT PAPERS...
AND THEY'RE BRINGING THEIR CARS TOO, SO NOW YOU CAN'T FIND PARKING ANYWHERE, AM I RIGHT?
I DON'T HAVE ANYTHING AGAINST THEM, OF COURSE, BUT...
BUT PEOPLE WHO ARE FROM HERE SHOULD GET TO PARK FIRST, AND IF THERE'S SPACE LEFT OVER...
EXACTLY! PARKING IS FOR SPANIARDS.
I LIKE YOU.

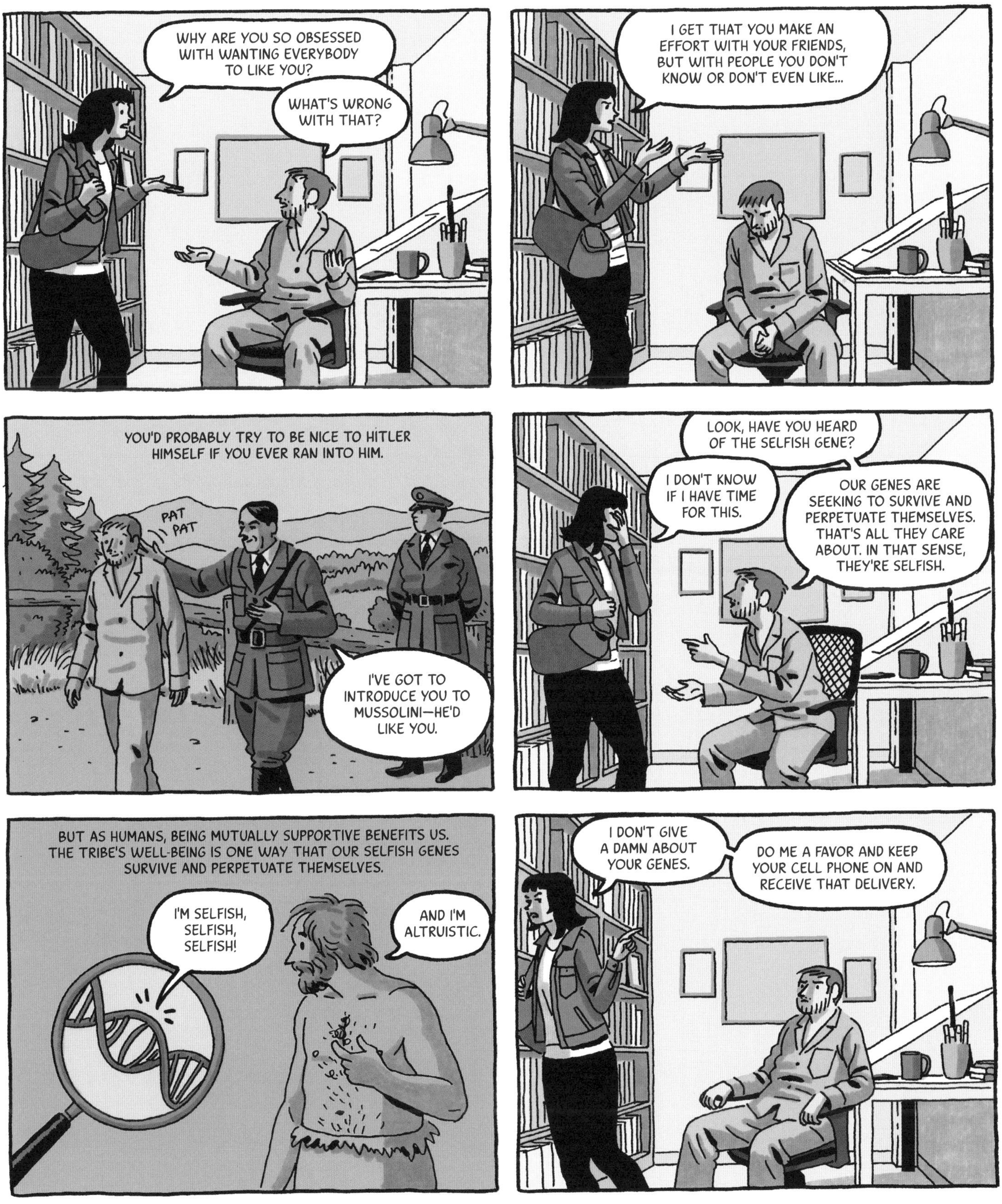
WHY ARE YOU SO OBSESSED WITH WANTING EVERYBODY TO LIKE YOU?
WHAT'S WRONG WITH THAT?
I GET THAT YOU MAKE AN EFFORT WITH YOUR FRIENDS, BUT WITH PEOPLE YOU DON'T KNOW OR DON'T EVEN LIKE...
YOU'D PROBABLY TRY TO BE NICE TO HITLER HIMSELF IF YOU EVER RAN INTO HIM.
PAT PAT
I'VE GOT TO INTRODUCE YOU TO MUSSOLINI—HE'D LIKE YOU.
LOOK, HAVE YOU HEARD OF THE SELFISH GENE?
I DON'T KNOW IF I HAVE TIME FOR THIS.
OUR GENES ARE SEEKING TO SURVIVE AND PERPETUATE THEMSELVES. THAT'S ALL THEY CARE ABOUT. IN THAT SENSE, THEY'RE SELFISH.
BUT AS HUMANS, BEING MUTUALLY SUPPORTIVE BENEFITS US. THE TRIBE'S WELL-BEING IS ONE WAY THAT OUR SELFISH GENES SURVIVE AND PERPETUATE THEMSELVES.
I'M SELFISH, SELFISH, SELFISH!
AND I'M ALTRUISTIC.
I DON'T GIVE A DAMN ABOUT YOUR GENES.
DO ME A FAVOR AND KEEP YOUR CELL PHONE ON AND RECEIVE THAT DELIVERY.

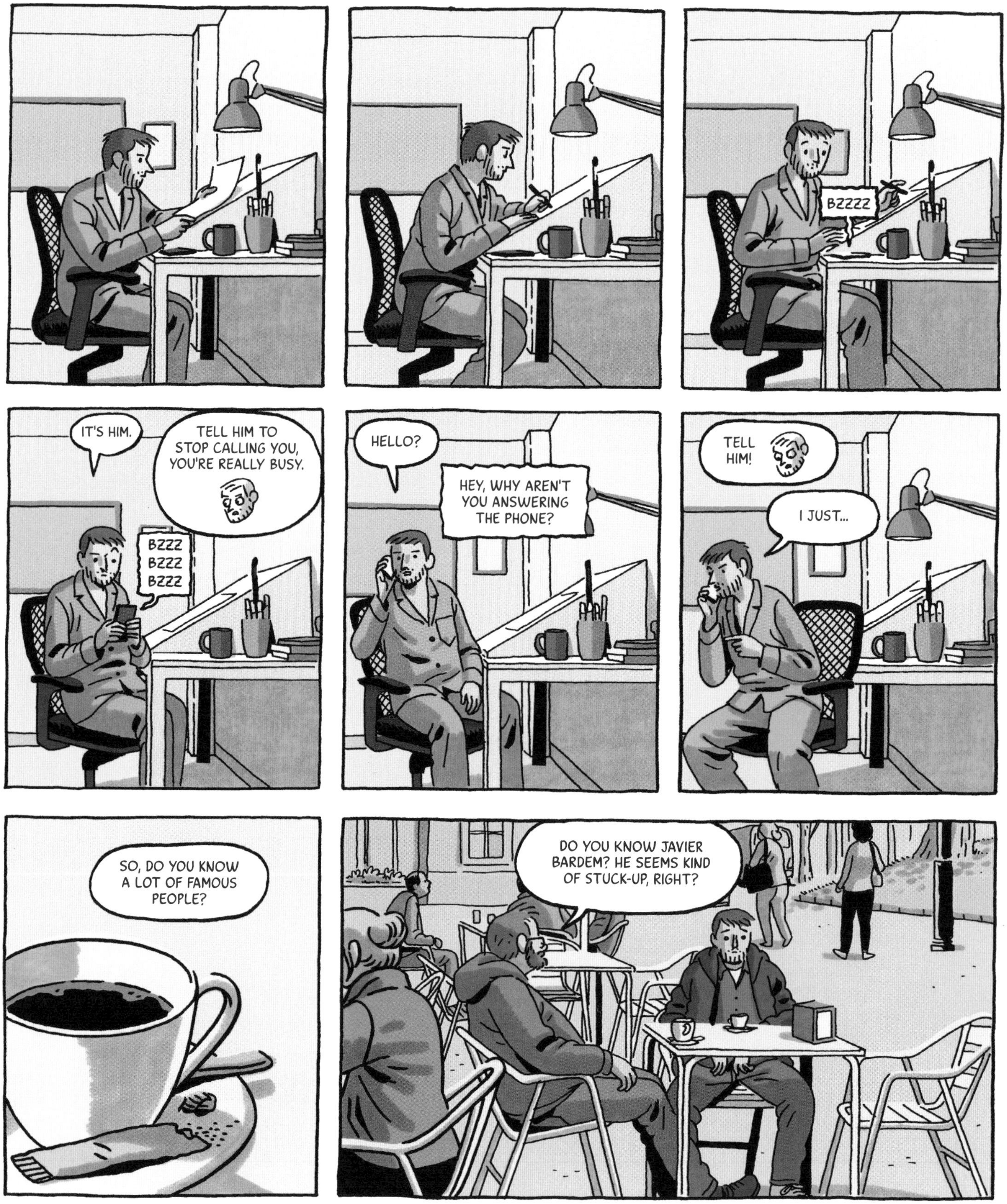
BZZZZ
IT'S HIM.
TELL HIM TO STOP CALLING YOU, YOU'RE REALLY BUSY.
BZZZ BZZZ BZZZ
HELLO?
HEY, WHY AREN'T YOU ANSWERING THE PHONE?
TELL HIM!
I JUST...
SO, DO YOU KNOW A LOT OF FAMOUS PEOPLE?
DO YOU KNOW JAVIER BARDEM? HE SEEMS KIND OF STUCK-UP, RIGHT?

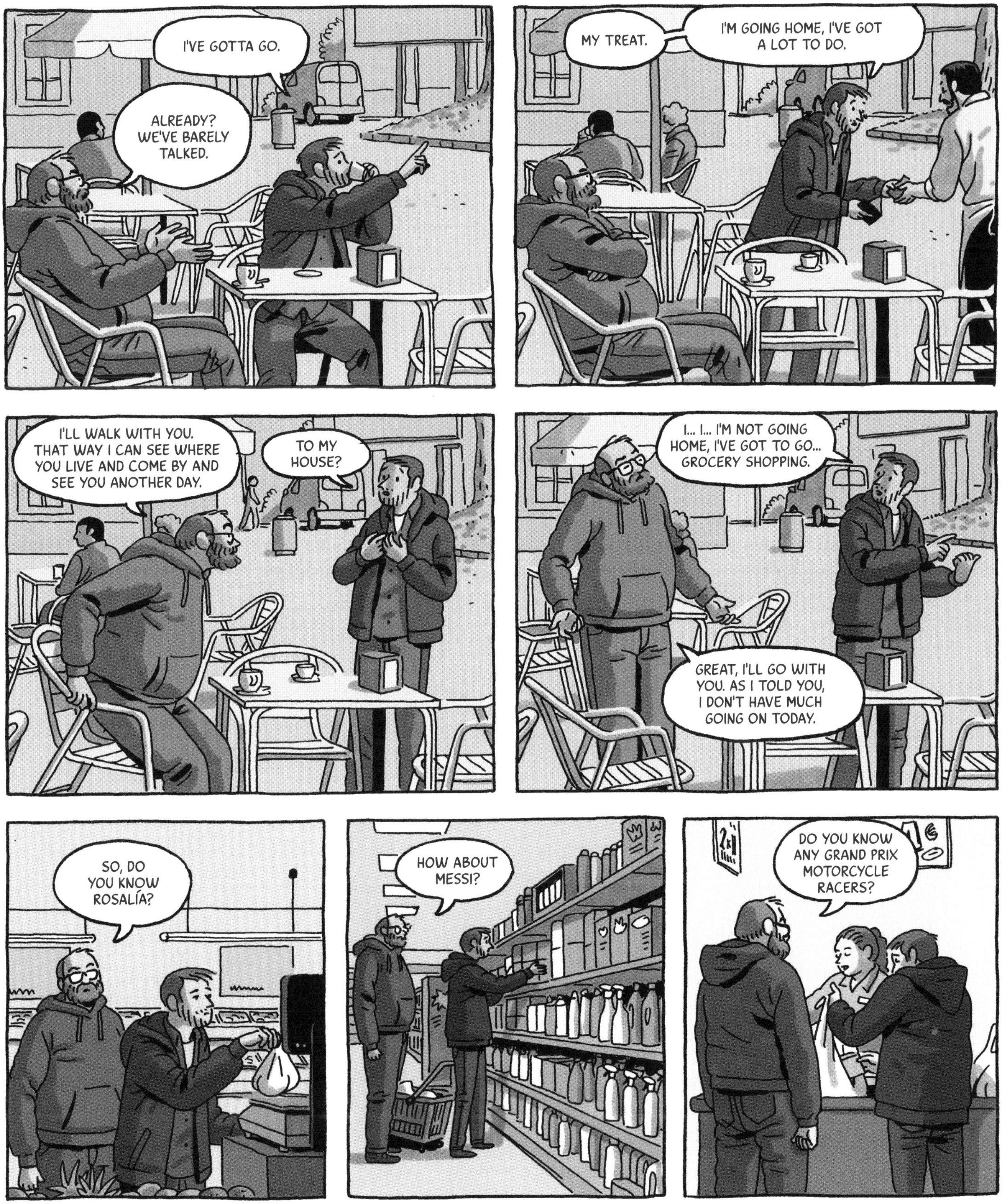
I'VE GOTTA GO.
ALREADY? WE'VE BARELY TALKED.
MY TREAT.
I'M GOING HOME, I'VE GOT A LOT TO DO.
I'LL WALK WITH YOU. THAT WAY I CAN SEE WHERE YOU LIVE AND COME BY AND SEE YOU ANOTHER DAY.
TO MY HOUSE?
I... I... I'M NOT GOING HOME, I'VE GOT TO GO... GROCERY SHOPPING.
GREAT, I'LL GO WITH YOU. AS I TOLD YOU, I DON'T HAVE MUCH GOING ON TODAY.
SO, DO YOU KNOW ROSALÍA?
HOW ABOUT MESSI?
DO YOU KNOW ANY GRAND PRIX MOTORCYCLE RACERS?

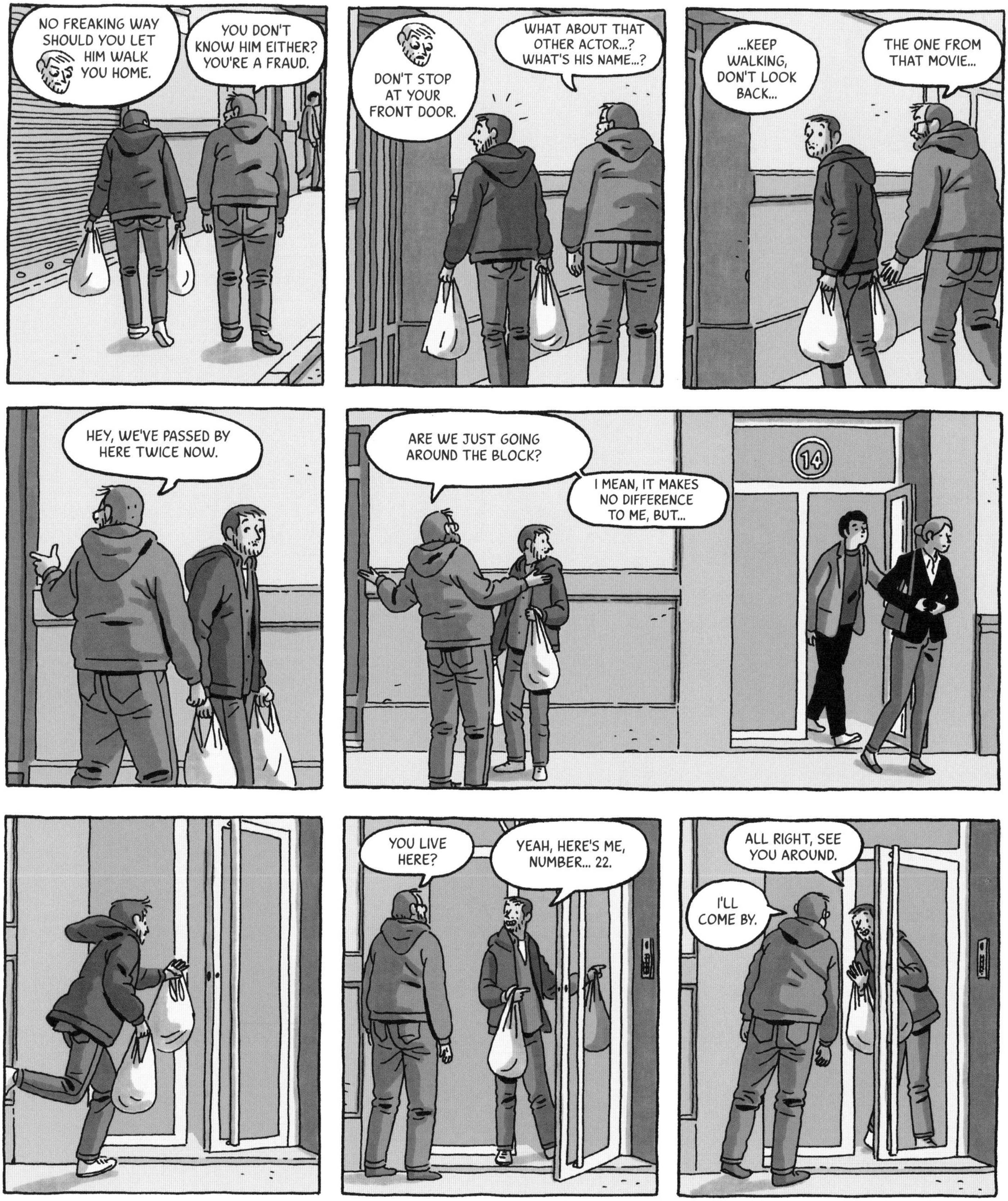
NO FREAKING WAY SHOULD YOU LET HIM WALK YOU HOME.
YOU DON'T KNOW HIM EITHER? YOU'RE A FRAUD.
DON'T STOP AT YOUR FRONT DOOR.
WHAT ABOUT THAT OTHER ACTOR...? WHAT'S HIS NAME...?
...KEEP WALKING, DON'T LOOK BACK...
THE ONE FROM THAT MOVIE...
HEY, WE'VE PASSED BY HERE TWICE NOW.
ARE WE JUST GOING AROUND THE BLOCK?
I MEAN, IT MAKES NO DIFFERENCE TO ME, BUT...
14
YOU LIVE HERE?
YEAH, HERE'S ME, NUMBER... 22.
ALL RIGHT, SEE YOU AROUND.
I'LL COME BY.

W-WHAT IS HE DOING HERE?

DAMN IT! SHIT! SHIT! SHIT!

NOV 23 AT 7:0
RESIDEN
MEETIN
AGENDA

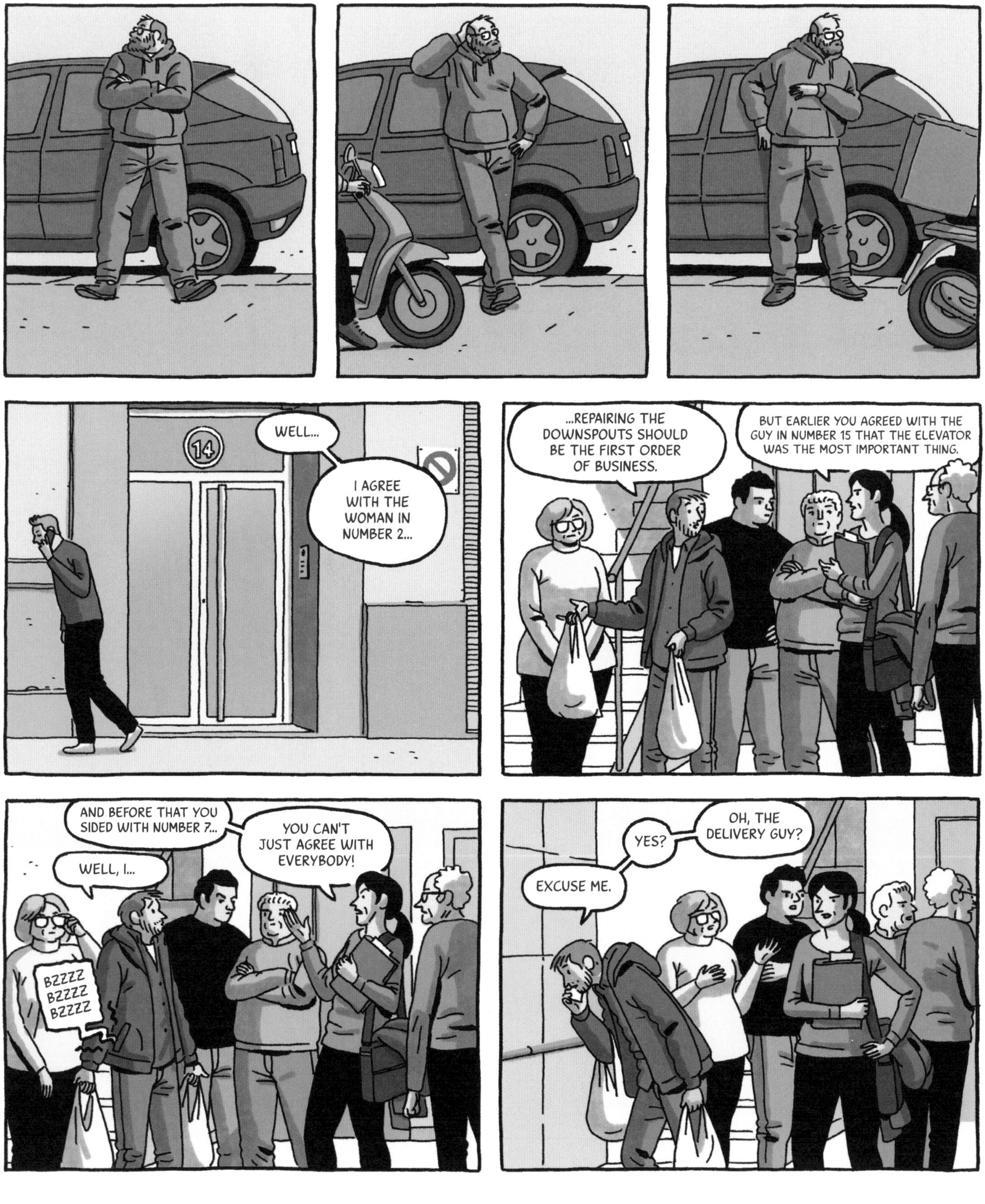
WELL...
I AGREE WITH THE WOMAN IN NUMBER 2...
...REPAIRING THE DOWNSPOUTS SHOULD BE THE FIRST ORDER OF BUSINESS.
BUT EARLIER YOU AGREED WITH THE GUY IN NUMBER 15 THAT THE ELEVATOR WAS THE MOST IMPORTANT THING.
AND BEFORE THAT YOU SIDED WITH NUMBER 7...
WELL, I...
YOU CAN'T JUST AGREE WITH EVERYBODY!
BZZZZ BZZZZ BZZZZ
EXCUSE ME.
YES?
OH, THE DELIVERY GUY?

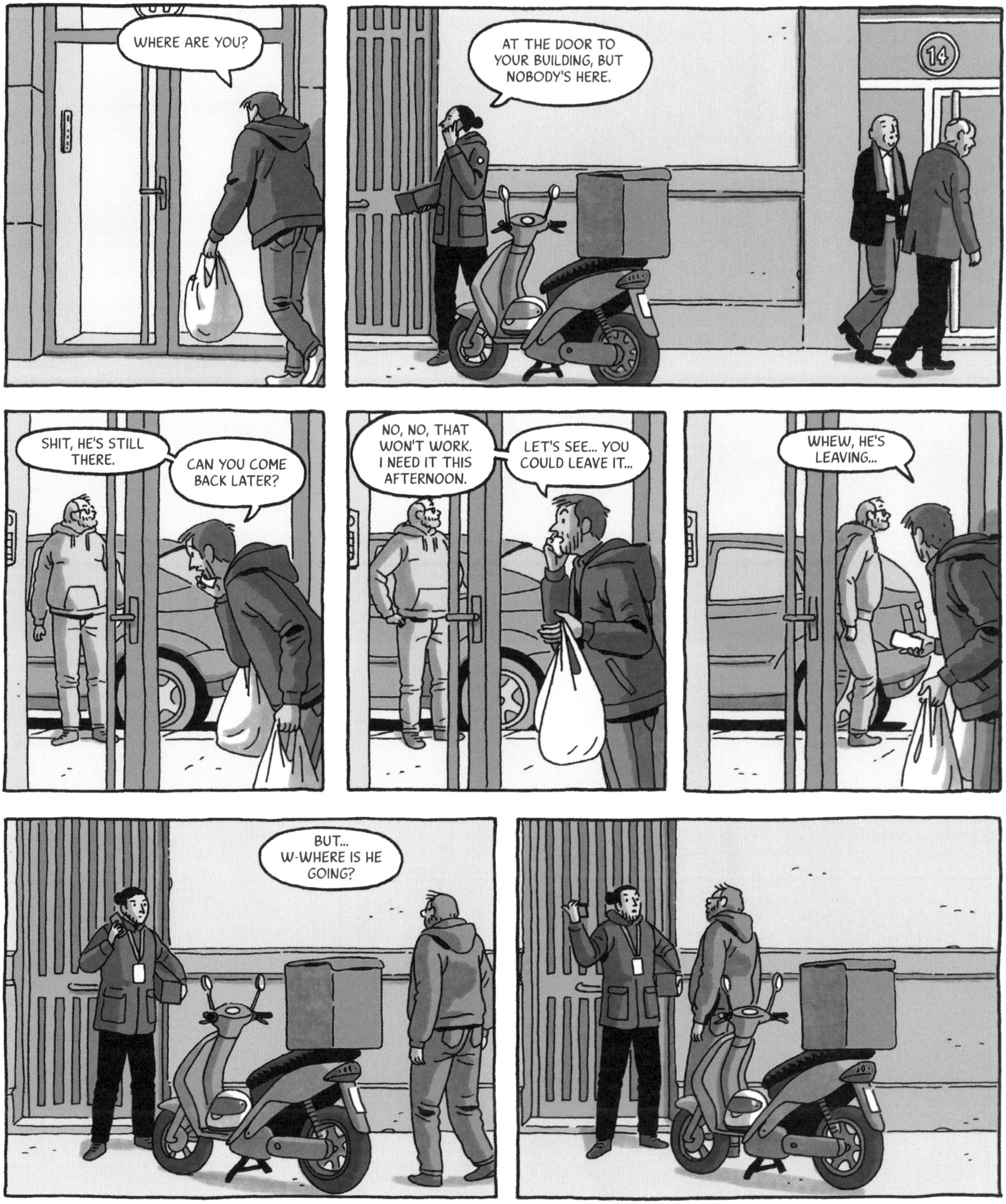
WHERE ARE YOU?
AT THE DOOR TO YOUR BUILDING, BUT NOBODY'S HERE.
SHIT, HE'S STILL THERE.
CAN YOU COME BACK LATER?
NO, NO, THAT WON'T WORK. I NEED IT THIS AFTERNOON.
LET'S SEE... YOU COULD LEAVE IT...
WHEW, HE'S LEAVING...
BUT... W-WHERE IS HE GOING?

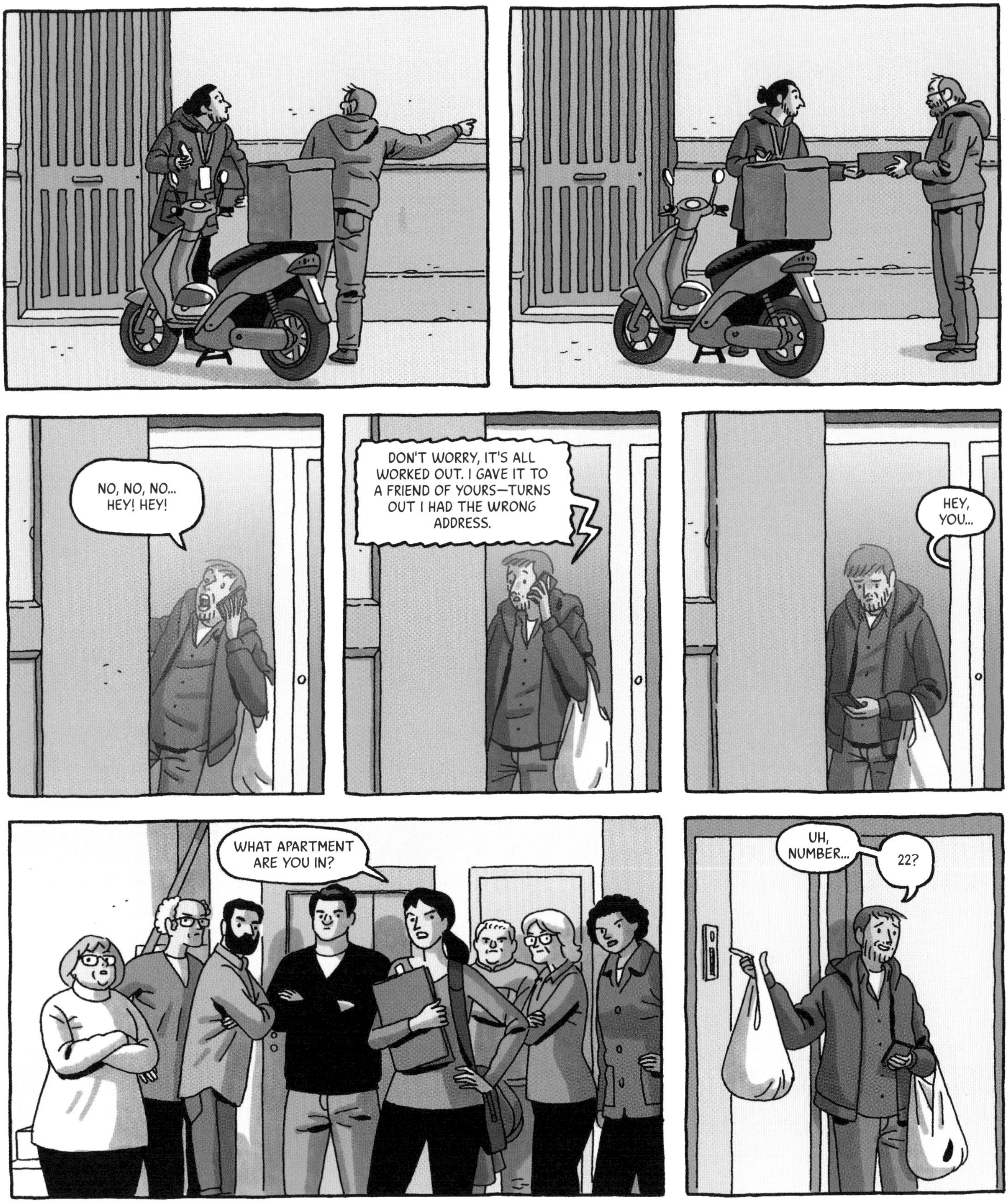
NO, NO, NO...
HEY! HEY!
DON'T WORRY, IT'S ALL WORKED OUT. I GAVE IT TO A FRIEND OF YOURS—TURNS OUT I HAD THE WRONG ADDRESS.
HEY, YOU...
WHAT APARTMENT ARE YOU IN?
UH, NUMBER...
22?

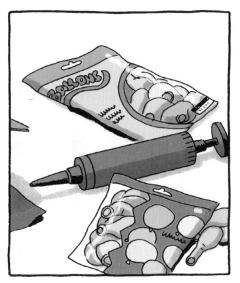

SEE? HE'S REALLY GOOD AT MAKING BALLOON ANIMALS.

PLUS, IT LOOKS LIKE HE'S REALLY HIT IT OFF WITH ANA'S FATHER.

HE INVITED HIM TO HIS DAUGHTER'S BIRTHDAY PARTY, HOW ABOUT THAT?

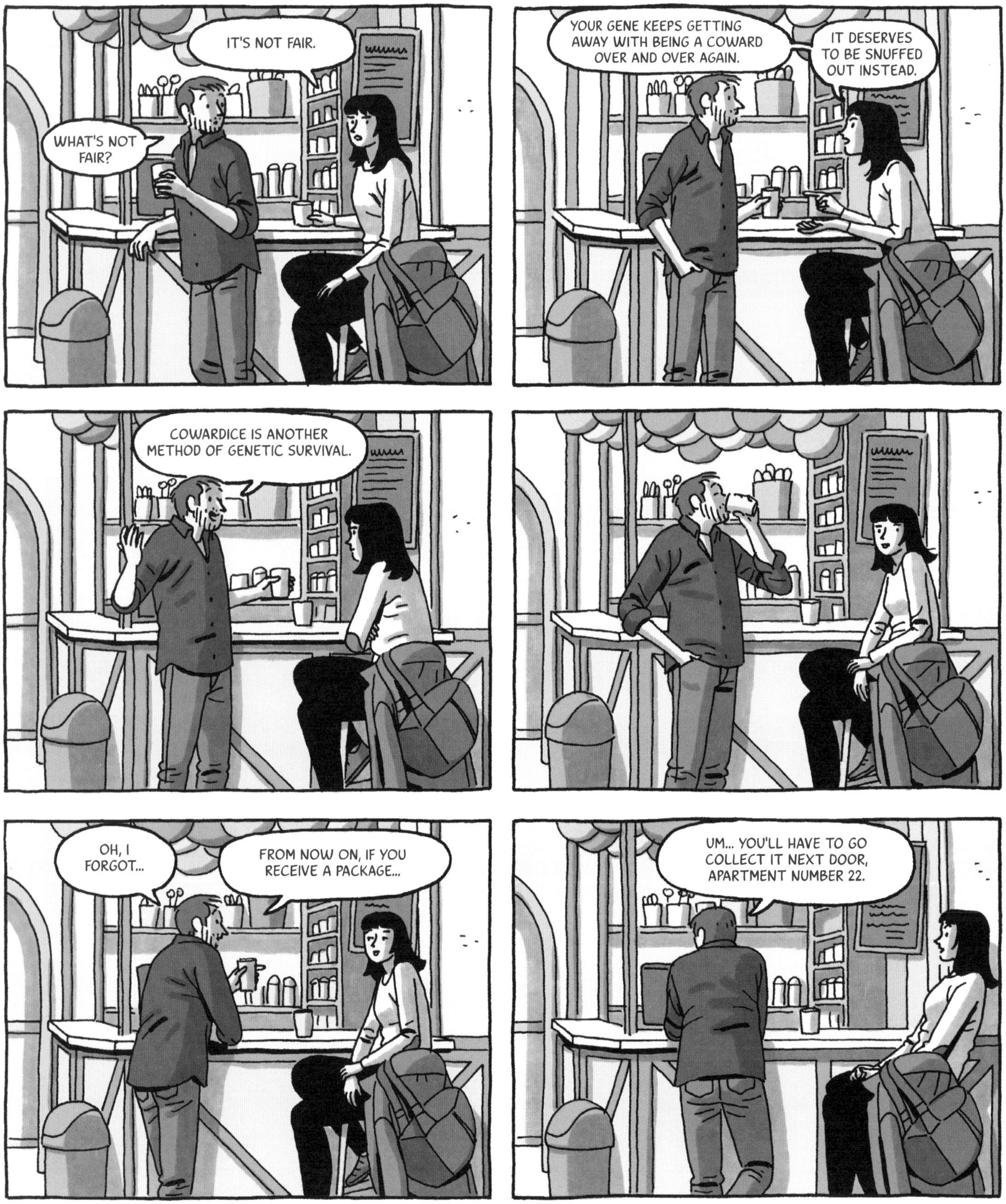
IT'S NOT FAIR.
WHAT'S NOT FAIR?
YOUR GENE KEEPS GETTING AWAY WITH BEING A COWARD OVER AND OVER AGAIN.
IT DESERVES TO BE SNUFFED OUT INSTEAD.
COWARDICE IS ANOTHER METHOD OF GENETIC SURVIVAL.
OH, I FORGOT...
FROM NOW ON, IF YOU RECEIVE A PACKAGE...
UM... YOU'LL HAVE TO GO COLLECT IT NEXT DOOR, APARTMENT NUMBER 22.

MY CHILDHOOD DREAM

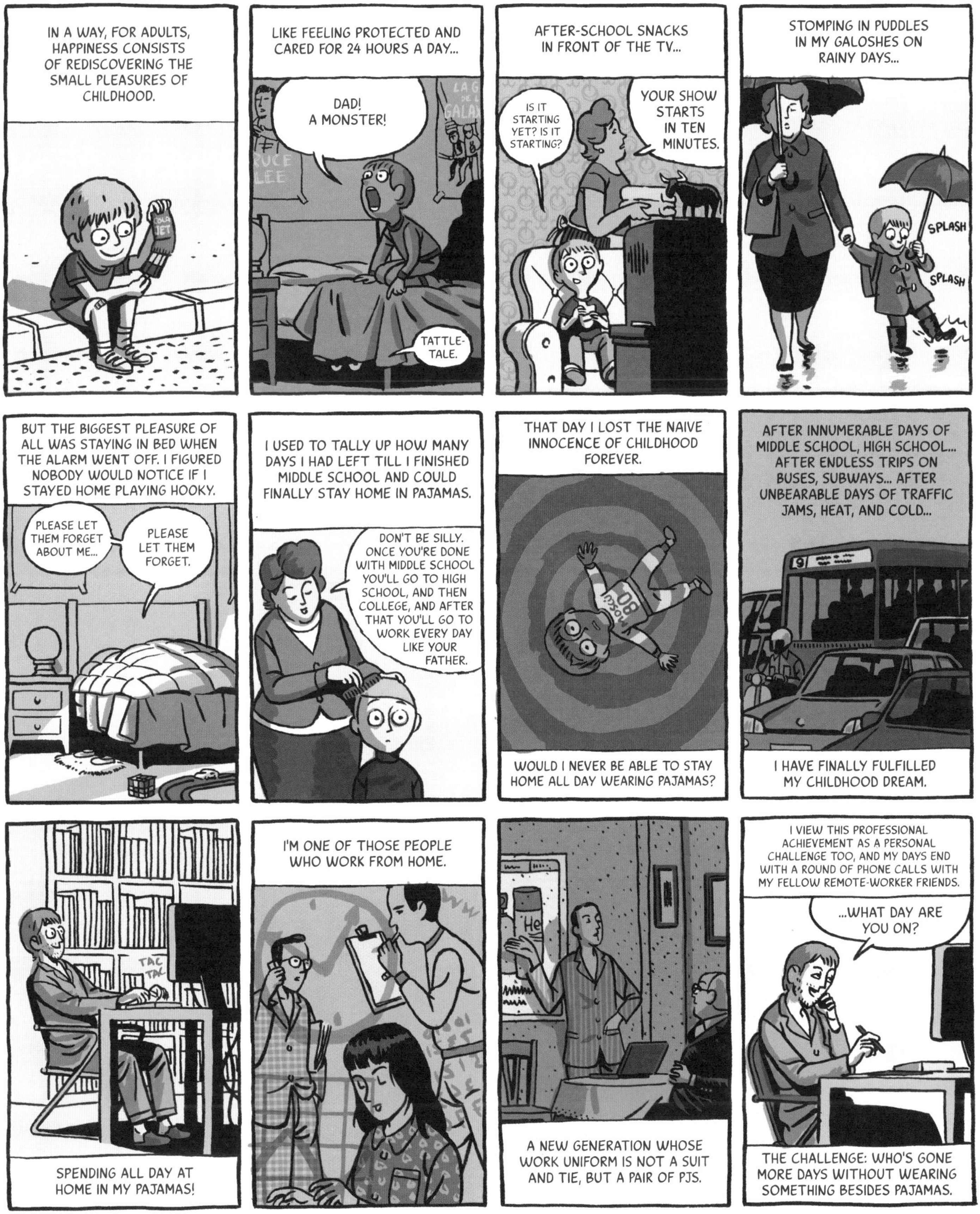

IN A WAY, FOR ADULTS, HAPPINESS CONSISTS OF REDISCOVERING THE SMALL PLEASURES OF CHILDHOOD.
LIKE FEELING PROTECTED AND CARED FOR 24 HOURS A DAY...
DAD! A MONSTER!
TATTLE-TALE.
AFTER-SCHOOL SNACKS IN FRONT OF THE TV...
IS IT STARTING YET? IS IT STARTING?
YOUR SHOW STARTS IN TEN MINUTES.
STOMPING IN PUDDLES IN MY GALOSHES ON RAINY DAYS...
SPLASH
SPLASH
BUT THE BIGGEST PLEASURE OF ALL WAS STAYING IN BED WHEN THE ALARM WENT OFF. I FIGURED NOBODY WOULD NOTICE IF I STAYED HOME PLAYING HOOKY.
PLEASE LET THEM FORGET ABOUT ME...
PLEASE LET THEM FORGET.
I USED TO TALLY UP HOW MANY DAYS I HAD LEFT TILL I FINISHED MIDDLE SCHOOL AND COULD FINALLY STAY HOME IN PAJAMAS.
DON'T BE SILLY. ONCE YOU'RE DONE WITH MIDDLE SCHOOL YOU'LL GO TO HIGH SCHOOL, AND THEN COLLEGE, AND AFTER THAT YOU'LL GO TO WORK EVERY DAY LIKE YOUR FATHER.
THAT DAY I LOST THE NAIVE INNOCENCE OF CHILDHOOD FOREVER.
WOULD I NEVER BE ABLE TO STAY HOME ALL DAY WEARING PAJAMAS?
AFTER INNUMERABLE DAYS OF MIDDLE SCHOOL, HIGH SCHOOL... AFTER ENDLESS TRIPS ON BUSES, SUBWAYS... AFTER UNBEARABLE DAYS OF TRAFFIC JAMS, HEAT, AND COLD...
I HAVE FINALLY FULFILLED MY CHILDHOOD DREAM.
TAC TAC
SPENDING ALL DAY AT HOME IN MY PAJAMAS!
I'M ONE OF THOSE PEOPLE WHO WORK FROM HOME.
A NEW GENERATION WHOSE WORK UNIFORM IS NOT A SUIT AND TIE, BUT A PAIR OF PJS.
I VIEW THIS PROFESSIONAL ACHIEVEMENT AS A PERSONAL CHALLENGE TOO, AND MY DAYS END WITH A ROUND OF PHONE CALLS WITH MY FELLOW REMOTE-WORKER FRIENDS.
...WHAT DAY ARE YOU ON?
THE CHALLENGE: WHO'S GONE MORE DAYS WITHOUT WEARING SOMETHING BESIDES PAJAMAS.

PACO THE TINKERABLE

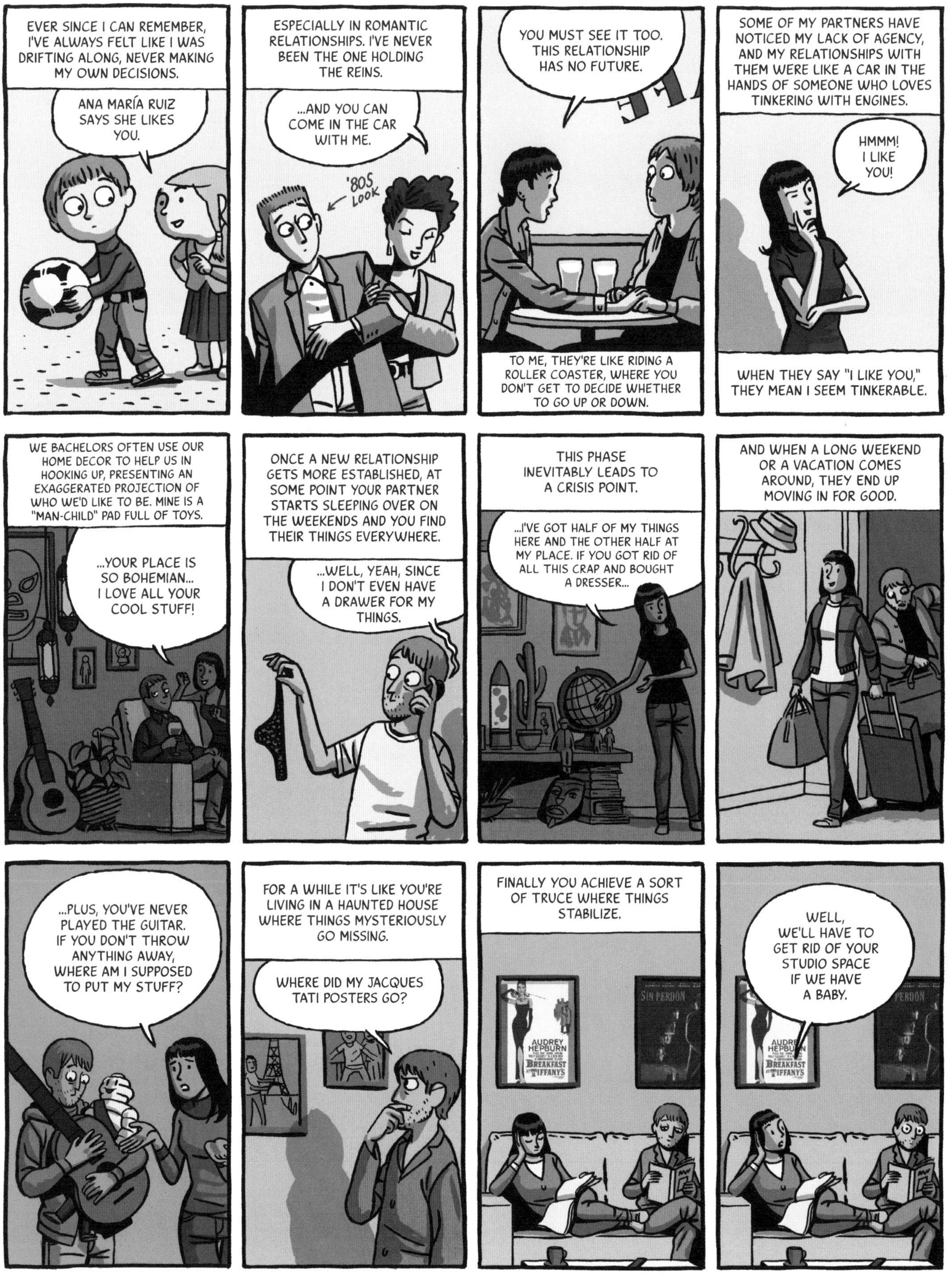

EVER SINCE I CAN REMEMBER, I'VE ALWAYS FELT LIKE I WAS DRIFTING ALONG, NEVER MAKING MY OWN DECISIONS.
ANA MARÍA RUIZ SAYS SHE LIKES YOU.
ESPECIALLY IN ROMANTIC RELATIONSHIPS. I'VE NEVER BEEN THE ONE HOLDING THE REINS.
...AND YOU CAN COME IN THE CAR WITH ME.
'80S LOOK
YOU MUST SEE IT TOO. THIS RELATIONSHIP HAS NO FUTURE.
TO ME, THEY'RE LIKE RIDING A ROLLER COASTER, WHERE YOU DON'T GET TO DECIDE WHETHER TO GO UP OR DOWN.
SOME OF MY PARTNERS HAVE NOTICED MY LACK OF AGENCY, AND MY RELATIONSHIPS WITH THEM WERE LIKE A CAR IN THE HANDS OF SOMEONE WHO LOVES TINKERING WITH ENGINES.
HMMM! I LIKE YOU!
WHEN THEY SAY "I LIKE YOU," THEY MEAN I SEEM TINKERABLE.
WE BACHELORS OFTEN USE OUR HOME DECOR TO HELP US IN HOOKING UP, PRESENTING AN EXAGGERATED PROJECTION OF WHO WE'D LIKE TO BE. MINE IS A "MAN-CHILD" PAD FULL OF TOYS.
...YOUR PLACE IS SO BOHEMIAN... I LOVE ALL YOUR COOL STUFF!
ONCE A NEW RELATIONSHIP GETS MORE ESTABLISHED, AT SOME POINT YOUR PARTNER STARTS SLEEPING OVER ON THE WEEKENDS AND YOU FIND THEIR THINGS EVERYWHERE.
...WELL, YEAH, SINCE I DON'T EVEN HAVE A DRAWER FOR MY THINGS.
THIS PHASE INEVITABLY LEADS TO A CRISIS POINT.
...I'VE GOT HALF OF MY THINGS HERE AND THE OTHER HALF AT MY PLACE. IF YOU GOT RID OF ALL THIS CRAP AND BOUGHT A DRESSER...
AND WHEN A LONG WEEKEND OR A VACATION COMES AROUND, THEY END UP MOVING IN FOR GOOD.
...PLUS, YOU'VE NEVER PLAYED THE GUITAR. IF YOU DON'T THROW ANYTHING AWAY, WHERE AM I SUPPOSED TO PUT MY STUFF?
FOR A WHILE IT'S LIKE YOU'RE LIVING IN A HAUNTED HOUSE WHERE THINGS MYSTERIOUSLY GO MISSING.
WHERE DID MY JACQUES TATI POSTERS GO?
FINALLY YOU ACHIEVE A SORT OF TRUCE WHERE THINGS STABILIZE.
AUDREY HEPBURN
BREAKFAST AT TIFFANY'S
SIN PERDÓN
WELL, WE'LL HAVE TO GET RID OF YOUR STUDIO SPACE IF WE HAVE A BABY.

THE ALPHA MALE

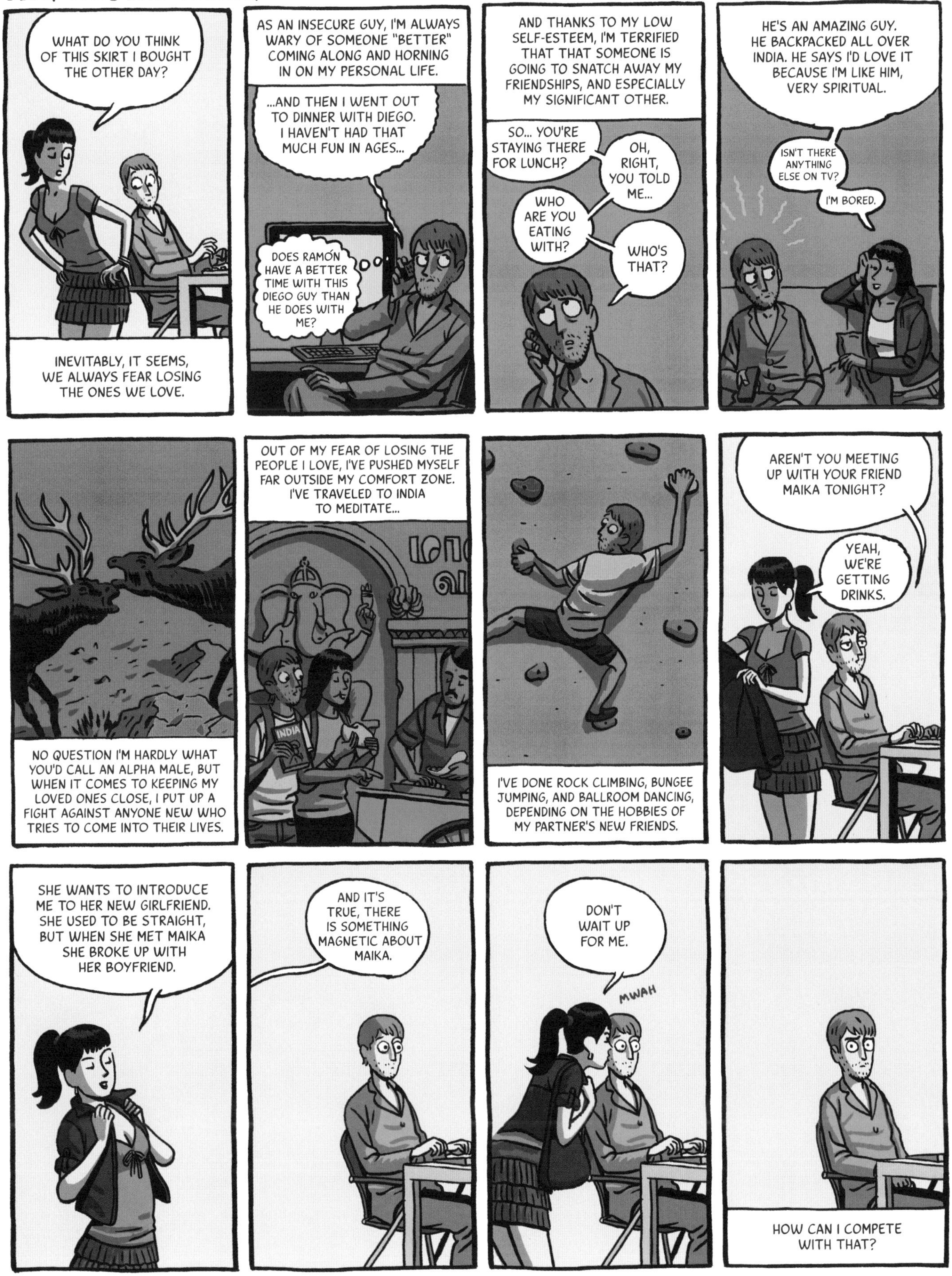

WHAT DO YOU THINK OF THIS SKIRT I BOUGHT THE OTHER DAY?
INEVITABLY, IT SEEMS, WE ALWAYS FEAR LOSING THE ONES WE LOVE.
AS AN INSECURE GUY, I'M ALWAYS WARY OF SOMEONE "BETTER" COMING ALONG AND HORNING IN ON MY PERSONAL LIFE.
...AND THEN I WENT OUT TO DINNER WITH DIEGO. I HAVEN'T HAD THAT MUCH FUN IN AGES...
DOES RAMÓN HAVE A BETTER TIME WITH THIS DIEGO GUY THAN HE DOES WITH ME?
AND THANKS TO MY LOW SELF-ESTEEM, I'M TERRIFIED THAT THAT SOMEONE IS GOING TO SNATCH AWAY MY FRIENDSHIPS, AND ESPECIALLY MY SIGNIFICANT OTHER.
SO... YOU'RE STAYING THERE FOR LUNCH?
OH, RIGHT, YOU TOLD ME...
WHO ARE YOU EATING WITH?
WHO'S THAT?
HE'S AN AMAZING GUY. HE BACKPACKED ALL OVER INDIA. HE SAYS I'D LOVE IT BECAUSE I'M LIKE HIM, VERY SPIRITUAL.
ISN'T THERE ANYTHING ELSE ON TV?
I'M BORED.
NO QUESTION I'M HARDLY WHAT YOU'D CALL AN ALPHA MALE, BUT WHEN IT COMES TO KEEPING MY LOVED ONES CLOSE, I PUT UP A FIGHT AGAINST ANYONE NEW WHO TRIES TO COME INTO THEIR LIVES.
OUT OF MY FEAR OF LOSING THE PEOPLE I LOVE, I'VE PUSHED MYSELF FAR OUTSIDE MY COMFORT ZONE. I'VE TRAVELED TO INDIA TO MEDITATE...
INDIA
I'VE DONE ROCK CLIMBING, BUNGEE JUMPING, AND BALLROOM DANCING, DEPENDING ON THE HOBBIES OF MY PARTNER'S NEW FRIENDS.
AREN'T YOU MEETING UP WITH YOUR FRIEND MAIKA TONIGHT?
YEAH, WE'RE GETTING DRINKS.
SHE WANTS TO INTRODUCE ME TO HER NEW GIRLFRIEND. SHE USED TO BE STRAIGHT, BUT WHEN SHE MET MAIKA SHE BROKE UP WITH HER BOYFRIEND.
AND IT'S TRUE, THERE IS SOMETHING MAGNETIC ABOUT MAIKA.
DON'T WAIT UP FOR ME.
MWAH
HOW CAN I COMPETE WITH THAT?

THE COLD STREAK

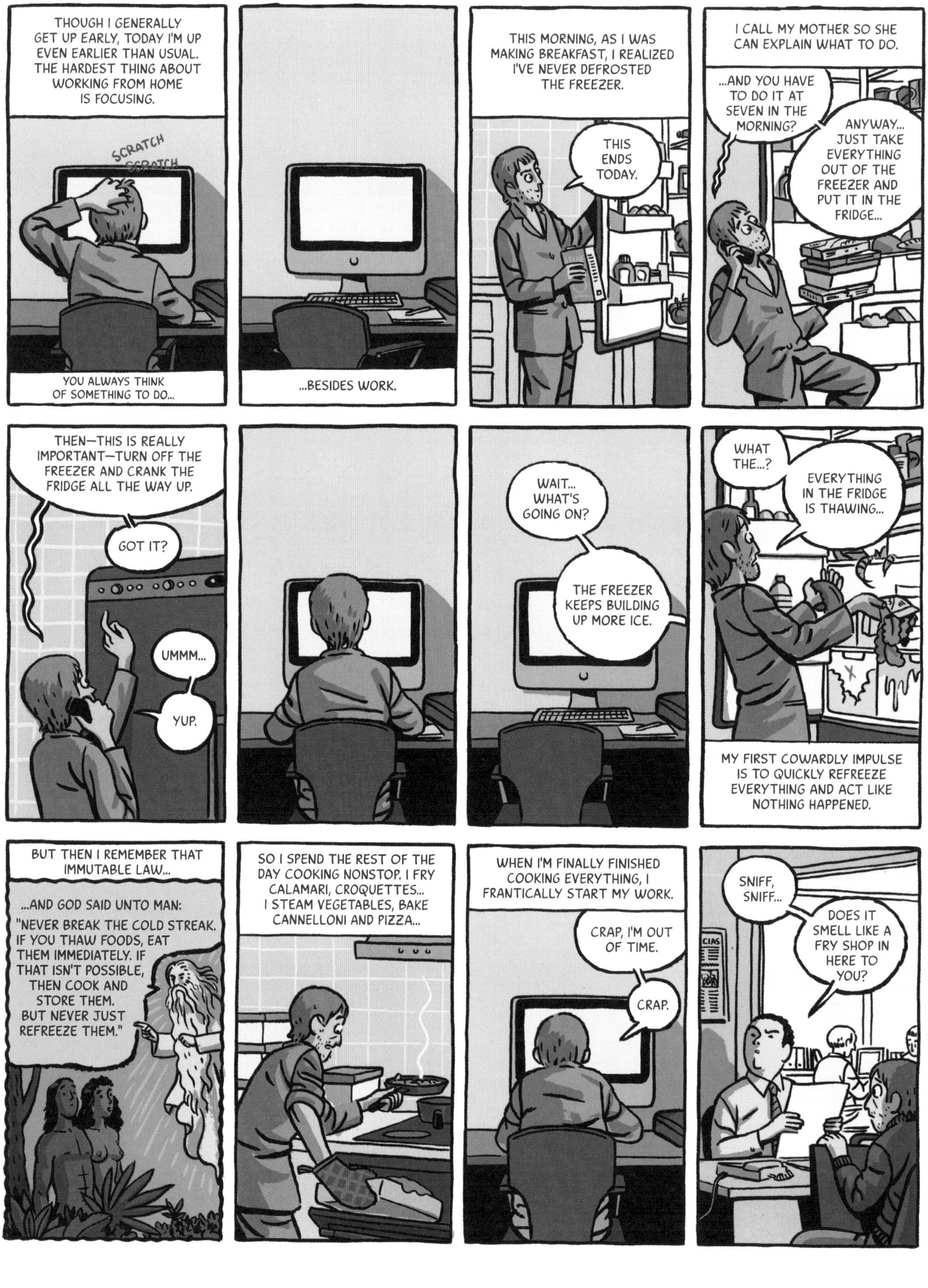
THOUGH I GENERALLY GET UP EARLY, TODAY I'M UP EVEN EARLIER THAN USUAL. THE HARDEST THING ABOUT WORKING FROM HOME IS FOCUSING.
SCRATCH
SCRATCH
YOU ALWAYS THINK OF SOMETHING TO DO...
...BESIDES WORK.
THIS MORNING, AS I WAS MAKING BREAKFAST, I REALIZED I'VE NEVER DEFROSTED THE FREEZER.
THIS ENDS TODAY.
I CALL MY MOTHER SO SHE CAN EXPLAIN WHAT TO DO.
...AND YOU HAVE TO DO IT AT SEVEN IN THE MORNING?
ANYWAY... JUST TAKE EVERYTHING OUT OF THE FREEZER AND PUT IT IN THE FRIDGE...
THEN—THIS IS REALLY IMPORTANT—TURN OFF THE FREEZER AND CRANK THE FRIDGE ALL THE WAY UP.
GOT IT?
UMMM...
YUP.
WAIT... WHAT'S GOING ON?
THE FREEZER KEEPS BUILDING UP MORE ICE.
WHAT THE...?
EVERYTHING IN THE FRIDGE IS THAWING...
MY FIRST COWARDLY IMPULSE IS TO QUICKLY REFREEZE EVERYTHING AND ACT LIKE NOTHING HAPPENED.
BUT THEN I REMEMBER THAT IMMUTABLE LAW...
...AND GOD SAID UNTO MAN:
"NEVER BREAK THE COLD STREAK. IF YOU THAW FOODS, EAT THEM IMMEDIATELY. IF THAT ISN'T POSSIBLE, THEN COOK AND STORE THEM. BUT NEVER JUST REFREEZE THEM."
SO I SPEND THE REST OF THE DAY COOKING NONSTOP. I FRY CALAMARI, CROQUETTES... I STEAM VEGETABLES, BAKE CANNELLONI AND PIZZA...
WHEN I'M FINALLY FINISHED COOKING EVERYTHING, I FRANTICALLY START MY WORK.
CRAP, I'M OUT OF TIME.
CRAP.
SNIFF, SNIFF...
DOES IT SMELL LIKE A FRY SHOP IN HERE TO YOU?

THE PARENT CULT

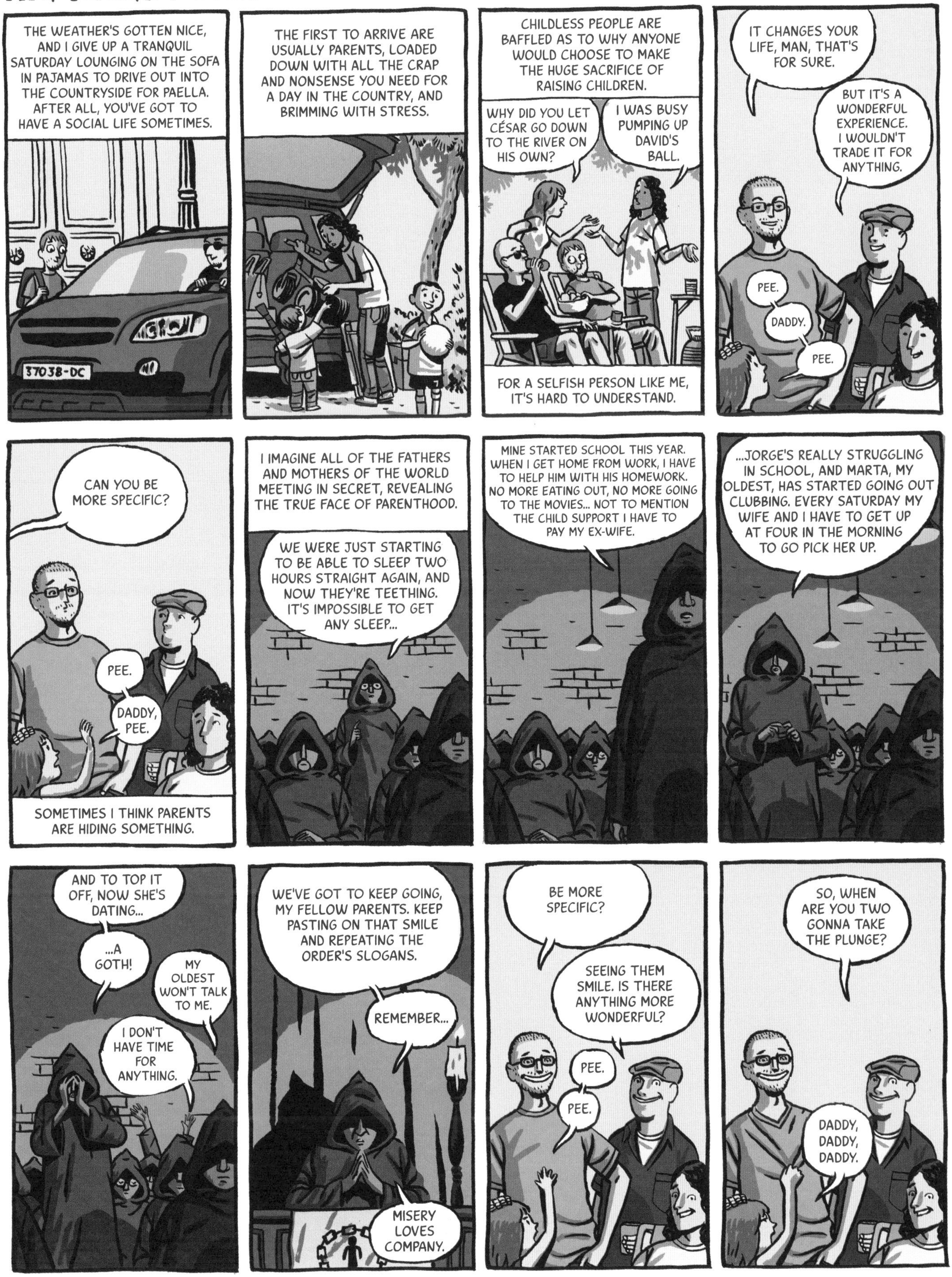
THE WEATHER'S GOTTEN NICE, AND I GIVE UP A TRANQUIL SATURDAY LOUNGING ON THE SOFA IN PAJAMAS TO DRIVE OUT INTO THE COUNTRYSIDE FOR PAELLA. AFTER ALL, YOU'VE GOT TO HAVE A SOCIAL LIFE SOMETIMES.
3703B-DC
THE FIRST TO ARRIVE ARE USUALLY PARENTS, LOADED DOWN WITH ALL THE CRAP AND NONSENSE YOU NEED FOR A DAY IN THE COUNTRY, AND BRIMMING WITH STRESS.
CHILDLESS PEOPLE ARE BAFFLED AS TO WHY ANYONE WOULD CHOOSE TO MAKE THE HUGE SACRIFICE OF RAISING CHILDREN.
WHY DID YOU LET CÉSAR GO DOWN TO THE RIVER ON HIS OWN?
I WAS BUSY PUMPING UP DAVID'S BALL.
FOR A SELFISH PERSON LIKE ME, IT'S HARD TO UNDERSTAND.
IT CHANGES YOUR LIFE, MAN, THAT'S FOR SURE.
BUT IT'S A WONDERFUL EXPERIENCE. I WOULDN'T TRADE IT FOR ANYTHING.
PEE.
DADDY.
PEE.
CAN YOU BE MORE SPECIFIC?
PEE.
DADDY, PEE.
SOMETIMES I THINK PARENTS ARE HIDING SOMETHING.
I IMAGINE ALL OF THE FATHERS AND MOTHERS OF THE WORLD MEETING IN SECRET, REVEALING THE TRUE FACE OF PARENTHOOD.
WE WERE JUST STARTING TO BE ABLE TO SLEEP TWO HOURS STRAIGHT AGAIN, AND NOW THEY'RE TEETHING. IT'S IMPOSSIBLE TO GET ANY SLEEP...
MINE STARTED SCHOOL THIS YEAR. WHEN I GET HOME FROM WORK, I HAVE TO HELP HIM WITH HIS HOMEWORK. NO MORE EATING OUT, NO MORE GOING TO THE MOVIES... NOT TO MENTION THE CHILD SUPPORT I HAVE TO PAY MY EX-WIFE.
...JORGE'S REALLY STRUGGLING IN SCHOOL, AND MARTA, MY OLDEST, HAS STARTED GOING OUT CLUBBING. EVERY SATURDAY MY WIFE AND I HAVE TO GET UP AT FOUR IN THE MORNING TO GO PICK HER UP.
AND TO TOP IT OFF, NOW SHE'S DATING...
...A GOTH!
MY OLDEST WON'T TALK TO ME.
I DON'T HAVE TIME FOR ANYTHING.
WE'VE GOT TO KEEP GOING, MY FELLOW PARENTS. KEEP PASTING ON THAT SMILE AND REPEATING THE ORDER'S SLOGANS.
REMEMBER...
MISERY LOVES COMPANY.
BE MORE SPECIFIC?
SEEING THEM SMILE. IS THERE ANYTHING MORE WONDERFUL?
PEE.
PEE.
SO, WHEN ARE YOU TWO GONNA TAKE THE PLUNGE?
DADDY, DADDY, DADDY.

DON'T SAY IT!

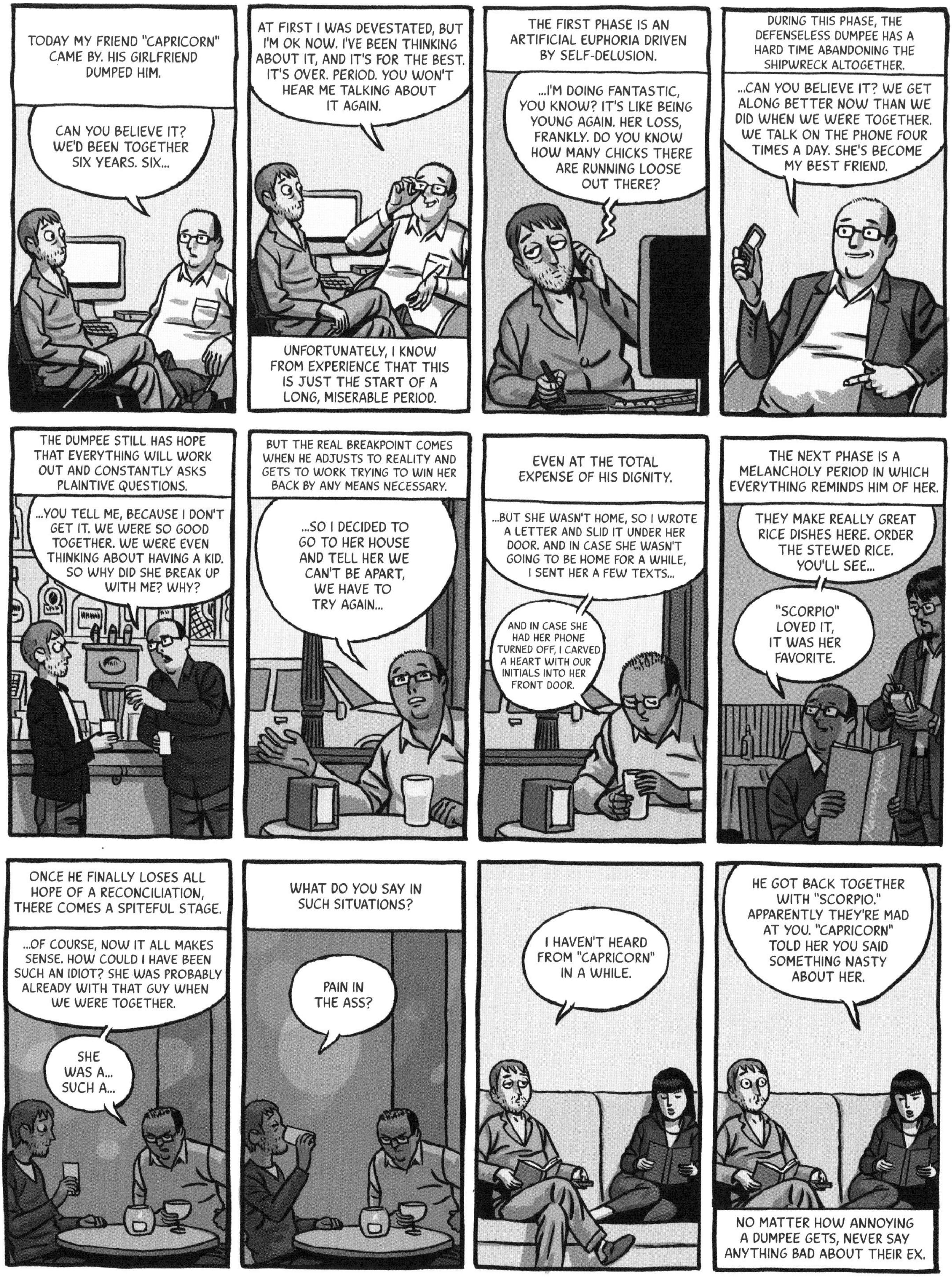

TODAY MY FRIEND "CAPRICORN" CAME BY. HIS GIRLFRIEND DUMPED HIM.
CAN YOU BELIEVE IT? WE'D BEEN TOGETHER SIX YEARS. SIX...
AT FIRST I WAS DEVESTATED, BUT I'M OK NOW. I'VE BEEN THINKING ABOUT IT, AND IT'S FOR THE BEST. IT'S OVER. PERIOD. YOU WON'T HEAR ME TALKING ABOUT IT AGAIN.
UNFORTUNATELY, I KNOW FROM EXPERIENCE THAT THIS IS JUST THE START OF A LONG, MISERABLE PERIOD.
THE FIRST PHASE IS AN ARTIFICIAL EUPHORIA DRIVEN BY SELF-DELUSION.
...I'M DOING FANTASTIC, YOU KNOW? IT'S LIKE BEING YOUNG AGAIN. HER LOSS, FRANKLY. DO YOU KNOW HOW MANY CHICKS THERE ARE RUNNING LOOSE OUT THERE?
DURING THIS PHASE, THE DEFENSELESS DUMPEE HAS A HARD TIME ABANDONING THE SHIPWRECK ALTOGETHER.
...CAN YOU BELIEVE IT? WE GET ALONG BETTER NOW THAN WE DID WHEN WE WERE TOGETHER. WE TALK ON THE PHONE FOUR TIMES A DAY. SHE'S BECOME MY BEST FRIEND.
THE DUMPEE STILL HAS HOPE THAT EVERYTHING WILL WORK OUT AND CONSTANTLY ASKS PLAINTIVE QUESTIONS.
...YOU TELL ME, BECAUSE I DON'T GET IT. WE WERE SO GOOD TOGETHER. WE WERE EVEN THINKING ABOUT HAVING A KID. SO WHY DID SHE BREAK UP WITH ME? WHY?
BUT THE REAL BREAKPOINT COMES WHEN HE ADJUSTS TO REALITY AND GETS TO WORK TRYING TO WIN HER BACK BY ANY MEANS NECESSARY.
...SO I DECIDED TO GO TO HER HOUSE AND TELL HER WE CAN'T BE APART, WE HAVE TO TRY AGAIN...
EVEN AT THE TOTAL EXPENSE OF HIS DIGNITY.
...BUT SHE WASN'T HOME, SO I WROTE A LETTER AND SLID IT UNDER HER DOOR. AND IN CASE SHE WASN'T GOING TO BE HOME FOR A WHILE, I SENT HER A FEW TEXTS...
AND IN CASE SHE HAD HER PHONE TURNED OFF, I CARVED A HEART WITH OUR INITIALS INTO HER FRONT DOOR.
THE NEXT PHASE IS A MELANCHOLY PERIOD IN WHICH EVERYTHING REMINDS HIM OF HER.
THEY MAKE REALLY GREAT RICE DISHES HERE. ORDER THE STEWED RICE. YOU'LL SEE...
"SCORPIO" LOVED IT, IT WAS HER FAVORITE.
ONCE HE FINALLY LOSES ALL HOPE OF A RECONCILIATION, THERE COMES A SPITEFUL STAGE.
...OF COURSE, NOW IT ALL MAKES SENSE. HOW COULD I HAVE BEEN SUCH AN IDIOT? SHE WAS PROBABLY ALREADY WITH THAT GUY WHEN WE WERE TOGETHER.
SHE WAS A... SUCH A...
WHAT DO YOU SAY IN SUCH SITUATIONS?
PAIN IN THE ASS?
I HAVEN'T HEARD FROM "CAPRICORN" IN A WHILE.
HE GOT BACK TOGETHER WITH "SCORPIO." APPARENTLY THEY'RE MAD AT YOU. "CAPRICORN" TOLD HER YOU SAID SOMETHING NASTY ABOUT HER.
NO MATTER HOW ANNOYING A DUMPEE GETS, NEVER SAY ANYTHING BAD ABOUT THEIR EX.

THE HUMAN WEATHER VANE

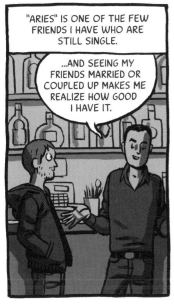

"ARIES" IS ONE OF THE FEW FRIENDS I HAVE WHO ARE STILL SINGLE.
...AND SEEING MY FRIENDS MARRIED OR COUPLED UP MAKES ME REALIZE HOW GOOD I HAVE IT.
STOP! STOP! NO MORE GIN. I GET A LITTLE FRISKY UNDER THE INFLUENCE.
WELL, YOU COULD FRISK ME IF YOU'D LIKE...
THE MAN'S TALENT FOR GETTING POINTS ON THE BOARD IS ASTONISHING.
THE TRICK IS TO PROJECT CONFIDENCE. YOU CAN'T LET THEM KNOW YOU'RE DYING TO GET LAID, YOU KNOW?
SOUNDS EASY...
EASY IF YOU'RE TALL, HANDSOME, AND CHARMING.
THE REST OF US HOMELY MORTALS HAVE HAD TO STRUGGLE HARD IN LIFE TO SCORE.
IF YOU COME OVER, I'LL DO THE DRAWINGS FOR YOUR HISTORY PROJECT.
AND THE ESSAY ON "DON QUIJOTE" TOO?
OVER THE YEARS I'VE BEEN REFINING MY TECHNIQUES FOR PICKING UP GIRLS...
...I MEAN, ALL THEIR SONGS ARE GOOD. I LOVE MECANO.
AC DC
MECANO'S MY FAVORITE BAND TOO! I HAVE ALL OF THEIR RECORDS.
THIS IS THEIR ONLY ONE.
RIGHT, BUT I'VE LISTENED TO IT SO MANY TIMES... MY OTHER FAVORITE GROUP IS OLÉ-OLÉ.
I'M NOT INTO OLÉ-OLÉ.
YEAH, I MEAN, THEY'RE JUST OK.
MY STYLE IS NOT TO HAVE A STYLE.
I SHARE GROUCHO MARX'S WORLDVIEW.
THOSE ARE MY PRINCIPLES, BUT IF YOU DON'T LIKE THEM, I HAVE OTHERS.
SINCE I LACK THE ASSETS THAT MY FRIEND "ARIES" ENJOYS...
BLAH
BLAH
BLAH
...I'VE BECOME A HUMAN WEATHER VANE.
BEING A WEATHER VANE HAS MEANT DELVING INTO TOPICS THAT NEVER WOULD HAVE INTERESTED ME OTHERWISE: THE DIHEDRAL SYSTEM, AVANT-GARDE FILM SCREENINGS, MACROBIOTIC COOKING CLASSES...
GR
SALS
CLASSES
TODAY
FIL
AUTEUR
POLISH FILM SERIE
HEY, DID YOU SCOPE OUT THE MELONS ON THE WAITRESS?
I WOULDN'T SAY MELONS, THEY'RE MORE LIKE A DRUPE FROM A COCOS NUCIFERA, DON'T YOU THINK?
UM...
IT'S JUST... I TRIED TO DATE A BOTANIST ONCE...
MY APPROACH TO DATING HAS MADE ME A RENAISSANCE MAN.

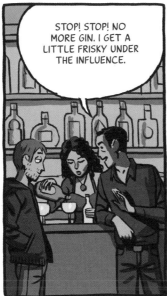

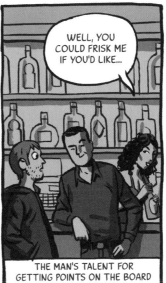

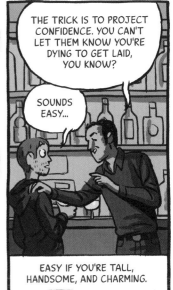

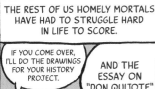

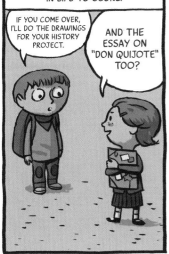

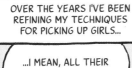

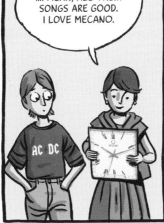

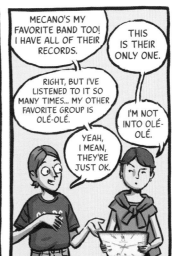

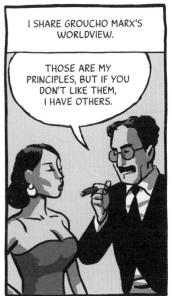

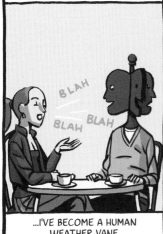

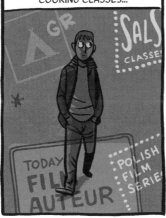

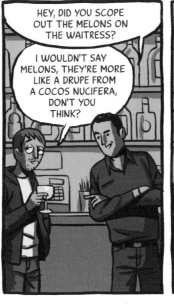

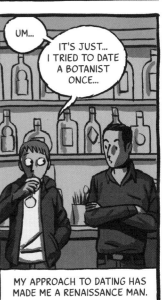

THE HEIGHTS OF FAME

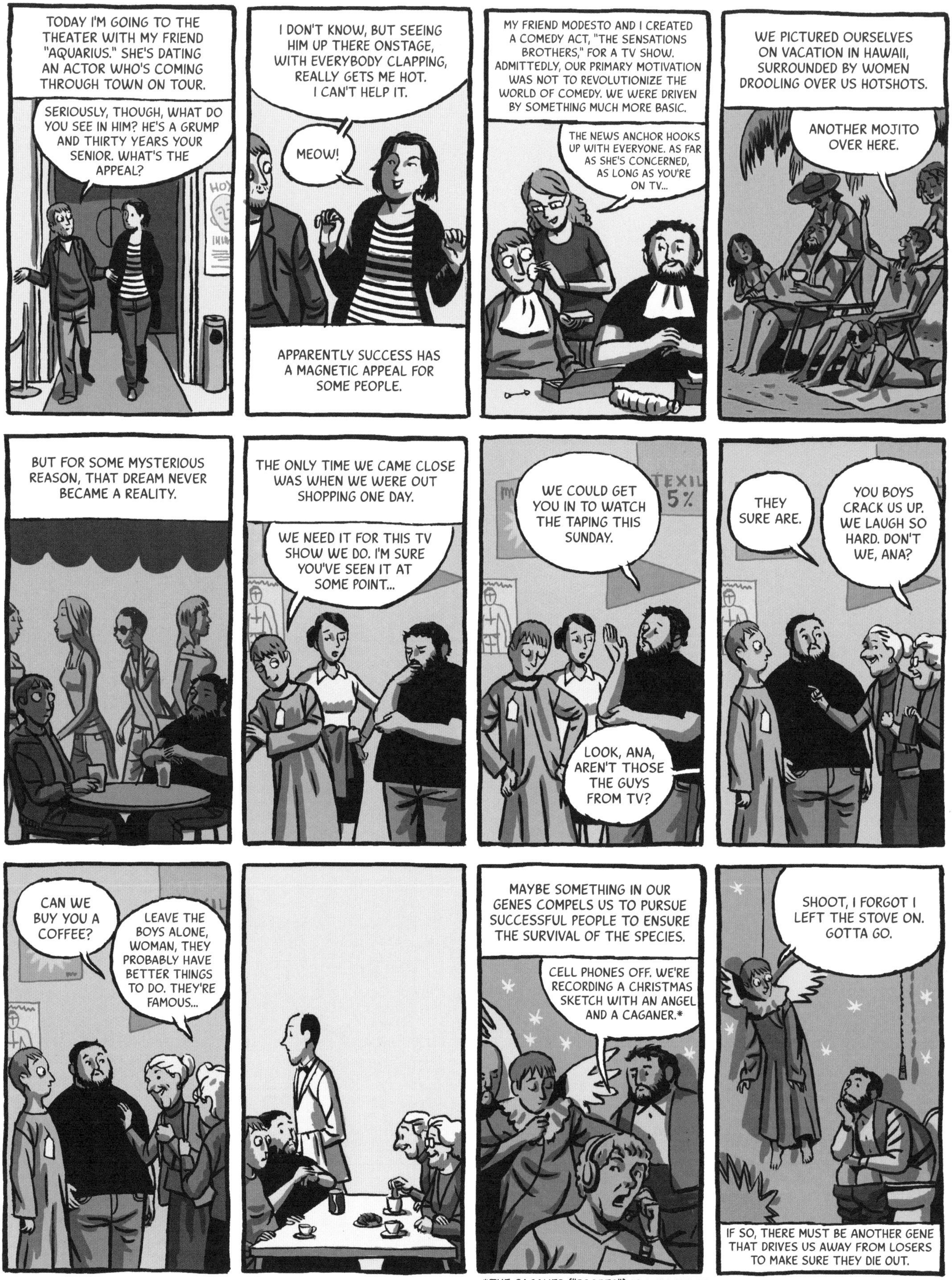
TODAY I'M GOING TO THE THEATER WITH MY FRIEND "AQUARIUS." SHE'S DATING AN ACTOR WHO'S COMING THROUGH TOWN ON TOUR.
SERIOUSLY, THOUGH, WHAT DO YOU SEE IN HIM? HE'S A GRUMP AND THIRTY YEARS YOUR SENIOR. WHAT'S THE APPEAL?
I DON'T KNOW, BUT SEEING HIM UP THERE ONSTAGE, WITH EVERYBODY CLAPPING, REALLY GETS ME HOT. I CAN'T HELP IT.
MEOW!
APPARENTLY SUCCESS HAS A MAGNETIC APPEAL FOR SOME PEOPLE.
MY FRIEND MODESTO AND I CREATED A COMEDY ACT, "THE SENSATIONS BROTHERS," FOR A TV SHOW. ADMITTEDLY, OUR PRIMARY MOTIVATION WAS NOT TO REVOLUTIONIZE THE WORLD OF COMEDY. WE WERE DRIVEN BY SOMETHING MUCH MORE BASIC.
THE NEWS ANCHOR HOOKS UP WITH EVERYONE. AS FAR AS SHE'S CONCERNED, AS LONG AS YOU'RE ON TV...
WE PICTURED OURSELVES ON VACATION IN HAWAII, SURROUNDED BY WOMEN DROOLING OVER US HOTSHOTS.
ANOTHER MOJITO OVER HERE.
BUT FOR SOME MYSTERIOUS REASON, THAT DREAM NEVER BECAME A REALITY.
THE ONLY TIME WE CAME CLOSE WAS WHEN WE WERE OUT SHOPPING ONE DAY.
WE NEED IT FOR THIS TV SHOW WE DO. I'M SURE YOU'VE SEEN IT AT SOME POINT...
WE COULD GET YOU IN TO WATCH THE TAPING THIS SUNDAY.
LOOK, ANA, AREN'T THOSE THE GUYS FROM TV?
THEY SURE ARE.
YOU BOYS CRACK US UP. WE LAUGH SO HARD. DON'T WE, ANA?
CAN WE BUY YOU A COFFEE?
LEAVE THE BOYS ALONE, WOMAN, THEY PROBABLY HAVE BETTER THINGS TO DO. THEY'RE FAMOUS...
MAYBE SOMETHING IN OUR GENES COMPELS US TO PURSUE SUCCESSFUL PEOPLE TO ENSURE THE SURVIVAL OF THE SPECIES.
CELL PHONES OFF. WE'RE RECORDING A CHRISTMAS SKETCH WITH AN ANGEL AND A CAGANER.*
SHOOT, I FORGOT I LEFT THE STOVE ON. GOTTA GO.
IF SO, THERE MUST BE ANOTHER GENE THAT DRIVES US AWAY FROM LOSERS TO MAKE SURE THEY DIE OUT.

*THE CAGANER ("POOPER") IS A FIGURE COMMONLY FOUND IN NATIVITY SCENES FROM CATALONIA, VALENCIA, AND OTHER AREAS OF NORTHEASTERN SPAIN.

MIDLIFE CRISIS

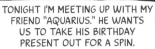

TONIGHT I'M MEETING UP WITH MY FRIEND "AQUARIUS." HE WANTS US TO TAKE HIS BIRTHDAY PRESENT OUT FOR A SPIN.

I DEBATED WHETHER TO BUY A FAT BOY OR A CAYENNE...

I KNOW NOTHING ABOUT THE SUBJECT, SO I HAVE NO IDEA WHICH ONE HE ULTIMATELY CHOSE.

"AQUARIUS" JUST TURNED FORTY, AND HE'S AT THAT STAGE WHERE YOU FEEL LIKE YOU'VE STARTED TO SLIDE DOWNHILL WITHOUT ANY BRAKES.

UP UNTIL A FEW MONTHS AGO HE WAS A "NORMAL" PERSON WITH A "NORMAL" LIFE.

BUT ALL OF A SUDDEN AN ALARM WENT OFF INSIDE HIM, AND HIS HORMONES STARTED RAGING AGAIN LIKE THEY DID WHEN HE WAS EIGHTEEN.

HE'D NEVER SET FOOT INSIDE A GYM, BUT NOW HE'S NOT ONLY JOINED ONE...

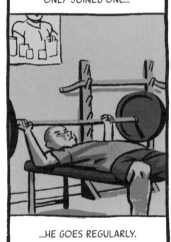

...HE GOES REGULARLY.

HE'S GROWING HIS HAIR OUT LIKE WHEN HE WAS YOUNG, AND HE GOT THE TATTOO HE ALWAYS WANTED.

HE'S ADOPTED A NEW WAY OF DRESSING AND NOW WEARS HIS PANTS SEVERAL CENTIMETERS LOWER THAN HE USED TO.

AND WHEREAS A FEW YEARS AGO HIS WEEKENDS CONSISTED OF MOVIES ON THE COUCH, LATELY HE'S BEEN INSISTING THAT WE GO OUT FOR DRINKS.

REMEMBER THAT DJ AT THE BAR WE USED TO GO TO? WELL, NOW HE PLAYS IN A DIVE NEAR HERE. COME ON, MAN... JUST ONE DRINK. AND I CAN SHOW YOU THE MOTORCYCLE I BOUGHT.

AT TWENTY-SOMETHING, "AQUARIUS" WAS AT THE CREST OF THE WAVE; HE WAS A PLAYER. HE'S USING HIS NEW LOOK AND HIS NEW BIKE TO TRY TO GET THAT MOMENT BACK. HE WANTS TO FEEL WANTED AGAIN.

VROOM VROOM

DAMN, MAN, THAT'S A SWEET BIKE. I USED TO HAVE A HARLEY TOO, BUT I HAD TO SELL IT WHEN I GOT MARRIED...

WHEN WE SPLIT, I SOLD THE MINIVAN AND BOUGHT A CONVERTIBLE. BUT I'VE ALWAYS LOVED MOTORCYCLES...

IS THAT A REAL LEATHER JACKET?

HOW DID IT GO?

"AQUARIUS" IS A MAGNET FOR MEN WHO ARE GOING THROUGH MIDLIFE CRISES.

THE INFERNAL MACHINE

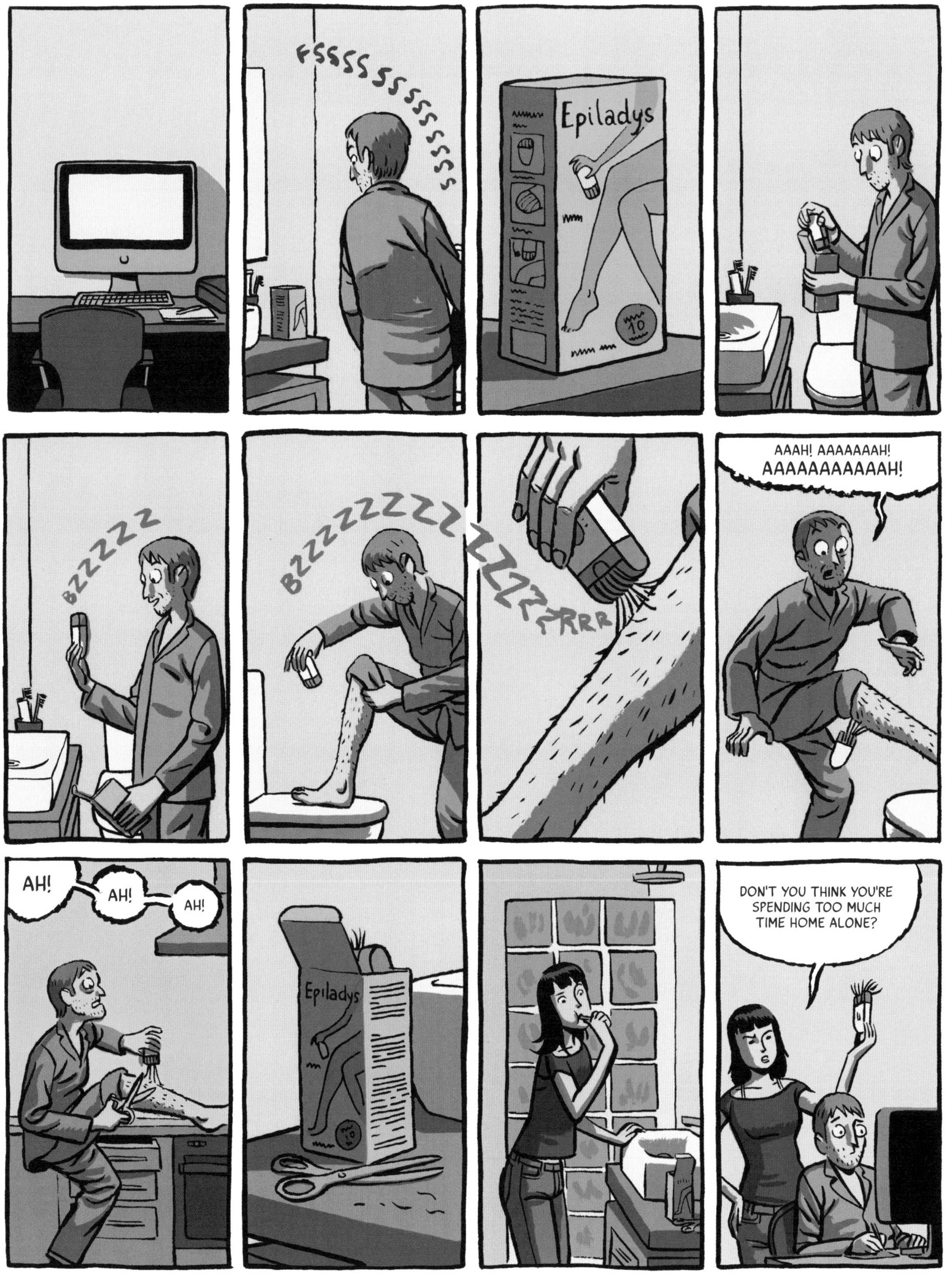
FSSSSSSSSSSSSSSSSS
Epiladys
10
BZZZZZ
BZZZZZZZZZZZZZZZZZZRRR
AAAH! AAAAAAAH!
AAAAAAAAAAAH!
AH!
AH!
AH!
Epiladys
10
DON'T YOU THINK YOU'RE SPENDING TOO MUCH TIME HOME ALONE?

THE GREAT OUTDOORS

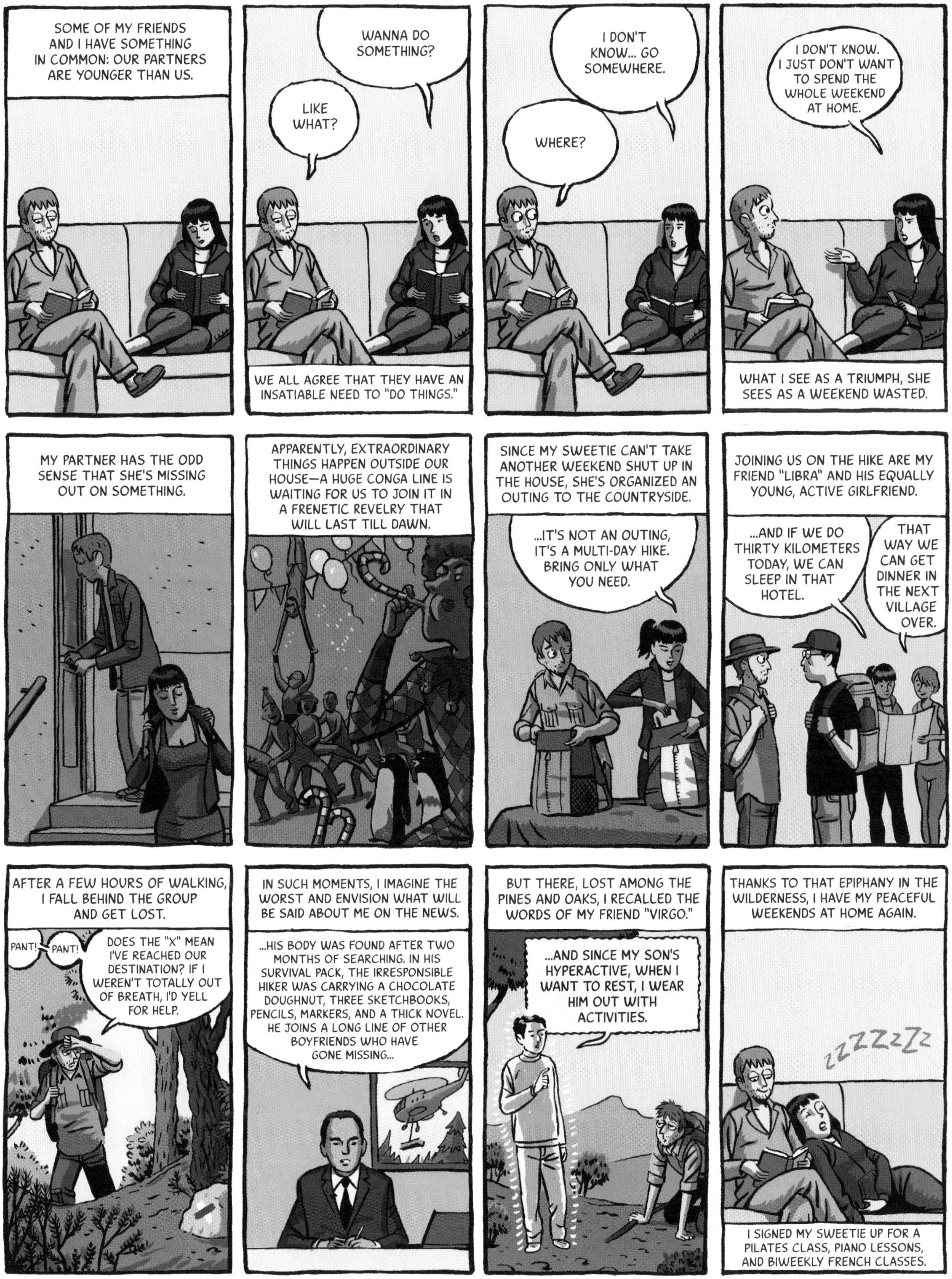
SOME OF MY FRIENDS AND I HAVE SOMETHING IN COMMON: OUR PARTNERS ARE YOUNGER THAN US.
WANNA DO SOMETHING?
LIKE WHAT?
WE ALL AGREE THAT THEY HAVE AN INSATIABLE NEED TO "DO THINGS."
I DON'T KNOW... GO SOMEWHERE.
WHERE?
I DON'T KNOW. I JUST DON'T WANT TO SPEND THE WHOLE WEEKEND AT HOME.
WHAT I SEE AS A TRIUMPH, SHE SEES AS A WEEKEND WASTED.
MY PARTNER HAS THE ODD SENSE THAT SHE'S MISSING OUT ON SOMETHING.
APPARENTLY, EXTRAORDINARY THINGS HAPPEN OUTSIDE OUR HOUSE—A HUGE CONGA LINE IS WAITING FOR US TO JOIN IT IN A FRENETIC REVELRY THAT WILL LAST TILL DAWN.
SINCE MY SWEETIE CAN'T TAKE ANOTHER WEEKEND SHUT UP IN THE HOUSE, SHE'S ORGANIZED AN OUTING TO THE COUNTRYSIDE.
...IT'S NOT AN OUTING, IT'S A MULTI-DAY HIKE. BRING ONLY WHAT YOU NEED.
JOINING US ON THE HIKE ARE MY FRIEND "LIBRA" AND HIS EQUALLY YOUNG, ACTIVE GIRLFRIEND.
...AND IF WE DO THIRTY KILOMETERS TODAY, WE CAN SLEEP IN THAT HOTEL.
THAT WAY WE CAN GET DINNER IN THE NEXT VILLAGE OVER.
AFTER A FEW HOURS OF WALKING, I FALL BEHIND THE GROUP AND GET LOST.
PANT! PANT!
DOES THE "X" MEAN I'VE REACHED OUR DESTINATION? IF I WEREN'T TOTALLY OUT OF BREATH, I'D YELL FOR HELP.
IN SUCH MOMENTS, I IMAGINE THE WORST AND ENVISION WHAT WILL BE SAID ABOUT ME ON THE NEWS.
...HIS BODY WAS FOUND AFTER TWO MONTHS OF SEARCHING. IN HIS SURVIVAL PACK, THE IRRESPONSIBLE HIKER WAS CARRYING A CHOCOLATE DOUGHNUT, THREE SKETCHBOOKS, PENCILS, MARKERS, AND A THICK NOVEL. HE JOINS A LONG LINE OF OTHER BOYFRIENDS WHO HAVE GONE MISSING...
BUT THERE, LOST AMONG THE PINES AND OAKS, I RECALLED THE WORDS OF MY FRIEND "VIRGO."
...AND SINCE MY SON'S HYPERACTIVE, WHEN I WANT TO REST, I WEAR HIM OUT WITH ACTIVITIES.
THANKS TO THAT EPIPHANY IN THE WILDERNESS, I HAVE MY PEACEFUL WEEKENDS AT HOME AGAIN.
ZZZZZZZ
I SIGNED MY SWEETIE UP FOR A PILATES CLASS, PIANO LESSONS, AND BIWEEKLY FRENCH CLASSES.

AND THERE WAS LIGHT

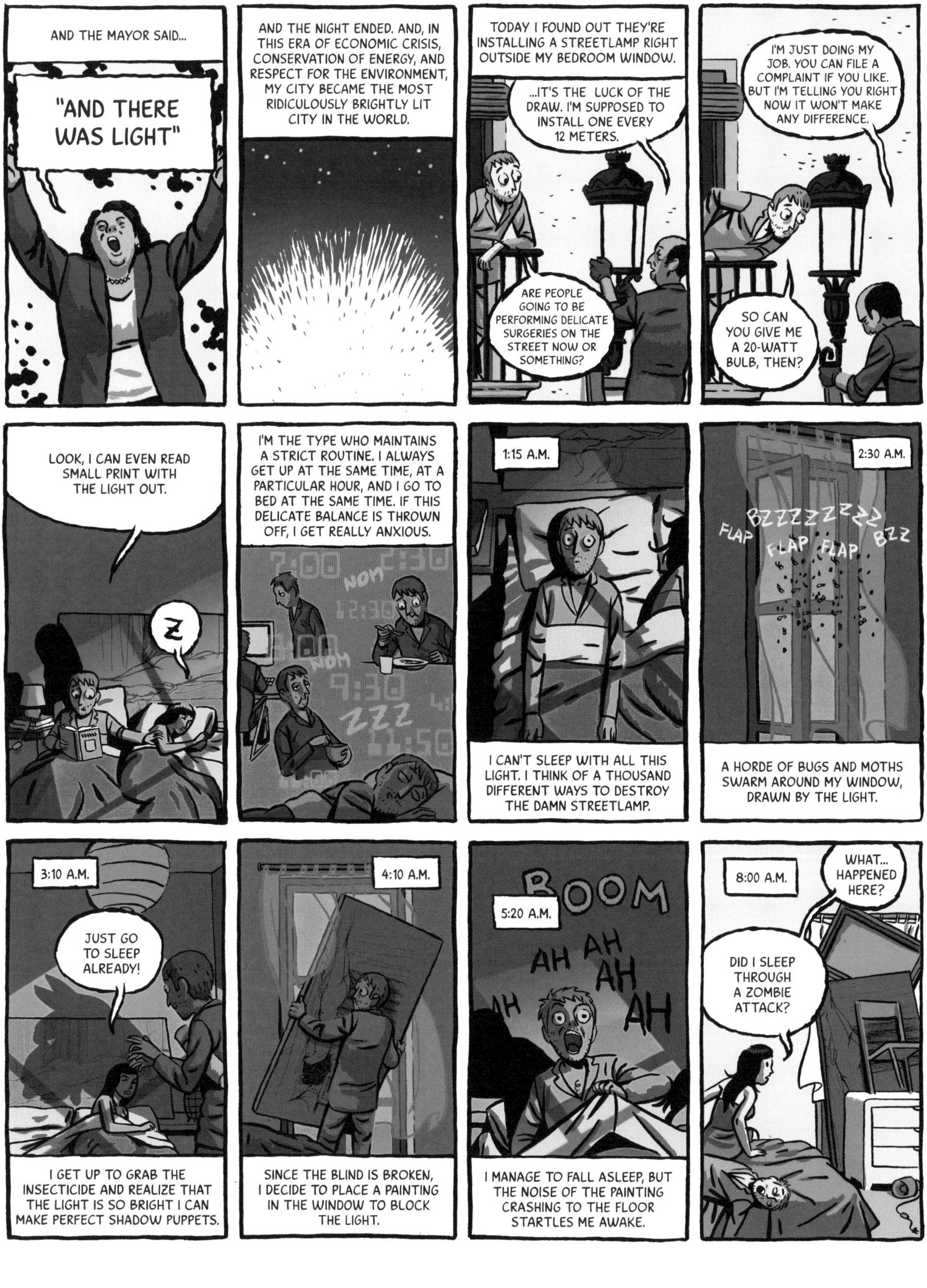

AND THE MAYOR SAID...
"AND THERE WAS LIGHT"
AND THE NIGHT ENDED. AND, IN THIS ERA OF ECONOMIC CRISIS, CONSERVATION OF ENERGY, AND RESPECT FOR THE ENVIRONMENT, MY CITY BECAME THE MOST RIDICULOUSLY BRIGHTLY LIT CITY IN THE WORLD.
TODAY I FOUND OUT THEY'RE INSTALLING A STREETLAMP RIGHT OUTSIDE MY BEDROOM WINDOW.
...IT'S THE LUCK OF THE DRAW. I'M SUPPOSED TO INSTALL ONE EVERY 12 METERS.
ARE PEOPLE GOING TO BE PERFORMING DELICATE SURGERIES ON THE STREET NOW OR SOMETHING?
I'M JUST DOING MY JOB. YOU CAN FILE A COMPLAINT IF YOU LIKE. BUT I'M TELLING YOU RIGHT NOW IT WON'T MAKE ANY DIFFERENCE.
SO CAN YOU GIVE ME A 20-WATT BULB, THEN?
LOOK, I CAN EVEN READ SMALL PRINT WITH THE LIGHT OUT.
Z
I'M THE TYPE WHO MAINTAINS A STRICT ROUTINE. I ALWAYS GET UP AT THE SAME TIME, AT A PARTICULAR HOUR, AND I GO TO BED AT THE SAME TIME. IF THIS DELICATE BALANCE IS THROWN OFF, I GET REALLY ANXIOUS.
7:00
2:30
NOM
12:30
NOM
9:30
ZZZ
1:15 A.M.
I CAN'T SLEEP WITH ALL THIS LIGHT. I THINK OF A THOUSAND DIFFERENT WAYS TO DESTROY THE DAMN STREETLAMP.
2:30 A.M.
BZZZZZZZZ
FLAP
FLAP
FLAP
BZZ
A HORDE OF BUGS AND MOTHS SWARM AROUND MY WINDOW, DRAWN BY THE LIGHT.
3:10 A.M.
JUST GO TO SLEEP ALREADY!
I GET UP TO GRAB THE INSECTICIDE AND REALIZE THAT THE LIGHT IS SO BRIGHT I CAN MAKE PERFECT SHADOW PUPPETS.
4:10 A.M.
SINCE THE BLIND IS BROKEN, I DECIDE TO PLACE A PAINTING IN THE WINDOW TO BLOCK THE LIGHT.
BOOM
5:20 A.M.
AH AH AH AH
AH
I MANAGE TO FALL ASLEEP, BUT THE NOISE OF THE PAINTING CRASHING TO THE FLOOR STARTLES ME AWAKE.
8:00 A.M.
WHAT... HAPPENED HERE?
DID I SLEEP THROUGH A ZOMBIE ATTACK?

THE RIGHT FINGER

I CAN ASSURE YOU I'VE BEEN IN UNPLEASANT SITUATIONS BEFORE...
BUT THIS HAS UNQUESTIONABLY BEEN THE MOST HUMILIATING EXPERIENCE OF MY LIFE.
WHY IS THIS SO TRAUMATIC FOR US?
YOU CAN PULL UP YOUR PANTS NOW.
SERIOUSLY?
HA HA HA!
THE UROLOGIST STUCK HIS FINGER UP YOU?
AT OUR AGE, IT'S VITAL FOR DISEASE PREVENTION.
DON'T TELL ME YOU'VE NEVER HAD A RECTAL EXAM.
...SO I TOLD HIM...
DID YOU MAKE AN APPOINTMENT WITH THE UROLOGIST YET?
I-I'M WORKING ON IT...
I'M LOOKING FOR THE FINEST PROFESSIONAL THERE IS.
...GOOD MORNING. IS THIS DR. PERELLÓ'S OFFICE? UM... WHAT IS THE DOCTOR LIKE? YES... RIGHT... I MEAN PHYSICALLY... JUST ONE MORE QUESTION... HIS HANDS...
YES, HIS HANDS—HOW BIG ARE THEY? I SEE. THANKS SO MUCH.
GUÍA MÉDICA
UROLOGISTS
Clinica Tarancón
Calle Denia, 7 Tel. 9657341
Doctor Quintanilla
Avda. Los Naranjos Tel. 961117
Doctor Perelló
Calle Colón Tel.
Bandrés
Giorgeta
Doctor Falom
Plaza España
Doctor Azpitarte
Tel.
ODON
Diego
Calle

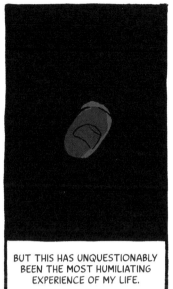

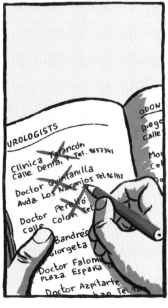

THE PERFECT PERSON

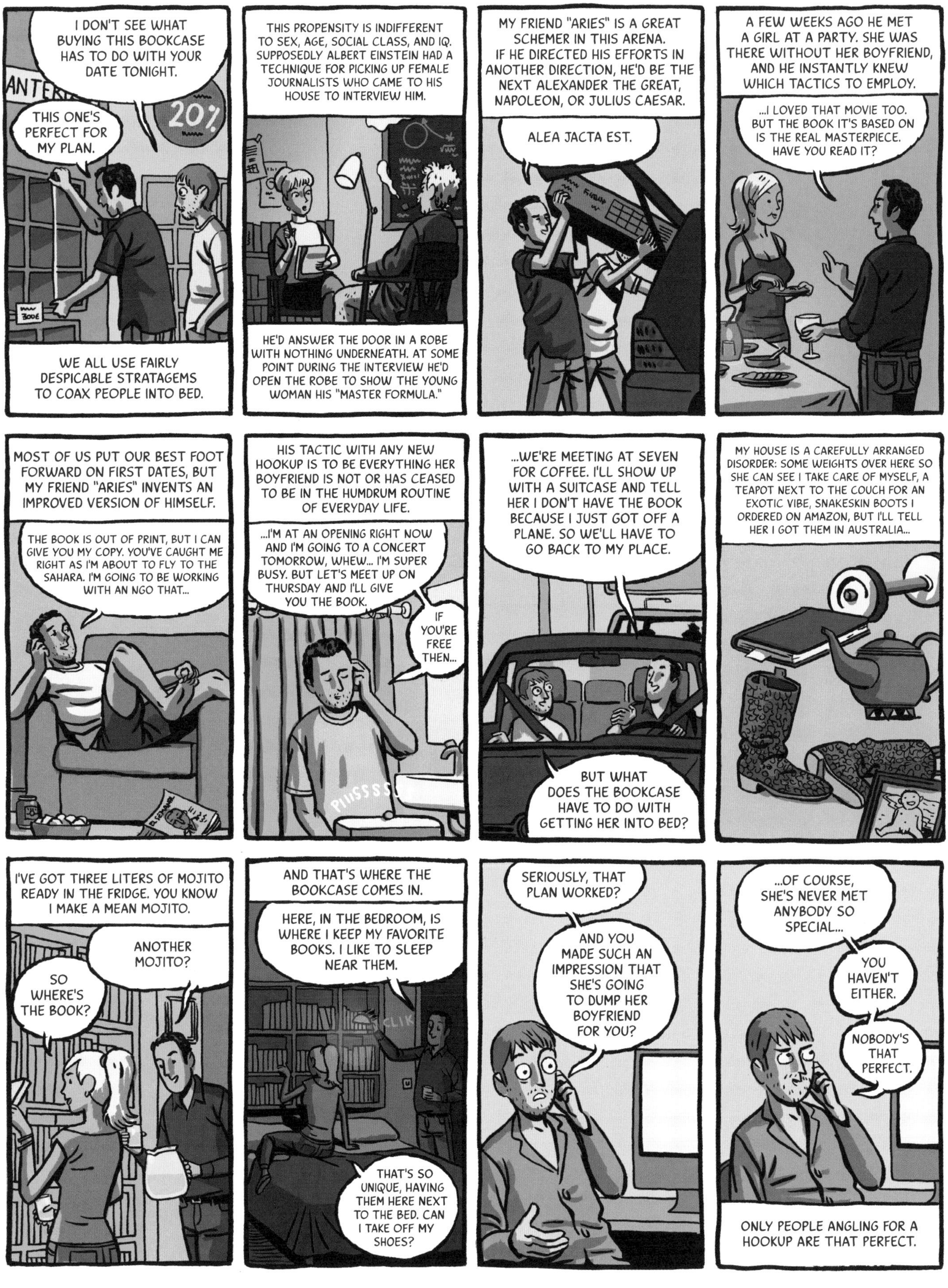

I DON'T SEE WHAT BUYING THIS BOOKCASE HAS TO DO WITH YOUR DATE TONIGHT.
THIS ONE'S PERFECT FOR MY PLAN.
WE ALL USE FAIRLY DESPICABLE STRATAGEMS TO COAX PEOPLE INTO BED.
THIS PROPENSITY IS INDIFFERENT TO SEX, AGE, SOCIAL CLASS, AND IQ. SUPPOSEDLY ALBERT EINSTEIN HAD A TECHNIQUE FOR PICKING UP FEMALE JOURNALISTS WHO CAME TO HIS HOUSE TO INTERVIEW HIM.
HE'D ANSWER THE DOOR IN A ROBE WITH NOTHING UNDERNEATH. AT SOME POINT DURING THE INTERVIEW HE'D OPEN THE ROBE TO SHOW THE YOUNG WOMAN HIS "MASTER FORMULA."
MY FRIEND "ARIES" IS A GREAT SCHEMER IN THIS ARENA. IF HE DIRECTED HIS EFFORTS IN ANOTHER DIRECTION, HE'D BE THE NEXT ALEXANDER THE GREAT, NAPOLEON, OR JULIUS CAESAR.
ALEA JACTA EST.
A FEW WEEKS AGO HE MET A GIRL AT A PARTY. SHE WAS THERE WITHOUT HER BOYFRIEND, AND HE INSTANTLY KNEW WHICH TACTICS TO EMPLOY.
...I LOVED THAT MOVIE TOO. BUT THE BOOK IT'S BASED ON IS THE REAL MASTERPIECE. HAVE YOU READ IT?
MOST OF US PUT OUR BEST FOOT FORWARD ON FIRST DATES, BUT MY FRIEND "ARIES" INVENTS AN IMPROVED VERSION OF HIMSELF.
THE BOOK IS OUT OF PRINT, BUT I CAN GIVE YOU MY COPY. YOU'VE CAUGHT ME RIGHT AS I'M ABOUT TO FLY TO THE SAHARA. I'M GOING TO BE WORKING WITH AN NGO THAT...
HIS TACTIC WITH ANY NEW HOOKUP IS TO BE EVERYTHING HER BOYFRIEND IS NOT OR HAS CEASED TO BE IN THE HUMDRUM ROUTINE OF EVERYDAY LIFE.
...I'M AT AN OPENING RIGHT NOW AND I'M GOING TO A CONCERT TOMORROW, WHEW... I'M SUPER BUSY. BUT LET'S MEET UP ON THURSDAY AND I'LL GIVE YOU THE BOOK.
IF YOU'RE FREE THEN...
...WE'RE MEETING AT SEVEN FOR COFFEE. I'LL SHOW UP WITH A SUITCASE AND TELL HER I DON'T HAVE THE BOOK BECAUSE I JUST GOT OFF A PLANE. SO WE'LL HAVE TO GO BACK TO MY PLACE.
BUT WHAT DOES THE BOOKCASE HAVE TO DO WITH GETTING HER INTO BED?
MY HOUSE IS A CAREFULLY ARRANGED DISORDER: SOME WEIGHTS OVER HERE SO SHE CAN SEE I TAKE CARE OF MYSELF, A TEAPOT NEXT TO THE COUCH FOR AN EXOTIC VIBE, SNAKESKIN BOOTS I ORDERED ON AMAZON, BUT I'LL TELL HER I GOT THEM IN AUSTRALIA...
I'VE GOT THREE LITERS OF MOJITO READY IN THE FRIDGE. YOU KNOW I MAKE A MEAN MOJITO.
SO WHERE'S THE BOOK?
ANOTHER MOJITO?
AND THAT'S WHERE THE BOOKCASE COMES IN.
HERE, IN THE BEDROOM, IS WHERE I KEEP MY FAVORITE BOOKS. I LIKE TO SLEEP NEAR THEM.
CLIK
THAT'S SO UNIQUE, HAVING THEM HERE NEXT TO THE BED. CAN I TAKE OFF MY SHOES?
SERIOUSLY, THAT PLAN WORKED?
AND YOU MADE SUCH AN IMPRESSION THAT SHE'S GOING TO DUMP HER BOYFRIEND FOR YOU?
...OF COURSE, SHE'S NEVER MET ANYBODY SO SPECIAL...
YOU HAVEN'T EITHER.
NOBODY'S THAT PERFECT.
ONLY PEOPLE ANGLING FOR A HOOKUP ARE THAT PERFECT.

CRISIS OF FAITH

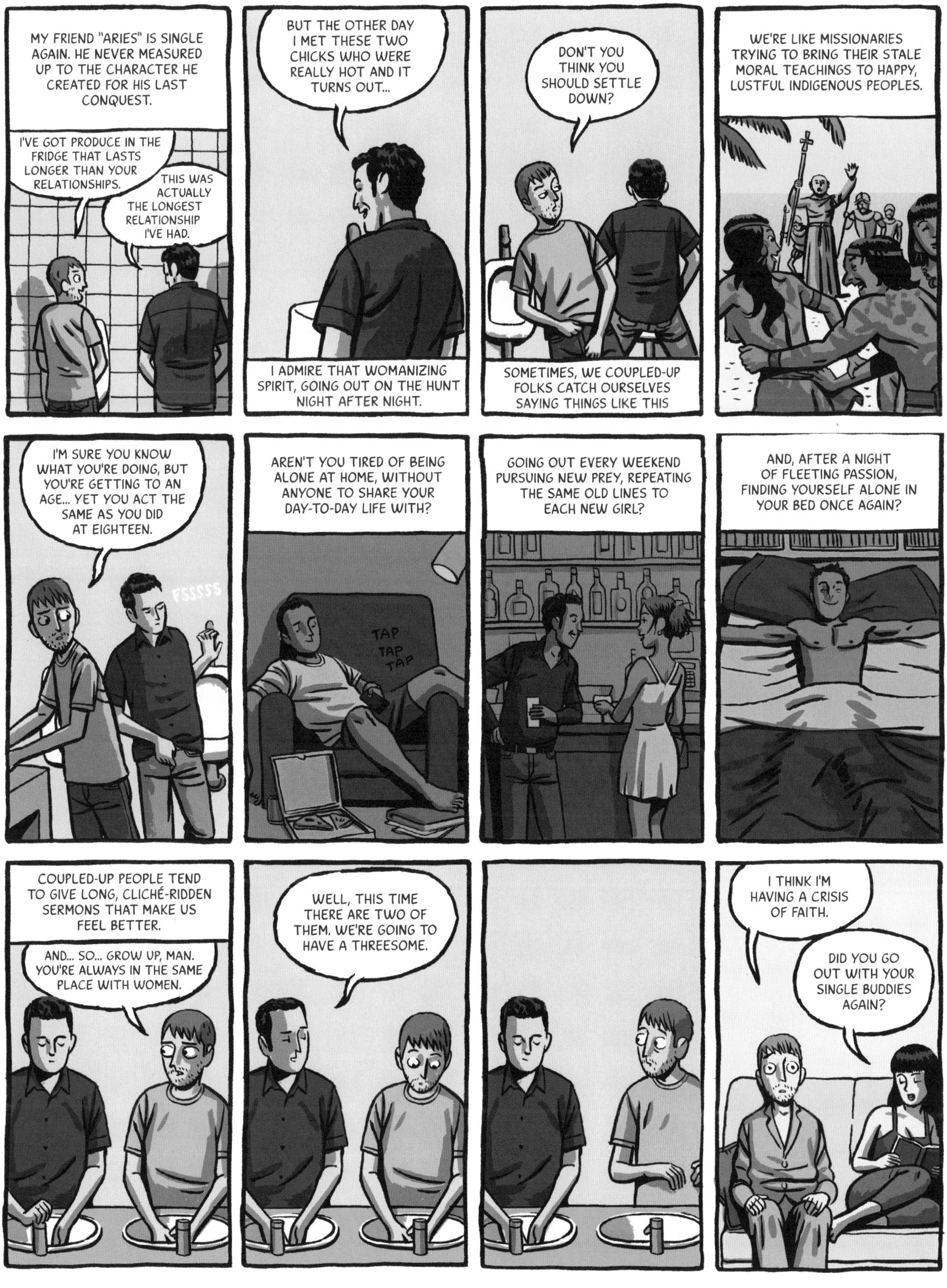

MY FRIEND "ARIES" IS SINGLE AGAIN. HE NEVER MEASURED UP TO THE CHARACTER HE CREATED FOR HIS LAST CONQUEST.
I'VE GOT PRODUCE IN THE FRIDGE THAT LASTS LONGER THAN YOUR RELATIONSHIPS.
THIS WAS ACTUALLY THE LONGEST RELATIONSHIP I'VE HAD.
BUT THE OTHER DAY I MET THESE TWO CHICKS WHO WERE REALLY HOT AND IT TURNS OUT...
I ADMIRE THAT WOMANIZING SPIRIT, GOING OUT ON THE HUNT NIGHT AFTER NIGHT.
DON'T YOU THINK YOU SHOULD SETTLE DOWN?
SOMETIMES, WE COUPLED-UP FOLKS CATCH OURSELVES SAYING THINGS LIKE THIS
WE'RE LIKE MISSIONARIES TRYING TO BRING THEIR STALE MORAL TEACHINGS TO HAPPY, LUSTFUL INDIGENOUS PEOPLES.
I'M SURE YOU KNOW WHAT YOU'RE DOING, BUT YOU'RE GETTING TO AN AGE... YET YOU ACT THE SAME AS YOU DID AT EIGHTEEN.
FSSSSS
AREN'T YOU TIRED OF BEING ALONE AT HOME, WITHOUT ANYONE TO SHARE YOUR DAY-TO-DAY LIFE WITH?
TAP TAP TAP
GOING OUT EVERY WEEKEND PURSUING NEW PREY, REPEATING THE SAME OLD LINES TO EACH NEW GIRL?
AND, AFTER A NIGHT OF FLEETING PASSION, FINDING YOURSELF ALONE IN YOUR BED ONCE AGAIN?
COUPLED-UP PEOPLE TEND TO GIVE LONG, CLICHÉ-RIDDEN SERMONS THAT MAKE US FEEL BETTER.
AND... SO... GROW UP, MAN. YOU'RE ALWAYS IN THE SAME PLACE WITH WOMEN.
WELL, THIS TIME THERE ARE TWO OF THEM. WE'RE GOING TO HAVE A THREESOME.
I THINK I'M HAVING A CRISIS OF FAITH.
DID YOU GO OUT WITH YOUR SINGLE BUDDIES AGAIN?

MANTERVENTION

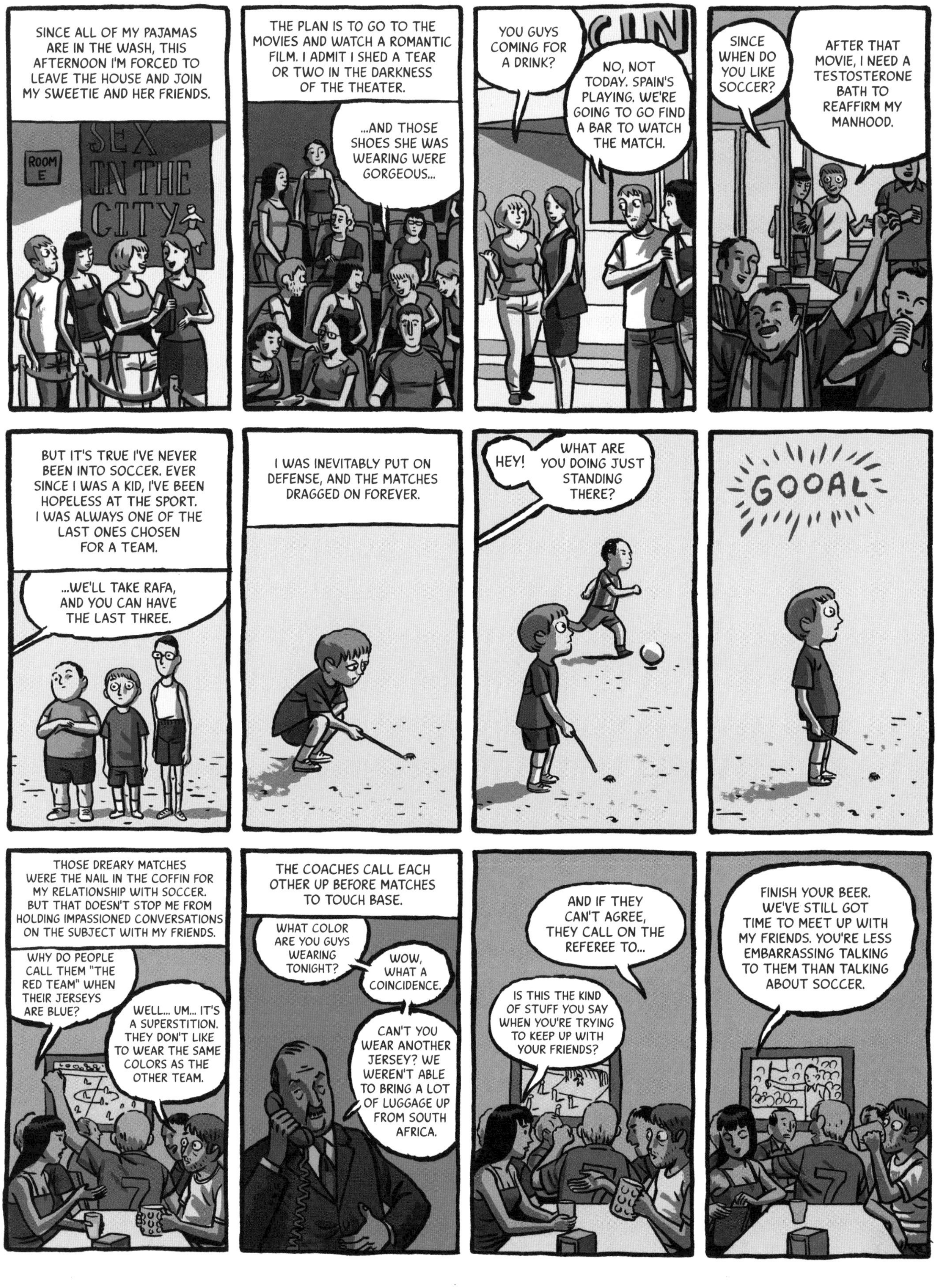
SINCE ALL OF MY PAJAMAS ARE IN THE WASH, THIS AFTERNOON I'M FORCED TO LEAVE THE HOUSE AND JOIN MY SWEETIE AND HER FRIENDS.
ROOM E
SEX IN THE CITY
THE PLAN IS TO GO TO THE MOVIES AND WATCH A ROMANTIC FILM. I ADMIT I SHED A TEAR OR TWO IN THE DARKNESS OF THE THEATER.
...AND THOSE SHOES SHE WAS WEARING WERE GORGEOUS...
YOU GUYS COMING FOR A DRINK?
NO, NOT TODAY. SPAIN'S PLAYING. WE'RE GOING TO GO FIND A BAR TO WATCH THE MATCH.
SINCE WHEN DO YOU LIKE SOCCER?
AFTER THAT MOVIE, I NEED A TESTOSTERONE BATH TO REAFFIRM MY MANHOOD.
BUT IT'S TRUE I'VE NEVER BEEN INTO SOCCER. EVER SINCE I WAS A KID, I'VE BEEN HOPELESS AT THE SPORT. I WAS ALWAYS ONE OF THE LAST ONES CHOSEN FOR A TEAM.
...WE'LL TAKE RAFA, AND YOU CAN HAVE THE LAST THREE.
I WAS INEVITABLY PUT ON DEFENSE, AND THE MATCHES DRAGGED ON FOREVER.
HEY!
WHAT ARE YOU DOING JUST STANDING THERE?
GOOAL
THOSE DREARY MATCHES WERE THE NAIL IN THE COFFIN FOR MY RELATIONSHIP WITH SOCCER. BUT THAT DOESN'T STOP ME FROM HOLDING IMPASSIONED CONVERSATIONS ON THE SUBJECT WITH MY FRIENDS.
WHY DO PEOPLE CALL THEM "THE RED TEAM" WHEN THEIR JERSEYS ARE BLUE?
WELL... UM... IT'S A SUPERSTITION. THEY DON'T LIKE TO WEAR THE SAME COLORS AS THE OTHER TEAM.
THE COACHES CALL EACH OTHER UP BEFORE MATCHES TO TOUCH BASE.
WHAT COLOR ARE YOU GUYS WEARING TONIGHT?
WOW, WHAT A COINCIDENCE.
CAN'T YOU WEAR ANOTHER JERSEY? WE WEREN'T ABLE TO BRING A LOT OF LUGGAGE UP FROM SOUTH AFRICA.
AND IF THEY CAN'T AGREE, THEY CALL ON THE REFEREE TO...
IS THIS THE KIND OF STUFF YOU SAY WHEN YOU'RE TRYING TO KEEP UP WITH YOUR FRIENDS?
FINISH YOUR BEER. WE'VE STILL GOT TIME TO MEET UP WITH MY FRIENDS. YOU'RE LESS EMBARRASSING TALKING TO THEM THAN TALKING ABOUT SOCCER.

CENSORED TALK

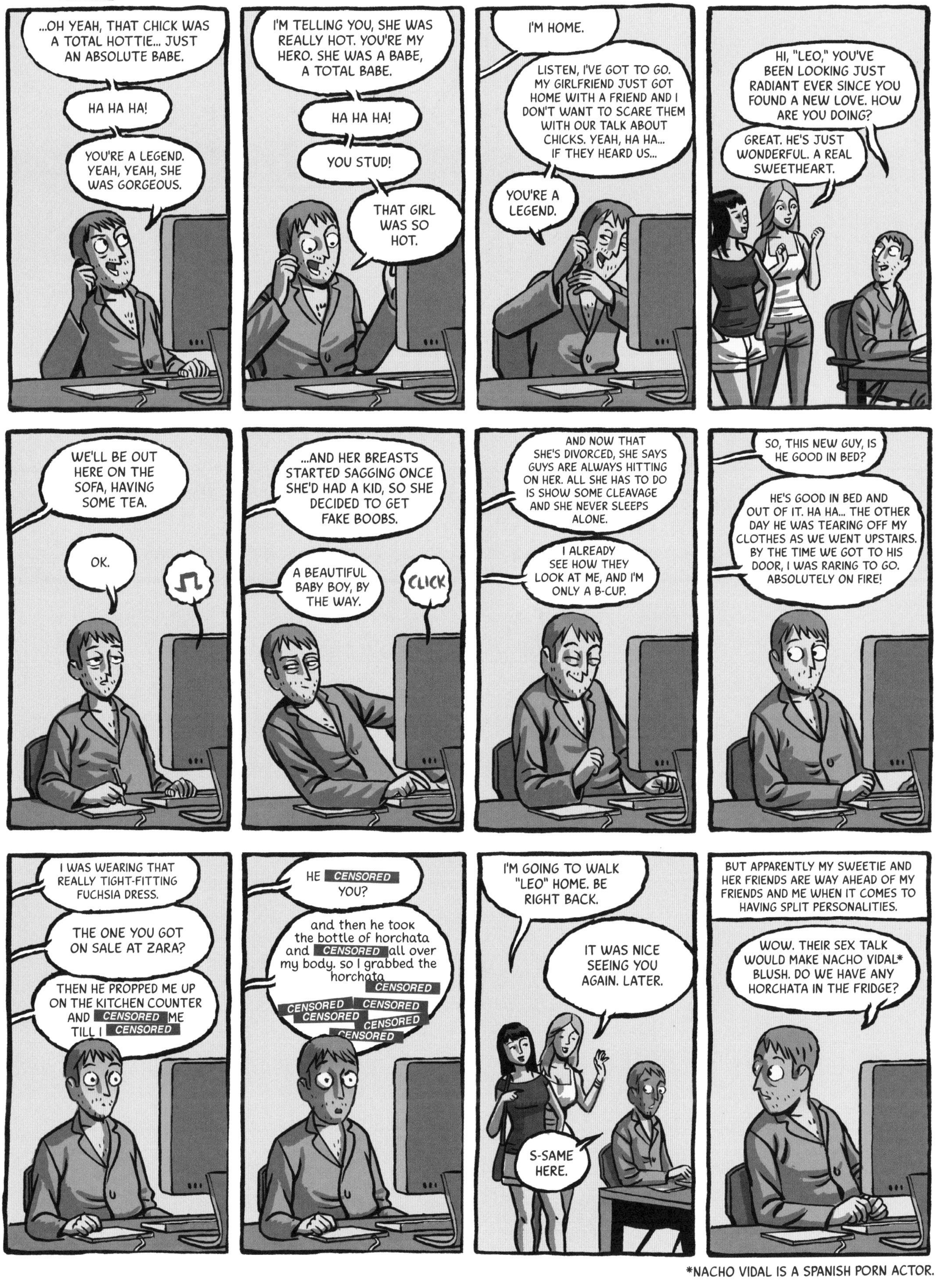

...OH YEAH, THAT CHICK WAS A TOTAL HOTTIE... JUST AN ABSOLUTE BABE.
HA HA HA!
YOU'RE A LEGEND. YEAH, YEAH, SHE WAS GORGEOUS.
I'M TELLING YOU, SHE WAS REALLY HOT. YOU'RE MY HERO. SHE WAS A BABE, A TOTAL BABE.
HA HA HA!
YOU STUD!
THAT GIRL WAS SO HOT.
I'M HOME.
LISTEN, I'VE GOT TO GO. MY GIRLFRIEND JUST GOT HOME WITH A FRIEND AND I DON'T WANT TO SCARE THEM WITH OUR TALK ABOUT CHICKS. YEAH, HA HA... IF THEY HEARD US...
YOU'RE A LEGEND.
HI, "LEO," YOU'VE BEEN LOOKING JUST RADIANT EVER SINCE YOU FOUND A NEW LOVE. HOW ARE YOU DOING?
GREAT. HE'S JUST WONDERFUL. A REAL SWEETHEART.
WE'LL BE OUT HERE ON THE SOFA, HAVING SOME TEA.
OK.
...AND HER BREASTS STARTED SAGGING ONCE SHE'D HAD A KID, SO SHE DECIDED TO GET FAKE BOOBS.
A BEAUTIFUL BABY BOY, BY THE WAY.
CLICK
AND NOW THAT SHE'S DIVORCED, SHE SAYS GUYS ARE ALWAYS HITTING ON HER. ALL SHE HAS TO DO IS SHOW SOME CLEAVAGE AND SHE NEVER SLEEPS ALONE.
I ALREADY SEE HOW THEY LOOK AT ME, AND I'M ONLY A B-CUP.
SO, THIS NEW GUY, IS HE GOOD IN BED?
HE'S GOOD IN BED AND OUT OF IT. HA HA... THE OTHER DAY HE WAS TEARING OFF MY CLOTHES AS WE WENT UPSTAIRS. BY THE TIME WE GOT TO HIS DOOR, I WAS RARING TO GO. ABSOLUTELY ON FIRE!
I WAS WEARING THAT REALLY TIGHT-FITTING FUCHSIA DRESS.
THE ONE YOU GOT ON SALE AT ZARA?
THEN HE PROPPED ME UP ON THE KITCHEN COUNTER AND CENSORED ME TILL I CENSORED
HE CENSORED YOU?
and then he took the bottle of horchata and CENSORED all over my body. so I grabbed the horchata CENSORED CENSORED CENSORED CENSORED CENSORED CENSORED
I'M GOING TO WALK "LEO" HOME. BE RIGHT BACK.
IT WAS NICE SEEING YOU AGAIN. LATER.
S-SAME HERE.
BUT APPARENTLY MY SWEETIE AND HER FRIENDS ARE WAY AHEAD OF MY FRIENDS AND ME WHEN IT COMES TO HAVING SPLIT PERSONALITIES.
WOW. THEIR SEX TALK WOULD MAKE NACHO VIDAL* BLUSH. DO WE HAVE ANY HORCHATA IN THE FRIDGE?

*NACHO VIDAL IS A SPANISH PORN ACTOR.

THE FEUD

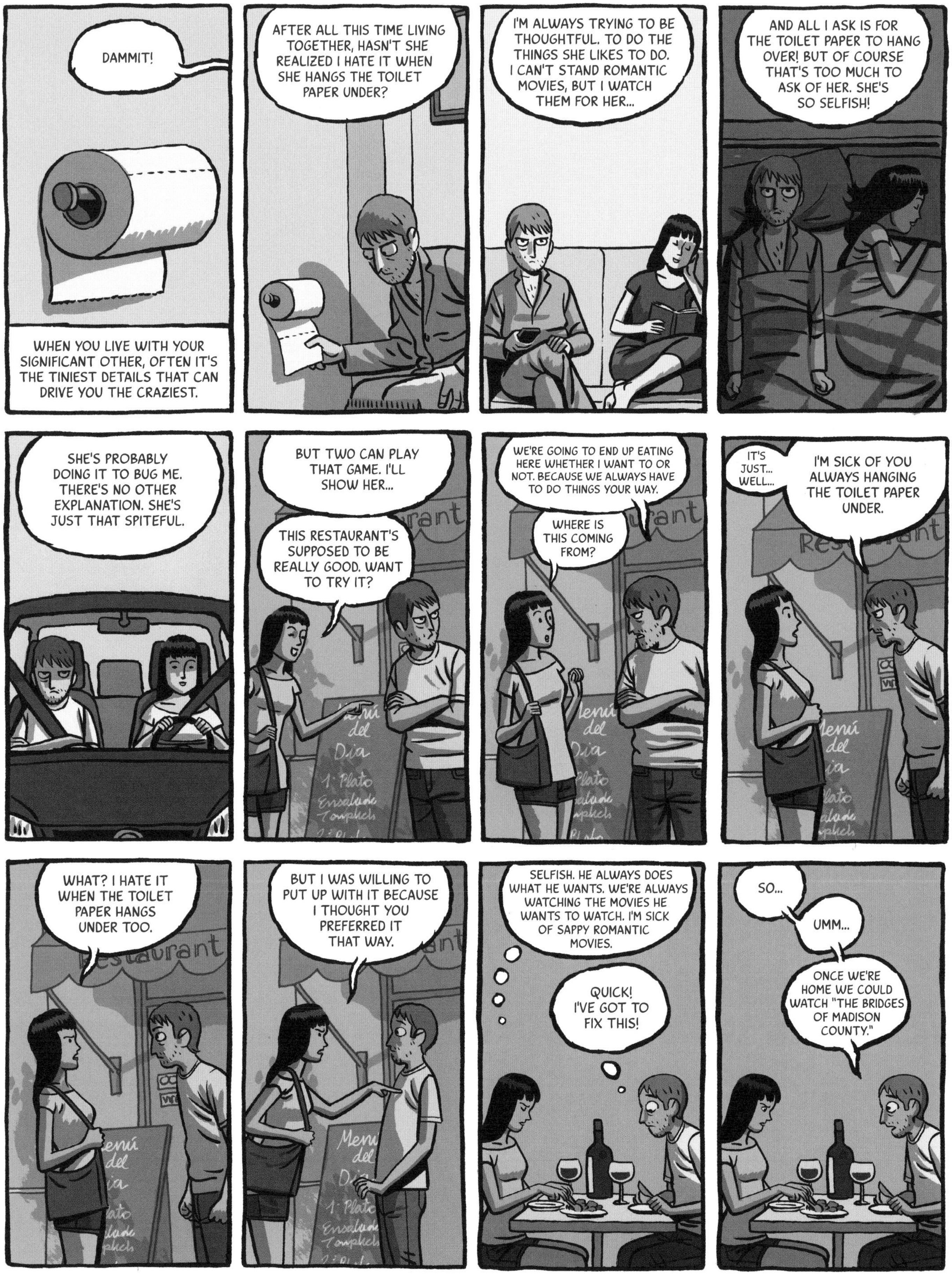
DAMMIT!
WHEN YOU LIVE WITH YOUR SIGNIFICANT OTHER, OFTEN IT'S THE TINIEST DETAILS THAT CAN DRIVE YOU THE CRAZIEST.
AFTER ALL THIS TIME LIVING TOGETHER, HASN'T SHE REALIZED I HATE IT WHEN SHE HANGS THE TOILET PAPER UNDER?
I'M ALWAYS TRYING TO BE THOUGHTFUL. TO DO THE THINGS SHE LIKES TO DO. I CAN'T STAND ROMANTIC MOVIES, BUT I WATCH THEM FOR HER...
AND ALL I ASK IS FOR THE TOILET PAPER TO HANG OVER! BUT OF COURSE THAT'S TOO MUCH TO ASK OF HER. SHE'S SO SELFISH!
SHE'S PROBABLY DOING IT TO BUG ME. THERE'S NO OTHER EXPLANATION. SHE'S JUST THAT SPITEFUL.
BUT TWO CAN PLAY THAT GAME. I'LL SHOW HER...
THIS RESTAURANT'S SUPPOSED TO BE REALLY GOOD. WANT TO TRY IT?
WE'RE GOING TO END UP EATING HERE WHETHER I WANT TO OR NOT. BECAUSE WE ALWAYS HAVE TO DO THINGS YOUR WAY.
WHERE IS THIS COMING FROM?
IT'S JUST... WELL...
I'M SICK OF YOU ALWAYS HANGING THE TOILET PAPER UNDER.
WHAT? I HATE IT WHEN THE TOILET PAPER HANGS UNDER TOO.
BUT I WAS WILLING TO PUT UP WITH IT BECAUSE I THOUGHT YOU PREFERRED IT THAT WAY.
SELFISH. HE ALWAYS DOES WHAT HE WANTS. WE'RE ALWAYS WATCHING THE MOVIES HE WANTS TO WATCH. I'M SICK OF SAPPY ROMANTIC MOVIES.
QUICK! I'VE GOT TO FIX THIS!
SO...
UMM...
ONCE WE'RE HOME WE COULD WATCH "THE BRIDGES OF MADISON COUNTY."

MY FRIENDS THE ELVES

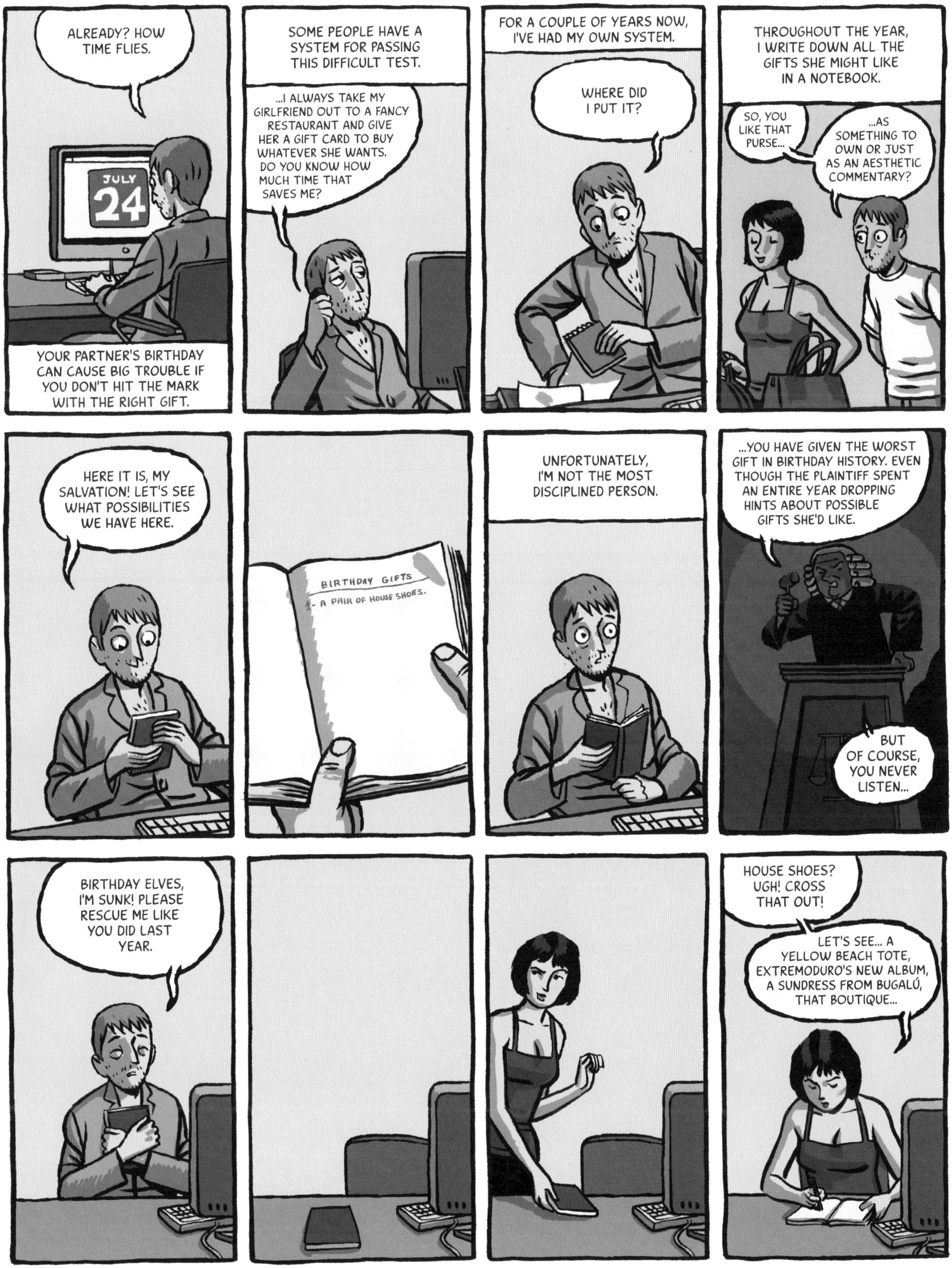

ALREADY? HOW TIME FLIES.
JULY
24
YOUR PARTNER'S BIRTHDAY CAN CAUSE BIG TROUBLE IF YOU DON'T HIT THE MARK WITH THE RIGHT GIFT.
SOME PEOPLE HAVE A SYSTEM FOR PASSING THIS DIFFICULT TEST.
...I ALWAYS TAKE MY GIRLFRIEND OUT TO A FANCY RESTAURANT AND GIVE HER A GIFT CARD TO BUY WHATEVER SHE WANTS. DO YOU KNOW HOW MUCH TIME THAT SAVES ME?
FOR A COUPLE OF YEARS NOW, I'VE HAD MY OWN SYSTEM.
WHERE DID I PUT IT?
THROUGHOUT THE YEAR, I WRITE DOWN ALL THE GIFTS SHE MIGHT LIKE IN A NOTEBOOK.
SO, YOU LIKE THAT PURSE...
...AS SOMETHING TO OWN OR JUST AS AN AESTHETIC COMMENTARY?
HERE IT IS, MY SALVATION! LET'S SEE WHAT POSSIBILITIES WE HAVE HERE.
BIRTHDAY GIFTS
1- A PAIR OF HOUSE SHOES.
UNFORTUNATELY, I'M NOT THE MOST DISCIPLINED PERSON.
...YOU HAVE GIVEN THE WORST GIFT IN BIRTHDAY HISTORY. EVEN THOUGH THE PLAINTIFF SPENT AN ENTIRE YEAR DROPPING HINTS ABOUT POSSIBLE GIFTS SHE'D LIKE.
BUT OF COURSE, YOU NEVER LISTEN...
BIRTHDAY ELVES, I'M SUNK! PLEASE RESCUE ME LIKE YOU DID LAST YEAR.
HOUSE SHOES? UGH! CROSS THAT OUT!
LET'S SEE... A YELLOW BEACH TOTE, EXTREMODURO'S NEW ALBUM, A SUNDRESS FROM BUGALÚ, THAT BOUTIQUE...

THE NEVER-ENDING JOURNEY

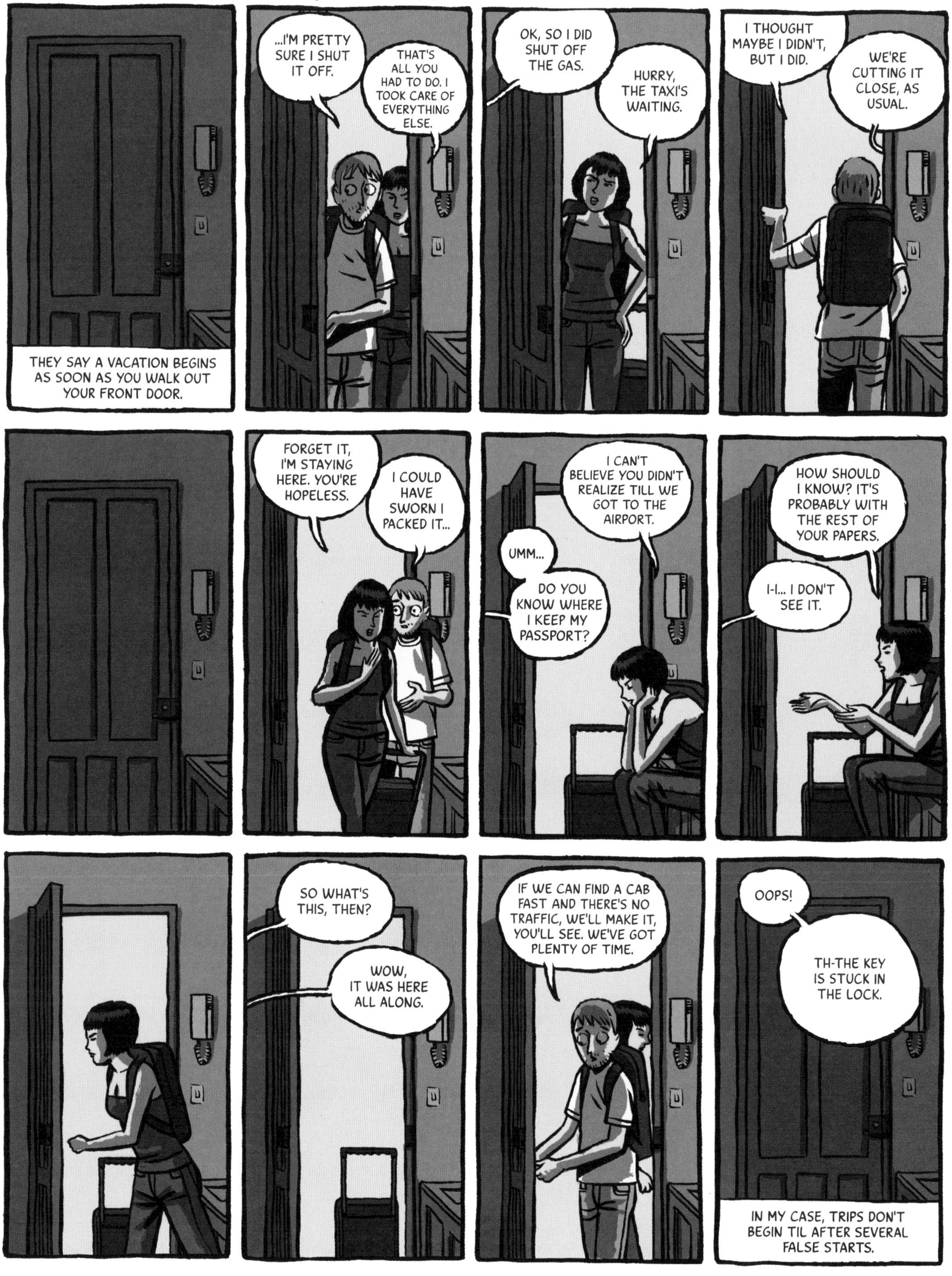

THEY SAY A VACATION BEGINS AS SOON AS YOU WALK OUT YOUR FRONT DOOR.
...I'M PRETTY SURE I SHUT IT OFF.
THAT'S ALL YOU HAD TO DO. I TOOK CARE OF EVERYTHING ELSE.
OK, SO I DID SHUT OFF THE GAS.
HURRY, THE TAXI'S WAITING.
I THOUGHT MAYBE I DIDN'T, BUT I DID.
WE'RE CUTTING IT CLOSE, AS USUAL.
FORGET IT, I'M STAYING HERE. YOU'RE HOPELESS.
I COULD HAVE SWORN I PACKED IT...
I CAN'T BELIEVE YOU DIDN'T REALIZE TILL WE GOT TO THE AIRPORT.
UMM...
DO YOU KNOW WHERE I KEEP MY PASSPORT?
HOW SHOULD I KNOW? IT'S PROBABLY WITH THE REST OF YOUR PAPERS.
I-I... I DON'T SEE IT.
SO WHAT'S THIS, THEN?
WOW, IT WAS HERE ALL ALONG.
IF WE CAN FIND A CAB FAST AND THERE'S NO TRAFFIC, WE'LL MAKE IT, YOU'LL SEE. WE'VE GOT PLENTY OF TIME.
OOPS!
TH-THE KEY IS STUCK IN THE LOCK.
IN MY CASE, TRIPS DON'T BEGIN TIL AFTER SEVERAL FALSE STARTS.

TIME TRAVEL

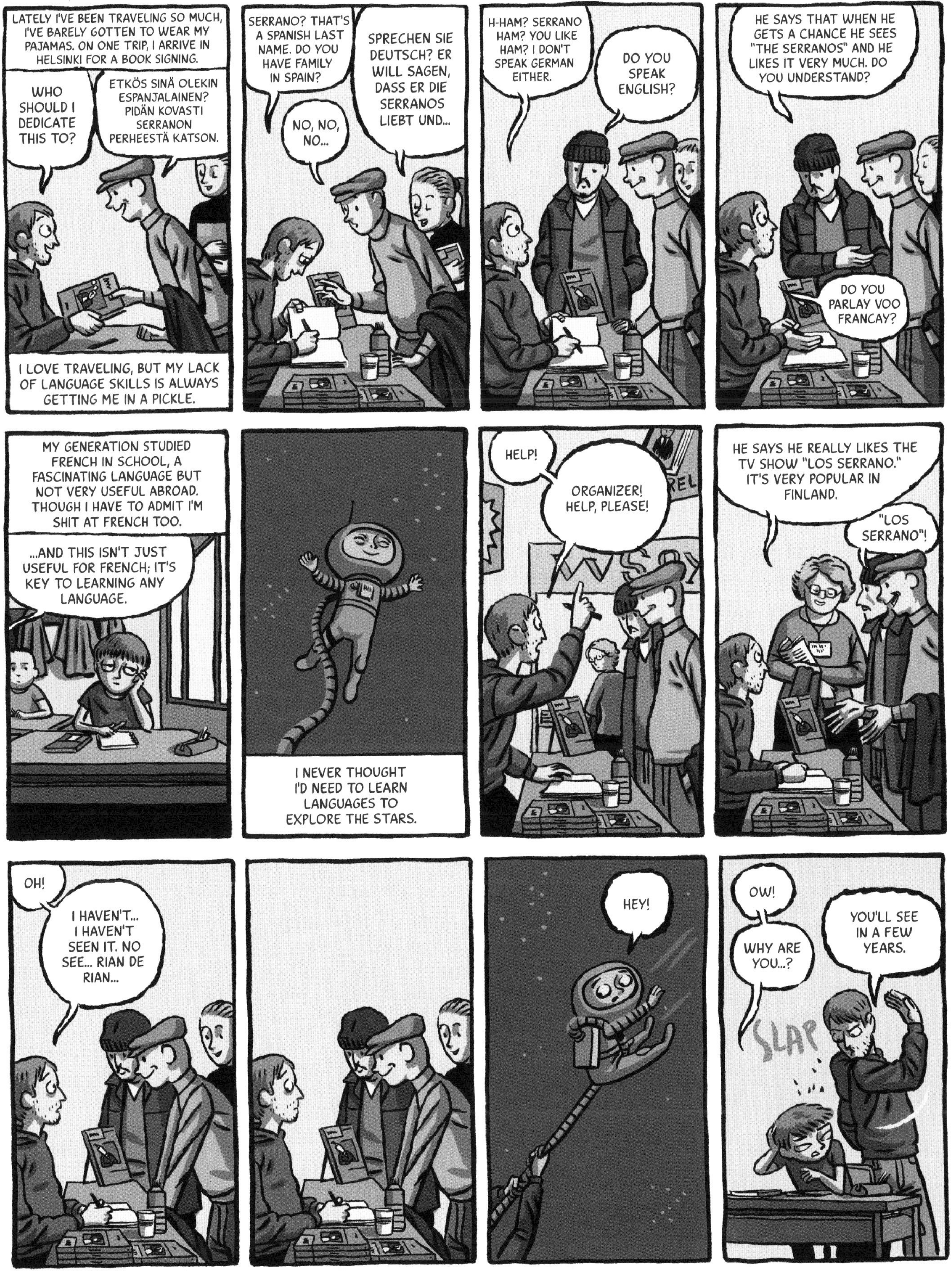
LATELY I'VE BEEN TRAVELING SO MUCH, I'VE BARELY GOTTEN TO WEAR MY PAJAMAS. ON ONE TRIP, I ARRIVE IN HELSINKI FOR A BOOK SIGNING.
WHO SHOULD I DEDICATE THIS TO?
ETKÖS SINÄ OLEKIN ESPANJALAINEN? PIDÄN KOVASTI SERRANON PERHEESTÄ KATSON.
I LOVE TRAVELING, BUT MY LACK OF LANGUAGE SKILLS IS ALWAYS GETTING ME IN A PICKLE.
SERRANO? THAT'S A SPANISH LAST NAME. DO YOU HAVE FAMILY IN SPAIN?
NO, NO, NO...
SPRECHEN SIE DEUTSCH? ER WILL SAGEN, DASS ER DIE SERRANOS LIEBT UND...
H-HAM? SERRANO HAM? YOU LIKE HAM? I DON'T SPEAK GERMAN EITHER.
DO YOU SPEAK ENGLISH?
HE SAYS THAT WHEN HE GETS A CHANCE HE SEES "THE SERRANOS" AND HE LIKES IT VERY MUCH. DO YOU UNDERSTAND?
DO YOU PARLAY VOO FRANCAY?
MY GENERATION STUDIED FRENCH IN SCHOOL, A FASCINATING LANGUAGE BUT NOT VERY USEFUL ABROAD. THOUGH I HAVE TO ADMIT I'M SHIT AT FRENCH TOO.
...AND THIS ISN'T JUST USEFUL FOR FRENCH; IT'S KEY TO LEARNING ANY LANGUAGE.
I NEVER THOUGHT I'D NEED TO LEARN LANGUAGES TO EXPLORE THE STARS.
HELP!
ORGANIZER! HELP, PLEASE!
HE SAYS HE REALLY LIKES THE TV SHOW "LOS SERRANO." IT'S VERY POPULAR IN FINLAND.
"LOS SERRANO"!
OH!
I HAVEN'T... I HAVEN'T SEEN IT. NO SEE... RIAN DE RIAN...
HEY!
OW!
WHY ARE YOU...?
YOU'LL SEE IN A FEW YEARS.
SLAP

CRACK

AFTER THE RADIO SHOW I'VE DONE EVERY FRIDAY FOR THE PAST FIFTEEN YEARS, WE USUALLY GO OUT TO EAT TOGETHER.

THERE'S ALWAYS AN EXTRA FRIEND WHO TAGS ALONG AT THE LAST MINUTE. THIS FRIDAY "SAGITTARIUS" HAS BROUGHT A BUDDY.

THE CHICK WAS A HOTTIE. SO I WENT UP AND OFFERED HER A DRINK.

THIS DUDE'S A LEGEND.

WE ENDED UP DOING IT RIGHT THERE IN THE CLUB BATHROOM.

THUMP THUMP THUMP

CENSORED CENSORED CENSORED CENSORED

HA HA HA...

DIDN'T I SAY HE'S A LEGEND? TOLD YOU.

SO THERE I WAS, POUNDING AWAY, HOLDING HER UP AGAINST THE WALL, BUT EVENTUALLY I STARTED GETTING WORN OUT.

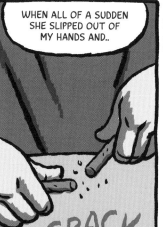

WHEN ALL OF A SUDDEN SHE SLIPPED OUT OF MY HANDS AND..

CRACK

YOUR... IT...

NO, NO WAY!

YOU BROKE IT?

I PASSED OUT RIGHT THERE.

I SWEAR, I'D NEVER FELT PAIN LIKE THAT BEFORE.

WHEN I CAME TO, I WAS SURROUNDED BY PARAMEDICS. THEY RUSHED ME OUT OF THE CLUB.

...THERE'S NO TIME TO GET HIM TO THE HOSPITAL. WE'VE GOT TO CUT OPEN HIS PENIS RIGHT HERE OR IT'LL BURST.

I GOT FIFTEEN STITCHES AND THEY NEARLY HAD TO AMPUTATE. RUPTURE OF THE CORPUS CAVERNOSUM WITH CONCOMITANT URETHRAL INJURY. I'VE BEEN DRUGGED UP FOR WEEKS. YOU CAN'T IMAGINE HOW MUCH IT HURTS.

...I DON'T KNOW WHAT'S UP WITH HIM, GIRL, BUT FOR WEEKS NOW WE'VE ONLY BEEN DOING IT MISSIONARY STYLE, AND SO GENTLY IT'S LIKE I'M FUCKING A TELETUBBY.

THE CHANGE

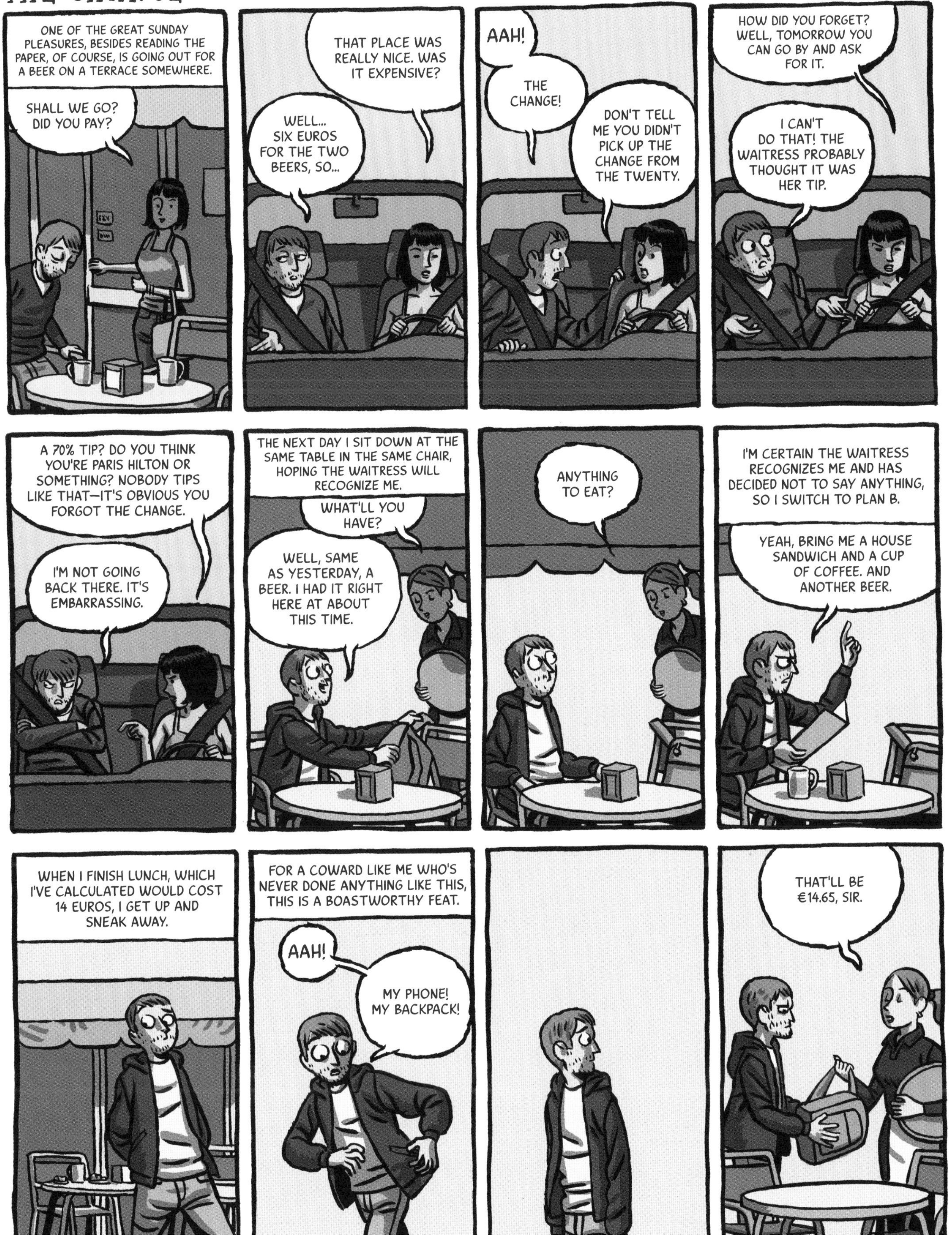

ONE OF THE GREAT SUNDAY PLEASURES, BESIDES READING THE PAPER, OF COURSE, IS GOING OUT FOR A BEER ON A TERRACE SOMEWHERE.
SHALL WE GO? DID YOU PAY?
THAT PLACE WAS REALLY NICE. WAS IT EXPENSIVE?
WELL... SIX EUROS FOR THE TWO BEERS, SO...
AAH!
THE CHANGE!
DON'T TELL ME YOU DIDN'T PICK UP THE CHANGE FROM THE TWENTY.
HOW DID YOU FORGET? WELL, TOMORROW YOU CAN GO BY AND ASK FOR IT.
I CAN'T DO THAT! THE WAITRESS PROBABLY THOUGHT IT WAS HER TIP.
A 70% TIP? DO YOU THINK YOU'RE PARIS HILTON OR SOMETHING? NOBODY TIPS LIKE THAT—IT'S OBVIOUS YOU FORGOT THE CHANGE.
I'M NOT GOING BACK THERE. IT'S EMBARRASSING.
THE NEXT DAY I SIT DOWN AT THE SAME TABLE IN THE SAME CHAIR, HOPING THE WAITRESS WILL RECOGNIZE ME.
WHAT'LL YOU HAVE?
WELL, SAME AS YESTERDAY, A BEER. I HAD IT RIGHT HERE AT ABOUT THIS TIME.
ANYTHING TO EAT?
I'M CERTAIN THE WAITRESS RECOGNIZES ME AND HAS DECIDED NOT TO SAY ANYTHING, SO I SWITCH TO PLAN B.
YEAH, BRING ME A HOUSE SANDWICH AND A CUP OF COFFEE. AND ANOTHER BEER.
WHEN I FINISH LUNCH, WHICH I'VE CALCULATED WOULD COST 14 EUROS, I GET UP AND SNEAK AWAY.
FOR A COWARD LIKE ME WHO'S NEVER DONE ANYTHING LIKE THIS, THIS IS A BOASTWORTHY FEAT.
AAH!
MY PHONE! MY BACKPACK!
THAT'LL BE €14.65, SIR.

THE SUIT

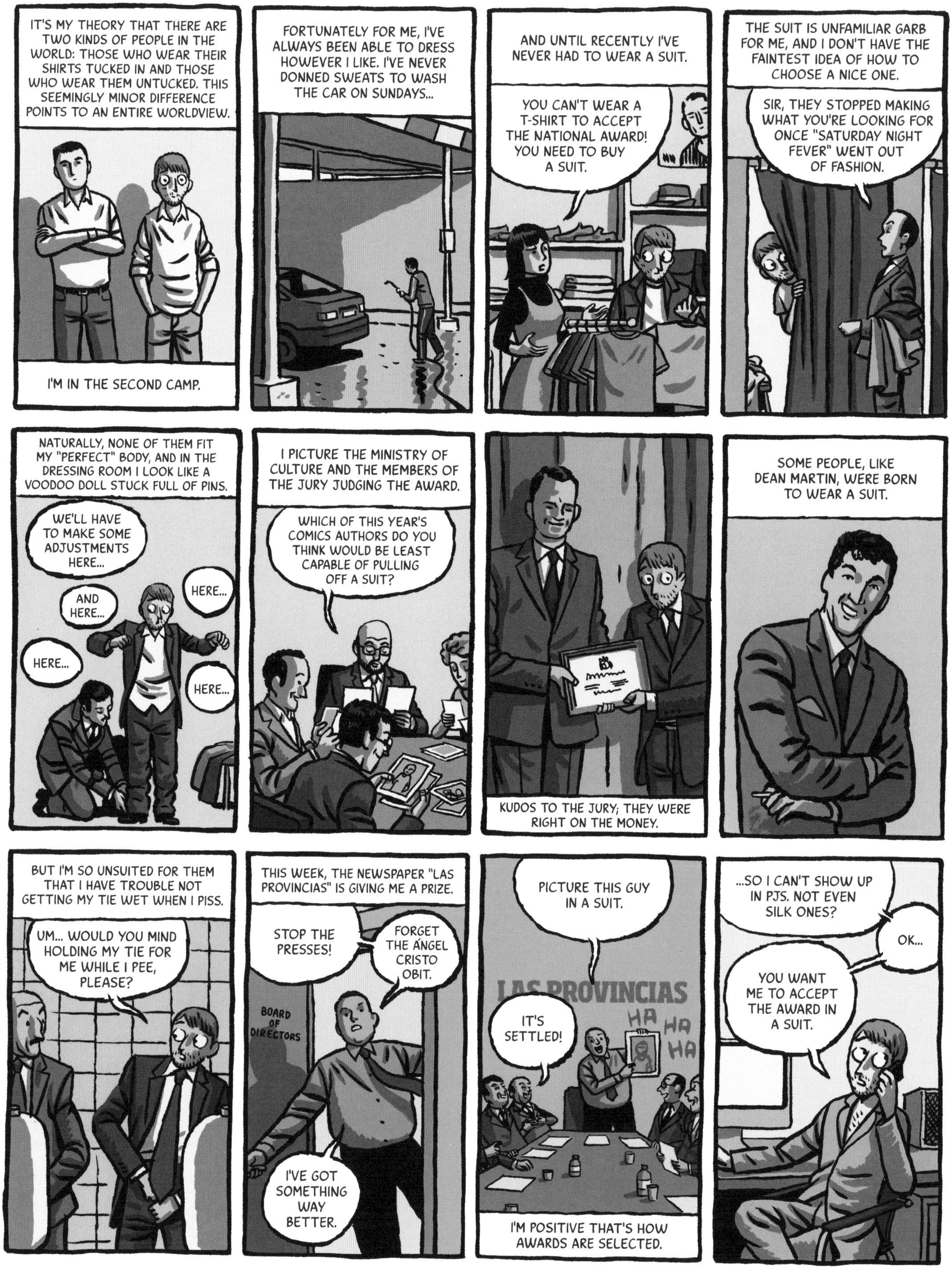
IT'S MY THEORY THAT THERE ARE TWO KINDS OF PEOPLE IN THE WORLD: THOSE WHO WEAR THEIR SHIRTS TUCKED IN AND THOSE WHO WEAR THEM UNTUCKED. THIS SEEMINGLY MINOR DIFFERENCE POINTS TO AN ENTIRE WORLDVIEW.
I'M IN THE SECOND CAMP.
FORTUNATELY FOR ME, I'VE ALWAYS BEEN ABLE TO DRESS HOWEVER I LIKE. I'VE NEVER DONNED SWEATS TO WASH THE CAR ON SUNDAYS...
AND UNTIL RECENTLY I'VE NEVER HAD TO WEAR A SUIT.
YOU CAN'T WEAR A T-SHIRT TO ACCEPT THE NATIONAL AWARD! YOU NEED TO BUY A SUIT.
THE SUIT IS UNFAMILIAR GARB FOR ME, AND I DON'T HAVE THE FAINTEST IDEA OF HOW TO CHOOSE A NICE ONE.
SIR, THEY STOPPED MAKING WHAT YOU'RE LOOKING FOR ONCE "SATURDAY NIGHT FEVER" WENT OUT OF FASHION.
NATURALLY, NONE OF THEM FIT MY "PERFECT" BODY, AND IN THE DRESSING ROOM I LOOK LIKE A VOODOO DOLL STUCK FULL OF PINS.
WE'LL HAVE TO MAKE SOME ADJUSTMENTS HERE...
AND HERE...
HERE...
HERE...
HERE...
I PICTURE THE MINISTRY OF CULTURE AND THE MEMBERS OF THE JURY JUDGING THE AWARD.
WHICH OF THIS YEAR'S COMICS AUTHORS DO YOU THINK WOULD BE LEAST CAPABLE OF PULLING OFF A SUIT?
KUDOS TO THE JURY; THEY WERE RIGHT ON THE MONEY.
SOME PEOPLE, LIKE DEAN MARTIN, WERE BORN TO WEAR A SUIT.
BUT I'M SO UNSUITED FOR THEM THAT I HAVE TROUBLE NOT GETTING MY TIE WET WHEN I PISS.
UM... WOULD YOU MIND HOLDING MY TIE FOR ME WHILE I PEE, PLEASE?
THIS WEEK, THE NEWSPAPER "LAS PROVINCIAS" IS GIVING ME A PRIZE.
STOP THE PRESSES!
FORGET THE ÁNGEL CRISTO OBIT.
BOARD OF DIRECTORS
I'VE GOT SOMETHING WAY BETTER.
PICTURE THIS GUY IN A SUIT.
LAS PROVINCIAS
IT'S SETTLED!
HA HA HA
I'M POSITIVE THAT'S HOW AWARDS ARE SELECTED.
...SO I CAN'T SHOW UP IN PJS. NOT EVEN SILK ONES?
OK...
YOU WANT ME TO ACCEPT THE AWARD IN A SUIT.

STOP THE TRAIN!

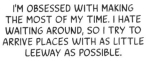

I'M OBSESSED WITH MAKING THE MOST OF MY TIME. I HATE WAITING AROUND, SO I TRY TO ARRIVE PLACES WITH AS LITTLE LEEWAY AS POSSIBLE.

...WEREN'T YOU SUPPOSED TO CATCH A TRAIN THIS MORNING?

WHAT TIME IS IT?

OBVIOUSLY THIS OBSESSION HAS LED ME TO MISS SEVERAL TRAINS AND THE OCCASIONAL FLIGHT. BUT TODAY IT'S REALLY IMPORTANT TO ARRIVE ON TIME. I HAVE A BOOK SIGNING IN MADRID, AND IT WOULD BE UNFORGIVABLE NOT TO SHOW UP.

SHIT! SHIT!

SHIT, I'M GOING TO MISS IT. SOME LEEWAY WOULD BE HANDY RIGHT NOW.

OOF! I'M THE LAST TO BOARD, RIGHT? T-TIME G-GOT AWAY FROM ME AND I ALMOST DIDN'T MAKE IT.

YOU'RE IN PLENTY OF TIME, SIR. A WHOLE DAY EARLY, IN FACT. THESE TICKETS ARE FOR THE 20TH, AND TODAY IS THE 19TH.

TH-THAT'S IMPOSSIBLE. I HAVE A BOOK SIGNING TODAY IN MADRID AND... THEY MUST HAVE MADE A MISTAKE WITH THE TICKETS. I HAVE TO BE ON THAT TRAIN. I CAN'T MISS MY OWN BOOK SIGNING.

RUN OVER TO THE TICKET COUNTER AND TELL THEM TO EXCHANGE IT. NOT JUST ANY COUNTER, THE ONE FOR IMMINENT DEPARTURES. HURRY!

W- WHERE?

COME WITH ME, QUICK. I'LL TELL THE CONDUCTOR TO WAIT A MINUTE.

THE LINE IS HUGE! YOU'LL NEVER MAKE IT, SON. MAYBE WE CAN...

EXCUSE ME, PAULA. THIS GENTLEMAN NEEDS TO BE ON THE TRAIN THAT'S ABOUT TO LEAVE AND WE NEED TO EXCHANGE HIS TICKET.

THE QUICKEST WAY IS TO GO TO CUSTOMER SERVICE AND TALK TO SONIA.

I'LL GO WITH YOU AND TALK TO HER TO SPEED THINGS ALONG SO YOU DON'T HAVE TO WAIT.

THE TRAIN'S WAITING, BUT JUST FOR A MINUTE.

I-I HAVE AN IMPORTANT BOOK SIGNING TONIGHT AND I CAN'T MISS IT.

...THE TRAIN IS WAITING, BUT IT NEEDS TO LEAVE ASAP.

THERE'S BEEN A MISTAKE. HE'S GOT A TICKET FOR TOMORROW AND...

ELENA, QUICK, CHANGE THIS TICKET FOR THE TRAIN THAT'S WAITING ON THE TRACK.

SO, I NEED TO CHANGE THE TICKET FOR THE 20TH TO THE TRAIN FOR TODAY, THE 19TH, RIGHT?

YES, I-I'VE GOT A VERY IMPORTANT BOOK SIGNING TONIGHT IN MADRID. I-I CAN'T MISS IT A-AND I GOT ISSUED A TICKET FOR THE 20TH...

...AND LOOK, THE EVENT AT THE FNAC ON CALLAO IS ON...

THE 20...

UM...

IS THERE A BACK WAY OUT?

41

ONE NUMBER 7 RIGHT HERE...

FOR ME, ONE OF THE MEALS I FIND MOST STRESSFUL TO EAT IS THE COMBINATION PLATTER.

THE DIVINE SALVADOR DALÍ ONCE SAID SOMETHING ALONG THE LINES OF THAT THE WAY WE EAT INDICATES OUR APPROACH TO LIFE.

SOME PEOPLE EAT ENTHUSIASTICALLY AND TAKE LIFE ON IN A PASSIONATE, NO-HOLDS-BARRED MANNER.

OTHERS ARE MORE FINICKY AT MEALTIME, AND THEIR LIVES ARE FULL OF QUIRKS AND OBSESSIONS.

AND SOME PEOPLE ARE TOTAL SLOBS WITH FOOD. THEY LIVE LAWLESSLY AND IN CONSTANT EXISTENTIAL CHAOS.

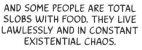

MY APPROACH TO THE COMBINATION PLATTER IS A GOOD INDICATOR OF MY WORLDVIEW TOO. FIRST I CAST AN ANALYTICAL EYE OVER THE PLATE.

ONCE ALL OF THE ELEMENTS HAVE BEEN IDENTIFIED, I START BY EATING THE ONE I LIKE LEAST. IN THIS CASE, BROCCOLI.

ONCE BROCCOLI HAS BEEN ELIMINATED FROM THE EQUATION, I TALLY UP THE REST IN MY HEAD.

15 FRENCH FRIES.

4 SLICES OF EGGPLANT.

2 MUSHROOMS.

STEAK. 10 SLICES WORTH.

EACH BITE IS THE EQUIVALENT OF 1 PART OF STEAK, 1.5 OF FRENCH FRIES, .4 OF EGGPLANT, AND .2 OF MUSHROOM.

NATURALLY, I PROCEED BY SELECTING THE WORST BITS AT THE BEGINNING AND SAVE THE BEST FOR MY VERY LAST BITE. THE FINAL PRIZE.

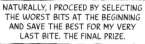

THESE KINDS OF THINGS SHOULD MAKE ME RECONSIDER MY APPROACH TO LIFE.

ALL YOU CAN EAT

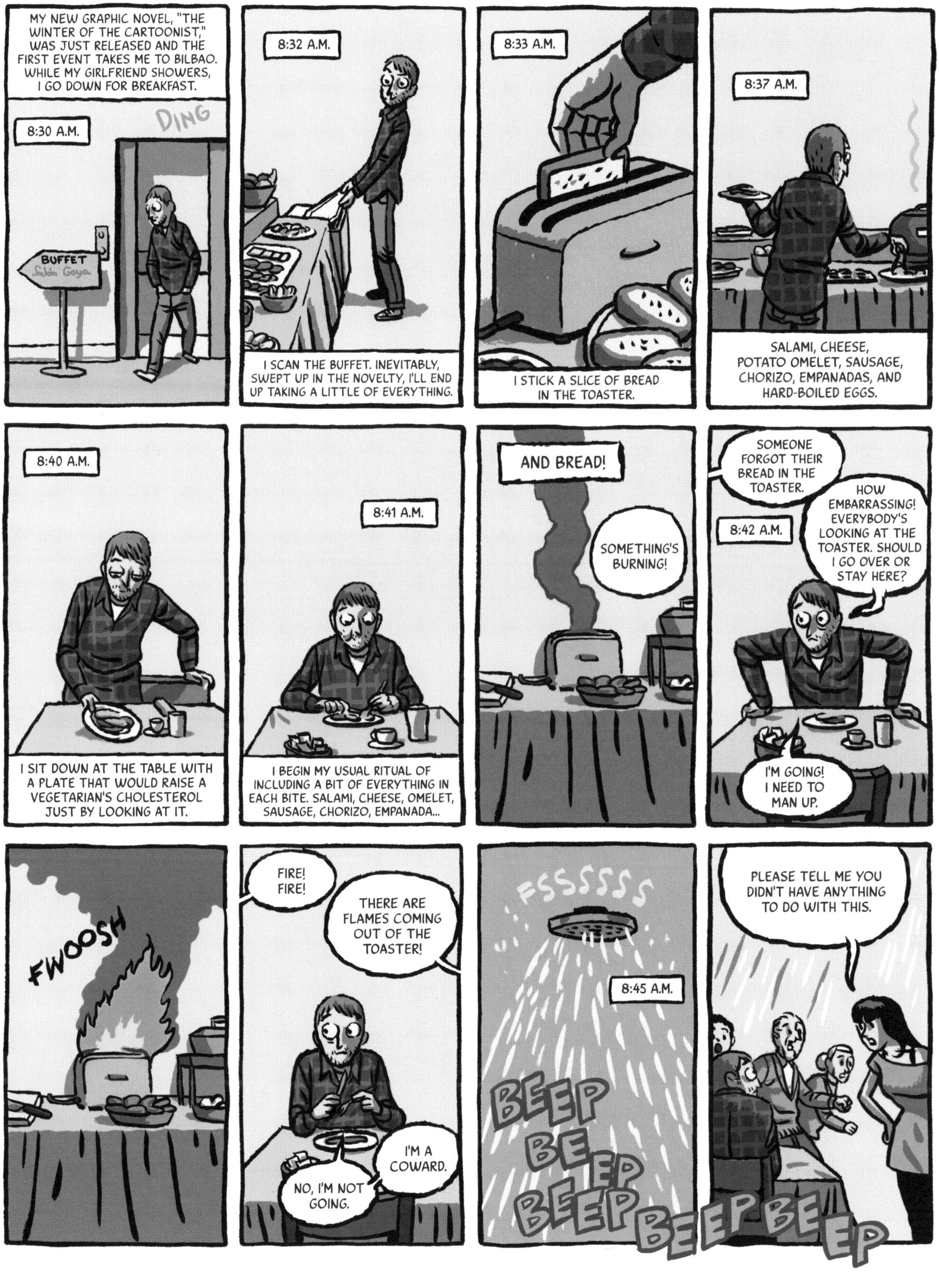

MY NEW GRAPHIC NOVEL, "THE WINTER OF THE CARTOONIST," WAS JUST RELEASED AND THE FIRST EVENT TAKES ME TO BILBAO. WHILE MY GIRLFRIEND SHOWERS, I GO DOWN FOR BREAKFAST.
8:30 A.M.
DING
BUFFET
Salón Goya
8:32 A.M.
I SCAN THE BUFFET. INEVITABLY, SWEPT UP IN THE NOVELTY, I'LL END UP TAKING A LITTLE OF EVERYTHING.
8:33 A.M.
I STICK A SLICE OF BREAD IN THE TOASTER.
8:37 A.M.
SALAMI, CHEESE, POTATO OMELET, SAUSAGE, CHORIZO, EMPANADAS, AND HARD-BOILED EGGS.
8:40 A.M.
I SIT DOWN AT THE TABLE WITH A PLATE THAT WOULD RAISE A VEGETARIAN'S CHOLESTEROL JUST BY LOOKING AT IT.
8:41 A.M.
I BEGIN MY USUAL RITUAL OF INCLUDING A BIT OF EVERYTHING IN EACH BITE. SALAMI, CHEESE, OMELET, SAUSAGE, CHORIZO, EMPANADA...
AND BREAD!
SOMETHING'S BURNING!
SOMEONE FORGOT THEIR BREAD IN THE TOASTER.
8:42 A.M.
HOW EMBARRASSING! EVERYBODY'S LOOKING AT THE TOASTER. SHOULD I GO OVER OR STAY HERE?
I'M GOING! I NEED TO MAN UP.
FWOOSH
FIRE! FIRE!
THERE ARE FLAMES COMING OUT OF THE TOASTER!
I'M A COWARD.
NO, I'M NOT GOING.
FSSSSSS
8:45 A.M.
BEEP BEEP BEEP BEEP BEEP BEEP
PLEASE TELL ME YOU DIDN'T HAVE ANYTHING TO DO WITH THIS.

DO YOUR LEAST

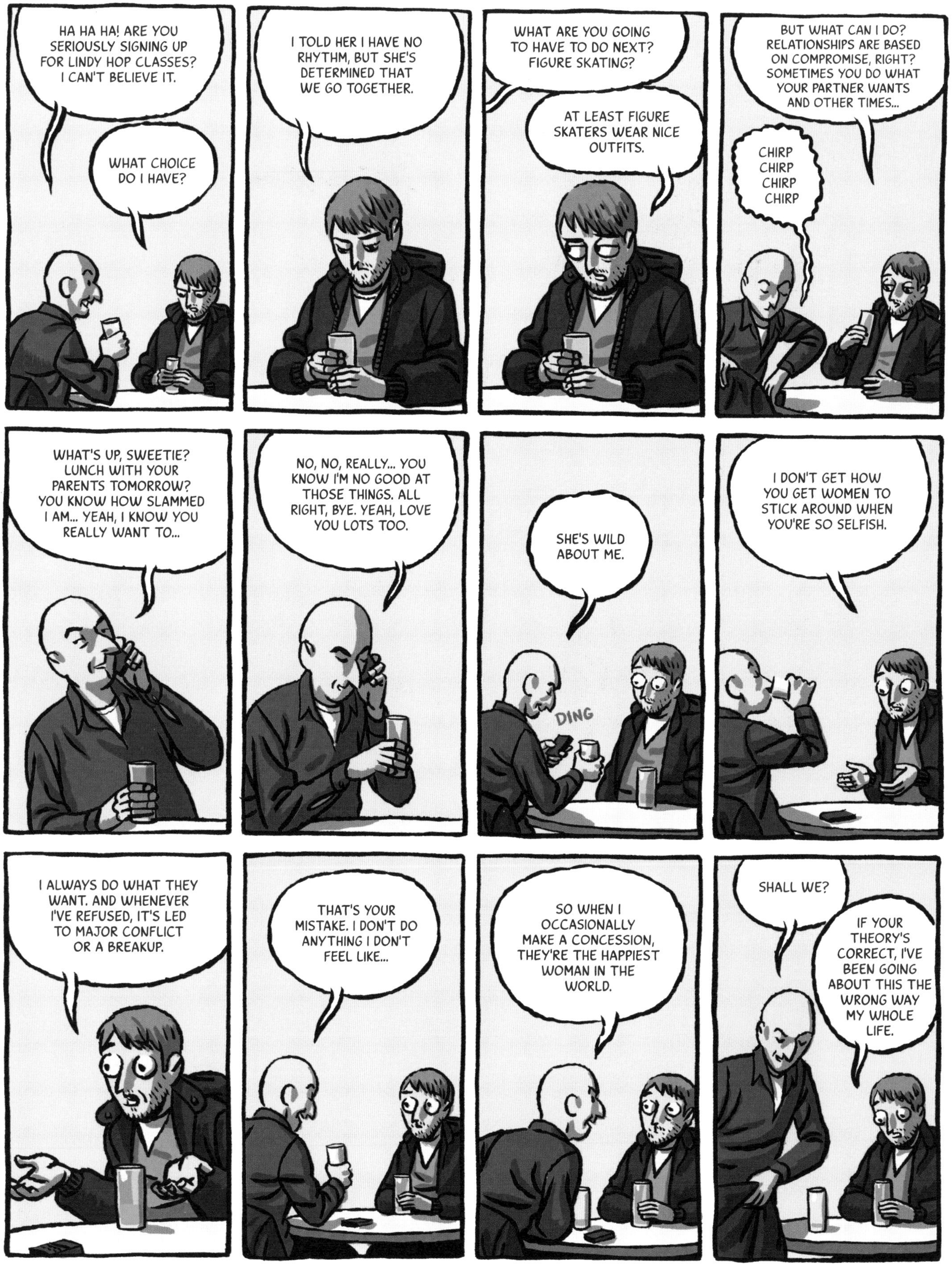

HA HA HA! ARE YOU SERIOUSLY SIGNING UP FOR LINDY HOP CLASSES? I CAN'T BELIEVE IT.
WHAT CHOICE DO I HAVE?
I TOLD HER I HAVE NO RHYTHM, BUT SHE'S DETERMINED THAT WE GO TOGETHER.
WHAT ARE YOU GOING TO HAVE TO DO NEXT? FIGURE SKATING?
AT LEAST FIGURE SKATERS WEAR NICE OUTFITS.
BUT WHAT CAN I DO? RELATIONSHIPS ARE BASED ON COMPROMISE, RIGHT? SOMETIMES YOU DO WHAT YOUR PARTNER WANTS AND OTHER TIMES...
CHIRP CHIRP CHIRP CHIRP
WHAT'S UP, SWEETIE? LUNCH WITH YOUR PARENTS TOMORROW? YOU KNOW HOW SLAMMED I AM... YEAH, I KNOW YOU REALLY WANT TO...
NO, NO, REALLY... YOU KNOW I'M NO GOOD AT THOSE THINGS. ALL RIGHT, BYE. YEAH, LOVE YOU LOTS TOO.
DING
SHE'S WILD ABOUT ME.
I DON'T GET HOW YOU GET WOMEN TO STICK AROUND WHEN YOU'RE SO SELFISH.
I ALWAYS DO WHAT THEY WANT. AND WHENEVER I'VE REFUSED, IT'S LED TO MAJOR CONFLICT OR A BREAKUP.
THAT'S YOUR MISTAKE. I DON'T DO ANYTHING I DON'T FEEL LIKE...
SO WHEN I OCCASIONALLY MAKE A CONCESSION, THEY'RE THE HAPPIEST WOMAN IN THE WORLD.
SHALL WE?
IF YOUR THEORY'S CORRECT, I'VE BEEN GOING ABOUT THIS THE WRONG WAY MY WHOLE LIFE.

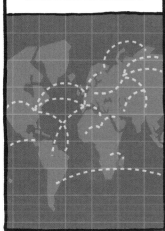

ON OUR PLANET, THERE'S ONE TYPE OF CIRCULATION THAT OUTMATCHES AIR TRAFFIC IN VOLUME AND COMPLEXITY.

...NO, MA, I ONLY HAVE THREE TUPPERWARE CONTAINERS. LIKE I SAID...

IN THE FREEZER? WHY WOULD I HAVE ONE IN THE FREEZER?

WOW, YOU WERE RIGHT. IT'S THE PAELLA YOU GAVE ME LAST WEEK.

MOTHERS HAVE DEVELOPED A KEENLY HONED SENSE ABOUT THEIR TUPPERWARE.

...THREE HEADING BACK HOME, READY FOR REFUELING.

ONE OF STUFFED PEPPERS IS TAKING OFF. RED LID.

THEY KNOW WHERE THEY ARE AT EVERY MOMENT, AND IT'S RARE THAT ONE GOES MISSING.

EVERY DAY MILLIONS OF PLASTIC CONTAINERS MOVE AROUND THE WORLD, BEING FILLED BY MOTHERS OR EMPTIED BY THEIR CHILDREN.

MOST OF US CHILDREN DON'T EVEN KNOW WHERE TO BUY THEM...

...THE BRAINCHILD OF INVENTOR EARL TUPPER AND SALESWOMAN BROWNIE WISE, THE MOTHERS OF THE WORLD HAVE GIVEN THIS CREATION A USE BEYOND MERELY TRANSPORTING FOOD.

...AND THIS ONE IS LASAGNA.

IF YOU DON'T EAT IT THIS WEEK, FREEZE IT.

MUAH

MOTHERS USE TUPPERWARE TO SEE MORE OF THEIR CHILDREN.

AND COME BACK ON TUESDAY FOR SOME RICE CASSEROLE.

THE SEATMATE

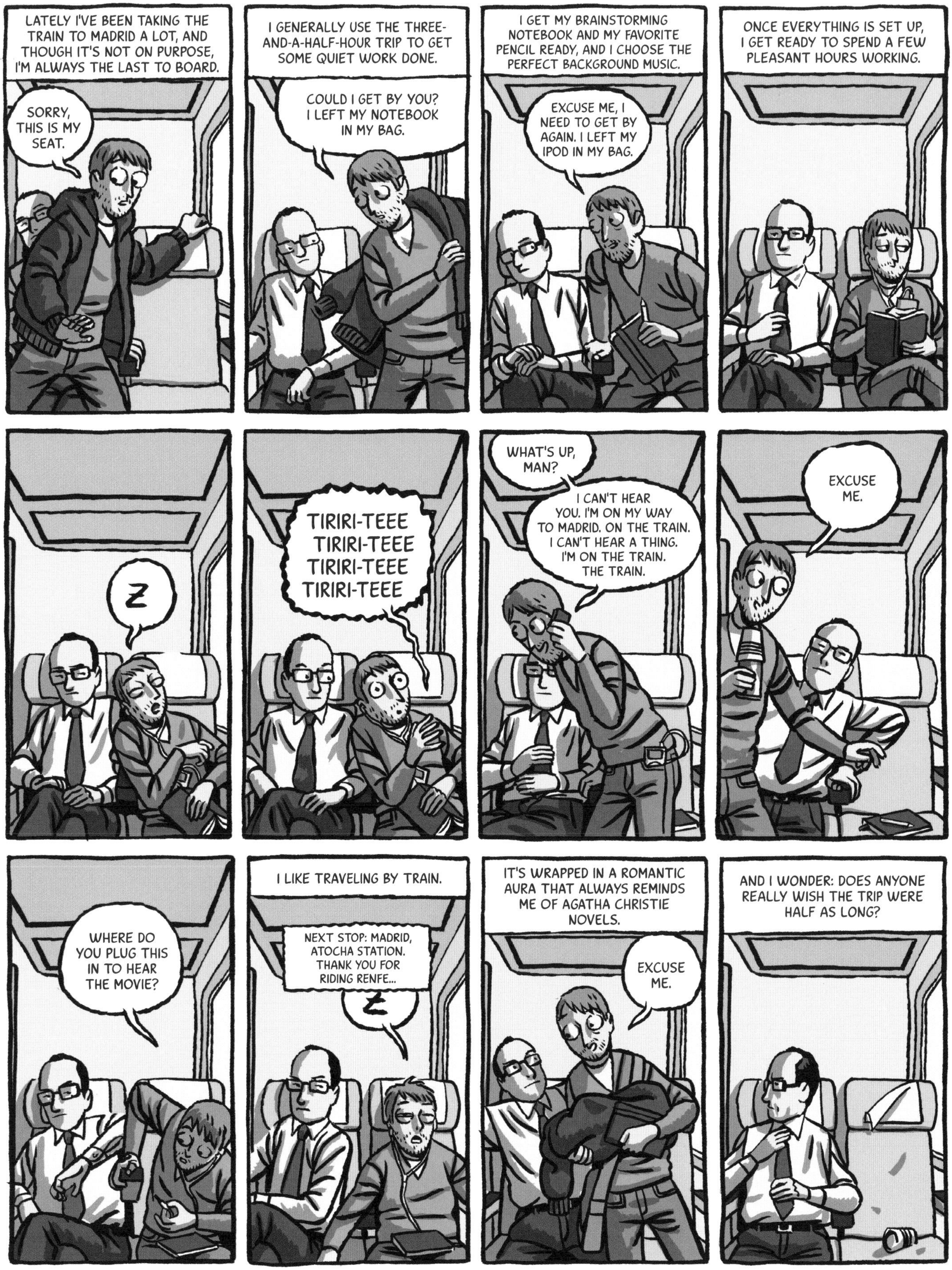

LATELY I'VE BEEN TAKING THE TRAIN TO MADRID A LOT, AND THOUGH IT'S NOT ON PURPOSE, I'M ALWAYS THE LAST TO BOARD.
SORRY, THIS IS MY SEAT.
I GENERALLY USE THE THREE-AND-A-HALF-HOUR TRIP TO GET SOME QUIET WORK DONE.
COULD I GET BY YOU? I LEFT MY NOTEBOOK IN MY BAG.
I GET MY BRAINSTORMING NOTEBOOK AND MY FAVORITE PENCIL READY, AND I CHOOSE THE PERFECT BACKGROUND MUSIC.
EXCUSE ME, I NEED TO GET BY AGAIN. I LEFT MY IPOD IN MY BAG.
ONCE EVERYTHING IS SET UP, I GET READY TO SPEND A FEW PLEASANT HOURS WORKING.
Z
TIRIRI-TEEE TIRIRI-TEEE TIRIRI-TEEE TIRIRI-TEEE
WHAT'S UP, MAN?
I CAN'T HEAR YOU. I'M ON MY WAY TO MADRID. ON THE TRAIN. I CAN'T HEAR A THING. I'M ON THE TRAIN. THE TRAIN.
EXCUSE ME.
WHERE DO YOU PLUG THIS IN TO HEAR THE MOVIE?
I LIKE TRAVELING BY TRAIN.
NEXT STOP: MADRID, ATOCHA STATION. THANK YOU FOR RIDING RENFE...
Z
IT'S WRAPPED IN A ROMANTIC AURA THAT ALWAYS REMINDS ME OF AGATHA CHRISTIE NOVELS.
EXCUSE ME.
AND I WONDER: DOES ANYONE REALLY WISH THE TRIP WERE HALF AS LONG?

THE IMPORTANCE OF MEMORIES

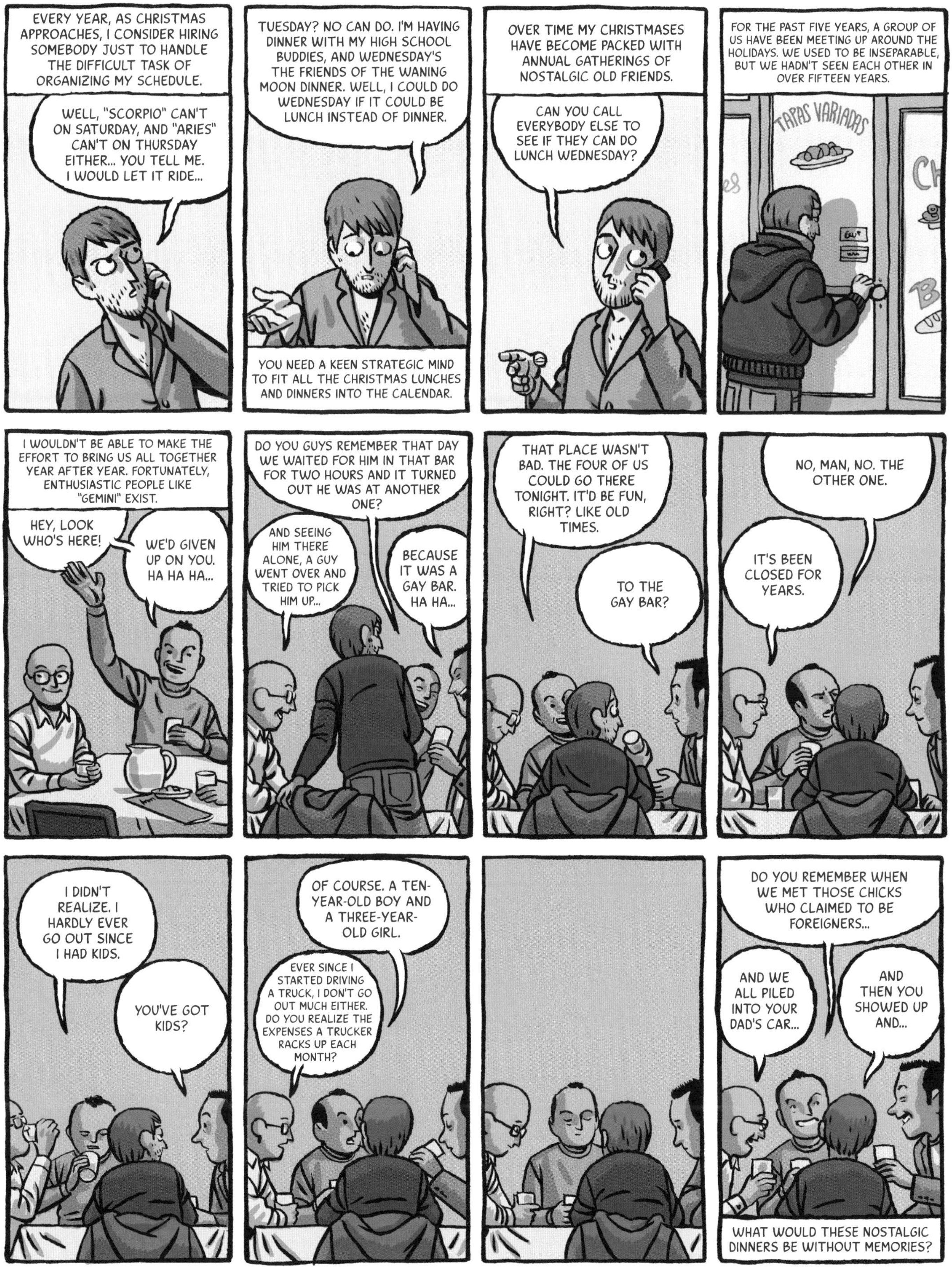
EVERY YEAR, AS CHRISTMAS APPROACHES, I CONSIDER HIRING SOMEBODY JUST TO HANDLE THE DIFFICULT TASK OF ORGANIZING MY SCHEDULE.
WELL, "SCORPIO" CAN'T ON SATURDAY, AND "ARIES" CAN'T ON THURSDAY EITHER... YOU TELL ME. I WOULD LET IT RIDE...
TUESDAY? NO CAN DO. I'M HAVING DINNER WITH MY HIGH SCHOOL BUDDIES, AND WEDNESDAY'S THE FRIENDS OF THE WANING MOON DINNER. WELL, I COULD DO WEDNESDAY IF IT COULD BE LUNCH INSTEAD OF DINNER.
YOU NEED A KEEN STRATEGIC MIND TO FIT ALL THE CHRISTMAS LUNCHES AND DINNERS INTO THE CALENDAR.
OVER TIME MY CHRISTMASES HAVE BECOME PACKED WITH ANNUAL GATHERINGS OF NOSTALGIC OLD FRIENDS.
CAN YOU CALL EVERYBODY ELSE TO SEE IF THEY CAN DO LUNCH WEDNESDAY?
FOR THE PAST FIVE YEARS, A GROUP OF US HAVE BEEN MEETING UP AROUND THE HOLIDAYS. WE USED TO BE INSEPARABLE, BUT WE HADN'T SEEN EACH OTHER IN OVER FIFTEEN YEARS.
TAPAS VARIADAS
I WOULDN'T BE ABLE TO MAKE THE EFFORT TO BRING US ALL TOGETHER YEAR AFTER YEAR. FORTUNATELY, ENTHUSIASTIC PEOPLE LIKE "GEMINI" EXIST.
HEY, LOOK WHO'S HERE!
WE'D GIVEN UP ON YOU. HA HA HA...
DO YOU GUYS REMEMBER THAT DAY WE WAITED FOR HIM IN THAT BAR FOR TWO HOURS AND IT TURNED OUT HE WAS AT ANOTHER ONE?
AND SEEING HIM THERE ALONE, A GUY WENT OVER AND TRIED TO PICK HIM UP...
BECAUSE IT WAS A GAY BAR. HA HA...
THAT PLACE WASN'T BAD. THE FOUR OF US COULD GO THERE TONIGHT. IT'D BE FUN, RIGHT? LIKE OLD TIMES.
TO THE GAY BAR?
NO, MAN, NO. THE OTHER ONE.
IT'S BEEN CLOSED FOR YEARS.
I DIDN'T REALIZE. I HARDLY EVER GO OUT SINCE I HAD KIDS.
YOU'VE GOT KIDS?
OF COURSE. A TEN-YEAR-OLD BOY AND A THREE-YEAR-OLD GIRL.
EVER SINCE I STARTED DRIVING A TRUCK, I DON'T GO OUT MUCH EITHER. DO YOU REALIZE THE EXPENSES A TRUCKER RACKS UP EACH MONTH?
DO YOU REMEMBER WHEN WE MET THOSE CHICKS WHO CLAIMED TO BE FOREIGNERS...
AND WE ALL PILED INTO YOUR DAD'S CAR...
AND THEN YOU SHOWED UP AND...
WHAT WOULD THESE NOSTALGIC DINNERS BE WITHOUT MEMORIES?

WAITING FOR THE CALL

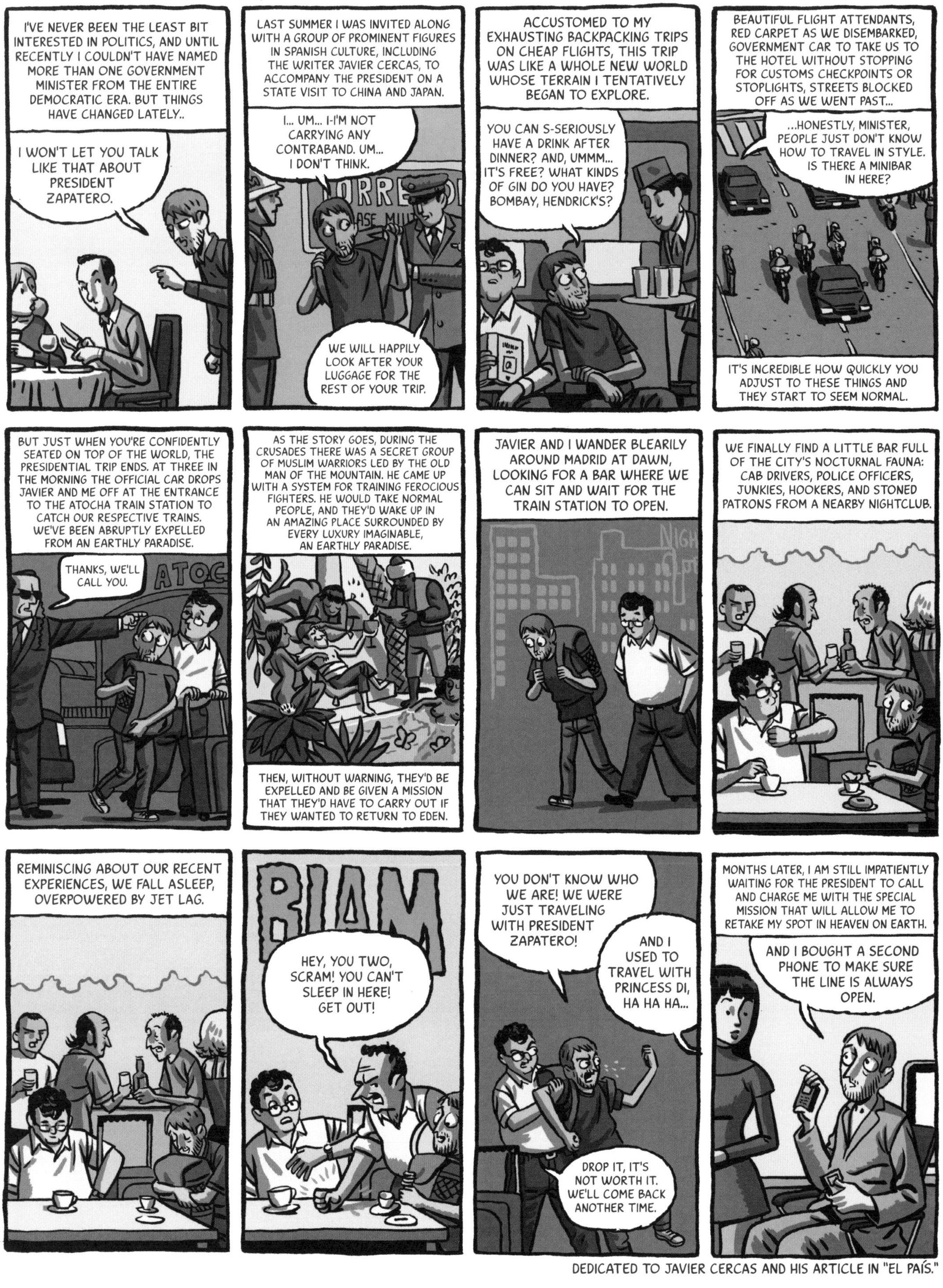
I'VE NEVER BEEN THE LEAST BIT INTERESTED IN POLITICS, AND UNTIL RECENTLY I COULDN'T HAVE NAMED MORE THAN ONE GOVERNMENT MINISTER FROM THE ENTIRE DEMOCRATIC ERA. BUT THINGS HAVE CHANGED LATELY..
I WON'T LET YOU TALK LIKE THAT ABOUT PRESIDENT ZAPATERO.
LAST SUMMER I WAS INVITED ALONG WITH A GROUP OF PROMINENT FIGURES IN SPANISH CULTURE, INCLUDING THE WRITER JAVIER CERCAS, TO ACCOMPANY THE PRESIDENT ON A STATE VISIT TO CHINA AND JAPAN.
I... UM... I-I'M NOT CARRYING ANY CONTRABAND. UM... I DON'T THINK.
WE WILL HAPPILY LOOK AFTER YOUR LUGGAGE FOR THE REST OF YOUR TRIP.
ACCUSTOMED TO MY EXHAUSTING BACKPACKING TRIPS ON CHEAP FLIGHTS, THIS TRIP WAS LIKE A WHOLE NEW WORLD WHOSE TERRAIN I TENTATIVELY BEGAN TO EXPLORE.
YOU CAN S-SERIOUSLY HAVE A DRINK AFTER DINNER? AND, UMMM... IT'S FREE? WHAT KINDS OF GIN DO YOU HAVE? BOMBAY, HENDRICK'S?
BEAUTIFUL FLIGHT ATTENDANTS, RED CARPET AS WE DISEMBARKED, GOVERNMENT CAR TO TAKE US TO THE HOTEL WITHOUT STOPPING FOR CUSTOMS CHECKPOINTS OR STOPLIGHTS, STREETS BLOCKED OFF AS WE WENT PAST...
...HONESTLY, MINISTER, PEOPLE JUST DON'T KNOW HOW TO TRAVEL IN STYLE. IS THERE A MINIBAR IN HERE?
IT'S INCREDIBLE HOW QUICKLY YOU ADJUST TO THESE THINGS AND THEY START TO SEEM NORMAL.
BUT JUST WHEN YOU'RE CONFIDENTLY SEATED ON TOP OF THE WORLD, THE PRESIDENTIAL TRIP ENDS. AT THREE IN THE MORNING THE OFFICIAL CAR DROPS JAVIER AND ME OFF AT THE ENTRANCE TO THE ATOCHA TRAIN STATION TO CATCH OUR RESPECTIVE TRAINS. WE'VE BEEN ABRUPTLY EXPELLED FROM AN EARTHLY PARADISE.
THANKS, WE'LL CALL YOU.
ATOC
AS THE STORY GOES, DURING THE CRUSADES THERE WAS A SECRET GROUP OF MUSLIM WARRIORS LED BY THE OLD MAN OF THE MOUNTAIN. HE CAME UP WITH A SYSTEM FOR TRAINING FEROCIOUS FIGHTERS. HE WOULD TAKE NORMAL PEOPLE, AND THEY'D WAKE UP IN AN AMAZING PLACE SURROUNDED BY EVERY LUXURY IMAGINABLE, AN EARTHLY PARADISE.
THEN, WITHOUT WARNING, THEY'D BE EXPELLED AND BE GIVEN A MISSION THAT THEY'D HAVE TO CARRY OUT IF THEY WANTED TO RETURN TO EDEN.
JAVIER AND I WANDER BLEARILY AROUND MADRID AT DAWN, LOOKING FOR A BAR WHERE WE CAN SIT AND WAIT FOR THE TRAIN STATION TO OPEN.
WE FINALLY FIND A LITTLE BAR FULL OF THE CITY'S NOCTURNAL FAUNA: CAB DRIVERS, POLICE OFFICERS, JUNKIES, HOOKERS, AND STONED PATRONS FROM A NEARBY NIGHTCLUB.
REMINISCING ABOUT OUR RECENT EXPERIENCES, WE FALL ASLEEP, OVERPOWERED BY JET LAG.
BLAM
HEY, YOU TWO, SCRAM! YOU CAN'T SLEEP IN HERE! GET OUT!
YOU DON'T KNOW WHO WE ARE! WE WERE JUST TRAVELING WITH PRESIDENT ZAPATERO!
AND I USED TO TRAVEL WITH PRINCESS DI, HA HA HA...
DROP IT, IT'S NOT WORTH IT. WE'LL COME BACK ANOTHER TIME.
MONTHS LATER, I AM STILL IMPATIENTLY WAITING FOR THE PRESIDENT TO CALL AND CHARGE ME WITH THE SPECIAL MISSION THAT WILL ALLOW ME TO RETAKE MY SPOT IN HEAVEN ON EARTH.
AND I BOUGHT A SECOND PHONE TO MAKE SURE THE LINE IS ALWAYS OPEN.

DEDICATED TO JAVIER CERCAS AND HIS ARTICLE IN "EL PAÍS."

SYMBIOSIS

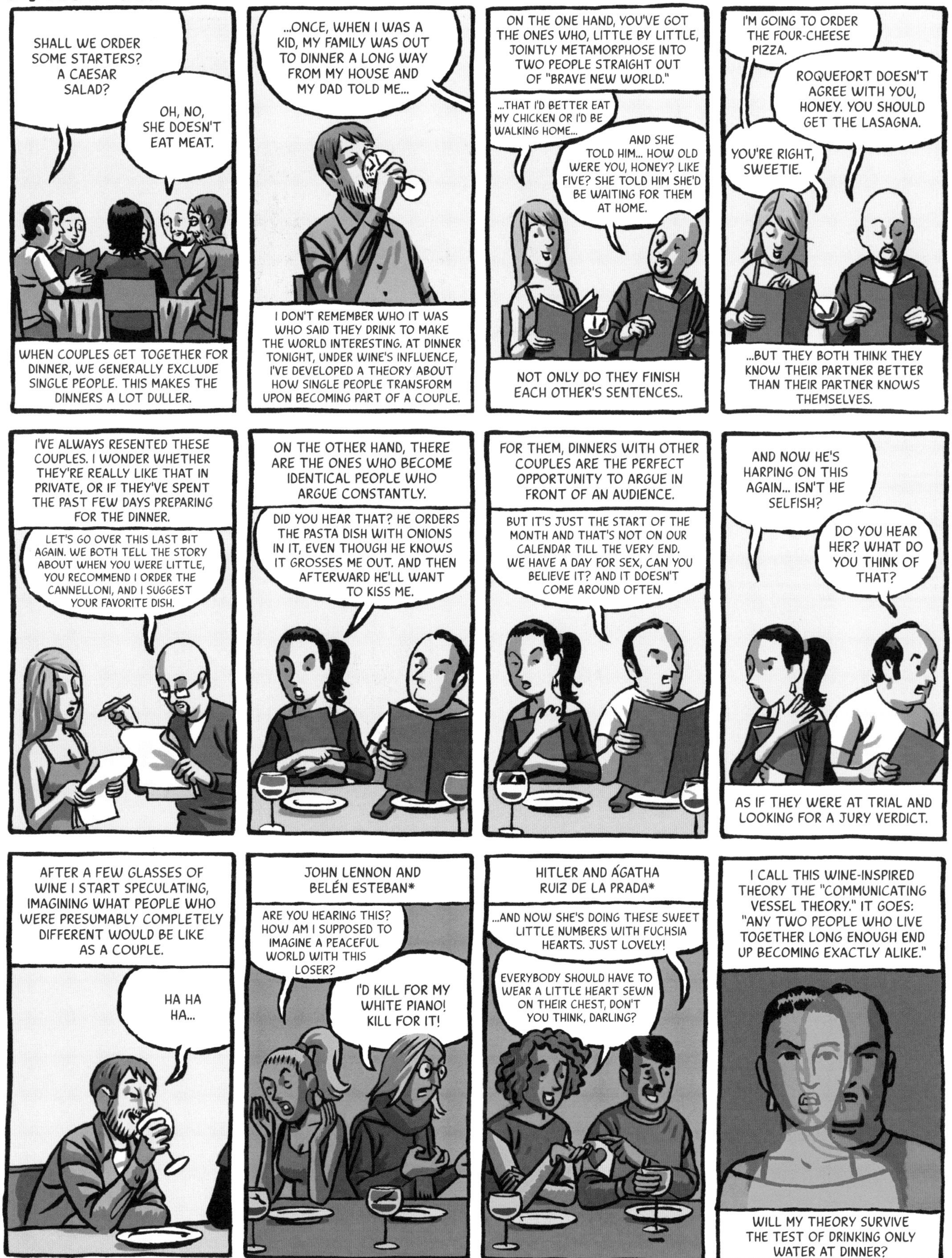
SHALL WE ORDER SOME STARTERS? A CAESAR SALAD?
OH, NO, SHE DOESN'T EAT MEAT.
WHEN COUPLES GET TOGETHER FOR DINNER, WE GENERALLY EXCLUDE SINGLE PEOPLE. THIS MAKES THE DINNERS A LOT DULLER.
...ONCE, WHEN I WAS A KID, MY FAMILY WAS OUT TO DINNER A LONG WAY FROM MY HOUSE AND MY DAD TOLD ME...
I DON'T REMEMBER WHO IT WAS WHO SAID THEY DRINK TO MAKE THE WORLD INTERESTING. AT DINNER TONIGHT, UNDER WINE'S INFLUENCE, I'VE DEVELOPED A THEORY ABOUT HOW SINGLE PEOPLE TRANSFORM UPON BECOMING PART OF A COUPLE.
ON THE ONE HAND, YOU'VE GOT THE ONES WHO, LITTLE BY LITTLE, JOINTLY METAMORPHOSE INTO TWO PEOPLE STRAIGHT OUT OF "BRAVE NEW WORLD."
...THAT I'D BETTER EAT MY CHICKEN OR I'D BE WALKING HOME...
AND SHE TOLD HIM... HOW OLD WERE YOU, HONEY? LIKE FIVE? SHE TOLD HIM SHE'D BE WAITING FOR THEM AT HOME.
NOT ONLY DO THEY FINISH EACH OTHER'S SENTENCES..
I'M GOING TO ORDER THE FOUR-CHEESE PIZZA.
ROQUEFORT DOESN'T AGREE WITH YOU, HONEY. YOU SHOULD GET THE LASAGNA.
YOU'RE RIGHT, SWEETIE.
...BUT THEY BOTH THINK THEY KNOW THEIR PARTNER BETTER THAN THEIR PARTNER KNOWS THEMSELVES.
I'VE ALWAYS RESENTED THESE COUPLES. I WONDER WHETHER THEY'RE REALLY LIKE THAT IN PRIVATE, OR IF THEY'VE SPENT THE PAST FEW DAYS PREPARING FOR THE DINNER.
LET'S GO OVER THIS LAST BIT AGAIN. WE BOTH TELL THE STORY ABOUT WHEN YOU WERE LITTLE, YOU RECOMMEND I ORDER THE CANNELLONI, AND I SUGGEST YOUR FAVORITE DISH.
ON THE OTHER HAND, THERE ARE THE ONES WHO BECOME IDENTICAL PEOPLE WHO ARGUE CONSTANTLY.
DID YOU HEAR THAT? HE ORDERS THE PASTA DISH WITH ONIONS IN IT, EVEN THOUGH HE KNOWS IT GROSSES ME OUT. AND THEN AFTERWARD HE'LL WANT TO KISS ME.
FOR THEM, DINNERS WITH OTHER COUPLES ARE THE PERFECT OPPORTUNITY TO ARGUE IN FRONT OF AN AUDIENCE.
BUT IT'S JUST THE START OF THE MONTH AND THAT'S NOT ON OUR CALENDAR TILL THE VERY END. WE HAVE A DAY FOR SEX, CAN YOU BELIEVE IT? AND IT DOESN'T COME AROUND OFTEN.
AND NOW HE'S HARPING ON THIS AGAIN... ISN'T HE SELFISH?
DO YOU HEAR HER? WHAT DO YOU THINK OF THAT?
AS IF THEY WERE AT TRIAL AND LOOKING FOR A JURY VERDICT.
AFTER A FEW GLASSES OF WINE I START SPECULATING, IMAGINING WHAT PEOPLE WHO WERE PRESUMABLY COMPLETELY DIFFERENT WOULD BE LIKE AS A COUPLE.
HA HA HA...
JOHN LENNON AND BELÉN ESTEBAN*
ARE YOU HEARING THIS? HOW AM I SUPPOSED TO IMAGINE A PEACEFUL WORLD WITH THIS LOSER?
I'D KILL FOR MY WHITE PIANO! KILL FOR IT!
HITLER AND ÁGATHA RUIZ DE LA PRADA*
...AND NOW SHE'S DOING THESE SWEET LITTLE NUMBERS WITH FUCHSIA HEARTS. JUST LOVELY!
EVERYBODY SHOULD HAVE TO WEAR A LITTLE HEART SEWN ON THEIR CHEST, DON'T YOU THINK, DARLING?
I CALL THIS WINE-INSPIRED THEORY THE "COMMUNICATING VESSEL THEORY." IT GOES: "ANY TWO PEOPLE WHO LIVE TOGETHER LONG ENOUGH END UP BECOMING EXACTLY ALIKE."
WILL MY THEORY SURVIVE THE TEST OF DRINKING ONLY WATER AT DINNER?

* BELÉN ESTEBAN IS A SPANISH TELEVISION PERSONALITY. IN A DISPUTE WITH THE JOURNALIST KARMELE MARCHANTE THAT BECAME GOSSIP-RAG FODDER, ESTEBAN ACCUSED MARCHANTE'S HUSBAND OF STEALING HER JEWELRY AND MARCHANTE REPORTEDLY REPLIED, "I'D KILL FOR MY HUSBAND. KILL FOR HIM."

* ÁGATHA RUIZ DE LA PRADA IS A SPANISH FASHION DESIGNER KNOWN FOR HER USE OF BRIGHT COLORS AND PATTERNS SUCH AS STRIPES, POLKA DOTS, AND, YES, HEARTS.

THE BET

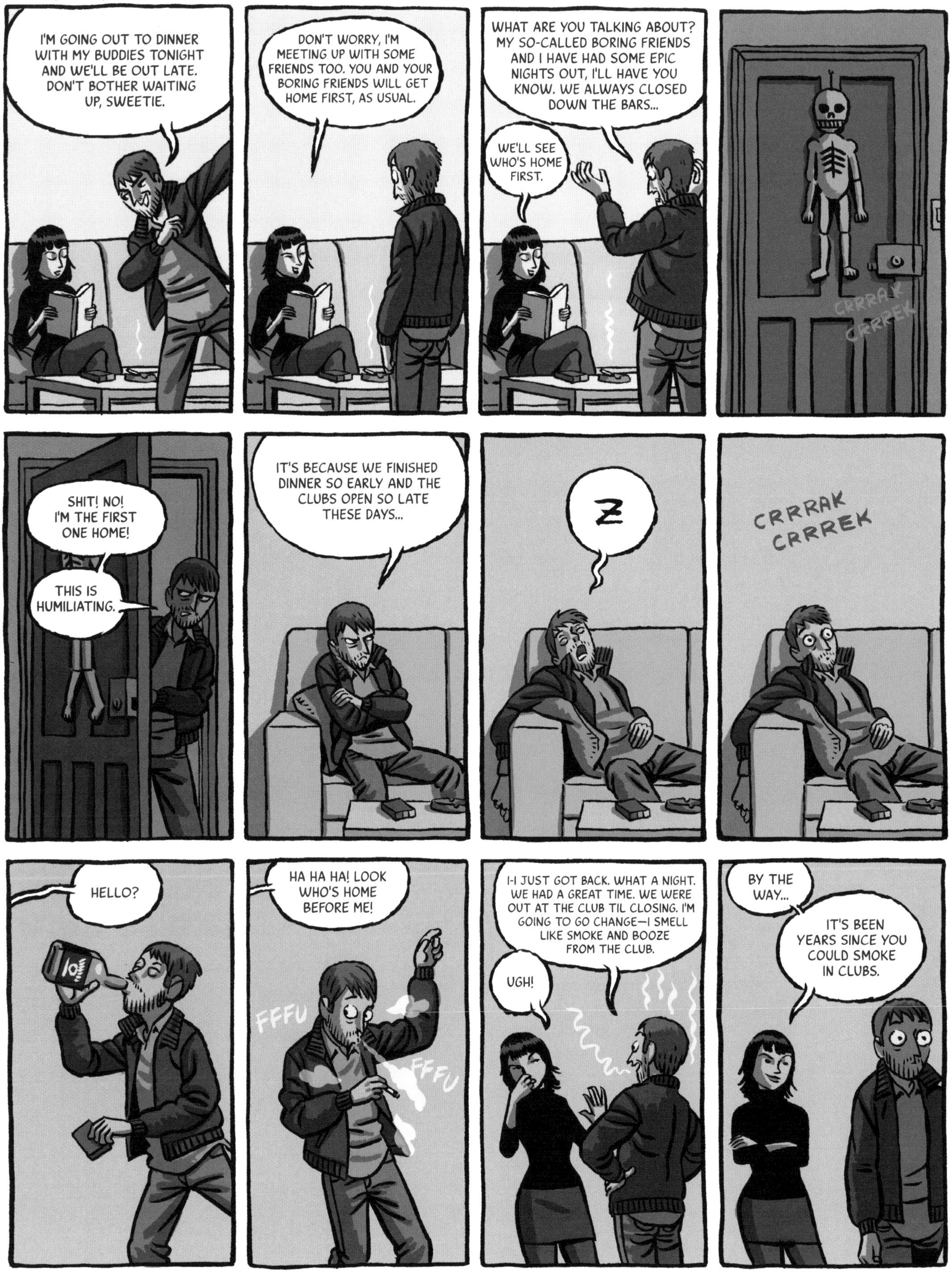
I'M GOING OUT TO DINNER WITH MY BUDDIES TONIGHT AND WE'LL BE OUT LATE. DON'T BOTHER WAITING UP, SWEETIE.
DON'T WORRY, I'M MEETING UP WITH SOME FRIENDS TOO. YOU AND YOUR BORING FRIENDS WILL GET HOME FIRST, AS USUAL.
WHAT ARE YOU TALKING ABOUT? MY SO-CALLED BORING FRIENDS AND I HAVE HAD SOME EPIC NIGHTS OUT, I'LL HAVE YOU KNOW. WE ALWAYS CLOSED DOWN THE BARS...
WE'LL SEE WHO'S HOME FIRST.
CRRRAK CRRREK
SHIT! NO! I'M THE FIRST ONE HOME!
THIS IS HUMILIATING.
IT'S BECAUSE WE FINISHED DINNER SO EARLY AND THE CLUBS OPEN SO LATE THESE DAYS...
Z
CRRRAK CRRREK
HELLO?
HA HA HA! LOOK WHO'S HOME BEFORE ME!
FFFU
FFFU
I-I JUST GOT BACK. WHAT A NIGHT. WE HAD A GREAT TIME. WE WERE OUT AT THE CLUB TIL CLOSING. I'M GOING TO GO CHANGE—I SMELL LIKE SMOKE AND BOOZE FROM THE CLUB.
UGH!
BY THE WAY...
IT'S BEEN YEARS SINCE YOU COULD SMOKE IN CLUBS.

PINEAPPLE PORK ROAST

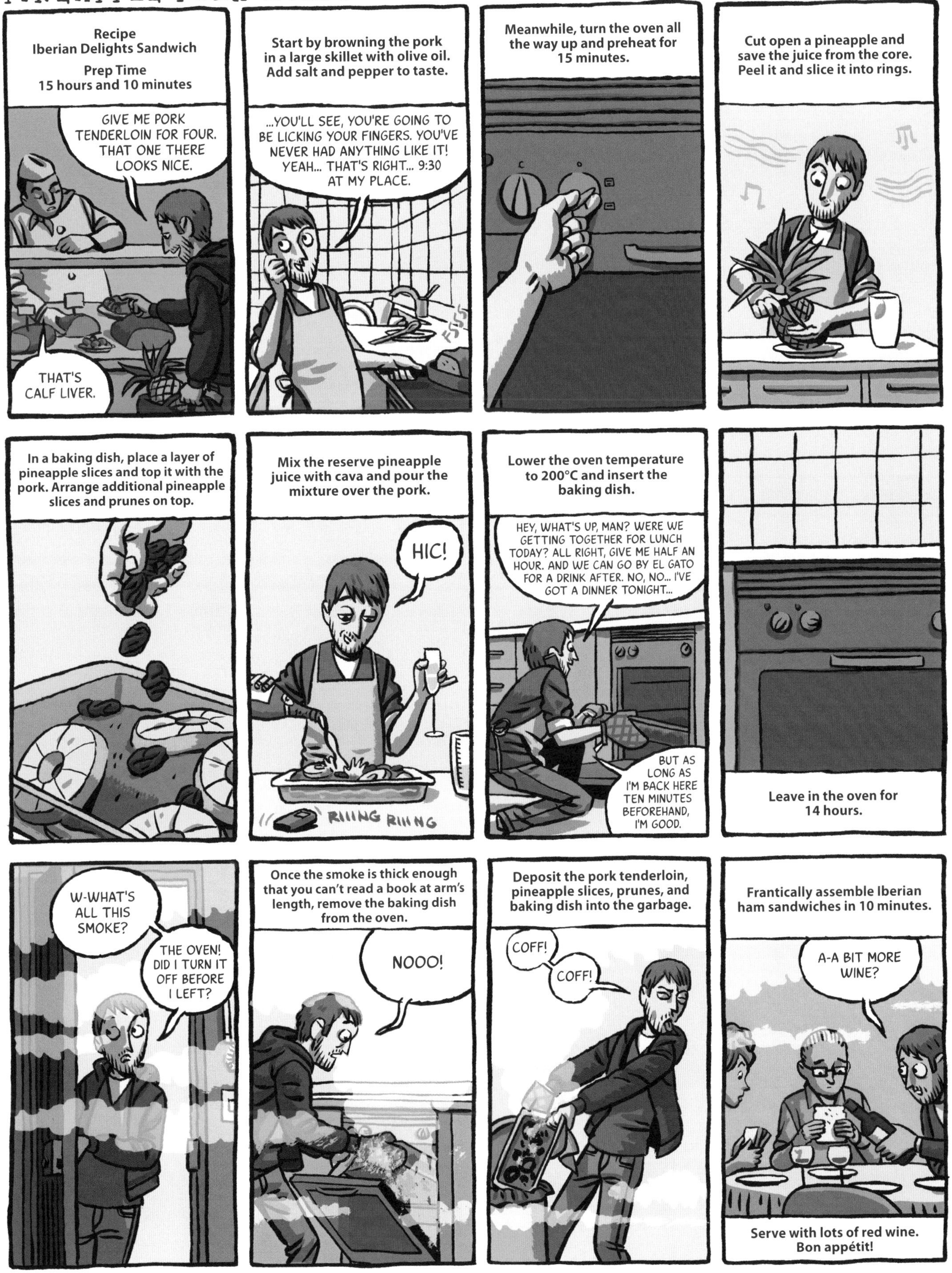

Recipe
Iberian Delights Sandwich
Prep Time
15 hours and 10 minutes
GIVE ME PORK TENDERLOIN FOR FOUR. THAT ONE THERE LOOKS NICE.
THAT'S CALF LIVER.
Start by browning the pork in a large skillet with olive oil. Add salt and pepper to taste.
...YOU'LL SEE, YOU'RE GOING TO BE LICKING YOUR FINGERS. YOU'VE NEVER HAD ANYTHING LIKE IT! YEAH... THAT'S RIGHT... 9:30 AT MY PLACE.
Meanwhile, turn the oven all the way up and preheat for 15 minutes.
Cut open a pineapple and save the juice from the core. Peel it and slice it into rings.
In a baking dish, place a layer of pineapple slices and top it with the pork. Arrange additional pineapple slices and prunes on top.
Mix the reserve pineapple juice with cava and pour the mixture over the pork.
HIC!
RIIING RIIING
Lower the oven temperature to 200°C and insert the baking dish.
HEY, WHAT'S UP, MAN? WERE WE GETTING TOGETHER FOR LUNCH TODAY? ALL RIGHT, GIVE ME HALF AN HOUR. AND WE CAN GO BY EL GATO FOR A DRINK AFTER. NO, NO... I'VE GOT A DINNER TONIGHT...
BUT AS LONG AS I'M BACK HERE TEN MINUTES BEFOREHAND, I'M GOOD.
Leave in the oven for 14 hours.
W-WHAT'S ALL THIS SMOKE?
THE OVEN! DID I TURN IT OFF BEFORE I LEFT?
Once the smoke is thick enough that you can't read a book at arm's length, remove the baking dish from the oven.
NOOO!
Deposit the pork tenderloin, pineapple slices, prunes, and baking dish into the garbage.
COFF!
COFF!
Frantically assemble Iberian ham sandwiches in 10 minutes.
A-A BIT MORE WINE?
Serve with lots of red wine. Bon appétit!

A RELAXING EVENING

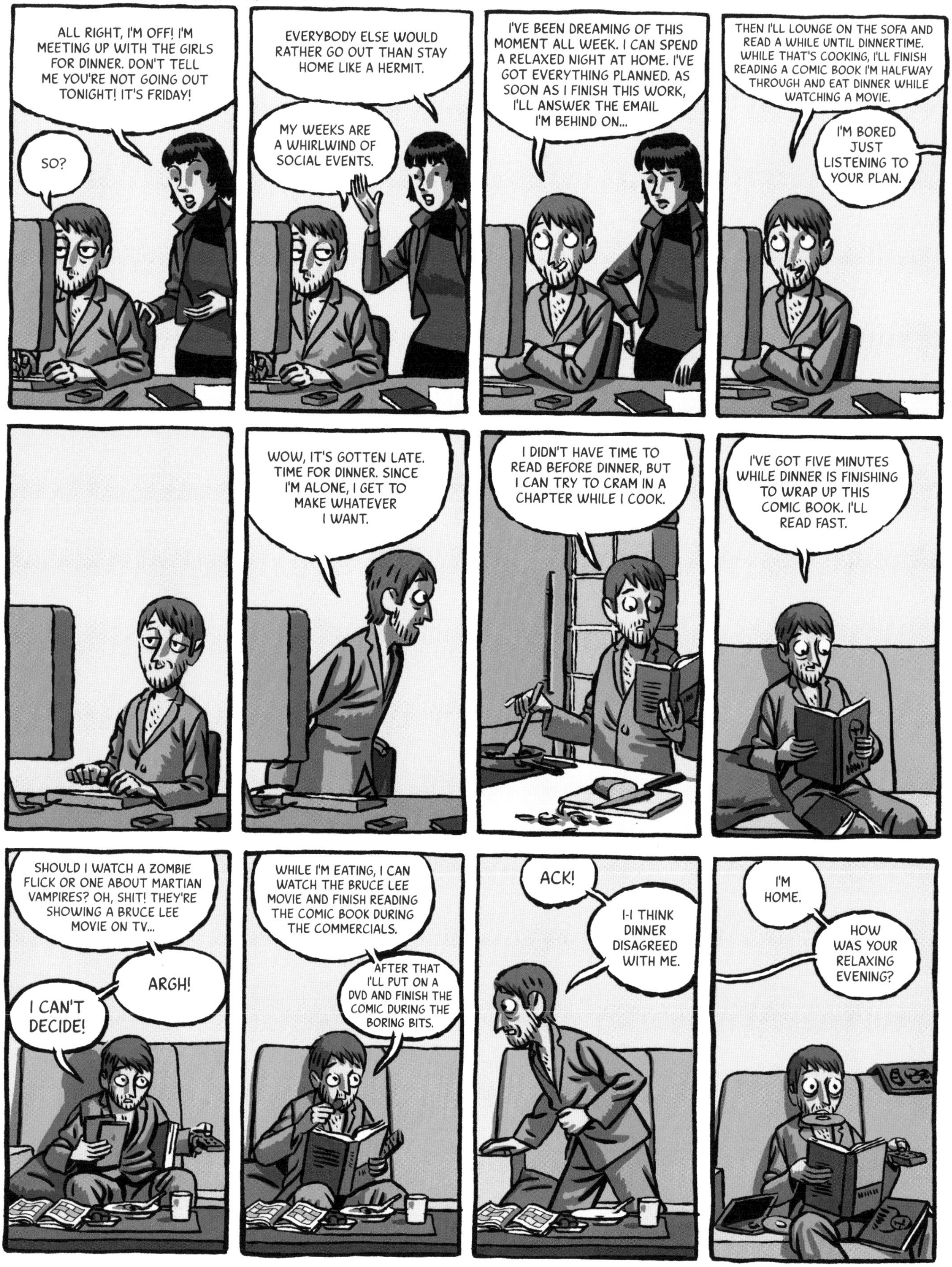
ALL RIGHT, I'M OFF! I'M MEETING UP WITH THE GIRLS FOR DINNER. DON'T TELL ME YOU'RE NOT GOING OUT TONIGHT! IT'S FRIDAY!
SO?
EVERYBODY ELSE WOULD RATHER GO OUT THAN STAY HOME LIKE A HERMIT.
MY WEEKS ARE A WHIRLWIND OF SOCIAL EVENTS.
I'VE BEEN DREAMING OF THIS MOMENT ALL WEEK. I CAN SPEND A RELAXED NIGHT AT HOME. I'VE GOT EVERYTHING PLANNED. AS SOON AS I FINISH THIS WORK, I'LL ANSWER THE EMAIL I'M BEHIND ON...
THEN I'LL LOUNGE ON THE SOFA AND READ A WHILE UNTIL DINNERTIME. WHILE THAT'S COOKING, I'LL FINISH READING A COMIC BOOK I'M HALFWAY THROUGH AND EAT DINNER WHILE WATCHING A MOVIE.
I'M BORED JUST LISTENING TO YOUR PLAN.
WOW, IT'S GOTTEN LATE. TIME FOR DINNER. SINCE I'M ALONE, I GET TO MAKE WHATEVER I WANT.
I DIDN'T HAVE TIME TO READ BEFORE DINNER, BUT I CAN TRY TO CRAM IN A CHAPTER WHILE I COOK.
I'VE GOT FIVE MINUTES WHILE DINNER IS FINISHING TO WRAP UP THIS COMIC BOOK. I'LL READ FAST.
SHOULD I WATCH A ZOMBIE FLICK OR ONE ABOUT MARTIAN VAMPIRES? OH, SHIT! THEY'RE SHOWING A BRUCE LEE MOVIE ON TV...
ARGH!
I CAN'T DECIDE!
WHILE I'M EATING, I CAN WATCH THE BRUCE LEE MOVIE AND FINISH READING THE COMIC BOOK DURING THE COMMERCIALS.
AFTER THAT I'LL PUT ON A DVD AND FINISH THE COMIC DURING THE BORING BITS.
ACK!
I-I THINK DINNER DISAGREED WITH ME.
I'M HOME.
HOW WAS YOUR RELAXING EVENING?

FOR THE FIFTH TIME IN MY LIFE, I'VE SIGNED UP FOR A GYM MEMBERSHIP. ON THE FOUR PREVIOUS OCCASIONS, UNFORTUNATELY, THE ONLY PART OF MY BODY THAT GOT ANY BIGGER WAS THE SOLES OF MY FEET THANKS TO FOOT FUNGUS.

ONE

TWO

THREE

AND FOUR!

THIS TIME I'M WORKING HARD FOR THINGS TO BE DIFFERENT.

ONE

T-TWO

AND...

AND THHREEE!

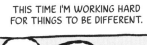

YOU BE AT GYM MUCH?

ARGH ARGH

OH, NO...

BUT I'VE ALWAYS WORKED OUT AND...

YOU BE WHAT WE IN MY COUNTRY CALL WOLF AMONG FLOCK. BACK AND FORTH AND NOT DO NOTHING. BEGINNER IMPATIENCE YOU HAVE.

I'VE BEEN WEARING MYSELF OUT EVERY DAY FOR THE PAST TWO MONTHS!

LOT OF WEIGHT AND LOT OF REPETITIONS. BE CALM.

HOW LONG HAVE YOU BEEN LIFTING WEIGHTS?

TWENTY OR THIRTY.

THIRTY YEARS? SO IF I'M LUCKY I CAN BE THE STRONGEST GUY IN THE NURSING HOME.

THERE IS MORE SIMPLE SOLUTION.

TAKE STEROIDS.

HA HA HA... OF COURSE. IF YOU SEE THE GYM DEALER, SEND HIM MY WAY, OK?

M-MY BODY IS A TEMPLE. SCRAWNY, BUT A TEMPLE. BUT I'LL KEEP IT IN MIND.

THAT IS THE QUESTION. WHETHER TO BE A GYM JUNKIE OR SUFFER FROM FOOT FUNGUS FOR THIRTY YEARS.

ONLINE SHOPPING

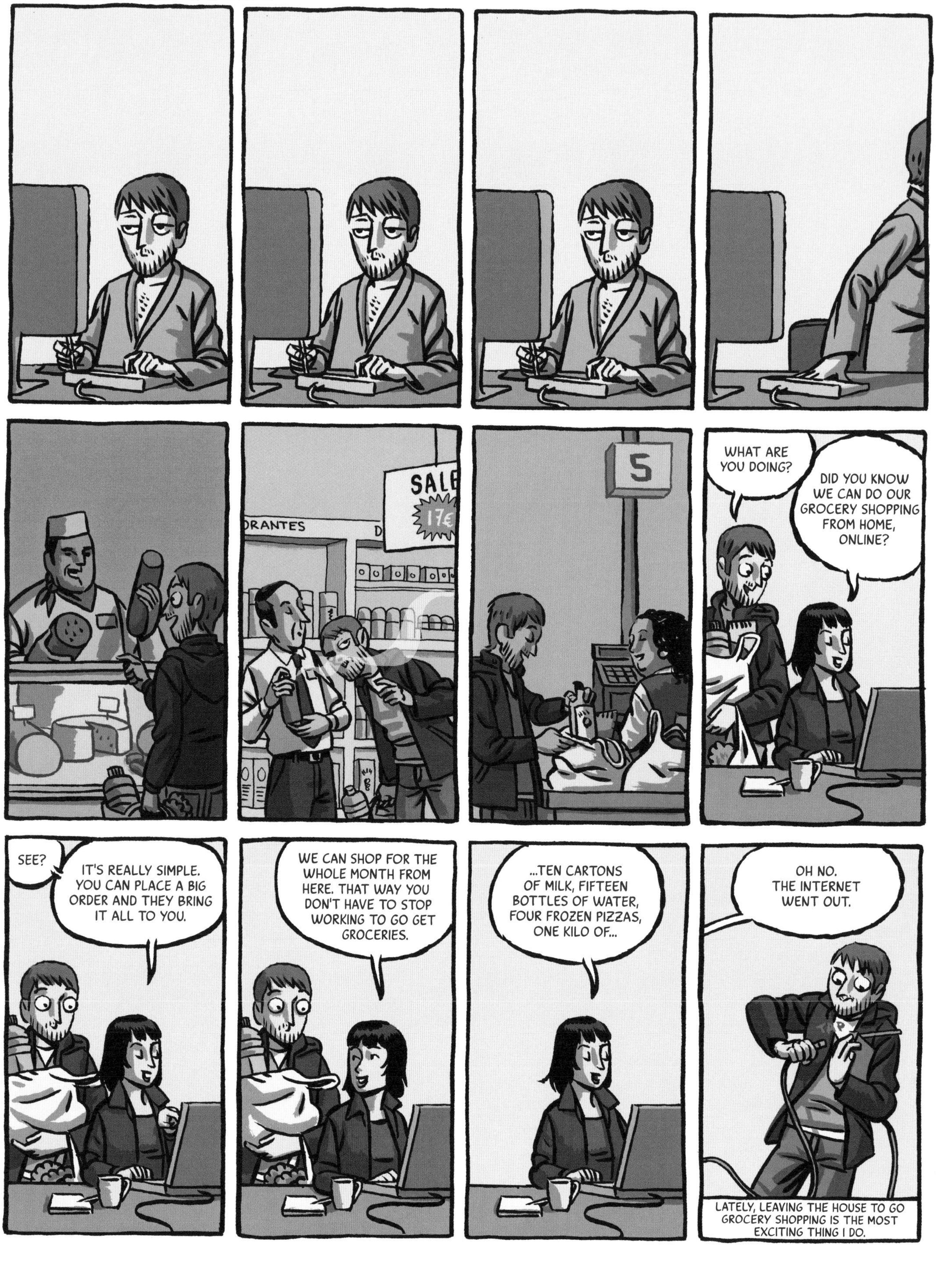
SALE
17€
5
WHAT ARE YOU DOING?
DID YOU KNOW WE CAN DO OUR GROCERY SHOPPING FROM HOME, ONLINE?
SEE?
IT'S REALLY SIMPLE. YOU CAN PLACE A BIG ORDER AND THEY BRING IT ALL TO YOU.
WE CAN SHOP FOR THE WHOLE MONTH FROM HERE. THAT WAY YOU DON'T HAVE TO STOP WORKING TO GO GET GROCERIES.
...TEN CARTONS OF MILK, FIFTEEN BOTTLES OF WATER, FOUR FROZEN PIZZAS, ONE KILO OF...
OH NO. THE INTERNET WENT OUT.
LATELY, LEAVING THE HOUSE TO GO GROCERY SHOPPING IS THE MOST EXCITING THING I DO.

THE FRAUD

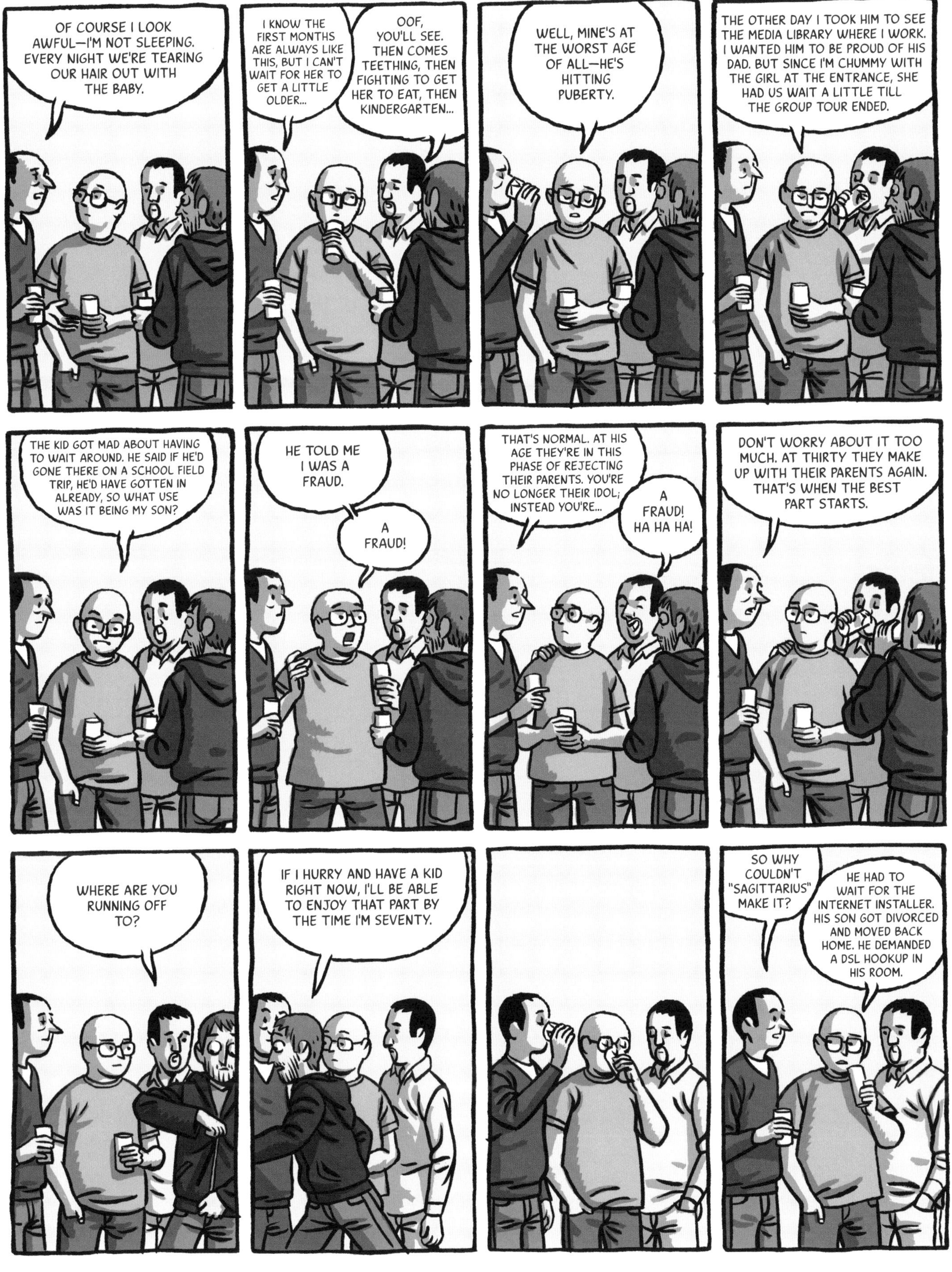

OF COURSE I LOOK AWFUL—I'M NOT SLEEPING. EVERY NIGHT WE'RE TEARING OUR HAIR OUT WITH THE BABY.
I KNOW THE FIRST MONTHS ARE ALWAYS LIKE THIS, BUT I CAN'T WAIT FOR HER TO GET A LITTLE OLDER...
OOF, YOU'LL SEE. THEN COMES TEETHING, THEN FIGHTING TO GET HER TO EAT, THEN KINDERGARTEN...
WELL, MINE'S AT THE WORST AGE OF ALL—HE'S HITTING PUBERTY.
THE OTHER DAY I TOOK HIM TO SEE THE MEDIA LIBRARY WHERE I WORK. I WANTED HIM TO BE PROUD OF HIS DAD. BUT SINCE I'M CHUMMY WITH THE GIRL AT THE ENTRANCE, SHE HAD US WAIT A LITTLE TILL THE GROUP TOUR ENDED.
THE KID GOT MAD ABOUT HAVING TO WAIT AROUND. HE SAID IF HE'D GONE THERE ON A SCHOOL FIELD TRIP, HE'D HAVE GOTTEN IN ALREADY, SO WHAT USE WAS IT BEING MY SON?
HE TOLD ME I WAS A FRAUD.
A FRAUD!
THAT'S NORMAL. AT HIS AGE THEY'RE IN THIS PHASE OF REJECTING THEIR PARENTS. YOU'RE NO LONGER THEIR IDOL; INSTEAD YOU'RE...
A FRAUD! HA HA HA!
DON'T WORRY ABOUT IT TOO MUCH. AT THIRTY THEY MAKE UP WITH THEIR PARENTS AGAIN. THAT'S WHEN THE BEST PART STARTS.
WHERE ARE YOU RUNNING OFF TO?
IF I HURRY AND HAVE A KID RIGHT NOW, I'LL BE ABLE TO ENJOY THAT PART BY THE TIME I'M SEVENTY.
SO WHY COULDN'T "SAGITTARIUS" MAKE IT?
HE HAD TO WAIT FOR THE INTERNET INSTALLER. HIS SON GOT DIVORCED AND MOVED BACK HOME. HE DEMANDED A DSL HOOKUP IN HIS ROOM.

THE PIECE THAT DOESN'T FIT

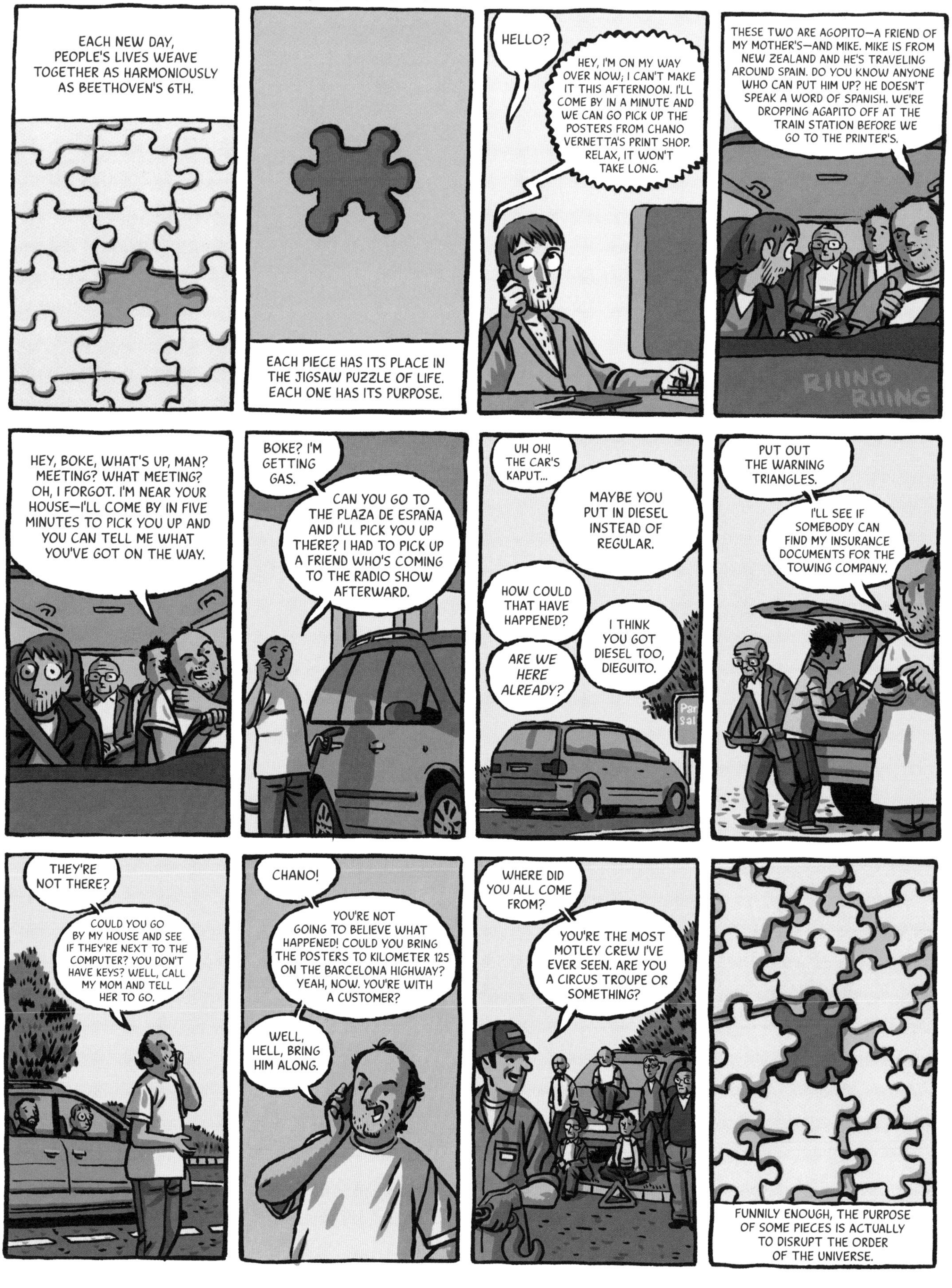

EACH NEW DAY, PEOPLE'S LIVES WEAVE TOGETHER AS HARMONIOUSLY AS BEETHOVEN'S 6TH.
EACH PIECE HAS ITS PLACE IN THE JIGSAW PUZZLE OF LIFE. EACH ONE HAS ITS PURPOSE.
HELLO?
HEY, I'M ON MY WAY OVER NOW; I CAN'T MAKE IT THIS AFTERNOON. I'LL COME BY IN A MINUTE AND WE CAN GO PICK UP THE POSTERS FROM CHANO VERNETTA'S PRINT SHOP. RELAX, IT WON'T TAKE LONG.
THESE TWO ARE AGOPITO—A FRIEND OF MY MOTHER'S—AND MIKE. MIKE IS FROM NEW ZEALAND AND HE'S TRAVELING AROUND SPAIN. DO YOU KNOW ANYONE WHO CAN PUT HIM UP? HE DOESN'T SPEAK A WORD OF SPANISH. WE'RE DROPPING AGAPITO OFF AT THE TRAIN STATION BEFORE WE GO TO THE PRINTER'S.
RIIING RIIING
HEY, BOKE, WHAT'S UP, MAN? MEETING? WHAT MEETING? OH, I FORGOT. I'M NEAR YOUR HOUSE—I'LL COME BY IN FIVE MINUTES TO PICK YOU UP AND YOU CAN TELL ME WHAT YOU'VE GOT ON THE WAY.
BOKE? I'M GETTING GAS.
CAN YOU GO TO THE PLAZA DE ESPAÑA AND I'LL PICK YOU UP THERE? I HAD TO PICK UP A FRIEND WHO'S COMING TO THE RADIO SHOW AFTERWARD.
UH OH! THE CAR'S KAPUT...
MAYBE YOU PUT IN DIESEL INSTEAD OF REGULAR.
HOW COULD THAT HAVE HAPPENED?
I THINK YOU GOT DIESEL TOO, DIEGUITO.
ARE WE HERE ALREADY?
PUT OUT THE WARNING TRIANGLES.
I'LL SEE IF SOMEBODY CAN FIND MY INSURANCE DOCUMENTS FOR THE TOWING COMPANY.
THEY'RE NOT THERE?
COULD YOU GO BY MY HOUSE AND SEE IF THEY'RE NEXT TO THE COMPUTER? YOU DON'T HAVE KEYS? WELL, CALL MY MOM AND TELL HER TO GO.
CHANO!
YOU'RE NOT GOING TO BELIEVE WHAT HAPPENED! COULD YOU BRING THE POSTERS TO KILOMETER 125 ON THE BARCELONA HIGHWAY? YEAH, NOW. YOU'RE WITH A CUSTOMER?
WELL, HELL, BRING HIM ALONG.
WHERE DID YOU ALL COME FROM?
YOU'RE THE MOST MOTLEY CREW I'VE EVER SEEN. ARE YOU A CIRCUS TROUPE OR SOMETHING?
FUNNILY ENOUGH, THE PURPOSE OF SOME PIECES IS ACTUALLY TO DISRUPT THE ORDER OF THE UNIVERSE.

EXISTENTIAL VOID

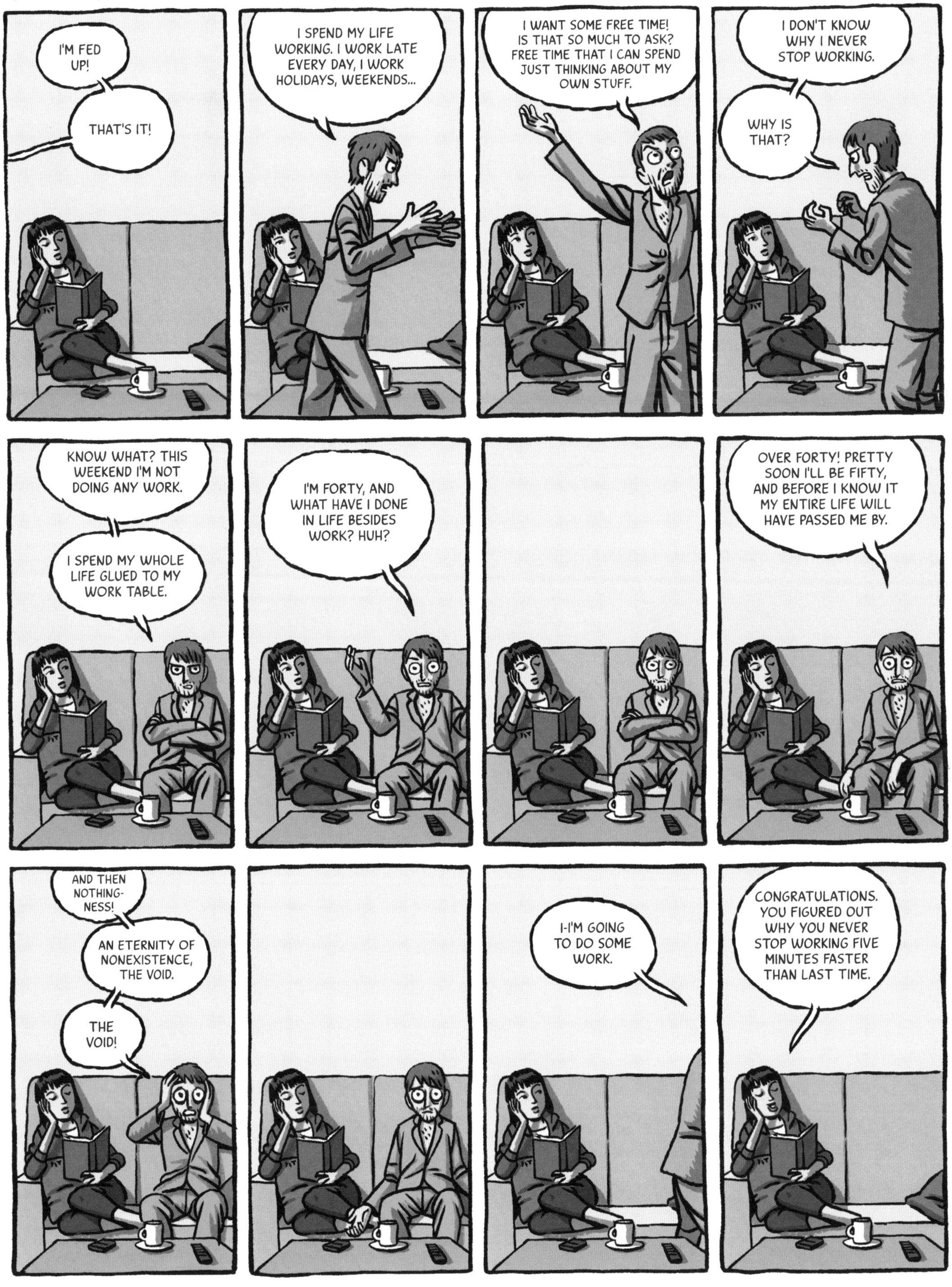
I'M FED UP!
THAT'S IT!
I SPEND MY LIFE WORKING. I WORK LATE EVERY DAY, I WORK HOLIDAYS, WEEKENDS...
I WANT SOME FREE TIME! IS THAT SO MUCH TO ASK? FREE TIME THAT I CAN SPEND JUST THINKING ABOUT MY OWN STUFF.
I DON'T KNOW WHY I NEVER STOP WORKING.
WHY IS THAT?
KNOW WHAT? THIS WEEKEND I'M NOT DOING ANY WORK.
I SPEND MY WHOLE LIFE GLUED TO MY WORK TABLE.
I'M FORTY, AND WHAT HAVE I DONE IN LIFE BESIDES WORK? HUH?
OVER FORTY! PRETTY SOON I'LL BE FIFTY, AND BEFORE I KNOW IT MY ENTIRE LIFE WILL HAVE PASSED ME BY.
AND THEN NOTHING-NESS!
AN ETERNITY OF NONEXISTENCE, THE VOID.
THE VOID!
I-I'M GOING TO DO SOME WORK.
CONGRATULATIONS. YOU FIGURED OUT WHY YOU NEVER STOP WORKING FIVE MINUTES FASTER THAN LAST TIME.

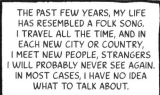

THE PAST FEW YEARS, MY LIFE HAS RESEMBLED A FOLK SONG. I TRAVEL ALL THE TIME, AND IN EACH NEW CITY OR COUNTRY, I MEET NEW PEOPLE, STRANGERS I WILL PROBABLY NEVER SEE AGAIN. IN MOST CASES, I HAVE NO IDEA WHAT TO TALK ABOUT.

MONSIEUR, HOW MANY INHABITANTS DOES SPAIN HAVE? C'EST PLUS GRAND QUE FRANCE?

UMMM... I-I HAVE NO IDEA. DESOLÉ.

THERE ARE A LOT OF LONG, AWKWARD SILENCES.

HOW IS CRISIS IN SPAIN? WHAT PERCENTAGE UNEMPLOYMENT?

OVER TIME I'VE LEARNED NOT TO LET A POTENTIAL CONVERSATION GO TO WASTE. NOT EVEN ON SUBJECTS I KNOW NOTHING ABOUT.

IT'S PROBABLY ABOUT 40%. BUT DON'T LISTEN TO ME. I DON'T KNOW MUCH ABOUT THESE THINGS.

NIE MOŻE BYĆ! THAT MORE THAN POLAND!

CAN YOU EXPLAIN THAT? VALENCIA HAS THE MOST DEBT OF ANY SPANISH CITY. PLUS, YOU'VE GOT A PRESIDENT WHO'S LINKED TO A WHOLE NETWORK OF CORRUPTION. HOW CAN YOU STAND IT? WHY DON'T YOU ALL DO SOMETHING?

OVER TIME I'VE REALIZED THAT WHEN YOU'RE ABROAD, NOBODY KNOWS ENOUGH TO CONTRADICT YOU. YOU BECOME AN EXPERT ON YOUR HOMELAND.

THE PRESIDENT CO-OPTED OUR FLAG! IN MY CITY THAT'S BASICALLY SACRED. THERE'S NOTHING WE CAN DO. NOTHING!

AND I'VE STARTED FILLING THOSE AWKWARD SILENCES WITH WILD FLIGHTS OF IMAGINATION.

NO WAY! THEY STOPPED CONSTRUCTION ON VALENCIA'S STADIUM BECAUSE THEY FOUND ROMAN RUINS AND HAVE TO EXCAVATE. WHENEVER YOU DIG A DITCH AROUND THERE...

...WE'VE BEEN CELEBRATING THE MOORS AND CHRISTIANS FESTIVAL SINCE IBERIAN TIMES. ONCE A YEAR ALL ACROSS SPAIN, PEOPLE BEAT EACH OTHER UP. YOU DON'T HAVE ANYTHING LIKE THAT HERE IN ITALY?

HI! I'M HOME!

DID YOU KNOW THAT ONCE A YEAR THE SICILIAN MAFIA AND THE CAMORRA FACE OFF IN A KNIFE FIGHT IN THE ROMAN COLISEUM? I HEARD IT FROM THIS ITALIAN WOMAN.

NOBODY SHOULD BE GIVEN A PASSPORT WITHOUT FIRST HAVING TO PASS A TEST ON THEIR LOCAL CULTURE.

THE CHEATER

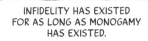

"ARIES" IS A CHARMING AND ATTRACTIVE FRIEND. "ARIES" IS A CHEATER.

...AND I ALWAYS HAVE BEEN, MIND YOU...

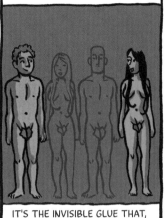

INFIDELITY HAS EXISTED FOR AS LONG AS MONOGAMY HAS EXISTED.

IT'S THE INVISIBLE GLUE THAT, FOR MILLENNIA, HAS KEPT COUPLES TOGETHER.

PROBABLY NONE OF OUR ANCESTORS FELT GUILTY ABOUT IT. BUT THAT'S STARTING TO CHANGE...

...BUT THIS TIME IS DIFFERENT. I'M REALLY INTO HER, AND I THINK MY WIFE SUSPECTS. AND IF SHE CATCHES ME, BETWEEN THE DIVORCE AND CHILD SUPPORT, SHE'LL DESTROY ME.

BUT THAT GIRL IS A VOLCANO! SHE GAVE ME AN ULTIMATUM. IT'S A TOUGH DECISION.

I'M HAPPY WITH MY WIFE AND DAUGHTER. I DON'T WANT TO THROW IT ALL AWAY... SO I DECIDED TO CALL OFF THE AFFAIR. I HAVEN'T SEEN HER OR CALLED HER IN A WEEK.

HAVE YOU DELETED HER FROM YOUR CONTACTS?

UMMM... WELL, NO... BUT I DON'T INTEND TO CALL.

HA! THAT'S THE KEY. I'LL TELL YOU WHAT'S NEXT.

OVER THE NEXT FEW DAYS (THREE AT MOST), YOU'LL FIND AN EXCUSE TO CALL OR TEXT HER—SOME MEMORY, SOMETHING YOU NEED TO SHARE WITH HER. COMMUNICATION WILL START UP AGAIN, AND YOU'LL MEET UP THE FOLLOWING WEEKEND (AS FRIENDS, YOU'LL SAY). AND YOU'LL END UP IN BED.

YOU'LL DECIDE TO CONTINUE THE RELATIONSHIP. YOU'LL REMAIN MORE OR LESS HAPPY WITH YOUR DOUBLE LIFE, AND YOU WON'T WANT TO LEAVE YOUR WIFE. BUT YOUR LOVER WILL TRY TO GET YOU TO LEAVE HER BY INDIRECT MEANS, GIVING YOU EVERYTHING YOUR WIFE DOESN'T PROVIDE. FINALLY SHE'LL GET SICK OF THE SITUATION AND LOOK FOR ANOTHER MAN (TO MAKE YOU JEALOUS).

YOU'LL THEN BECOME DESPERATE AND REALIZE SHE'S THE ONE YOU WANT. SO YOU'LL LEAVE YOUR WIFE.

YOU'LL GET BACK TOGETHER WITH YOUR LOVER (NOW YOUR PARTNER), BUT NOTHING WILL BE LIKE IT USED TO BE. YOU'LL START ARGUING, AND AFTER A FEW MONTHS YOU'LL BREAK UP.

YOU'LL PATHETICALLY HAUNT NIGHT-CLUBS FOR 40-SOMETHINGS AND SOCIAL MEDIA PLATFORMS.

THAT'S YOUR FUTURE IF YOU DON'T DELETE HER NUMBER RIGHT NOW.

HOW DO YOU KNOW SO MUCH ABOUT INFIDELITY? DON'T TELL ME YOU'VE CHEATED TOO.

YOU GUYS ARE PATHETIC. YOU HAVE NO WILLPOWER TO RESIST.

I WOULD NEVER CHEAT ON MY WIFE.

SADLY, THE DEGREE OF A COUPLE'S FAITHFULNESS IS INVERSELY PROPORTIONAL TO THE NUMBER OF OPPORTUNITIES THEY'VE HAD.

HOW MANY CHANCES TO CHEAT HAVE YOU HAD?

RECEIVED, APPRECIATED, AND FORGOTTEN

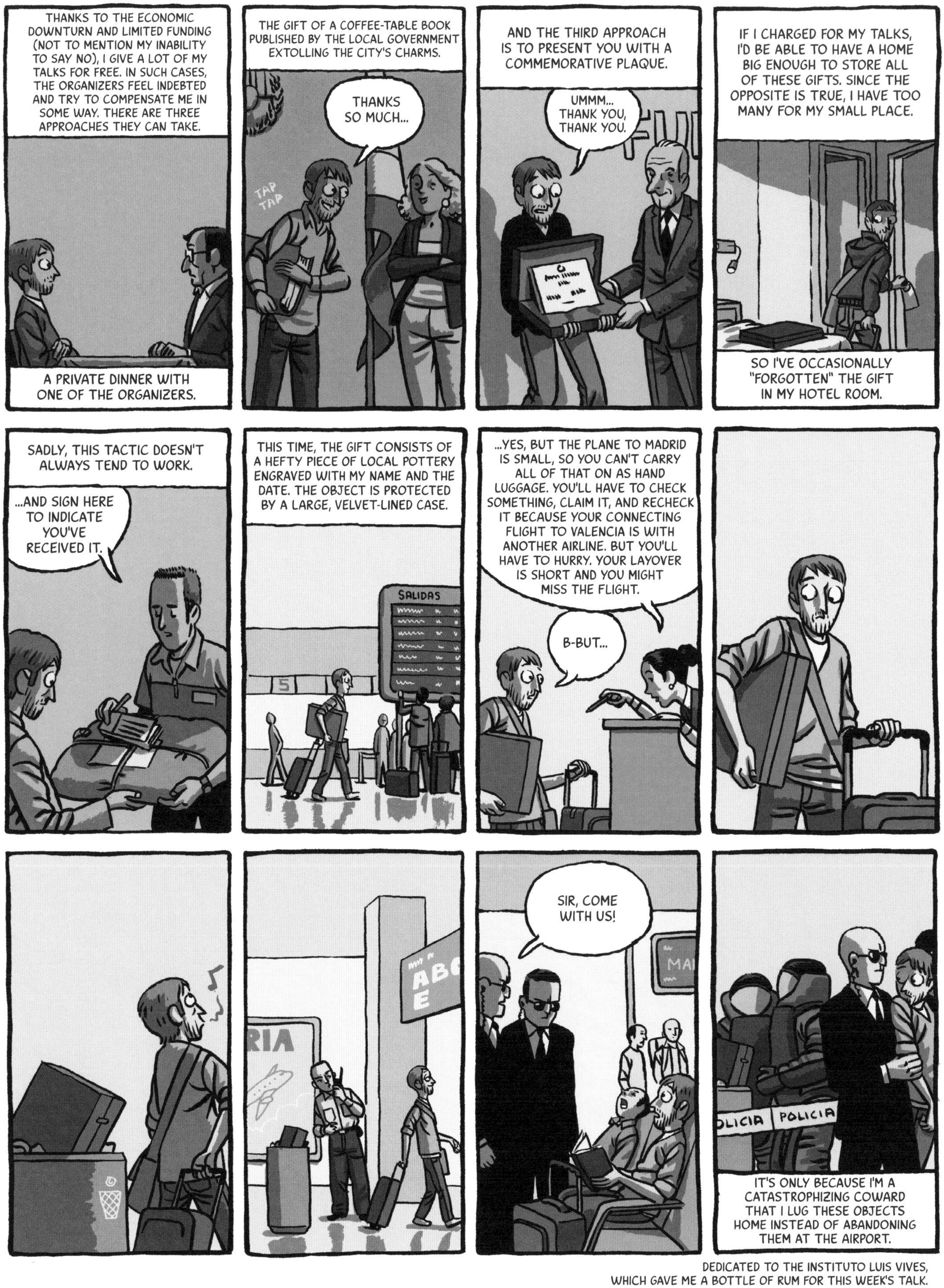
THANKS TO THE ECONOMIC DOWNTURN AND LIMITED FUNDING (NOT TO MENTION MY INABILITY TO SAY NO), I GIVE A LOT OF MY TALKS FOR FREE. IN SUCH CASES, THE ORGANIZERS FEEL INDEBTED AND TRY TO COMPENSATE ME IN SOME WAY. THERE ARE THREE APPROACHES THEY CAN TAKE.
A PRIVATE DINNER WITH ONE OF THE ORGANIZERS.
THE GIFT OF A COFFEE-TABLE BOOK PUBLISHED BY THE LOCAL GOVERNMENT EXTOLLING THE CITY'S CHARMS.
THANKS SO MUCH...
TAP TAP
AND THE THIRD APPROACH IS TO PRESENT YOU WITH A COMMEMORATIVE PLAQUE.
UMMM... THANK YOU, THANK YOU.
IF I CHARGED FOR MY TALKS, I'D BE ABLE TO HAVE A HOME BIG ENOUGH TO STORE ALL OF THESE GIFTS. SINCE THE OPPOSITE IS TRUE, I HAVE TOO MANY FOR MY SMALL PLACE.
SO I'VE OCCASIONALLY "FORGOTTEN" THE GIFT IN MY HOTEL ROOM.
SADLY, THIS TACTIC DOESN'T ALWAYS TEND TO WORK.
...AND SIGN HERE TO INDICATE YOU'VE RECEIVED IT.
THIS TIME, THE GIFT CONSISTS OF A HEFTY PIECE OF LOCAL POTTERY ENGRAVED WITH MY NAME AND THE DATE. THE OBJECT IS PROTECTED BY A LARGE, VELVET-LINED CASE.
SALIDAS
5
...YES, BUT THE PLANE TO MADRID IS SMALL, SO YOU CAN'T CARRY ALL OF THAT ON AS HAND LUGGAGE. YOU'LL HAVE TO CHECK SOMETHING, CLAIM IT, AND RECHECK IT BECAUSE YOUR CONNECTING FLIGHT TO VALENCIA IS WITH ANOTHER AIRLINE. BUT YOU'LL HAVE TO HURRY. YOUR LAYOVER IS SHORT AND YOU MIGHT MISS THE FLIGHT.
B-BUT...
RIA
SIR, COME WITH US!
POLICIA
IT'S ONLY BECAUSE I'M A CATASTROPHIZING COWARD THAT I LUG THESE OBJECTS HOME INSTEAD OF ABANDONING THEM AT THE AIRPORT.

DEDICATED TO THE INSTITUTO LUIS VIVES, WHICH GAVE ME A BOTTLE OF RUM FOR THIS WEEK'S TALK.

...WHILE WE'RE AT IT, I'M GOING TO RUN A FULL BLOOD PANEL. OK?

I-IS IT REALLY THAT SERIOUS?

WHEN WAS THE LAST TIME YOU HAD BLOODWORK DONE?

I REMEMBER EXACTLY WHEN IT WAS. IT WAS THE WORLD CUP. SANTILLANA SCORED A HEADER.

THE '82 WORLD CUP?

YOU HAVEN'T HAD BLOODWORK DONE IN THIRTY YEARS? THAT'S INSANE. AT YOUR AGE YOU NEED TO GET TESTED MORE REGULARLY.

HAS IT BEEN A WHILE SINCE YOU'VE GOTTEN A BLOOD TEST?

NAH... SINCE THE WORLD CUP.

THE RESULTS WILL BE BACK ON MONDAY. AND DON'T WORRY, A LITTLE DIZZINESS IS NORMAL. IT HAPPENS TO A LOT OF PEOPLE.

W-WHAT ABOUT PASSING OUT?

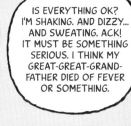

IS EVERYTHING OK? I'M SHAKING. AND DIZZY... AND SWEATING. ACK! IT MUST BE SOMETHING SERIOUS. I THINK MY GREAT-GREAT-GRAND-FATHER DIED OF FEVER OR SOMETHING.

THEY TOOK A LONG TIME BRINGING ME MY RESULTS, AND WHEN THE NURSE HANDED THEM OVER, SHE GAVE ME A PITYING LOOK.

ANALISIS

...SOME HARD-TO-CURE DISEASE. THAT'S OBVIOUS. IT MUST BE SOMETHING TERMINAL. IT'S ALL OVER. I HAD SO MANY THINGS LEFT TO DO. TWO COLLECTIONS OF STRIPS TO FINISH! WHY?!

GOD, I'VE NEVER ASKED YOU FOR ANYTHING, PARTLY BECAUSE I NEVER BELIEVED IN YOU. BUT IF I COME THROUGH THIS, I PROMISE TO LIVE A HEALTHY LIFE. I'LL WORK OUT MORE, GO MACROBIOTIC, EAT BETTER, STOP DRINKING...

YOU CAN COME IN.

...WELL, EVERYTHING LOOKS GOOD. NO CAUSE FOR CONCERN.

...I'LL SKIP THE GYM.

YEAH, LET'S MEET AT THE SAME DIVEY BAR AS ALWAYS... AND ORDER ME A BEER. WE'VE GOT TO CELEBRATE THE GOOD NEWS.

MY ENTERTAINING PAJAMAS

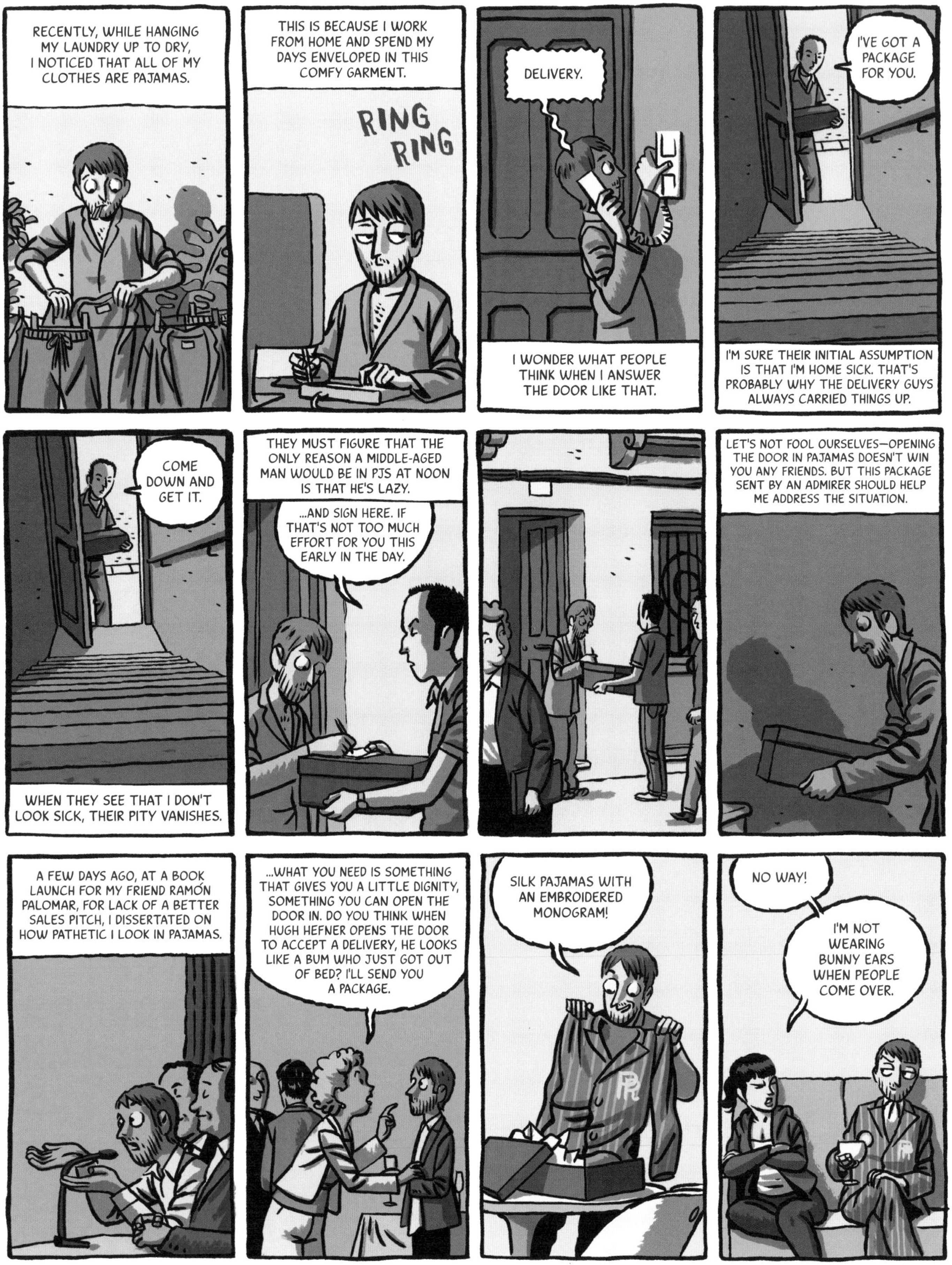
RECENTLY, WHILE HANGING MY LAUNDRY UP TO DRY, I NOTICED THAT ALL OF MY CLOTHES ARE PAJAMAS.
THIS IS BECAUSE I WORK FROM HOME AND SPEND MY DAYS ENVELOPED IN THIS COMFY GARMENT.
RING RING
DELIVERY.
I WONDER WHAT PEOPLE THINK WHEN I ANSWER THE DOOR LIKE THAT.
I'VE GOT A PACKAGE FOR YOU.
I'M SURE THEIR INITIAL ASSUMPTION IS THAT I'M HOME SICK. THAT'S PROBABLY WHY THE DELIVERY GUYS ALWAYS CARRIED THINGS UP.
COME DOWN AND GET IT.
WHEN THEY SEE THAT I DON'T LOOK SICK, THEIR PITY VANISHES.
THEY MUST FIGURE THAT THE ONLY REASON A MIDDLE-AGED MAN WOULD BE IN PJS AT NOON IS THAT HE'S LAZY.
...AND SIGN HERE. IF THAT'S NOT TOO MUCH EFFORT FOR YOU THIS EARLY IN THE DAY.
LET'S NOT FOOL OURSELVES—OPENING THE DOOR IN PAJAMAS DOESN'T WIN YOU ANY FRIENDS. BUT THIS PACKAGE SENT BY AN ADMIRER SHOULD HELP ME ADDRESS THE SITUATION.
A FEW DAYS AGO, AT A BOOK LAUNCH FOR MY FRIEND RAMÓN PALOMAR, FOR LACK OF A BETTER SALES PITCH, I DISSERTATED ON HOW PATHETIC I LOOK IN PAJAMAS.
...WHAT YOU NEED IS SOMETHING THAT GIVES YOU A LITTLE DIGNITY, SOMETHING YOU CAN OPEN THE DOOR IN. DO YOU THINK WHEN HUGH HEFNER OPENS THE DOOR TO ACCEPT A DELIVERY, HE LOOKS LIKE A BUM WHO JUST GOT OUT OF BED? I'LL SEND YOU A PACKAGE.
SILK PAJAMAS WITH AN EMBROIDERED MONOGRAM!
NO WAY!
I'M NOT WEARING BUNNY EARS WHEN PEOPLE COME OVER.

THE GREAT THINKER

IF I HAD TO ADMIT MY BIGGEST FLAW, IT WOULD HAVE TO BE "THINKING." I FIND IT A PLEASURABLE ACTIVITY: WRINGING OUT MY NEURONS, CONTEMPLATING UNIFICATION THEORY, MACROECONOMICS...
AT THE GYM, BETWEEN EXERCISES, I THINK ABOUT THOSE SORTS OF THINGS.
WATCHING EVERYBODY RUNNING ON TREADMILLS OR RIDING STATIONARY BIKES, I WONDER HOW MANY PEOPLE IN THE WORLD ARE DOING THE VERY SAME THING RIGHT NOW.
THIS MIDSIZE GYM HAS FIFTY TREADMILLS AND BIKES. IF A CITY LIKE VALENCIA, WITH A POPULATION OF 800,000, HAS ABOUT A HUNDRED GYMS...
WE COULD EXTRAPOLATE THAT SPAIN HAS SOME 5,600 GYMS.
THE WORLD POPULATION IS 6.5 BILLION. IF WE COUNT ONLY THE PEOPLE WHO LIVE IN DEVELOPED COUNTRIES, THAT WOULD MEAN THERE ARE ABOUT 300,000 GYMS IN THE WORLD.
AND IF EACH GYM HAS AN AVERAGE OF FIFTY TREADMILLS AND BIKES, THAT MEANS THAT RIGHT THIS MINUTE THERE ARE MORE THAN 15 MILLION PEOPLE BURNING CALORIES.
CONVERTING PHYSICAL EFFORT INTO ENERGY! EIGHTEEN HOURS A DAY, SIX DAYS A WEEK. EVERY MONTH OF THE YEAR, RAIN OR SHINE...
UNTIL OUR SOCIETY LEARNS TO LIVE WITHOUT SQUANDERING ENERGY...
...THE ENERGY PRODUCED BY GYMS, IF WE MADE GOOD USE OF IT, COULD REPLACE NUCLEAR ENERGY.
GYMS
COAL
OTHER
OIL
NATURAL GAS
CLEAN, RENEWABLE ENERGY.
HEY, ARE YOU GOING TO JUST SIT THERE DOING NOTHING FOR MUCH LONGER?
SCIENCE IS MISSING OUT ON A SUPERIOR INTELLECT.

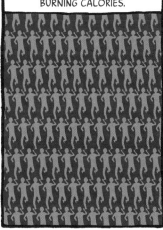

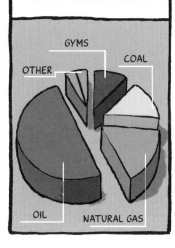

MY THRILLING ROUTINE

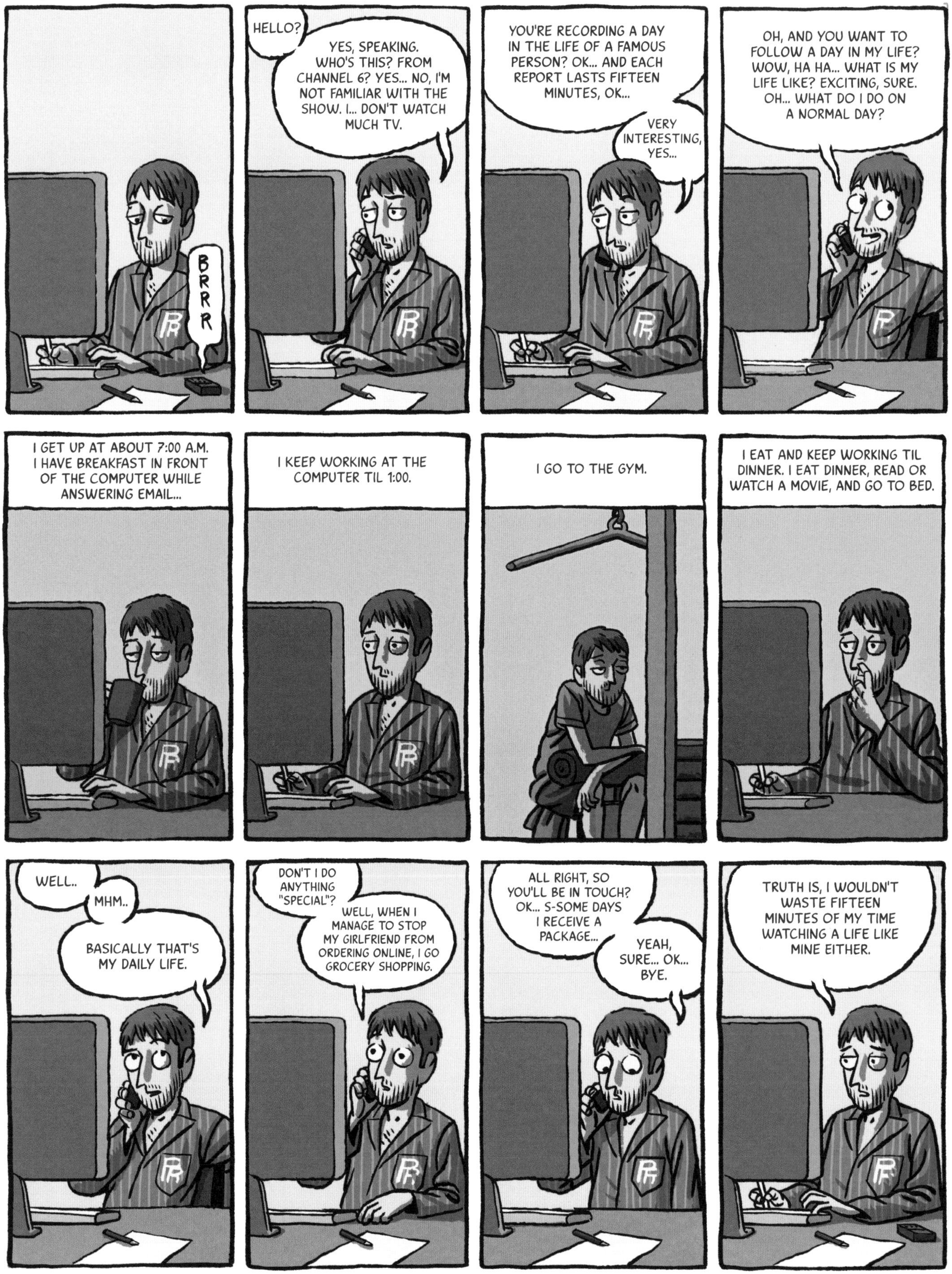
BRRR
HELLO?
YES, SPEAKING. WHO'S THIS? FROM CHANNEL 6? YES... NO, I'M NOT FAMILIAR WITH THE SHOW. I... DON'T WATCH MUCH TV.
YOU'RE RECORDING A DAY IN THE LIFE OF A FAMOUS PERSON? OK... AND EACH REPORT LASTS FIFTEEN MINUTES, OK...
VERY INTERESTING, YES...
OH, AND YOU WANT TO FOLLOW A DAY IN MY LIFE? WOW, HA HA... WHAT IS MY LIFE LIKE? EXCITING, SURE. OH... WHAT DO I DO ON A NORMAL DAY?
I GET UP AT ABOUT 7:00 A.M. I HAVE BREAKFAST IN FRONT OF THE COMPUTER WHILE ANSWERING EMAIL...
I KEEP WORKING AT THE COMPUTER TIL 1:00.
I GO TO THE GYM.
I EAT AND KEEP WORKING TIL DINNER. I EAT DINNER, READ OR WATCH A MOVIE, AND GO TO BED.
WELL..
MHM..
BASICALLY THAT'S MY DAILY LIFE.
DON'T I DO ANYTHING "SPECIAL"?
WELL, WHEN I MANAGE TO STOP MY GIRLFRIEND FROM ORDERING ONLINE, I GO GROCERY SHOPPING.
ALL RIGHT, SO YOU'LL BE IN TOUCH? OK... S-SOME DAYS I RECEIVE A PACKAGE...
YEAH, SURE... OK... BYE.
TRUTH IS, I WOULDN'T WASTE FIFTEEN MINUTES OF MY TIME WATCHING A LIFE LIKE MINE EITHER.

MODERN COMMUNICATION

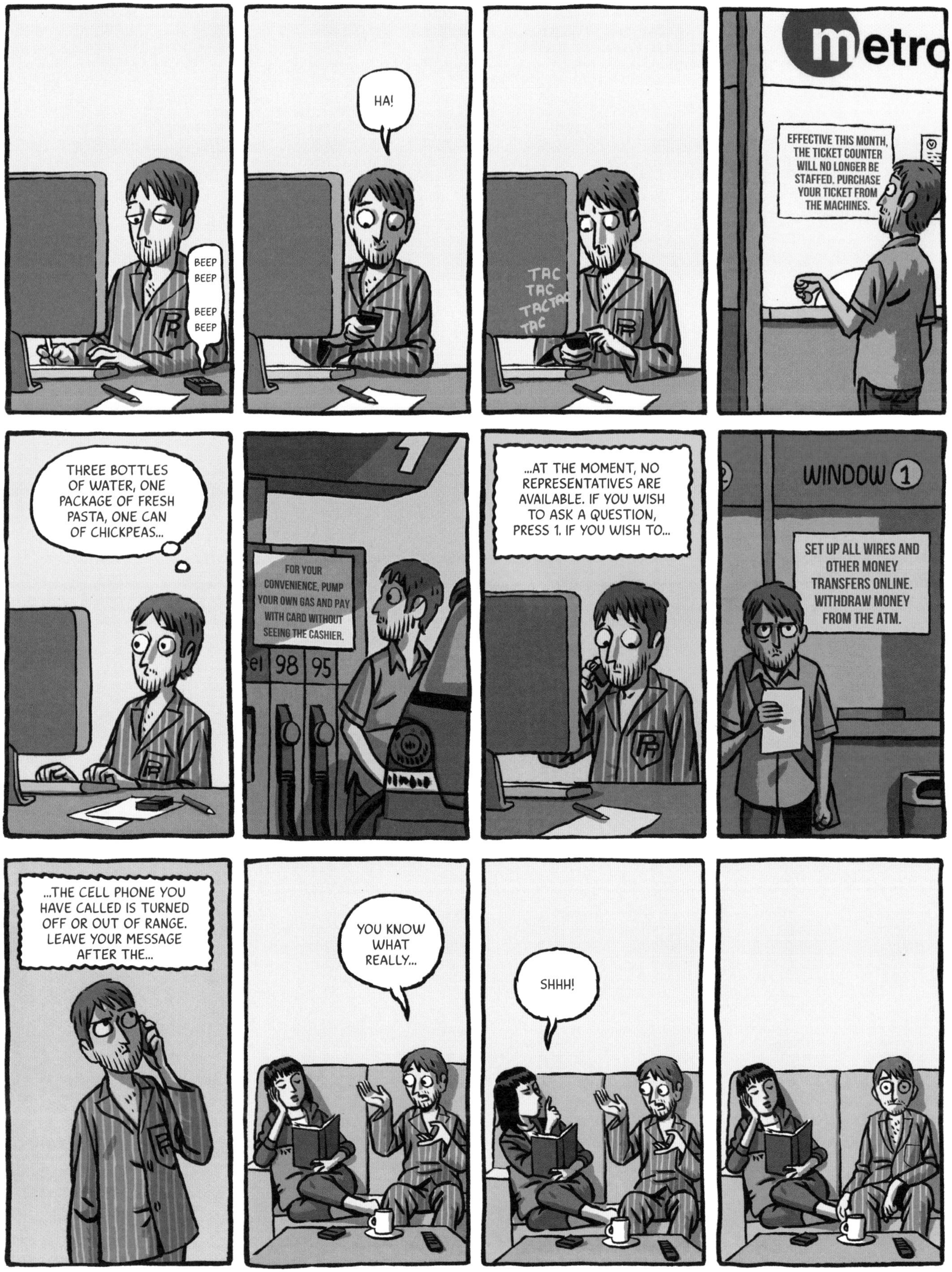

BEEP BEEP BEEP BEEP
HA!
TAC TAC TACTAC TAC
metro
EFFECTIVE THIS MONTH, THE TICKET COUNTER WILL NO LONGER BE STAFFED. PURCHASE YOUR TICKET FROM THE MACHINES.
THREE BOTTLES OF WATER, ONE PACKAGE OF FRESH PASTA, ONE CAN OF CHICKPEAS...
1
FOR YOUR CONVENIENCE, PUMP YOUR OWN GAS AND PAY WITH CARD WITHOUT SEEING THE CASHIER.
98 95
...AT THE MOMENT, NO REPRESENTATIVES ARE AVAILABLE. IF YOU WISH TO ASK A QUESTION, PRESS 1. IF YOU WISH TO...
WINDOW 1
SET UP ALL WIRES AND OTHER MONEY TRANSFERS ONLINE. WITHDRAW MONEY FROM THE ATM.
...THE CELL PHONE YOU HAVE CALLED IS TURNED OFF OR OUT OF RANGE. LEAVE YOUR MESSAGE AFTER THE...
YOU KNOW WHAT REALLY...
SHHH!

THE DEATH OF POSTPRANDIAL CONVERSATION

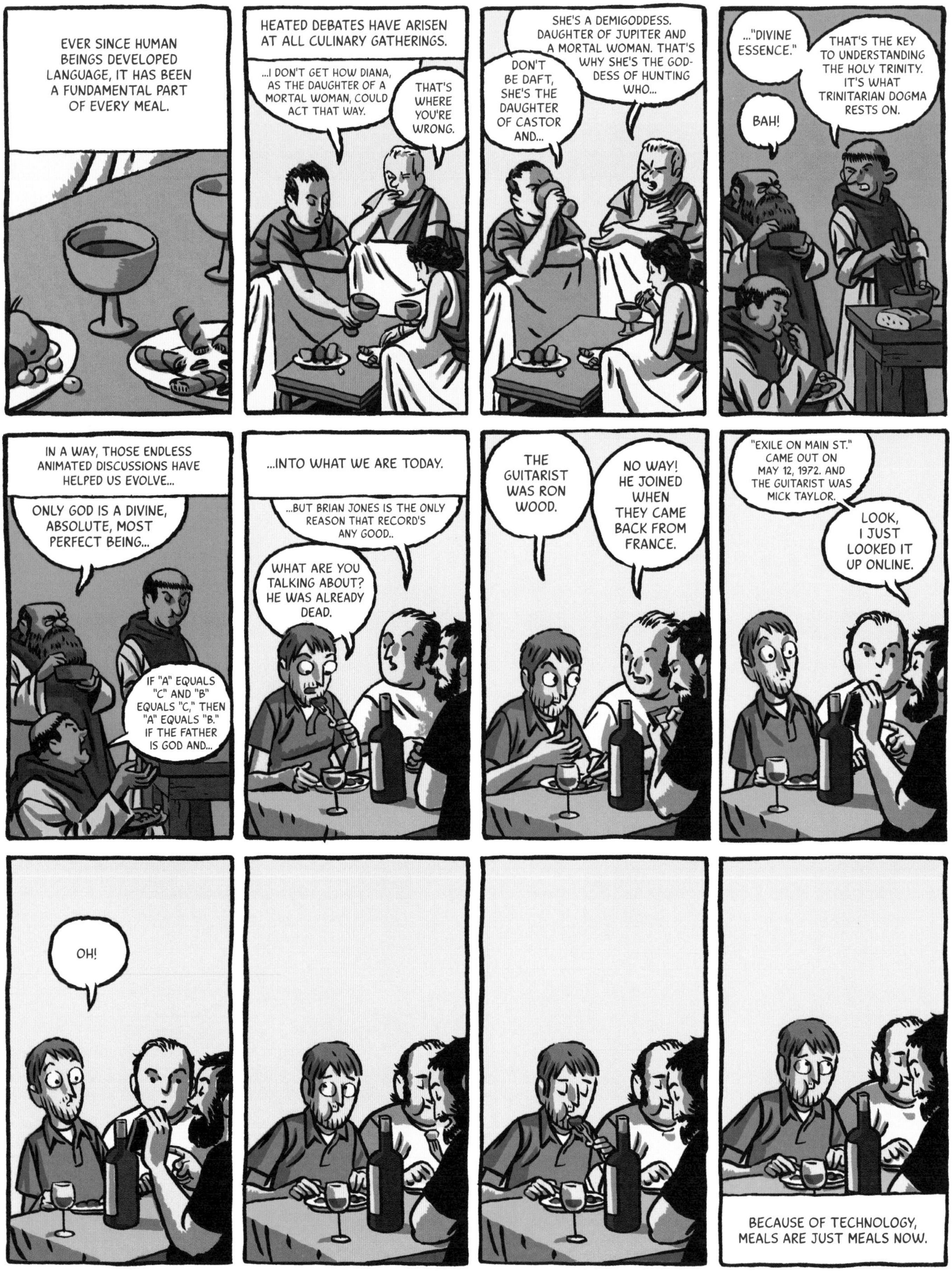

EVER SINCE HUMAN BEINGS DEVELOPED LANGUAGE, IT HAS BEEN A FUNDAMENTAL PART OF EVERY MEAL.
HEATED DEBATES HAVE ARISEN AT ALL CULINARY GATHERINGS.
...I DON'T GET HOW DIANA, AS THE DAUGHTER OF A MORTAL WOMAN, COULD ACT THAT WAY.
THAT'S WHERE YOU'RE WRONG.
SHE'S A DEMIGODDESS. DAUGHTER OF JUPITER AND A MORTAL WOMAN. THAT'S WHY SHE'S THE GODDESS OF HUNTING WHO...
DON'T BE DAFT, SHE'S THE DAUGHTER OF CASTOR AND...
..."DIVINE ESSENCE."
THAT'S THE KEY TO UNDERSTANDING THE HOLY TRINITY. IT'S WHAT TRINITARIAN DOGMA RESTS ON.
BAH!
IN A WAY, THOSE ENDLESS ANIMATED DISCUSSIONS HAVE HELPED US EVOLVE...
ONLY GOD IS A DIVINE, ABSOLUTE, MOST PERFECT BEING...
IF "A" EQUALS "C" AND "B" EQUALS "C," THEN "A" EQUALS "B." IF THE FATHER IS GOD AND...
...INTO WHAT WE ARE TODAY.
...BUT BRIAN JONES IS THE ONLY REASON THAT RECORD'S ANY GOOD..
WHAT ARE YOU TALKING ABOUT? HE WAS ALREADY DEAD.
THE GUITARIST WAS RON WOOD.
NO WAY! HE JOINED WHEN THEY CAME BACK FROM FRANCE.
"EXILE ON MAIN ST." CAME OUT ON MAY 12, 1972. AND THE GUITARIST WAS MICK TAYLOR.
LOOK, I JUST LOOKED IT UP ONLINE.
OH!
BECAUSE OF TECHNOLOGY, MEALS ARE JUST MEALS NOW.

MY SELF AND I

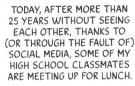

TODAY, AFTER MORE THAN 25 YEARS WITHOUT SEEING EACH OTHER, THANKS TO (OR THROUGH THE FAULT OF) SOCIAL MEDIA, SOME OF MY HIGH SCHOOL CLASSMATES ARE MEETING UP FOR LUNCH.

...YOU LOOK THE SAME AS EVER...

...AND YOU LOOK EVEN YOUNGER...

THOUGH WE TELL EACH OTHER WHITE LIES, IT'S OBVIOUS THAT TIME HAS LEFT A MARK ON ALL OF US. I HAD A HARD TIME RECOGNIZING SOME OF MY FORMER CLASSMATES.

WE'RE NOT YOUR AVERAGE 40-SOMETHINGS. WE'VE AGED WELL.

WE TAKE CARE OF OUR-SELVES...

I'D LIKE TO SIT ACROSS FROM HIGH-SCHOOL ME SO I COULD COMPARE.

ONE OF MY FAVORITE BORGES STORIES IS THE ONE WHERE THE AUTHOR, AS AN OLD MAN, DESCRIBES A "HYPOTHETICAL" ENCOUNTER WITH HIS YOUNGER SELF. THEY CHAT AMIABLY BESIDE THE SEINE, AND THE ELDERLY BORGES TELLS THE YOUNG MAN HOW MUCH HE HAS LEARNED OVER THE COURSE OF HIS LONG LIFE.

I WONDER WHAT A SIMILAR ENCOUNTER WITH MYSELF FROM 25 YEARS AGO WOULD BE LIKE.

YOU LOOK SO... SO... WEIRD. YOU LOOK LIKE AN OLD MAN— LIKE DAD.

SERIOUSLY? TO ME I ALWAYS LOOK THE SAME. WHEREAS YOU LOOK LIKE... LIKE A KID.

SO TELL ME, WHAT DO YOU DO? OR, I GUESS, WHAT DO WE DO?

THAT'S THE BEST PART!

I'VE FULFILLED OUR DREAM.

WE'RE A RICH AND FAMOUS ARTIST LIKE PICASSO?! WE GET ALL THE CHICKS!?

UMMM... WELLLL, NO.

WE EARN A LIVING DRAWING COMICS AND STUFF...

THAT WAS OUR DREAM, RIGHT?

WELL...

THAT'S COOL...

BUT THE OTHER VERSION SOUNDS WAY COOLER.

NOW THAT YOU'RE 25 YEARS OLDER, WHAT HAVE YOU LEARNED?

LET'S SEE...

WELL... FOR EXAMPLE, PUTTING A SPOON IN THE MOUTH OF A BOTTLE OF CHAMPAGNE DOESN'T KEEP IT FROM GOING FLAT. AND DRINKING TONIC WATER AFTER BAILEY'S WON'T MAKE YOU SICK. I KNOW YOU'RE CONCERNED ABOUT THAT...

I'M NOT QUITE CLEAR ON THE THING ABOUT WAITING TWO HOURS AFTER MEALS BEFORE SWIMMING, SO FOLLOW IT JUST IN CASE. AND ABOVE ALL—AND THIS IS THE MOST IMPORTANT BIT—AVOID '80S FASHION AS MUCH AS POSSIBLE, OR YOU'LL REGRET IT WHEN YOU SEE THE PHOTOS LATER ON.

OK.

WHAT ABOUT GIRLS? ANY ADVICE?

SURE, OF COURSE. THAT'S IMPORTANT AT YOUR AGE... WELL... ON A DATE, IT'S BETTER TO LET THEM TALK. WHAT ELSE...

JEEZ, CONSIDERING YOU'RE 25 YEARS OLDER THAN ME, IT DOESN'T SEEM LIKE YOU'VE LEARNED MUCH ABOUT LIFE.

TAKE CARE OF YOURSELF, MAN, YOU'RE LOOKING HAGGARD.

OH, ONE LAST BIT OF ADVICE.

TELL MA NOT TO BOTHER LEAVING EXTRA FABRIC INSIDE YOUR PANTS HEM, BECAUSE YOU WON'T BE HITTING A GROWTH SPURT. GET USED TO IT.

JERK!

RELATIVITY

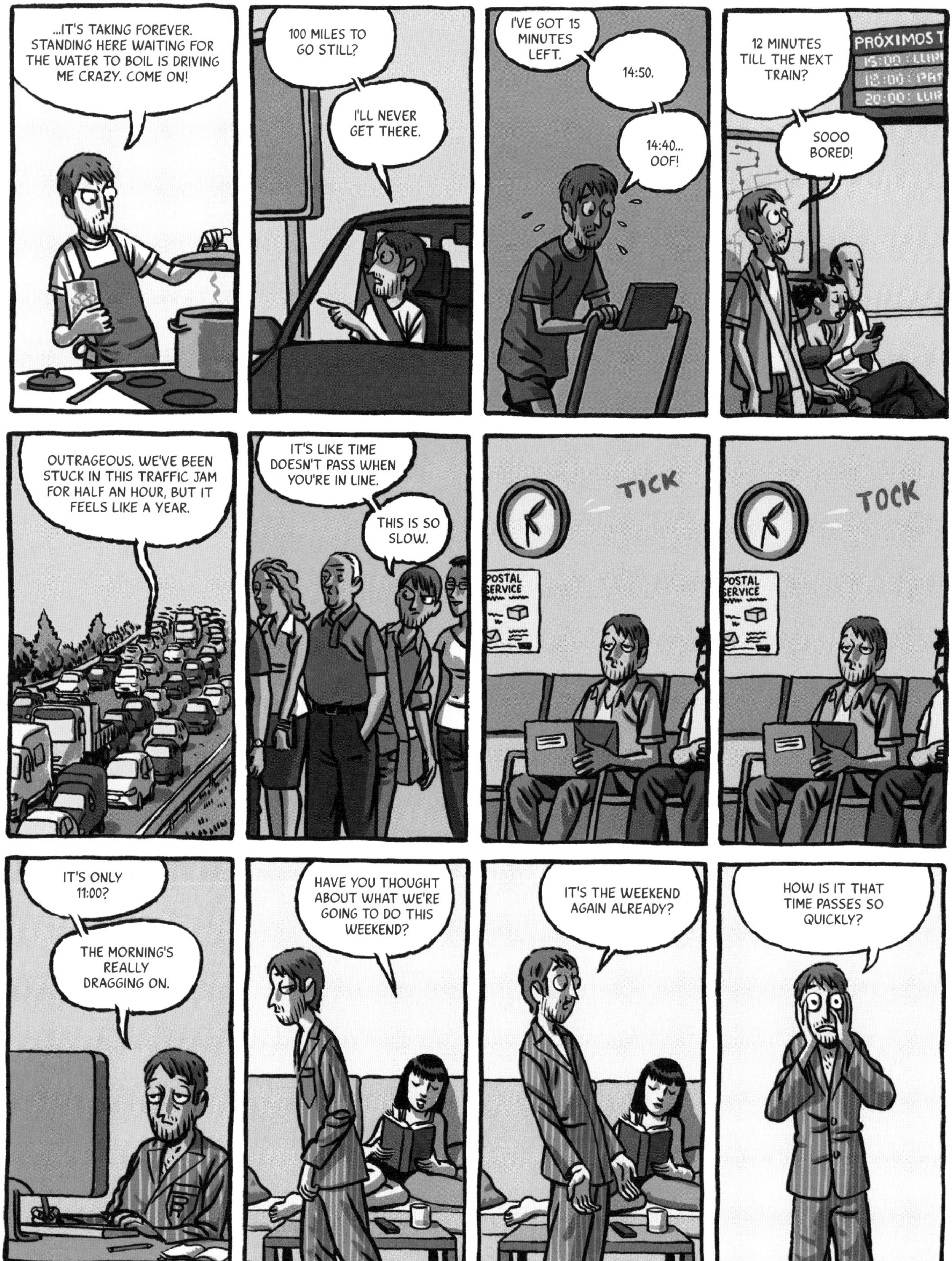

...IT'S TAKING FOREVER. STANDING HERE WAITING FOR THE WATER TO BOIL IS DRIVING ME CRAZY. COME ON!
100 MILES TO GO STILL?
I'LL NEVER GET THERE.
I'VE GOT 15 MINUTES LEFT.
14:50.
14:40... OOF!
12 MINUTES TILL THE NEXT TRAIN?
SOOO BORED!
OUTRAGEOUS. WE'VE BEEN STUCK IN THIS TRAFFIC JAM FOR HALF AN HOUR, BUT IT FEELS LIKE A YEAR.
IT'S LIKE TIME DOESN'T PASS WHEN YOU'RE IN LINE.
THIS IS SO SLOW.
TICK
POSTAL SERVICE
TOCK
POSTAL SERVICE
IT'S ONLY 11:00?
THE MORNING'S REALLY DRAGGING ON.
HAVE YOU THOUGHT ABOUT WHAT WE'RE GOING TO DO THIS WEEKEND?
IT'S THE WEEKEND AGAIN ALREADY?
HOW IS IT THAT TIME PASSES SO QUICKLY?

PRIVACY, PLEASE

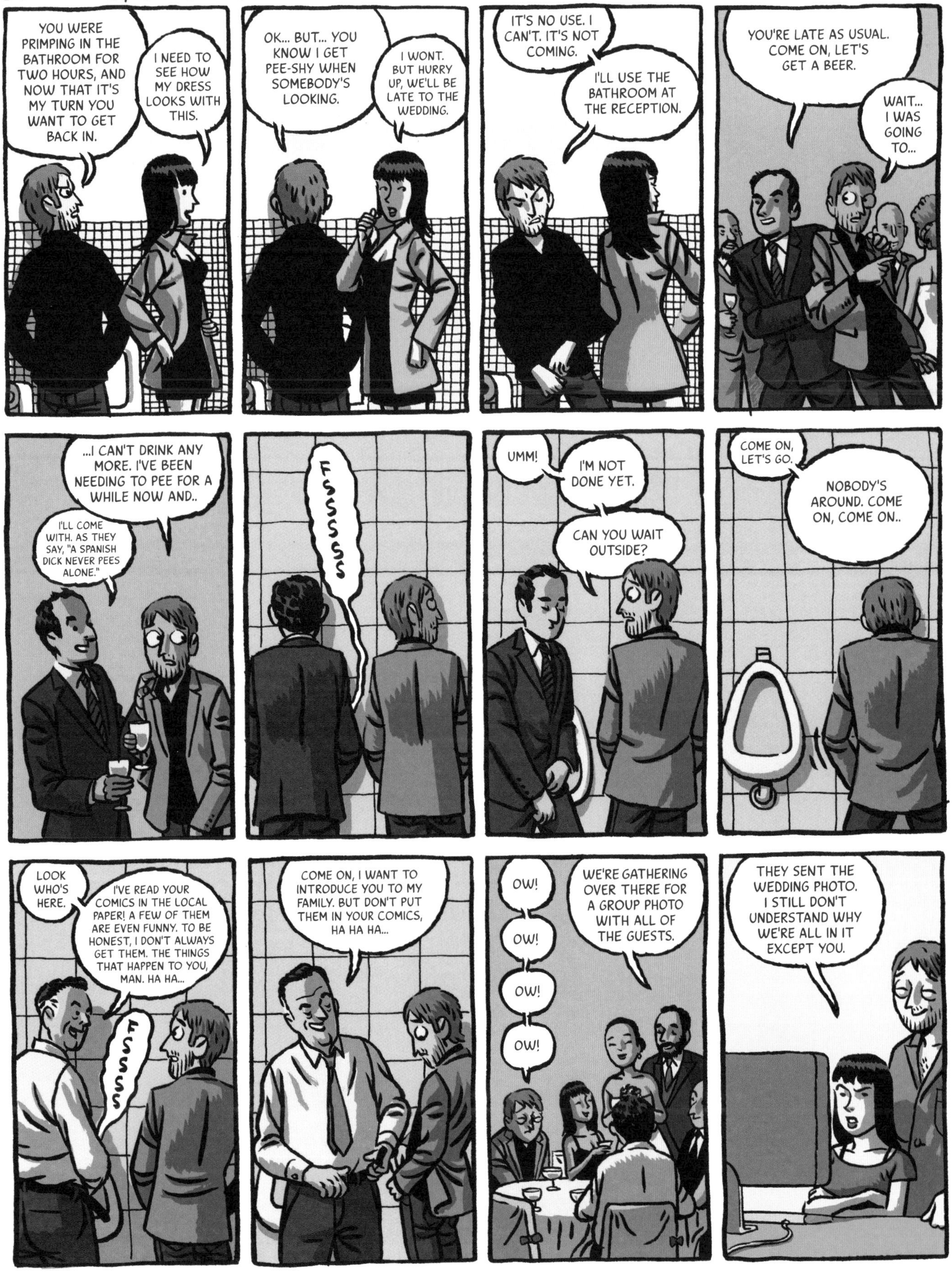
YOU WERE PRIMPING IN THE BATHROOM FOR TWO HOURS, AND NOW THAT IT'S MY TURN YOU WANT TO GET BACK IN.
I NEED TO SEE HOW MY DRESS LOOKS WITH THIS.
OK... BUT... YOU KNOW I GET PEE-SHY WHEN SOMEBODY'S LOOKING.
I WONT. BUT HURRY UP, WE'LL BE LATE TO THE WEDDING.
IT'S NO USE. I CAN'T. IT'S NOT COMING.
I'LL USE THE BATHROOM AT THE RECEPTION.
YOU'RE LATE AS USUAL. COME ON, LET'S GET A BEER.
WAIT... I WAS GOING TO...
...I CAN'T DRINK ANY MORE. I'VE BEEN NEEDING TO PEE FOR A WHILE NOW AND..
I'LL COME WITH. AS THEY SAY, "A SPANISH DICK NEVER PEES ALONE."
FSSSSSS
UMM!
I'M NOT DONE YET.
CAN YOU WAIT OUTSIDE?
COME ON, LET'S GO.
NOBODY'S AROUND. COME ON, COME ON..
LOOK WHO'S HERE.
I'VE READ YOUR COMICS IN THE LOCAL PAPER! A FEW OF THEM ARE EVEN FUNNY. TO BE HONEST, I DON'T ALWAYS GET THEM. THE THINGS THAT HAPPEN TO YOU, MAN. HA HA...
FSSSS
COME ON, I WANT TO INTRODUCE YOU TO MY FAMILY. BUT DON'T PUT THEM IN YOUR COMICS, HA HA HA...
OW!
OW!
OW!
OW!
WE'RE GATHERING OVER THERE FOR A GROUP PHOTO WITH ALL OF THE GUESTS.
THEY SENT THE WEDDING PHOTO. I STILL DON'T UNDERSTAND WHY WE'RE ALL IN IT EXCEPT YOU.

THE 15-M MOVEMENT

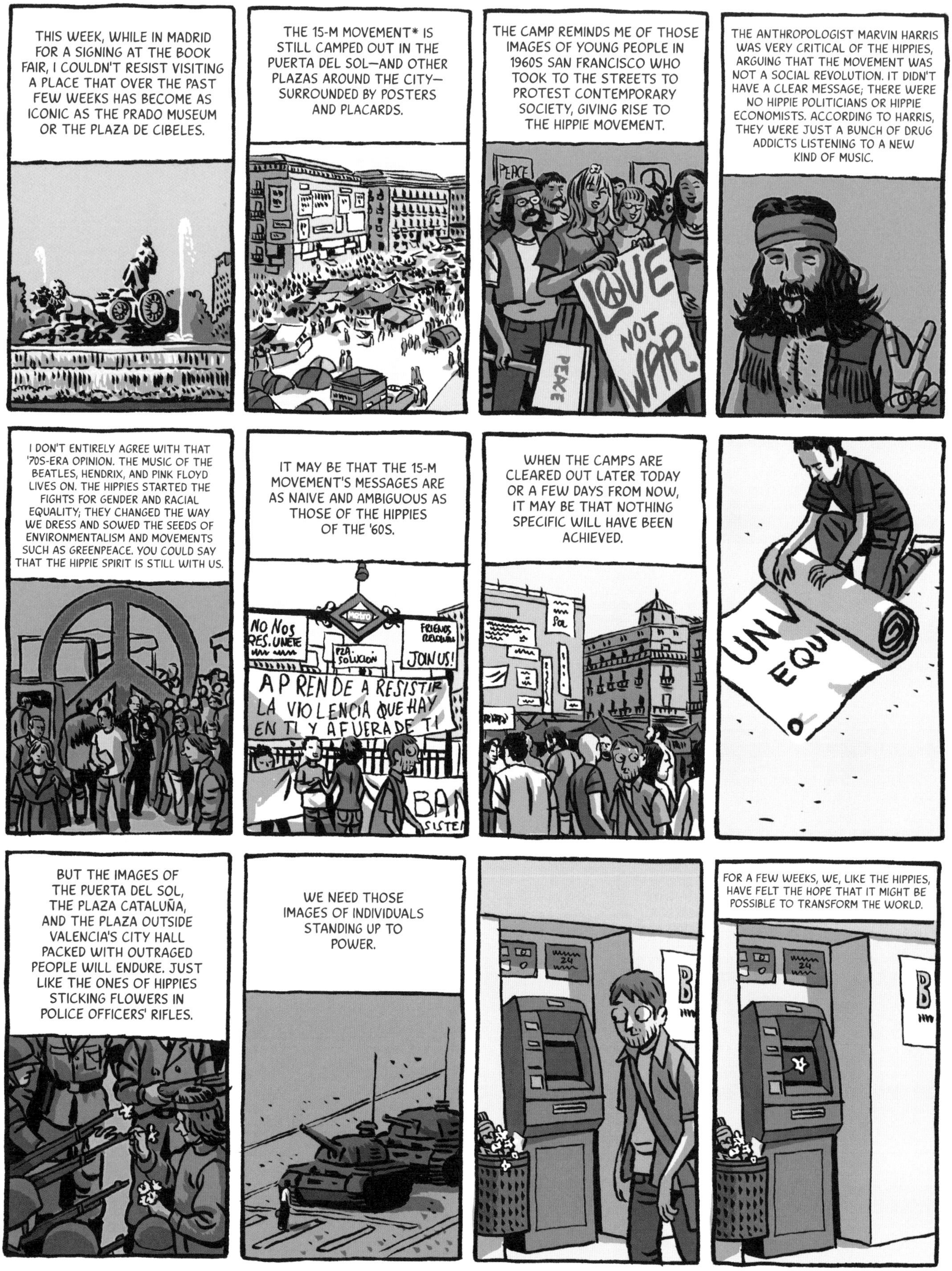
THIS WEEK, WHILE IN MADRID FOR A SIGNING AT THE BOOK FAIR, I COULDN'T RESIST VISITING A PLACE THAT OVER THE PAST FEW WEEKS HAS BECOME AS ICONIC AS THE PRADO MUSEUM OR THE PLAZA DE CIBELES.
THE 15-M MOVEMENT* IS STILL CAMPED OUT IN THE PUERTA DEL SOL—AND OTHER PLAZAS AROUND THE CITY—SURROUNDED BY POSTERS AND PLACARDS.
THE CAMP REMINDS ME OF THOSE IMAGES OF YOUNG PEOPLE IN 1960S SAN FRANCISCO WHO TOOK TO THE STREETS TO PROTEST CONTEMPORARY SOCIETY, GIVING RISE TO THE HIPPIE MOVEMENT.
PEACE
LOVE NOT WAR
PEACE
THE ANTHROPOLOGIST MARVIN HARRIS WAS VERY CRITICAL OF THE HIPPIES, ARGUING THAT THE MOVEMENT WAS NOT A SOCIAL REVOLUTION. IT DIDN'T HAVE A CLEAR MESSAGE; THERE WERE NO HIPPIE POLITICIANS OR HIPPIE ECONOMISTS. ACCORDING TO HARRIS, THEY WERE JUST A BUNCH OF DRUG ADDICTS LISTENING TO A NEW KIND OF MUSIC.
I DON'T ENTIRELY AGREE WITH THAT '70S-ERA OPINION. THE MUSIC OF THE BEATLES, HENDRIX, AND PINK FLOYD LIVES ON. THE HIPPIES STARTED THE FIGHTS FOR GENDER AND RACIAL EQUALITY; THEY CHANGED THE WAY WE DRESS AND SOWED THE SEEDS OF ENVIRONMENTALISM AND MOVEMENTS SUCH AS GREENPEACE. YOU COULD SAY THAT THE HIPPIE SPIRIT IS STILL WITH US.
IT MAY BE THAT THE 15-M MOVEMENT'S MESSAGES ARE AS NAIVE AND AMBIGUOUS AS THOSE OF THE HIPPIES OF THE '60S.
NO NOS RES. UNETE
Metro
PZA. SOLUCION
JOIN US!
APRENDE A RESISTIR LA VIOLENCIA QUE HAY EN TI Y AFUERA DE TI
WHEN THE CAMPS ARE CLEARED OUT LATER TODAY OR A FEW DAYS FROM NOW, IT MAY BE THAT NOTHING SPECIFIC WILL HAVE BEEN ACHIEVED.
SOL
BUT THE IMAGES OF THE PUERTA DEL SOL, THE PLAZA CATALUÑA, AND THE PLAZA OUTSIDE VALENCIA'S CITY HALL PACKED WITH OUTRAGED PEOPLE WILL ENDURE. JUST LIKE THE ONES OF HIPPIES STICKING FLOWERS IN POLICE OFFICERS' RIFLES.
WE NEED THOSE IMAGES OF INDIVIDUALS STANDING UP TO POWER.
FOR A FEW WEEKS, WE, LIKE THE HIPPIES, HAVE FELT THE HOPE THAT IT MIGHT BE POSSIBLE TO TRANSFORM THE WORLD.

*A WIDESPREAD ANTI-AUSTERITY MOVEMENT IN SPAIN THAT AROSE IN MAY 2011. THE MOVEMENT CONSISTED OF A SERIES OF LARGE DEMONSTRATIONS AND OCCUPATIONS REGARDING PRIMARILY ECONOMIC ISSUES AFTER THE 2008 ONSET OF CRUSHING FINANCIAL CRISIS AND RECORD UNEMPLOYMENT IN SPAIN.

MISSION IMPOSSIBLE

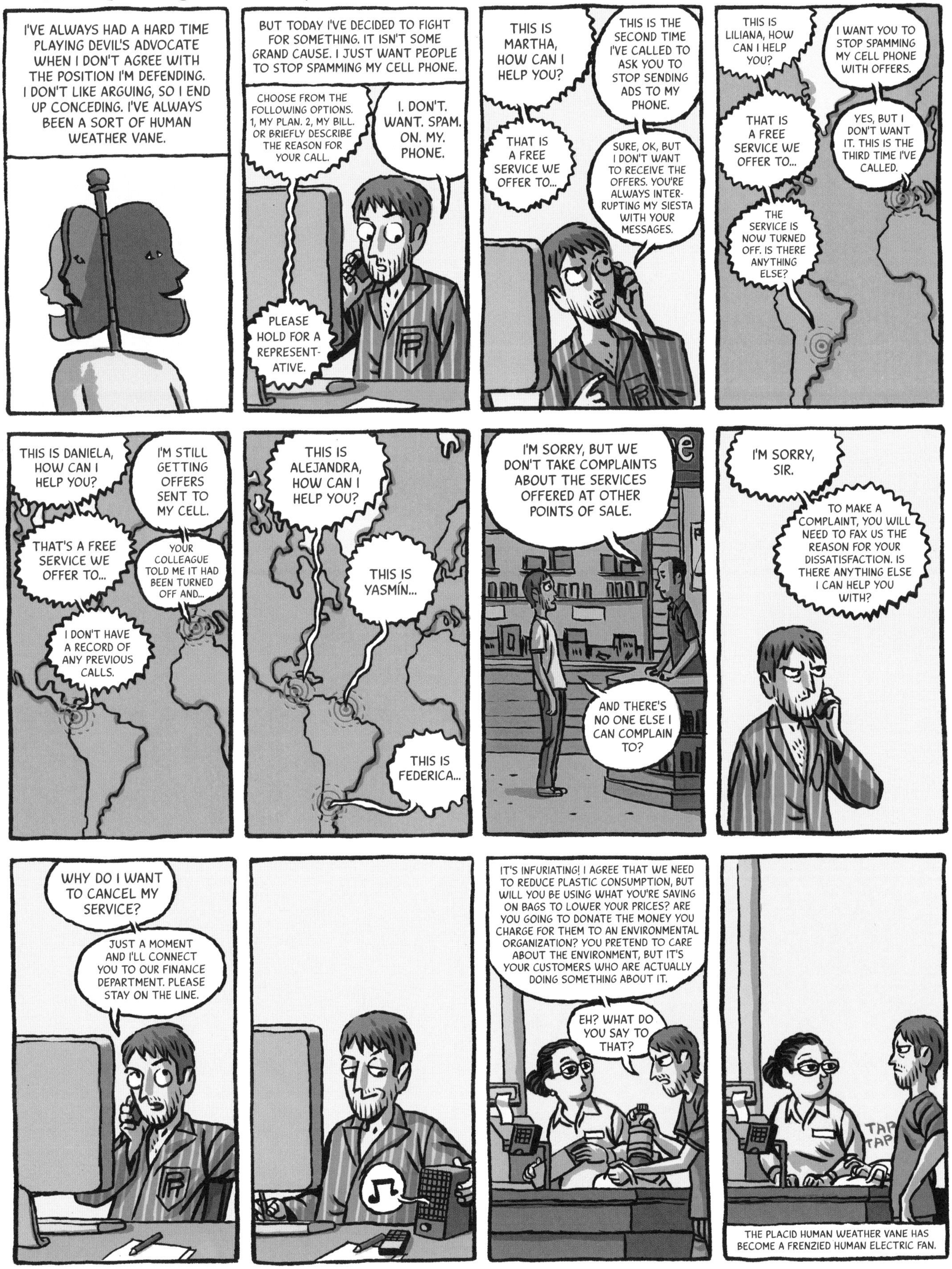

I'VE ALWAYS HAD A HARD TIME PLAYING DEVIL'S ADVOCATE WHEN I DON'T AGREE WITH THE POSITION I'M DEFENDING. I DON'T LIKE ARGUING, SO I END UP CONCEDING. I'VE ALWAYS BEEN A SORT OF HUMAN WEATHER VANE.
BUT TODAY I'VE DECIDED TO FIGHT FOR SOMETHING. IT ISN'T SOME GRAND CAUSE. I JUST WANT PEOPLE TO STOP SPAMMING MY CELL PHONE.
CHOOSE FROM THE FOLLOWING OPTIONS. 1, MY PLAN. 2, MY BILL. OR BRIEFLY DESCRIBE THE REASON FOR YOUR CALL.
I. DON'T. WANT. SPAM. ON. MY. PHONE.
PLEASE HOLD FOR A REPRESENT-ATIVE.
THIS IS MARTHA, HOW CAN I HELP YOU?
THIS IS THE SECOND TIME I'VE CALLED TO ASK YOU TO STOP SENDING ADS TO MY PHONE.
THAT IS A FREE SERVICE WE OFFER TO...
SURE, OK, BUT I DON'T WANT TO RECEIVE THE OFFERS. YOU'RE ALWAYS INTER-RUPTING MY SIESTA WITH YOUR MESSAGES.
THIS IS LILIANA, HOW CAN I HELP YOU?
I WANT YOU TO STOP SPAMMING MY CELL PHONE WITH OFFERS.
THAT IS A FREE SERVICE WE OFFER TO...
YES, BUT I DON'T WANT IT. THIS IS THE THIRD TIME I'VE CALLED.
THE SERVICE IS NOW TURNED OFF. IS THERE ANYTHING ELSE?
THIS IS DANIELA, HOW CAN I HELP YOU?
I'M STILL GETTING OFFERS SENT TO MY CELL.
THAT'S A FREE SERVICE WE OFFER TO...
YOUR COLLEAGUE TOLD ME IT HAD BEEN TURNED OFF AND...
I DON'T HAVE A RECORD OF ANY PREVIOUS CALLS.
THIS IS ALEJANDRA, HOW CAN I HELP YOU?
THIS IS YASMÍN...
THIS IS FEDERICA...
I'M SORRY, BUT WE DON'T TAKE COMPLAINTS ABOUT THE SERVICES OFFERED AT OTHER POINTS OF SALE.
AND THERE'S NO ONE ELSE I CAN COMPLAIN TO?
I'M SORRY, SIR.
TO MAKE A COMPLAINT, YOU WILL NEED TO FAX US THE REASON FOR YOUR DISSATISFACTION. IS THERE ANYTHING ELSE I CAN HELP YOU WITH?
WHY DO I WANT TO CANCEL MY SERVICE?
JUST A MOMENT AND I'LL CONNECT YOU TO OUR FINANCE DEPARTMENT. PLEASE STAY ON THE LINE.
IT'S INFURIATING! I AGREE THAT WE NEED TO REDUCE PLASTIC CONSUMPTION, BUT WILL YOU BE USING WHAT YOU'RE SAVING ON BAGS TO LOWER YOUR PRICES? ARE YOU GOING TO DONATE THE MONEY YOU CHARGE FOR THEM TO AN ENVIRONMENTAL ORGANIZATION? YOU PRETEND TO CARE ABOUT THE ENVIRONMENT, BUT IT'S YOUR CUSTOMERS WHO ARE ACTUALLY DOING SOMETHING ABOUT IT.
EH? WHAT DO YOU SAY TO THAT?
TAP TAP
THE PLACID HUMAN WEATHER VANE HAS BECOME A FRENZIED HUMAN ELECTRIC FAN.

THE SENSOR

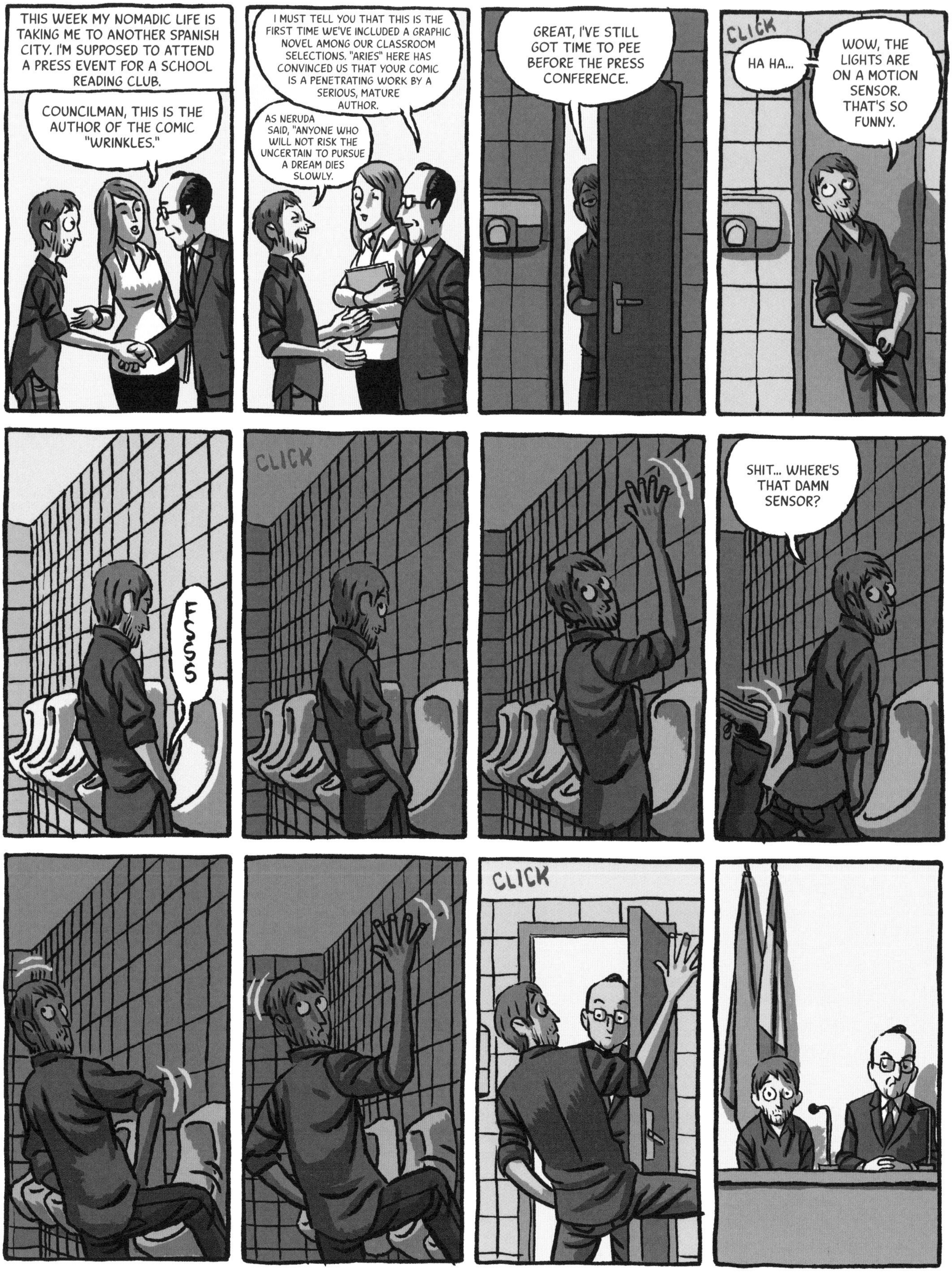

THIS WEEK MY NOMADIC LIFE IS TAKING ME TO ANOTHER SPANISH CITY. I'M SUPPOSED TO ATTEND A PRESS EVENT FOR A SCHOOL READING CLUB.
COUNCILMAN, THIS IS THE AUTHOR OF THE COMIC "WRINKLES."
I MUST TELL YOU THAT THIS IS THE FIRST TIME WE'VE INCLUDED A GRAPHIC NOVEL AMONG OUR CLASSROOM SELECTIONS. "ARIES" HERE HAS CONVINCED US THAT YOUR COMIC IS A PENETRATING WORK BY A SERIOUS, MATURE AUTHOR.
AS NERUDA SAID, "ANYONE WHO WILL NOT RISK THE UNCERTAIN TO PURSUE A DREAM DIES SLOWLY.
GREAT, I'VE STILL GOT TIME TO PEE BEFORE THE PRESS CONFERENCE.
CLICK
HA HA...
WOW, THE LIGHTS ARE ON A MOTION SENSOR. THAT'S SO FUNNY.
FSSSS
CLICK
SHIT... WHERE'S THAT DAMN SENSOR?
CLICK

A LIGHT REMODEL

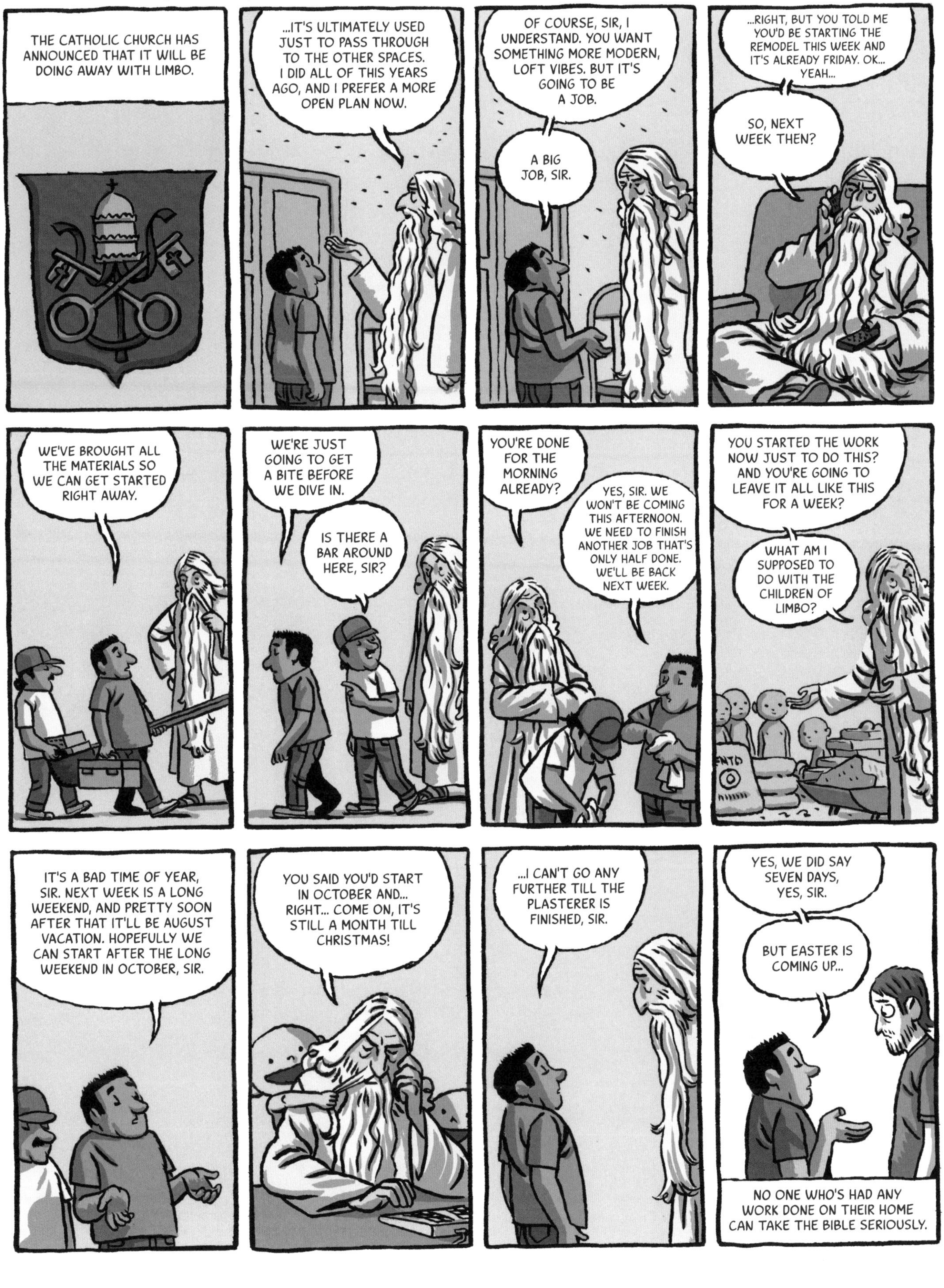

THE CATHOLIC CHURCH HAS ANNOUNCED THAT IT WILL BE DOING AWAY WITH LIMBO.
...IT'S ULTIMATELY USED JUST TO PASS THROUGH TO THE OTHER SPACES. I DID ALL OF THIS YEARS AGO, AND I PREFER A MORE OPEN PLAN NOW.
OF COURSE, SIR, I UNDERSTAND. YOU WANT SOMETHING MORE MODERN, LOFT VIBES. BUT IT'S GOING TO BE A JOB.
A BIG JOB, SIR.
...RIGHT, BUT YOU TOLD ME YOU'D BE STARTING THE REMODEL THIS WEEK AND IT'S ALREADY FRIDAY. OK... YEAH...
SO, NEXT WEEK THEN?
WE'VE BROUGHT ALL THE MATERIALS SO WE CAN GET STARTED RIGHT AWAY.
WE'RE JUST GOING TO GET A BITE BEFORE WE DIVE IN.
IS THERE A BAR AROUND HERE, SIR?
YOU'RE DONE FOR THE MORNING ALREADY?
YES, SIR. WE WON'T BE COMING THIS AFTERNOON. WE NEED TO FINISH ANOTHER JOB THAT'S ONLY HALF DONE. WE'LL BE BACK NEXT WEEK.
YOU STARTED THE WORK NOW JUST TO DO THIS? AND YOU'RE GOING TO LEAVE IT ALL LIKE THIS FOR A WEEK?
WHAT AM I SUPPOSED TO DO WITH THE CHILDREN OF LIMBO?
IT'S A BAD TIME OF YEAR, SIR. NEXT WEEK IS A LONG WEEKEND, AND PRETTY SOON AFTER THAT IT'LL BE AUGUST VACATION. HOPEFULLY WE CAN START AFTER THE LONG WEEKEND IN OCTOBER, SIR.
YOU SAID YOU'D START IN OCTOBER AND... RIGHT... COME ON, IT'S STILL A MONTH TILL CHRISTMAS!
...I CAN'T GO ANY FURTHER TILL THE PLASTERER IS FINISHED, SIR.
YES, WE DID SAY SEVEN DAYS, YES, SIR.
BUT EASTER IS COMING UP...
NO ONE WHO'S HAD ANY WORK DONE ON THEIR HOME CAN TAKE THE BIBLE SERIOUSLY.

OUT OF OPTIONS

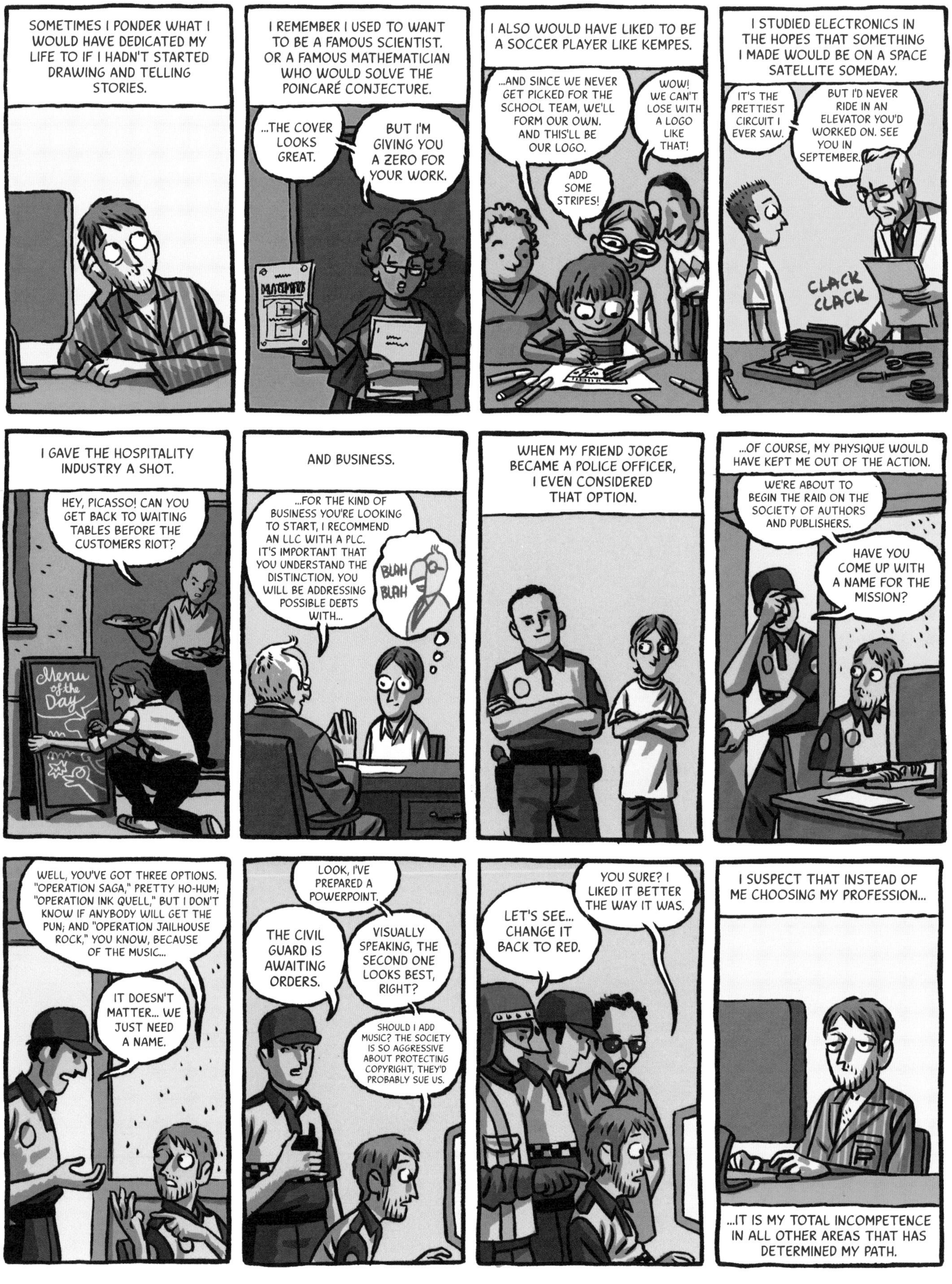

SOMETIMES I PONDER WHAT I WOULD HAVE DEDICATED MY LIFE TO IF I HADN'T STARTED DRAWING AND TELLING STORIES.
I REMEMBER I USED TO WANT TO BE A FAMOUS SCIENTIST. OR A FAMOUS MATHEMATICIAN WHO WOULD SOLVE THE POINCARÉ CONJECTURE.
...THE COVER LOOKS GREAT.
BUT I'M GIVING YOU A ZERO FOR YOUR WORK.
I ALSO WOULD HAVE LIKED TO BE A SOCCER PLAYER LIKE KEMPES.
...AND SINCE WE NEVER GET PICKED FOR THE SCHOOL TEAM, WE'LL FORM OUR OWN. AND THIS'LL BE OUR LOGO.
WOW! WE CAN'T LOSE WITH A LOGO LIKE THAT!
ADD SOME STRIPES!
I STUDIED ELECTRONICS IN THE HOPES THAT SOMETHING I MADE WOULD BE ON A SPACE SATELLITE SOMEDAY.
IT'S THE PRETTIEST CIRCUIT I EVER SAW.
BUT I'D NEVER RIDE IN AN ELEVATOR YOU'D WORKED ON. SEE YOU IN SEPTEMBER.
CLACK CLACK
I GAVE THE HOSPITALITY INDUSTRY A SHOT.
HEY, PICASSO! CAN YOU GET BACK TO WAITING TABLES BEFORE THE CUSTOMERS RIOT?
Menu of the Day
AND BUSINESS.
...FOR THE KIND OF BUSINESS YOU'RE LOOKING TO START, I RECOMMEND AN LLC WITH A PLC. IT'S IMPORTANT THAT YOU UNDERSTAND THE DISTINCTION. YOU WILL BE ADDRESSING POSSIBLE DEBTS WITH...
BLAH BLAH
WHEN MY FRIEND JORGE BECAME A POLICE OFFICER, I EVEN CONSIDERED THAT OPTION.
...OF COURSE, MY PHYSIQUE WOULD HAVE KEPT ME OUT OF THE ACTION.
WE'RE ABOUT TO BEGIN THE RAID ON THE SOCIETY OF AUTHORS AND PUBLISHERS.
HAVE YOU COME UP WITH A NAME FOR THE MISSION?
WELL, YOU'VE GOT THREE OPTIONS. "OPERATION SAGA," PRETTY HO-HUM; "OPERATION INK QUELL," BUT I DON'T KNOW IF ANYBODY WILL GET THE PUN; AND "OPERATION JAILHOUSE ROCK," YOU KNOW, BECAUSE OF THE MUSIC...
IT DOESN'T MATTER... WE JUST NEED A NAME.
LOOK, I'VE PREPARED A POWERPOINT.
THE CIVIL GUARD IS AWAITING ORDERS.
VISUALLY SPEAKING, THE SECOND ONE LOOKS BEST, RIGHT?
SHOULD I ADD MUSIC? THE SOCIETY IS SO AGGRESSIVE ABOUT PROTECTING COPYRIGHT, THEY'D PROBABLY SUE US.
LET'S SEE... CHANGE IT BACK TO RED.
YOU SURE? I LIKED IT BETTER THE WAY IT WAS.
I SUSPECT THAT INSTEAD OF ME CHOOSING MY PROFESSION...
...IT IS MY TOTAL INCOMPETENCE IN ALL OTHER AREAS THAT HAS DETERMINED MY PATH.

WATCH OUT FOR THE SHORT ONES

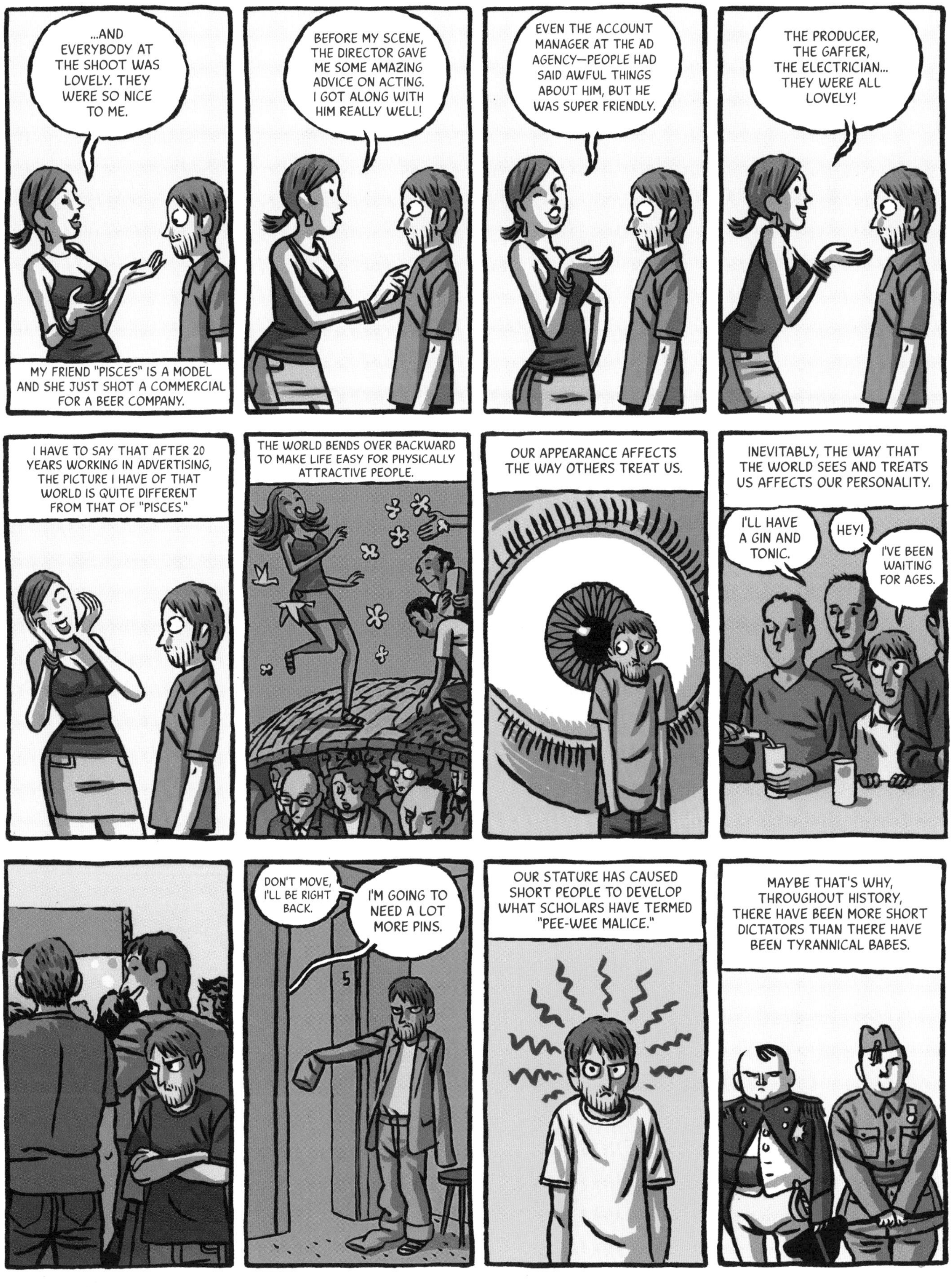
...AND EVERYBODY AT THE SHOOT WAS LOVELY. THEY WERE SO NICE TO ME.
MY FRIEND "PISCES" IS A MODEL AND SHE JUST SHOT A COMMERCIAL FOR A BEER COMPANY.
BEFORE MY SCENE, THE DIRECTOR GAVE ME SOME AMAZING ADVICE ON ACTING. I GOT ALONG WITH HIM REALLY WELL!
EVEN THE ACCOUNT MANAGER AT THE AD AGENCY—PEOPLE HAD SAID AWFUL THINGS ABOUT HIM, BUT HE WAS SUPER FRIENDLY.
THE PRODUCER, THE GAFFER, THE ELECTRICIAN... THEY WERE ALL LOVELY!
I HAVE TO SAY THAT AFTER 20 YEARS WORKING IN ADVERTISING, THE PICTURE I HAVE OF THAT WORLD IS QUITE DIFFERENT FROM THAT OF "PISCES."
THE WORLD BENDS OVER BACKWARD TO MAKE LIFE EASY FOR PHYSICALLY ATTRACTIVE PEOPLE.
OUR APPEARANCE AFFECTS THE WAY OTHERS TREAT US.
INEVITABLY, THE WAY THAT THE WORLD SEES AND TREATS US AFFECTS OUR PERSONALITY.
I'LL HAVE A GIN AND TONIC.
HEY!
I'VE BEEN WAITING FOR AGES.
DON'T MOVE, I'LL BE RIGHT BACK.
I'M GOING TO NEED A LOT MORE PINS.
5
OUR STATURE HAS CAUSED SHORT PEOPLE TO DEVELOP WHAT SCHOLARS HAVE TERMED "PEE-WEE MALICE."
MAYBE THAT'S WHY, THROUGHOUT HISTORY, THERE HAVE BEEN MORE SHORT DICTATORS THAN THERE HAVE BEEN TYRANNICAL BABES.

IF IDEAS DON'T COME, GO AFTER THEM

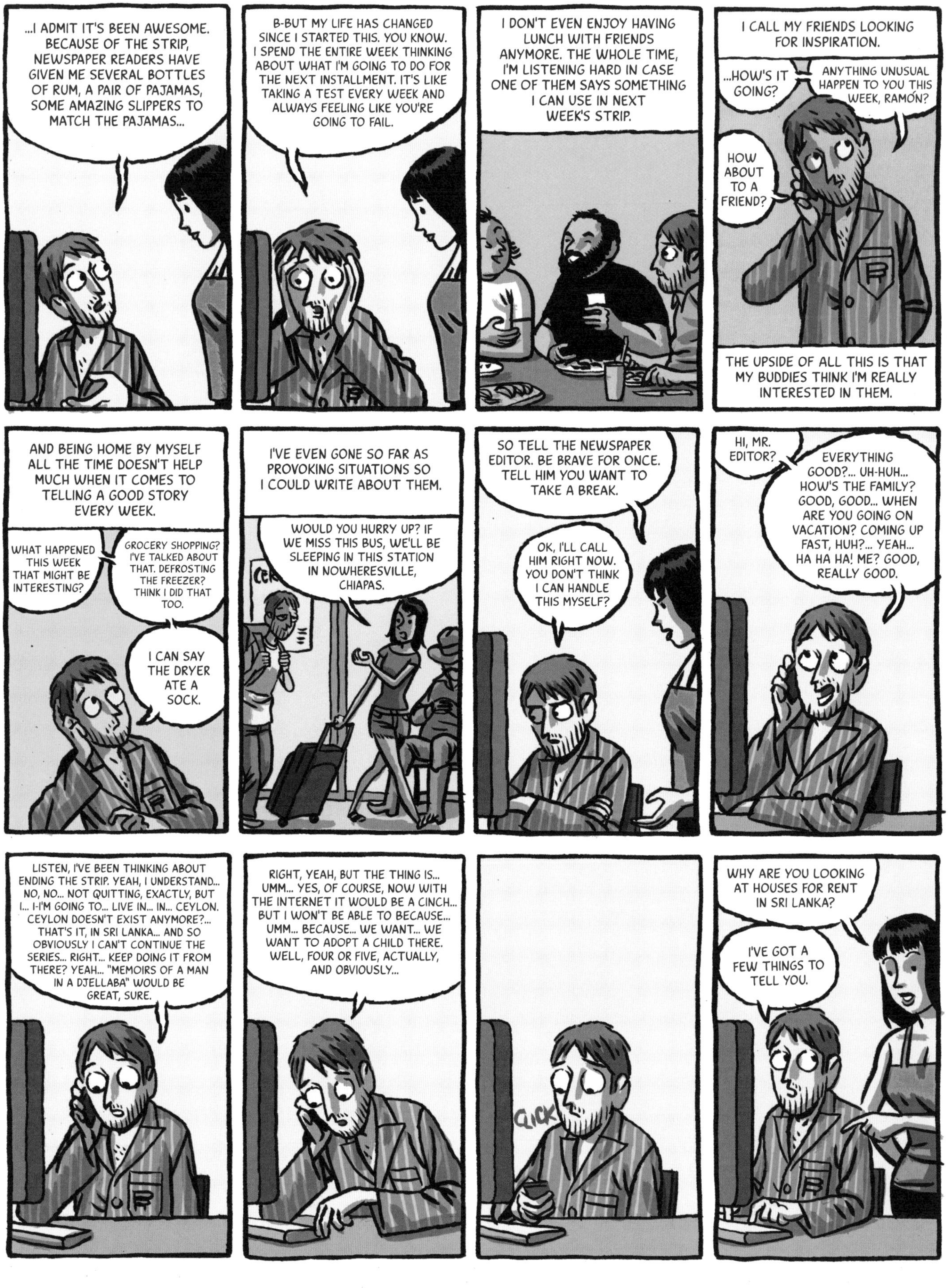

...I ADMIT IT'S BEEN AWESOME. BECAUSE OF THE STRIP, NEWSPAPER READERS HAVE GIVEN ME SEVERAL BOTTLES OF RUM, A PAIR OF PAJAMAS, SOME AMAZING SLIPPERS TO MATCH THE PAJAMAS...
B-BUT MY LIFE HAS CHANGED SINCE I STARTED THIS. YOU KNOW. I SPEND THE ENTIRE WEEK THINKING ABOUT WHAT I'M GOING TO DO FOR THE NEXT INSTALLMENT. IT'S LIKE TAKING A TEST EVERY WEEK AND ALWAYS FEELING LIKE YOU'RE GOING TO FAIL.
I DON'T EVEN ENJOY HAVING LUNCH WITH FRIENDS ANYMORE. THE WHOLE TIME, I'M LISTENING HARD IN CASE ONE OF THEM SAYS SOMETHING I CAN USE IN NEXT WEEK'S STRIP.
I CALL MY FRIENDS LOOKING FOR INSPIRATION.
...HOW'S IT GOING?
ANYTHING UNUSUAL HAPPEN TO YOU THIS WEEK, RAMÓN?
HOW ABOUT TO A FRIEND?
THE UPSIDE OF ALL THIS IS THAT MY BUDDIES THINK I'M REALLY INTERESTED IN THEM.
AND BEING HOME BY MYSELF ALL THE TIME DOESN'T HELP MUCH WHEN IT COMES TO TELLING A GOOD STORY EVERY WEEK.
WHAT HAPPENED THIS WEEK THAT MIGHT BE INTERESTING?
GROCERY SHOPPING? I'VE TALKED ABOUT THAT. DEFROSTING THE FREEZER? THINK I DID THAT TOO.
I CAN SAY THE DRYER ATE A SOCK.
I'VE EVEN GONE SO FAR AS PROVOKING SITUATIONS SO I COULD WRITE ABOUT THEM.
WOULD YOU HURRY UP? IF WE MISS THIS BUS, WE'LL BE SLEEPING IN THIS STATION IN NOWHERESVILLE, CHIAPAS.
SO TELL THE NEWSPAPER EDITOR. BE BRAVE FOR ONCE. TELL HIM YOU WANT TO TAKE A BREAK.
OK, I'LL CALL HIM RIGHT NOW. YOU DON'T THINK I CAN HANDLE THIS MYSELF?
HI, MR. EDITOR?
EVERYTHING GOOD?... UH-HUH... HOW'S THE FAMILY? GOOD, GOOD... WHEN ARE YOU GOING ON VACATION? COMING UP FAST, HUH?... YEAH... HA HA HA! ME? GOOD, REALLY GOOD.
LISTEN, I'VE BEEN THINKING ABOUT ENDING THE STRIP. YEAH, I UNDERSTAND... NO, NO... NOT QUITTING, EXACTLY, BUT I... I-I'M GOING TO... LIVE IN... IN... CEYLON. CEYLON DOESN'T EXIST ANYMORE?... THAT'S IT, IN SRI LANKA... AND SO OBVIOUSLY I CAN'T CONTINUE THE SERIES... RIGHT... KEEP DOING IT FROM THERE? YEAH... "MEMOIRS OF A MAN IN A DJELLABA" WOULD BE GREAT, SURE.
RIGHT, YEAH, BUT THE THING IS... UMM... YES, OF COURSE, NOW WITH THE INTERNET IT WOULD BE A CINCH... BUT I WON'T BE ABLE TO BECAUSE... UMM... BECAUSE... WE WANT... WE WANT TO ADOPT A CHILD THERE. WELL, FOUR OR FIVE, ACTUALLY, AND OBVIOUSLY...
CLICK
WHY ARE YOU LOOKING AT HOUSES FOR RENT IN SRI LANKA?
I'VE GOT A FEW THINGS TO TELL YOU.

FLEETING GENIUS

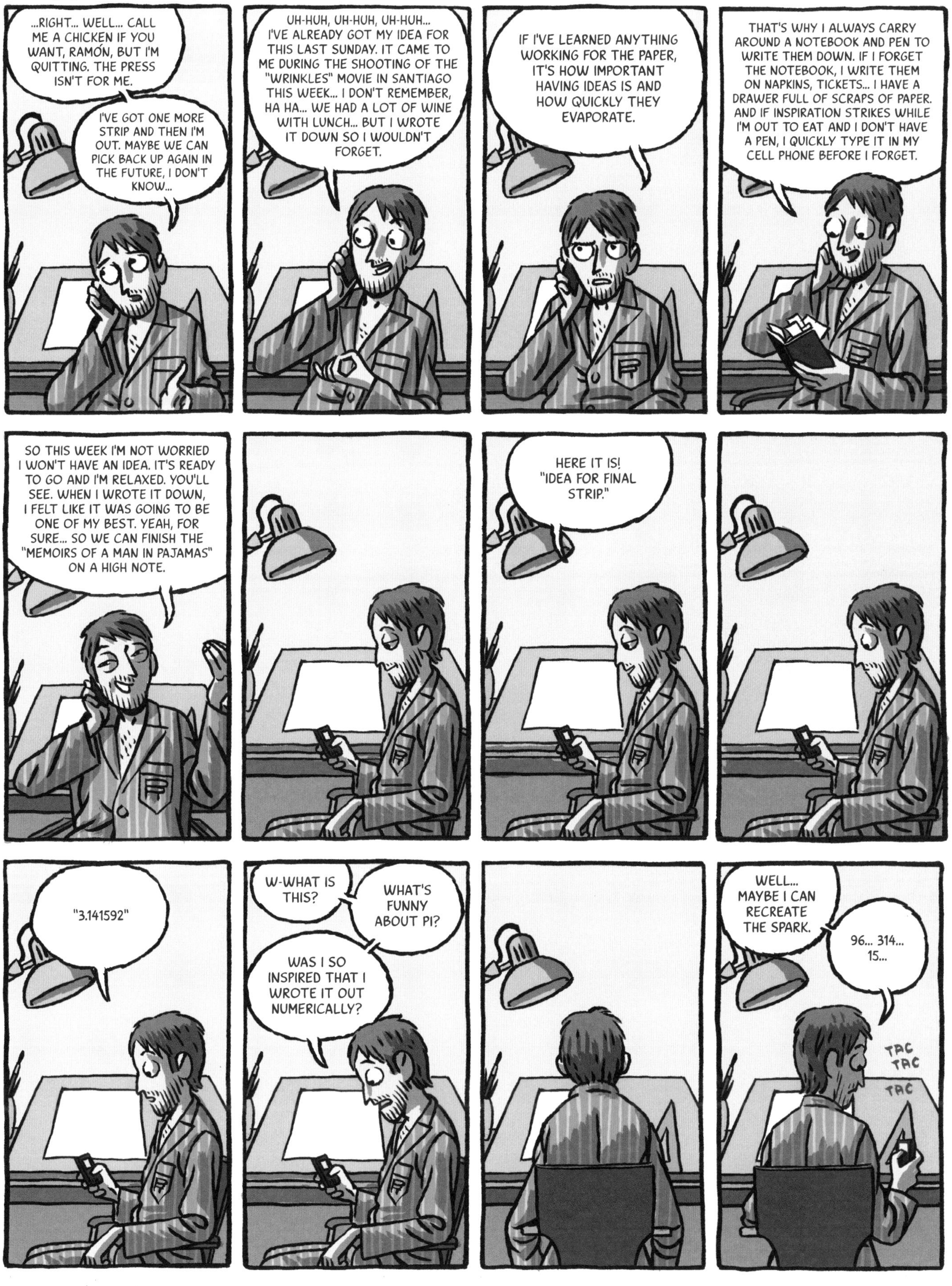
...RIGHT... WELL... CALL ME A CHICKEN IF YOU WANT, RAMÓN, BUT I'M QUITTING. THE PRESS ISN'T FOR ME.
I'VE GOT ONE MORE STRIP AND THEN I'M OUT. MAYBE WE CAN PICK BACK UP AGAIN IN THE FUTURE, I DON'T KNOW...
UH-HUH, UH-HUH, UH-HUH... I'VE ALREADY GOT MY IDEA FOR THIS LAST SUNDAY. IT CAME TO ME DURING THE SHOOTING OF THE "WRINKLES" MOVIE IN SANTIAGO THIS WEEK... I DON'T REMEMBER, HA HA... WE HAD A LOT OF WINE WITH LUNCH... BUT I WROTE IT DOWN SO I WOULDN'T FORGET.
IF I'VE LEARNED ANYTHING WORKING FOR THE PAPER, IT'S HOW IMPORTANT HAVING IDEAS IS AND HOW QUICKLY THEY EVAPORATE.
THAT'S WHY I ALWAYS CARRY AROUND A NOTEBOOK AND PEN TO WRITE THEM DOWN. IF I FORGET THE NOTEBOOK, I WRITE THEM ON NAPKINS, TICKETS... I HAVE A DRAWER FULL OF SCRAPS OF PAPER. AND IF INSPIRATION STRIKES WHILE I'M OUT TO EAT AND I DON'T HAVE A PEN, I QUICKLY TYPE IT IN MY CELL PHONE BEFORE I FORGET.
SO THIS WEEK I'M NOT WORRIED I WON'T HAVE AN IDEA. IT'S READY TO GO AND I'M RELAXED. YOU'LL SEE. WHEN I WROTE IT DOWN, I FELT LIKE IT WAS GOING TO BE ONE OF MY BEST. YEAH, FOR SURE... SO WE CAN FINISH THE "MEMOIRS OF A MAN IN PAJAMAS" ON A HIGH NOTE.
HERE IT IS! "IDEA FOR FINAL STRIP."
"3.141592"
W-WHAT IS THIS?
WHAT'S FUNNY ABOUT PI?
WAS I SO INSPIRED THAT I WROTE IT OUT NUMERICALLY?
WELL... MAYBE I CAN RECREATE THE SPARK.
96... 314... 15...
TAC TAC
TAC

II

THE (TEMPORAL) LAWS OF THE MARKET

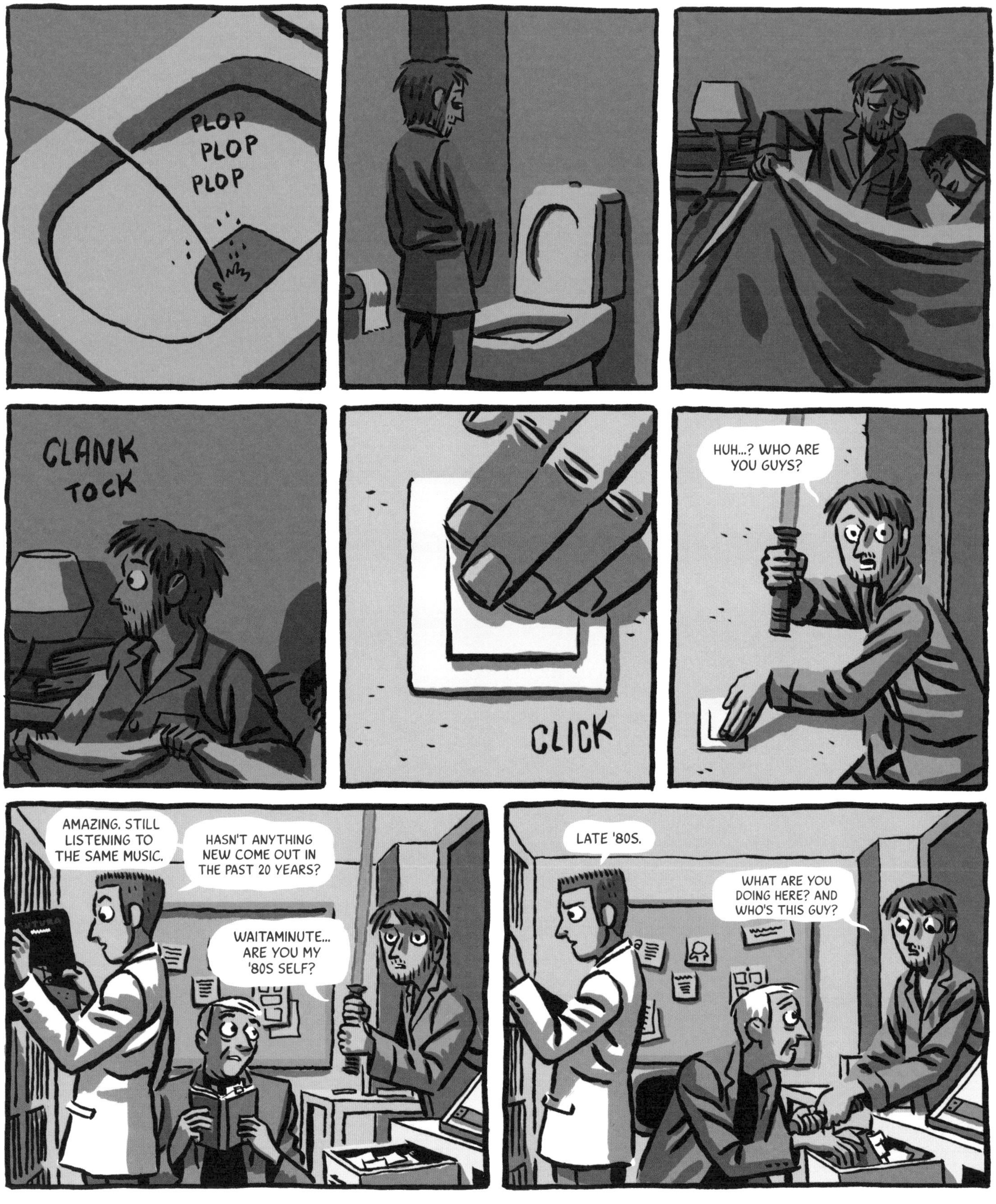
PLOP
PLOP
PLOP
CLANK
TOCK
CLICK
HUH...? WHO ARE YOU GUYS?
AMAZING. STILL LISTENING TO THE SAME MUSIC.
HASN'T ANYTHING NEW COME OUT IN THE PAST 20 YEARS?
WAITAMINUTE... ARE YOU MY '80S SELF?
LATE '80S.
WHAT ARE YOU DOING HERE? AND WHO'S THIS GUY?

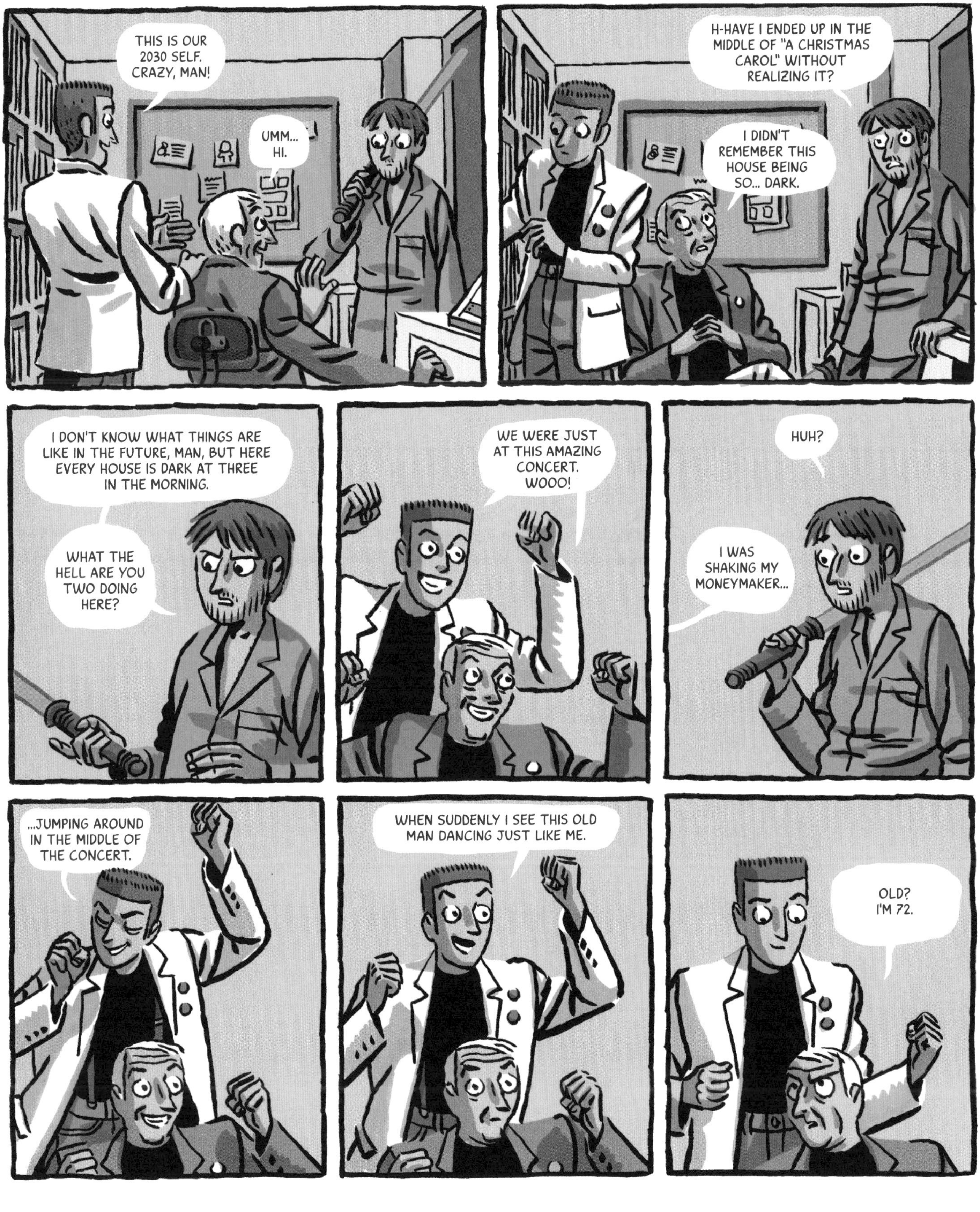
THIS IS OUR 2030 SELF. CRAZY, MAN!
UMM... HI.
H-HAVE I ENDED UP IN THE MIDDLE OF "A CHRISTMAS CAROL" WITHOUT REALIZING IT?
I DIDN'T REMEMBER THIS HOUSE BEING SO... DARK.
I DON'T KNOW WHAT THINGS ARE LIKE IN THE FUTURE, MAN, BUT HERE EVERY HOUSE IS DARK AT THREE IN THE MORNING.
WHAT THE HELL ARE YOU TWO DOING HERE?
WE WERE JUST AT THIS AMAZING CONCERT. WOOO!
HUH?
I WAS SHAKING MY MONEYMAKER...
...JUMPING AROUND IN THE MIDDLE OF THE CONCERT.
WHEN SUDDENLY I SEE THIS OLD MAN DANCING JUST LIKE ME.
OLD? I'M 72.

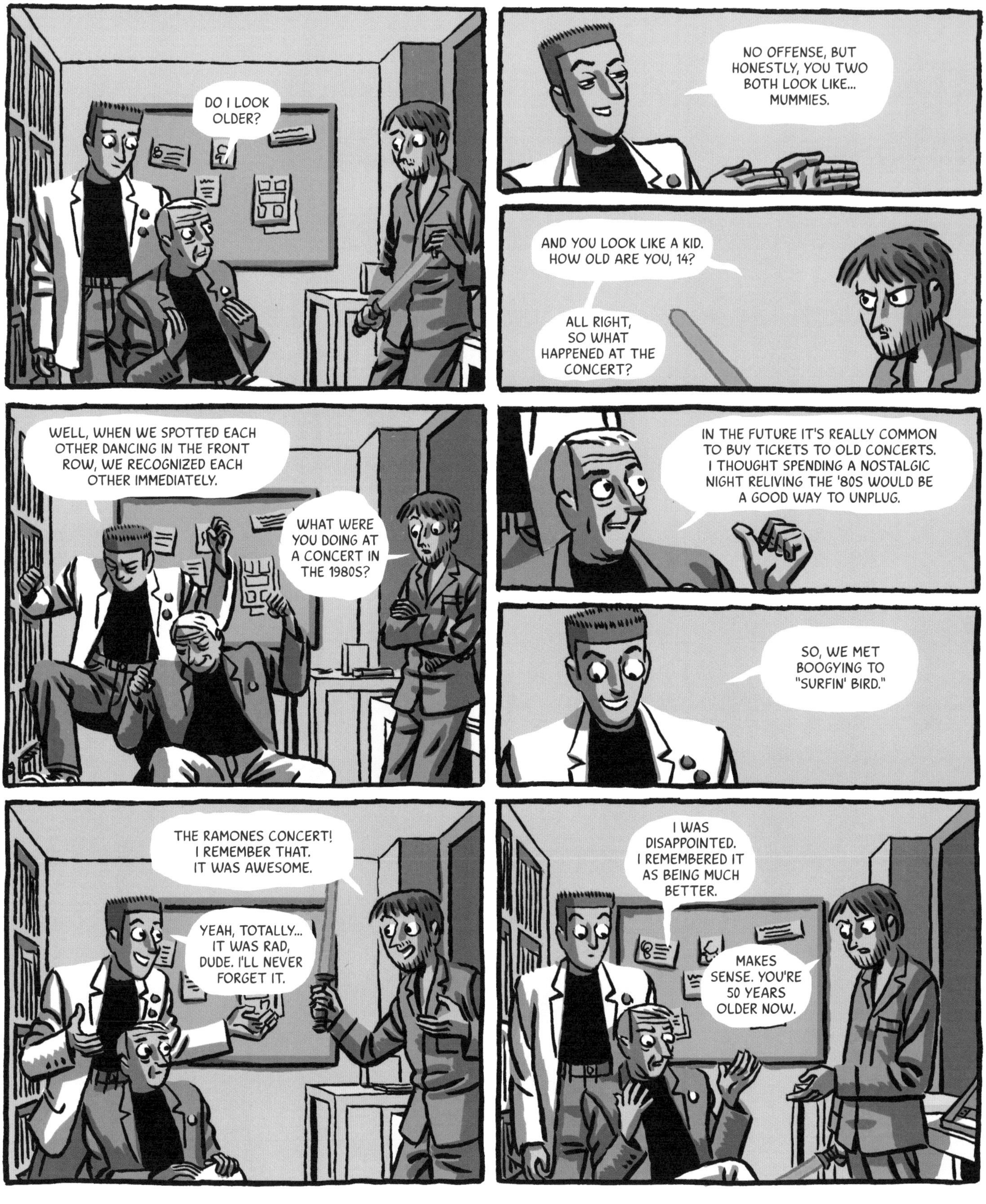
DO I LOOK OLDER?
NO OFFENSE, BUT HONESTLY, YOU TWO BOTH LOOK LIKE... MUMMIES.
AND YOU LOOK LIKE A KID. HOW OLD ARE YOU, 14?
ALL RIGHT, SO WHAT HAPPENED AT THE CONCERT?
WELL, WHEN WE SPOTTED EACH OTHER DANCING IN THE FRONT ROW, WE RECOGNIZED EACH OTHER IMMEDIATELY.
WHAT WERE YOU DOING AT A CONCERT IN THE 1980S?
IN THE FUTURE IT'S REALLY COMMON TO BUY TICKETS TO OLD CONCERTS. I THOUGHT SPENDING A NOSTALGIC NIGHT RELIVING THE '80S WOULD BE A GOOD WAY TO UNPLUG.
SO, WE MET BOOGYING TO "SURFIN' BIRD."
THE RAMONES CONCERT! I REMEMBER THAT. IT WAS AWESOME.
YEAH, TOTALLY... IT WAS RAD, DUDE. I'LL NEVER FORGET IT.
I WAS DISAPPOINTED. I REMEMBERED IT AS BEING MUCH BETTER.
MAKES SENSE. YOU'RE 50 YEARS OLDER NOW.

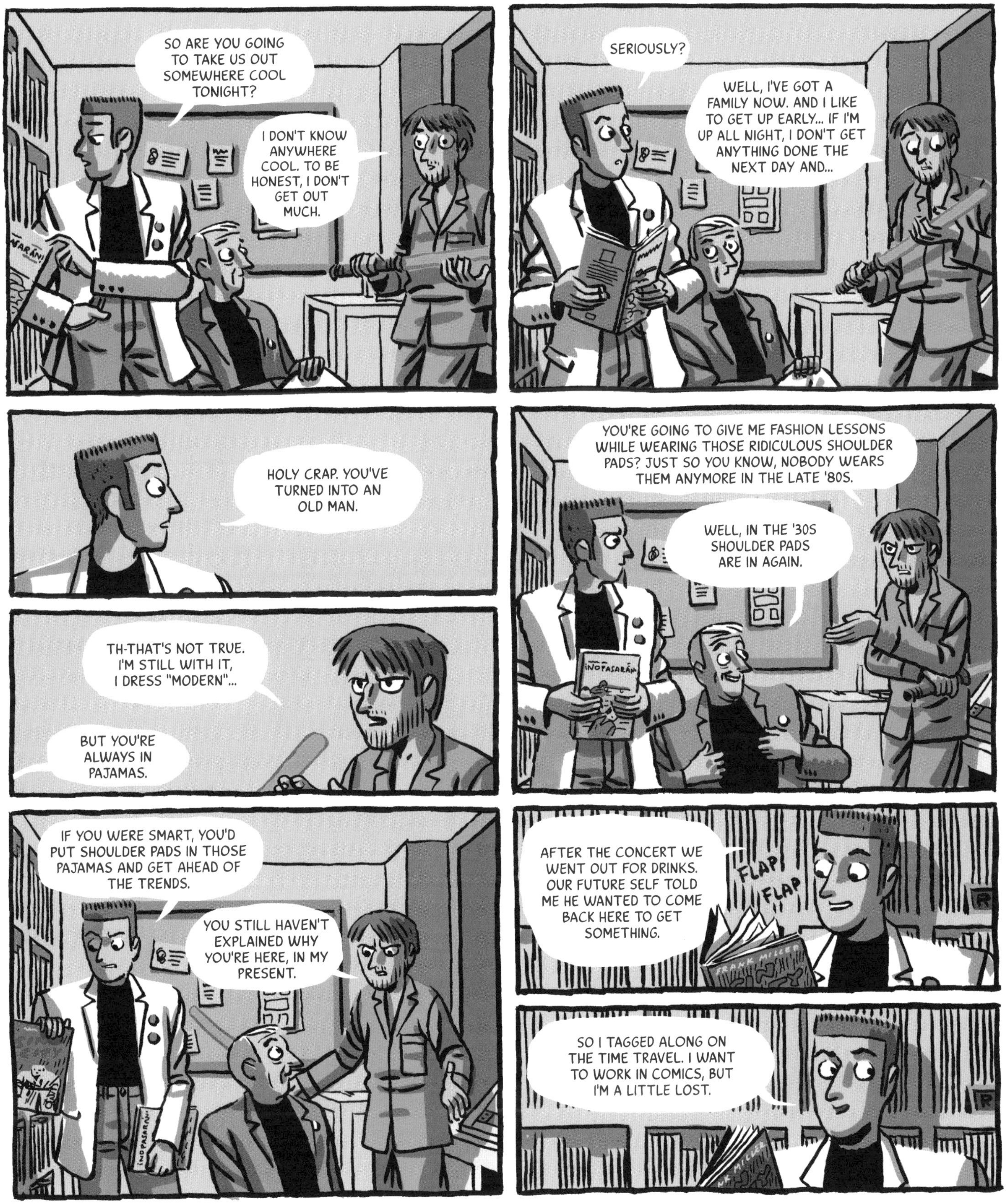
SO ARE YOU GOING TO TAKE US OUT SOMEWHERE COOL TONIGHT?
I DON'T KNOW ANYWHERE COOL. TO BE HONEST, I DON'T GET OUT MUCH.
SERIOUSLY?
WELL, I'VE GOT A FAMILY NOW. AND I LIKE TO GET UP EARLY... IF I'M UP ALL NIGHT, I DON'T GET ANYTHING DONE THE NEXT DAY AND...
HOLY CRAP. YOU'VE TURNED INTO AN OLD MAN.
TH-THAT'S NOT TRUE. I'M STILL WITH IT, I DRESS "MODERN"...
BUT YOU'RE ALWAYS IN PAJAMAS.
YOU'RE GOING TO GIVE ME FASHION LESSONS WHILE WEARING THOSE RIDICULOUS SHOULDER PADS? JUST SO YOU KNOW, NOBODY WEARS THEM ANYMORE IN THE LATE '80S.
WELL, IN THE '30S SHOULDER PADS ARE IN AGAIN.
IF YOU WERE SMART, YOU'D PUT SHOULDER PADS IN THOSE PAJAMAS AND GET AHEAD OF THE TRENDS.
YOU STILL HAVEN'T EXPLAINED WHY YOU'RE HERE, IN MY PRESENT.
AFTER THE CONCERT WE WENT OUT FOR DRINKS. OUR FUTURE SELF TOLD ME HE WANTED TO COME BACK HERE TO GET SOMETHING.
FLAP FLAP
SO I TAGGED ALONG ON THE TIME TRAVEL. I WANT TO WORK IN COMICS, BUT I'M A LITTLE LOST.

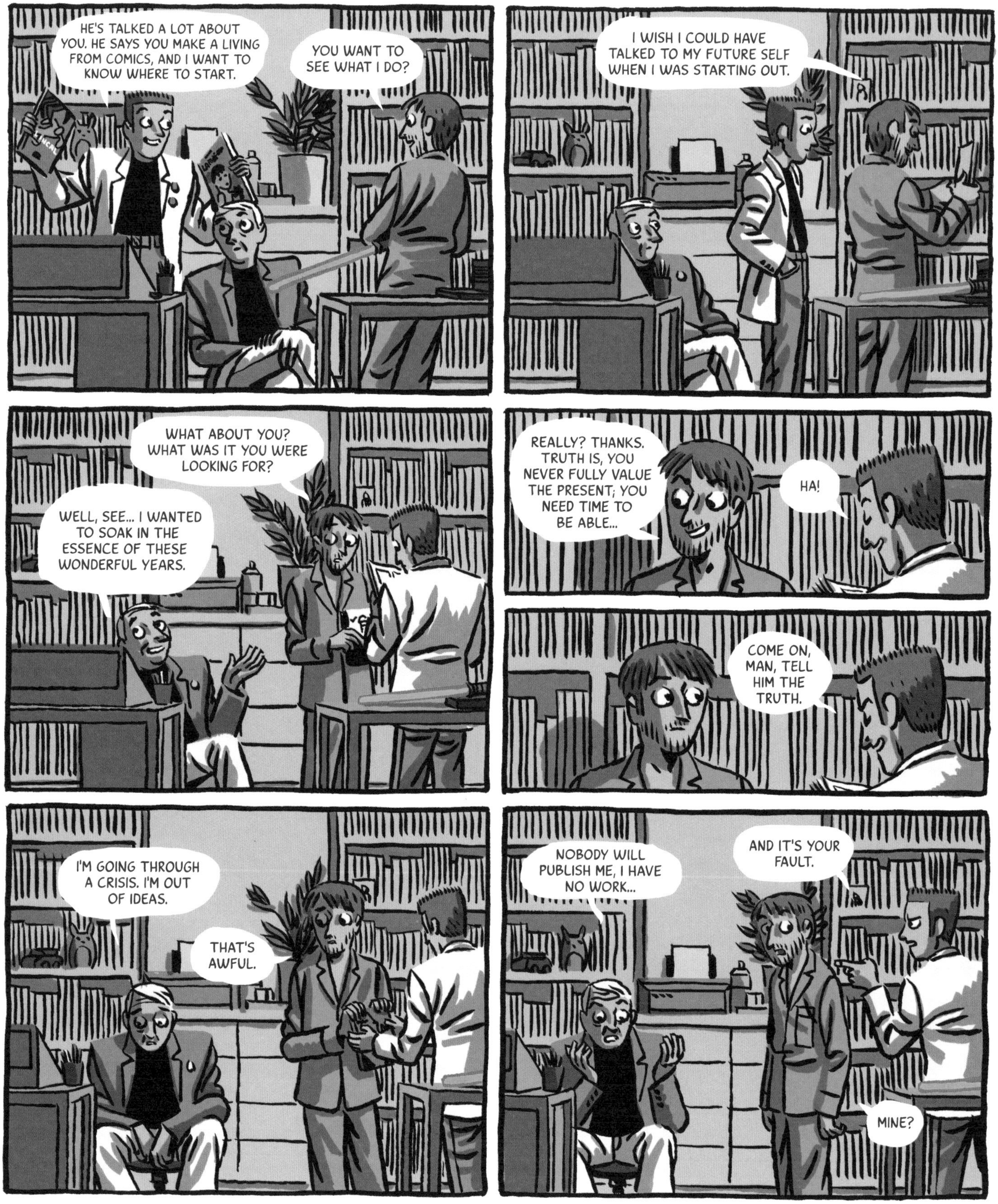
HE'S TALKED A LOT ABOUT YOU. HE SAYS YOU MAKE A LIVING FROM COMICS, AND I WANT TO KNOW WHERE TO START.
YOU WANT TO SEE WHAT I DO?
I WISH I COULD HAVE TALKED TO MY FUTURE SELF WHEN I WAS STARTING OUT.
WHAT ABOUT YOU? WHAT WAS IT YOU WERE LOOKING FOR?
WELL, SEE... I WANTED TO SOAK IN THE ESSENCE OF THESE WONDERFUL YEARS.
REALLY? THANKS. TRUTH IS, YOU NEVER FULLY VALUE THE PRESENT; YOU NEED TIME TO BE ABLE...
HA!
COME ON, MAN, TELL HIM THE TRUTH.
I'M GOING THROUGH A CRISIS. I'M OUT OF IDEAS.
THAT'S AWFUL.
NOBODY WILL PUBLISH ME, I HAVE NO WORK...
AND IT'S YOUR FAULT.
MINE?

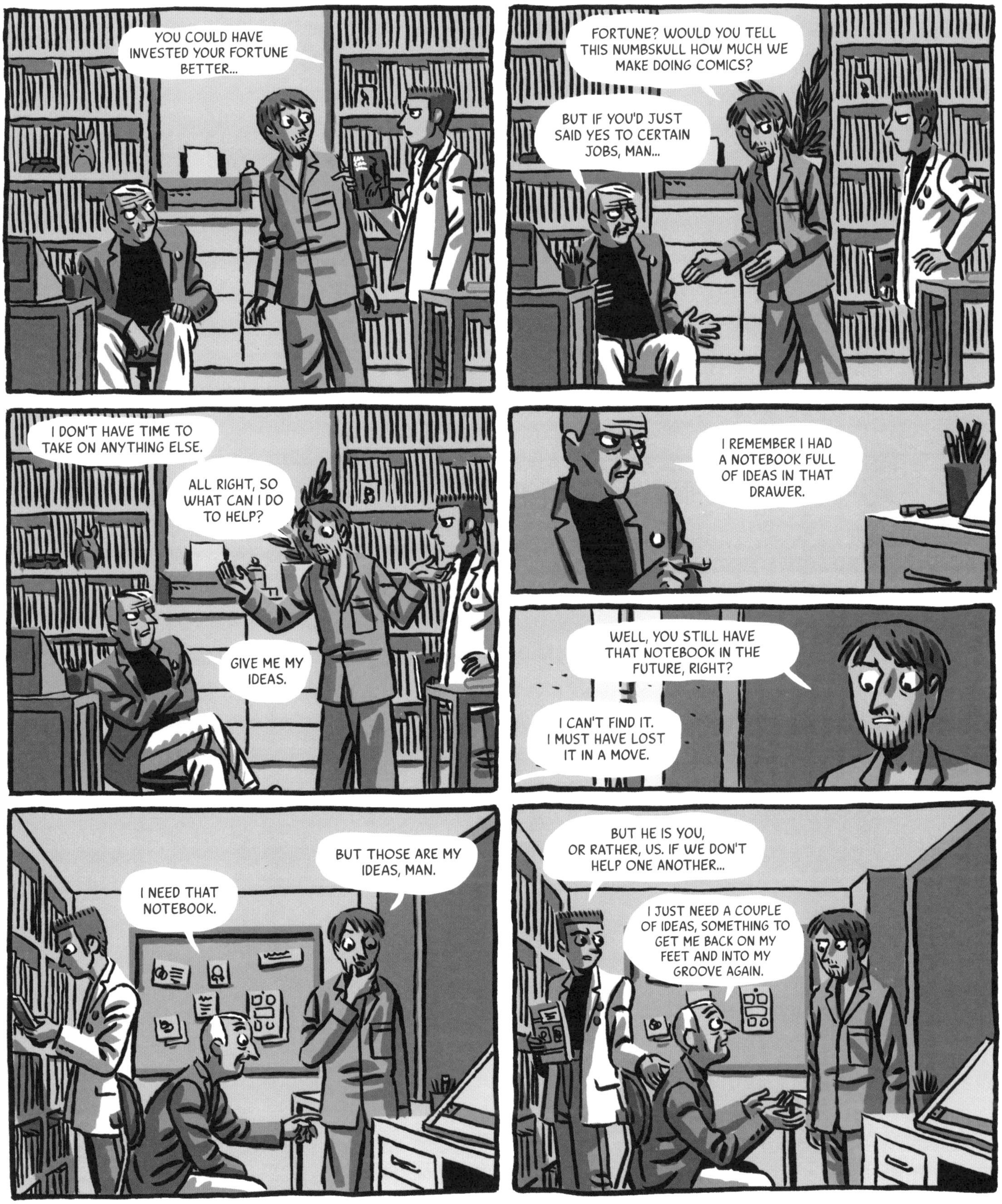
YOU COULD HAVE INVESTED YOUR FORTUNE BETTER...
FORTUNE? WOULD YOU TELL THIS NUMBSKULL HOW MUCH WE MAKE DOING COMICS?
BUT IF YOU'D JUST SAID YES TO CERTAIN JOBS, MAN...
I DON'T HAVE TIME TO TAKE ON ANYTHING ELSE.
ALL RIGHT, SO WHAT CAN I DO TO HELP?
GIVE ME MY IDEAS.
I REMEMBER I HAD A NOTEBOOK FULL OF IDEAS IN THAT DRAWER.
WELL, YOU STILL HAVE THAT NOTEBOOK IN THE FUTURE, RIGHT?
I CAN'T FIND IT. I MUST HAVE LOST IT IN A MOVE.
I NEED THAT NOTEBOOK.
BUT THOSE ARE MY IDEAS, MAN.
BUT HE IS YOU, OR RATHER, US. IF WE DON'T HELP ONE ANOTHER...
I JUST NEED A COUPLE OF IDEAS, SOMETHING TO GET ME BACK ON MY FEET AND INTO MY GROOVE AGAIN.

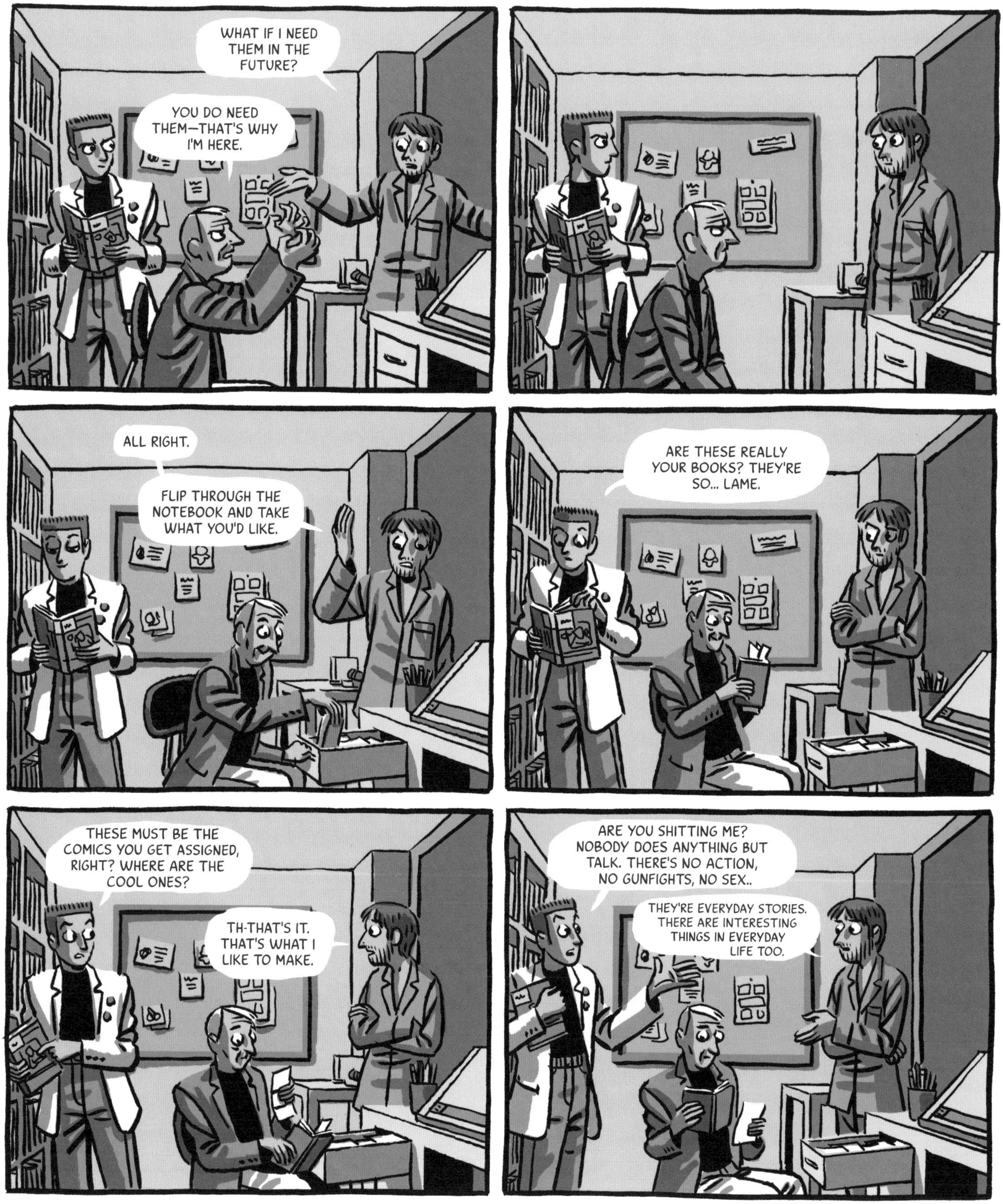
WHAT IF I NEED THEM IN THE FUTURE?
YOU DO NEED THEM—THAT'S WHY I'M HERE.
ALL RIGHT.
FLIP THROUGH THE NOTEBOOK AND TAKE WHAT YOU'D LIKE.
ARE THESE REALLY YOUR BOOKS? THEY'RE SO... LAME.
THESE MUST BE THE COMICS YOU GET ASSIGNED, RIGHT? WHERE ARE THE COOL ONES?
TH-THAT'S IT. THAT'S WHAT I LIKE TO MAKE.
ARE YOU SHITTING ME? NOBODY DOES ANYTHING BUT TALK. THERE'S NO ACTION, NO GUNFIGHTS, NO SEX..
THEY'RE EVERYDAY STORIES. THERE ARE INTERESTING THINGS IN EVERYDAY LIFE TOO.

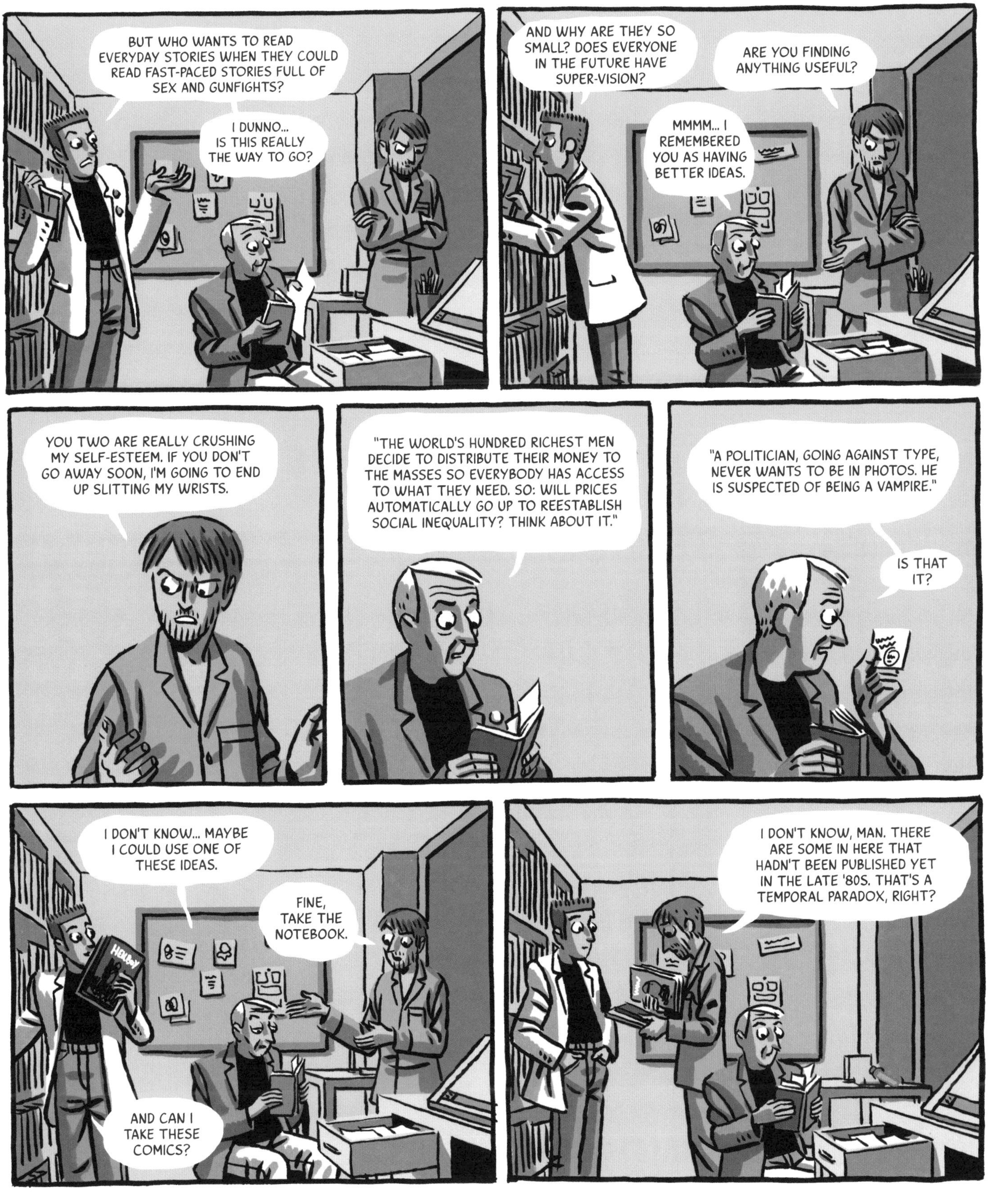
BUT WHO WANTS TO READ EVERYDAY STORIES WHEN THEY COULD READ FAST-PACED STORIES FULL OF SEX AND GUNFIGHTS?
I DUNNO... IS THIS REALLY THE WAY TO GO?
AND WHY ARE THEY SO SMALL? DOES EVERYONE IN THE FUTURE HAVE SUPER-VISION?
ARE YOU FINDING ANYTHING USEFUL?
MMMM... I REMEMBERED YOU AS HAVING BETTER IDEAS.
YOU TWO ARE REALLY CRUSHING MY SELF-ESTEEM. IF YOU DON'T GO AWAY SOON, I'M GOING TO END UP SLITTING MY WRISTS.
"THE WORLD'S HUNDRED RICHEST MEN DECIDE TO DISTRIBUTE THEIR MONEY TO THE MASSES SO EVERYBODY HAS ACCESS TO WHAT THEY NEED. SO: WILL PRICES AUTOMATICALLY GO UP TO REESTABLISH SOCIAL INEQUALITY? THINK ABOUT IT."
"A POLITICIAN, GOING AGAINST TYPE, NEVER WANTS TO BE IN PHOTOS. HE IS SUSPECTED OF BEING A VAMPIRE."
IS THAT IT?
I DON'T KNOW... MAYBE I COULD USE ONE OF THESE IDEAS.
FINE, TAKE THE NOTEBOOK.
AND CAN I TAKE THESE COMICS?
I DON'T KNOW, MAN. THERE ARE SOME IN HERE THAT HADN'T BEEN PUBLISHED YET IN THE LATE '80S. THAT'S A TEMPORAL PARADOX, RIGHT?

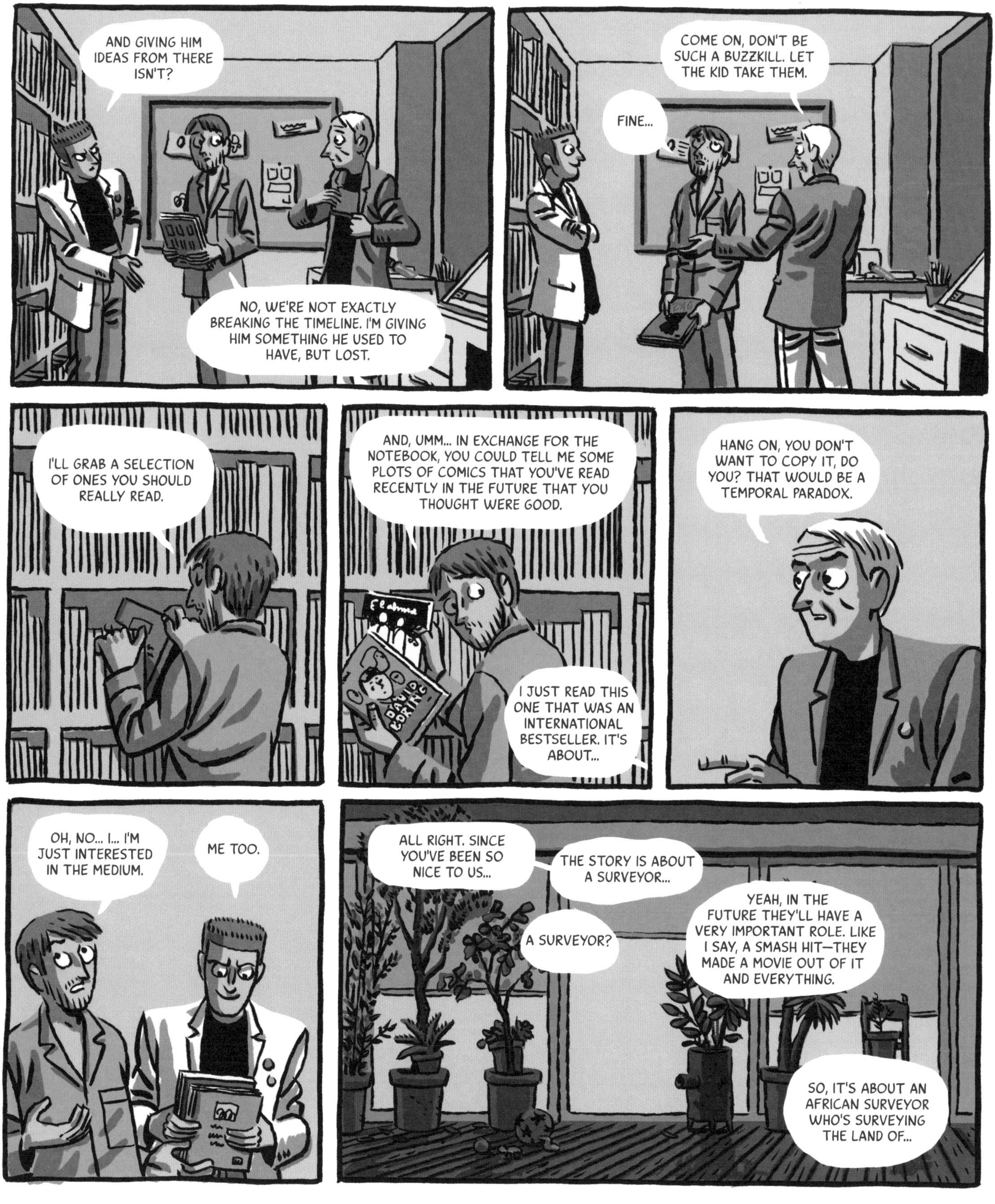
AND GIVING HIM IDEAS FROM THERE ISN'T?
NO, WE'RE NOT EXACTLY BREAKING THE TIMELINE. I'M GIVING HIM SOMETHING HE USED TO HAVE, BUT LOST.
COME ON, DON'T BE SUCH A BUZZKILL. LET THE KID TAKE THEM.
FINE...
I'LL GRAB A SELECTION OF ONES YOU SHOULD REALLY READ.
AND, UMM... IN EXCHANGE FOR THE NOTEBOOK, YOU COULD TELL ME SOME PLOTS OF COMICS THAT YOU'VE READ RECENTLY IN THE FUTURE THAT YOU THOUGHT WERE GOOD.
I JUST READ THIS ONE THAT WAS AN INTERNATIONAL BESTSELLER. IT'S ABOUT...
HANG ON, YOU DON'T WANT TO COPY IT, DO YOU? THAT WOULD BE A TEMPORAL PARADOX.
OH, NO... I... I'M JUST INTERESTED IN THE MEDIUM.
ME TOO.
ALL RIGHT. SINCE YOU'VE BEEN SO NICE TO US...
THE STORY IS ABOUT A SURVEYOR...
A SURVEYOR?
YEAH, IN THE FUTURE THEY'LL HAVE A VERY IMPORTANT ROLE. LIKE I SAY, A SMASH HIT—THEY MADE A MOVIE OUT OF IT AND EVERYTHING.
SO, IT'S ABOUT AN AFRICAN SURVEYOR WHO'S SURVEYING THE LAND OF...

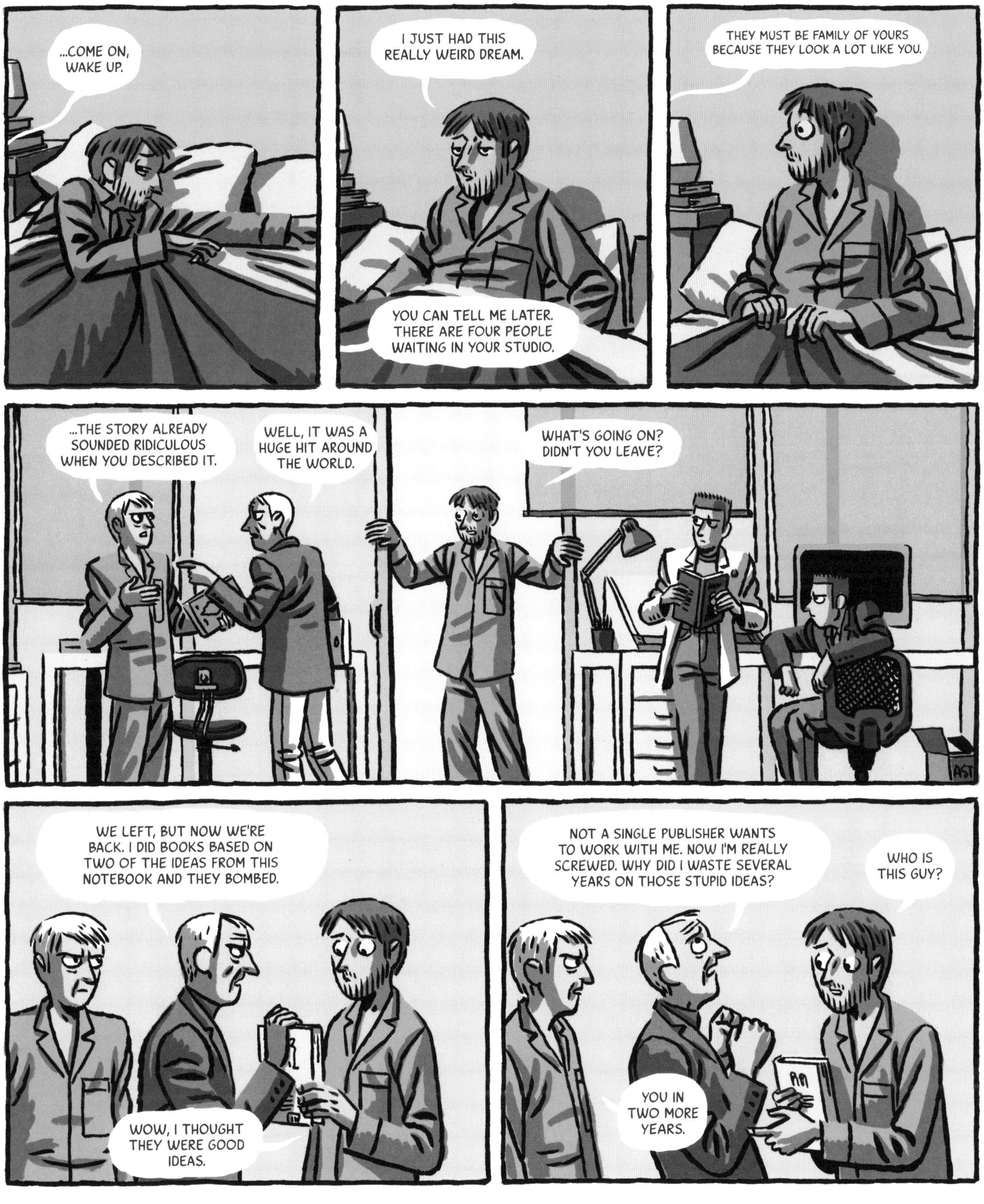
...COME ON, WAKE UP.
I JUST HAD THIS REALLY WEIRD DREAM.
YOU CAN TELL ME LATER. THERE ARE FOUR PEOPLE WAITING IN YOUR STUDIO.
THEY MUST BE FAMILY OF YOURS BECAUSE THEY LOOK A LOT LIKE YOU.
...THE STORY ALREADY SOUNDED RIDICULOUS WHEN YOU DESCRIBED IT.
WELL, IT WAS A HUGE HIT AROUND THE WORLD.
WHAT'S GOING ON? DIDN'T YOU LEAVE?
AST
WE LEFT, BUT NOW WE'RE BACK. I DID BOOKS BASED ON TWO OF THE IDEAS FROM THIS NOTEBOOK AND THEY BOMBED.
WOW, I THOUGHT THEY WERE GOOD IDEAS.
NOT A SINGLE PUBLISHER WANTS TO WORK WITH ME. NOW I'M REALLY SCREWED. WHY DID I WASTE SEVERAL YEARS ON THOSE STUPID IDEAS?
WHO IS THIS GUY?
YOU IN TWO MORE YEARS.

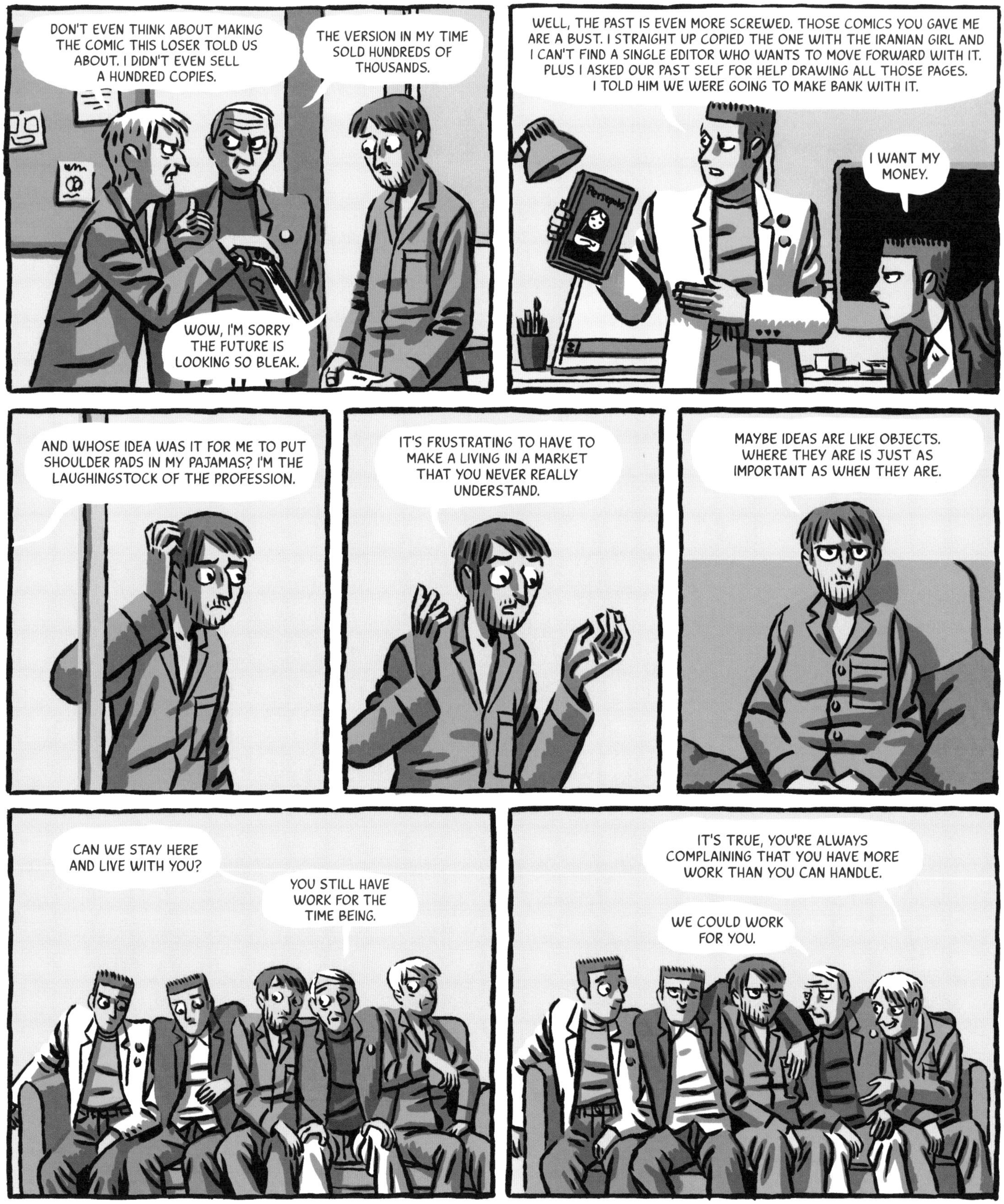
DON'T EVEN THINK ABOUT MAKING THE COMIC THIS LOSER TOLD US ABOUT. I DIDN'T EVEN SELL A HUNDRED COPIES.
THE VERSION IN MY TIME SOLD HUNDREDS OF THOUSANDS.
WOW, I'M SORRY THE FUTURE IS LOOKING SO BLEAK.
WELL, THE PAST IS EVEN MORE SCREWED. THOSE COMICS YOU GAVE ME ARE A BUST. I STRAIGHT UP COPIED THE ONE WITH THE IRANIAN GIRL AND I CAN'T FIND A SINGLE EDITOR WHO WANTS TO MOVE FORWARD WITH IT. PLUS I ASKED OUR PAST SELF FOR HELP DRAWING ALL THOSE PAGES. I TOLD HIM WE WERE GOING TO MAKE BANK WITH IT.
I WANT MY MONEY.
AND WHOSE IDEA WAS IT FOR ME TO PUT SHOULDER PADS IN MY PAJAMAS? I'M THE LAUGHINGSTOCK OF THE PROFESSION.
IT'S FRUSTRATING TO HAVE TO MAKE A LIVING IN A MARKET THAT YOU NEVER REALLY UNDERSTAND.
MAYBE IDEAS ARE LIKE OBJECTS. WHERE THEY ARE IS JUST AS IMPORTANT AS WHEN THEY ARE.
CAN WE STAY HERE AND LIVE WITH YOU?
YOU STILL HAVE WORK FOR THE TIME BEING.
IT'S TRUE, YOU'RE ALWAYS COMPLAINING THAT YOU HAVE MORE WORK THAN YOU CAN HANDLE.
WE COULD WORK FOR YOU.

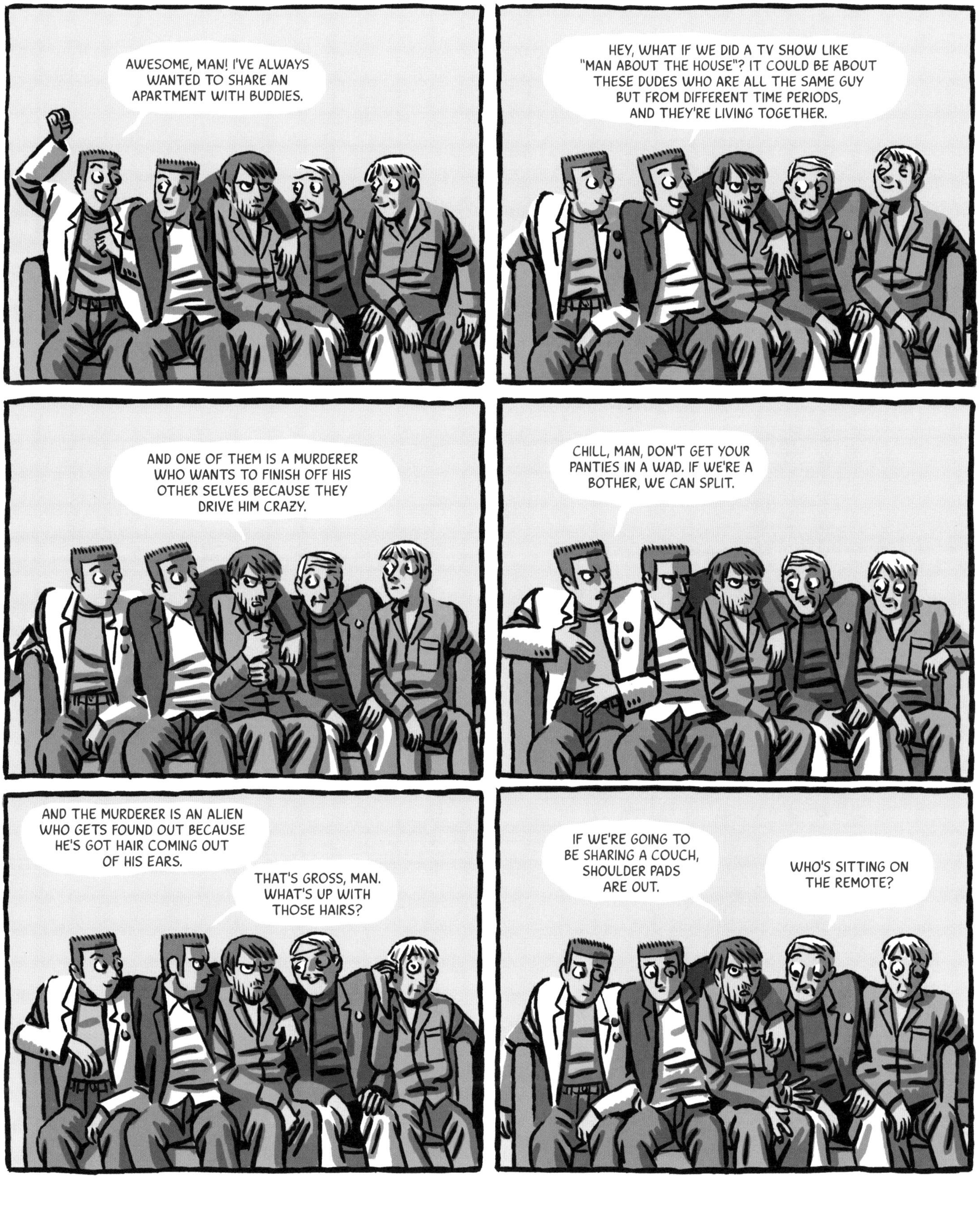
AWESOME, MAN! I'VE ALWAYS WANTED TO SHARE AN APARTMENT WITH BUDDIES.
HEY, WHAT IF WE DID A TV SHOW LIKE "MAN ABOUT THE HOUSE"? IT COULD BE ABOUT THESE DUDES WHO ARE ALL THE SAME GUY BUT FROM DIFFERENT TIME PERIODS, AND THEY'RE LIVING TOGETHER.
AND ONE OF THEM IS A MURDERER WHO WANTS TO FINISH OFF HIS OTHER SELVES BECAUSE THEY DRIVE HIM CRAZY.
CHILL, MAN, DON'T GET YOUR PANTIES IN A WAD. IF WE'RE A BOTHER, WE CAN SPLIT.
AND THE MURDERER IS AN ALIEN WHO GETS FOUND OUT BECAUSE HE'S GOT HAIR COMING OUT OF HIS EARS.
THAT'S GROSS, MAN. WHAT'S UP WITH THOSE HAIRS?
IF WE'RE GOING TO BE SHARING A COUCH, SHOULDER PADS ARE OUT.
WHO'S SITTING ON THE REMOTE?

ABANDON SHIP

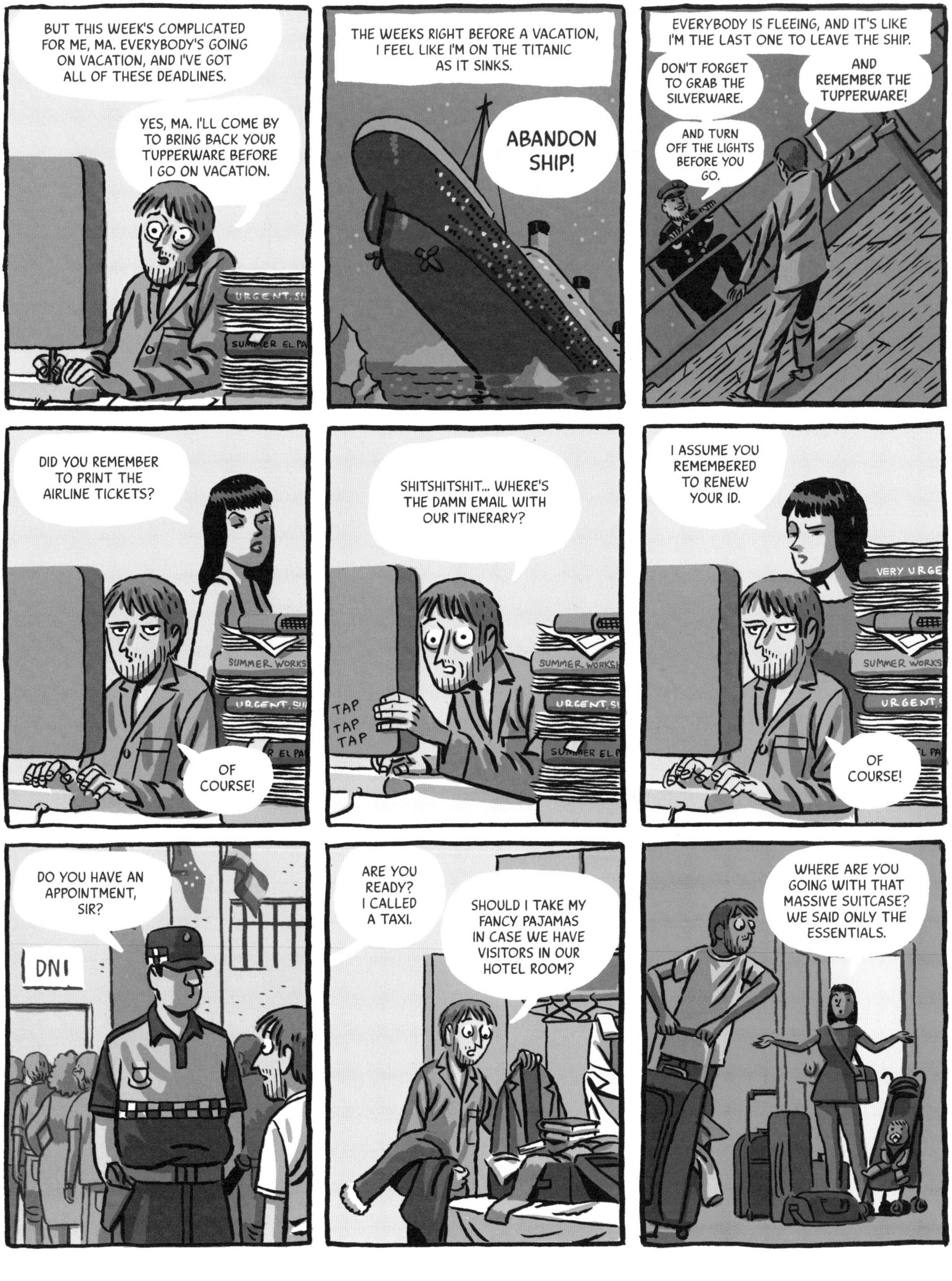
BUT THIS WEEK'S COMPLICATED FOR ME, MA. EVERYBODY'S GOING ON VACATION, AND I'VE GOT ALL OF THESE DEADLINES.
YES, MA. I'LL COME BY TO BRING BACK YOUR TUPPERWARE BEFORE I GO ON VACATION.
URGENT, SU
SUMMER EL PA
THE WEEKS RIGHT BEFORE A VACATION, I FEEL LIKE I'M ON THE TITANIC AS IT SINKS.
ABANDON SHIP!
EVERYBODY IS FLEEING, AND IT'S LIKE I'M THE LAST ONE TO LEAVE THE SHIP.
DON'T FORGET TO GRAB THE SILVERWARE.
AND REMEMBER THE TUPPERWARE!
AND TURN OFF THE LIGHTS BEFORE YOU GO.
DID YOU REMEMBER TO PRINT THE AIRLINE TICKETS?
SUMMER WORKS
URGENT, SU
R EL PA
OF COURSE!
SHITSHITSHIT... WHERE'S THE DAMN EMAIL WITH OUR ITINERARY?
TAP TAP TAP
SUMMER WORKSH
URGENT, SU
SUMMER EL P
I ASSUME YOU REMEMBERED TO RENEW YOUR ID.
VERY URGE
SUMMER WORKS
URGENT,
L PA
OF COURSE!
DO YOU HAVE AN APPOINTMENT, SIR?
DNI
ARE YOU READY? I CALLED A TAXI.
SHOULD I TAKE MY FANCY PAJAMAS IN CASE WE HAVE VISITORS IN OUR HOTEL ROOM?
WHERE ARE YOU GOING WITH THAT MASSIVE SUITCASE? WE SAID ONLY THE ESSENTIALS.

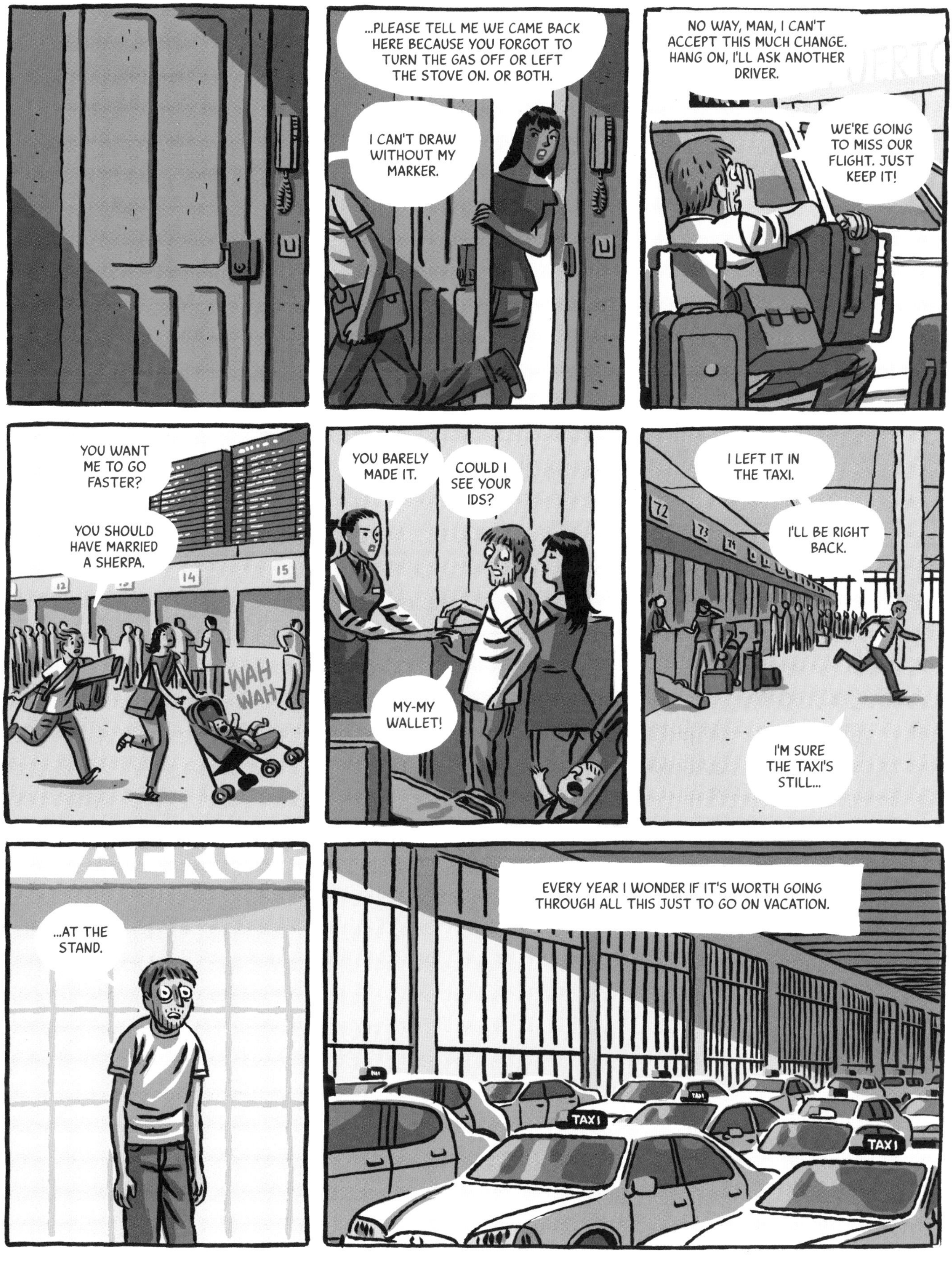
...PLEASE TELL ME WE CAME BACK HERE BECAUSE YOU FORGOT TO TURN THE GAS OFF OR LEFT THE STOVE ON. OR BOTH.
I CAN'T DRAW WITHOUT MY MARKER.
NO WAY, MAN, I CAN'T ACCEPT THIS MUCH CHANGE. HANG ON, I'LL ASK ANOTHER DRIVER.
WE'RE GOING TO MISS OUR FLIGHT. JUST KEEP IT!
YOU WANT ME TO GO FASTER?
YOU SHOULD HAVE MARRIED A SHERPA.
WAH WAH
YOU BARELY MADE IT.
COULD I SEE YOUR IDS?
MY-MY WALLET!
I LEFT IT IN THE TAXI.
I'LL BE RIGHT BACK.
I'M SURE THE TAXI'S STILL...
...AT THE STAND.
EVERY YEAR I WONDER IF IT'S WORTH GOING THROUGH ALL THIS JUST TO GO ON VACATION.
TAXI
TAXI

YOU'RE GOING TO GET A STOMACH CRAMP!

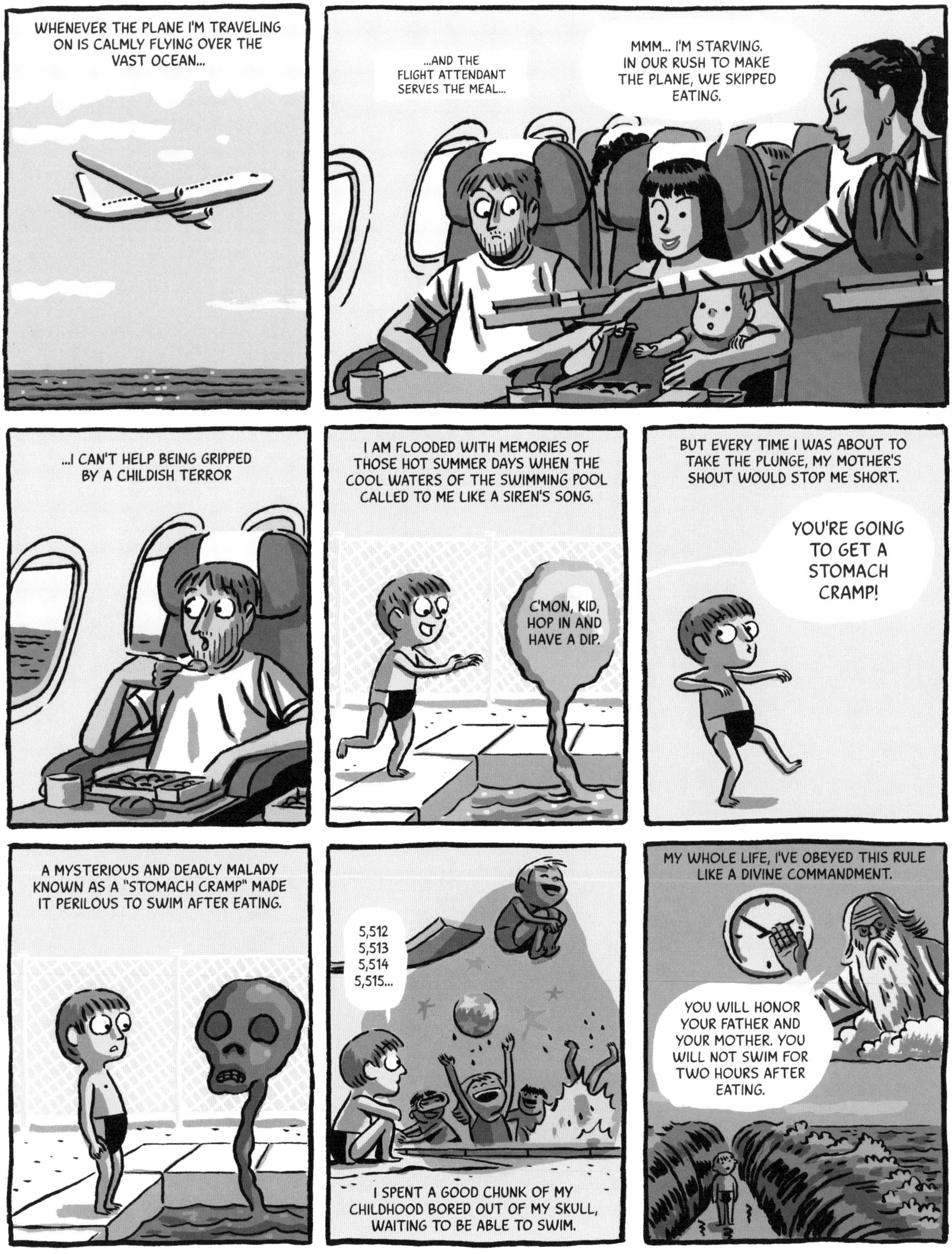
WHENEVER THE PLANE I'M TRAVELING ON IS CALMLY FLYING OVER THE VAST OCEAN...
...AND THE FLIGHT ATTENDANT SERVES THE MEAL...
MMM... I'M STARVING. IN OUR RUSH TO MAKE THE PLANE, WE SKIPPED EATING.
...I CAN'T HELP BEING GRIPPED BY A CHILDISH TERROR
I AM FLOODED WITH MEMORIES OF THOSE HOT SUMMER DAYS WHEN THE COOL WATERS OF THE SWIMMING POOL CALLED TO ME LIKE A SIREN'S SONG.
C'MON, KID, HOP IN AND HAVE A DIP.
BUT EVERY TIME I WAS ABOUT TO TAKE THE PLUNGE, MY MOTHER'S SHOUT WOULD STOP ME SHORT.
YOU'RE GOING TO GET A STOMACH CRAMP!
A MYSTERIOUS AND DEADLY MALADY KNOWN AS A "STOMACH CRAMP" MADE IT PERILOUS TO SWIM AFTER EATING.
5,512 5,513 5,514 5,515...
I SPENT A GOOD CHUNK OF MY CHILDHOOD BORED OUT OF MY SKULL, WAITING TO BE ABLE TO SWIM.
MY WHOLE LIFE, I'VE OBEYED THIS RULE LIKE A DIVINE COMMANDMENT.
YOU WILL HONOR YOUR FATHER AND YOUR MOTHER. YOU WILL NOT SWIM FOR TWO HOURS AFTER EATING.

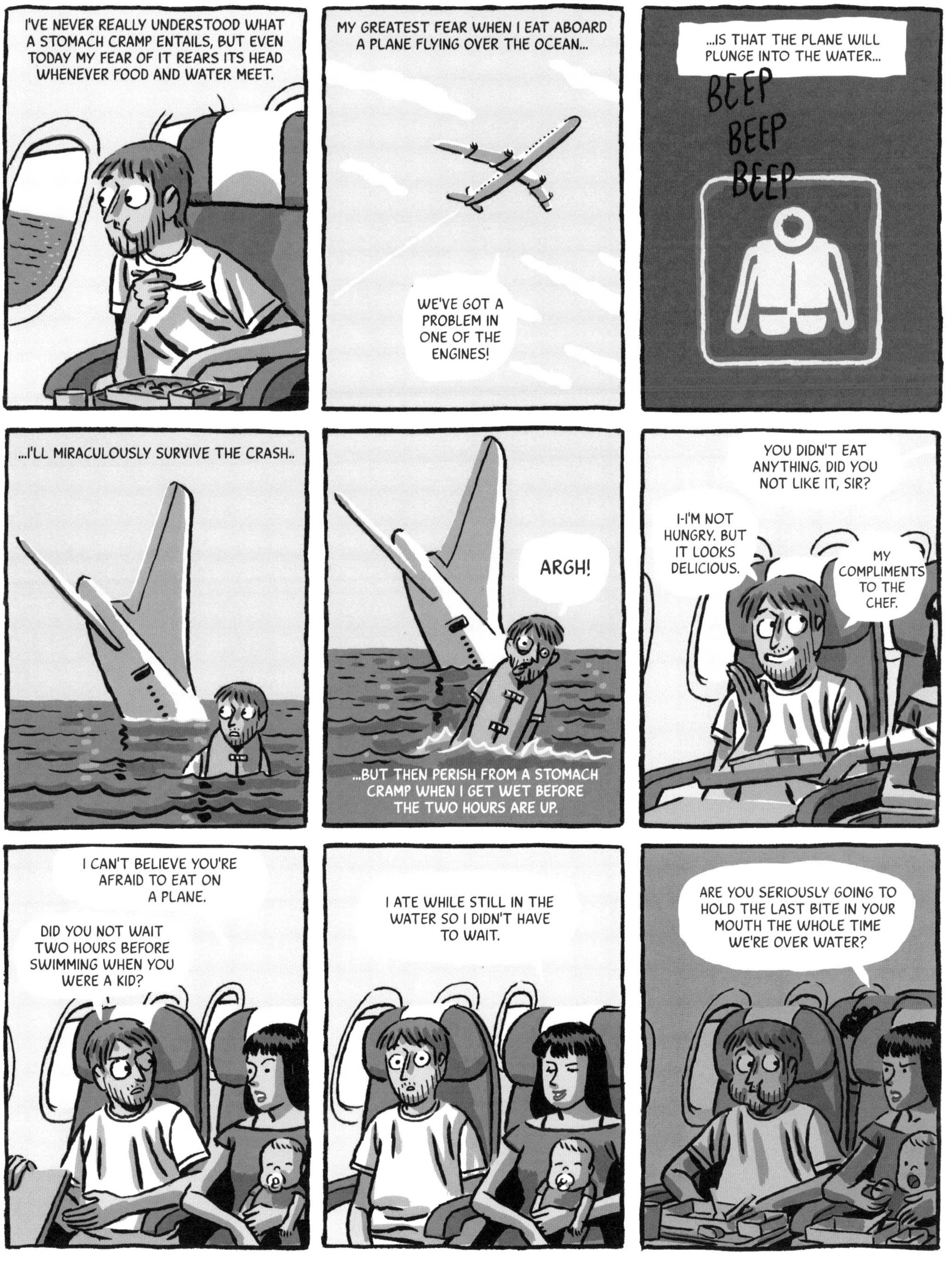
I'VE NEVER REALLY UNDERSTOOD WHAT A STOMACH CRAMP ENTAILS, BUT EVEN TODAY MY FEAR OF IT REARS ITS HEAD WHENEVER FOOD AND WATER MEET.
MY GREATEST FEAR WHEN I EAT ABOARD A PLANE FLYING OVER THE OCEAN...
WE'VE GOT A PROBLEM IN ONE OF THE ENGINES!
...IS THAT THE PLANE WILL PLUNGE INTO THE WATER...
BEEP
BEEP
BEEP
...I'LL MIRACULOUSLY SURVIVE THE CRASH..
ARGH!
...BUT THEN PERISH FROM A STOMACH CRAMP WHEN I GET WET BEFORE THE TWO HOURS ARE UP.
YOU DIDN'T EAT ANYTHING. DID YOU NOT LIKE IT, SIR?
I-I'M NOT HUNGRY. BUT IT LOOKS DELICIOUS.
MY COMPLIMENTS TO THE CHEF.
I CAN'T BELIEVE YOU'RE AFRAID TO EAT ON A PLANE.
DID YOU NOT WAIT TWO HOURS BEFORE SWIMMING WHEN YOU WERE A KID?
I ATE WHILE STILL IN THE WATER SO I DIDN'T HAVE TO WAIT.
ARE YOU SERIOUSLY GOING TO HOLD THE LAST BITE IN YOUR MOUTH THE WHOLE TIME WE'RE OVER WATER?

PUTTING OUR ABILITIES TO THE TEST

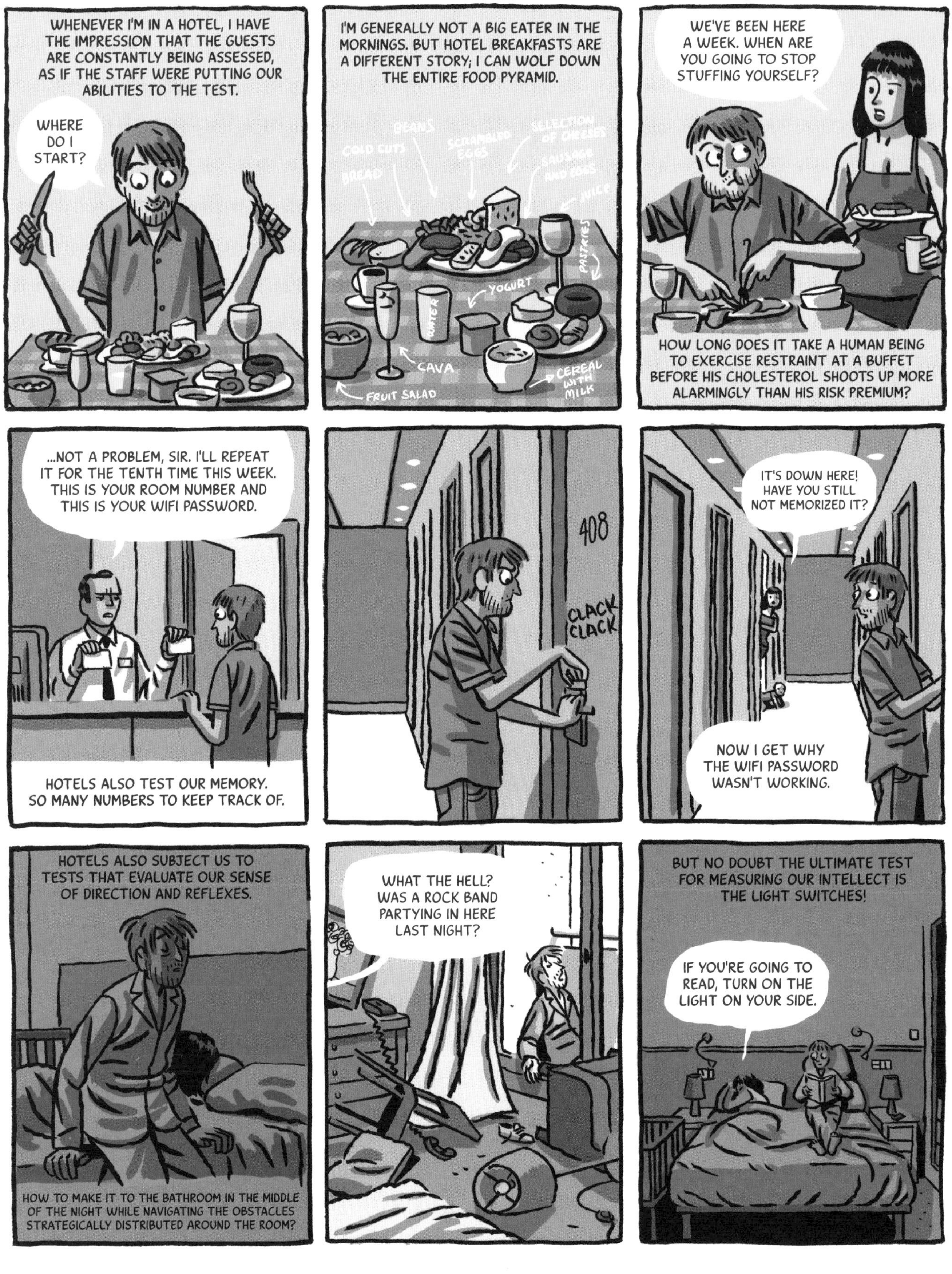
WHENEVER I'M IN A HOTEL, I HAVE THE IMPRESSION THAT THE GUESTS ARE CONSTANTLY BEING ASSESSED, AS IF THE STAFF WERE PUTTING OUR ABILITIES TO THE TEST.
WHERE DO I START?
I'M GENERALLY NOT A BIG EATER IN THE MORNINGS. BUT HOTEL BREAKFASTS ARE A DIFFERENT STORY; I CAN WOLF DOWN THE ENTIRE FOOD PYRAMID.
BEANS
COLD CUTS
SCRAMBLED EGGS
SELECTION OF CHEESES
SAUSAGE AND EGGS
BREAD
JUICE
PASTRIES
YOGURT
WATER
CAVA
CEREAL WITH MILK
FRUIT SALAD
WE'VE BEEN HERE A WEEK. WHEN ARE YOU GOING TO STOP STUFFING YOURSELF?
HOW LONG DOES IT TAKE A HUMAN BEING TO EXERCISE RESTRAINT AT A BUFFET BEFORE HIS CHOLESTEROL SHOOTS UP MORE ALARMINGLY THAN HIS RISK PREMIUM?
...NOT A PROBLEM, SIR. I'LL REPEAT IT FOR THE TENTH TIME THIS WEEK. THIS IS YOUR ROOM NUMBER AND THIS IS YOUR WIFI PASSWORD.
HOTELS ALSO TEST OUR MEMORY. SO MANY NUMBERS TO KEEP TRACK OF.
408
CLACK CLACK
IT'S DOWN HERE! HAVE YOU STILL NOT MEMORIZED IT?
NOW I GET WHY THE WIFI PASSWORD WASN'T WORKING.
HOTELS ALSO SUBJECT US TO TESTS THAT EVALUATE OUR SENSE OF DIRECTION AND REFLEXES.
HOW TO MAKE IT TO THE BATHROOM IN THE MIDDLE OF THE NIGHT WHILE NAVIGATING THE OBSTACLES STRATEGICALLY DISTRIBUTED AROUND THE ROOM?
WHAT THE HELL? WAS A ROCK BAND PARTYING IN HERE LAST NIGHT?
BUT NO DOUBT THE ULTIMATE TEST FOR MEASURING OUR INTELLECT IS THE LIGHT SWITCHES!
IF YOU'RE GOING TO READ, TURN ON THE LIGHT ON YOUR SIDE.

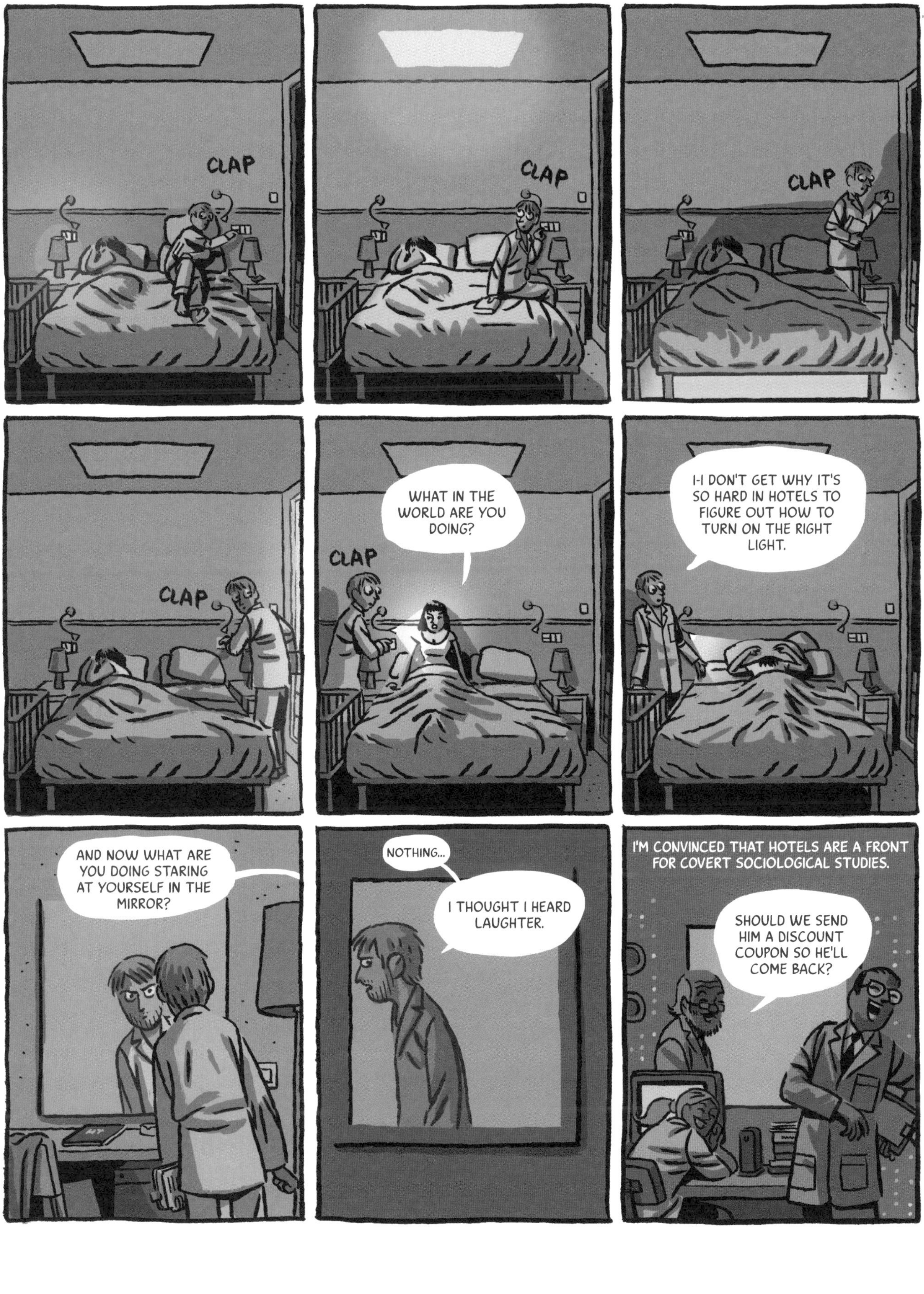
CLAP
CLAP
CLAP
CLAP
CLAP
WHAT IN THE WORLD ARE YOU DOING?
I-I DON'T GET WHY IT'S SO HARD IN HOTELS TO FIGURE OUT HOW TO TURN ON THE RIGHT LIGHT.
AND NOW WHAT ARE YOU DOING STARING AT YOURSELF IN THE MIRROR?
NOTHING...
I THOUGHT I HEARD LAUGHTER.
I'M CONVINCED THAT HOTELS ARE A FRONT FOR COVERT SOCIOLOGICAL STUDIES.
SHOULD WE SEND HIM A DISCOUNT COUPON SO HE'LL COME BACK?

THE HALFWAY POINT

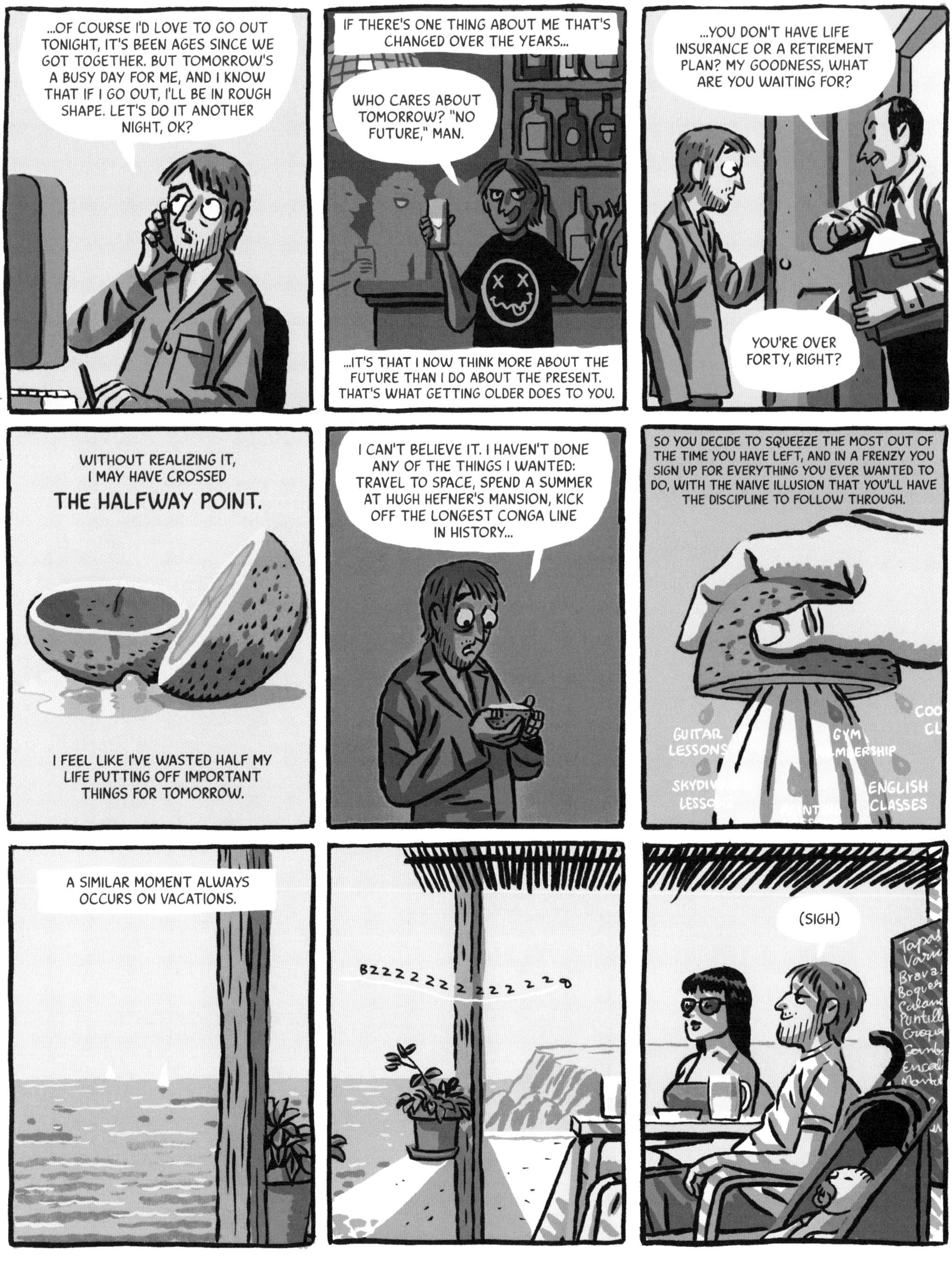

...OF COURSE I'D LOVE TO GO OUT TONIGHT, IT'S BEEN AGES SINCE WE GOT TOGETHER. BUT TOMORROW'S A BUSY DAY FOR ME, AND I KNOW THAT IF I GO OUT, I'LL BE IN ROUGH SHAPE. LET'S DO IT ANOTHER NIGHT, OK?
IF THERE'S ONE THING ABOUT ME THAT'S CHANGED OVER THE YEARS...
WHO CARES ABOUT TOMORROW? "NO FUTURE," MAN.
...IT'S THAT I NOW THINK MORE ABOUT THE FUTURE THAN I DO ABOUT THE PRESENT. THAT'S WHAT GETTING OLDER DOES TO YOU.
...YOU DON'T HAVE LIFE INSURANCE OR A RETIREMENT PLAN? MY GOODNESS, WHAT ARE YOU WAITING FOR?
YOU'RE OVER FORTY, RIGHT?
WITHOUT REALIZING IT, I MAY HAVE CROSSED
THE HALFWAY POINT.
I FEEL LIKE I'VE WASTED HALF MY LIFE PUTTING OFF IMPORTANT THINGS FOR TOMORROW.
I CAN'T BELIEVE IT. I HAVEN'T DONE ANY OF THE THINGS I WANTED: TRAVEL TO SPACE, SPEND A SUMMER AT HUGH HEFNER'S MANSION, KICK OFF THE LONGEST CONGA LINE IN HISTORY...
SO YOU DECIDE TO SQUEEZE THE MOST OUT OF THE TIME YOU HAVE LEFT, AND IN A FRENZY YOU SIGN UP FOR EVERYTHING YOU EVER WANTED TO DO, WITH THE NAIVE ILLUSION THAT YOU'LL HAVE THE DISCIPLINE TO FOLLOW THROUGH.
GUITAR LESSONS
ENGLISH CLASSES
A SIMILAR MOMENT ALWAYS OCCURS ON VACATIONS.
BZZZZZZZZZZZZZZZ
(SIGH)

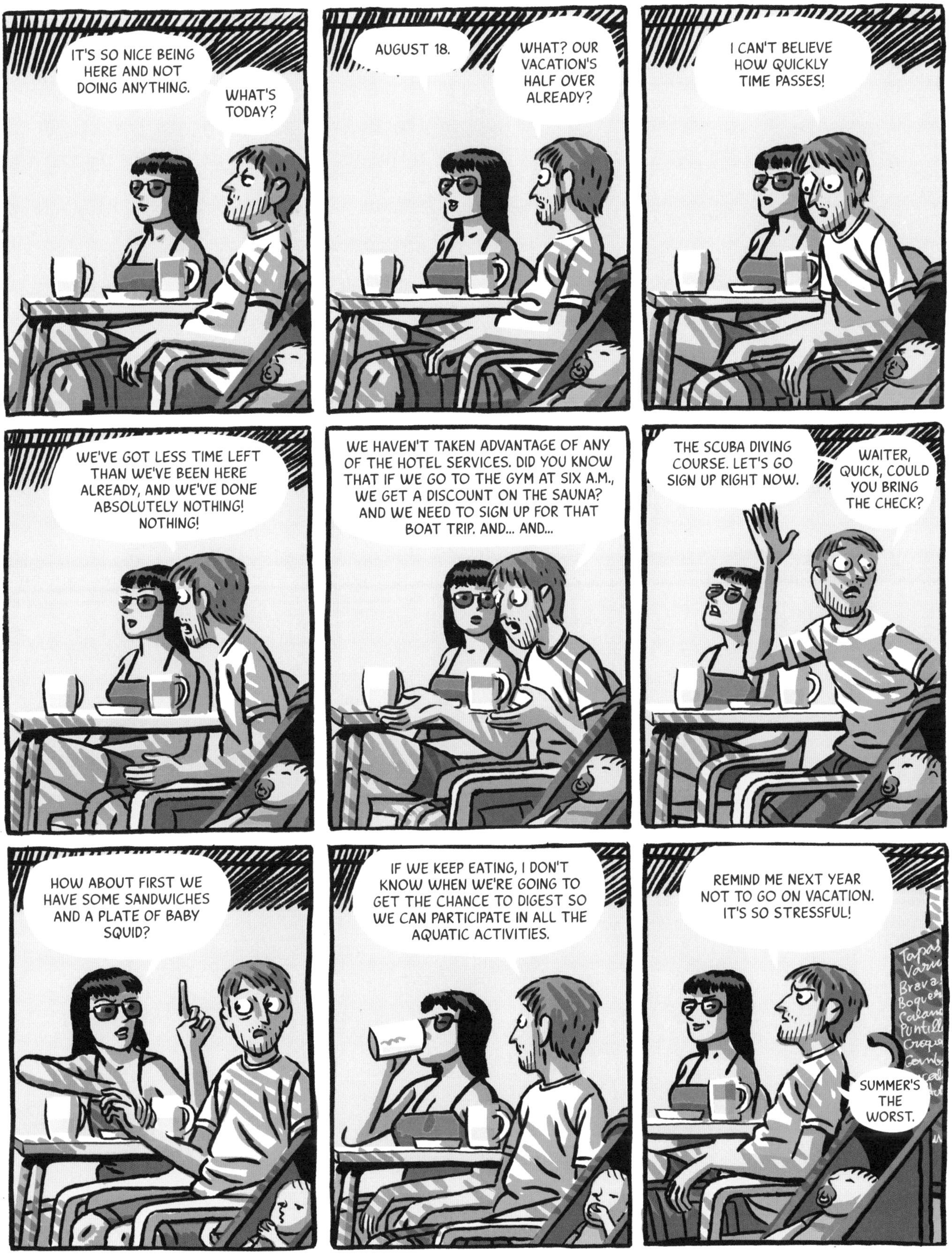
IT'S SO NICE BEING HERE AND NOT DOING ANYTHING.
WHAT'S TODAY?
AUGUST 18.
WHAT? OUR VACATION'S HALF OVER ALREADY?
I CAN'T BELIEVE HOW QUICKLY TIME PASSES!
WE'VE GOT LESS TIME LEFT THAN WE'VE BEEN HERE ALREADY, AND WE'VE DONE ABSOLUTELY NOTHING! NOTHING!
WE HAVEN'T TAKEN ADVANTAGE OF ANY OF THE HOTEL SERVICES. DID YOU KNOW THAT IF WE GO TO THE GYM AT SIX A.M., WE GET A DISCOUNT ON THE SAUNA? AND WE NEED TO SIGN UP FOR THAT BOAT TRIP. AND... AND...
THE SCUBA DIVING COURSE. LET'S GO SIGN UP RIGHT NOW.
WAITER, QUICK, COULD YOU BRING THE CHECK?
HOW ABOUT FIRST WE HAVE SOME SANDWICHES AND A PLATE OF BABY SQUID?
IF WE KEEP EATING, I DON'T KNOW WHEN WE'RE GOING TO GET THE CHANCE TO DIGEST SO WE CAN PARTICIPATE IN ALL THE AQUATIC ACTIVITIES.
REMIND ME NEXT YEAR NOT TO GO ON VACATION. IT'S SO STRESSFUL!
SUMMER'S THE WORST.

THE POST-VACATION GROWTH SPURT

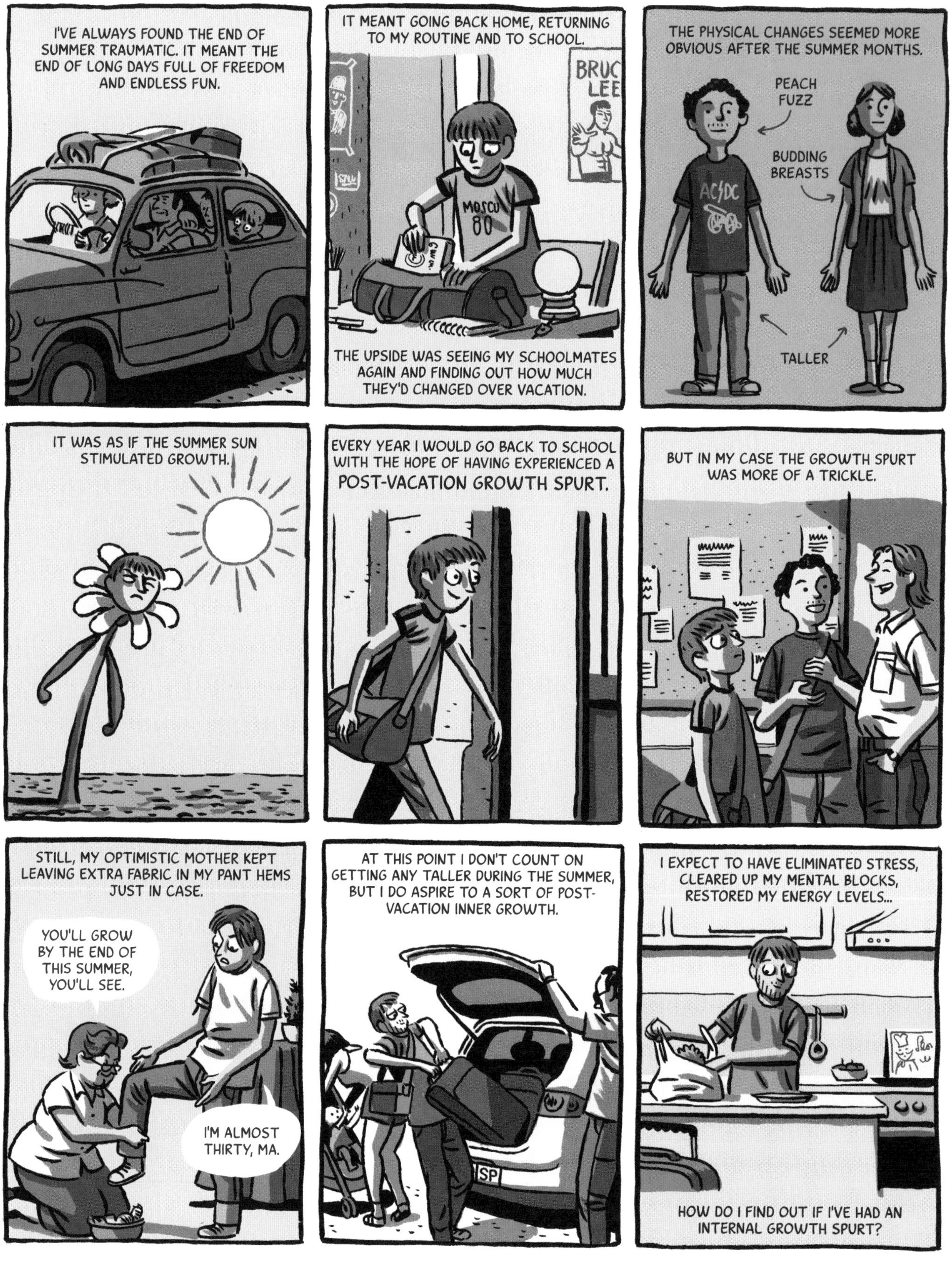

I'VE ALWAYS FOUND THE END OF SUMMER TRAUMATIC. IT MEANT THE END OF LONG DAYS FULL OF FREEDOM AND ENDLESS FUN.
IT MEANT GOING BACK HOME, RETURNING TO MY ROUTINE AND TO SCHOOL.
MOSCU 80
THE UPSIDE WAS SEEING MY SCHOOLMATES AGAIN AND FINDING OUT HOW MUCH THEY'D CHANGED OVER VACATION.
THE PHYSICAL CHANGES SEEMED MORE OBVIOUS AFTER THE SUMMER MONTHS.
PEACH FUZZ
BUDDING BREASTS
AC/DC
TALLER
IT WAS AS IF THE SUMMER SUN STIMULATED GROWTH.
EVERY YEAR I WOULD GO BACK TO SCHOOL WITH THE HOPE OF HAVING EXPERIENCED A POST-VACATION GROWTH SPURT.
BUT IN MY CASE THE GROWTH SPURT WAS MORE OF A TRICKLE.
STILL, MY OPTIMISTIC MOTHER KEPT LEAVING EXTRA FABRIC IN MY PANT HEMS JUST IN CASE.
YOU'LL GROW BY THE END OF THIS SUMMER, YOU'LL SEE.
I'M ALMOST THIRTY, MA.
AT THIS POINT I DON'T COUNT ON GETTING ANY TALLER DURING THE SUMMER, BUT I DO ASPIRE TO A SORT OF POST-VACATION INNER GROWTH.
SP
I EXPECT TO HAVE ELIMINATED STRESS, CLEARED UP MY MENTAL BLOCKS, RESTORED MY ENERGY LEVELS...
HOW DO I FIND OUT IF I'VE HAD AN INTERNAL GROWTH SPURT?

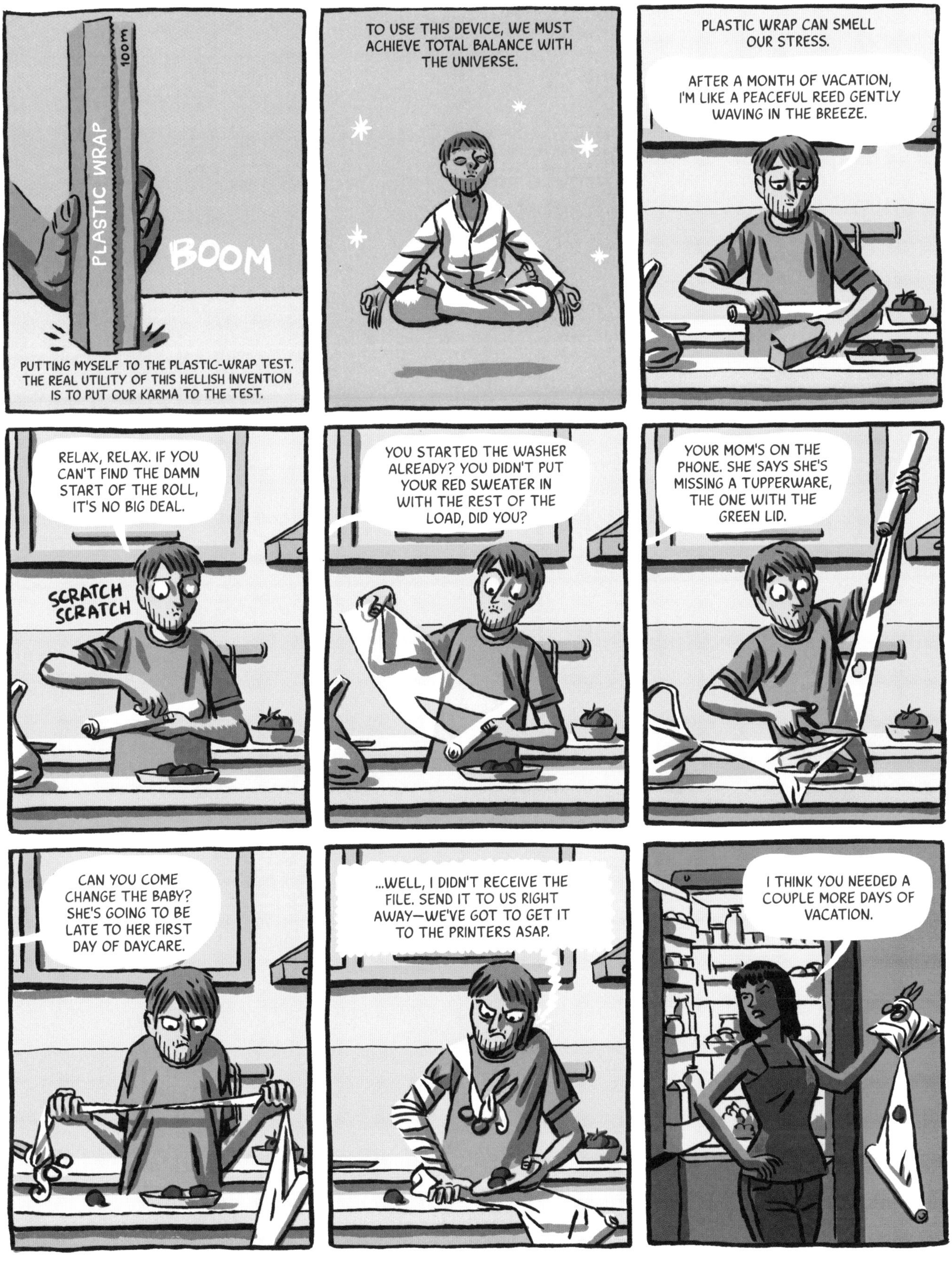
100m
PLASTIC WRAP
BOOM
PUTTING MYSELF TO THE PLASTIC-WRAP TEST. THE REAL UTILITY OF THIS HELLISH INVENTION IS TO PUT OUR KARMA TO THE TEST.
TO USE THIS DEVICE, WE MUST ACHIEVE TOTAL BALANCE WITH THE UNIVERSE.
PLASTIC WRAP CAN SMELL OUR STRESS.
AFTER A MONTH OF VACATION, I'M LIKE A PEACEFUL REED GENTLY WAVING IN THE BREEZE.
RELAX, RELAX. IF YOU CAN'T FIND THE DAMN START OF THE ROLL, IT'S NO BIG DEAL.
SCRATCH SCRATCH
YOU STARTED THE WASHER ALREADY? YOU DIDN'T PUT YOUR RED SWEATER IN WITH THE REST OF THE LOAD, DID YOU?
YOUR MOM'S ON THE PHONE. SHE SAYS SHE'S MISSING A TUPPERWARE, THE ONE WITH THE GREEN LID.
CAN YOU COME CHANGE THE BABY? SHE'S GOING TO BE LATE TO HER FIRST DAY OF DAYCARE.
...WELL, I DIDN'T RECEIVE THE FILE. SEND IT TO US RIGHT AWAY—WE'VE GOT TO GET IT TO THE PRINTERS ASAP.
I THINK YOU NEEDED A COUPLE MORE DAYS OF VACATION.

ARTISTIC FREEDOM

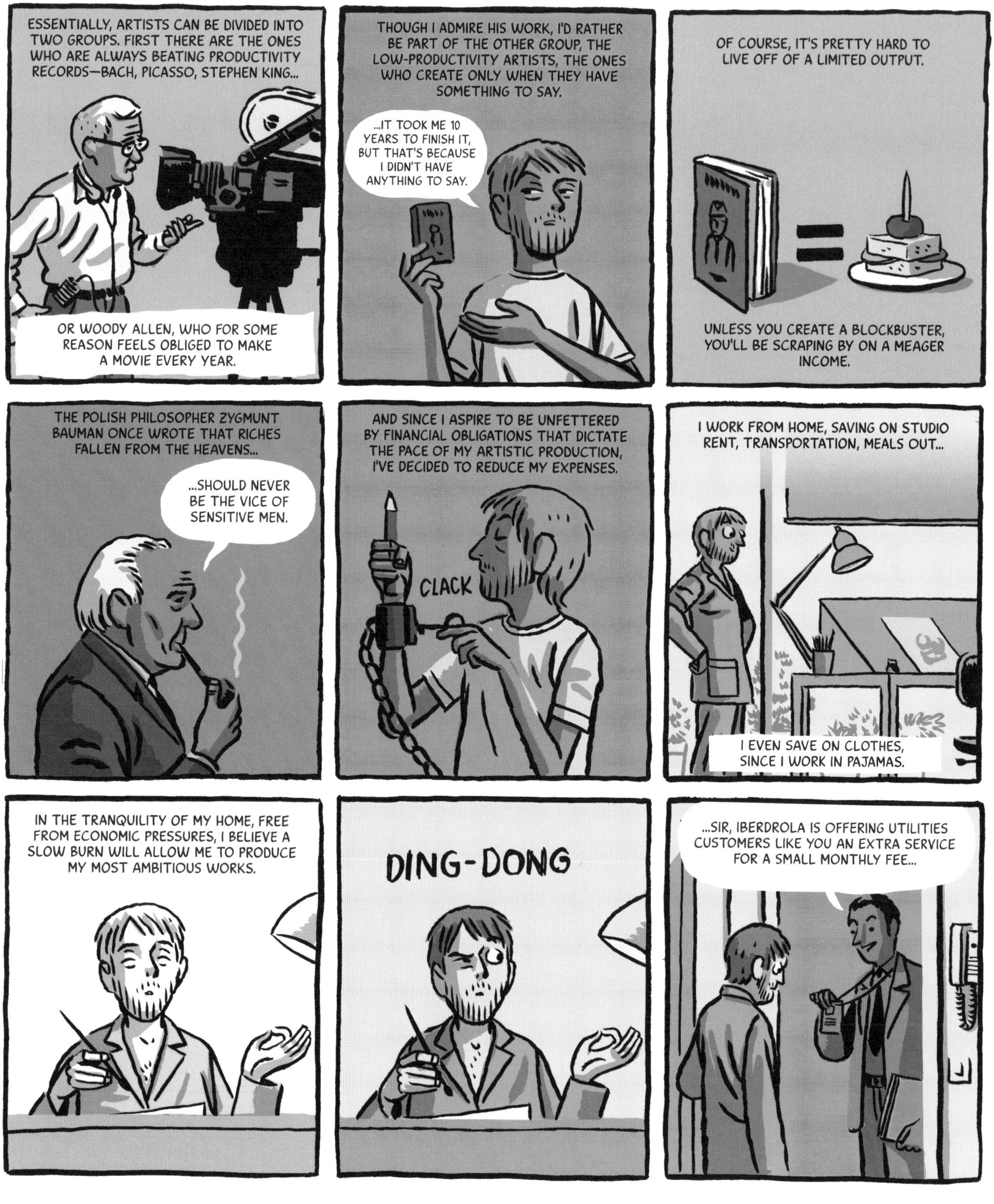
ESSENTIALLY, ARTISTS CAN BE DIVIDED INTO TWO GROUPS. FIRST THERE ARE THE ONES WHO ARE ALWAYS BEATING PRODUCTIVITY RECORDS—BACH, PICASSO, STEPHEN KING...
OR WOODY ALLEN, WHO FOR SOME REASON FEELS OBLIGED TO MAKE A MOVIE EVERY YEAR.
THOUGH I ADMIRE HIS WORK, I'D RATHER BE PART OF THE OTHER GROUP, THE LOW-PRODUCTIVITY ARTISTS, THE ONES WHO CREATE ONLY WHEN THEY HAVE SOMETHING TO SAY.
...IT TOOK ME 10 YEARS TO FINISH IT, BUT THAT'S BECAUSE I DIDN'T HAVE ANYTHING TO SAY.
OF COURSE, IT'S PRETTY HARD TO LIVE OFF OF A LIMITED OUTPUT.
UNLESS YOU CREATE A BLOCKBUSTER, YOU'LL BE SCRAPING BY ON A MEAGER INCOME.
THE POLISH PHILOSOPHER ZYGMUNT BAUMAN ONCE WROTE THAT RICHES FALLEN FROM THE HEAVENS...
...SHOULD NEVER BE THE VICE OF SENSITIVE MEN.
AND SINCE I ASPIRE TO BE UNFETTERED BY FINANCIAL OBLIGATIONS THAT DICTATE THE PACE OF MY ARTISTIC PRODUCTION, I'VE DECIDED TO REDUCE MY EXPENSES.
CLACK
I WORK FROM HOME, SAVING ON STUDIO RENT, TRANSPORTATION, MEALS OUT...
I EVEN SAVE ON CLOTHES, SINCE I WORK IN PAJAMAS.
IN THE TRANQUILITY OF MY HOME, FREE FROM ECONOMIC PRESSURES, I BELIEVE A SLOW BURN WILL ALLOW ME TO PRODUCE MY MOST AMBITIOUS WORKS.
DING-DONG
...SIR, IBERDROLA IS OFFERING UTILITIES CUSTOMERS LIKE YOU AN EXTRA SERVICE FOR A SMALL MONTHLY FEE...

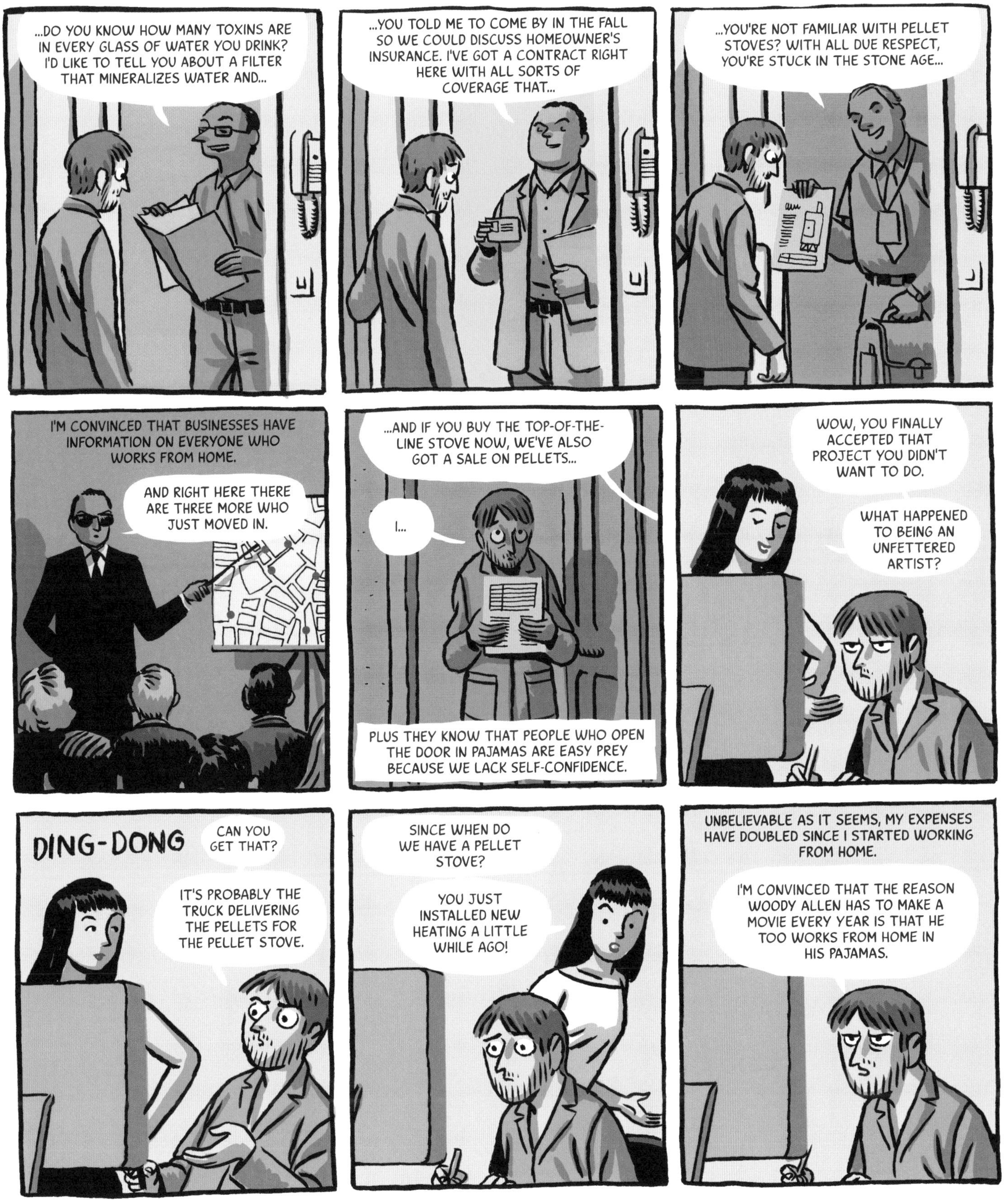
...DO YOU KNOW HOW MANY TOXINS ARE IN EVERY GLASS OF WATER YOU DRINK? I'D LIKE TO TELL YOU ABOUT A FILTER THAT MINERALIZES WATER AND...
...YOU TOLD ME TO COME BY IN THE FALL SO WE COULD DISCUSS HOMEOWNER'S INSURANCE. I'VE GOT A CONTRACT RIGHT HERE WITH ALL SORTS OF COVERAGE THAT...
...YOU'RE NOT FAMILIAR WITH PELLET STOVES? WITH ALL DUE RESPECT, YOU'RE STUCK IN THE STONE AGE...
I'M CONVINCED THAT BUSINESSES HAVE INFORMATION ON EVERYONE WHO WORKS FROM HOME.
AND RIGHT HERE THERE ARE THREE MORE WHO JUST MOVED IN.
...AND IF YOU BUY THE TOP-OF-THE-LINE STOVE NOW, WE'VE ALSO GOT A SALE ON PELLETS...
I...
PLUS THEY KNOW THAT PEOPLE WHO OPEN THE DOOR IN PAJAMAS ARE EASY PREY BECAUSE WE LACK SELF-CONFIDENCE.
WOW, YOU FINALLY ACCEPTED THAT PROJECT YOU DIDN'T WANT TO DO.
WHAT HAPPENED TO BEING AN UNFETTERED ARTIST?
DING-DONG
CAN YOU GET THAT?
IT'S PROBABLY THE TRUCK DELIVERING THE PELLETS FOR THE PELLET STOVE.
SINCE WHEN DO WE HAVE A PELLET STOVE?
YOU JUST INSTALLED NEW HEATING A LITTLE WHILE AGO!
UNBELIEVABLE AS IT SEEMS, MY EXPENSES HAVE DOUBLED SINCE I STARTED WORKING FROM HOME.
I'M CONVINCED THAT THE REASON WOODY ALLEN HAS TO MAKE A MOVIE EVERY YEAR IS THAT HE TOO WORKS FROM HOME IN HIS PAJAMAS.

SAVINGS PLAN

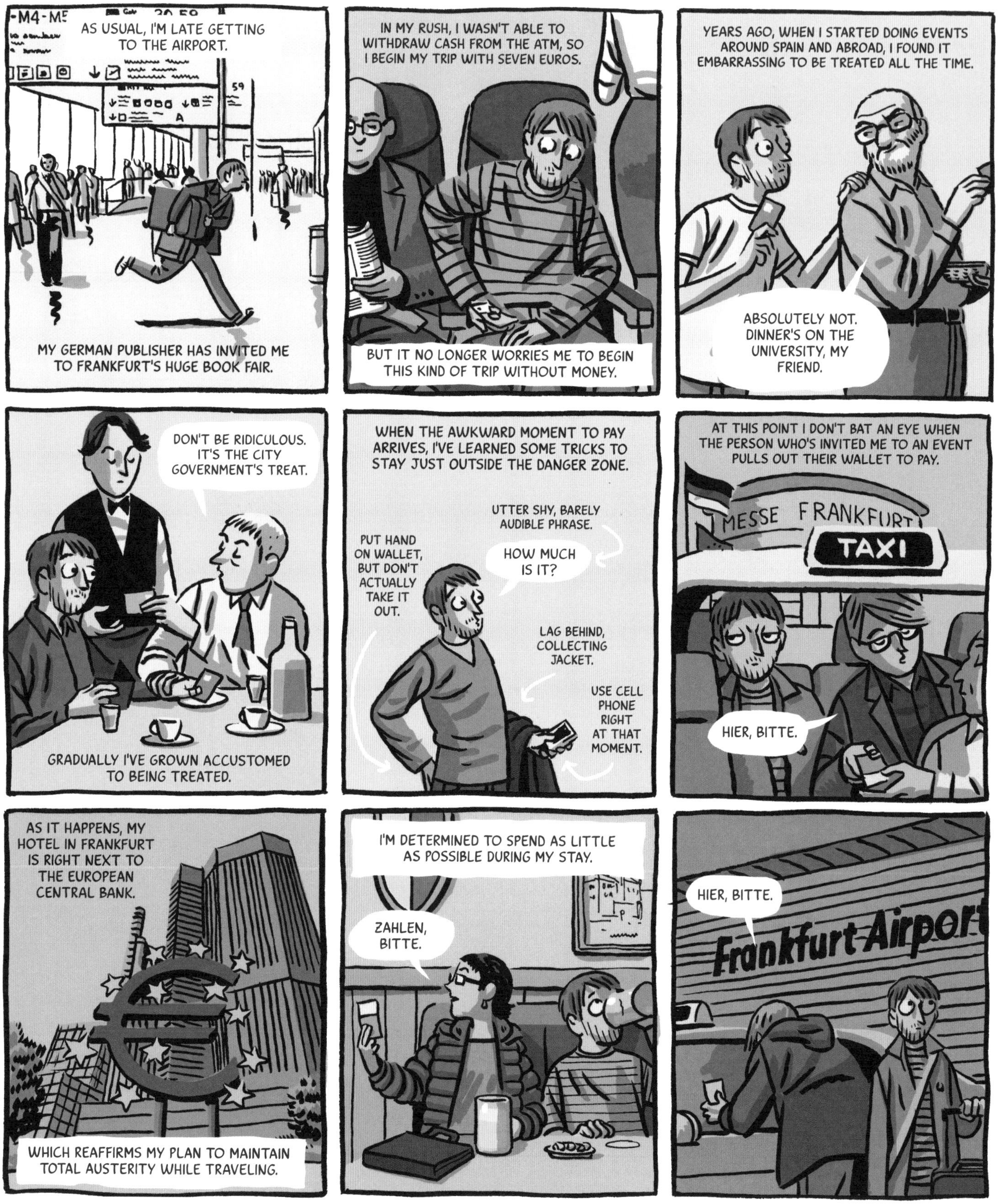

AS USUAL, I'M LATE GETTING TO THE AIRPORT.
MY GERMAN PUBLISHER HAS INVITED ME TO FRANKFURT'S HUGE BOOK FAIR.
IN MY RUSH, I WASN'T ABLE TO WITHDRAW CASH FROM THE ATM, SO I BEGIN MY TRIP WITH SEVEN EUROS.
BUT IT NO LONGER WORRIES ME TO BEGIN THIS KIND OF TRIP WITHOUT MONEY.
YEARS AGO, WHEN I STARTED DOING EVENTS AROUND SPAIN AND ABROAD, I FOUND IT EMBARRASSING TO BE TREATED ALL THE TIME.
ABSOLUTELY NOT. DINNER'S ON THE UNIVERSITY, MY FRIEND.
DON'T BE RIDICULOUS. IT'S THE CITY GOVERNMENT'S TREAT.
GRADUALLY I'VE GROWN ACCUSTOMED TO BEING TREATED.
WHEN THE AWKWARD MOMENT TO PAY ARRIVES, I'VE LEARNED SOME TRICKS TO STAY JUST OUTSIDE THE DANGER ZONE.
PUT HAND ON WALLET, BUT DON'T ACTUALLY TAKE IT OUT.
UTTER SHY, BARELY AUDIBLE PHRASE.
HOW MUCH IS IT?
LAG BEHIND, COLLECTING JACKET.
USE CELL PHONE RIGHT AT THAT MOMENT.
AT THIS POINT I DON'T BAT AN EYE WHEN THE PERSON WHO'S INVITED ME TO AN EVENT PULLS OUT THEIR WALLET TO PAY.
MESSE FRANKFURT
TAXI
HIER, BITTE.
AS IT HAPPENS, MY HOTEL IN FRANKFURT IS RIGHT NEXT TO THE EUROPEAN CENTRAL BANK.
WHICH REAFFIRMS MY PLAN TO MAINTAIN TOTAL AUSTERITY WHILE TRAVELING.
I'M DETERMINED TO SPEND AS LITTLE AS POSSIBLE DURING MY STAY.
ZAHLEN, BITTE.
HIER, BITTE.
Frankfurt Airport

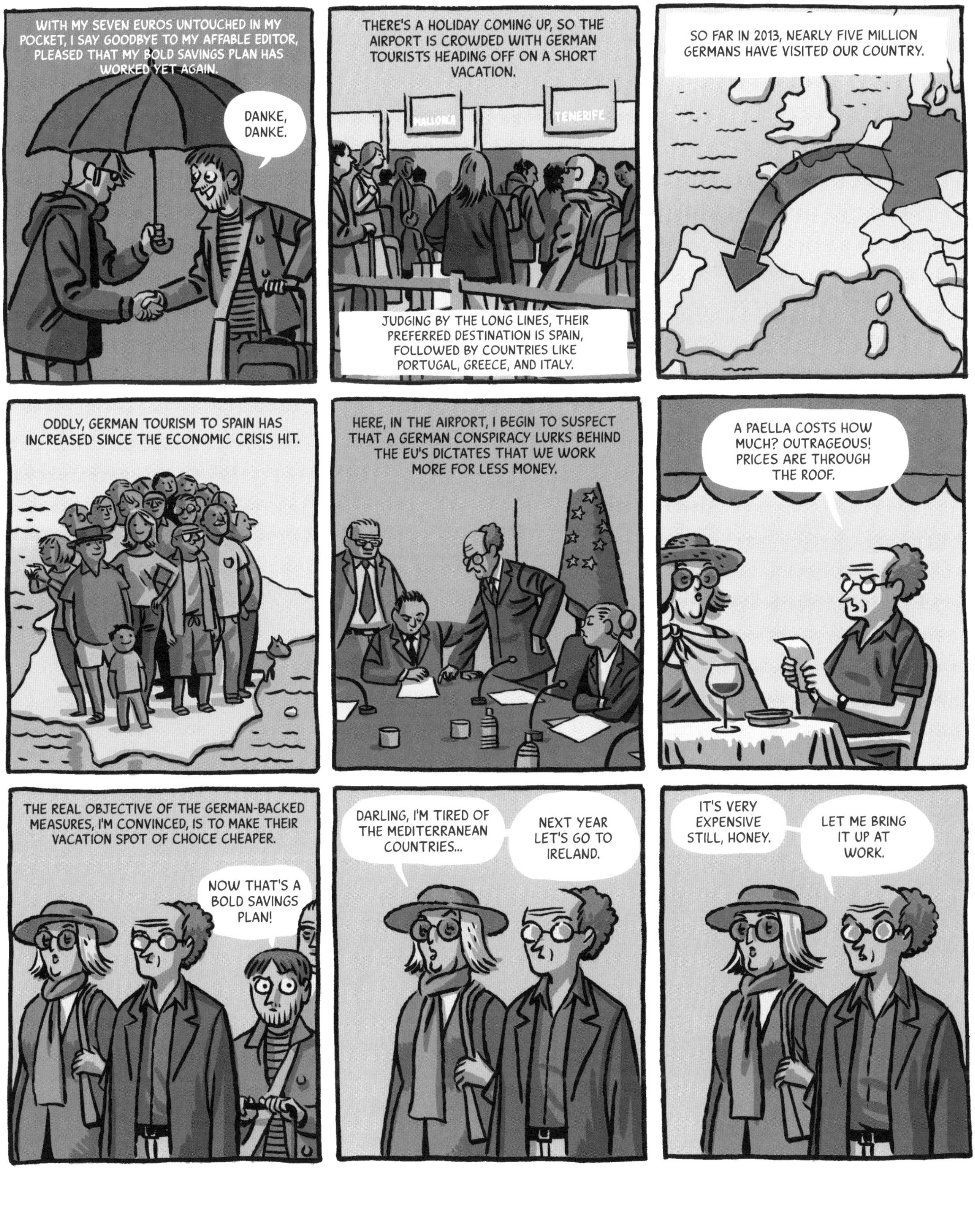
WITH MY SEVEN EUROS UNTOUCHED IN MY POCKET, I SAY GOODBYE TO MY AFFABLE EDITOR, PLEASED THAT MY BOLD SAVINGS PLAN HAS WORKED YET AGAIN.
DANKE, DANKE.
THERE'S A HOLIDAY COMING UP, SO THE AIRPORT IS CROWDED WITH GERMAN TOURISTS HEADING OFF ON A SHORT VACATION.
MALLORCA
TENERIFE
JUDGING BY THE LONG LINES, THEIR PREFERRED DESTINATION IS SPAIN, FOLLOWED BY COUNTRIES LIKE PORTUGAL, GREECE, AND ITALY.
SO FAR IN 2013, NEARLY FIVE MILLION GERMANS HAVE VISITED OUR COUNTRY.
ODDLY, GERMAN TOURISM TO SPAIN HAS INCREASED SINCE THE ECONOMIC CRISIS HIT.
HERE, IN THE AIRPORT, I BEGIN TO SUSPECT THAT A GERMAN CONSPIRACY LURKS BEHIND THE EU'S DICTATES THAT WE WORK MORE FOR LESS MONEY.
A PAELLA COSTS HOW MUCH? OUTRAGEOUS! PRICES ARE THROUGH THE ROOF.
THE REAL OBJECTIVE OF THE GERMAN-BACKED MEASURES, I'M CONVINCED, IS TO MAKE THEIR VACATION SPOT OF CHOICE CHEAPER.
NOW THAT'S A BOLD SAVINGS PLAN!
DARLING, I'M TIRED OF THE MEDITERRANEAN COUNTRIES...
NEXT YEAR LET'S GO TO IRELAND.
IT'S VERY EXPENSIVE STILL, HONEY.
LET ME BRING IT UP AT WORK.

WHAT PHONE COMPANIES JOIN TOGETHER...

SINCE THE INVENTION OF THE MOBILE PHONE IN THE 1980S, TELECOMMUNICATIONS HAS BEEN ONE OF THE FASTEST-GROWING INDUSTRIES.

IN SPAIN WE'VE GONE FROM HAVING ONE TELEPHONE PER FAMILY TO HAVING MORE PHONE LINES THAN INHABITANTS.

WITH THE MARKET OVERSATURATED, THE PHONE COMPANY WARS HAVE BEGUN. THE BIG ONES LOSE CUSTOMERS TO THE BETTER DEALS OFFERED BY THE SMALL ONES.

BUT... WHAT THE PHONE COMPANIES JOIN TOGETHER, LET NO MAN PUT ASUNDER.

...THE THING IS, THIS BILL ISN'T ON ME. I'VE BEEN WITH ANOTHER COMPANY FOR TWO MONTHS.

IT'S ANOTHER DEPARTMENT'S ISSUE? SO PUT ME THROUGH TO THEM.

I'LL HAVE TO CALL BACK?

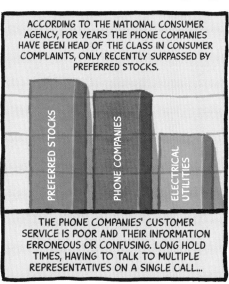

ACCORDING TO THE NATIONAL CONSUMER AGENCY, FOR YEARS THE PHONE COMPANIES HAVE BEEN HEAD OF THE CLASS IN CONSUMER COMPLAINTS, ONLY RECENTLY SURPASSED BY PREFERRED STOCKS.

PREFERRED STOCKS

PHONE COMPANIES

ELECTRICAL UTILITIES

THE PHONE COMPANIES' CUSTOMER SERVICE IS POOR AND THEIR INFORMATION ERRONEOUS OR CONFUSING. LONG HOLD TIMES, HAVING TO TALK TO MULTIPLE REPRESENTATIVES ON A SINGLE CALL...

AND IF WE'RE CALLING TO CANCEL OUR SERVICE, THE COMPANY WILL PUT UP ENDLESS ROADBLOCKS.

PLEASE TELL ME WHY YOU ARE CALLING...

ROSALINDA SPEAKING, HOW CAN I HELP YOU?

JAZMÍN SPEAKING.

PLEASE HOLD.

H-HELLO?

THERE'S NO DIRECT LINE CUSTOMERS CAN CALL TO RESOLVE PROBLEMS EFFICIENTLY.

NOT EVEN AN OFFICE THEY CAN GO TO. CELL PHONE STORES ARE THE COMPANIES' FIREWALL TO AVOID OFFERING PERSONAL ASSISTANCE.

I'M SORRY. WE DON'T HANDLE COMPLAINTS OR CANCELLATIONS OF SERVICE HERE. WE ONLY DO SIGNUPS.

YOU'LL HAVE TO CALL.

IS THERE NOBODY BEHIND THE COMPANIES, A PHYSICAL PERSON WE CAN COMPLAIN TO? BASED ON REPORTS OF THEIR EXORBITANT SALARIES, WE KNOW THEY HAVE PRESIDENTS AND CEOS AT THE VERY LEAST.

...IS ANYONE THERE? I... WANT TO CANCEL MY SERVICE...

GIVEN HOW HARD IT IS TO CANCEL SERVICE OR RESOLVE PROBLEMS, IT'S UNDERSTANDABLE THAT MANY CUSTOMERS, FED UP WITH THE KAFKAESQUE SITUATION, CHOOSE TO SIMPLY STOP PAYING.

WOW, I GOT A LOT OF CHRISTMAS CARDS THIS YEAR.

THAT'S WHEN THE COMPANY'S LEGAL HARASSMENT BEGINS. LETTERS FROM THEIR STABLE OF LAWYERS...

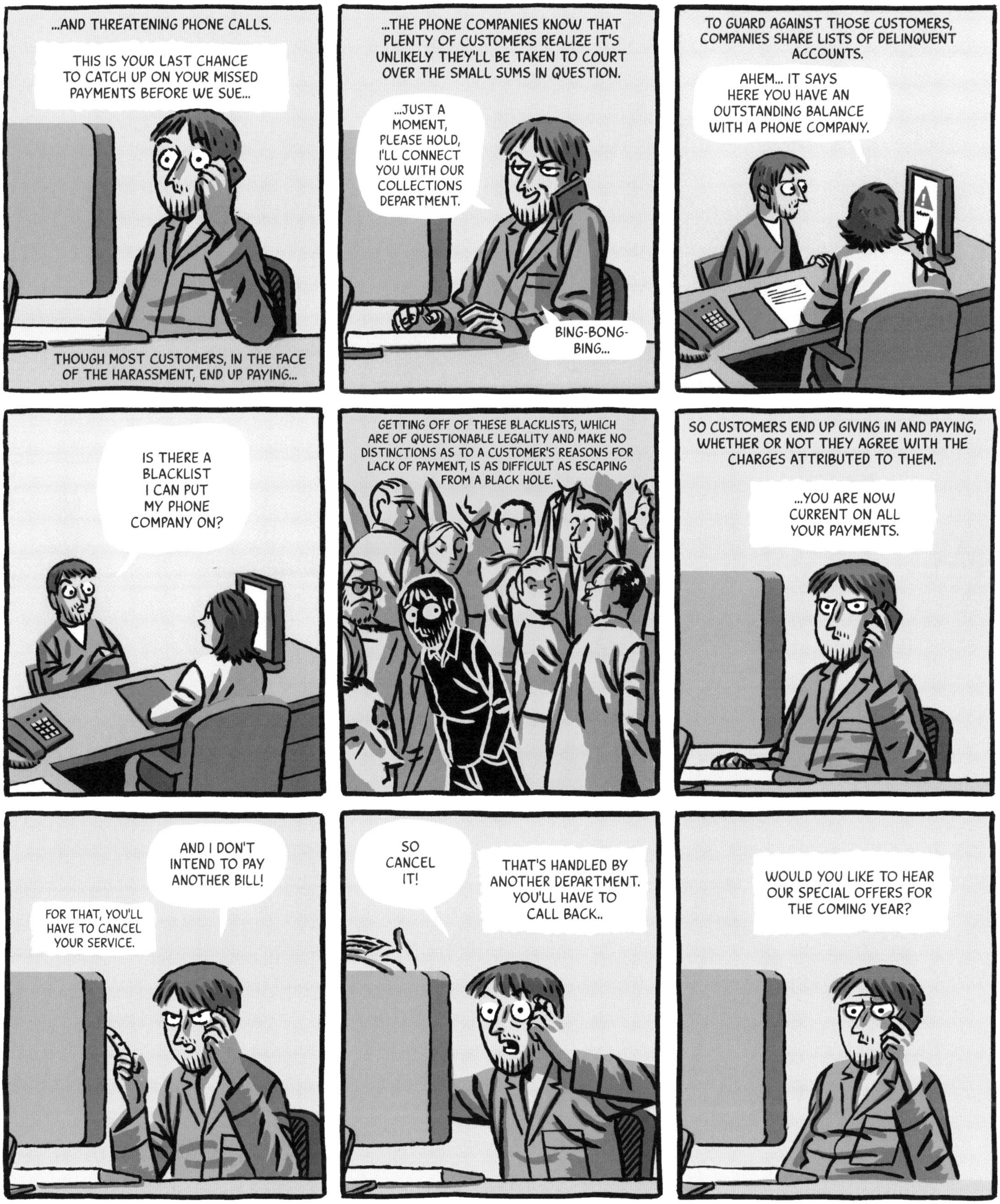
...AND THREATENING PHONE CALLS.
THIS IS YOUR LAST CHANCE TO CATCH UP ON YOUR MISSED PAYMENTS BEFORE WE SUE...
THOUGH MOST CUSTOMERS, IN THE FACE OF THE HARASSMENT, END UP PAYING...
...THE PHONE COMPANIES KNOW THAT PLENTY OF CUSTOMERS REALIZE IT'S UNLIKELY THEY'LL BE TAKEN TO COURT OVER THE SMALL SUMS IN QUESTION.
...JUST A MOMENT, PLEASE HOLD, I'LL CONNECT YOU WITH OUR COLLECTIONS DEPARTMENT.
BING-BONG-BING...
TO GUARD AGAINST THOSE CUSTOMERS, COMPANIES SHARE LISTS OF DELINQUENT ACCOUNTS.
AHEM... IT SAYS HERE YOU HAVE AN OUTSTANDING BALANCE WITH A PHONE COMPANY.
IS THERE A BLACKLIST I CAN PUT MY PHONE COMPANY ON?
GETTING OFF OF THESE BLACKLISTS, WHICH ARE OF QUESTIONABLE LEGALITY AND MAKE NO DISTINCTIONS AS TO A CUSTOMER'S REASONS FOR LACK OF PAYMENT, IS AS DIFFICULT AS ESCAPING FROM A BLACK HOLE.
SO CUSTOMERS END UP GIVING IN AND PAYING, WHETHER OR NOT THEY AGREE WITH THE CHARGES ATTRIBUTED TO THEM.
...YOU ARE NOW CURRENT ON ALL YOUR PAYMENTS.
AND I DON'T INTEND TO PAY ANOTHER BILL!
FOR THAT, YOU'LL HAVE TO CANCEL YOUR SERVICE.
SO CANCEL IT!
THAT'S HANDLED BY ANOTHER DEPARTMENT. YOU'LL HAVE TO CALL BACK..
WOULD YOU LIKE TO HEAR OUR SPECIAL OFFERS FOR THE COMING YEAR?

THE UNFAITHFUL PUBLIC

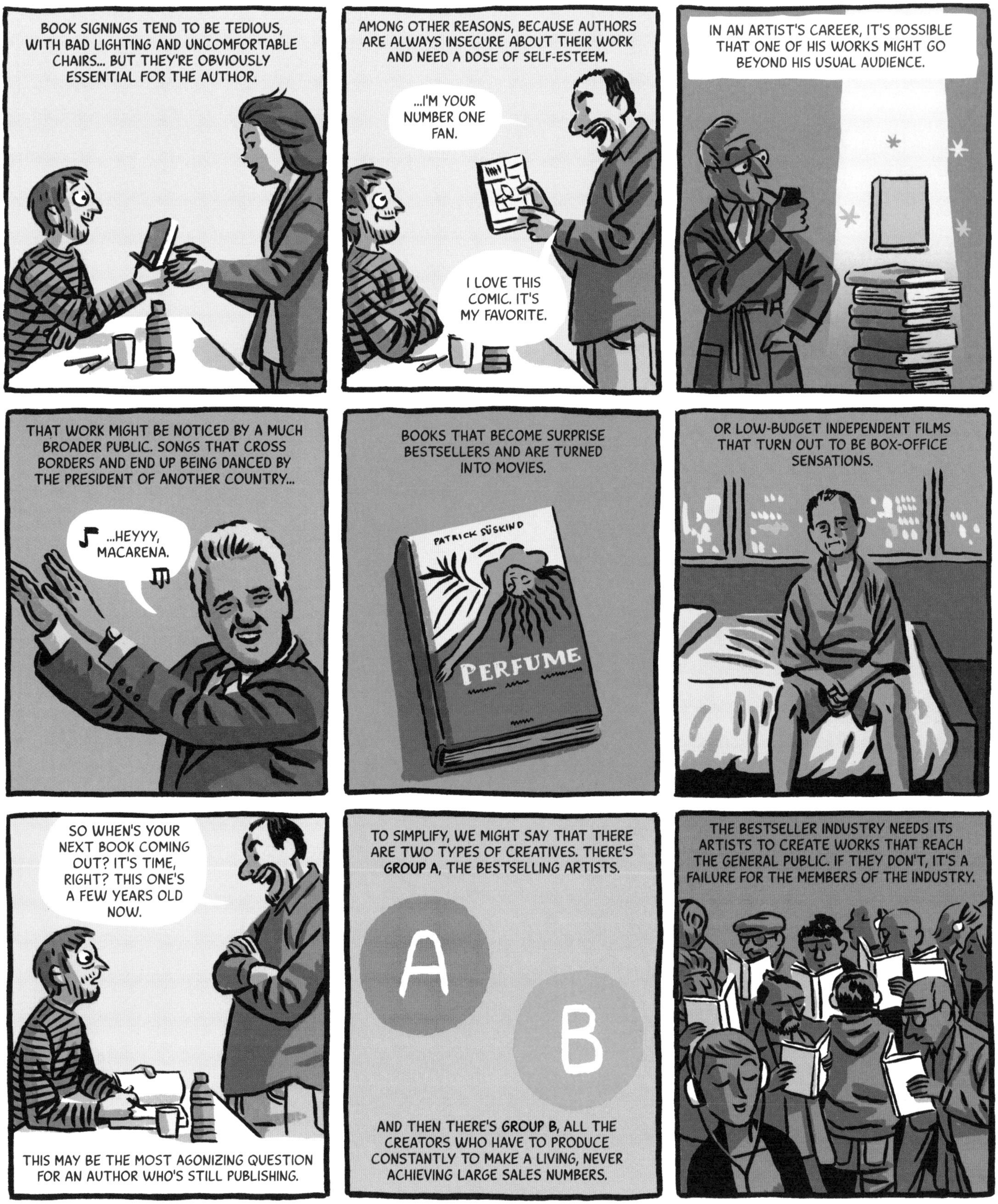
BOOK SIGNINGS TEND TO BE TEDIOUS, WITH BAD LIGHTING AND UNCOMFORTABLE CHAIRS... BUT THEY'RE OBVIOUSLY ESSENTIAL FOR THE AUTHOR.
AMONG OTHER REASONS, BECAUSE AUTHORS ARE ALWAYS INSECURE ABOUT THEIR WORK AND NEED A DOSE OF SELF-ESTEEM.
...I'M YOUR NUMBER ONE FAN.
I LOVE THIS COMIC. IT'S MY FAVORITE.
IN AN ARTIST'S CAREER, IT'S POSSIBLE THAT ONE OF HIS WORKS MIGHT GO BEYOND HIS USUAL AUDIENCE.
THAT WORK MIGHT BE NOTICED BY A MUCH BROADER PUBLIC. SONGS THAT CROSS BORDERS AND END UP BEING DANCED BY THE PRESIDENT OF ANOTHER COUNTRY...
...HEYYY, MACARENA.
BOOKS THAT BECOME SURPRISE BESTSELLERS AND ARE TURNED INTO MOVIES.
PATRICK SÜSKIND
PERFUME
OR LOW-BUDGET INDEPENDENT FILMS THAT TURN OUT TO BE BOX-OFFICE SENSATIONS.
SO WHEN'S YOUR NEXT BOOK COMING OUT? IT'S TIME, RIGHT? THIS ONE'S A FEW YEARS OLD NOW.
THIS MAY BE THE MOST AGONIZING QUESTION FOR AN AUTHOR WHO'S STILL PUBLISHING.
TO SIMPLIFY, WE MIGHT SAY THAT THERE ARE TWO TYPES OF CREATIVES. THERE'S **GROUP A**, THE BESTSELLING ARTISTS.
A
B
AND THEN THERE'S **GROUP B**, ALL THE CREATORS WHO HAVE TO PRODUCE CONSTANTLY TO MAKE A LIVING, NEVER ACHIEVING LARGE SALES NUMBERS.
THE BESTSELLER INDUSTRY NEEDS ITS ARTISTS TO CREATE WORKS THAT REACH THE GENERAL PUBLIC. IF THEY DON'T, IT'S A FAILURE FOR THE MEMBERS OF THE INDUSTRY.

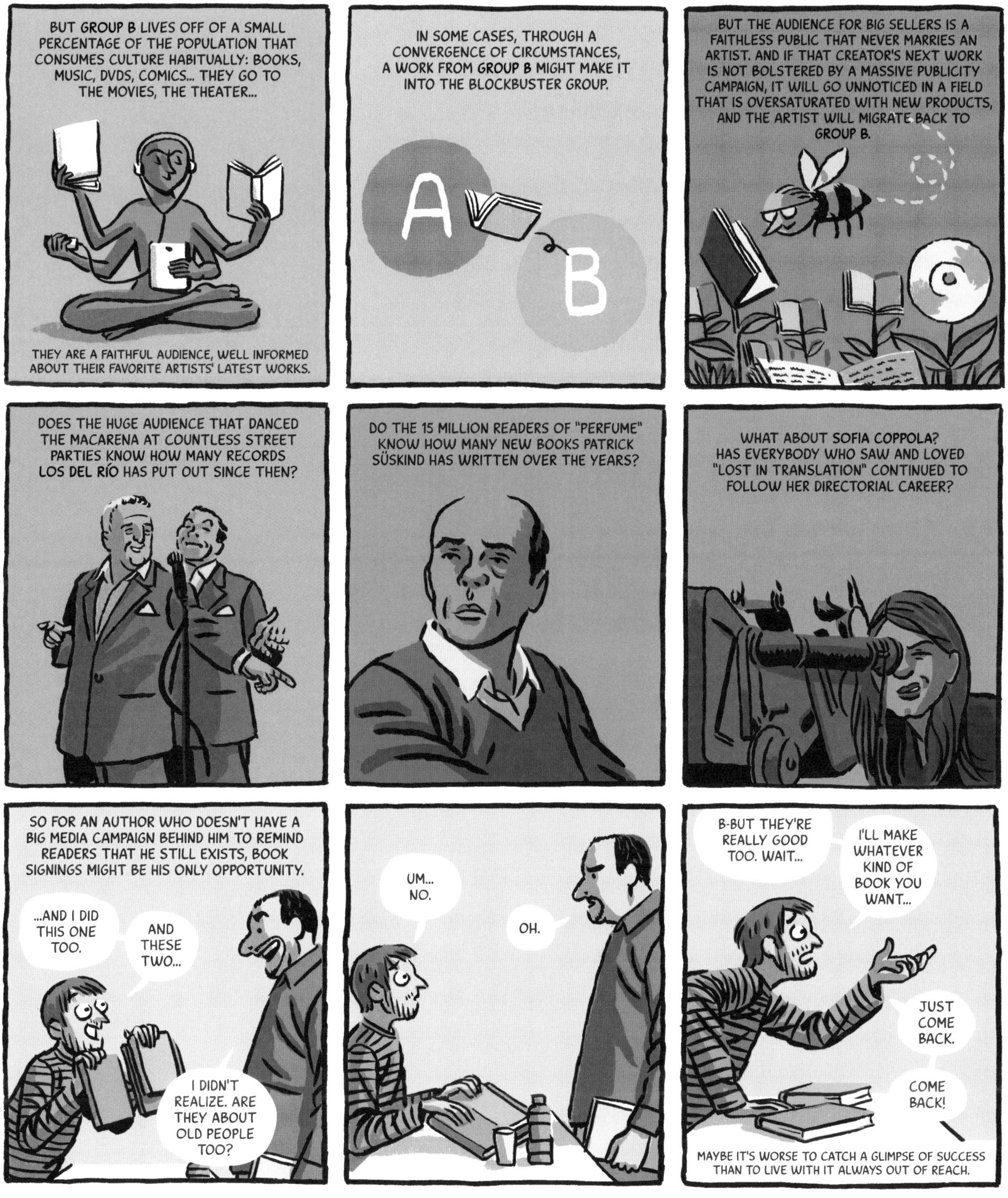
BUT GROUP B LIVES OFF OF A SMALL PERCENTAGE OF THE POPULATION THAT CONSUMES CULTURE HABITUALLY: BOOKS, MUSIC, DVDS, COMICS... THEY GO TO THE MOVIES, THE THEATER...
THEY ARE A FAITHFUL AUDIENCE, WELL INFORMED ABOUT THEIR FAVORITE ARTISTS' LATEST WORKS.
IN SOME CASES, THROUGH A CONVERGENCE OF CIRCUMSTANCES, A WORK FROM GROUP B MIGHT MAKE IT INTO THE BLOCKBUSTER GROUP.
A
B
BUT THE AUDIENCE FOR BIG SELLERS IS A FAITHLESS PUBLIC THAT NEVER MARRIES AN ARTIST. AND IF THAT CREATOR'S NEXT WORK IS NOT BOLSTERED BY A MASSIVE PUBLICITY CAMPAIGN, IT WILL GO UNNOTICED IN A FIELD THAT IS OVERSATURATED WITH NEW PRODUCTS, AND THE ARTIST WILL MIGRATE BACK TO GROUP B.
DOES THE HUGE AUDIENCE THAT DANCED THE MACARENA AT COUNTLESS STREET PARTIES KNOW HOW MANY RECORDS LOS DEL RÍO HAS PUT OUT SINCE THEN?
DO THE 15 MILLION READERS OF "PERFUME" KNOW HOW MANY NEW BOOKS PATRICK SÜSKIND HAS WRITTEN OVER THE YEARS?
WHAT ABOUT SOFIA COPPOLA? HAS EVERYBODY WHO SAW AND LOVED "LOST IN TRANSLATION" CONTINUED TO FOLLOW HER DIRECTORIAL CAREER?
SO FOR AN AUTHOR WHO DOESN'T HAVE A BIG MEDIA CAMPAIGN BEHIND HIM TO REMIND READERS THAT HE STILL EXISTS, BOOK SIGNINGS MIGHT BE HIS ONLY OPPORTUNITY.
...AND I DID THIS ONE TOO.
AND THESE TWO...
I DIDN'T REALIZE. ARE THEY ABOUT OLD PEOPLE TOO?
UM... NO.
OH.
B-BUT THEY'RE REALLY GOOD TOO. WAIT...
I'LL MAKE WHATEVER KIND OF BOOK YOU WANT...
JUST COME BACK.
COME BACK!
MAYBE IT'S WORSE TO CATCH A GLIMPSE OF SUCCESS THAN TO LIVE WITH IT ALWAYS OUT OF REACH.

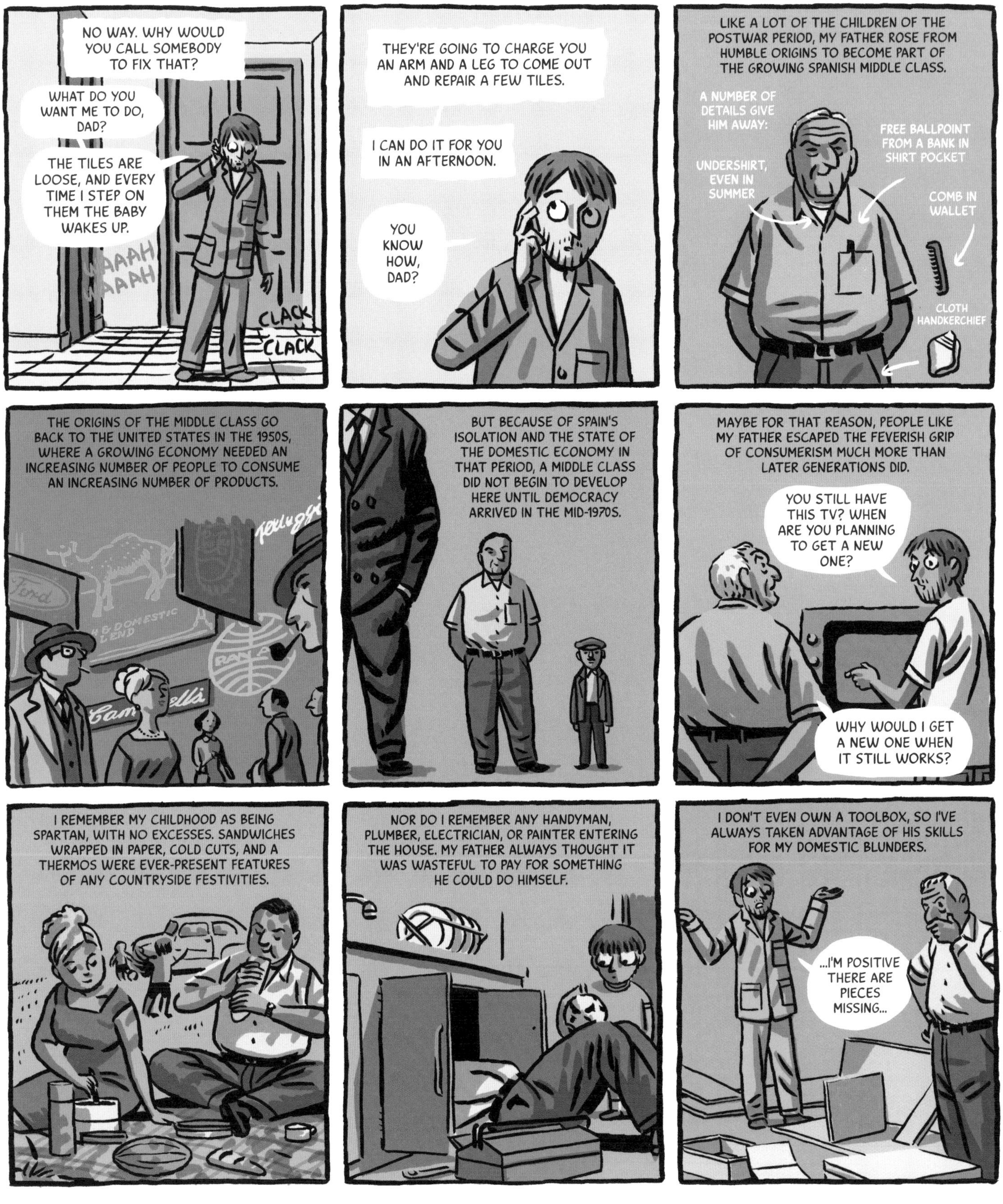
NO WAY. WHY WOULD YOU CALL SOMEBODY TO FIX THAT?
WHAT DO YOU WANT ME TO DO, DAD?
THE TILES ARE LOOSE, AND EVERY TIME I STEP ON THEM THE BABY WAKES UP.
WAAAH WAAAH
CLACK
CLACK
THEY'RE GOING TO CHARGE YOU AN ARM AND A LEG TO COME OUT AND REPAIR A FEW TILES.
I CAN DO IT FOR YOU IN AN AFTERNOON.
YOU KNOW HOW, DAD?
LIKE A LOT OF THE CHILDREN OF THE POSTWAR PERIOD, MY FATHER ROSE FROM HUMBLE ORIGINS TO BECOME PART OF THE GROWING SPANISH MIDDLE CLASS.
A NUMBER OF DETAILS GIVE HIM AWAY:
UNDERSHIRT, EVEN IN SUMMER
FREE BALLPOINT FROM A BANK IN SHIRT POCKET
COMB IN WALLET
CLOTH HANDKERCHIEF
THE ORIGINS OF THE MIDDLE CLASS GO BACK TO THE UNITED STATES IN THE 1950S, WHERE A GROWING ECONOMY NEEDED AN INCREASING NUMBER OF PEOPLE TO CONSUME AN INCREASING NUMBER OF PRODUCTS.
Ford
BUT BECAUSE OF SPAIN'S ISOLATION AND THE STATE OF THE DOMESTIC ECONOMY IN THAT PERIOD, A MIDDLE CLASS DID NOT BEGIN TO DEVELOP HERE UNTIL DEMOCRACY ARRIVED IN THE MID-1970S.
MAYBE FOR THAT REASON, PEOPLE LIKE MY FATHER ESCAPED THE FEVERISH GRIP OF CONSUMERISM MUCH MORE THAN LATER GENERATIONS DID.
YOU STILL HAVE THIS TV? WHEN ARE YOU PLANNING TO GET A NEW ONE?
WHY WOULD I GET A NEW ONE WHEN IT STILL WORKS?
I REMEMBER MY CHILDHOOD AS BEING SPARTAN, WITH NO EXCESSES. SANDWICHES WRAPPED IN PAPER, COLD CUTS, AND A THERMOS WERE EVER-PRESENT FEATURES OF ANY COUNTRYSIDE FESTIVITIES.
NOR DO I REMEMBER ANY HANDYMAN, PLUMBER, ELECTRICIAN, OR PAINTER ENTERING THE HOUSE. MY FATHER ALWAYS THOUGHT IT WAS WASTEFUL TO PAY FOR SOMETHING HE COULD DO HIMSELF.
I DON'T EVEN OWN A TOOLBOX, SO I'VE ALWAYS TAKEN ADVANTAGE OF HIS SKILLS FOR MY DOMESTIC BLUNDERS.
...I'M POSITIVE THERE ARE PIECES MISSING...

...GET A BAG OF SAND AND I'LL COME BY TOMORROW TO FIX THOSE TILES.
AND WHERE AM I SUPPOSED TO BUY A BAG OF SAND?
WASN'T THERE AN ABANDONED CONSTRUCTION SITE BY YOUR HOUSE? TAKE ONE OF THOSE.
WHAT? YOU WANT ME TO STEAL A BAG FROM THE SITE?
IT'S NOT STEALING. THOSE BAGS ARE GOING TO BE RUINED. WHY WASTE MONEY BUYING IT WHEN YOU CAN TAKE ONE FROM THERE?
CRACK
YOU'RE REALLY TIGHT TODAY!
WHAT DID YOU DO?
THIS IS GOING TO TAKE AT LEAST FIVE SESSIONS.
AND IT'S 50 EUROS A SESSION.
I'M FROM OF A GENERATION THAT'S GOING TO HAVE A HARD TIME ADAPTING TO THE CURRENT ECONOMIC REALITY.
...INSTEAD OF MUSIC CLASS, DO YOU HAVE A QUICK DIY HOME IMPROVEMENT COURSE I COULD ENROLL HER IN?
OUR ONLY HOPE IS FOR OUR CHILDREN TO START TAKING CARE OF US ASAP.

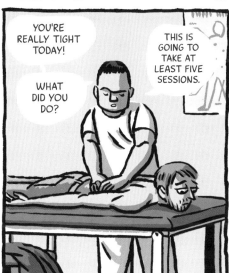

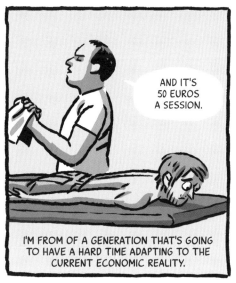

THE ENIGMA OF THE POLITICAL CLASS

FROM THE BEGINNING OF CIVILIZATION, A SMALL ELITE HAS RULED THE WORLD: SHAMANS, PHARAOHS, KINGS, SULTANS, CONQUISTADORS... ALL OF THEM FELT SUPERIOR TO THE REST OF THE COMMUNITY BECAUSE THEY WERE CONNECTED TO THE FORCES OF THE DIVINE.

THESE RULERS HAVE ALWAYS INITIATED EXPENSIVE PROJECTS WHOSE PRACTICAL PURPOSE I DOUBT THE CITIZENS UNDERSTOOD, WHETHER THEY WERE SLAVES, WORKERS, OR INVESTORS VIA TAXES.

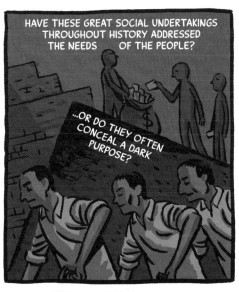

HAVE THESE GREAT SOCIAL UNDERTAKINGS THROUGHOUT HISTORY ADDRESSED THE NEEDS OF THE PEOPLE?

...OR DO THEY OFTEN CONCEAL A DARK PURPOSE?

A LITTLE WHILE BACK I WAS IN PUERTO RICO TO GIVE A FEW TALKS. DURING SOME DOWNTIME, LORETTA, MY CONTACT AT THE UNIVERSITY, TOOK ME TO SEE THE IMPRESSIVE ARECIBO OBSERVATORY.

...NOW THAT'S AN INTERGALACTIC ANTENNA!

BACK IN SAN JUAN, UNDER A CLEAR, STARRY SKY, WE ANIMATEDLY DISCUSSED THE VASTNESS OF THE COSMOS, THE SEARCH FOR EXTRATERRESTRIAL LIFE...

SAN JUAN 57

AND, OF COURSE, **UFOS.**

...A LOT OF PEOPLE HERE BELIEVE IN THEM. THERE ARE ALWAYS SIGHTINGS...

REINALDO RÍOS IS A PUERTO RICAN EXPERT ON UFOS AND THEIR EXTRATERRESTRIAL OCCUPANTS. THESE BEINGS HAVE BEEN VISITING US AND LIVING AMONG US FOR THOUSANDS OF YEARS.

BUT... TO WHAT END?

fig.1

REINALDO IS WORKING ON A UNIQUE PROJECT. HE'S BUILDING A LARGE AIRPORT, BUT... NOT FOR PLANES.

SUDDENLY, THERE IN THE MIDDLE OF THE NIGHT, I HAD AN EPIPHANY AND ALL THE PUZZLE PIECES FIT TOGETHER IN MY HEAD.

WHERE ELSE IN THE WORLD ARE AIRPORTS WITHOUT PLANES BEING BUILT?

SPAIN!

AND WHO IS BEHIND THE CONSTRUCTION OF THESE INTERSTELLAR AIRSTRIPS?

SO, ARE THE MEMBERS OF THE POLITICAL AND GOVERNING CLASS AN EXTRATERRESTRIAL RACE?

KUKILI KUKILI-KU.

THAT WOULD ACTUALLY EXPLAIN A LOT OF THINGS.

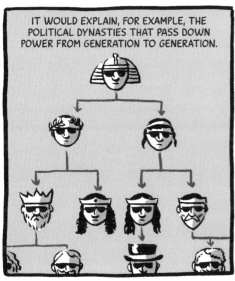

IT WOULD EXPLAIN, FOR EXAMPLE, THE POLITICAL DYNASTIES THAT PASS DOWN POWER FROM GENERATION TO GENERATION.

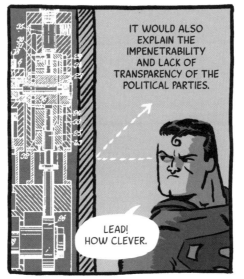

IT WOULD ALSO EXPLAIN THE IMPENETRABILITY AND LACK OF TRANSPARENCY OF THE POLITICAL PARTIES.

LEAD! HOW CLEVER.

AND OF COURSE, IT WOULD EXPLAIN THE LACK OF EMPATHY FOR THE EVERYDAY CITIZEN, WHICH ALWAYS MAKES IT SEEM LIKE POLITICIANS ARE SERVING THE PARTY RATHER THAN THE VOTER.

...THIS CONSPIRACY, WHICH FINALLY EXPLAINS THE MAJOR ENIGMAS OF THE POLITICAL CLASS, MAKES ME SHUDDER AND...

AHEM!

TAP TAP TAP

STOP TYPING AND COME WITH US.

WE'LL BE TAKING THAT COMPUTER AND WIPING THE HARD DRIVE.

RECORDING OR DRAWING AUTHORITIES AS THEY PERFORM THEIR DUTIES IS STRICTLY PROHIBITED!

IS IT TOO LATE TO DESTROY THIS AGE-OLD SCHEME?

POSTPARTUM DEPRESSION

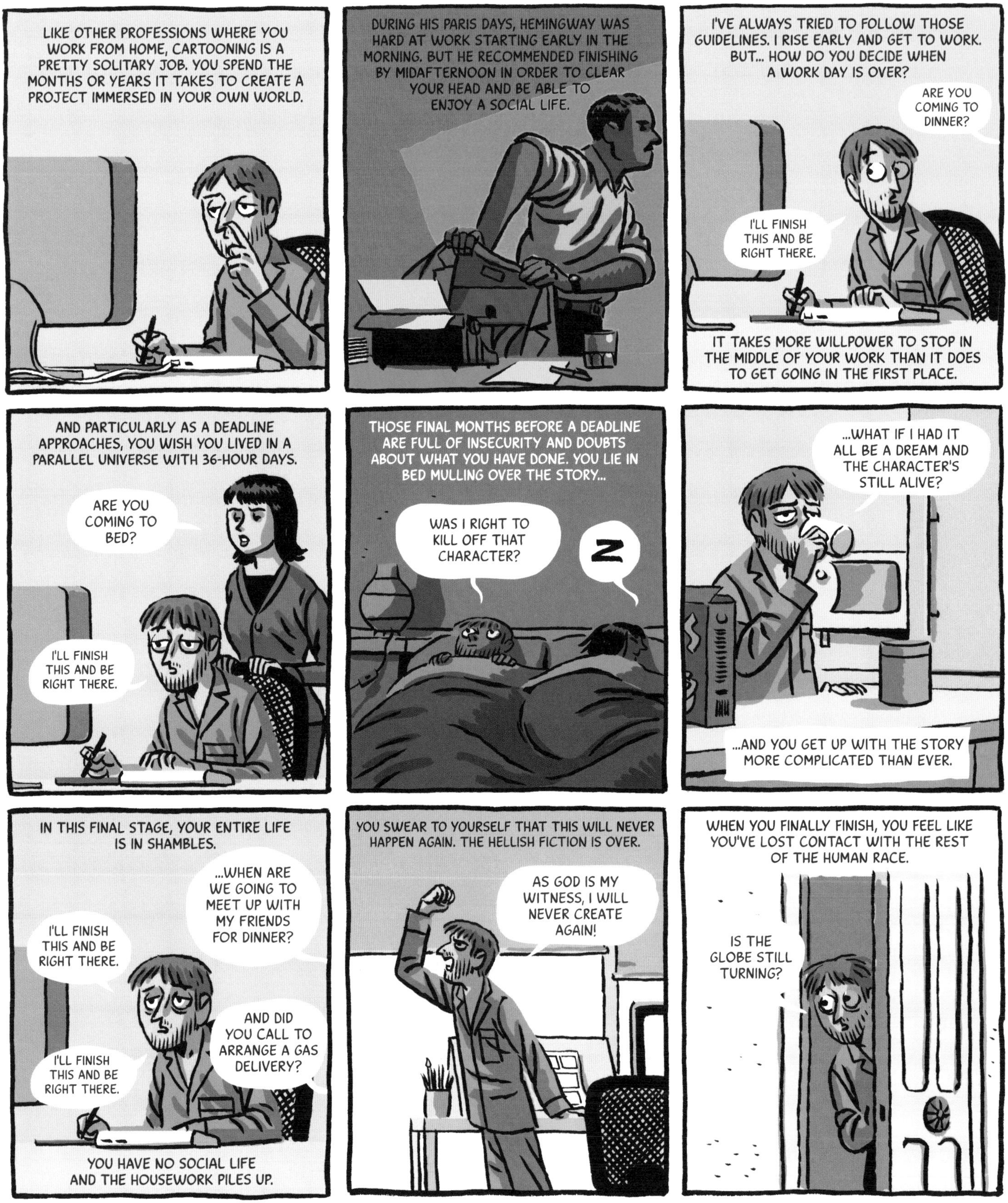
LIKE OTHER PROFESSIONS WHERE YOU WORK FROM HOME, CARTOONING IS A PRETTY SOLITARY JOB. YOU SPEND THE MONTHS OR YEARS IT TAKES TO CREATE A PROJECT IMMERSED IN YOUR OWN WORLD.
DURING HIS PARIS DAYS, HEMINGWAY WAS HARD AT WORK STARTING EARLY IN THE MORNING. BUT HE RECOMMENDED FINISHING BY MIDAFTERNOON IN ORDER TO CLEAR YOUR HEAD AND BE ABLE TO ENJOY A SOCIAL LIFE.
I'VE ALWAYS TRIED TO FOLLOW THOSE GUIDELINES. I RISE EARLY AND GET TO WORK. BUT... HOW DO YOU DECIDE WHEN A WORK DAY IS OVER?
ARE YOU COMING TO DINNER?
I'LL FINISH THIS AND BE RIGHT THERE.
IT TAKES MORE WILLPOWER TO STOP IN THE MIDDLE OF YOUR WORK THAN IT DOES TO GET GOING IN THE FIRST PLACE.
AND PARTICULARLY AS A DEADLINE APPROACHES, YOU WISH YOU LIVED IN A PARALLEL UNIVERSE WITH 36-HOUR DAYS.
ARE YOU COMING TO BED?
I'LL FINISH THIS AND BE RIGHT THERE.
THOSE FINAL MONTHS BEFORE A DEADLINE ARE FULL OF INSECURITY AND DOUBTS ABOUT WHAT YOU HAVE DONE. YOU LIE IN BED MULLING OVER THE STORY...
WAS I RIGHT TO KILL OFF THAT CHARACTER?
Z
...WHAT IF I HAD IT ALL BE A DREAM AND THE CHARACTER'S STILL ALIVE?
...AND YOU GET UP WITH THE STORY MORE COMPLICATED THAN EVER.
IN THIS FINAL STAGE, YOUR ENTIRE LIFE IS IN SHAMBLES.
...WHEN ARE WE GOING TO MEET UP WITH MY FRIENDS FOR DINNER?
I'LL FINISH THIS AND BE RIGHT THERE.
AND DID YOU CALL TO ARRANGE A GAS DELIVERY?
I'LL FINISH THIS AND BE RIGHT THERE.
YOU HAVE NO SOCIAL LIFE AND THE HOUSEWORK PILES UP.
YOU SWEAR TO YOURSELF THAT THIS WILL NEVER HAPPEN AGAIN. THE HELLISH FICTION IS OVER.
AS GOD IS MY WITNESS, I WILL NEVER CREATE AGAIN!
WHEN YOU FINALLY FINISH, YOU FEEL LIKE YOU'VE LOST CONTACT WITH THE REST OF THE HUMAN RACE.
IS THE GLOBE STILL TURNING?

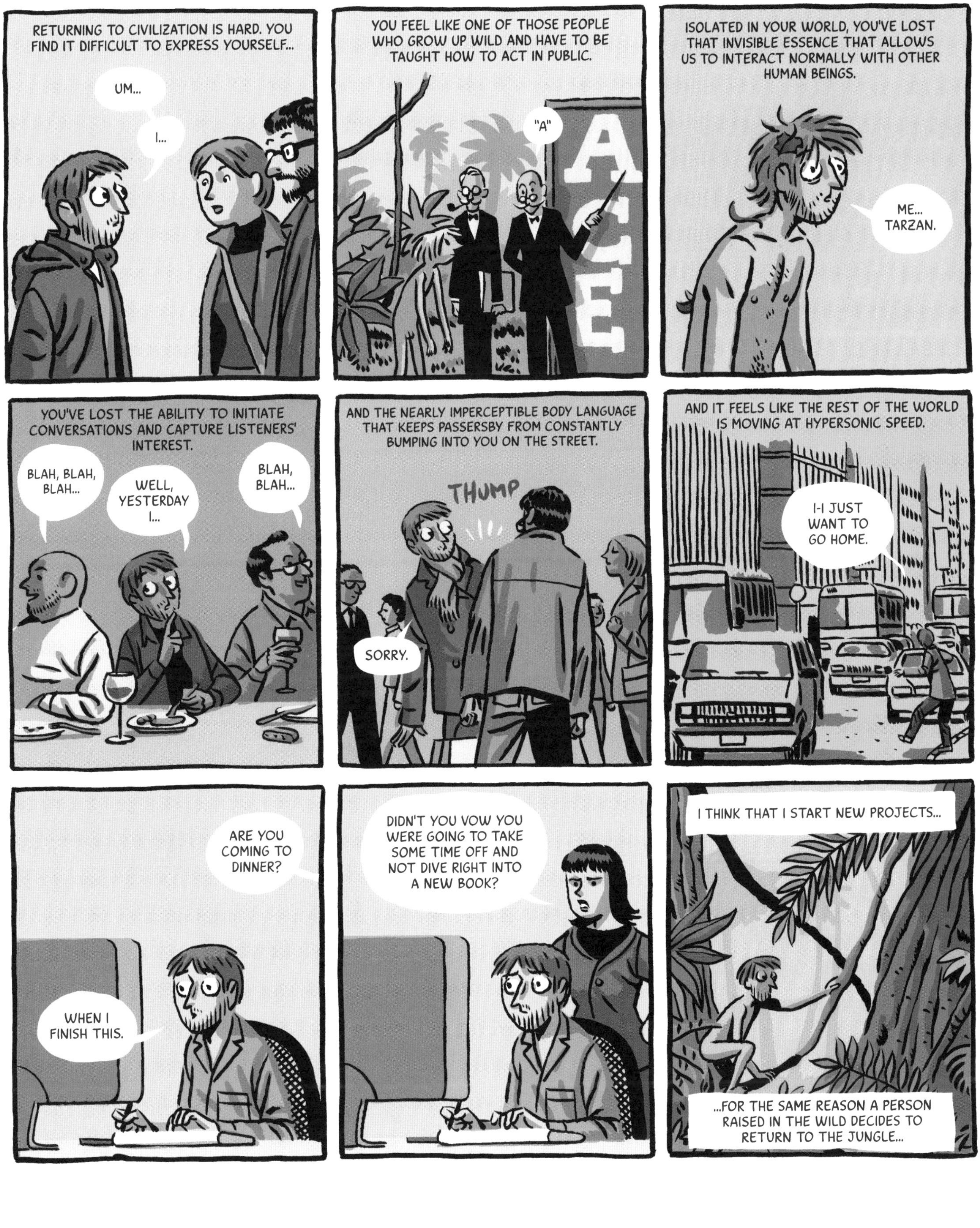
RETURNING TO CIVILIZATION IS HARD. YOU FIND IT DIFFICULT TO EXPRESS YOURSELF...
UM...
I...
YOU FEEL LIKE ONE OF THOSE PEOPLE WHO GROW UP WILD AND HAVE TO BE TAUGHT HOW TO ACT IN PUBLIC.
"A"
ACE
ISOLATED IN YOUR WORLD, YOU'VE LOST THAT INVISIBLE ESSENCE THAT ALLOWS US TO INTERACT NORMALLY WITH OTHER HUMAN BEINGS.
ME... TARZAN.
YOU'VE LOST THE ABILITY TO INITIATE CONVERSATIONS AND CAPTURE LISTENERS' INTEREST.
BLAH, BLAH, BLAH...
WELL, YESTERDAY I...
BLAH, BLAH...
AND THE NEARLY IMPERCEPTIBLE BODY LANGUAGE THAT KEEPS PASSERSBY FROM CONSTANTLY BUMPING INTO YOU ON THE STREET.
THUMP
SORRY.
AND IT FEELS LIKE THE REST OF THE WORLD IS MOVING AT HYPERSONIC SPEED.
I-I JUST WANT TO GO HOME.
ARE YOU COMING TO DINNER?
WHEN I FINISH THIS.
DIDN'T YOU VOW YOU WERE GOING TO TAKE SOME TIME OFF AND NOT DIVE RIGHT INTO A NEW BOOK?
I THINK THAT I START NEW PROJECTS...
...FOR THE SAME REASON A PERSON RAISED IN THE WILD DECIDES TO RETURN TO THE JUNGLE...

ETERNAL WRITING

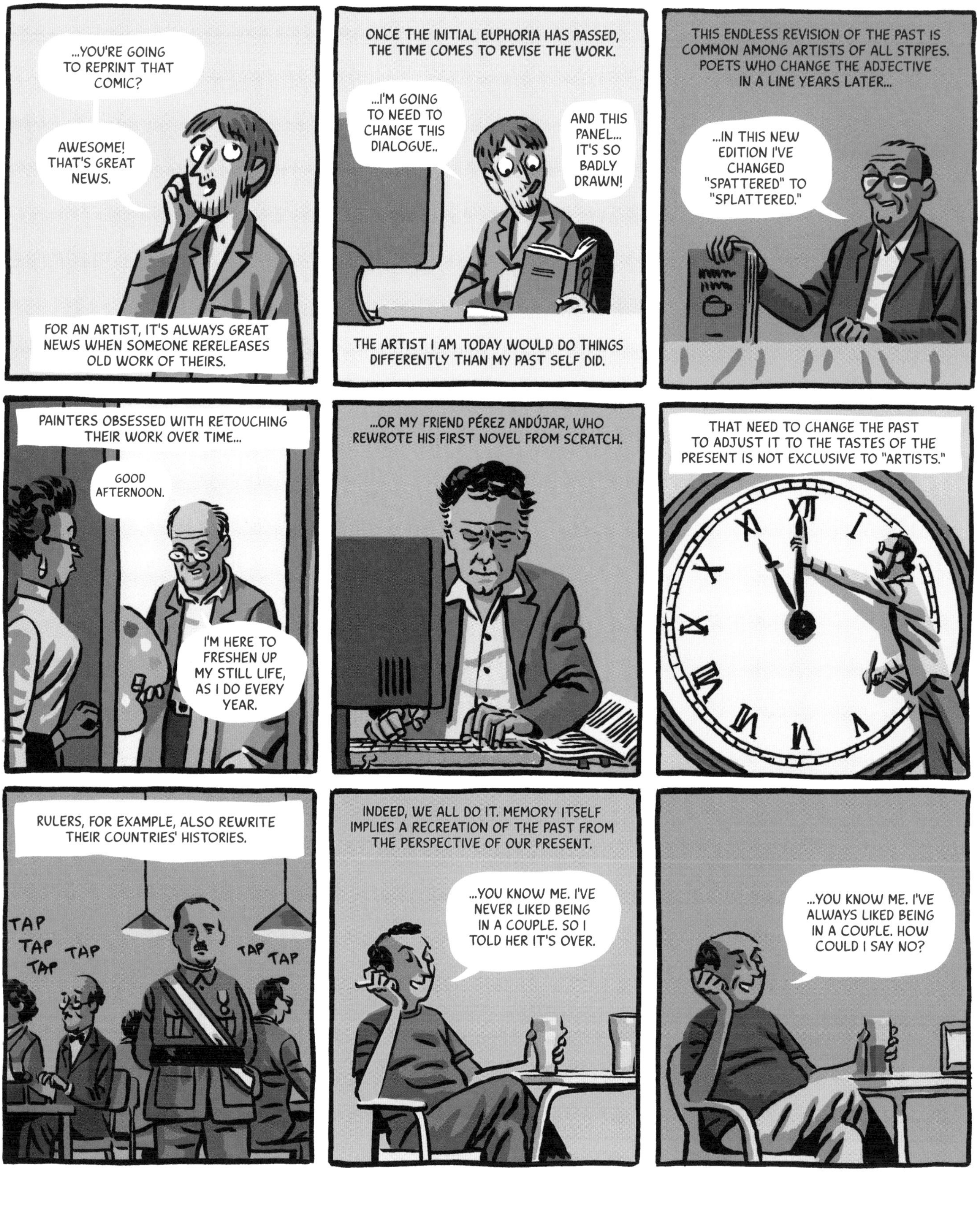
...YOU'RE GOING TO REPRINT THAT COMIC?
AWESOME! THAT'S GREAT NEWS.
FOR AN ARTIST, IT'S ALWAYS GREAT NEWS WHEN SOMEONE RERELEASES OLD WORK OF THEIRS.
ONCE THE INITIAL EUPHORIA HAS PASSED, THE TIME COMES TO REVISE THE WORK.
...I'M GOING TO NEED TO CHANGE THIS DIALOGUE..
AND THIS PANEL... IT'S SO BADLY DRAWN!
THE ARTIST I AM TODAY WOULD DO THINGS DIFFERENTLY THAN MY PAST SELF DID.
THIS ENDLESS REVISION OF THE PAST IS COMMON AMONG ARTISTS OF ALL STRIPES. POETS WHO CHANGE THE ADJECTIVE IN A LINE YEARS LATER...
...IN THIS NEW EDITION I'VE CHANGED "SPATTERED" TO "SPLATTERED."
PAINTERS OBSESSED WITH RETOUCHING THEIR WORK OVER TIME...
GOOD AFTERNOON.
I'M HERE TO FRESHEN UP MY STILL LIFE, AS I DO EVERY YEAR.
...OR MY FRIEND PÉREZ ANDÚJAR, WHO REWROTE HIS FIRST NOVEL FROM SCRATCH.
THAT NEED TO CHANGE THE PAST TO ADJUST IT TO THE TASTES OF THE PRESENT IS NOT EXCLUSIVE TO "ARTISTS."
RULERS, FOR EXAMPLE, ALSO REWRITE THEIR COUNTRIES' HISTORIES.
TAP TAP TAP TAP
TAP TAP
INDEED, WE ALL DO IT. MEMORY ITSELF IMPLIES A RECREATION OF THE PAST FROM THE PERSPECTIVE OF OUR PRESENT.
...YOU KNOW ME. I'VE NEVER LIKED BEING IN A COUPLE. SO I TOLD HER IT'S OVER.
...YOU KNOW ME. I'VE ALWAYS LIKED BEING IN A COUPLE. HOW COULD I SAY NO?

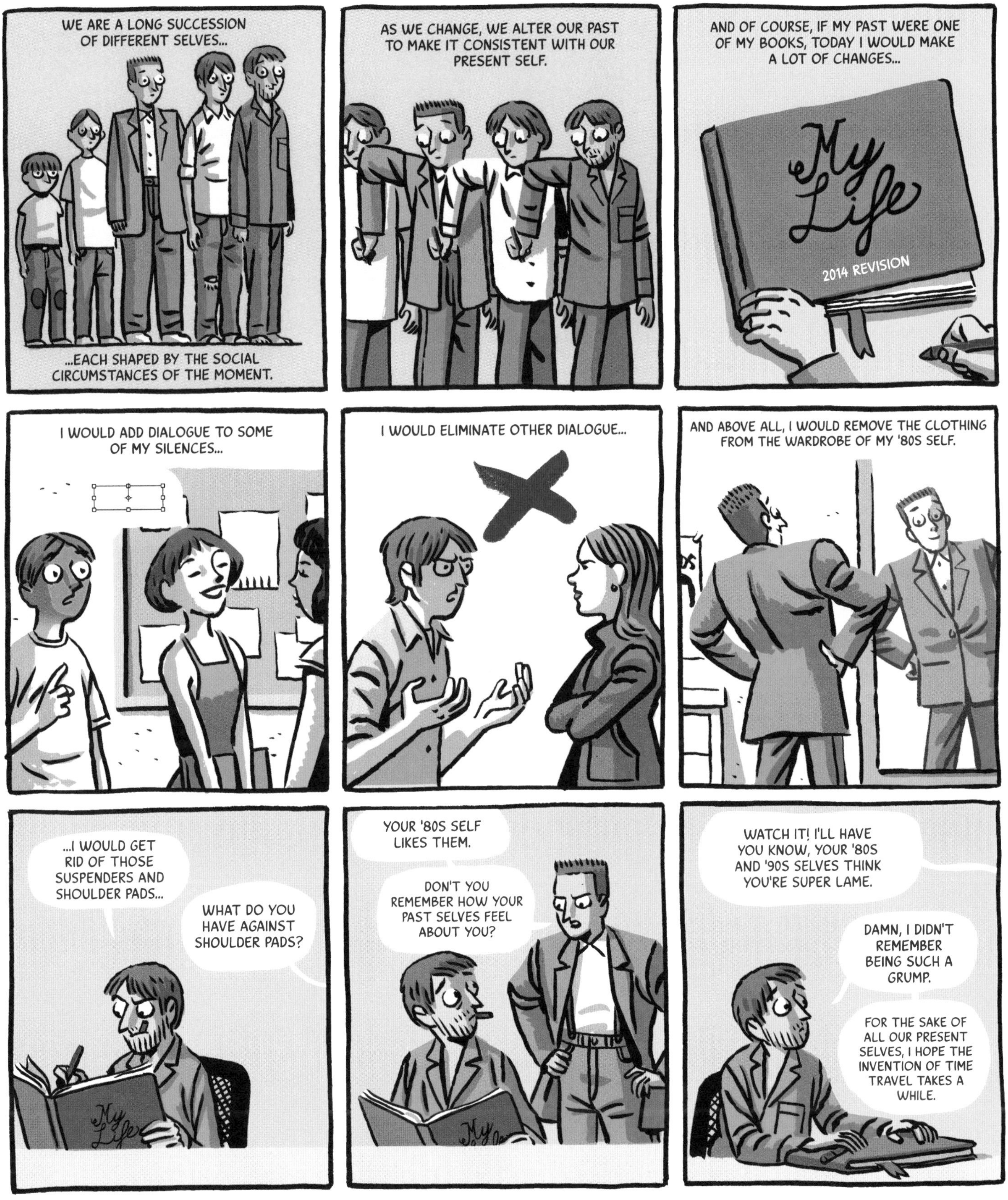
WE ARE A LONG SUCCESSION OF DIFFERENT SELVES...
...EACH SHAPED BY THE SOCIAL CIRCUMSTANCES OF THE MOMENT.
AS WE CHANGE, WE ALTER OUR PAST TO MAKE IT CONSISTENT WITH OUR PRESENT SELF.
AND OF COURSE, IF MY PAST WERE ONE OF MY BOOKS, TODAY I WOULD MAKE A LOT OF CHANGES...
My Life
2014 REVISION
I WOULD ADD DIALOGUE TO SOME OF MY SILENCES...
I WOULD ELIMINATE OTHER DIALOGUE...
AND ABOVE ALL, I WOULD REMOVE THE CLOTHING FROM THE WARDROBE OF MY '80S SELF.
...I WOULD GET RID OF THOSE SUSPENDERS AND SHOULDER PADS...
WHAT DO YOU HAVE AGAINST SHOULDER PADS?
My Life
YOUR '80S SELF LIKES THEM.
DON'T YOU REMEMBER HOW YOUR PAST SELVES FEEL ABOUT YOU?
WATCH IT! I'LL HAVE YOU KNOW, YOUR '80S AND '90S SELVES THINK YOU'RE SUPER LAME.
DAMN, I DIDN'T REMEMBER BEING SUCH A GRUMP.
FOR THE SAKE OF ALL OUR PRESENT SELVES, I HOPE THE INVENTION OF TIME TRAVEL TAKES A WHILE.

THE TRIUMPH OF CHAOS

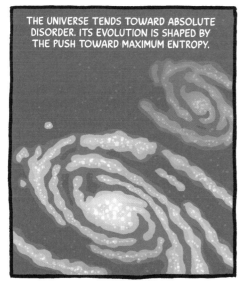

THE UNIVERSE TENDS TOWARD ABSOLUTE DISORDER. ITS EVOLUTION IS SHAPED BY THE PUSH TOWARD MAXIMUM ENTROPY.

WHEN THE TEMPERATURE OF ALL OF THE ELEMENTS OF THE UNIVERSE HAS EQUALIZED, THAT WILL MEAN THE UNIVERSE'S HEAT DEATH. IT'S LIKE WHAT HAPPENS WHEN OBJECTS EQUALIZE WITH THE AMBIENT TEMPERATURE.

ROOM TEMPERATURE **74°F**

104°F ⬇

54°F ⬆

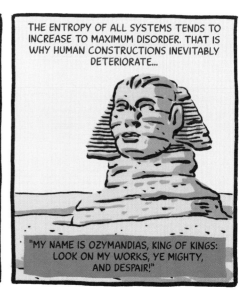

THE ENTROPY OF ALL SYSTEMS TENDS TO INCREASE TO MAXIMUM DISORDER. THAT IS WHY HUMAN CONSTRUCTIONS INEVITABLY DETERIORATE...

"MY NAME IS OZYMANDIAS, KING OF KINGS: LOOK ON MY WORKS, YE MIGHTY, AND DESPAIR!"

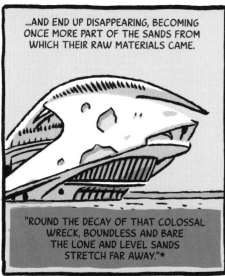

...AND END UP DISAPPEARING, BECOMING ONCE MORE PART OF THE SANDS FROM WHICH THEIR RAW MATERIALS CAME.

"ROUND THE DECAY OF THAT COLOSSAL WRECK, BOUNDLESS AND BARE THE LONE AND LEVEL SANDS STRETCH FAR AWAY."*

BUT MAN STUBBORNLY BATTLES THE DISORDER AND CHAOS TOWARD WHICH THE UNIVERSE TENDS.

WAITER, THIS CALAMARI'S COLD AND MY BEER'S WARM.

WE BATTLE IT EVERY DAY IN OUR HOMES...

...AND I ORGANIZE MY LPS CHRONOLOGICALLY.

NOT THE ORDER THEY WERE RECORDED IN, THOUGH...

...BUT THE TIME I FIRST LISTENED TO THEM.

WE TRY TO IMPOSE AN ORDER ON NATURE...

OH, IT'S A ZINNIA ELEGANS, FROM THE ASTERACEAE FAMILY.

PUT WORDS IN ORDER...

...THIS NEW WORD GOES BETWEEN "MANEUVER" AND "MANGANESE."

Ma...
Maneuver
Manga
Ma...nes
Manag
Manhandle

...OR IN MY CASE, MY EMAIL. THAT'S MY PERSONAL BATTLE AGAINST CHAOS.

PLINK!

ARE YOU COMING TO DINNER?

UMM... C-COMING.

FOR ME, ORDER IS KEEPING ON TOP OF MY EMAIL.

*FROM THE POEM "OZYMANDIAS" BY PERCY BYSSHE SHELLEY

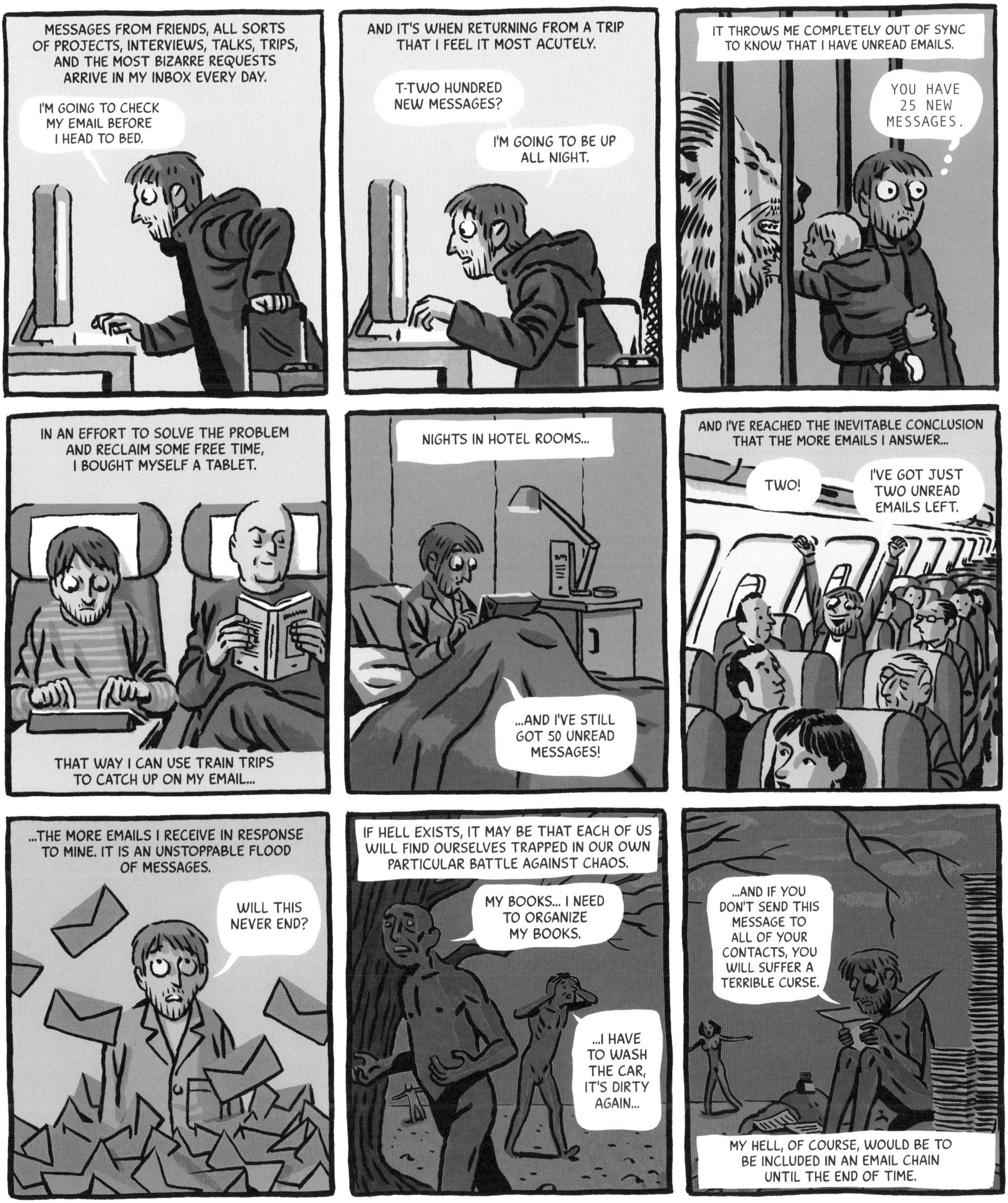
MESSAGES FROM FRIENDS, ALL SORTS OF PROJECTS, INTERVIEWS, TALKS, TRIPS, AND THE MOST BIZARRE REQUESTS ARRIVE IN MY INBOX EVERY DAY.
I'M GOING TO CHECK MY EMAIL BEFORE I HEAD TO BED.
AND IT'S WHEN RETURNING FROM A TRIP THAT I FEEL IT MOST ACUTELY.
T-TWO HUNDRED NEW MESSAGES?
I'M GOING TO BE UP ALL NIGHT.
IT THROWS ME COMPLETELY OUT OF SYNC TO KNOW THAT I HAVE UNREAD EMAILS.
YOU HAVE 25 NEW MESSAGES.
IN AN EFFORT TO SOLVE THE PROBLEM AND RECLAIM SOME FREE TIME, I BOUGHT MYSELF A TABLET.
THAT WAY I CAN USE TRAIN TRIPS TO CATCH UP ON MY EMAIL...
NIGHTS IN HOTEL ROOMS...
...AND I'VE STILL GOT 50 UNREAD MESSAGES!
AND I'VE REACHED THE INEVITABLE CONCLUSION THAT THE MORE EMAILS I ANSWER...
TWO!
I'VE GOT JUST TWO UNREAD EMAILS LEFT.
...THE MORE EMAILS I RECEIVE IN RESPONSE TO MINE. IT IS AN UNSTOPPABLE FLOOD OF MESSAGES.
WILL THIS NEVER END?
IF HELL EXISTS, IT MAY BE THAT EACH OF US WILL FIND OURSELVES TRAPPED IN OUR OWN PARTICULAR BATTLE AGAINST CHAOS.
MY BOOKS... I NEED TO ORGANIZE MY BOOKS.
...I HAVE TO WASH THE CAR, IT'S DIRTY AGAIN...
...AND IF YOU DON'T SEND THIS MESSAGE TO ALL OF YOUR CONTACTS, YOU WILL SUFFER A TERRIBLE CURSE.
MY HELL, OF COURSE, WOULD BE TO BE INCLUDED IN AN EMAIL CHAIN UNTIL THE END OF TIME.

THE OBLIGATION TO CREATE

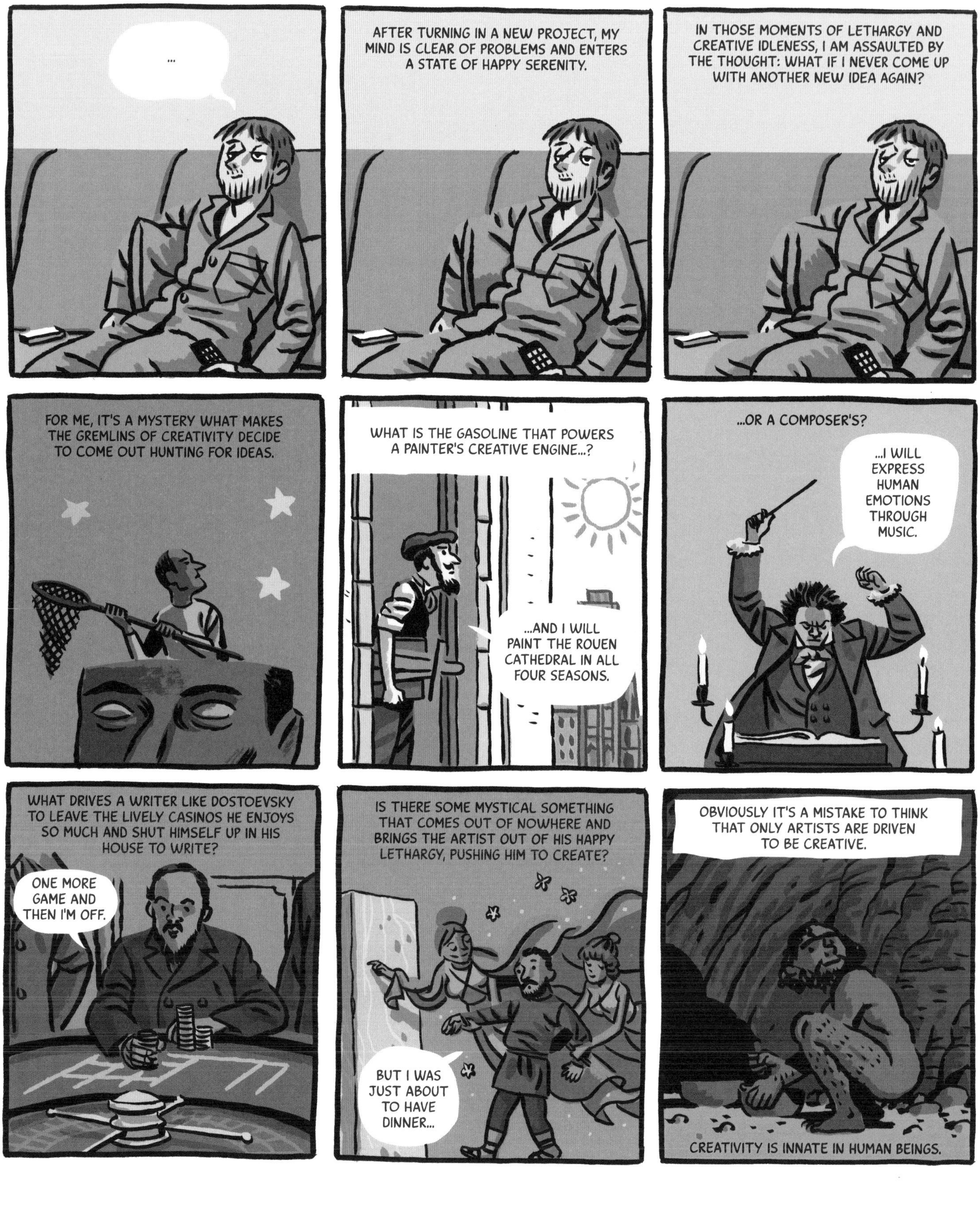
...
AFTER TURNING IN A NEW PROJECT, MY MIND IS CLEAR OF PROBLEMS AND ENTERS A STATE OF HAPPY SERENITY.
IN THOSE MOMENTS OF LETHARGY AND CREATIVE IDLENESS, I AM ASSAULTED BY THE THOUGHT: WHAT IF I NEVER COME UP WITH ANOTHER NEW IDEA AGAIN?
FOR ME, IT'S A MYSTERY WHAT MAKES THE GREMLINS OF CREATIVITY DECIDE TO COME OUT HUNTING FOR IDEAS.
WHAT IS THE GASOLINE THAT POWERS A PAINTER'S CREATIVE ENGINE...?
...AND I WILL PAINT THE ROUEN CATHEDRAL IN ALL FOUR SEASONS.
...OR A COMPOSER'S?
...I WILL EXPRESS HUMAN EMOTIONS THROUGH MUSIC.
WHAT DRIVES A WRITER LIKE DOSTOEVSKY TO LEAVE THE LIVELY CASINOS HE ENJOYS SO MUCH AND SHUT HIMSELF UP IN HIS HOUSE TO WRITE?
ONE MORE GAME AND THEN I'M OFF.
IS THERE SOME MYSTICAL SOMETHING THAT COMES OUT OF NOWHERE AND BRINGS THE ARTIST OUT OF HIS HAPPY LETHARGY, PUSHING HIM TO CREATE?
BUT I WAS JUST ABOUT TO HAVE DINNER...
OBVIOUSLY IT'S A MISTAKE TO THINK THAT ONLY ARTISTS ARE DRIVEN TO BE CREATIVE.
CREATIVITY IS INNATE IN HUMAN BEINGS.

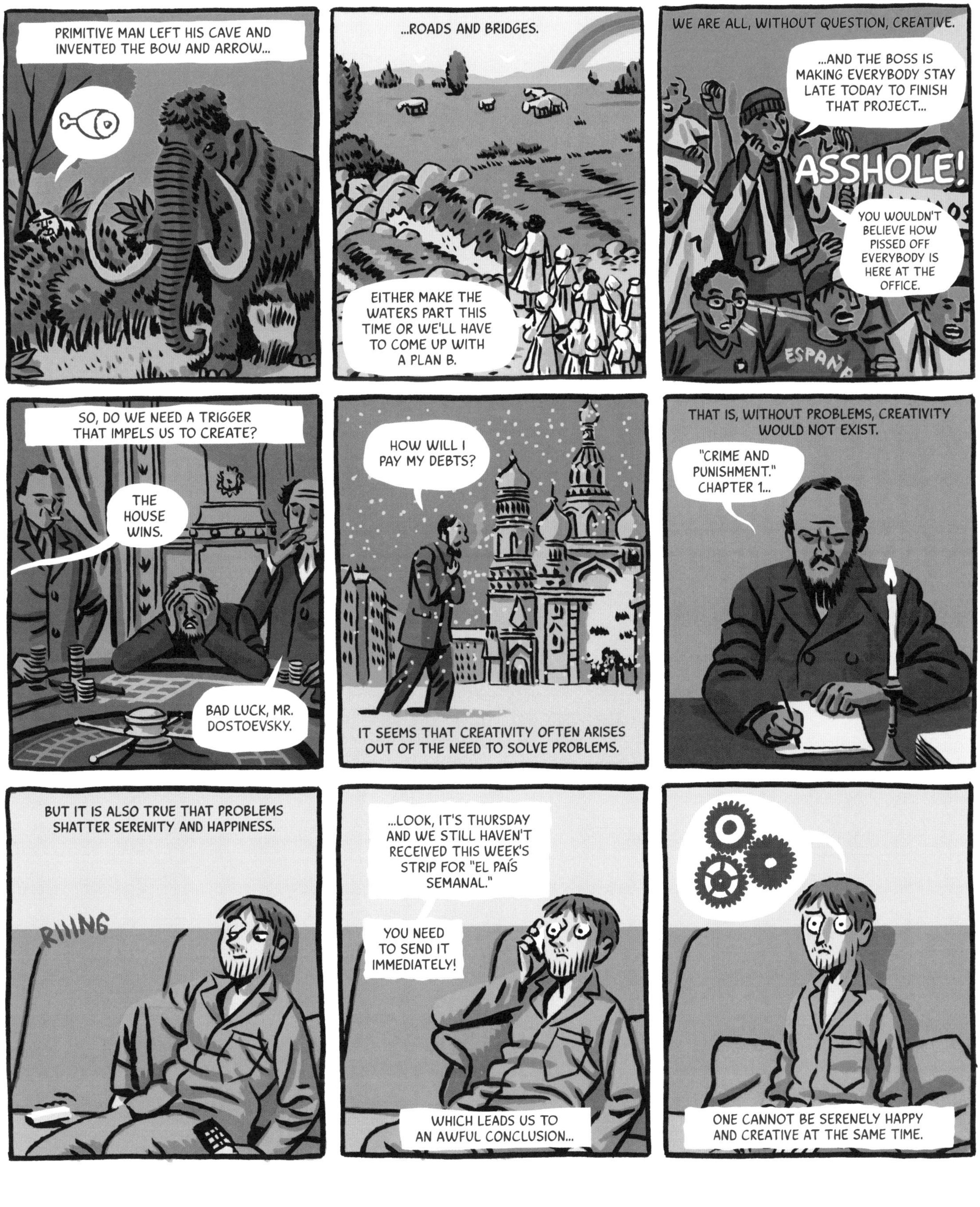
PRIMITIVE MAN LEFT HIS CAVE AND INVENTED THE BOW AND ARROW...
...ROADS AND BRIDGES.
EITHER MAKE THE WATERS PART THIS TIME OR WE'LL HAVE TO COME UP WITH A PLAN B.
WE ARE ALL, WITHOUT QUESTION, CREATIVE.
...AND THE BOSS IS MAKING EVERYBODY STAY LATE TODAY TO FINISH THAT PROJECT...
ASSHOLE!
YOU WOULDN'T BELIEVE HOW PISSED OFF EVERYBODY IS HERE AT THE OFFICE.
ESPAÑA
SO, DO WE NEED A TRIGGER THAT IMPELS US TO CREATE?
THE HOUSE WINS.
BAD LUCK, MR. DOSTOEVSKY.
HOW WILL I PAY MY DEBTS?
IT SEEMS THAT CREATIVITY OFTEN ARISES OUT OF THE NEED TO SOLVE PROBLEMS.
THAT IS, WITHOUT PROBLEMS, CREATIVITY WOULD NOT EXIST.
"CRIME AND PUNISHMENT." CHAPTER 1...
BUT IT IS ALSO TRUE THAT PROBLEMS SHATTER SERENITY AND HAPPINESS.
RIIING
...LOOK, IT'S THURSDAY AND WE STILL HAVEN'T RECEIVED THIS WEEK'S STRIP FOR "EL PAÍS SEMANAL."
YOU NEED TO SEND IT IMMEDIATELY!
WHICH LEADS US TO AN AWFUL CONCLUSION...
ONE CANNOT BE SERENELY HAPPY AND CREATIVE AT THE SAME TIME.

THE CALL OF ADVENTURE

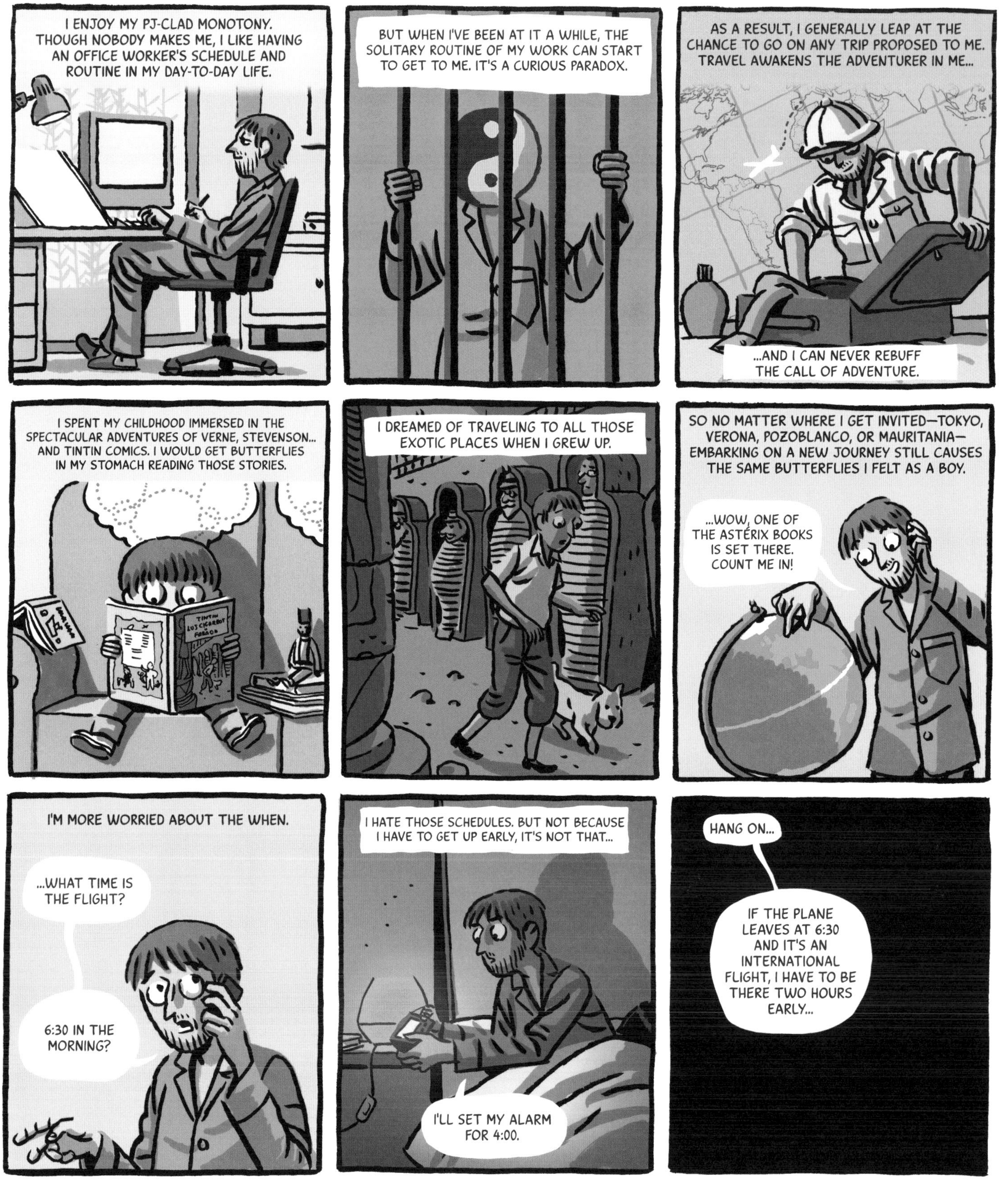

I ENJOY MY PJ-CLAD MONOTONY. THOUGH NOBODY MAKES ME, I LIKE HAVING AN OFFICE WORKER'S SCHEDULE AND ROUTINE IN MY DAY-TO-DAY LIFE.
BUT WHEN I'VE BEEN AT IT A WHILE, THE SOLITARY ROUTINE OF MY WORK CAN START TO GET TO ME. IT'S A CURIOUS PARADOX.
AS A RESULT, I GENERALLY LEAP AT THE CHANCE TO GO ON ANY TRIP PROPOSED TO ME. TRAVEL AWAKENS THE ADVENTURER IN ME...
...AND I CAN NEVER REBUFF THE CALL OF ADVENTURE.
I SPENT MY CHILDHOOD IMMERSED IN THE SPECTACULAR ADVENTURES OF VERNE, STEVENSON... AND TINTIN COMICS. I WOULD GET BUTTERFLIES IN MY STOMACH READING THOSE STORIES.
I DREAMED OF TRAVELING TO ALL THOSE EXOTIC PLACES WHEN I GREW UP.
SO NO MATTER WHERE I GET INVITED—TOKYO, VERONA, POZOBLANCO, OR MAURITANIA—EMBARKING ON A NEW JOURNEY STILL CAUSES THE SAME BUTTERFLIES I FELT AS A BOY.
...WOW, ONE OF THE ASTÉRIX BOOKS IS SET THERE. COUNT ME IN!
I'M MORE WORRIED ABOUT THE WHEN.
...WHAT TIME IS THE FLIGHT?
6:30 IN THE MORNING?
I HATE THOSE SCHEDULES. BUT NOT BECAUSE I HAVE TO GET UP EARLY, IT'S NOT THAT...
I'LL SET MY ALARM FOR 4:00.
HANG ON...
IF THE PLANE LEAVES AT 6:30 AND IT'S AN INTERNATIONAL FLIGHT, I HAVE TO BE THERE TWO HOURS EARLY...

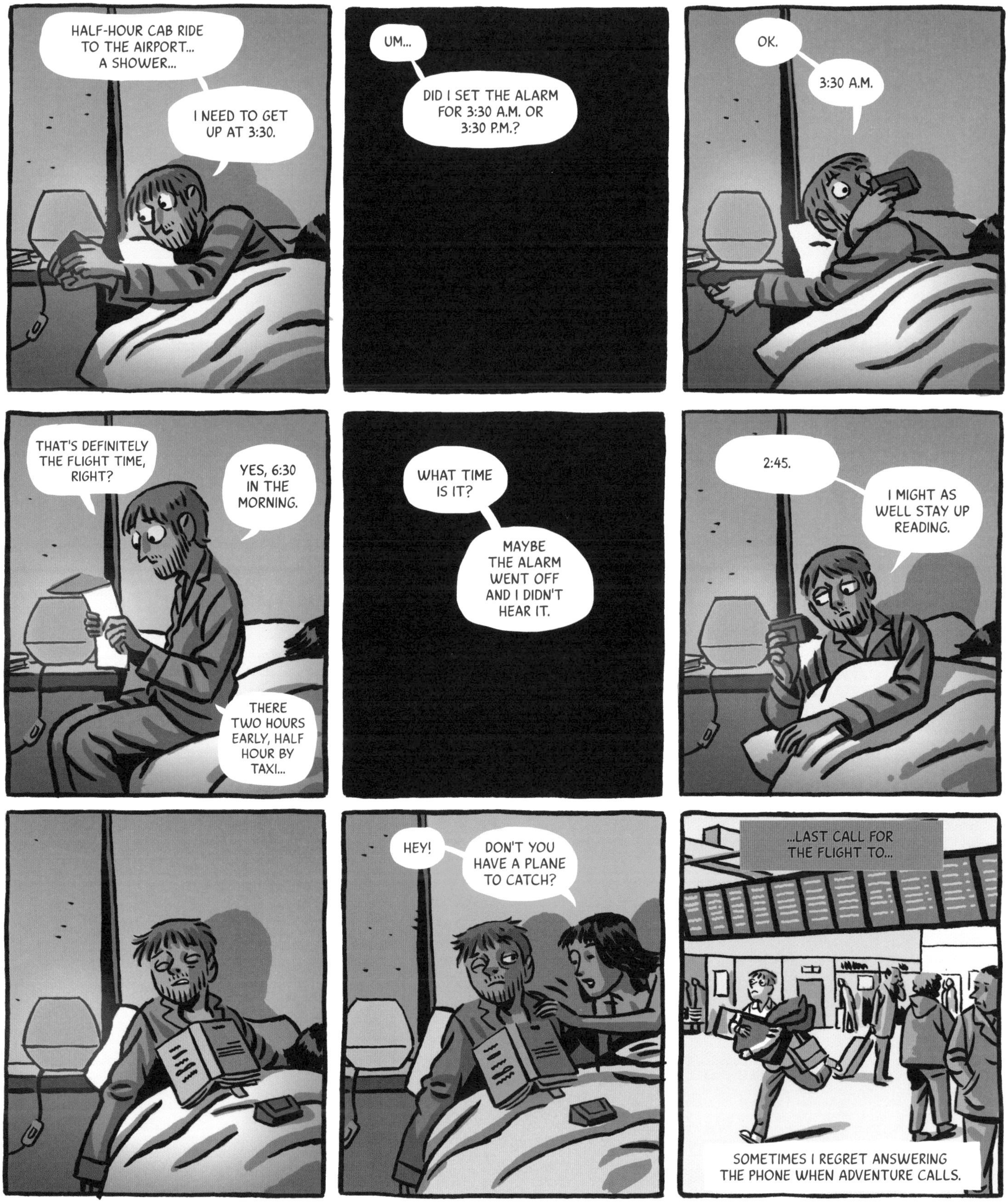
HALF-HOUR CAB RIDE TO THE AIRPORT... A SHOWER...
I NEED TO GET UP AT 3:30.
UM...
DID I SET THE ALARM FOR 3:30 A.M. OR 3:30 P.M.?
OK.
3:30 A.M.
THAT'S DEFINITELY THE FLIGHT TIME, RIGHT?
YES, 6:30 IN THE MORNING.
THERE TWO HOURS EARLY, HALF HOUR BY TAXI...
WHAT TIME IS IT?
MAYBE THE ALARM WENT OFF AND I DIDN'T HEAR IT.
2:45.
I MIGHT AS WELL STAY UP READING.
HEY!
DON'T YOU HAVE A PLANE TO CATCH?
...LAST CALL FOR THE FLIGHT TO...
SOMETIMES I REGRET ANSWERING THE PHONE WHEN ADVENTURE CALLS.

SECOND-HAND COUNTRY

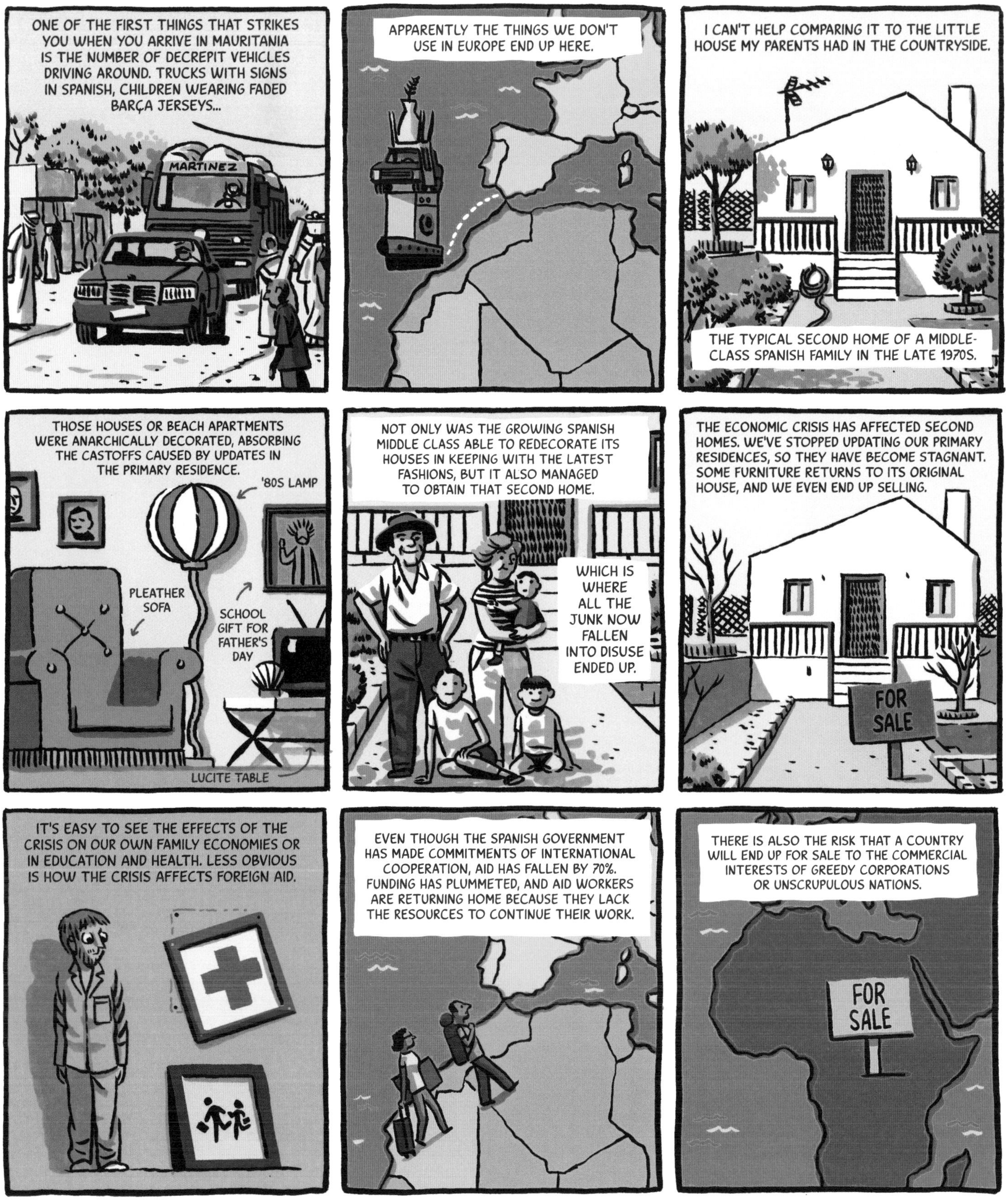
ONE OF THE FIRST THINGS THAT STRIKES YOU WHEN YOU ARRIVE IN MAURITANIA IS THE NUMBER OF DECREPIT VEHICLES DRIVING AROUND. TRUCKS WITH SIGNS IN SPANISH, CHILDREN WEARING FADED BARÇA JERSEYS...
MARTINEZ
APPARENTLY THE THINGS WE DON'T USE IN EUROPE END UP HERE.
I CAN'T HELP COMPARING IT TO THE LITTLE HOUSE MY PARENTS HAD IN THE COUNTRYSIDE.
THE TYPICAL SECOND HOME OF A MIDDLE-CLASS SPANISH FAMILY IN THE LATE 1970S.
THOSE HOUSES OR BEACH APARTMENTS WERE ANARCHICALLY DECORATED, ABSORBING THE CASTOFFS CAUSED BY UPDATES IN THE PRIMARY RESIDENCE.
'80S LAMP
PLEATHER SOFA
SCHOOL GIFT FOR FATHER'S DAY
LUCITE TABLE
NOT ONLY WAS THE GROWING SPANISH MIDDLE CLASS ABLE TO REDECORATE ITS HOUSES IN KEEPING WITH THE LATEST FASHIONS, BUT IT ALSO MANAGED TO OBTAIN THAT SECOND HOME.
WHICH IS WHERE ALL THE JUNK NOW FALLEN INTO DISUSE ENDED UP.
THE ECONOMIC CRISIS HAS AFFECTED SECOND HOMES. WE'VE STOPPED UPDATING OUR PRIMARY RESIDENCES, SO THEY HAVE BECOME STAGNANT. SOME FURNITURE RETURNS TO ITS ORIGINAL HOUSE, AND WE EVEN END UP SELLING.
FOR SALE
IT'S EASY TO SEE THE EFFECTS OF THE CRISIS ON OUR OWN FAMILY ECONOMIES OR IN EDUCATION AND HEALTH. LESS OBVIOUS IS HOW THE CRISIS AFFECTS FOREIGN AID.
EVEN THOUGH THE SPANISH GOVERNMENT HAS MADE COMMITMENTS OF INTERNATIONAL COOPERATION, AID HAS FALLEN BY 70%. FUNDING HAS PLUMMETED, AND AID WORKERS ARE RETURNING HOME BECAUSE THEY LACK THE RESOURCES TO CONTINUE THEIR WORK.
THERE IS ALSO THE RISK THAT A COUNTRY WILL END UP FOR SALE TO THE COMMERCIAL INTERESTS OF GREEDY CORPORATIONS OR UNSCRUPULOUS NATIONS.
FOR SALE

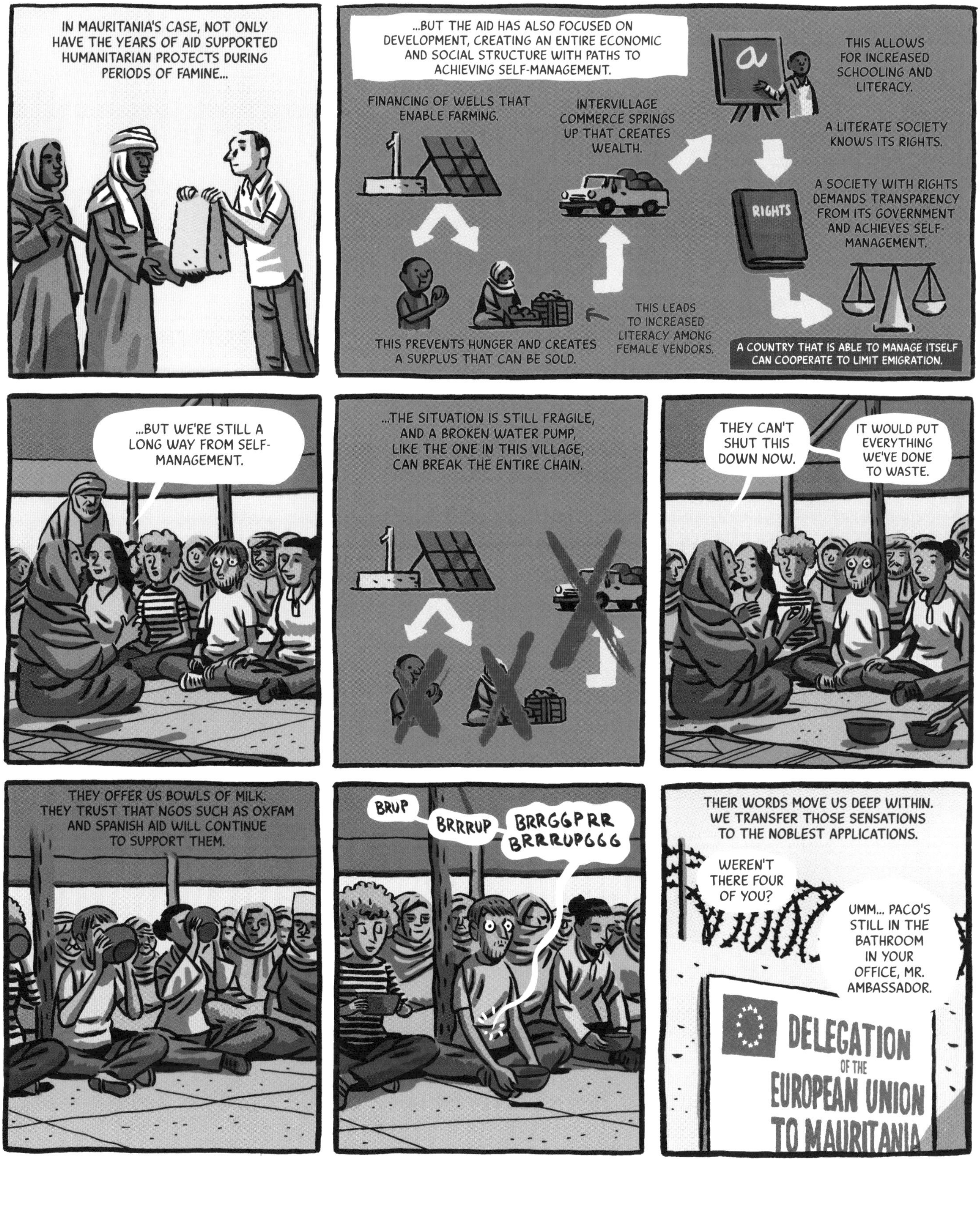
IN MAURITANIA'S CASE, NOT ONLY HAVE THE YEARS OF AID SUPPORTED HUMANITARIAN PROJECTS DURING PERIODS OF FAMINE...
...BUT THE AID HAS ALSO FOCUSED ON DEVELOPMENT, CREATING AN ENTIRE ECONOMIC AND SOCIAL STRUCTURE WITH PATHS TO ACHIEVING SELF-MANAGEMENT.
FINANCING OF WELLS THAT ENABLE FARMING.
THIS PREVENTS HUNGER AND CREATES A SURPLUS THAT CAN BE SOLD.
THIS LEADS TO INCREASED LITERACY AMONG FEMALE VENDORS.
INTERVILLAGE COMMERCE SPRINGS UP THAT CREATES WEALTH.
a
THIS ALLOWS FOR INCREASED SCHOOLING AND LITERACY.
A LITERATE SOCIETY KNOWS ITS RIGHTS.
RIGHTS
A SOCIETY WITH RIGHTS DEMANDS TRANSPARENCY FROM ITS GOVERNMENT AND ACHIEVES SELF-MANAGEMENT.
A COUNTRY THAT IS ABLE TO MANAGE ITSELF CAN COOPERATE TO LIMIT EMIGRATION.
...BUT WE'RE STILL A LONG WAY FROM SELF-MANAGEMENT.
...THE SITUATION IS STILL FRAGILE, AND A BROKEN WATER PUMP, LIKE THE ONE IN THIS VILLAGE, CAN BREAK THE ENTIRE CHAIN.
THEY CAN'T SHUT THIS DOWN NOW.
IT WOULD PUT EVERYTHING WE'VE DONE TO WASTE.
THEY OFFER US BOWLS OF MILK. THEY TRUST THAT NGOS SUCH AS OXFAM AND SPANISH AID WILL CONTINUE TO SUPPORT THEM.
BRUP
BRRRUP
BRRGGPRR BRRRUPGGG
THEIR WORDS MOVE US DEEP WITHIN. WE TRANSFER THOSE SENSATIONS TO THE NOBLEST APPLICATIONS.
WEREN'T THERE FOUR OF YOU?
UMM... PACO'S STILL IN THE BATHROOM IN YOUR OFFICE, MR. AMBASSADOR.
DELEGATION OF THE EUROPEAN UNION TO MAURITANIA

THE WISDOM OF NATURE

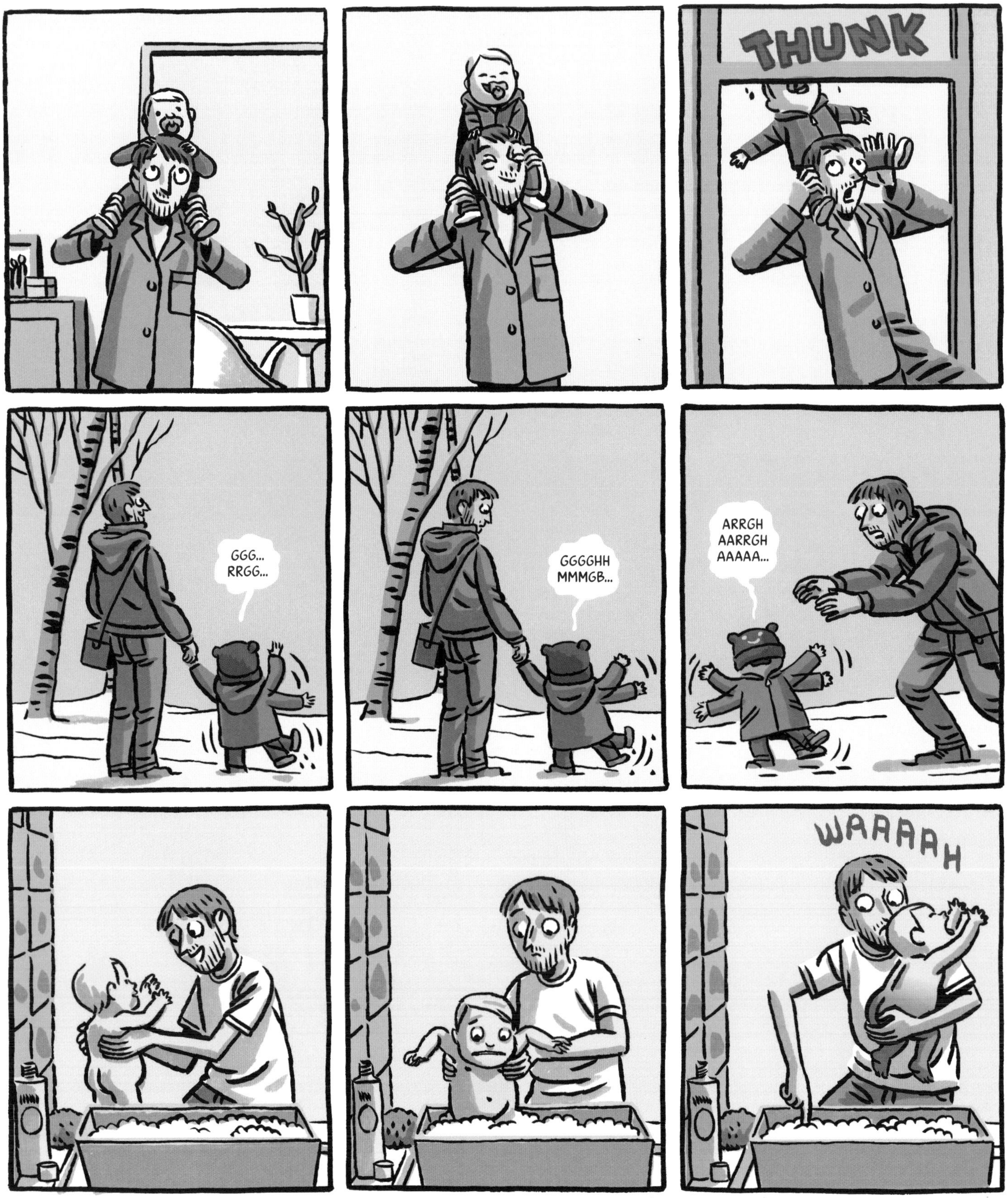
THUNK
GGG...
RRGG...
GGGGHH
MMMGB...
ARRGH
AARRGH
AAAAA...
WAAAAH

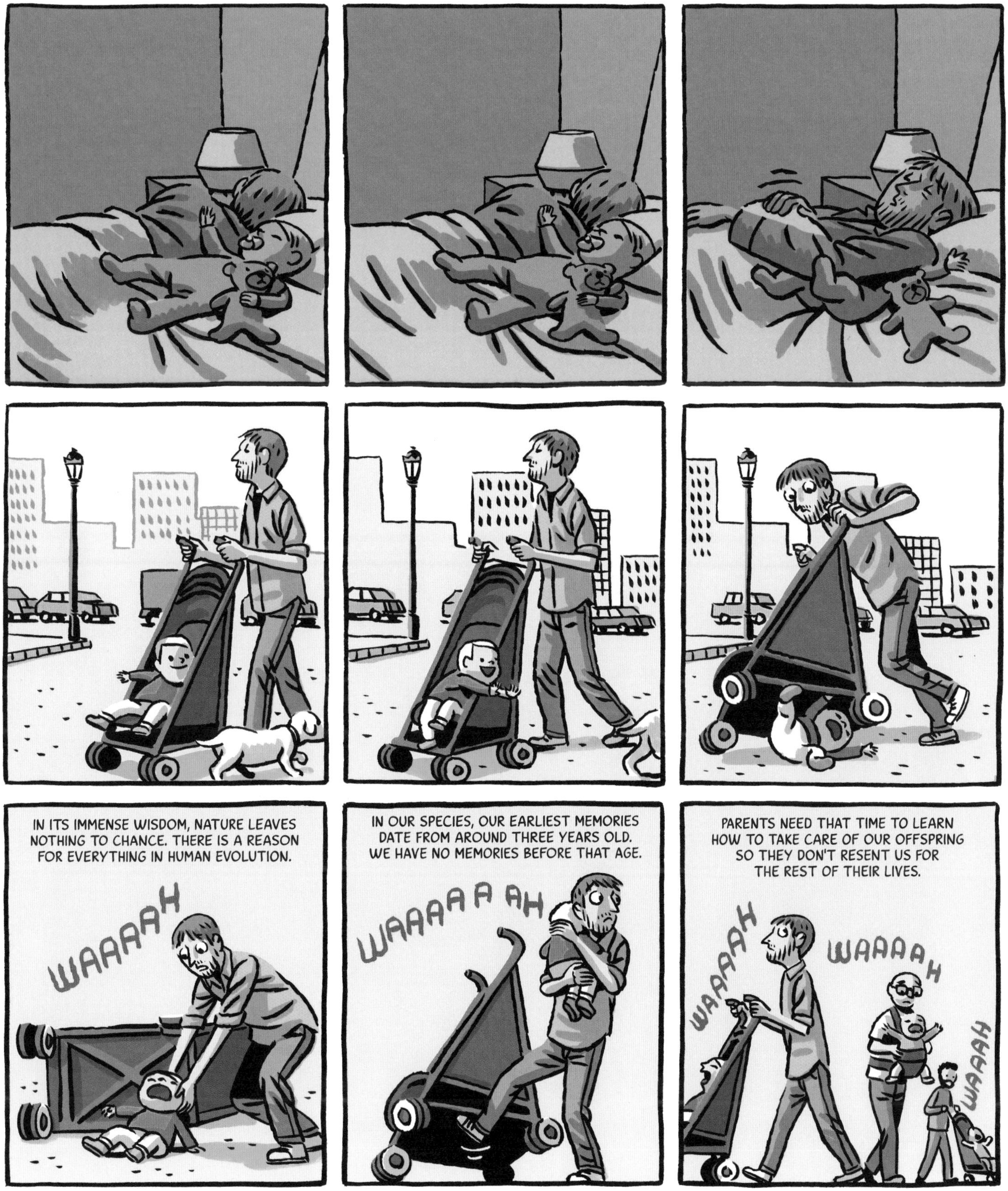
IN ITS IMMENSE WISDOM, NATURE LEAVES NOTHING TO CHANCE. THERE IS A REASON FOR EVERYTHING IN HUMAN EVOLUTION.
WAAAAH
IN OUR SPECIES, OUR EARLIEST MEMORIES DATE FROM AROUND THREE YEARS OLD. WE HAVE NO MEMORIES BEFORE THAT AGE.
WAAAA A AH
PARENTS NEED THAT TIME TO LEARN HOW TO TAKE CARE OF OUR OFFSPRING SO THEY DON'T RESENT US FOR THE REST OF THEIR LIVES.
WAAAAH
WAAAAAH
WAAAH

TAKING STOCK

MY CHILDHOOD SNACKS WERE CONSUMED IN FRONT OF THE TV WHILE IMPATIENTLY WAITING FOR THE BROADCAST TO START.

THE PROGRAMMING WAS FULL OF SHOWS AND MOVIES IN WHICH THE HEROES AND VILLAINS SUFFERED VIOLENT DEATHS.

BANG

BUT IN THOSE FINAL MOMENTS, THEY ALL HAD TIME TO RECITE A LENGTHY FINAL MONOLOGUE.

TH-THEY GOT ME...

DON'T TALK. YOU'RE GOING TO GET THROUGH THIS, BUDDY.

I-I SHOULD'VE WAITED FOR BACKUP.

IN THOSE FINAL WORDS, THEY TENDED TO TAKE STOCK OF THEIR LIVES.

I-I'VE BEEN A GOOD COP, YOU KNOW THAT. I NEVER TOOK BRIBES... I'VE LED A GOOD LIFE. I-I'VE BEEN A GOOD FATHER AND A FAITHFUL HUSBAND... TELL MY WIFE.

YOU'RE GOING TO TELL HER YOURSELF, MIKE.

THOSE FINAL MONOLOGUES HAD A BIG INFLUENCE ON ME. I WONDERED WHAT I WOULD SAY IN SUCH A MOMENT.

...IF I DON'T RECOVER FROM BEING HIT BY THAT SOCCER BALL, I WANT YOU TO KNOW THAT THIRD GRADE HAS BEEN THE BEST YEAR OF MY LIFE...

EVER SINCE THEN I'VE WONDERED: HOW DOES ONE TAKE FINAL STOCK OF AN ENTIRE LIFE?

?

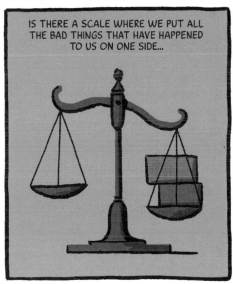

IS THERE A SCALE WHERE WE PUT ALL THE BAD THINGS THAT HAVE HAPPENED TO US ON ONE SIDE...

...AND THE GOOD EXPERIENCES ON THE OTHER?

OR IS THE PROCESS MORE AKIN TO CALCULATING A PENSION...

10

14 13 12 11 9 8 7 6 5 4 3 2 1

...AND IT'S THE QUALITY OF ONE'S FINAL YEARS THAT MATTERS?

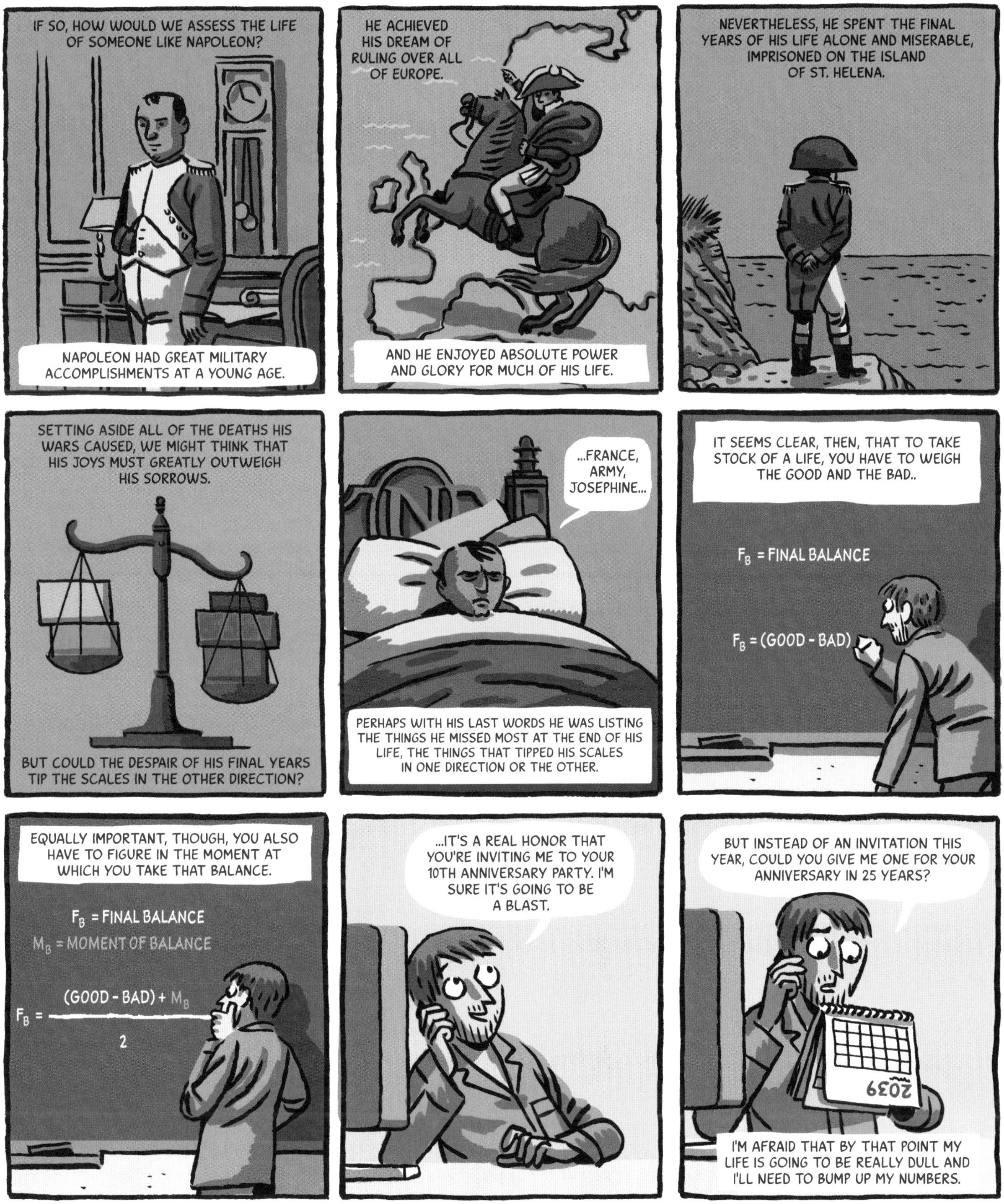
IF SO, HOW WOULD WE ASSESS THE LIFE OF SOMEONE LIKE NAPOLEON?
NAPOLEON HAD GREAT MILITARY ACCOMPLISHMENTS AT A YOUNG AGE.
HE ACHIEVED HIS DREAM OF RULING OVER ALL OF EUROPE.
AND HE ENJOYED ABSOLUTE POWER AND GLORY FOR MUCH OF HIS LIFE.
NEVERTHELESS, HE SPENT THE FINAL YEARS OF HIS LIFE ALONE AND MISERABLE, IMPRISONED ON THE ISLAND OF ST. HELENA.
SETTING ASIDE ALL OF THE DEATHS HIS WARS CAUSED, WE MIGHT THINK THAT HIS JOYS MUST GREATLY OUTWEIGH HIS SORROWS.
BUT COULD THE DESPAIR OF HIS FINAL YEARS TIP THE SCALES IN THE OTHER DIRECTION?
...FRANCE, ARMY, JOSEPHINE...
PERHAPS WITH HIS LAST WORDS HE WAS LISTING THE THINGS HE MISSED MOST AT THE END OF HIS LIFE, THE THINGS THAT TIPPED HIS SCALES IN ONE DIRECTION OR THE OTHER.
IT SEEMS CLEAR, THEN, THAT TO TAKE STOCK OF A LIFE, YOU HAVE TO WEIGH THE GOOD AND THE BAD..
F_B = FINAL BALANCE
F_B = (GOOD - BAD)
EQUALLY IMPORTANT, THOUGH, YOU ALSO HAVE TO FIGURE IN THE MOMENT AT WHICH YOU TAKE THAT BALANCE.
F_B = FINAL BALANCE
M_B = MOMENT OF BALANCE
$F_B = \frac{(GOOD - BAD) + M_B}{2}$
...IT'S A REAL HONOR THAT YOU'RE INVITING ME TO YOUR 10TH ANNIVERSARY PARTY. I'M SURE IT'S GOING TO BE A BLAST.
BUT INSTEAD OF AN INVITATION THIS YEAR, COULD YOU GIVE ME ONE FOR YOUR ANNIVERSARY IN 25 YEARS?
2039
I'M AFRAID THAT BY THAT POINT MY LIFE IS GOING TO BE REALLY DULL AND I'LL NEED TO BUMP UP MY NUMBERS.

GIVE ME A PLACE TO STAND...

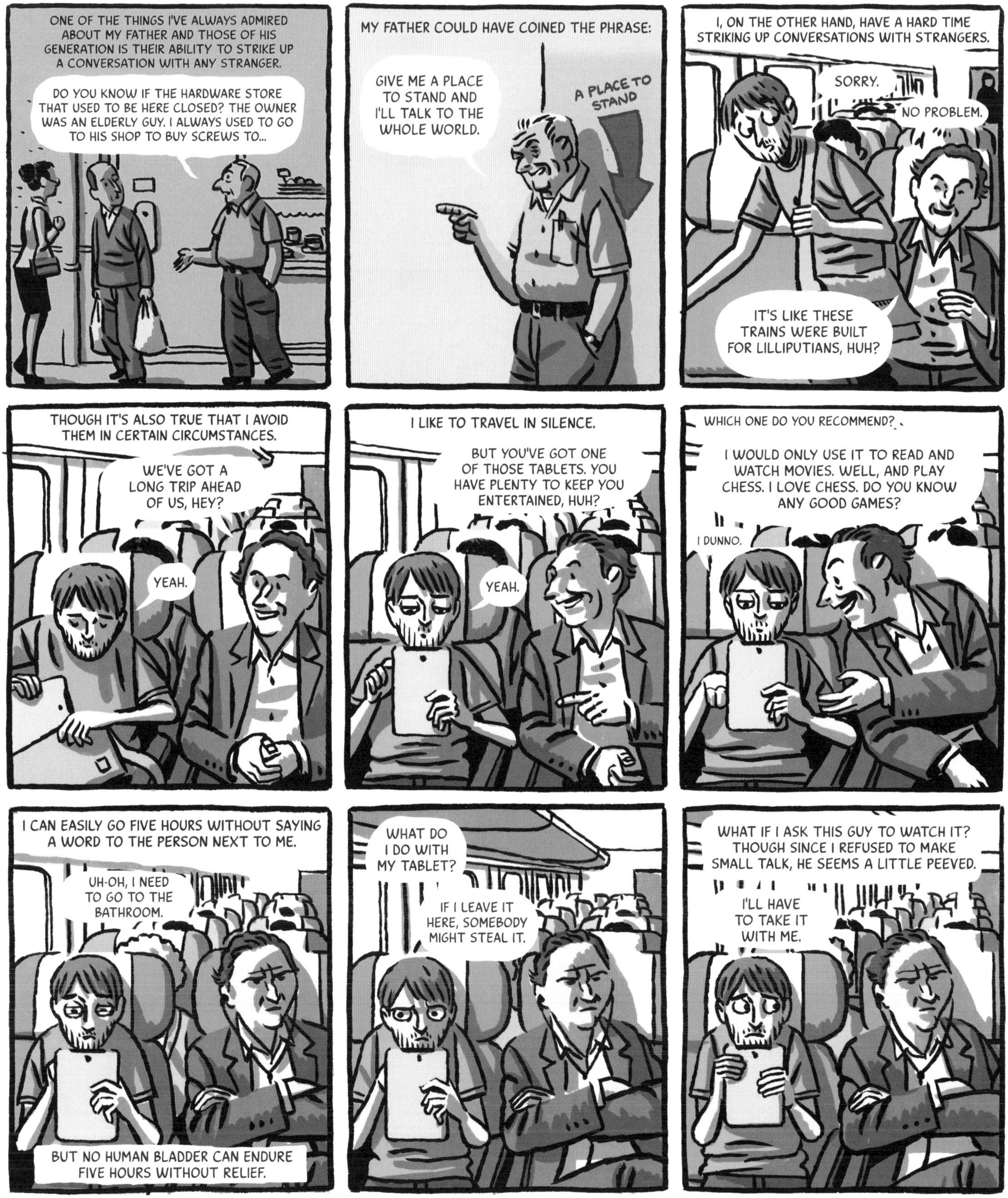

ONE OF THE THINGS I'VE ALWAYS ADMIRED ABOUT MY FATHER AND THOSE OF HIS GENERATION IS THEIR ABILITY TO STRIKE UP A CONVERSATION WITH ANY STRANGER.
DO YOU KNOW IF THE HARDWARE STORE THAT USED TO BE HERE CLOSED? THE OWNER WAS AN ELDERLY GUY. I ALWAYS USED TO GO TO HIS SHOP TO BUY SCREWS TO...
MY FATHER COULD HAVE COINED THE PHRASE:
GIVE ME A PLACE TO STAND AND I'LL TALK TO THE WHOLE WORLD.
A PLACE TO STAND
I, ON THE OTHER HAND, HAVE A HARD TIME STRIKING UP CONVERSATIONS WITH STRANGERS.
SORRY.
NO PROBLEM.
IT'S LIKE THESE TRAINS WERE BUILT FOR LILLIPUTIANS, HUH?
THOUGH IT'S ALSO TRUE THAT I AVOID THEM IN CERTAIN CIRCUMSTANCES.
WE'VE GOT A LONG TRIP AHEAD OF US, HEY?
YEAH.
I LIKE TO TRAVEL IN SILENCE.
BUT YOU'VE GOT ONE OF THOSE TABLETS. YOU HAVE PLENTY TO KEEP YOU ENTERTAINED, HUH?
YEAH.
WHICH ONE DO YOU RECOMMEND?
I WOULD ONLY USE IT TO READ AND WATCH MOVIES. WELL, AND PLAY CHESS. I LOVE CHESS. DO YOU KNOW ANY GOOD GAMES?
I DUNNO.
I CAN EASILY GO FIVE HOURS WITHOUT SAYING A WORD TO THE PERSON NEXT TO ME.
UH-OH, I NEED TO GO TO THE BATHROOM.
BUT NO HUMAN BLADDER CAN ENDURE FIVE HOURS WITHOUT RELIEF.
WHAT DO I DO WITH MY TABLET?
IF I LEAVE IT HERE, SOMEBODY MIGHT STEAL IT.
WHAT IF I ASK THIS GUY TO WATCH IT? THOUGH SINCE I REFUSED TO MAKE SMALL TALK, HE SEEMS A LITTLE PEEVED.
I'LL HAVE TO TAKE IT WITH ME.

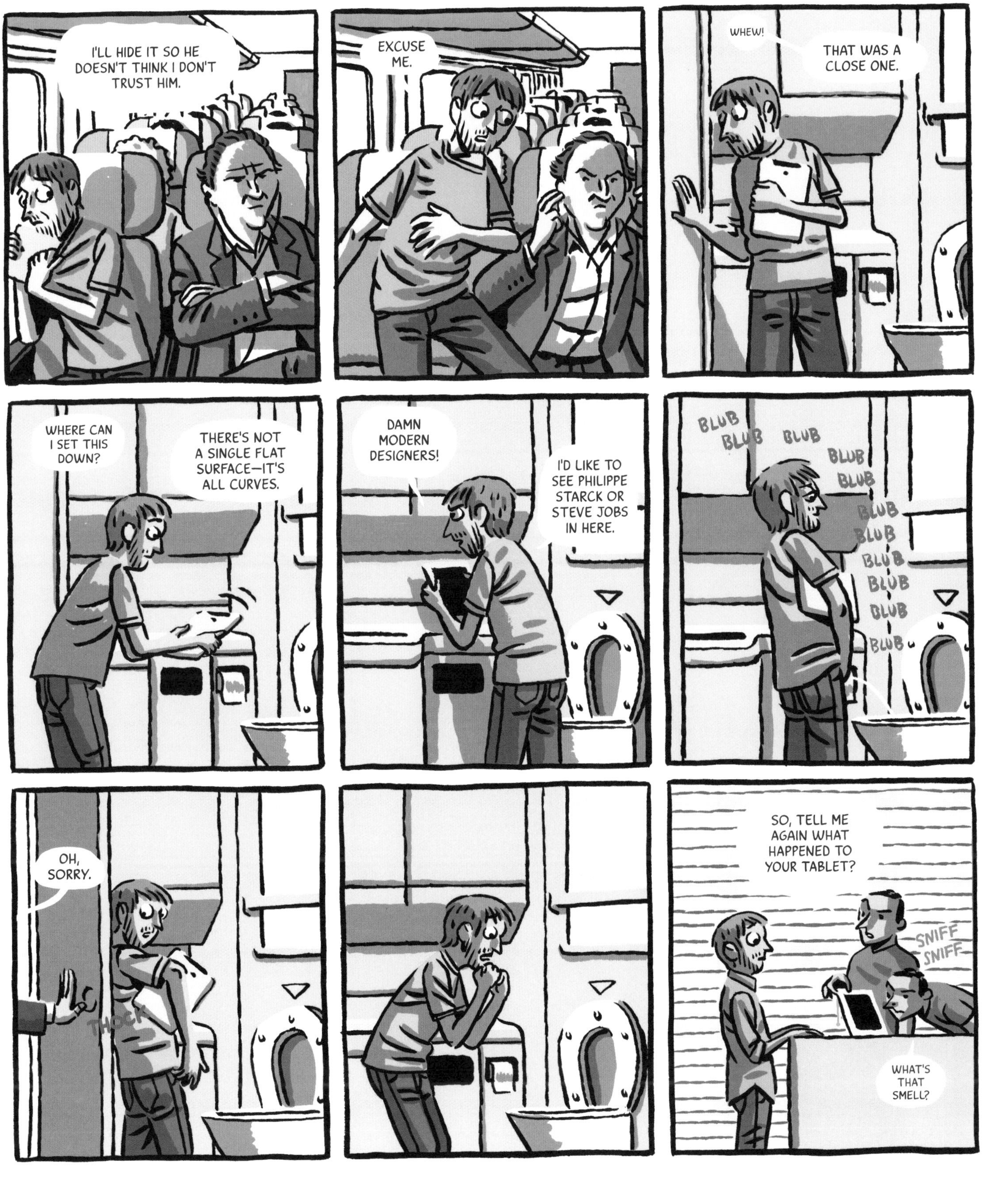
I'LL HIDE IT SO HE DOESN'T THINK I DON'T TRUST HIM.
EXCUSE ME.
WHEW!
THAT WAS A CLOSE ONE.
WHERE CAN I SET THIS DOWN?
THERE'S NOT A SINGLE FLAT SURFACE—IT'S ALL CURVES.
DAMN MODERN DESIGNERS!
I'D LIKE TO SEE PHILIPPE STARCK OR STEVE JOBS IN HERE.
BLUB BLUB BLUB BLUB BLUB BLUB BLUB BLUB BLUB BLUB BLUB
OH, SORRY.
THOCK
SO, TELL ME AGAIN WHAT HAPPENED TO YOUR TABLET?
SNIFF SNIFF
WHAT'S THAT SMELL?

FULL STOP

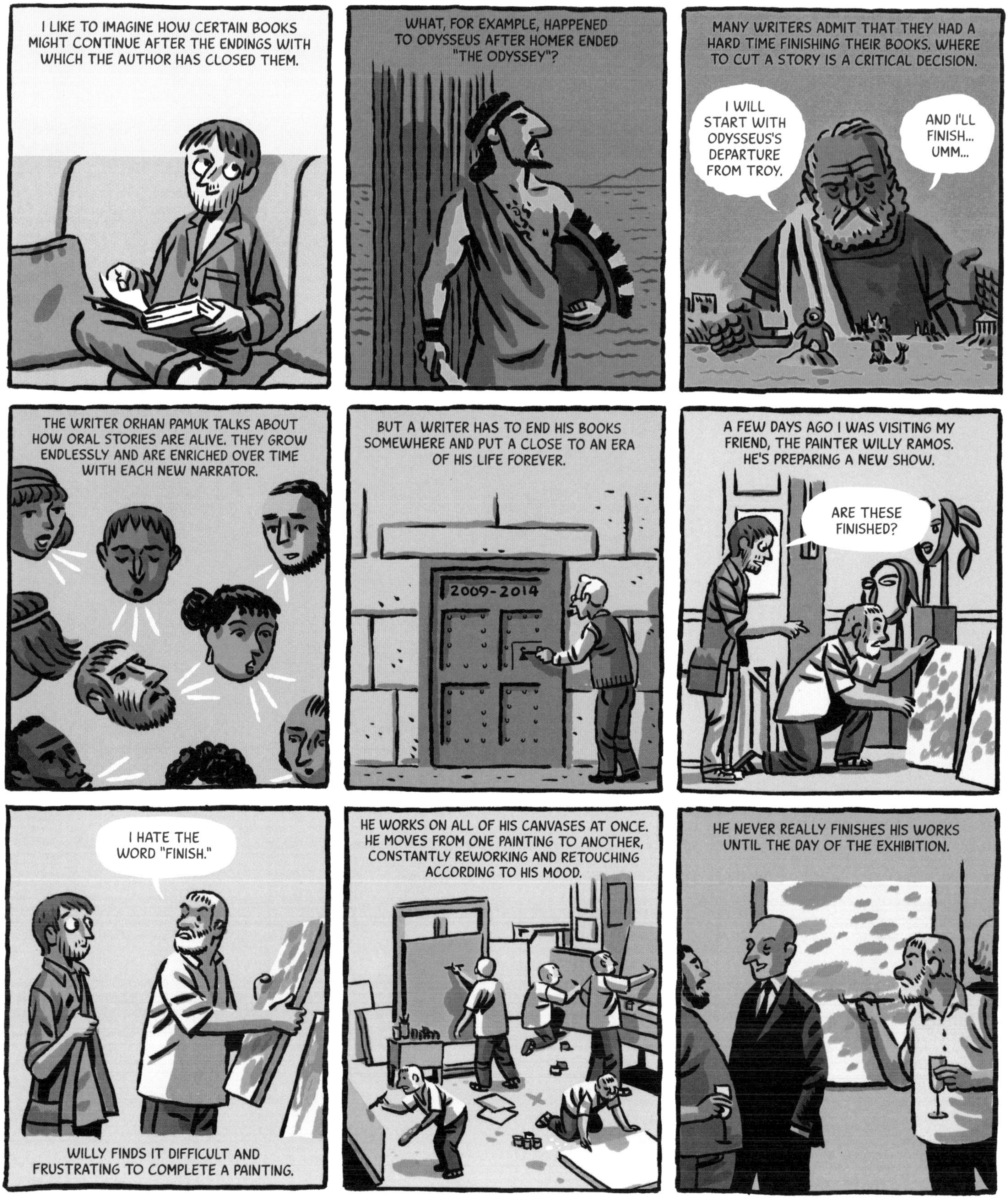
I LIKE TO IMAGINE HOW CERTAIN BOOKS MIGHT CONTINUE AFTER THE ENDINGS WITH WHICH THE AUTHOR HAS CLOSED THEM.
WHAT, FOR EXAMPLE, HAPPENED TO ODYSSEUS AFTER HOMER ENDED "THE ODYSSEY"?
MANY WRITERS ADMIT THAT THEY HAD A HARD TIME FINISHING THEIR BOOKS. WHERE TO CUT A STORY IS A CRITICAL DECISION.
I WILL START WITH ODYSSEUS'S DEPARTURE FROM TROY.
AND I'LL FINISH... UMM...
THE WRITER ORHAN PAMUK TALKS ABOUT HOW ORAL STORIES ARE ALIVE. THEY GROW ENDLESSLY AND ARE ENRICHED OVER TIME WITH EACH NEW NARRATOR.
BUT A WRITER HAS TO END HIS BOOKS SOMEWHERE AND PUT A CLOSE TO AN ERA OF HIS LIFE FOREVER.
2009-2014
A FEW DAYS AGO I WAS VISITING MY FRIEND, THE PAINTER WILLY RAMOS. HE'S PREPARING A NEW SHOW.
ARE THESE FINISHED?
I HATE THE WORD "FINISH."
WILLY FINDS IT DIFFICULT AND FRUSTRATING TO COMPLETE A PAINTING.
HE WORKS ON ALL OF HIS CANVASES AT ONCE. HE MOVES FROM ONE PAINTING TO ANOTHER, CONSTANTLY REWORKING AND RETOUCHING ACCORDING TO HIS MOOD.
HE NEVER REALLY FINISHES HIS WORKS UNTIL THE DAY OF THE EXHIBITION.

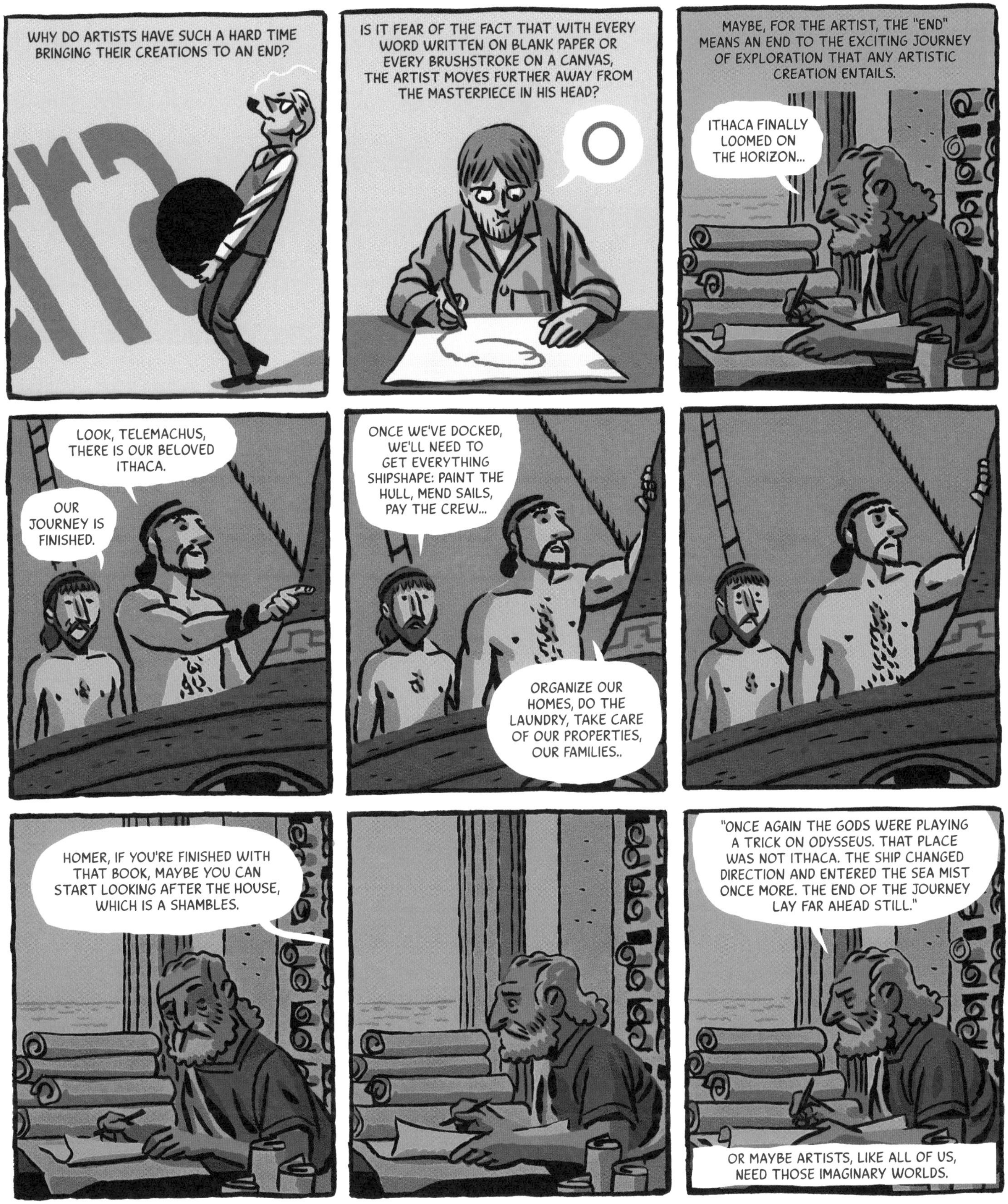
WHY DO ARTISTS HAVE SUCH A HARD TIME BRINGING THEIR CREATIONS TO AN END?
IS IT FEAR OF THE FACT THAT WITH EVERY WORD WRITTEN ON BLANK PAPER OR EVERY BRUSHSTROKE ON A CANVAS, THE ARTIST MOVES FURTHER AWAY FROM THE MASTERPIECE IN HIS HEAD?
MAYBE, FOR THE ARTIST, THE "END" MEANS AN END TO THE EXCITING JOURNEY OF EXPLORATION THAT ANY ARTISTIC CREATION ENTAILS.
ITHACA FINALLY LOOMED ON THE HORIZON...
LOOK, TELEMACHUS, THERE IS OUR BELOVED ITHACA.
OUR JOURNEY IS FINISHED.
ONCE WE'VE DOCKED, WE'LL NEED TO GET EVERYTHING SHIPSHAPE: PAINT THE HULL, MEND SAILS, PAY THE CREW...
ORGANIZE OUR HOMES, DO THE LAUNDRY, TAKE CARE OF OUR PROPERTIES, OUR FAMILIES..
HOMER, IF YOU'RE FINISHED WITH THAT BOOK, MAYBE YOU CAN START LOOKING AFTER THE HOUSE, WHICH IS A SHAMBLES.
"ONCE AGAIN THE GODS WERE PLAYING A TRICK ON ODYSSEUS. THAT PLACE WAS NOT ITHACA. THE SHIP CHANGED DIRECTION AND ENTERED THE SEA MIST ONCE MORE. THE END OF THE JOURNEY LAY FAR AHEAD STILL."
OR MAYBE ARTISTS, LIKE ALL OF US, NEED THOSE IMAGINARY WORLDS.

THE SNOWS OF TIME

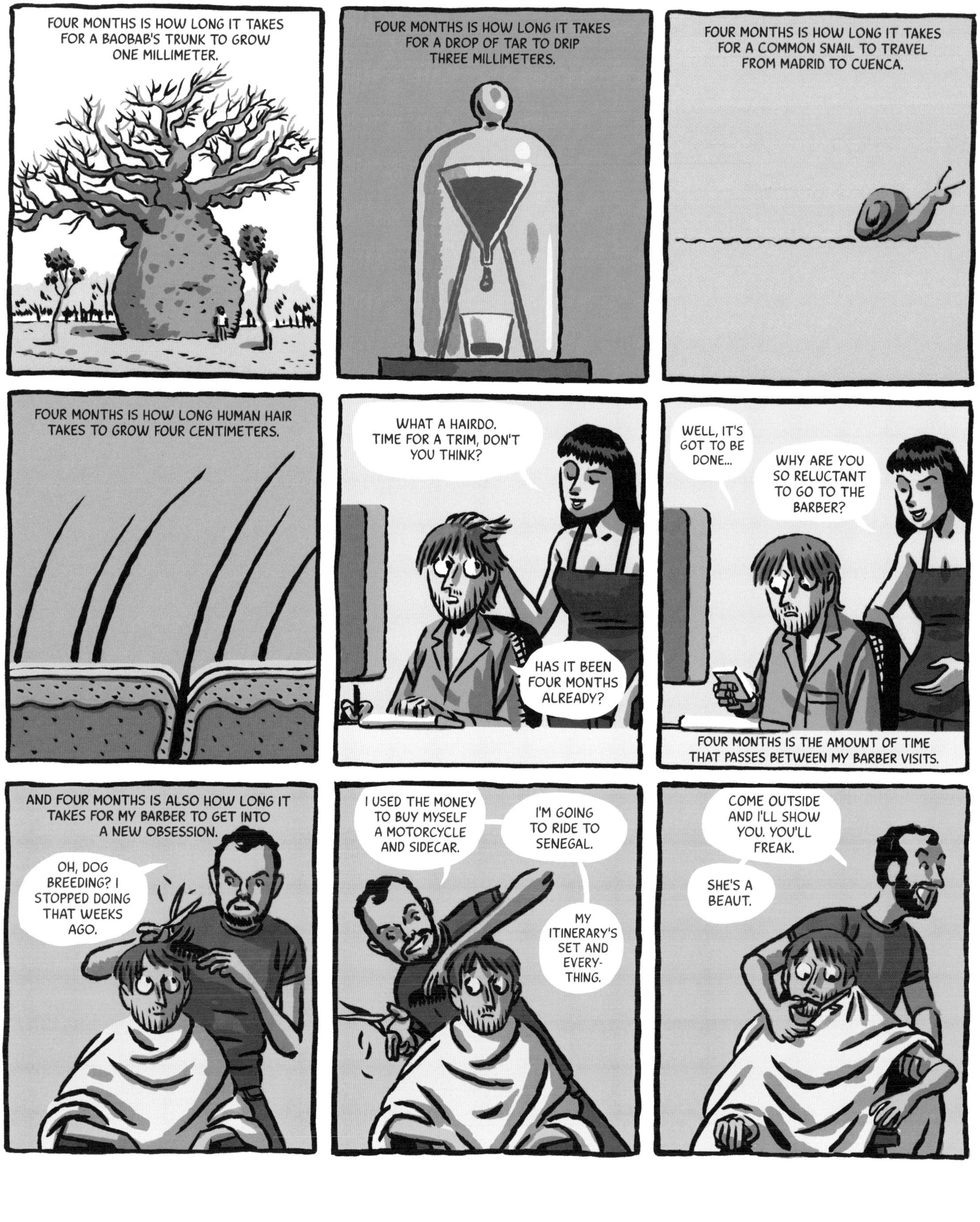
FOUR MONTHS IS HOW LONG IT TAKES FOR A BAOBAB'S TRUNK TO GROW ONE MILLIMETER.
FOUR MONTHS IS HOW LONG IT TAKES FOR A DROP OF TAR TO DRIP THREE MILLIMETERS.
FOUR MONTHS IS HOW LONG IT TAKES FOR A COMMON SNAIL TO TRAVEL FROM MADRID TO CUENCA.
FOUR MONTHS IS HOW LONG HUMAN HAIR TAKES TO GROW FOUR CENTIMETERS.
WHAT A HAIRDO. TIME FOR A TRIM, DON'T YOU THINK?
HAS IT BEEN FOUR MONTHS ALREADY?
WELL, IT'S GOT TO BE DONE...
WHY ARE YOU SO RELUCTANT TO GO TO THE BARBER?
FOUR MONTHS IS THE AMOUNT OF TIME THAT PASSES BETWEEN MY BARBER VISITS.
AND FOUR MONTHS IS ALSO HOW LONG IT TAKES FOR MY BARBER TO GET INTO A NEW OBSESSION.
OH, DOG BREEDING? I STOPPED DOING THAT WEEKS AGO.
I USED THE MONEY TO BUY MYSELF A MOTORCYCLE AND SIDECAR.
I'M GOING TO RIDE TO SENEGAL.
MY ITINERARY'S SET AND EVERY-THING.
COME OUTSIDE AND I'LL SHOW YOU. YOU'LL FREAK.
SHE'S A BEAUT.

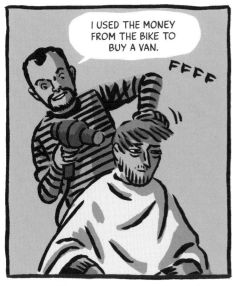

I USED THE MONEY FROM THE BIKE TO BUY A VAN.

FFFF

CHECK OUT THIS PHOTO. IT'S LIKE THE ONE FROM THE FREAK BROTHERS.

FFFF

THE PLAN IS TO SET UP A MOBILE BARBERSHOP IN FORMENTERA.

LEMME FIND ANOTHER PHOTO...

FFFFF

THESE ROLLERBLADES ARE SWEET, HUH?

IMAGINE CUTTING HAIR ON ROLLERBLADES.

TCHAK

...TO BE HONEST, I DON'T HAVE WRINKLES OR A SINGLE GRAY HAIR, BUT I'M DOING TAI CHI FOR RELAXATION.

LOOK, THIS IS THE YE MA FEN ZONG POSE...

CLEARLY THE SNOWS OF TIME HAVE LESS POWER OVER PEOPLE WHO ARE CONSTANTLY IN MOTION...

JESUS, EVERY TIME YOU COME BACK FROM THE BARBER YOU LOOK TEN YEARS OLDER.

BUT THEY BURY THOSE WHO LIVE IN FEAR.

135

DRIVEN TO DESPAIR

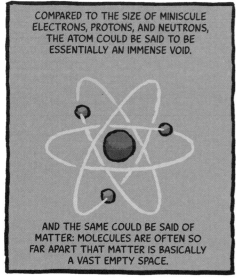

COMPARED TO THE SIZE OF MINISCULE ELECTRONS, PROTONS, AND NEUTRONS, THE ATOM COULD BE SAID TO BE ESSENTIALLY AN IMMENSE VOID.

AND THE SAME COULD BE SAID OF MATTER: MOLECULES ARE OFTEN SO FAR APART THAT MATTER IS BASICALLY A VAST EMPTY SPACE.

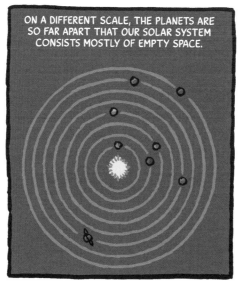

ON A DIFFERENT SCALE, THE PLANETS ARE SO FAR APART THAT OUR SOLAR SYSTEM CONSISTS MOSTLY OF EMPTY SPACE.

SOLAR SYSTEMS, GALAXIES, GLOBULAR CLUSTERS... THEY'RE SO FAR APART, THE COSMOS COULD BE SAID TO BE A VAST EMPTY SPACE.

EMPTINESS, THEN, IS THE NORM IN THE UNIVERSE.

SO IF EMPTINESS IS THE NORM IN THE UNIVERSE, WHY IS PARKING SO DIFFICULT?

DO YOU THINK I CAN FIT THERE?

NOT THERE EITHER, HUH? TIGHT SQUEEZE.

LIKE MY FATHER, I'M OBSESSED WITH PARKING.

THE MAIN PLEASURE MY FATHER DERIVED FROM HIS ADDITIONAL FREE TIME IN RETIREMENT WAS BEING ABLE TO PARK CLOSER TO HOME.

LOOK, THAT GUY'S LEAVING.

IT WAS LIKE A GAME FOR HIM TO SEE HOW CLOSE HE COULD GET TO HIS DOOR.

YOU CAME BY BUS LOADED DOWN LIKE THAT?

WHAT DO YOU WANT ME TO DO?

I'D MANAGED TO SNAG A PARKING SPACE RIGHT BY MY FRONT DOOR!

IT'S BECAUSE OF MY OWN OBSESSION WITH PARKING THAT I DON'T LIKE TO DRIVE. WHENEVER I'M ABOUT TO GET IN THE CAR, I'M SEIZED BY AN AWFUL FEAR...

WILL I FIND ANOTHER PARKING SPACE?

I'M TERRIFIED THAT I'LL NEVER BE ABLE TO PARK THE CAR AGAIN.

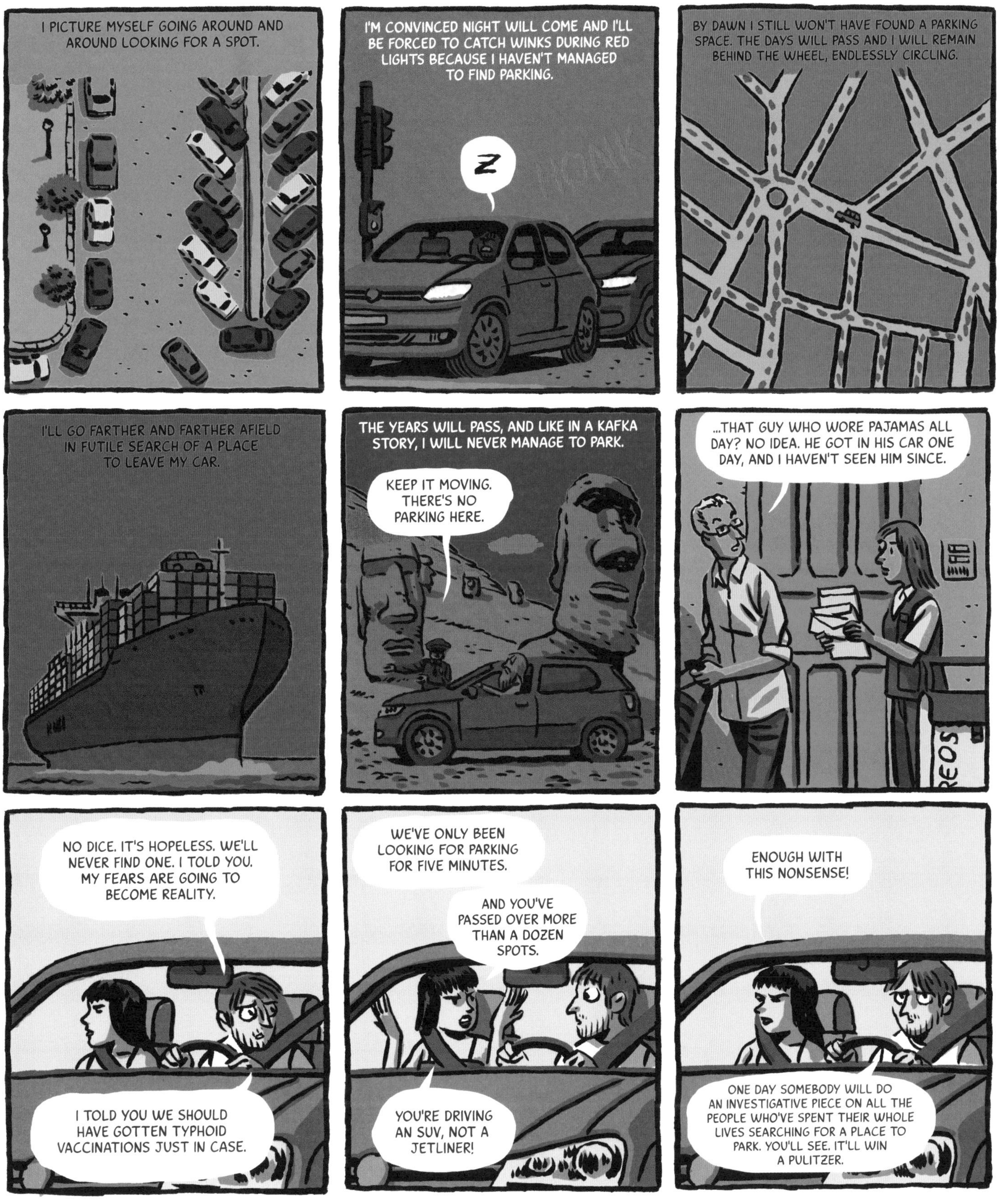
I PICTURE MYSELF GOING AROUND AND AROUND LOOKING FOR A SPOT.
I'M CONVINCED NIGHT WILL COME AND I'LL BE FORCED TO CATCH WINKS DURING RED LIGHTS BECAUSE I HAVEN'T MANAGED TO FIND PARKING.
Z
HONK
BY DAWN I STILL WON'T HAVE FOUND A PARKING SPACE. THE DAYS WILL PASS AND I WILL REMAIN BEHIND THE WHEEL, ENDLESSLY CIRCLING.
I'LL GO FARTHER AND FARTHER AFIELD IN FUTILE SEARCH OF A PLACE TO LEAVE MY CAR.
THE YEARS WILL PASS, AND LIKE IN A KAFKA STORY, I WILL NEVER MANAGE TO PARK.
KEEP IT MOVING. THERE'S NO PARKING HERE.
...THAT GUY WHO WORE PAJAMAS ALL DAY? NO IDEA. HE GOT IN HIS CAR ONE DAY, AND I HAVEN'T SEEN HIM SINCE.
NO DICE. IT'S HOPELESS. WE'LL NEVER FIND ONE. I TOLD YOU. MY FEARS ARE GOING TO BECOME REALITY.
I TOLD YOU WE SHOULD HAVE GOTTEN TYPHOID VACCINATIONS JUST IN CASE.
WE'VE ONLY BEEN LOOKING FOR PARKING FOR FIVE MINUTES.
AND YOU'VE PASSED OVER MORE THAN A DOZEN SPOTS.
YOU'RE DRIVING AN SUV, NOT A JETLINER!
ENOUGH WITH THIS NONSENSE!
ONE DAY SOMEBODY WILL DO AN INVESTIGATIVE PIECE ON ALL THE PEOPLE WHO'VE SPENT THEIR WHOLE LIVES SEARCHING FOR A PLACE TO PARK. YOU'LL SEE. IT'LL WIN A PULITZER.

SENTIMENTAL POSSESSION

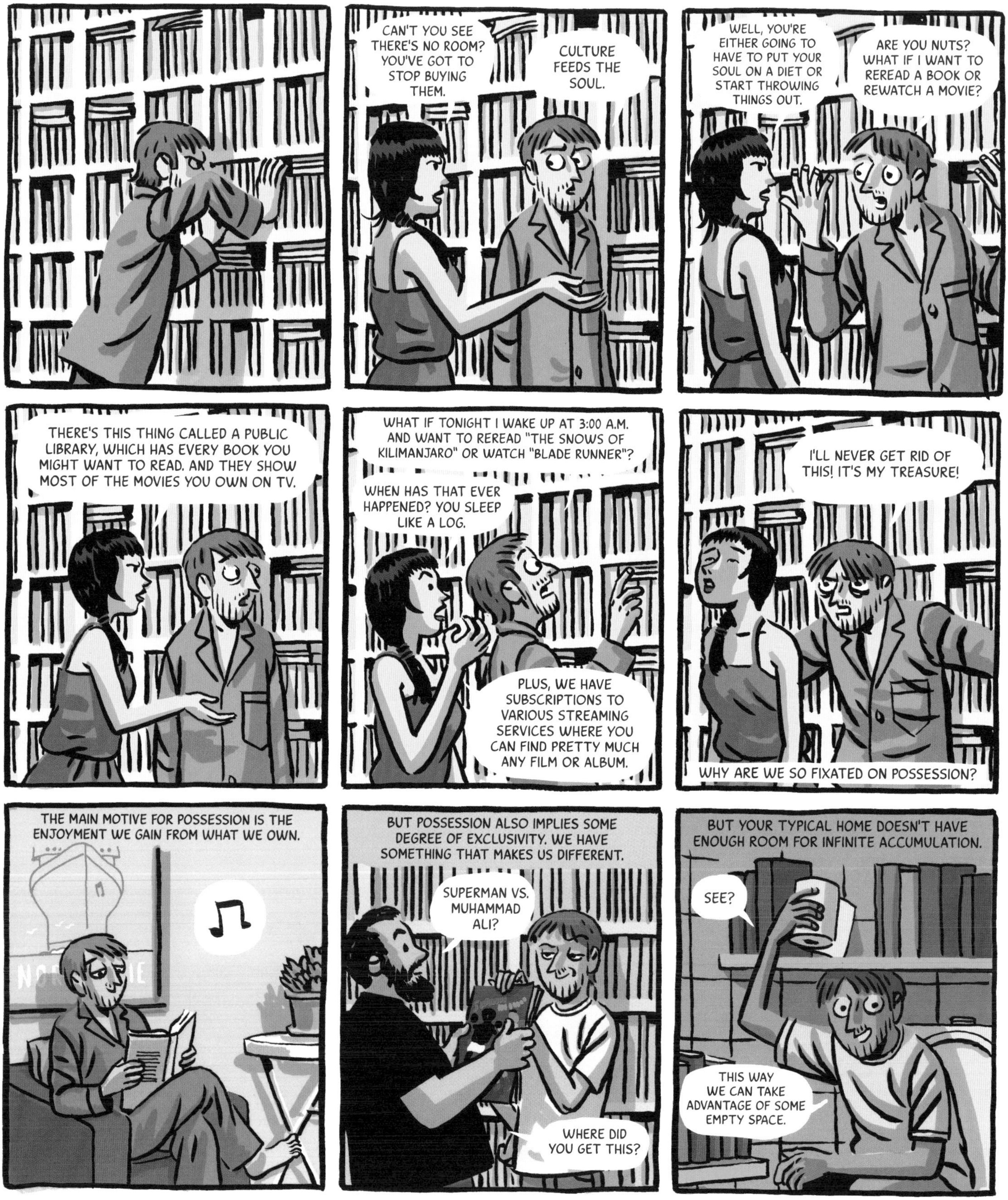

CAN'T YOU SEE THERE'S NO ROOM? YOU'VE GOT TO STOP BUYING THEM.
CULTURE FEEDS THE SOUL.
WELL, YOU'RE EITHER GOING TO HAVE TO PUT YOUR SOUL ON A DIET OR START THROWING THINGS OUT.
ARE YOU NUTS? WHAT IF I WANT TO REREAD A BOOK OR REWATCH A MOVIE?
THERE'S THIS THING CALLED A PUBLIC LIBRARY, WHICH HAS EVERY BOOK YOU MIGHT WANT TO READ. AND THEY SHOW MOST OF THE MOVIES YOU OWN ON TV.
WHAT IF TONIGHT I WAKE UP AT 3:00 A.M. AND WANT TO REREAD "THE SNOWS OF KILIMANJARO" OR WATCH "BLADE RUNNER"?
WHEN HAS THAT EVER HAPPENED? YOU SLEEP LIKE A LOG.
PLUS, WE HAVE SUBSCRIPTIONS TO VARIOUS STREAMING SERVICES WHERE YOU CAN FIND PRETTY MUCH ANY FILM OR ALBUM.
I'LL NEVER GET RID OF THIS! IT'S MY TREASURE!
WHY ARE WE SO FIXATED ON POSSESSION?
THE MAIN MOTIVE FOR POSSESSION IS THE ENJOYMENT WE GAIN FROM WHAT WE OWN.
BUT POSSESSION ALSO IMPLIES SOME DEGREE OF EXCLUSIVITY. WE HAVE SOMETHING THAT MAKES US DIFFERENT.
SUPERMAN VS. MUHAMMAD ALI?
WHERE DID YOU GET THIS?
BUT YOUR TYPICAL HOME DOESN'T HAVE ENOUGH ROOM FOR INFINITE ACCUMULATION.
SEE?
THIS WAY WE CAN TAKE ADVANTAGE OF SOME EMPTY SPACE.

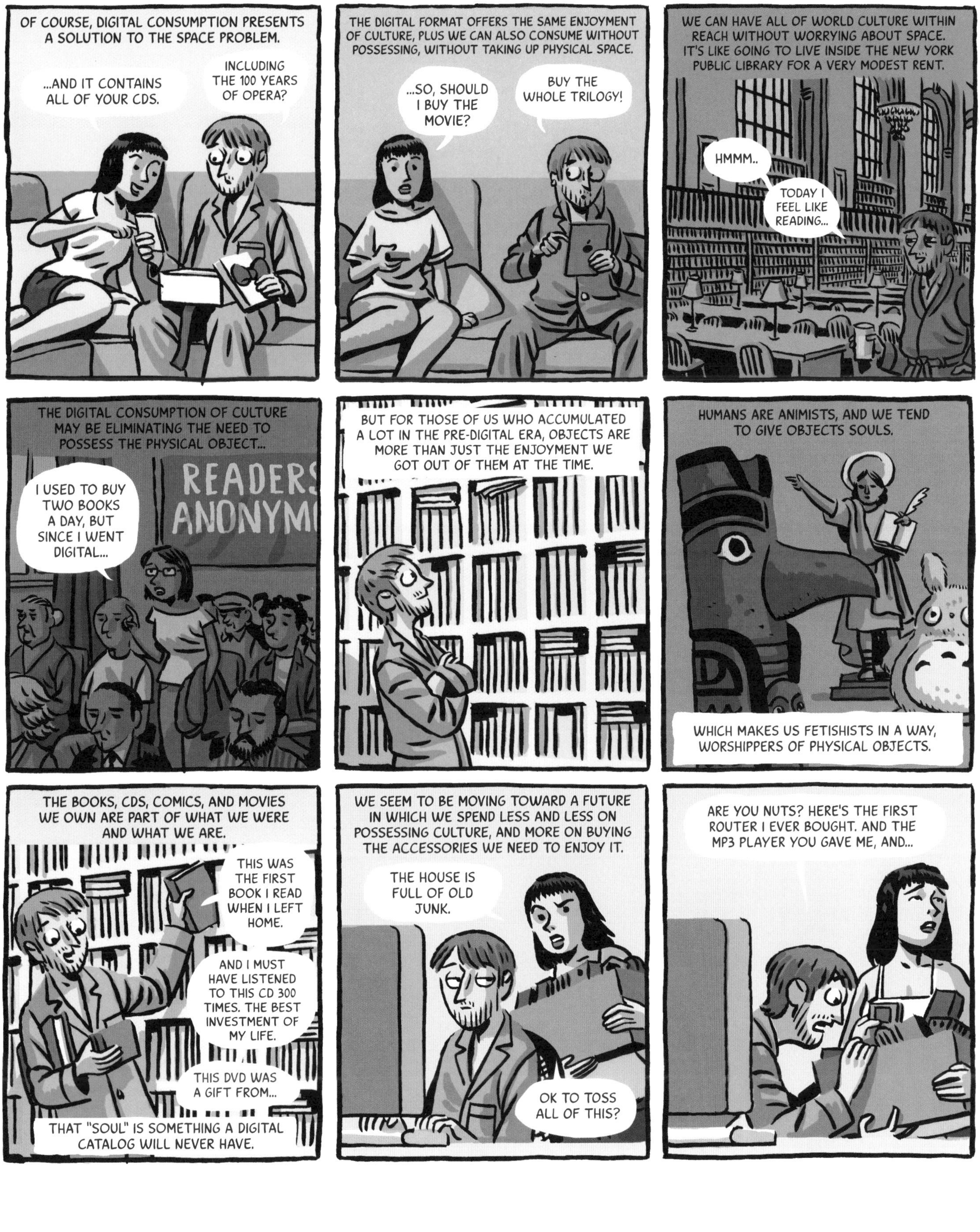

OF COURSE, DIGITAL CONSUMPTION PRESENTS A SOLUTION TO THE SPACE PROBLEM.
...AND IT CONTAINS ALL OF YOUR CDS.
INCLUDING THE 100 YEARS OF OPERA?
THE DIGITAL FORMAT OFFERS THE SAME ENJOYMENT OF CULTURE, PLUS WE CAN ALSO CONSUME WITHOUT POSSESSING, WITHOUT TAKING UP PHYSICAL SPACE.
...SO, SHOULD I BUY THE MOVIE?
BUY THE WHOLE TRILOGY!
WE CAN HAVE ALL OF WORLD CULTURE WITHIN REACH WITHOUT WORRYING ABOUT SPACE. IT'S LIKE GOING TO LIVE INSIDE THE NEW YORK PUBLIC LIBRARY FOR A VERY MODEST RENT.
HMMM..
TODAY I FEEL LIKE READING...
THE DIGITAL CONSUMPTION OF CULTURE MAY BE ELIMINATING THE NEED TO POSSESS THE PHYSICAL OBJECT...
READERS ANONYM
I USED TO BUY TWO BOOKS A DAY, BUT SINCE I WENT DIGITAL...
BUT FOR THOSE OF US WHO ACCUMULATED A LOT IN THE PRE-DIGITAL ERA, OBJECTS ARE MORE THAN JUST THE ENJOYMENT WE GOT OUT OF THEM AT THE TIME.
HUMANS ARE ANIMISTS, AND WE TEND TO GIVE OBJECTS SOULS.
WHICH MAKES US FETISHISTS IN A WAY, WORSHIPPERS OF PHYSICAL OBJECTS.
THE BOOKS, CDS, COMICS, AND MOVIES WE OWN ARE PART OF WHAT WE WERE AND WHAT WE ARE.
THIS WAS THE FIRST BOOK I READ WHEN I LEFT HOME.
AND I MUST HAVE LISTENED TO THIS CD 300 TIMES. THE BEST INVESTMENT OF MY LIFE.
THIS DVD WAS A GIFT FROM...
THAT "SOUL" IS SOMETHING A DIGITAL CATALOG WILL NEVER HAVE.
WE SEEM TO BE MOVING TOWARD A FUTURE IN WHICH WE SPEND LESS AND LESS ON POSSESSING CULTURE, AND MORE ON BUYING THE ACCESSORIES WE NEED TO ENJOY IT.
THE HOUSE IS FULL OF OLD JUNK.
OK TO TOSS ALL OF THIS?
ARE YOU NUTS? HERE'S THE FIRST ROUTER I EVER BOUGHT. AND THE MP3 PLAYER YOU GAVE ME, AND...

THE AUTHOR'S VOICE

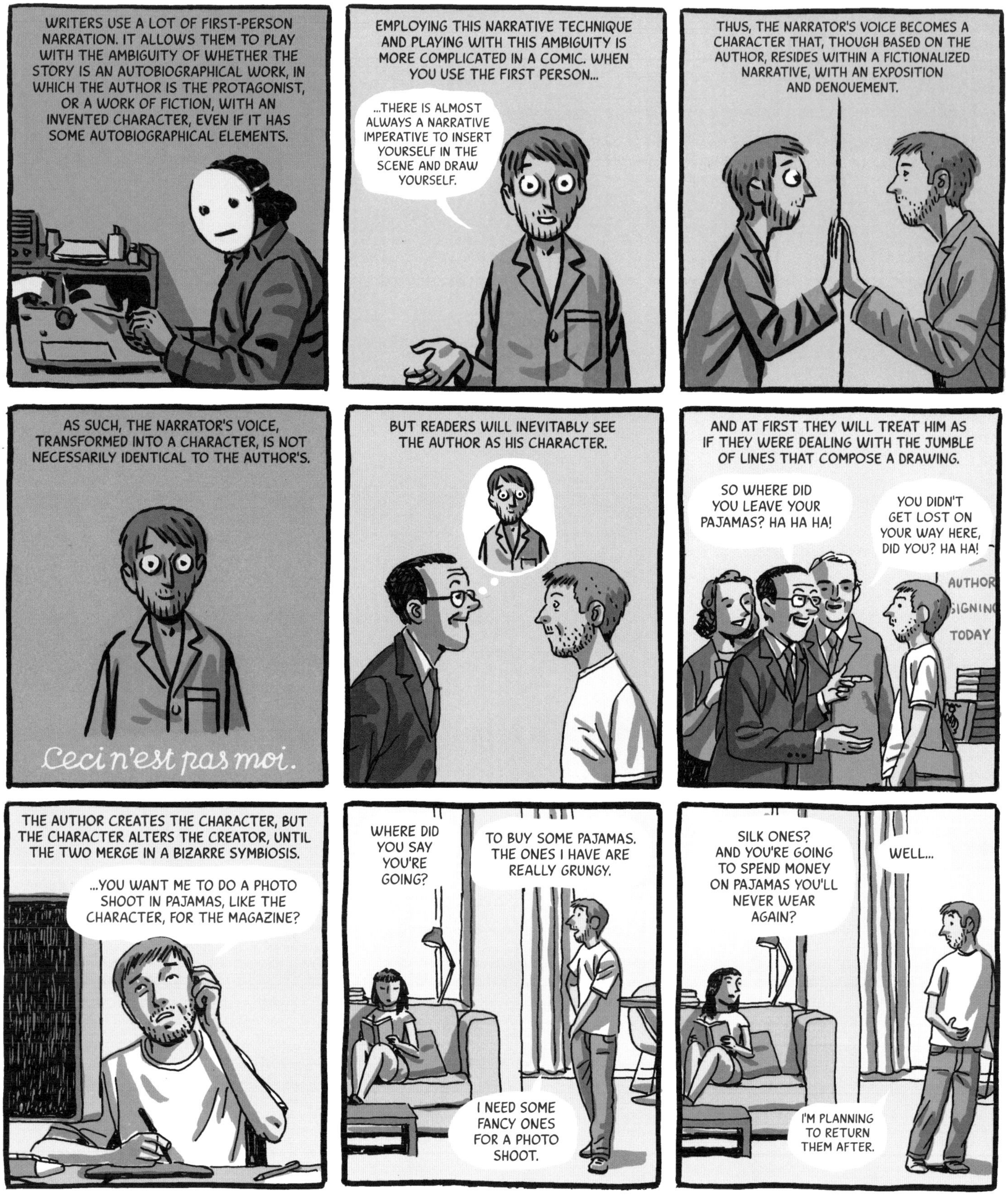

WRITERS USE A LOT OF FIRST-PERSON NARRATION. IT ALLOWS THEM TO PLAY WITH THE AMBIGUITY OF WHETHER THE STORY IS AN AUTOBIOGRAPHICAL WORK, IN WHICH THE AUTHOR IS THE PROTAGONIST, OR A WORK OF FICTION, WITH AN INVENTED CHARACTER, EVEN IF IT HAS SOME AUTOBIOGRAPHICAL ELEMENTS.
EMPLOYING THIS NARRATIVE TECHNIQUE AND PLAYING WITH THIS AMBIGUITY IS MORE COMPLICATED IN A COMIC. WHEN YOU USE THE FIRST PERSON...
...THERE IS ALMOST ALWAYS A NARRATIVE IMPERATIVE TO INSERT YOURSELF IN THE SCENE AND DRAW YOURSELF.
THUS, THE NARRATOR'S VOICE BECOMES A CHARACTER THAT, THOUGH BASED ON THE AUTHOR, RESIDES WITHIN A FICTIONALIZED NARRATIVE, WITH AN EXPOSITION AND DENOUEMENT.
AS SUCH, THE NARRATOR'S VOICE, TRANSFORMED INTO A CHARACTER, IS NOT NECESSARILY IDENTICAL TO THE AUTHOR'S.
Ceci n'est pas moi.
BUT READERS WILL INEVITABLY SEE THE AUTHOR AS HIS CHARACTER.
AND AT FIRST THEY WILL TREAT HIM AS IF THEY WERE DEALING WITH THE JUMBLE OF LINES THAT COMPOSE A DRAWING.
SO WHERE DID YOU LEAVE YOUR PAJAMAS? HA HA HA!
YOU DIDN'T GET LOST ON YOUR WAY HERE, DID YOU? HA HA!
AUTHOR SIGNING TODAY
THE AUTHOR CREATES THE CHARACTER, BUT THE CHARACTER ALTERS THE CREATOR, UNTIL THE TWO MERGE IN A BIZARRE SYMBIOSIS.
...YOU WANT ME TO DO A PHOTO SHOOT IN PAJAMAS, LIKE THE CHARACTER, FOR THE MAGAZINE?
WHERE DID YOU SAY YOU'RE GOING?
TO BUY SOME PAJAMAS. THE ONES I HAVE ARE REALLY GRUNGY.
I NEED SOME FANCY ONES FOR A PHOTO SHOOT.
SILK ONES? AND YOU'RE GOING TO SPEND MONEY ON PAJAMAS YOU'LL NEVER WEAR AGAIN?
WELL...
I'M PLANNING TO RETURN THEM AFTER.

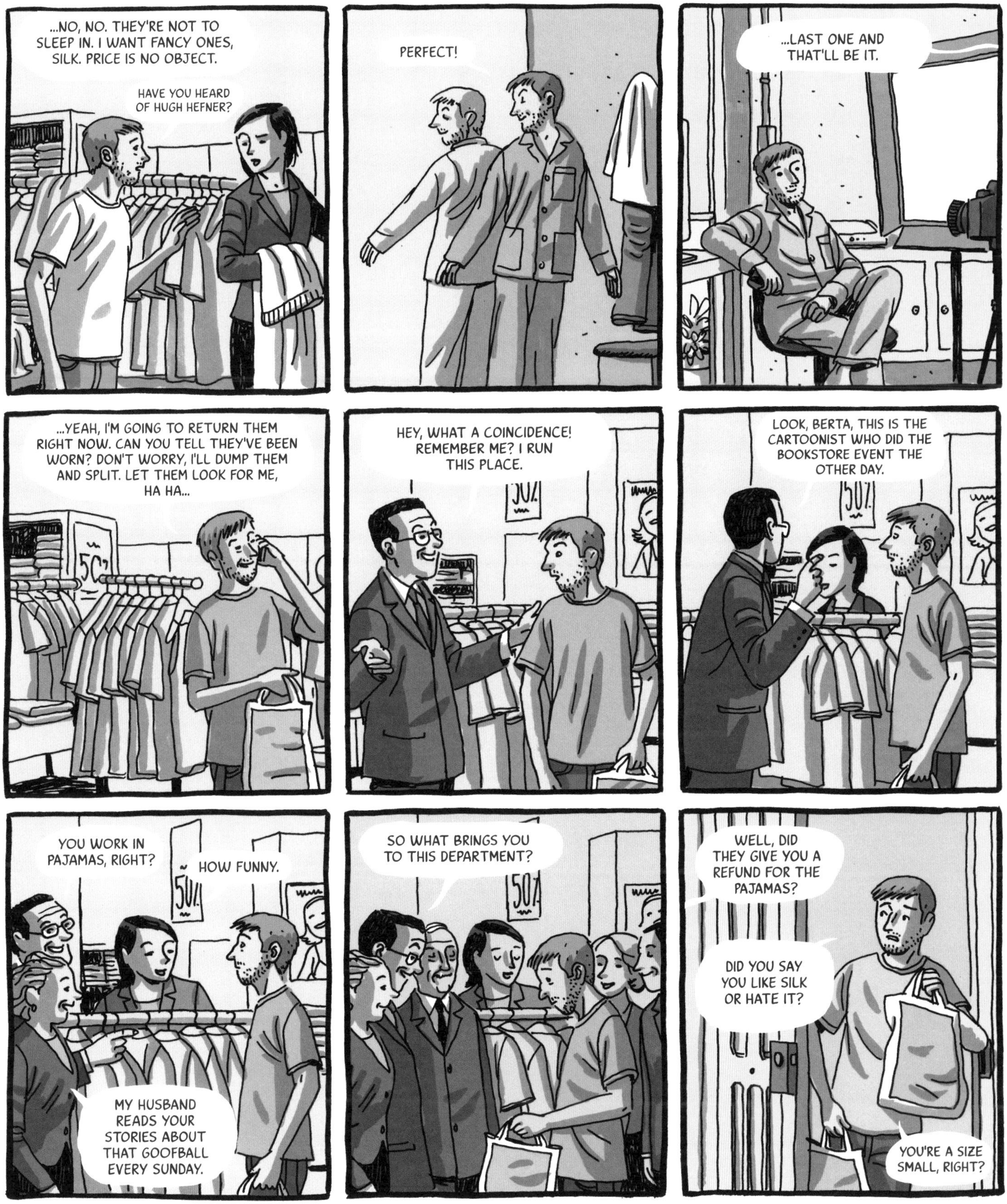
...NO, NO. THEY'RE NOT TO SLEEP IN. I WANT FANCY ONES, SILK. PRICE IS NO OBJECT.
HAVE YOU HEARD OF HUGH HEFNER?
PERFECT!
...LAST ONE AND THAT'LL BE IT.
...YEAH, I'M GOING TO RETURN THEM RIGHT NOW. CAN YOU TELL THEY'VE BEEN WORN? DON'T WORRY, I'LL DUMP THEM AND SPLIT. LET THEM LOOK FOR ME, HA HA...
50%
HEY, WHAT A COINCIDENCE! REMEMBER ME? I RUN THIS PLACE.
LOOK, BERTA, THIS IS THE CARTOONIST WHO DID THE BOOKSTORE EVENT THE OTHER DAY.
YOU WORK IN PAJAMAS, RIGHT?
HOW FUNNY.
MY HUSBAND READS YOUR STORIES ABOUT THAT GOOFBALL EVERY SUNDAY.
SO WHAT BRINGS YOU TO THIS DEPARTMENT?
WELL, DID THEY GIVE YOU A REFUND FOR THE PAJAMAS?
DID YOU SAY YOU LIKE SILK OR HATE IT?
YOU'RE A SIZE SMALL, RIGHT?

FREE PEOPLE'S TIME

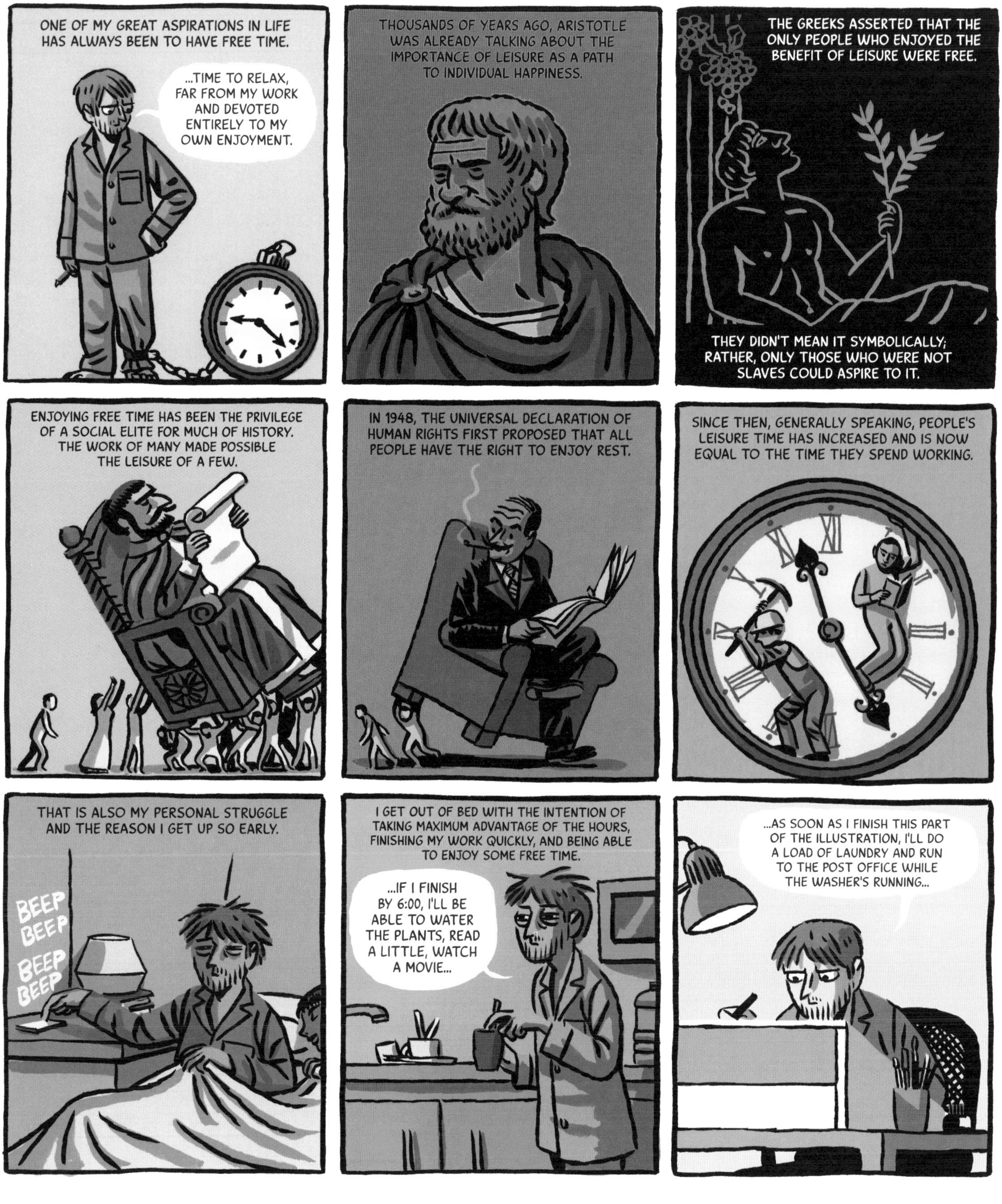
ONE OF MY GREAT ASPIRATIONS IN LIFE HAS ALWAYS BEEN TO HAVE FREE TIME.
...TIME TO RELAX, FAR FROM MY WORK AND DEVOTED ENTIRELY TO MY OWN ENJOYMENT.
THOUSANDS OF YEARS AGO, ARISTOTLE WAS ALREADY TALKING ABOUT THE IMPORTANCE OF LEISURE AS A PATH TO INDIVIDUAL HAPPINESS.
THE GREEKS ASSERTED THAT THE ONLY PEOPLE WHO ENJOYED THE BENEFIT OF LEISURE WERE FREE.
THEY DIDN'T MEAN IT SYMBOLICALLY; RATHER, ONLY THOSE WHO WERE NOT SLAVES COULD ASPIRE TO IT.
ENJOYING FREE TIME HAS BEEN THE PRIVILEGE OF A SOCIAL ELITE FOR MUCH OF HISTORY. THE WORK OF MANY MADE POSSIBLE THE LEISURE OF A FEW.
IN 1948, THE UNIVERSAL DECLARATION OF HUMAN RIGHTS FIRST PROPOSED THAT ALL PEOPLE HAVE THE RIGHT TO ENJOY REST.
SINCE THEN, GENERALLY SPEAKING, PEOPLE'S LEISURE TIME HAS INCREASED AND IS NOW EQUAL TO THE TIME THEY SPEND WORKING.
THAT IS ALSO MY PERSONAL STRUGGLE AND THE REASON I GET UP SO EARLY.
BEEP BEEP
BEEP BEEP
I GET OUT OF BED WITH THE INTENTION OF TAKING MAXIMUM ADVANTAGE OF THE HOURS, FINISHING MY WORK QUICKLY, AND BEING ABLE TO ENJOY SOME FREE TIME.
...IF I FINISH BY 6:00, I'LL BE ABLE TO WATER THE PLANTS, READ A LITTLE, WATCH A MOVIE...
...AS SOON AS I FINISH THIS PART OF THE ILLUSTRATION, I'LL DO A LOAD OF LAUNDRY AND RUN TO THE POST OFFICE WHILE THE WASHER'S RUNNING...

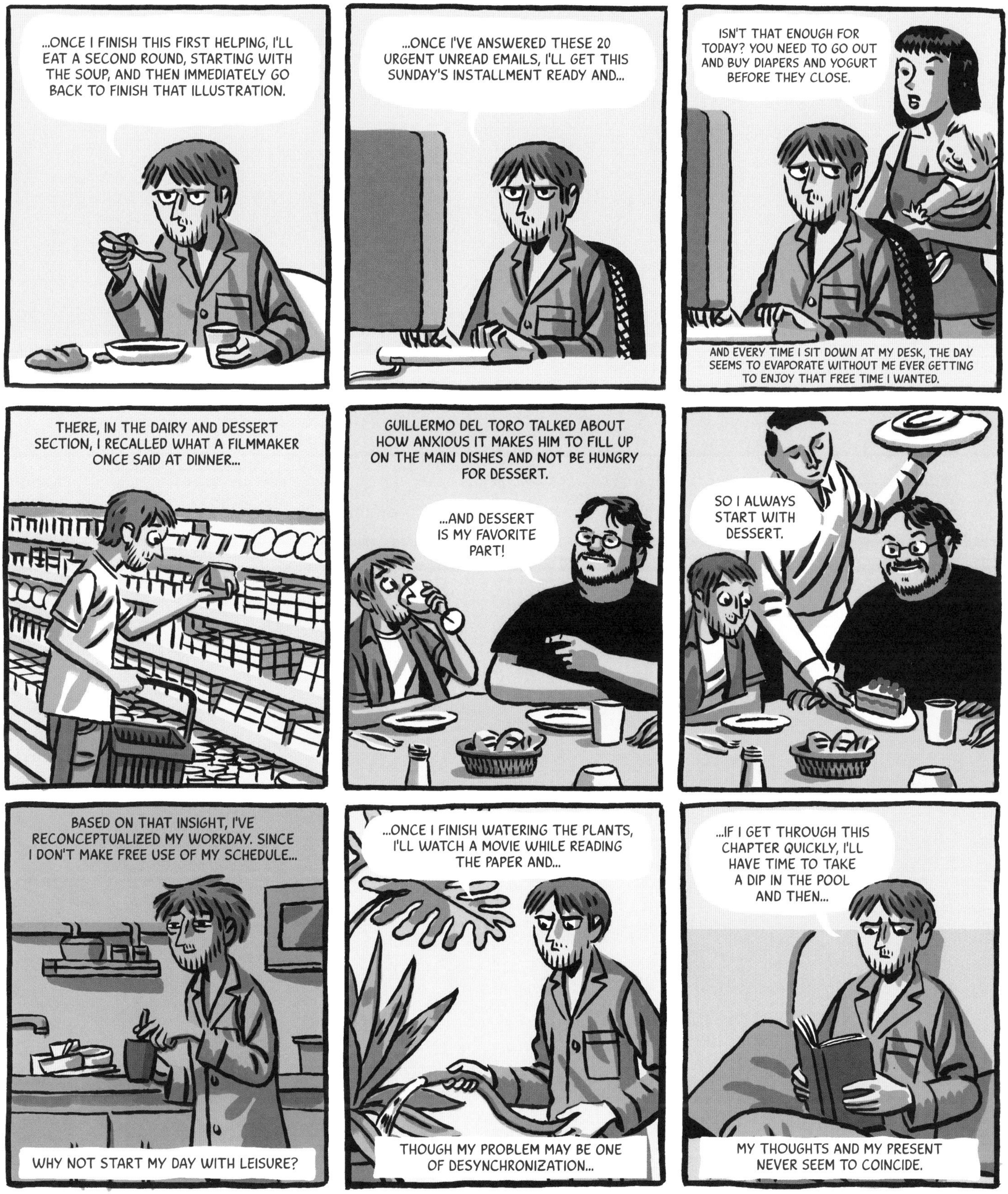
...ONCE I FINISH THIS FIRST HELPING, I'LL EAT A SECOND ROUND, STARTING WITH THE SOUP, AND THEN IMMEDIATELY GO BACK TO FINISH THAT ILLUSTRATION.
...ONCE I'VE ANSWERED THESE 20 URGENT UNREAD EMAILS, I'LL GET THIS SUNDAY'S INSTALLMENT READY AND...
ISN'T THAT ENOUGH FOR TODAY? YOU NEED TO GO OUT AND BUY DIAPERS AND YOGURT BEFORE THEY CLOSE.
AND EVERY TIME I SIT DOWN AT MY DESK, THE DAY SEEMS TO EVAPORATE WITHOUT ME EVER GETTING TO ENJOY THAT FREE TIME I WANTED.
THERE, IN THE DAIRY AND DESSERT SECTION, I RECALLED WHAT A FILMMAKER ONCE SAID AT DINNER...
GUILLERMO DEL TORO TALKED ABOUT HOW ANXIOUS IT MAKES HIM TO FILL UP ON THE MAIN DISHES AND NOT BE HUNGRY FOR DESSERT.
...AND DESSERT IS MY FAVORITE PART!
SO I ALWAYS START WITH DESSERT.
BASED ON THAT INSIGHT, I'VE RECONCEPTUALIZED MY WORKDAY. SINCE I DON'T MAKE FREE USE OF MY SCHEDULE...
WHY NOT START MY DAY WITH LEISURE?
...ONCE I FINISH WATERING THE PLANTS, I'LL WATCH A MOVIE WHILE READING THE PAPER AND...
THOUGH MY PROBLEM MAY BE ONE OF DESYNCHRONIZATION...
...IF I GET THROUGH THIS CHAPTER QUICKLY, I'LL HAVE TIME TO TAKE A DIP IN THE POOL AND THEN...
MY THOUGHTS AND MY PRESENT NEVER SEEM TO COINCIDE.

EXCLUSIVE PRODUCTS

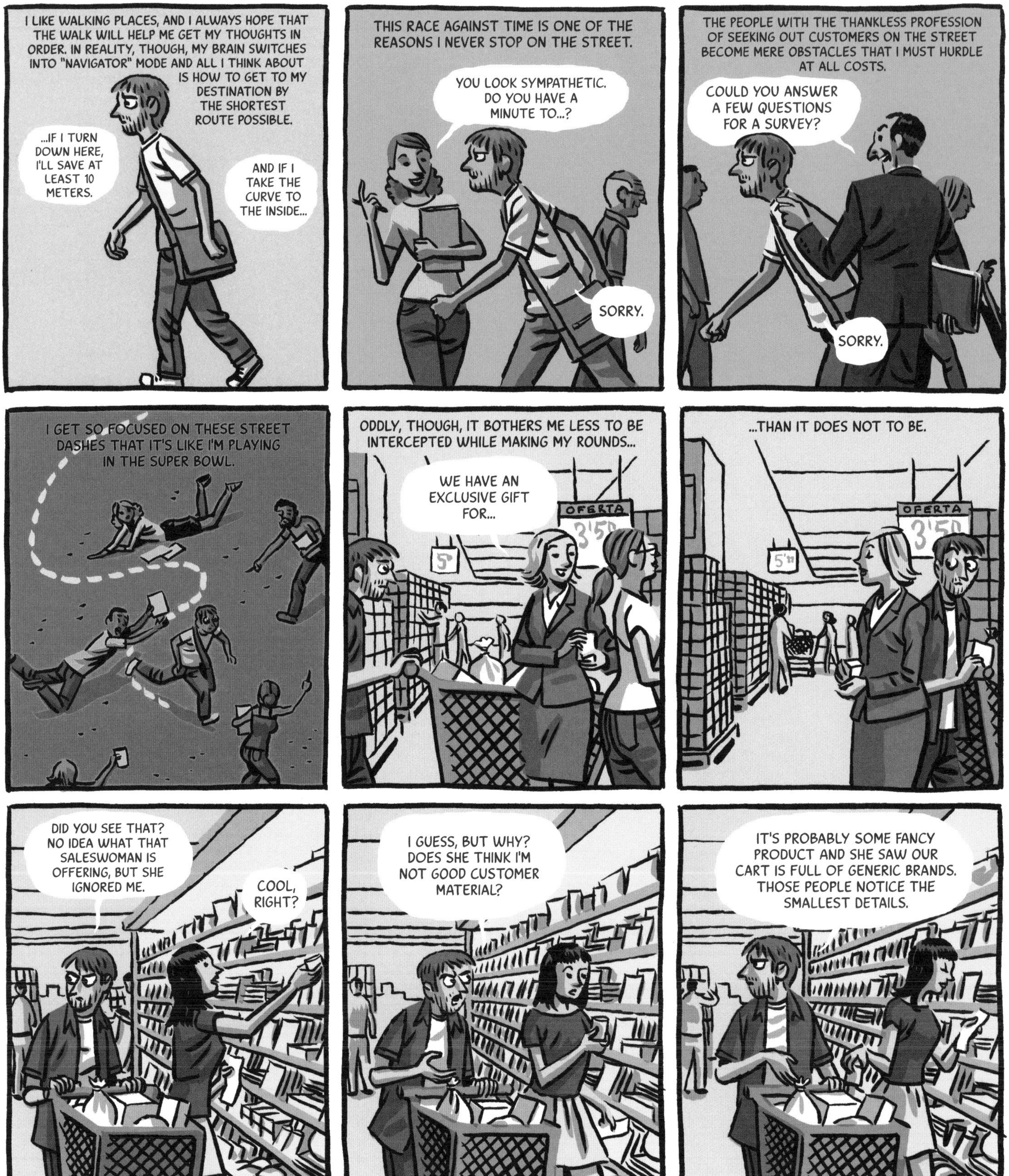

I LIKE WALKING PLACES, AND I ALWAYS HOPE THAT THE WALK WILL HELP ME GET MY THOUGHTS IN ORDER. IN REALITY, THOUGH, MY BRAIN SWITCHES INTO "NAVIGATOR" MODE AND ALL I THINK ABOUT IS HOW TO GET TO MY DESTINATION BY THE SHORTEST ROUTE POSSIBLE.
...IF I TURN DOWN HERE, I'LL SAVE AT LEAST 10 METERS.
AND IF I TAKE THE CURVE TO THE INSIDE...
THIS RACE AGAINST TIME IS ONE OF THE REASONS I NEVER STOP ON THE STREET.
YOU LOOK SYMPATHETIC. DO YOU HAVE A MINUTE TO...?
SORRY.
THE PEOPLE WITH THE THANKLESS PROFESSION OF SEEKING OUT CUSTOMERS ON THE STREET BECOME MERE OBSTACLES THAT I MUST HURDLE AT ALL COSTS.
COULD YOU ANSWER A FEW QUESTIONS FOR A SURVEY?
SORRY.
I GET SO FOCUSED ON THESE STREET DASHES THAT IT'S LIKE I'M PLAYING IN THE SUPER BOWL.
ODDLY, THOUGH, IT BOTHERS ME LESS TO BE INTERCEPTED WHILE MAKING MY ROUNDS...
WE HAVE AN EXCLUSIVE GIFT FOR...
OFERTA
...THAN IT DOES NOT TO BE.
OFERTA
DID YOU SEE THAT? NO IDEA WHAT THAT SALESWOMAN IS OFFERING, BUT SHE IGNORED ME.
COOL, RIGHT?
I GUESS, BUT WHY? DOES SHE THINK I'M NOT GOOD CUSTOMER MATERIAL?
IT'S PROBABLY SOME FANCY PRODUCT AND SHE SAW OUR CART IS FULL OF GENERIC BRANDS. THOSE PEOPLE NOTICE THE SMALLEST DETAILS.

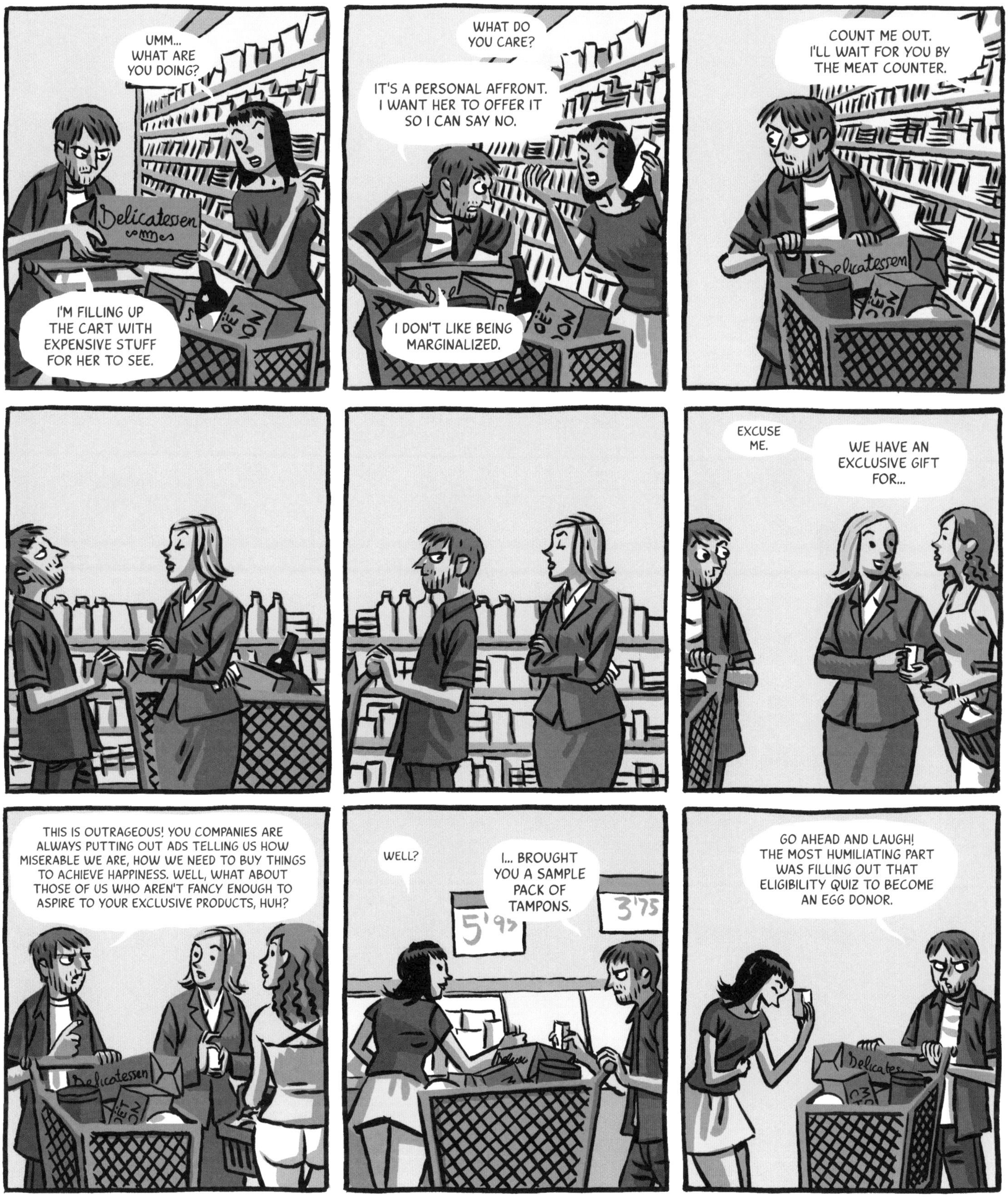
UMM... WHAT ARE YOU DOING?
I'M FILLING UP THE CART WITH EXPENSIVE STUFF FOR HER TO SEE.
WHAT DO YOU CARE?
IT'S A PERSONAL AFFRONT. I WANT HER TO OFFER IT SO I CAN SAY NO.
I DON'T LIKE BEING MARGINALIZED.
COUNT ME OUT. I'LL WAIT FOR YOU BY THE MEAT COUNTER.
EXCUSE ME.
WE HAVE AN EXCLUSIVE GIFT FOR...
THIS IS OUTRAGEOUS! YOU COMPANIES ARE ALWAYS PUTTING OUT ADS TELLING US HOW MISERABLE WE ARE, HOW WE NEED TO BUY THINGS TO ACHIEVE HAPPINESS. WELL, WHAT ABOUT THOSE OF US WHO AREN'T FANCY ENOUGH TO ASPIRE TO YOUR EXCLUSIVE PRODUCTS, HUH?
WELL?
I... BROUGHT YOU A SAMPLE PACK OF TAMPONS.
GO AHEAD AND LAUGH! THE MOST HUMILIATING PART WAS FILLING OUT THAT ELIGIBILITY QUIZ TO BECOME AN EGG DONOR.

AND CORPORATIONS CREATED LIFE

THE ANCIENT ROMAN DIET INCLUDED A LOT OF OLIVES.
THEY ATE THEM AS THEY MARCHED ACROSS HISPANIA, AND NATURALLY THEY TOSSED THE PITS ON THE GROUND.
POK
MANY OF THE OLIVE TREES THAT EVEN TODAY LINE THE VIA AUGUSTA MIGHT HAVE GROWN FROM THOSE PITS CASUALLY DISCARDED BY THE ANCIENT ROMANS.
OVER TIME, NATURE HAS COME UP WITH EFFECTIVE SOLUTIONS FOR PLANT REPRODUCTION. FRUITS, FOR EXAMPLE, FALL TO THE GROUND AND REPRODUCE THROUGH THEIR SEEDS.
OR THEY CAN BE EATEN BY ANIMALS, TRANSPORTED A LONG WAY IN THEIR STOMACHS, AND RETURNED TO THE SOIL—ALONG WITH A BONUS DEPOSIT OF USEFUL FERTILIZER.
2
1
3
4
A SYSTEM AS SEAMLESS AS A RING.
BUT EVER SINCE PEOPLE STARTED CULTIVATING THE LAND AND TRYING TO IMPROVE PRODUCTION, THINGS HAVE CHANGED.
FOR THOUSANDS OF YEARS THEY SELECTED THE BEST OF EACH HARVEST TO BE SOWN ANEW, AND THUS OBTAINED TENS OF THOUSANDS OF DIFFERENT HEIRLOOM VARIETIES.
IN THE 20TH CENTURY, NEW FASTER AND MORE EFFECTIVE SYSTEMS FOR IMPROVING SEEDS WERE DEVELOPED, COMBINING DIFFERENT VARIETIES OF A SINGLE CROP.
IN THE LATE 20TH CENTURY, THE PROCESS WENT A STEP FURTHER, AND MUTATIONS WERE INTRODUCED INTO THE SEEDS TO PRODUCE TRANSGENIC SEEDS.
TODAY, 90% OF SEEDS USED ARE TRANSGENIC.
THERE ARE JUST AS MANY ARGUMENTS IN FAVOR OF THIS SYSTEM AS THERE ARE AGAINST IT.

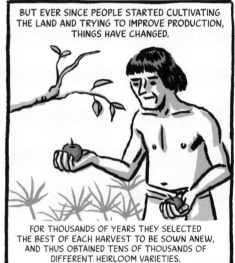

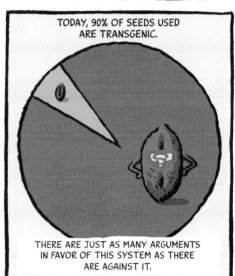

BUT ONE THING'S FOR SURE: THE SEEDS HAVE BECOME A HUGE BUSINESS THAT MOVES A LOT OF MONEY.

TEN COMPANIES CONTROL 73% OF THE MARKET. AND, AS USUAL, LARGE CORPORATIONS CAN NEVER EARN ENOUGH PROFITS. IN SOME CASES THEY ENGAGE IN NEFARIOUS PRACTICES.

MONSANTO, FOR EXAMPLE, TRIES TO PATENT VARIETIES OF HEIRLOOM SEEDS.

AND WHEN FARMERS USE THOSE SEEDS, AS THEY'VE DONE THEIR WHOLE LIVES, MONSANTO SUES THEM.

THE FIGHT AGAINST THESE BAD PRACTICES THAT LEAD TO SOCIAL INJUSTICE IS STARTING TO SHOW RESULTS. IN 2006 THE NGO OXFAM MANAGED TO FORCE STARBUCKS, WHICH HAD PATENTED AN HEIRLOOM COFFEE BEAN FROM ETHIOPIA, TO RETURN ITS PROPERTY TO THE ETHIOPIAN PEOPLE.

PATENTED SEED DO NOT USE

APPARENTLY AGRICULTURE IS NO LONGER SO SIMPLE AS EATING A FRUIT, TOSSING IT ON THE GROUND, AND WAITING FOR IT TO GROW.

IF WE DID THAT NOW WITH ANY FRUIT PURCHASED IN A SUPERMARKET, WE COULD SPEND AGES WATCHING AND NOTHING WOULD HAPPEN.

THE MORE A SEED IS "IMPROVED," THE MORE STERILE IT BECOMES.

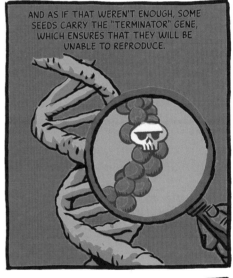

AND AS IF THAT WEREN'T ENOUGH, SOME SEEDS CARRY THE "TERMINATOR" GENE, WHICH ENSURES THAT THEY WILL BE UNABLE TO REPRODUCE.

ARE YOU COMING? WHAT ARE YOU DOING GOGGLING AT THE OLIVE PITS?

DO YOU REALIZE THAT IN THOUSANDS OF YEARS OUR DESCENDANTS WON'T BE ABLE TO TRACE THE ROUTES OF OUR HIGHWAYS BY THE FRUITS WE DROPPED ALONG THE WAY?

AT MOST THEY'LL TRACK US BY OUR PLASTIC RUBBISH.

SOME PEOPLE CLAIM THAT CREATING LIFE IS IN GOD'S HANDS ALONE. FOR NONBELIEVERS, CREATION IS NOW IN THE HANDS OF A FEW CORPORATIONS.

147

THE OTHER SHORE

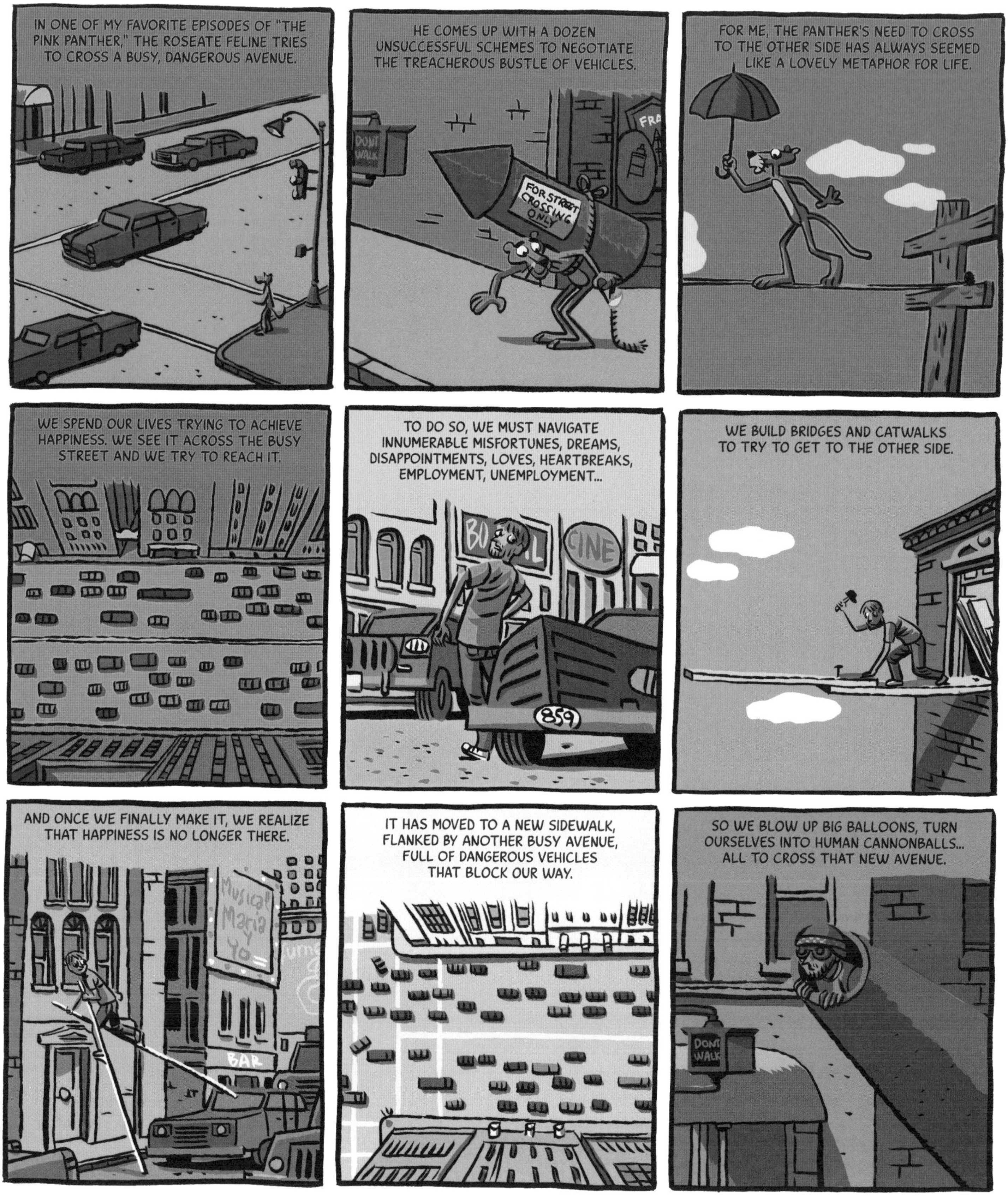
IN ONE OF MY FAVORITE EPISODES OF "THE PINK PANTHER," THE ROSEATE FELINE TRIES TO CROSS A BUSY, DANGEROUS AVENUE.
HE COMES UP WITH A DOZEN UNSUCCESSFUL SCHEMES TO NEGOTIATE THE TREACHEROUS BUSTLE OF VEHICLES.
DONT WALK
FOR STREET CROSSING ONLY
FOR ME, THE PANTHER'S NEED TO CROSS TO THE OTHER SIDE HAS ALWAYS SEEMED LIKE A LOVELY METAPHOR FOR LIFE.
WE SPEND OUR LIVES TRYING TO ACHIEVE HAPPINESS. WE SEE IT ACROSS THE BUSY STREET AND WE TRY TO REACH IT.
TO DO SO, WE MUST NAVIGATE INNUMERABLE MISFORTUNES, DREAMS, DISAPPOINTMENTS, LOVES, HEARTBREAKS, EMPLOYMENT, UNEMPLOYMENT...
CINE
859
WE BUILD BRIDGES AND CATWALKS TO TRY TO GET TO THE OTHER SIDE.
AND ONCE WE FINALLY MAKE IT, WE REALIZE THAT HAPPINESS IS NO LONGER THERE.
Musical Maria y Yo
BAR
IT HAS MOVED TO A NEW SIDEWALK, FLANKED BY ANOTHER BUSY AVENUE, FULL OF DANGEROUS VEHICLES THAT BLOCK OUR WAY.
SO WE BLOW UP BIG BALLOONS, TURN OURSELVES INTO HUMAN CANNONBALLS... ALL TO CROSS THAT NEW AVENUE.
DONT WALK

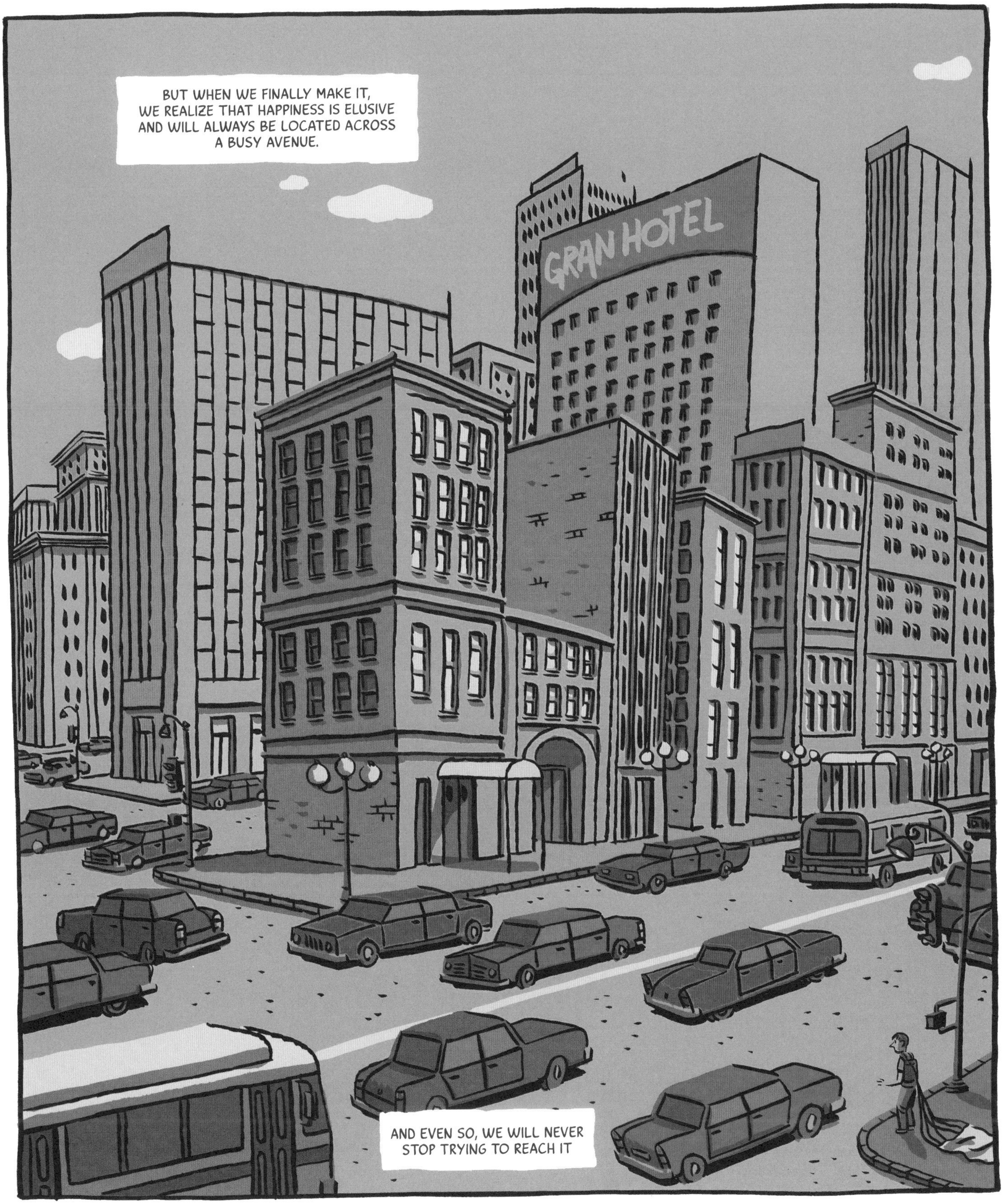
BUT WHEN WE FINALLY MAKE IT, WE REALIZE THAT HAPPINESS IS ELUSIVE AND WILL ALWAYS BE LOCATED ACROSS A BUSY AVENUE.
GRAN HOTEL
AND EVEN SO, WE WILL NEVER STOP TRYING TO REACH IT

III

STICKY DEBT

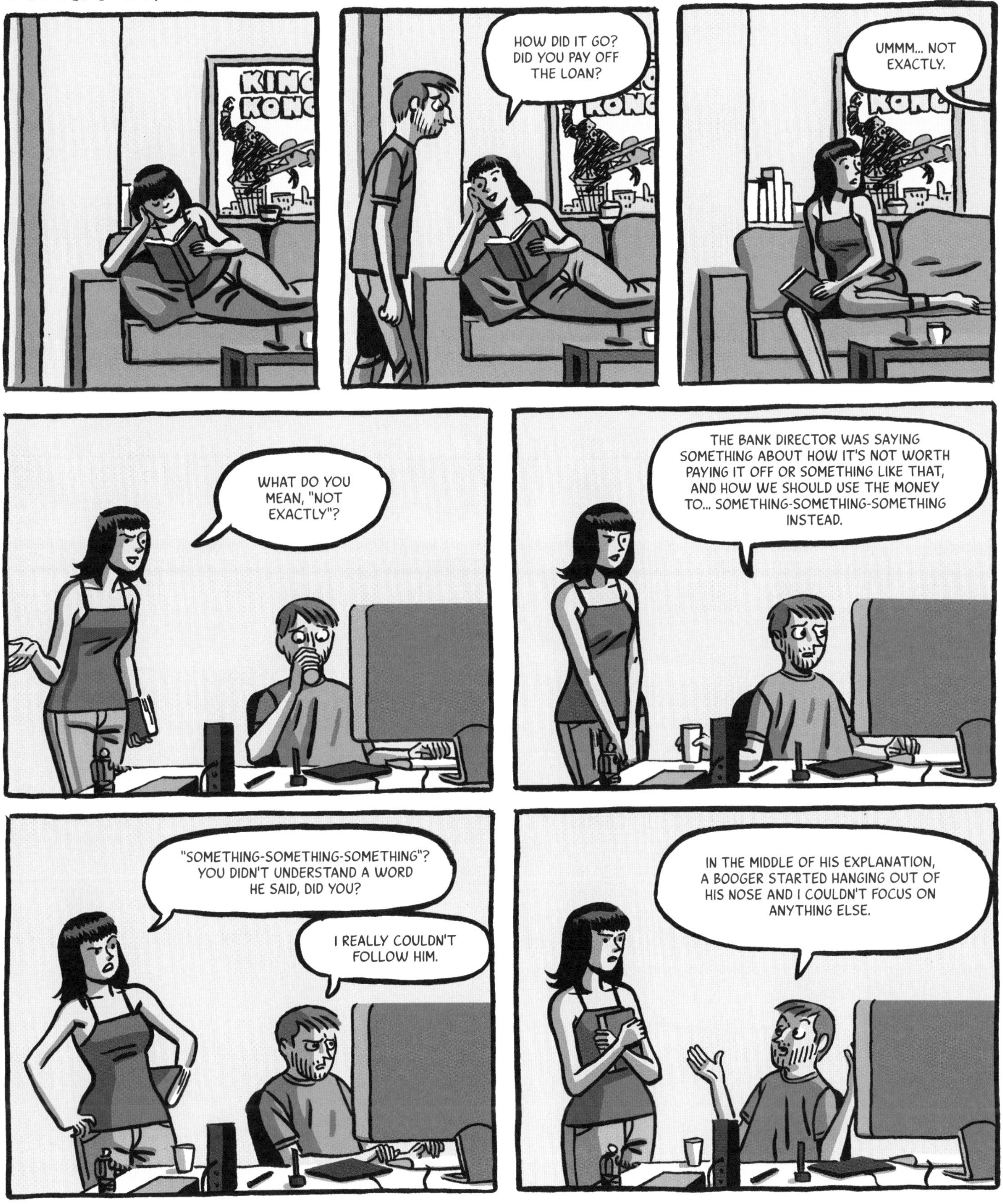
KING KONG
HOW DID IT GO? DID YOU PAY OFF THE LOAN?
UMMM... NOT EXACTLY.
WHAT DO YOU MEAN, "NOT EXACTLY"?
THE BANK DIRECTOR WAS SAYING SOMETHING ABOUT HOW IT'S NOT WORTH PAYING IT OFF OR SOMETHING LIKE THAT, AND HOW WE SHOULD USE THE MONEY TO... SOMETHING-SOMETHING-SOMETHING INSTEAD.
"SOMETHING-SOMETHING-SOMETHING"? YOU DIDN'T UNDERSTAND A WORD HE SAID, DID YOU?
I REALLY COULDN'T FOLLOW HIM.
IN THE MIDDLE OF HIS EXPLANATION, A BOOGER STARTED HANGING OUT OF HIS NOSE AND I COULDN'T FOCUS ON ANYTHING ELSE.

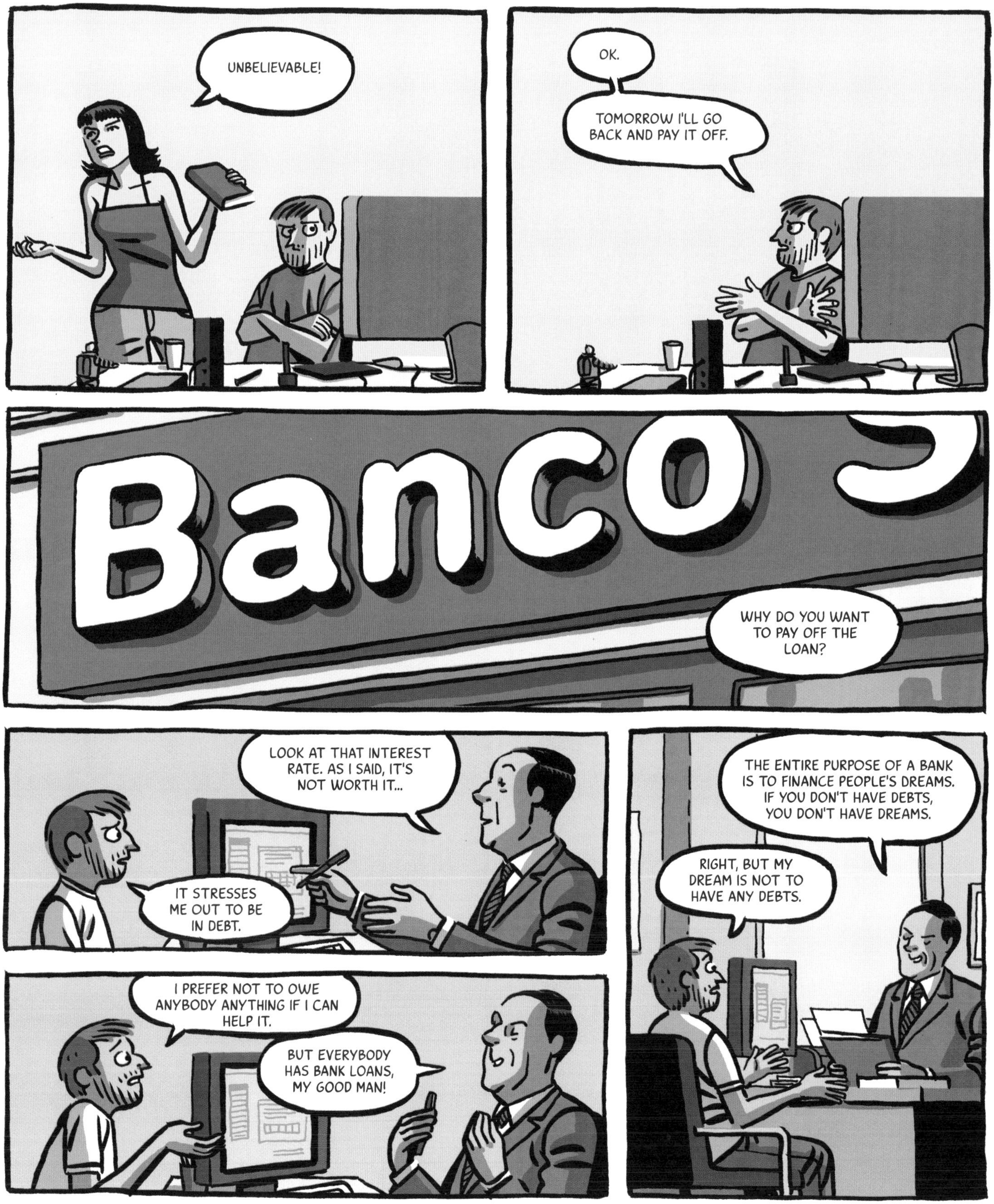
UNBELIEVABLE!
OK.
TOMORROW I'LL GO BACK AND PAY IT OFF.
Banco
WHY DO YOU WANT TO PAY OFF THE LOAN?
LOOK AT THAT INTEREST RATE. AS I SAID, IT'S NOT WORTH IT...
IT STRESSES ME OUT TO BE IN DEBT.
THE ENTIRE PURPOSE OF A BANK IS TO FINANCE PEOPLE'S DREAMS. IF YOU DON'T HAVE DEBTS, YOU DON'T HAVE DREAMS.
RIGHT, BUT MY DREAM IS NOT TO HAVE ANY DEBTS.
I PREFER NOT TO OWE ANYBODY ANYTHING IF I CAN HELP IT.
BUT EVERYBODY HAS BANK LOANS, MY GOOD MAN!

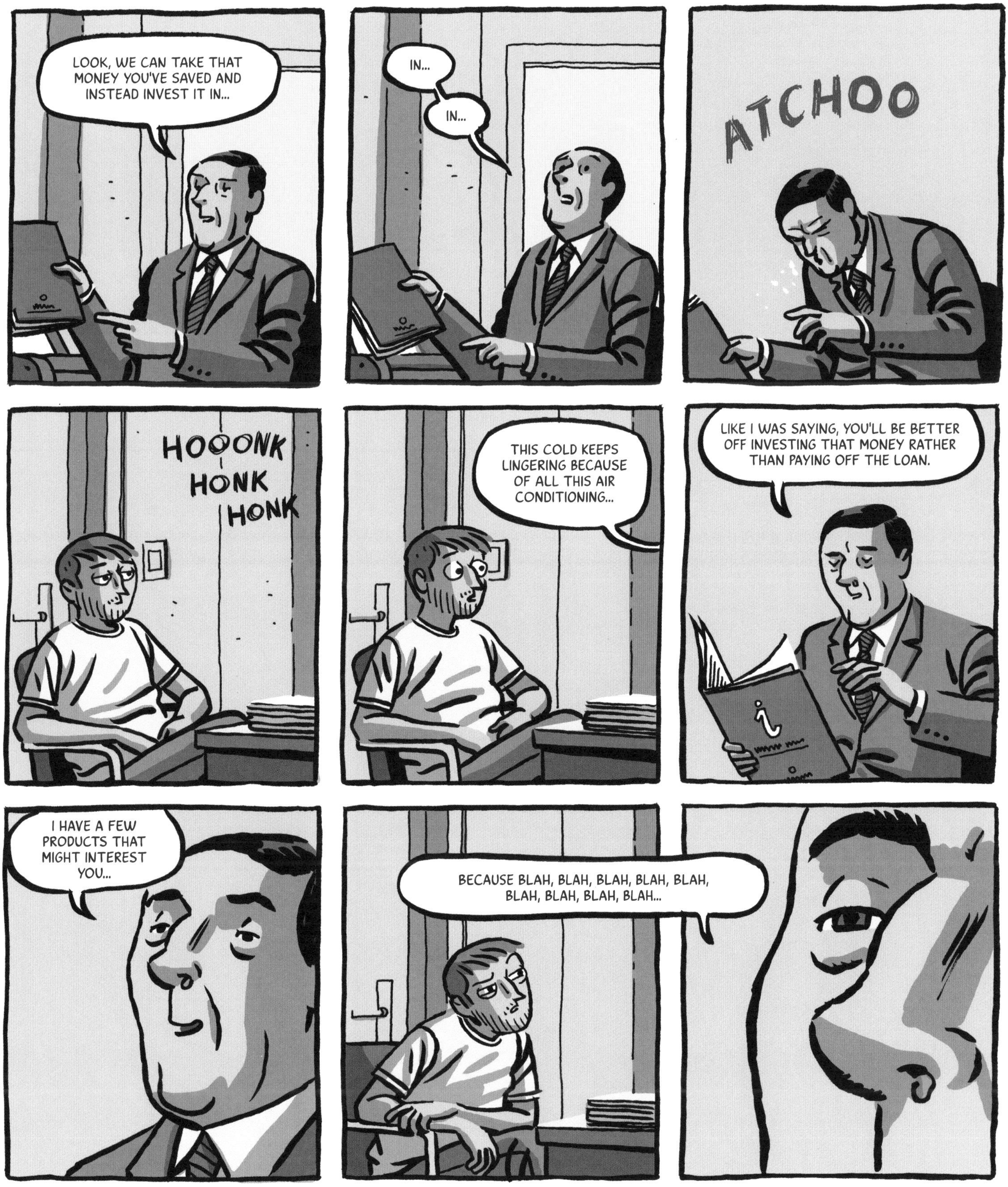
LOOK, WE CAN TAKE THAT MONEY YOU'VE SAVED AND INSTEAD INVEST IT IN...
IN...
IN...
ATCHOO
HOOOONK
HONK
HONK
THIS COLD KEEPS LINGERING BECAUSE OF ALL THIS AIR CONDITIONING...
LIKE I WAS SAYING, YOU'LL BE BETTER OFF INVESTING THAT MONEY RATHER THAN PAYING OFF THE LOAN.
I HAVE A FEW PRODUCTS THAT MIGHT INTEREST YOU...
BECAUSE BLAH, BLAH, BLAH, BLAH, BLAH, BLAH, BLAH, BLAH, BLAH, BLAH...

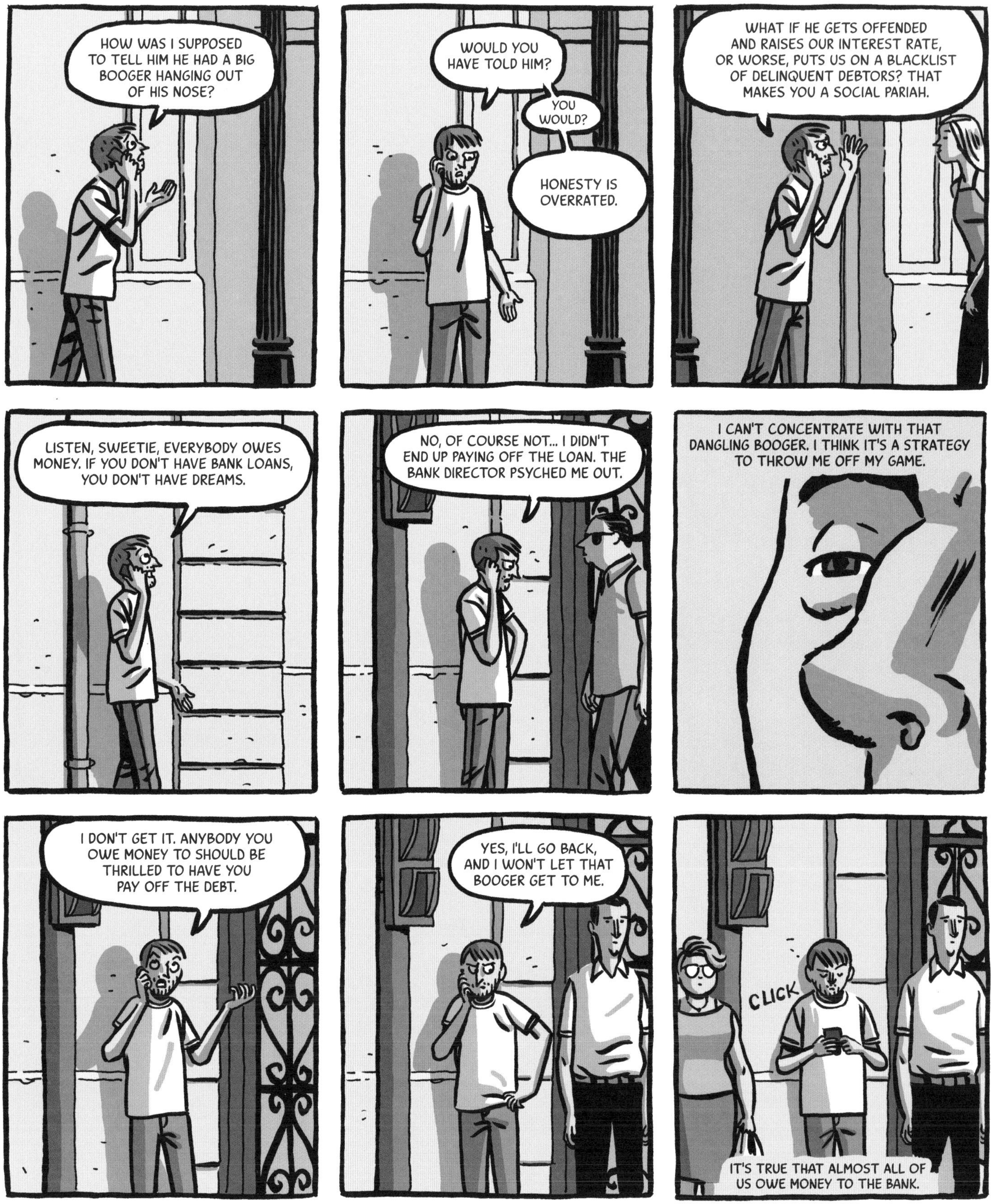
HOW WAS I SUPPOSED TO TELL HIM HE HAD A BIG BOOGER HANGING OUT OF HIS NOSE?
WOULD YOU HAVE TOLD HIM?
YOU WOULD?
HONESTY IS OVERRATED.
WHAT IF HE GETS OFFENDED AND RAISES OUR INTEREST RATE, OR WORSE, PUTS US ON A BLACKLIST OF DELINQUENT DEBTORS? THAT MAKES YOU A SOCIAL PARIAH.
LISTEN, SWEETIE, EVERYBODY OWES MONEY. IF YOU DON'T HAVE BANK LOANS, YOU DON'T HAVE DREAMS.
NO, OF COURSE NOT... I DIDN'T END UP PAYING OFF THE LOAN. THE BANK DIRECTOR PSYCHED ME OUT.
I CAN'T CONCENTRATE WITH THAT DANGLING BOOGER. I THINK IT'S A STRATEGY TO THROW ME OFF MY GAME.
I DON'T GET IT. ANYBODY YOU OWE MONEY TO SHOULD BE THRILLED TO HAVE YOU PAY OFF THE DEBT.
YES, I'LL GO BACK, AND I WON'T LET THAT BOOGER GET TO ME.
CLICK
IT'S TRUE THAT ALMOST ALL OF US OWE MONEY TO THE BANK.

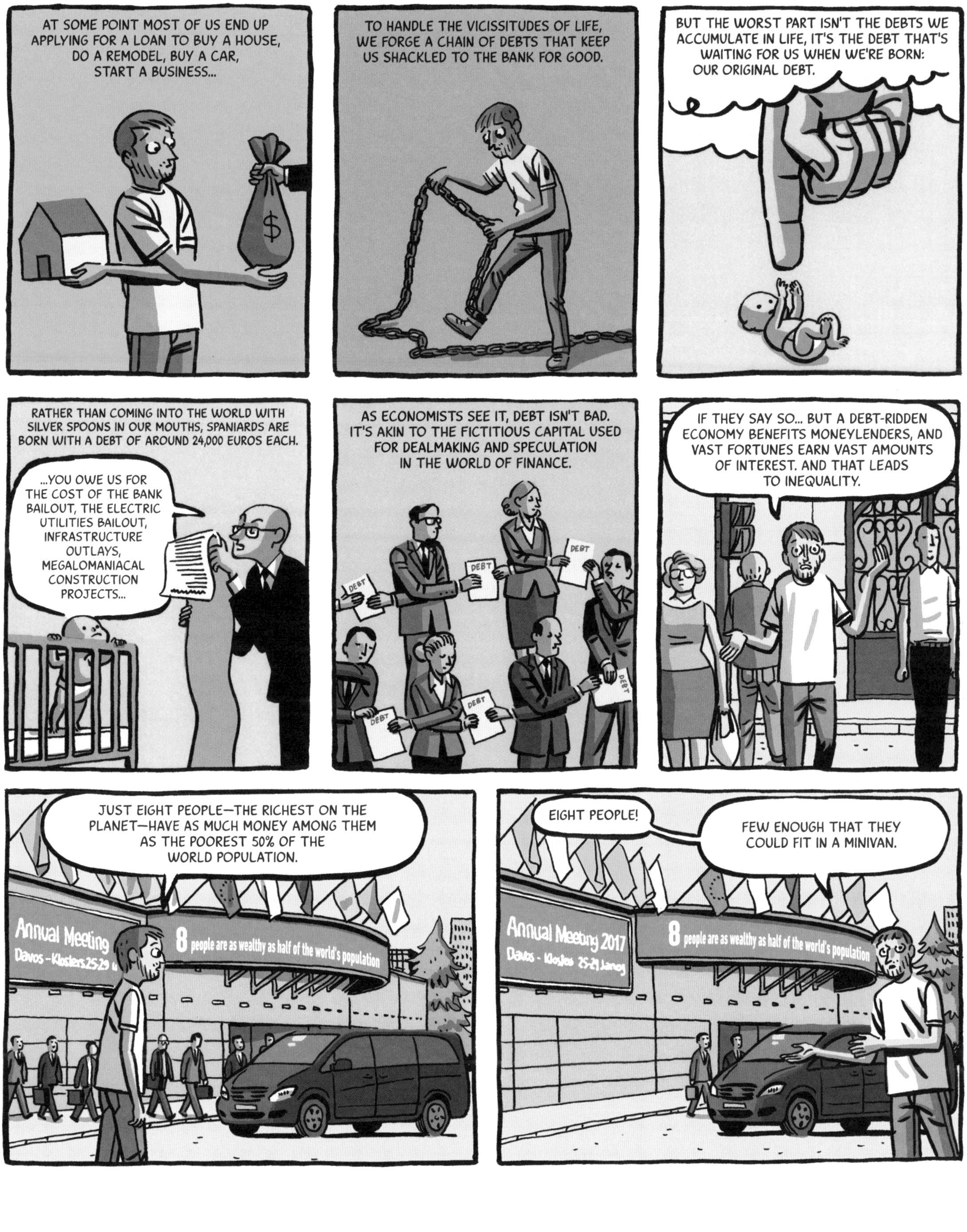
AT SOME POINT MOST OF US END UP APPLYING FOR A LOAN TO BUY A HOUSE, DO A REMODEL, BUY A CAR, START A BUSINESS...
$
TO HANDLE THE VICISSITUDES OF LIFE, WE FORGE A CHAIN OF DEBTS THAT KEEP US SHACKLED TO THE BANK FOR GOOD.
BUT THE WORST PART ISN'T THE DEBTS WE ACCUMULATE IN LIFE, IT'S THE DEBT THAT'S WAITING FOR US WHEN WE'RE BORN: OUR ORIGINAL DEBT.
RATHER THAN COMING INTO THE WORLD WITH SILVER SPOONS IN OUR MOUTHS, SPANIARDS ARE BORN WITH A DEBT OF AROUND 24,000 EUROS EACH.
...YOU OWE US FOR THE COST OF THE BANK BAILOUT, THE ELECTRIC UTILITIES BAILOUT, INFRASTRUCTURE OUTLAYS, MEGALOMANIACAL CONSTRUCTION PROJECTS...
AS ECONOMISTS SEE IT, DEBT ISN'T BAD. IT'S AKIN TO THE FICTITIOUS CAPITAL USED FOR DEALMAKING AND SPECULATION IN THE WORLD OF FINANCE.
DEBT
DEBT
DEBT
DEBT
DEBT
DEBT
IF THEY SAY SO... BUT A DEBT-RIDDEN ECONOMY BENEFITS MONEYLENDERS, AND VAST FORTUNES EARN VAST AMOUNTS OF INTEREST. AND THAT LEADS TO INEQUALITY.
JUST EIGHT PEOPLE—THE RICHEST ON THE PLANET—HAVE AS MUCH MONEY AMONG THEM AS THE POOREST 50% OF THE WORLD POPULATION.
Annual Meeting
8 people are as wealthy as half of the world's population
EIGHT PEOPLE!
FEW ENOUGH THAT THEY COULD FIT IN A MINIVAN.
Annual Meeting 2017
8 people are as wealthy as half of the world's population

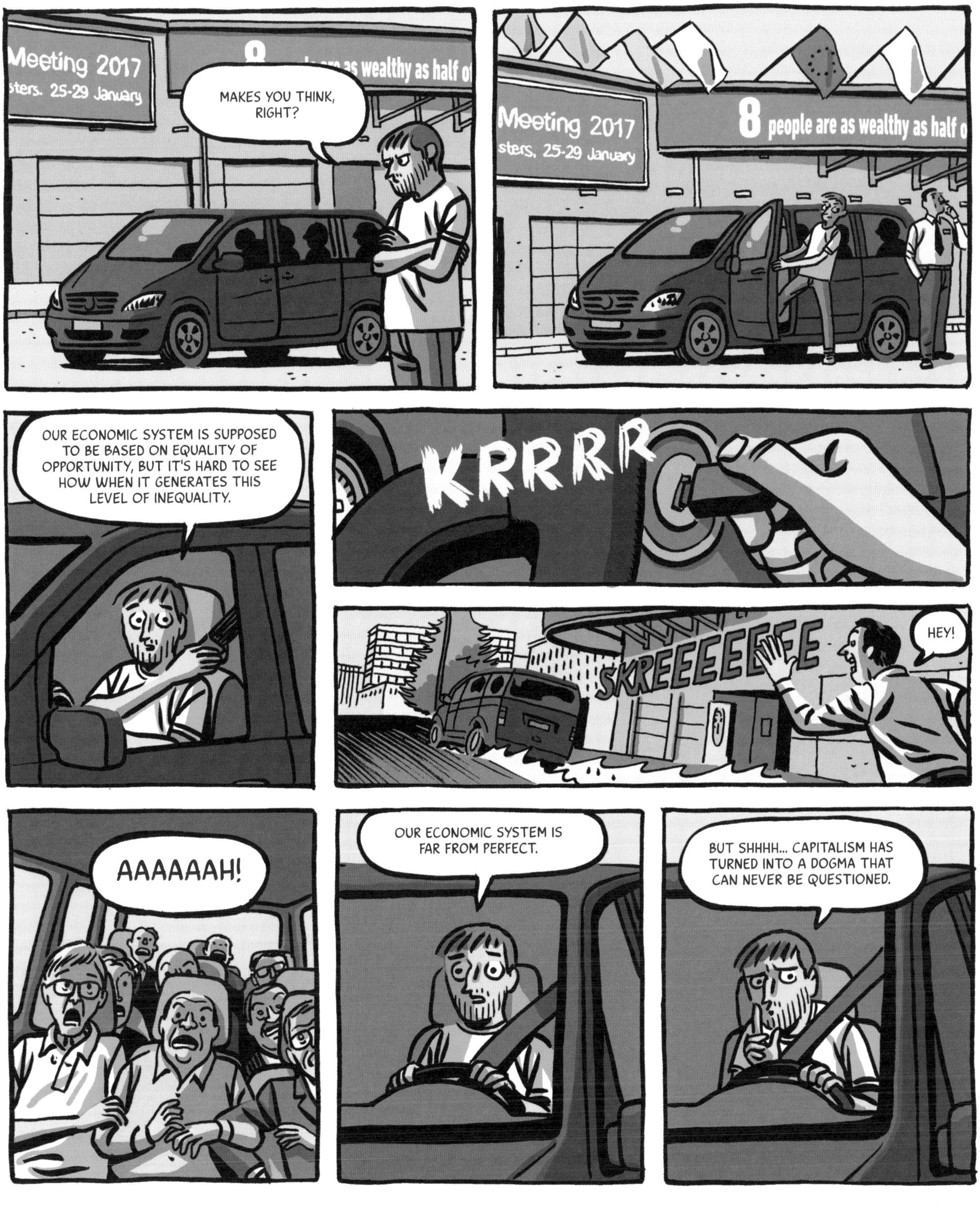
Meeting 2017
sters. 25-29 January
MAKES YOU THINK, RIGHT?
Meeting 2017
sters. 25-29 January
8 people are as wealthy as half o
OUR ECONOMIC SYSTEM IS SUPPOSED TO BE BASED ON EQUALITY OF OPPORTUNITY, BUT IT'S HARD TO SEE HOW WHEN IT GENERATES THIS LEVEL OF INEQUALITY.
KRRRR
SKREEEEEEEE
HEY!
AAAAAAH!
OUR ECONOMIC SYSTEM IS FAR FROM PERFECT.
BUT SHHHH... CAPITALISM HAS TURNED INTO A DOGMA THAT CAN NEVER BE QUESTIONED.

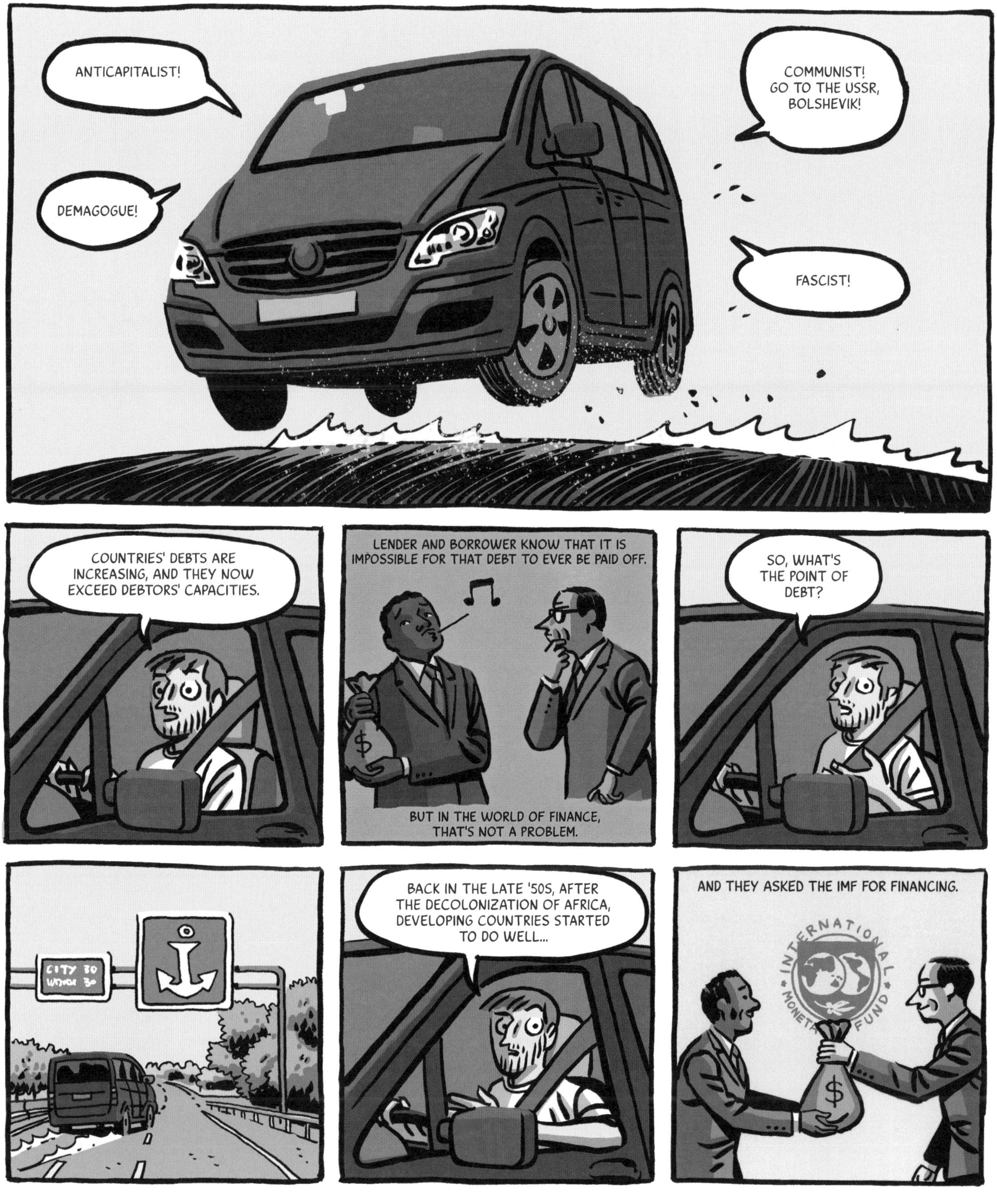
ANTICAPITALIST!
COMMUNIST! GO TO THE USSR, BOLSHEVIK!
DEMAGOGUE!
FASCIST!
COUNTRIES' DEBTS ARE INCREASING, AND THEY NOW EXCEED DEBTORS' CAPACITIES.
LENDER AND BORROWER KNOW THAT IT IS IMPOSSIBLE FOR THAT DEBT TO EVER BE PAID OFF.
BUT IN THE WORLD OF FINANCE, THAT'S NOT A PROBLEM.
SO, WHAT'S THE POINT OF DEBT?
BACK IN THE LATE '50S, AFTER THE DECOLONIZATION OF AFRICA, DEVELOPING COUNTRIES STARTED TO DO WELL...
AND THEY ASKED THE IMF FOR FINANCING.
INTERNATIONAL MONETARY FUND

LOANS WERE GRANTED IN EXCHANGE FOR THEIR ACCEPTING FREE TRADE AND FACILITATING THE ENTRY OF FOREIGN INVESTMENT.

THE CHEAP IMPORTATION OF CONSUMER GOODS BEGAN. FOR EXAMPLE, RICE WAS BROUGHT FROM THE US BECAUSE, THANKS TO SUBSIDIES THERE, IT WAS CHEAPER THAN WHAT LOCAL FARMERS COULD PRODUCE.

CLONK

THAT LED TO THE INDUSTRY'S COLLAPSE. AT THE SAME TIME, LOCAL BUSINESSES THAT WERE DOING WELL WERE SNAPPED UP BY FOREIGN INVESTORS.

AND, OF COURSE, LENDERS MADE SURE TO PLACE AS MANY OBSTACLES AS POSSIBLE IN THESE COUNTRIES' PATH TO SELF-SUFFICIENCY.

DEBT AND FREE TRADE AREN'T BAD IN AND OF THEMSELVES, BUT UNEVEN POWER DYNAMICS HAVE LED TO THE POVERTY AND SUFFERING OF MANY PEOPLE.

THOUGH THEY BENEFIT FROM A SYSTEM THAT FAVORS THE RICH OVER THE POOR, THESE EIGHT PEOPLE AREN'T THE DIRECT CAUSE OF ALL THAT SUFFERING.

BUT IF THEY CAME TOGETHER, THEY COULD WIPE OUT THE DEBT FOR THE ENTIRE CONTINENT OF AFRICA ALL BY THEMSELVES...

...AND STILL HAVE ENOUGH TO LIVE COMFORTABLY FOR THE REST OF THEIR DAYS.

DEBT HAS BECOME A MODERN FORM OF COLONIZATION.

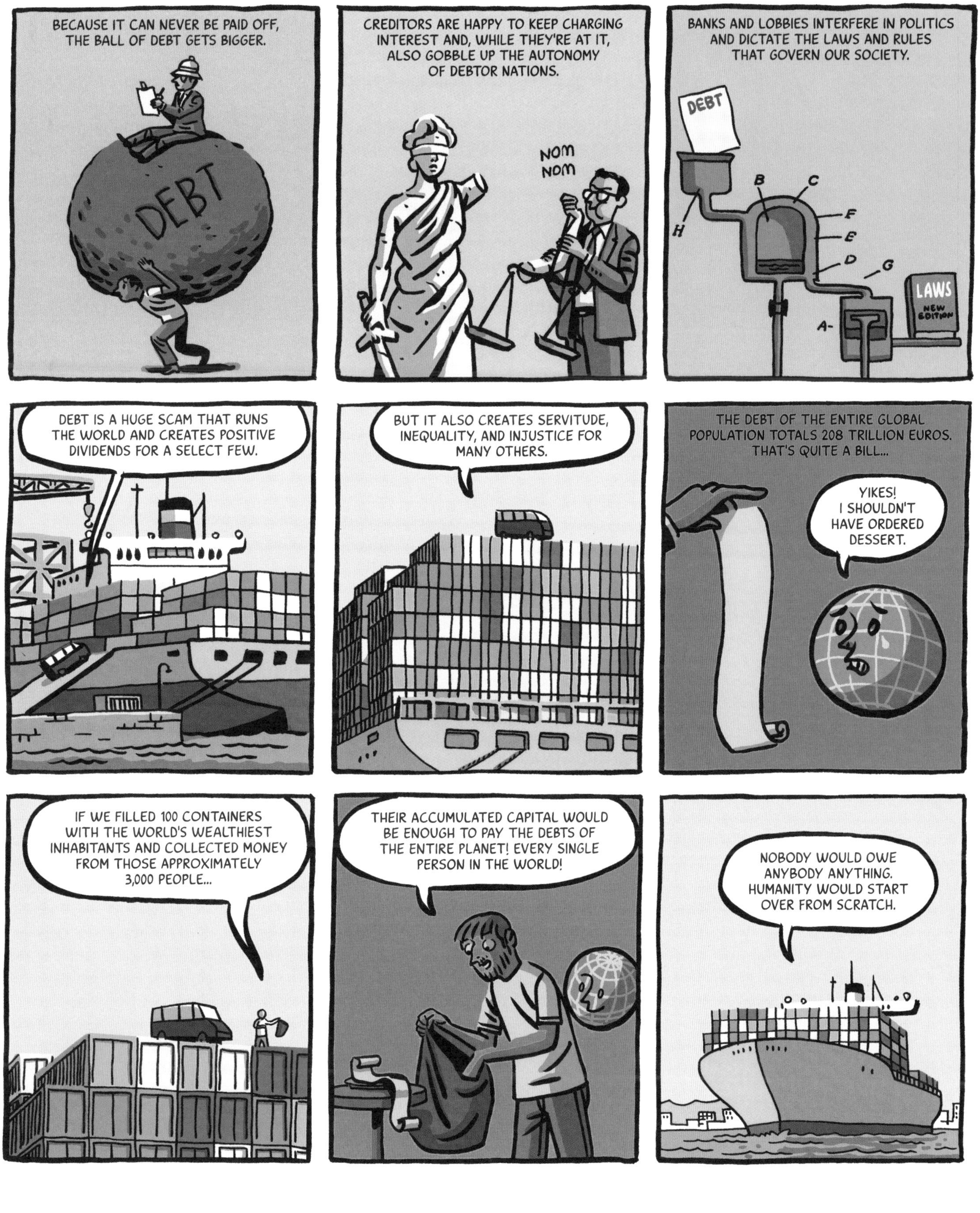
BECAUSE IT CAN NEVER BE PAID OFF, THE BALL OF DEBT GETS BIGGER.
DEBT
CREDITORS ARE HAPPY TO KEEP CHARGING INTEREST AND, WHILE THEY'RE AT IT, ALSO GOBBLE UP THE AUTONOMY OF DEBTOR NATIONS.
NOM NOM
BANKS AND LOBBIES INTERFERE IN POLITICS AND DICTATE THE LAWS AND RULES THAT GOVERN OUR SOCIETY.
DEBT
B
C
H
F
E
D
G
LAWS NEW EDITION
A-
DEBT IS A HUGE SCAM THAT RUNS THE WORLD AND CREATES POSITIVE DIVIDENDS FOR A SELECT FEW.
BUT IT ALSO CREATES SERVITUDE, INEQUALITY, AND INJUSTICE FOR MANY OTHERS.
THE DEBT OF THE ENTIRE GLOBAL POPULATION TOTALS 208 TRILLION EUROS. THAT'S QUITE A BILL...
YIKES! I SHOULDN'T HAVE ORDERED DESSERT.
IF WE FILLED 100 CONTAINERS WITH THE WORLD'S WEALTHIEST INHABITANTS AND COLLECTED MONEY FROM THOSE APPROXIMATELY 3,000 PEOPLE...
THEIR ACCUMULATED CAPITAL WOULD BE ENOUGH TO PAY THE DEBTS OF THE ENTIRE PLANET! EVERY SINGLE PERSON IN THE WORLD!
NOBODY WOULD OWE ANYBODY ANYTHING. HUMANITY WOULD START OVER FROM SCRATCH.

THANK YOU FOR YOUR GENEROSITY. NOW GO AND ENJOY THIS "PARADISE."
WHAT WOULD THAT NEW, DEBT-FREE WORLD BE LIKE?
IT WOULD GIVE US THE CHANCE TO PUT OTHER KINDS OF ECONOMIES INTO PRACTICE.
CREATING A SUSTAINABLE, MORE HUMANE, PEOPLE-CENTERED CAPITALISM IN WHICH SHORT-TERM PROFITS ARE NOT THE SOLE OBJECTIVE.
1 EURO
A GREEN ECONOMY, WITH LOCAL COMMERCE AND AGRICULTURE...
OR MAYBE A MORE RADICAL MODEL, A WORLD FULL OF NONHIERARCHICAL COLLECTIVES...
IN ANY CASE, IT WOULD BE DIFFERENT FROM THE ONE WE'VE BEEN LIVING IN, BECAUSE OUR SYSTEM IS UNSUSTAINABLE IN THE LONG TERM.

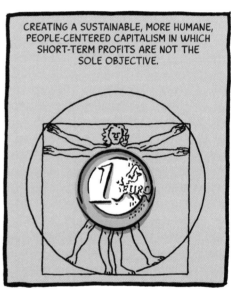

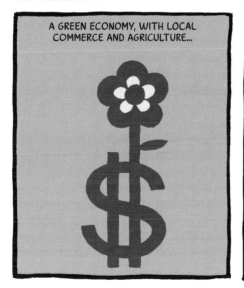

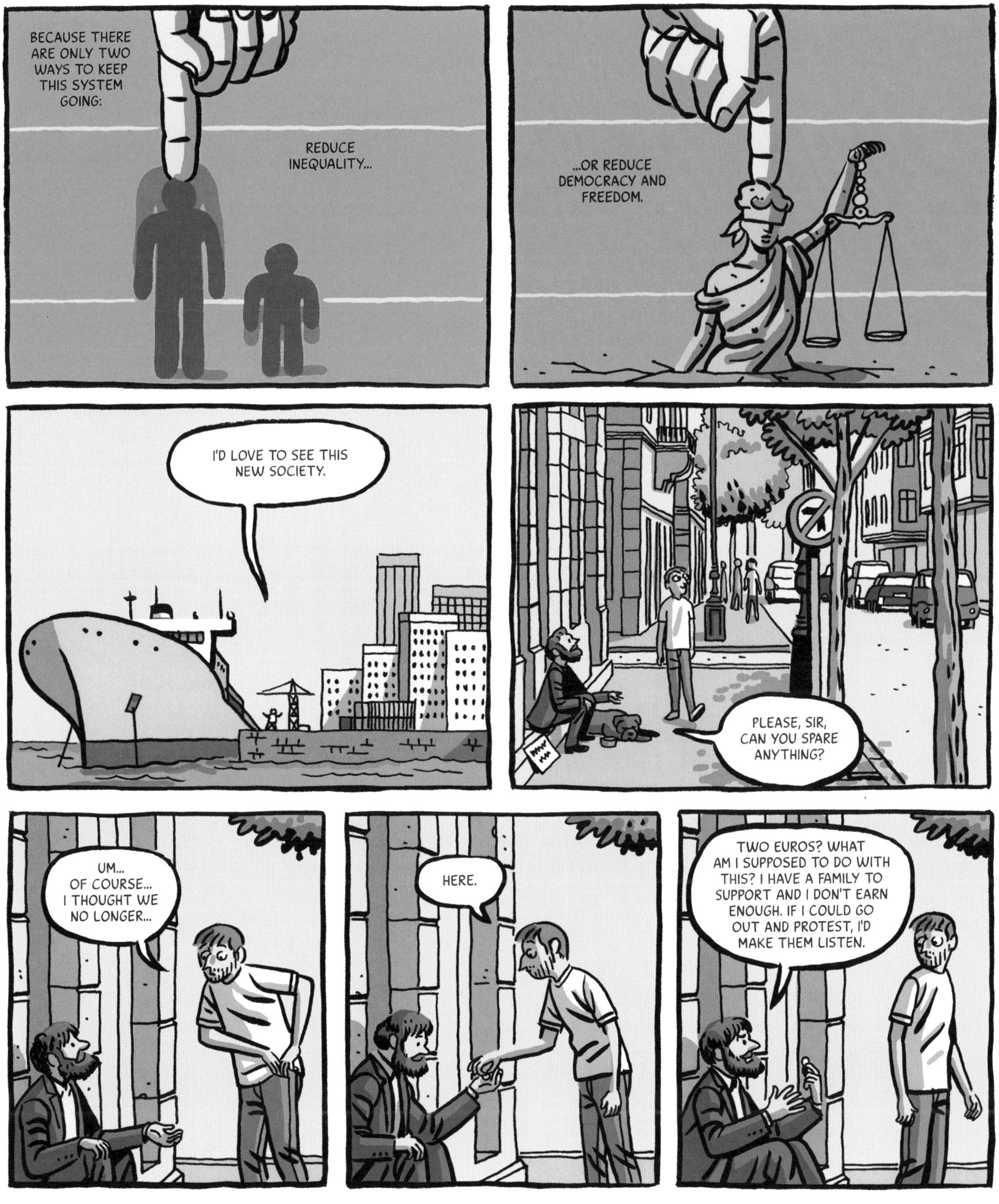
BECAUSE THERE ARE ONLY TWO WAYS TO KEEP THIS SYSTEM GOING:
REDUCE INEQUALITY...
...OR REDUCE DEMOCRACY AND FREEDOM.
I'D LOVE TO SEE THIS NEW SOCIETY.
PLEASE, SIR, CAN YOU SPARE ANYTHING?
UM... OF COURSE... I THOUGHT WE NO LONGER...
HERE.
TWO EUROS? WHAT AM I SUPPOSED TO DO WITH THIS? I HAVE A FAMILY TO SUPPORT AND I DON'T EARN ENOUGH. IF I COULD GO OUT AND PROTEST, I'D MAKE THEM LISTEN.

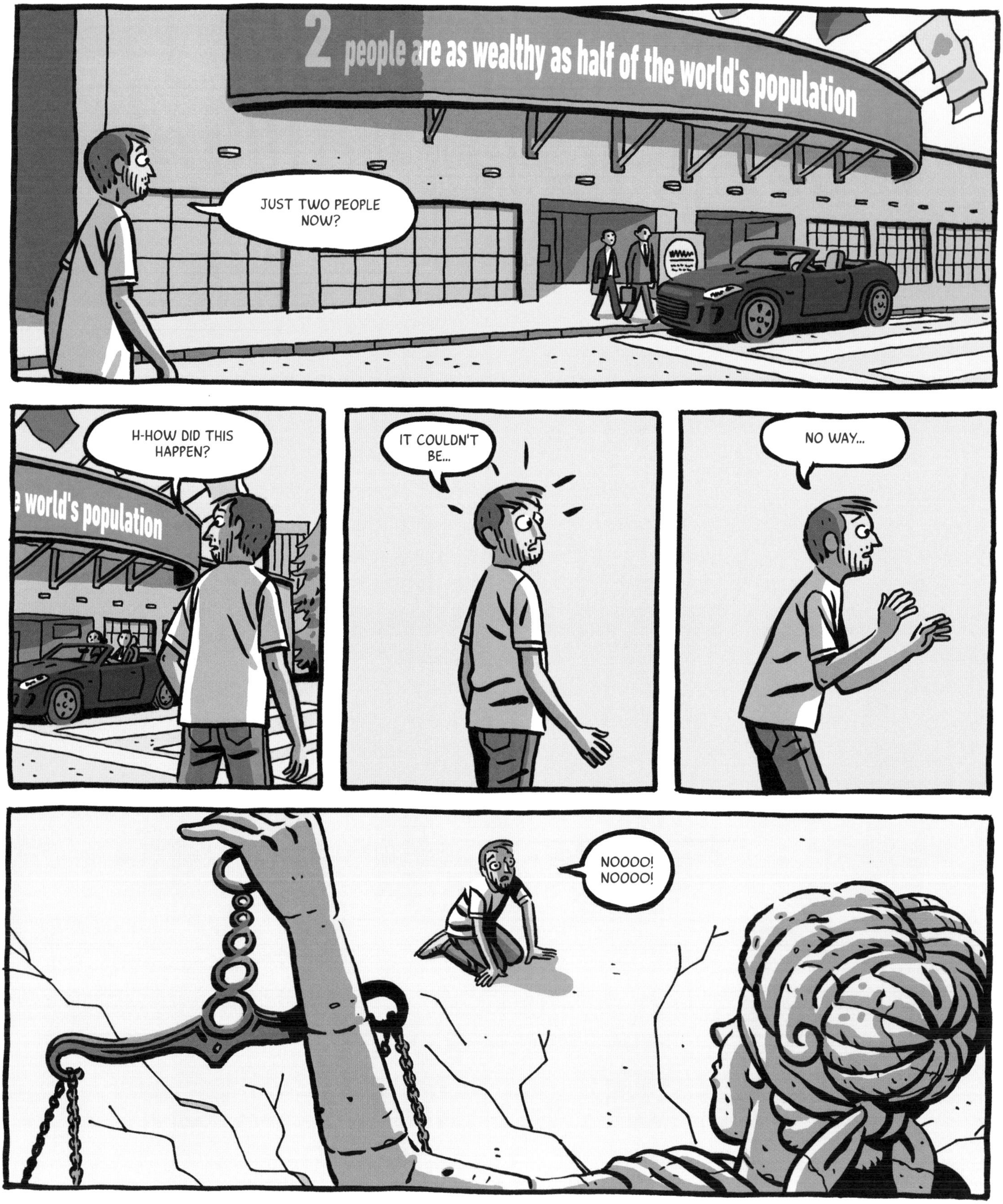
2 people are as wealthy as half of the world's population
JUST TWO PEOPLE NOW?
H-HOW DID THIS HAPPEN?
world's population
IT COULDN'T BE...
NO WAY...
NOOOO! NOOOO!

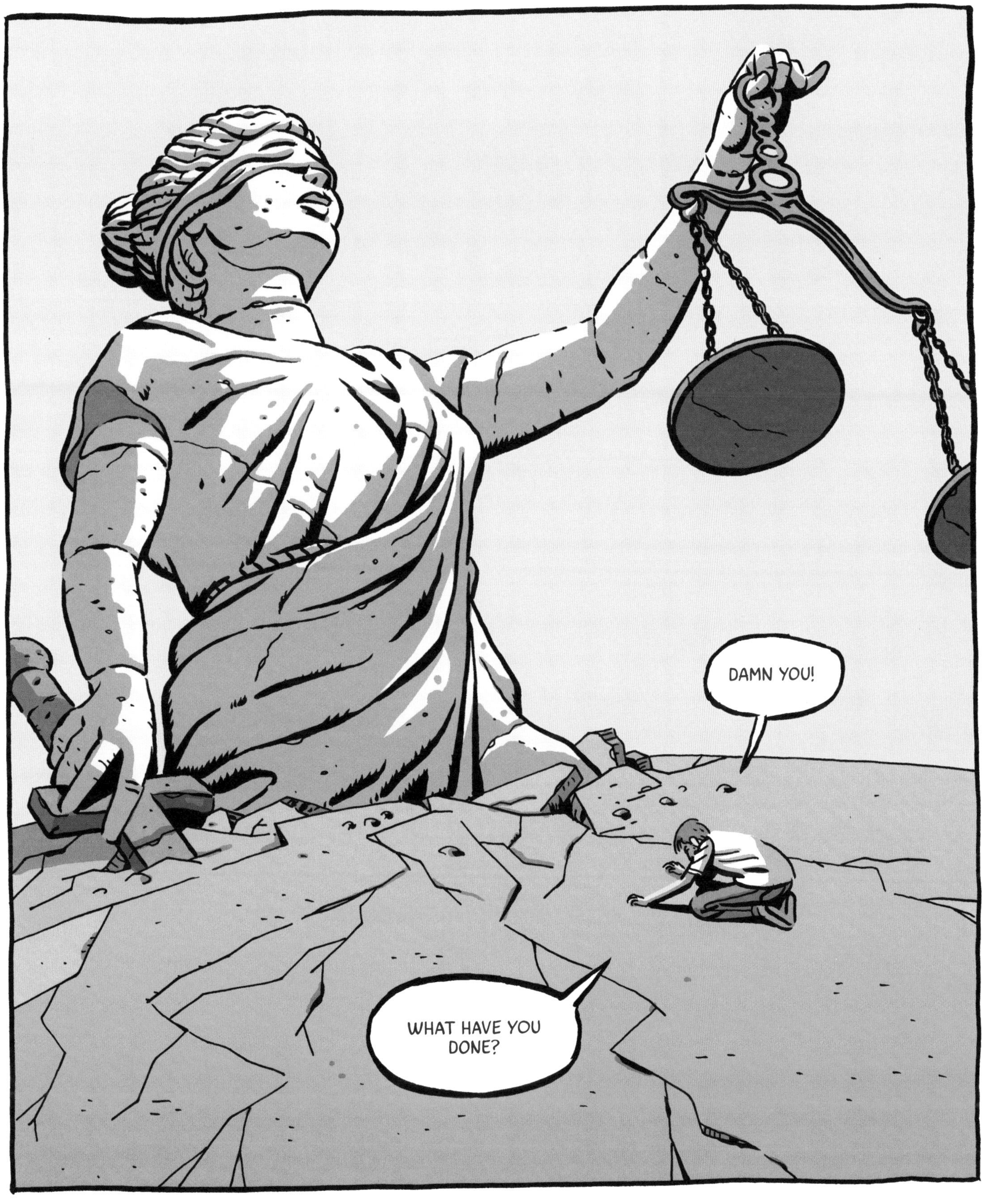
DAMN YOU!
WHAT HAVE YOU DONE?

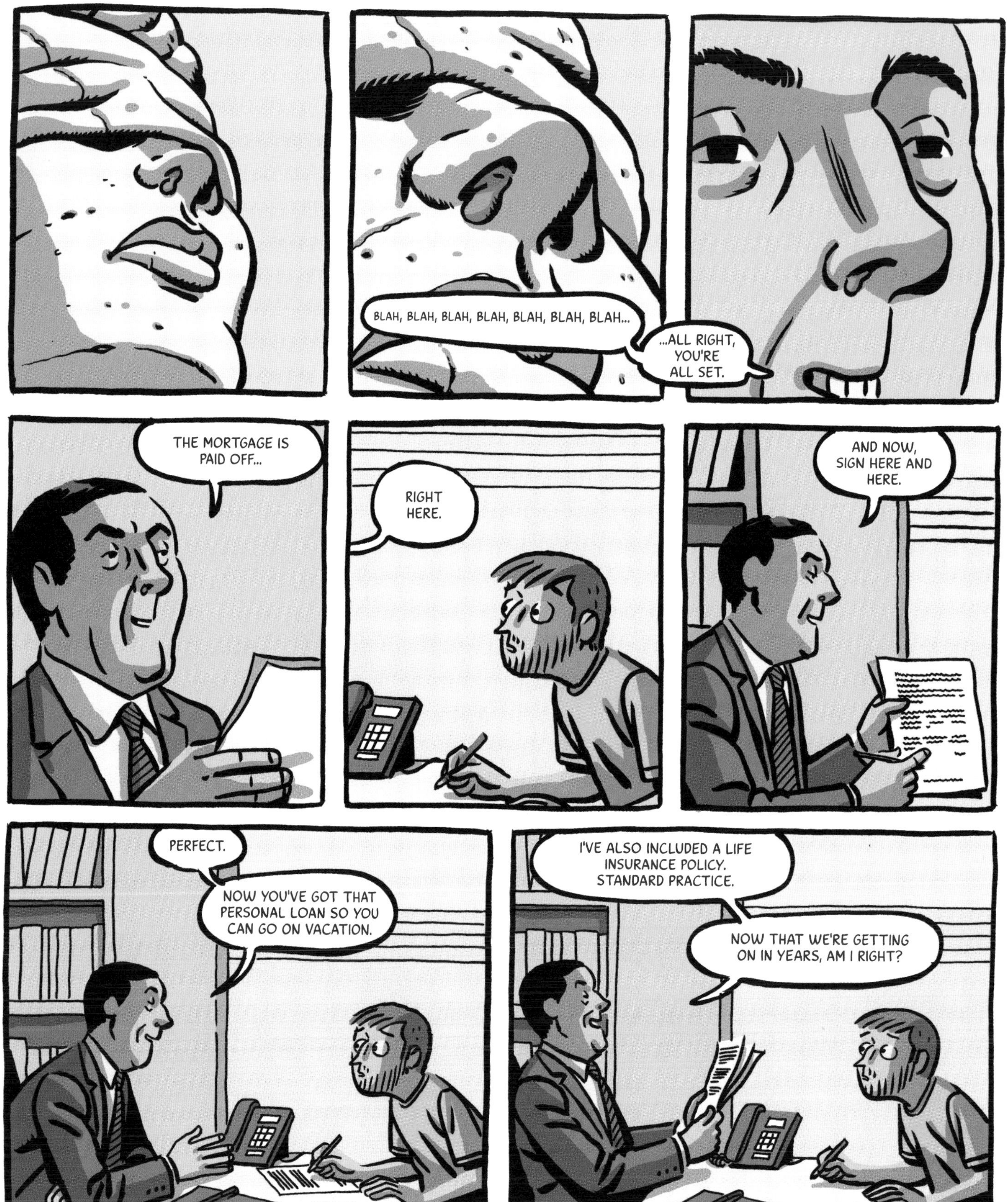

BLAH, BLAH, BLAH, BLAH, BLAH, BLAH, BLAH...
...ALL RIGHT, YOU'RE ALL SET.
THE MORTGAGE IS PAID OFF...
RIGHT HERE.
AND NOW, SIGN HERE AND HERE.
PERFECT.
NOW YOU'VE GOT THAT PERSONAL LOAN SO YOU CAN GO ON VACATION.
I'VE ALSO INCLUDED A LIFE INSURANCE POLICY. STANDARD PRACTICE.
NOW THAT WE'RE GETTING ON IN YEARS, AM I RIGHT?

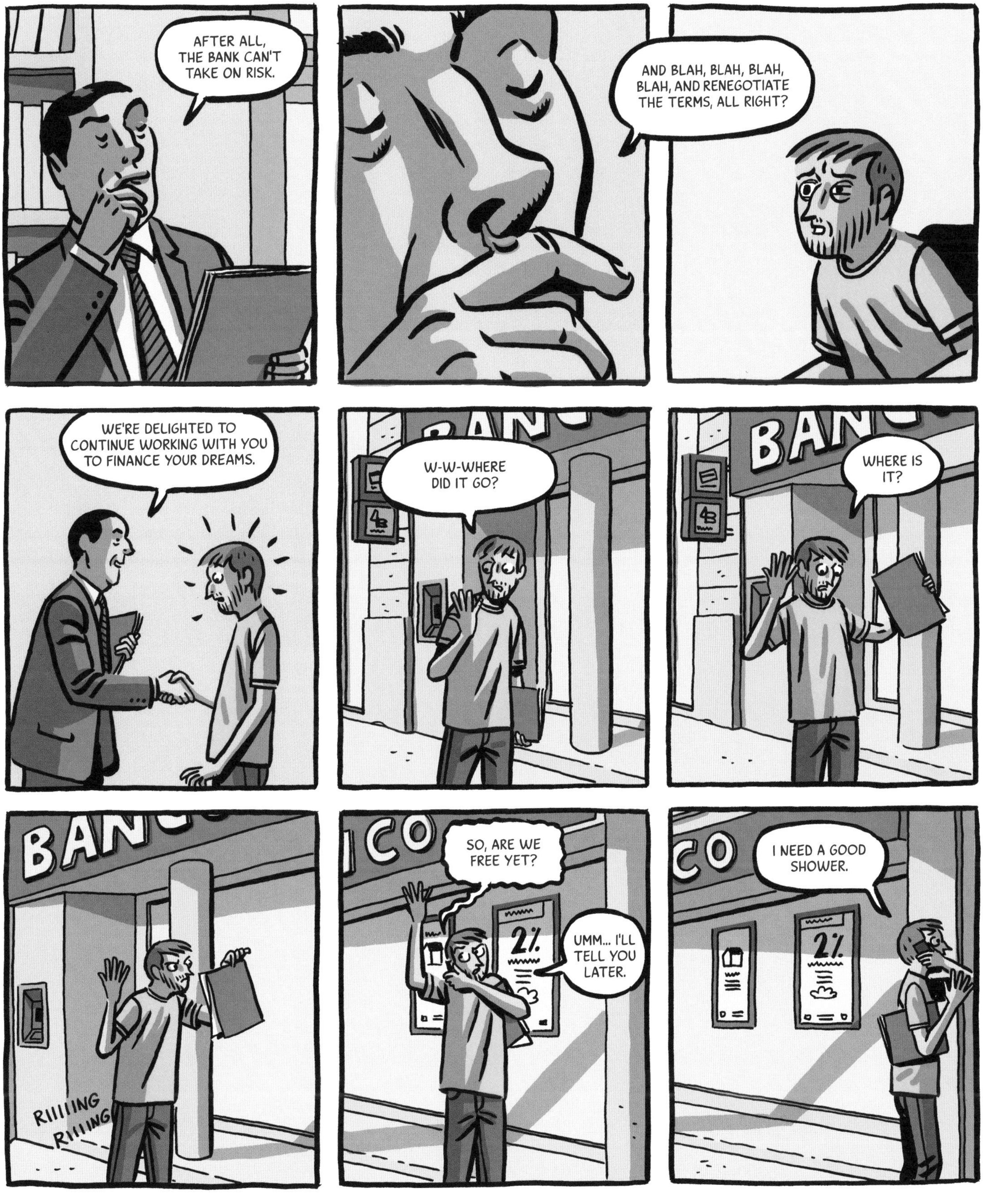
AFTER ALL, THE BANK CAN'T TAKE ON RISK.
AND BLAH, BLAH, BLAH, BLAH, AND RENEGOTIATE THE TERMS, ALL RIGHT?
WE'RE DELIGHTED TO CONTINUE WORKING WITH YOU TO FINANCE YOUR DREAMS.
BAN
W-W-WHERE DID IT GO?
BAN
WHERE IS IT?
BAN
RIIIING RIIIING
CO
SO, ARE WE FREE YET?
2%
UMM... I'LL TELL YOU LATER.
CO
I NEED A GOOD SHOWER.
2%

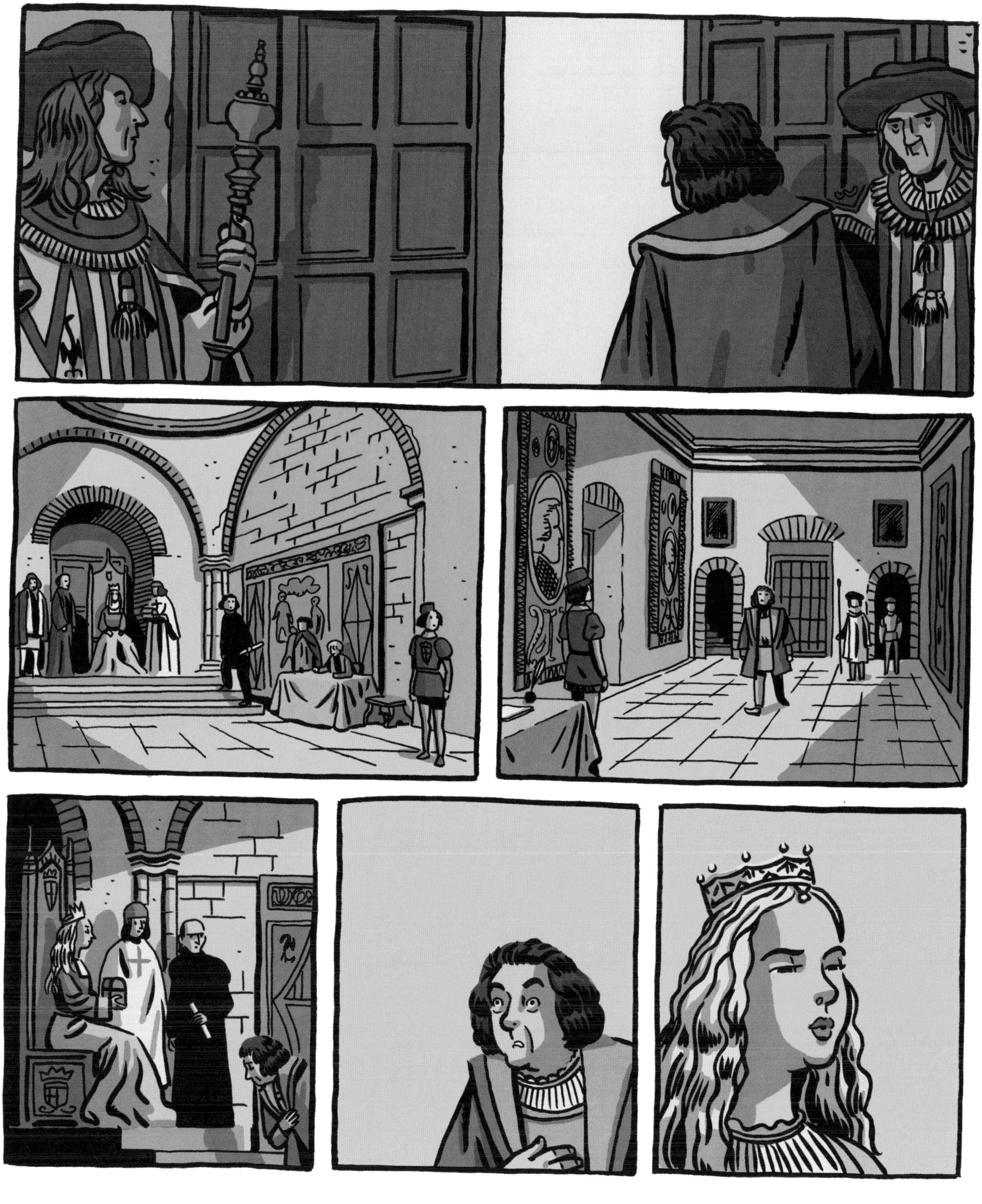

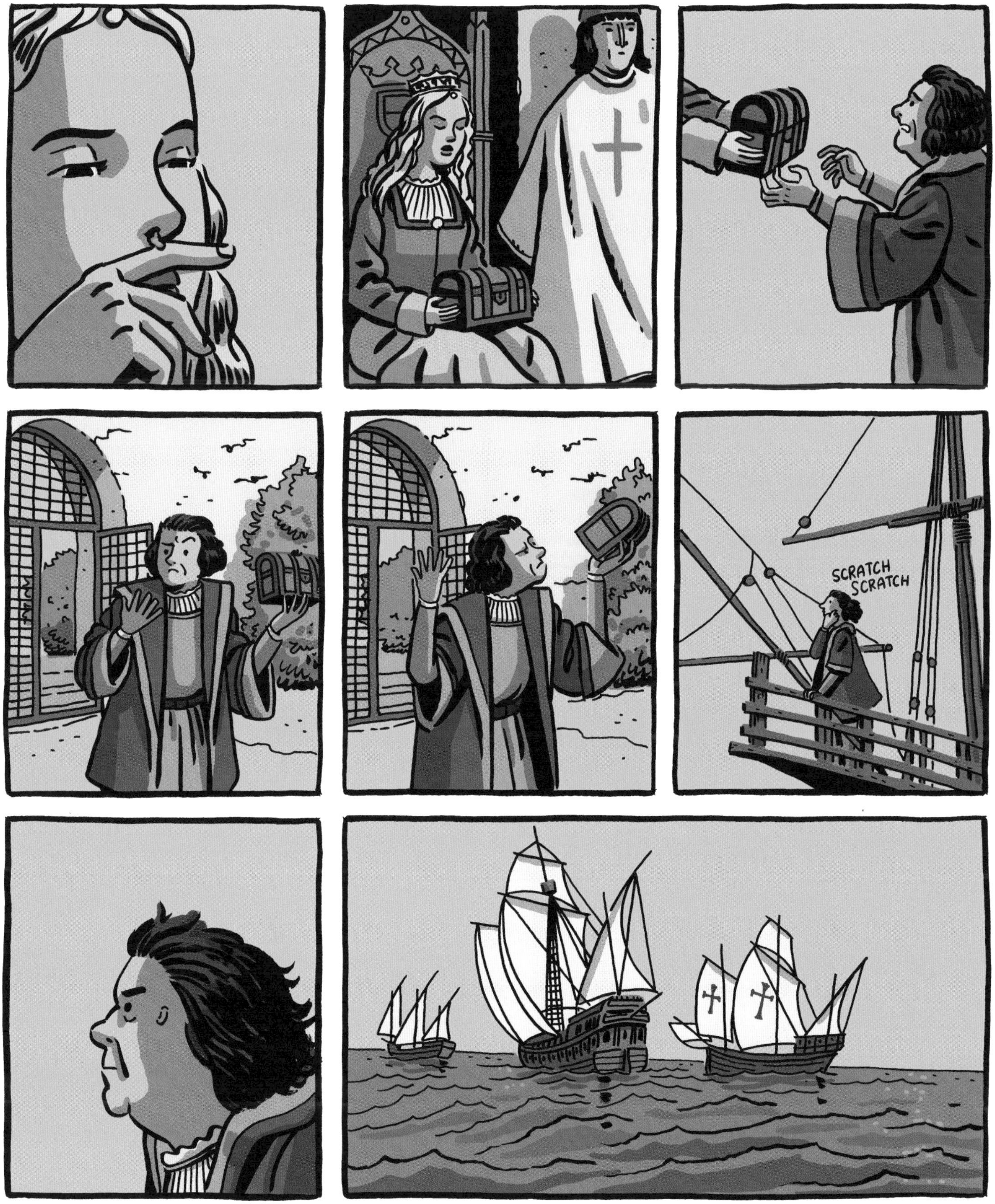
SCRATCH
SCRATCH

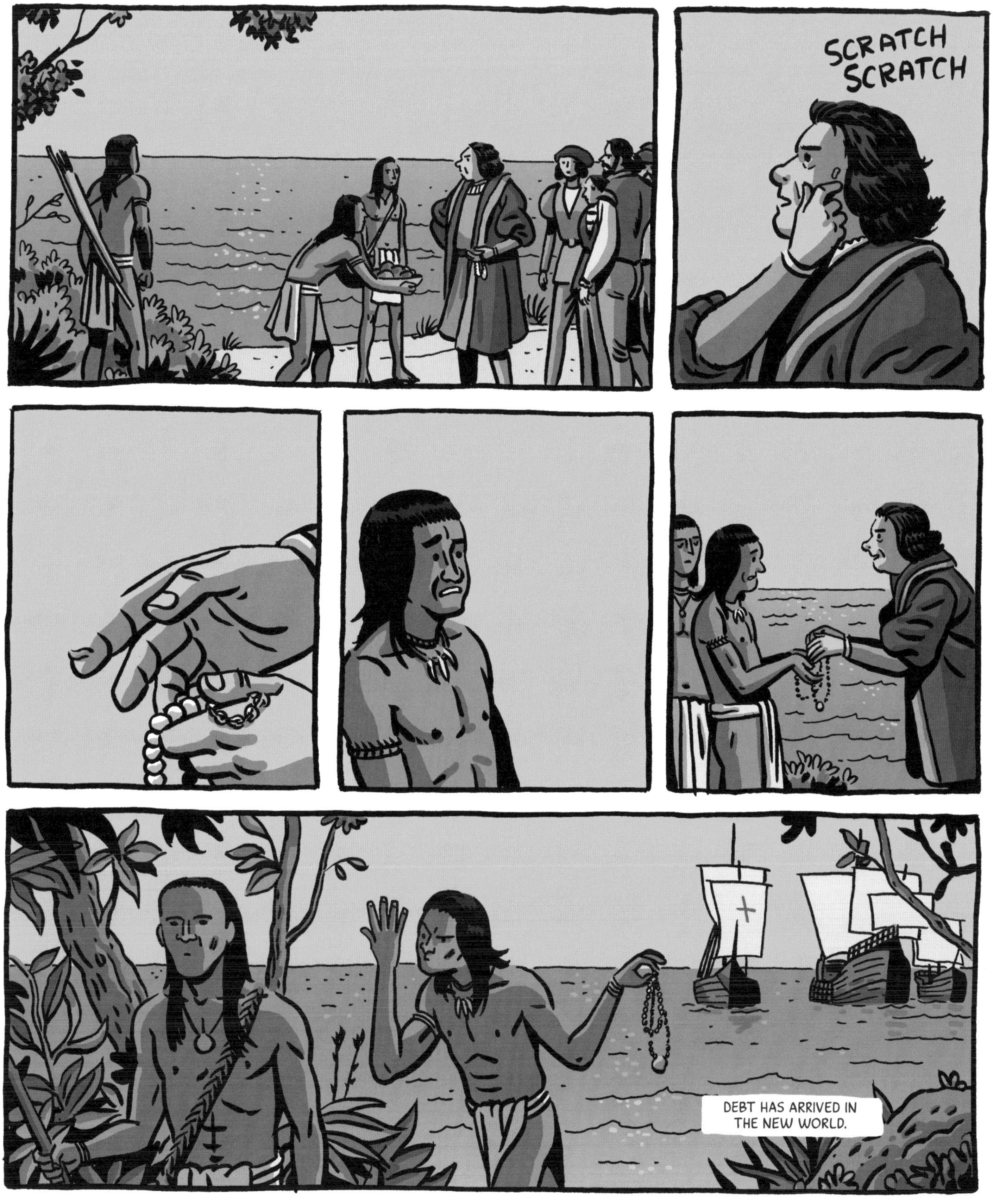
SCRATCH
SCRATCH
DEBT HAS ARRIVED IN
THE NEW WORLD.

REVOLT OF THE MACHINES

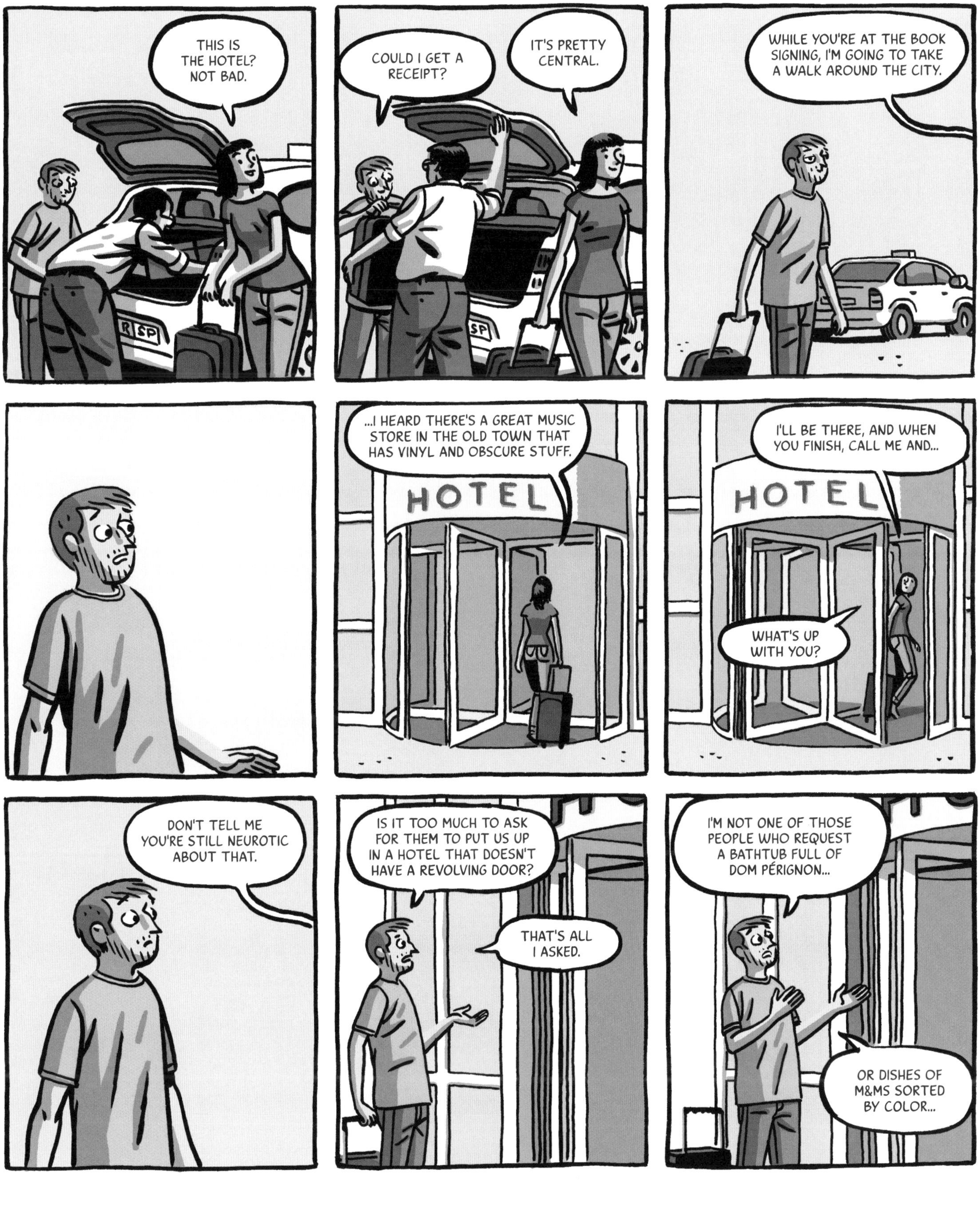
THIS IS THE HOTEL? NOT BAD.
COULD I GET A RECEIPT?
IT'S PRETTY CENTRAL.
WHILE YOU'RE AT THE BOOK SIGNING, I'M GOING TO TAKE A WALK AROUND THE CITY.
...I HEARD THERE'S A GREAT MUSIC STORE IN THE OLD TOWN THAT HAS VINYL AND OBSCURE STUFF.
HOTEL
I'LL BE THERE, AND WHEN YOU FINISH, CALL ME AND...
HOTEL
WHAT'S UP WITH YOU?
DON'T TELL ME YOU'RE STILL NEUROTIC ABOUT THAT.
IS IT TOO MUCH TO ASK FOR THEM TO PUT US UP IN A HOTEL THAT DOESN'T HAVE A REVOLVING DOOR?
THAT'S ALL I ASKED.
I'M NOT ONE OF THOSE PEOPLE WHO REQUEST A BATHTUB FULL OF DOM PÉRIGNON...
OR DISHES OF M&MS SORTED BY COLOR...

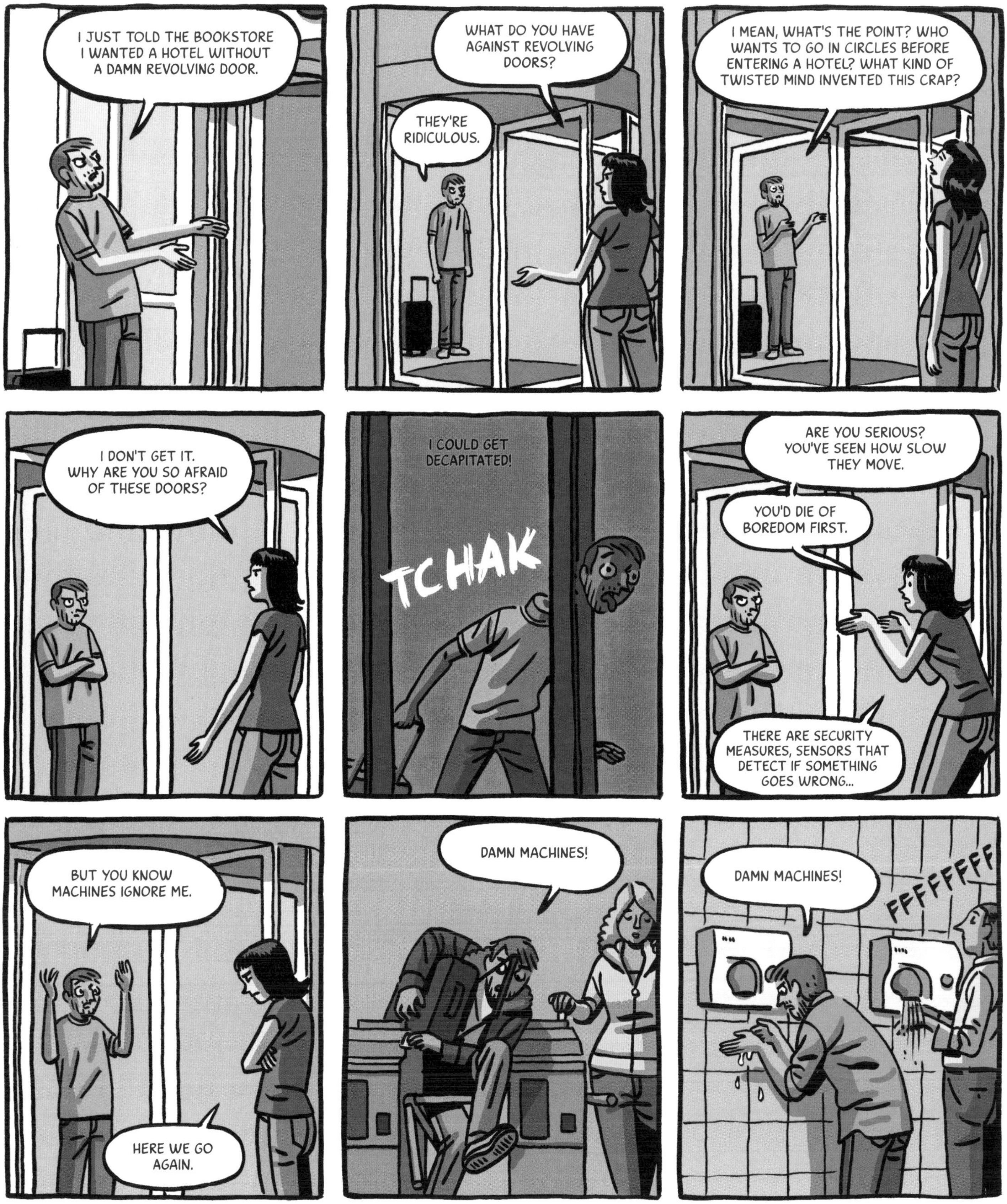
I JUST TOLD THE BOOKSTORE I WANTED A HOTEL WITHOUT A DAMN REVOLVING DOOR.
WHAT DO YOU HAVE AGAINST REVOLVING DOORS?
THEY'RE RIDICULOUS.
I MEAN, WHAT'S THE POINT? WHO WANTS TO GO IN CIRCLES BEFORE ENTERING A HOTEL? WHAT KIND OF TWISTED MIND INVENTED THIS CRAP?
I DON'T GET IT. WHY ARE YOU SO AFRAID OF THESE DOORS?
I COULD GET DECAPITATED!
TCHAK
ARE YOU SERIOUS? YOU'VE SEEN HOW SLOW THEY MOVE.
YOU'D DIE OF BOREDOM FIRST.
THERE ARE SECURITY MEASURES, SENSORS THAT DETECT IF SOMETHING GOES WRONG...
BUT YOU KNOW MACHINES IGNORE ME.
HERE WE GO AGAIN.
DAMN MACHINES!
DAMN MACHINES!
FFFFFFFF

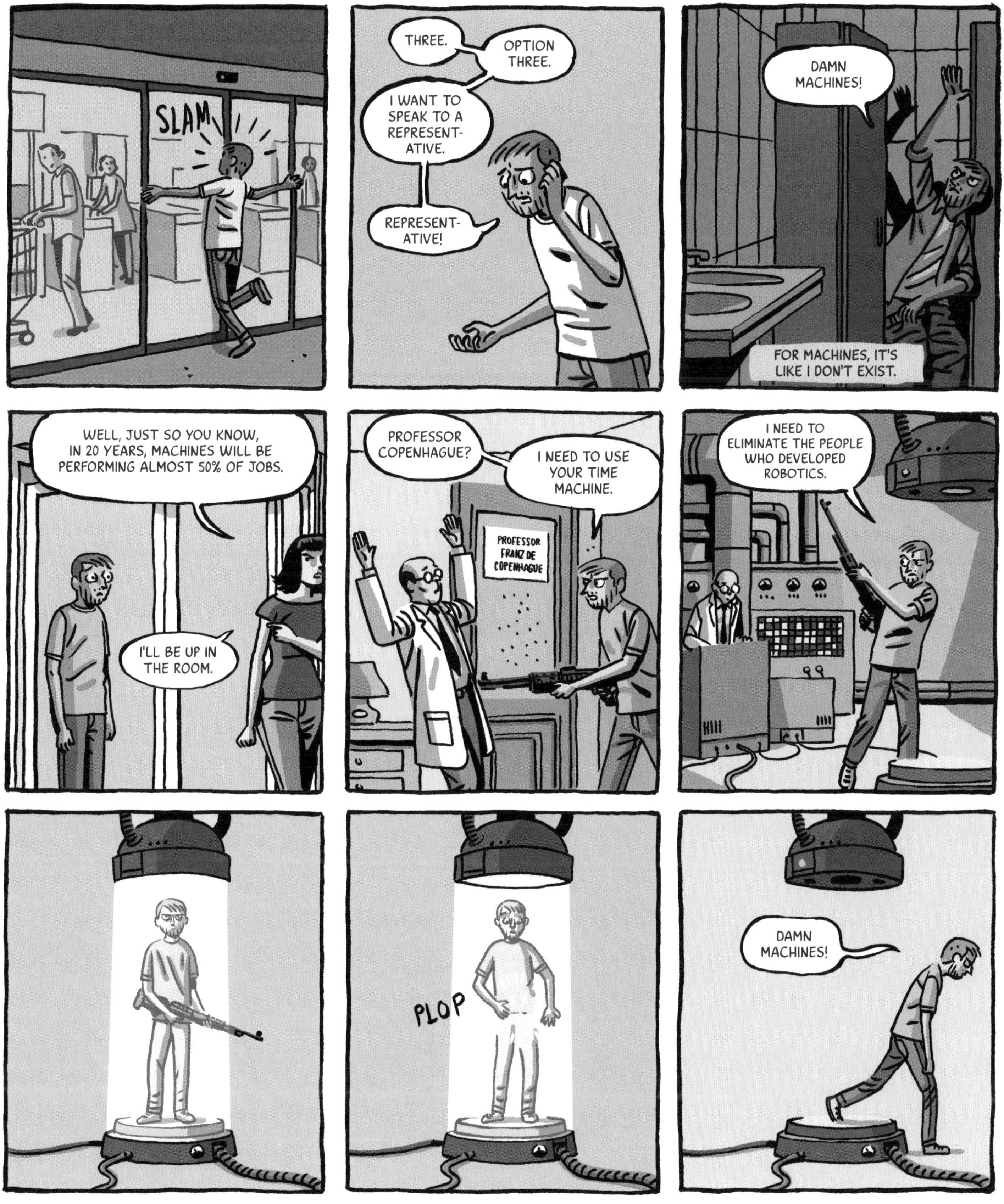

SLAM
THREE.
OPTION THREE.
I WANT TO SPEAK TO A REPRESENT-ATIVE.
REPRESENT-ATIVE!
DAMN MACHINES!
FOR MACHINES, IT'S LIKE I DON'T EXIST.
WELL, JUST SO YOU KNOW, IN 20 YEARS, MACHINES WILL BE PERFORMING ALMOST 50% OF JOBS.
I'LL BE UP IN THE ROOM.
PROFESSOR COPENHAGUE?
I NEED TO USE YOUR TIME MACHINE.
PROFESSOR FRANZ DE COPENHAGUE
I NEED TO ELIMINATE THE PEOPLE WHO DEVELOPED ROBOTICS.
PLOP
DAMN MACHINES!

A NEED-TO-FORGET BASIS

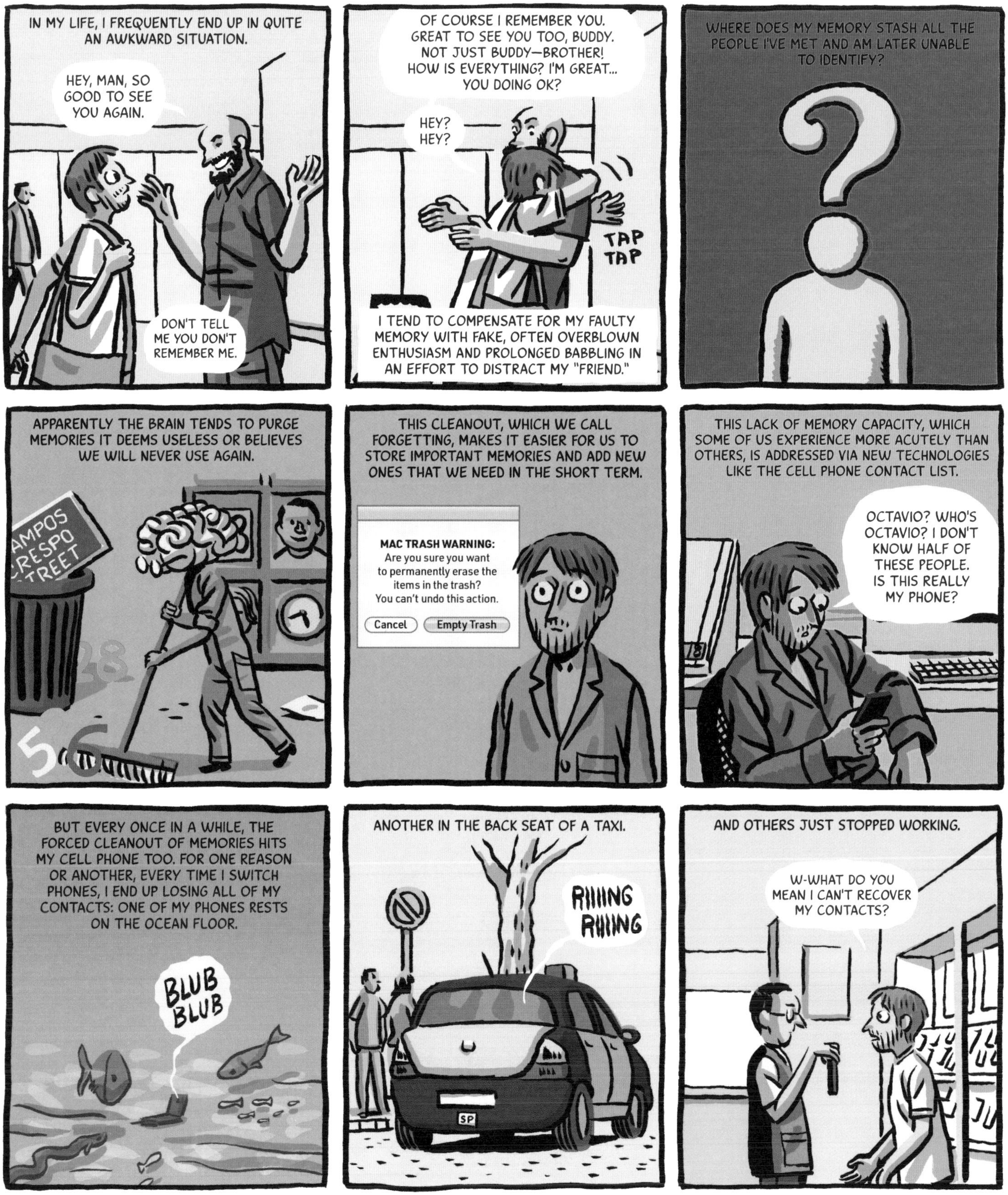

IN MY LIFE, I FREQUENTLY END UP IN QUITE AN AWKWARD SITUATION.
HEY, MAN, SO GOOD TO SEE YOU AGAIN.
DON'T TELL ME YOU DON'T REMEMBER ME.
OF COURSE I REMEMBER YOU. GREAT TO SEE YOU TOO, BUDDY. NOT JUST BUDDY—BROTHER! HOW IS EVERYTHING? I'M GREAT... YOU DOING OK?
HEY? HEY?
TAP TAP
I TEND TO COMPENSATE FOR MY FAULTY MEMORY WITH FAKE, OFTEN OVERBLOWN ENTHUSIASM AND PROLONGED BABBLING IN AN EFFORT TO DISTRACT MY "FRIEND."
WHERE DOES MY MEMORY STASH ALL THE PEOPLE I'VE MET AND AM LATER UNABLE TO IDENTIFY?
APPARENTLY THE BRAIN TENDS TO PURGE MEMORIES IT DEEMS USELESS OR BELIEVES WE WILL NEVER USE AGAIN.
AMPOS CRESPO STREET
THIS CLEANOUT, WHICH WE CALL FORGETTING, MAKES IT EASIER FOR US TO STORE IMPORTANT MEMORIES AND ADD NEW ONES THAT WE NEED IN THE SHORT TERM.
MAC TRASH WARNING:
Are you sure you want to permanently erase the items in the trash? You can't undo this action.
Cancel
Empty Trash
THIS LACK OF MEMORY CAPACITY, WHICH SOME OF US EXPERIENCE MORE ACUTELY THAN OTHERS, IS ADDRESSED VIA NEW TECHNOLOGIES LIKE THE CELL PHONE CONTACT LIST.
OCTAVIO? WHO'S OCTAVIO? I DON'T KNOW HALF OF THESE PEOPLE. IS THIS REALLY MY PHONE?
BUT EVERY ONCE IN A WHILE, THE FORCED CLEANOUT OF MEMORIES HITS MY CELL PHONE TOO. FOR ONE REASON OR ANOTHER, EVERY TIME I SWITCH PHONES, I END UP LOSING ALL OF MY CONTACTS: ONE OF MY PHONES RESTS ON THE OCEAN FLOOR.
BLUB BLUB
ANOTHER IN THE BACK SEAT OF A TAXI.
RIIIING RIIIING
SP
AND OTHERS JUST STOPPED WORKING.
W-WHAT DO YOU MEAN I CAN'T RECOVER MY CONTACTS?

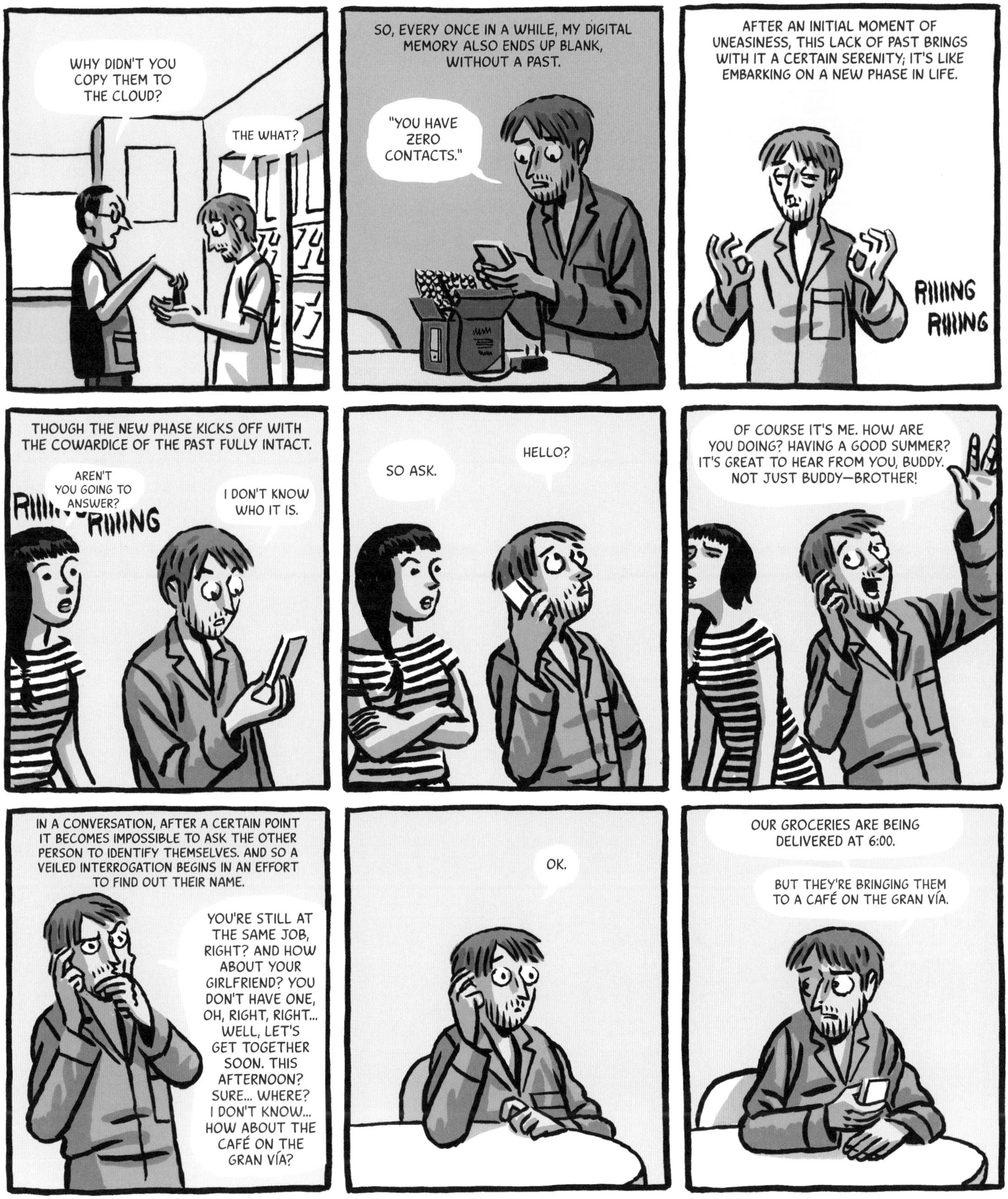
WHY DIDN'T YOU COPY THEM TO THE CLOUD?
THE WHAT?
SO, EVERY ONCE IN A WHILE, MY DIGITAL MEMORY ALSO ENDS UP BLANK, WITHOUT A PAST.
"YOU HAVE ZERO CONTACTS."
AFTER AN INITIAL MOMENT OF UNEASINESS, THIS LACK OF PAST BRINGS WITH IT A CERTAIN SERENITY; IT'S LIKE EMBARKING ON A NEW PHASE IN LIFE.
RIIIING
RIIIING
THOUGH THE NEW PHASE KICKS OFF WITH THE COWARDICE OF THE PAST FULLY INTACT.
AREN'T YOU GOING TO ANSWER?
RIIIING
I DON'T KNOW WHO IT IS.
SO ASK.
HELLO?
OF COURSE IT'S ME. HOW ARE YOU DOING? HAVING A GOOD SUMMER? IT'S GREAT TO HEAR FROM YOU, BUDDY. NOT JUST BUDDY—BROTHER!
IN A CONVERSATION, AFTER A CERTAIN POINT IT BECOMES IMPOSSIBLE TO ASK THE OTHER PERSON TO IDENTIFY THEMSELVES. AND SO A VEILED INTERROGATION BEGINS IN AN EFFORT TO FIND OUT THEIR NAME.
YOU'RE STILL AT THE SAME JOB, RIGHT? AND HOW ABOUT YOUR GIRLFRIEND? YOU DON'T HAVE ONE, OH, RIGHT, RIGHT... WELL, LET'S GET TOGETHER SOON. THIS AFTERNOON? SURE... WHERE? I DON'T KNOW... HOW ABOUT THE CAFÉ ON THE GRAN VÍA?
OK.
OUR GROCERIES ARE BEING DELIVERED AT 6:00.
BUT THEY'RE BRINGING THEM TO A CAFÉ ON THE GRAN VÍA.

COMMENTARY VERSION

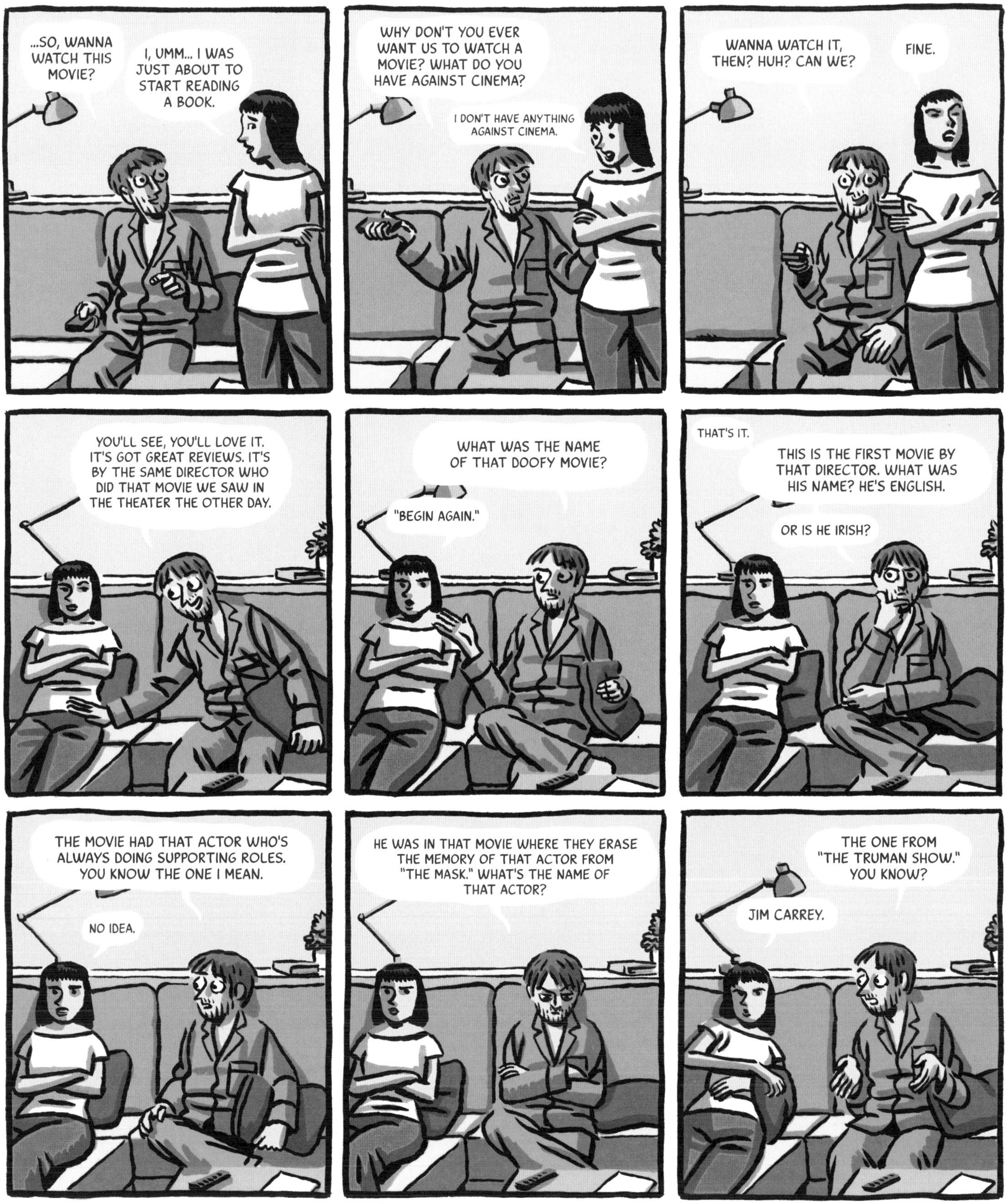
...SO, WANNA WATCH THIS MOVIE?
I, UMM... I WAS JUST ABOUT TO START READING A BOOK.
WHY DON'T YOU EVER WANT US TO WATCH A MOVIE? WHAT DO YOU HAVE AGAINST CINEMA?
I DON'T HAVE ANYTHING AGAINST CINEMA.
WANNA WATCH IT, THEN? HUH? CAN WE?
FINE.
YOU'LL SEE, YOU'LL LOVE IT. IT'S GOT GREAT REVIEWS. IT'S BY THE SAME DIRECTOR WHO DID THAT MOVIE WE SAW IN THE THEATER THE OTHER DAY.
WHAT WAS THE NAME OF THAT DOOFY MOVIE?
"BEGIN AGAIN."
THAT'S IT.
THIS IS THE FIRST MOVIE BY THAT DIRECTOR. WHAT WAS HIS NAME? HE'S ENGLISH.
OR IS HE IRISH?
THE MOVIE HAD THAT ACTOR WHO'S ALWAYS DOING SUPPORTING ROLES. YOU KNOW THE ONE I MEAN.
NO IDEA.
HE WAS IN THAT MOVIE WHERE THEY ERASE THE MEMORY OF THAT ACTOR FROM "THE MASK." WHAT'S THE NAME OF THAT ACTOR?
THE ONE FROM "THE TRUMAN SHOW." YOU KNOW?
JIM CARREY.

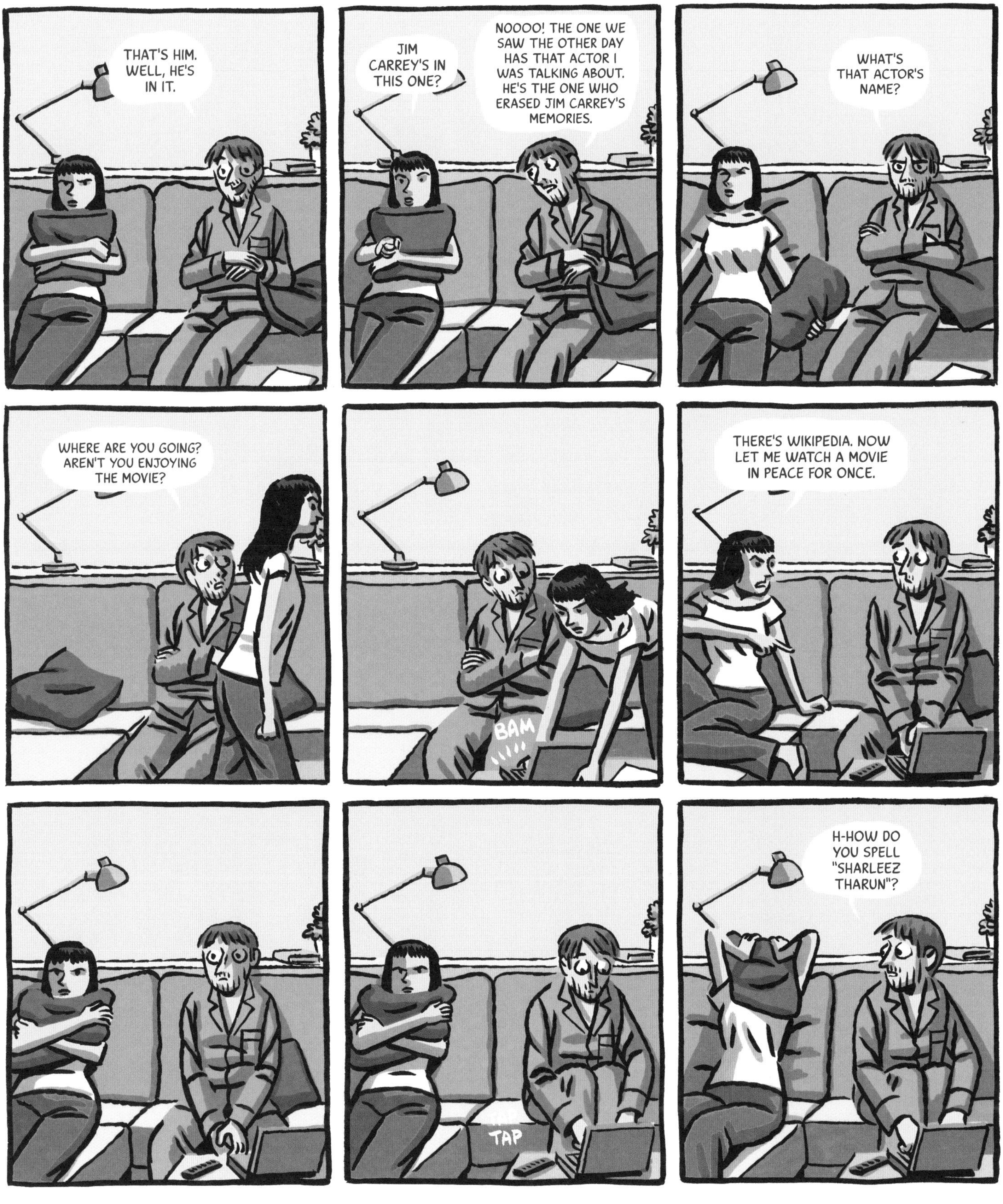
THAT'S HIM. WELL, HE'S IN IT.
JIM CARREY'S IN THIS ONE?
NOOOO! THE ONE WE SAW THE OTHER DAY HAS THAT ACTOR I WAS TALKING ABOUT. HE'S THE ONE WHO ERASED JIM CARREY'S MEMORIES.
WHAT'S THAT ACTOR'S NAME?
WHERE ARE YOU GOING? AREN'T YOU ENJOYING THE MOVIE?
BAM
THERE'S WIKIPEDIA. NOW LET ME WATCH A MOVIE IN PEACE FOR ONCE.
TAP
H-HOW DO YOU SPELL "SHARLEEZ THARUN"?

AN ONLINE ODYSSEY

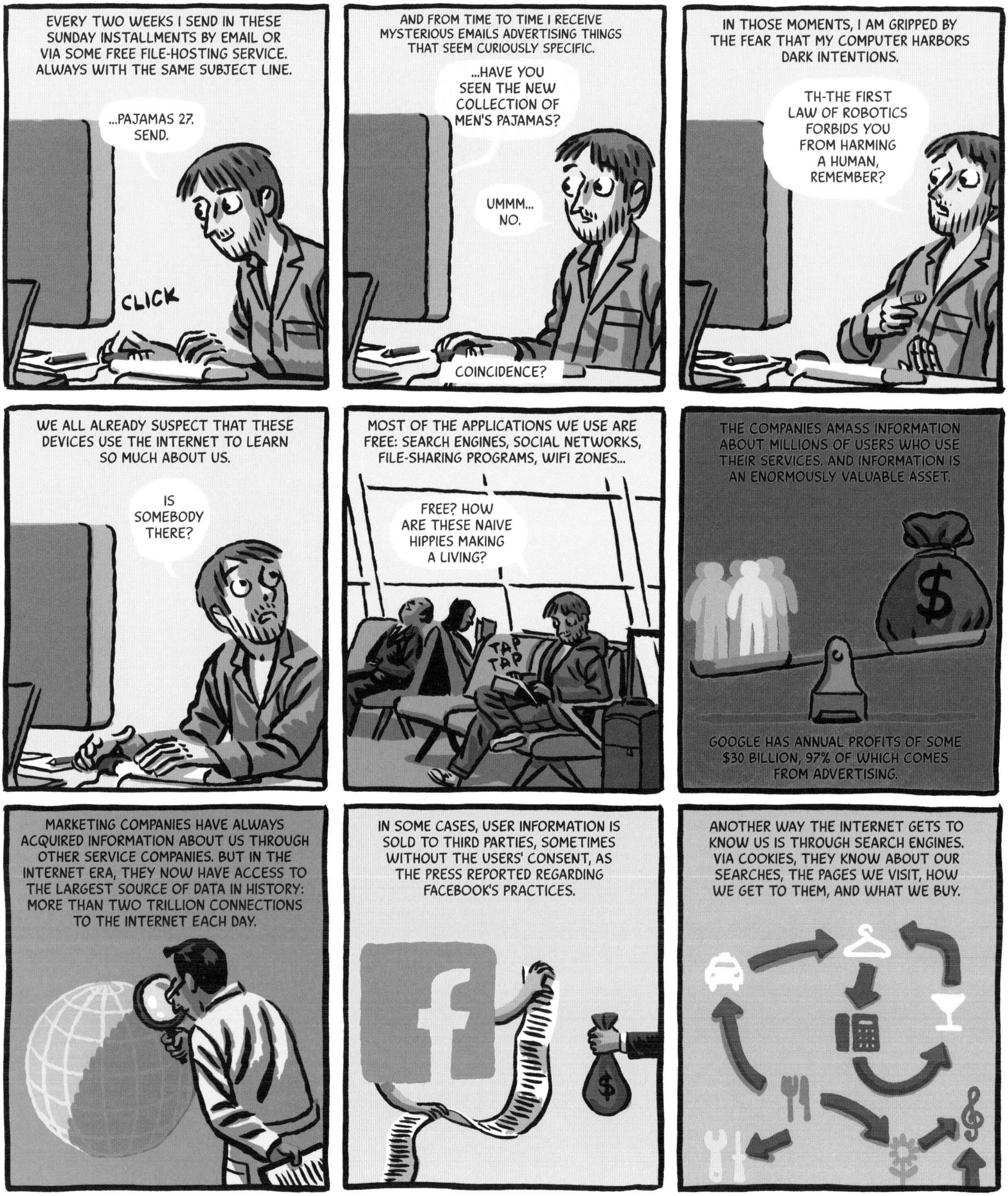
EVERY TWO WEEKS I SEND IN THESE SUNDAY INSTALLMENTS BY EMAIL OR VIA SOME FREE FILE-HOSTING SERVICE. ALWAYS WITH THE SAME SUBJECT LINE.
...PAJAMAS 27. SEND.
CLICK
AND FROM TIME TO TIME I RECEIVE MYSTERIOUS EMAILS ADVERTISING THINGS THAT SEEM CURIOUSLY SPECIFIC.
...HAVE YOU SEEN THE NEW COLLECTION OF MEN'S PAJAMAS?
UMMM... NO.
COINCIDENCE?
IN THOSE MOMENTS, I AM GRIPPED BY THE FEAR THAT MY COMPUTER HARBORS DARK INTENTIONS.
TH-THE FIRST LAW OF ROBOTICS FORBIDS YOU FROM HARMING A HUMAN, REMEMBER?
WE ALL ALREADY SUSPECT THAT THESE DEVICES USE THE INTERNET TO LEARN SO MUCH ABOUT US.
IS SOMEBODY THERE?
MOST OF THE APPLICATIONS WE USE ARE FREE: SEARCH ENGINES, SOCIAL NETWORKS, FILE-SHARING PROGRAMS, WIFI ZONES...
FREE? HOW ARE THESE NAIVE HIPPIES MAKING A LIVING?
TAP TAP
THE COMPANIES AMASS INFORMATION ABOUT MILLIONS OF USERS WHO USE THEIR SERVICES. AND INFORMATION IS AN ENORMOUSLY VALUABLE ASSET.
$
GOOGLE HAS ANNUAL PROFITS OF SOME $30 BILLION, 97% OF WHICH COMES FROM ADVERTISING.
MARKETING COMPANIES HAVE ALWAYS ACQUIRED INFORMATION ABOUT US THROUGH OTHER SERVICE COMPANIES. BUT IN THE INTERNET ERA, THEY NOW HAVE ACCESS TO THE LARGEST SOURCE OF DATA IN HISTORY: MORE THAN TWO TRILLION CONNECTIONS TO THE INTERNET EACH DAY.
IN SOME CASES, USER INFORMATION IS SOLD TO THIRD PARTIES, SOMETIMES WITHOUT THE USERS' CONSENT, AS THE PRESS REPORTED REGARDING FACEBOOK'S PRACTICES.
f
$
ANOTHER WAY THE INTERNET GETS TO KNOW US IS THROUGH SEARCH ENGINES. VIA COOKIES, THEY KNOW ABOUT OUR SEARCHES, THE PAGES WE VISIT, HOW WE GET TO THEM, AND WHAT WE BUY.

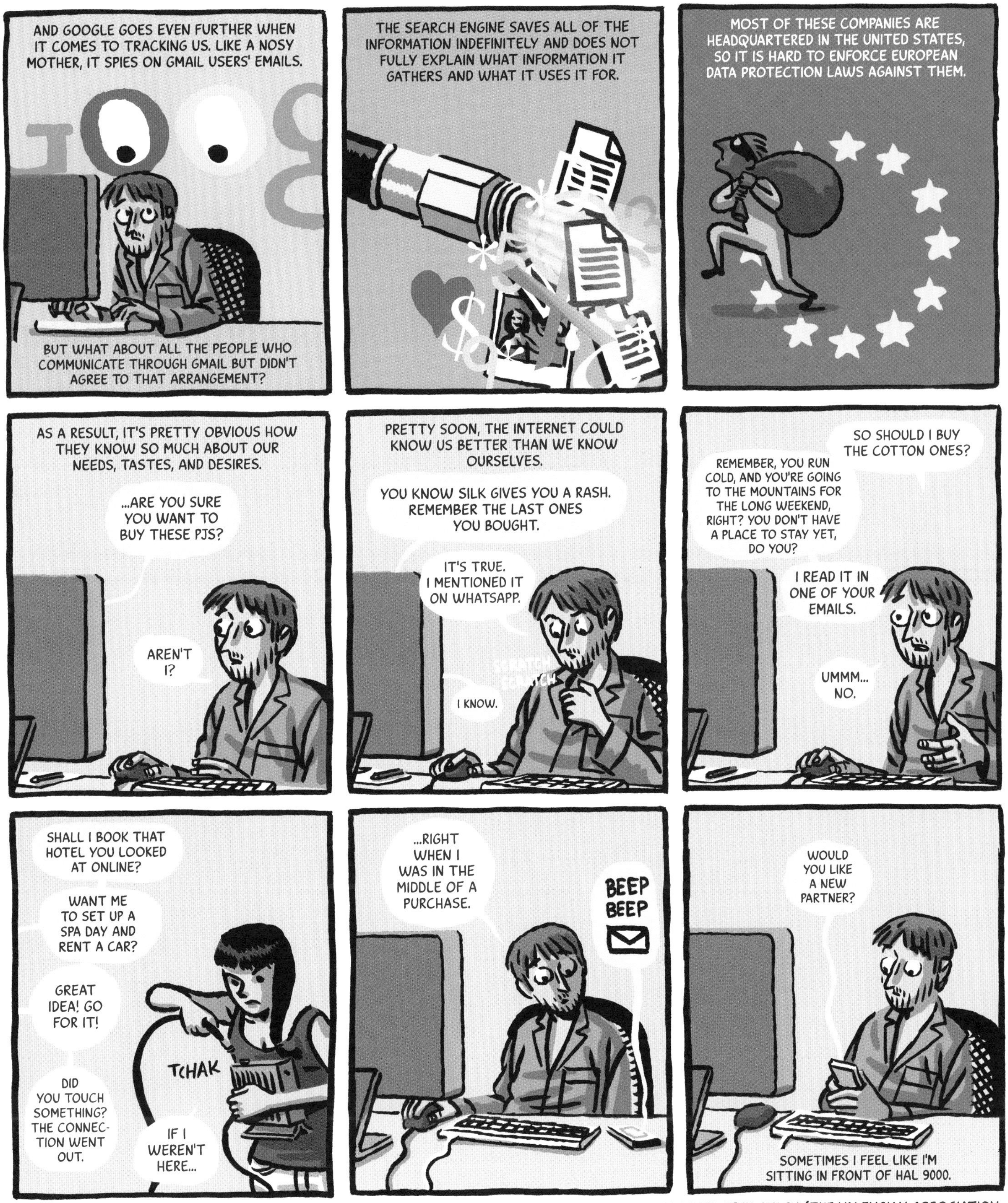
AND GOOGLE GOES EVEN FURTHER WHEN IT COMES TO TRACKING US. LIKE A NOSY MOTHER, IT SPIES ON GMAIL USERS' EMAILS.
BUT WHAT ABOUT ALL THE PEOPLE WHO COMMUNICATE THROUGH GMAIL BUT DIDN'T AGREE TO THAT ARRANGEMENT?
THE SEARCH ENGINE SAVES ALL OF THE INFORMATION INDEFINITELY AND DOES NOT FULLY EXPLAIN WHAT INFORMATION IT GATHERS AND WHAT IT USES IT FOR.
MOST OF THESE COMPANIES ARE HEADQUARTERED IN THE UNITED STATES, SO IT IS HARD TO ENFORCE EUROPEAN DATA PROTECTION LAWS AGAINST THEM.
AS A RESULT, IT'S PRETTY OBVIOUS HOW THEY KNOW SO MUCH ABOUT OUR NEEDS, TASTES, AND DESIRES.
...ARE YOU SURE YOU WANT TO BUY THESE PJS?
AREN'T I?
PRETTY SOON, THE INTERNET COULD KNOW US BETTER THAN WE KNOW OURSELVES.
YOU KNOW SILK GIVES YOU A RASH. REMEMBER THE LAST ONES YOU BOUGHT.
IT'S TRUE. I MENTIONED IT ON WHATSAPP.
SCRATCH SCRATCH
I KNOW.
SO SHOULD I BUY THE COTTON ONES?
REMEMBER, YOU RUN COLD, AND YOU'RE GOING TO THE MOUNTAINS FOR THE LONG WEEKEND, RIGHT? YOU DON'T HAVE A PLACE TO STAY YET, DO YOU?
I READ IT IN ONE OF YOUR EMAILS.
UMMM... NO.
SHALL I BOOK THAT HOTEL YOU LOOKED AT ONLINE?
WANT ME TO SET UP A SPA DAY AND RENT A CAR?
GREAT IDEA! GO FOR IT!
TCHAK
DID YOU TOUCH SOMETHING? THE CONNECTION WENT OUT.
IF I WEREN'T HERE...
...RIGHT WHEN I WAS IN THE MIDDLE OF A PURCHASE.
BEEP BEEP
WOULD YOU LIKE A NEW PARTNER?
SOMETIMES I FEEL LIKE I'M SITTING IN FRONT OF HAL 9000.

THANKS TO CECU-AVACU (THE VALENCIAN ASSOCIATION OF CONSUMERS AND USERS) FOR THEIR HELP.

UNCONSCIOUS, MIND YOUR OWN BUISNESS

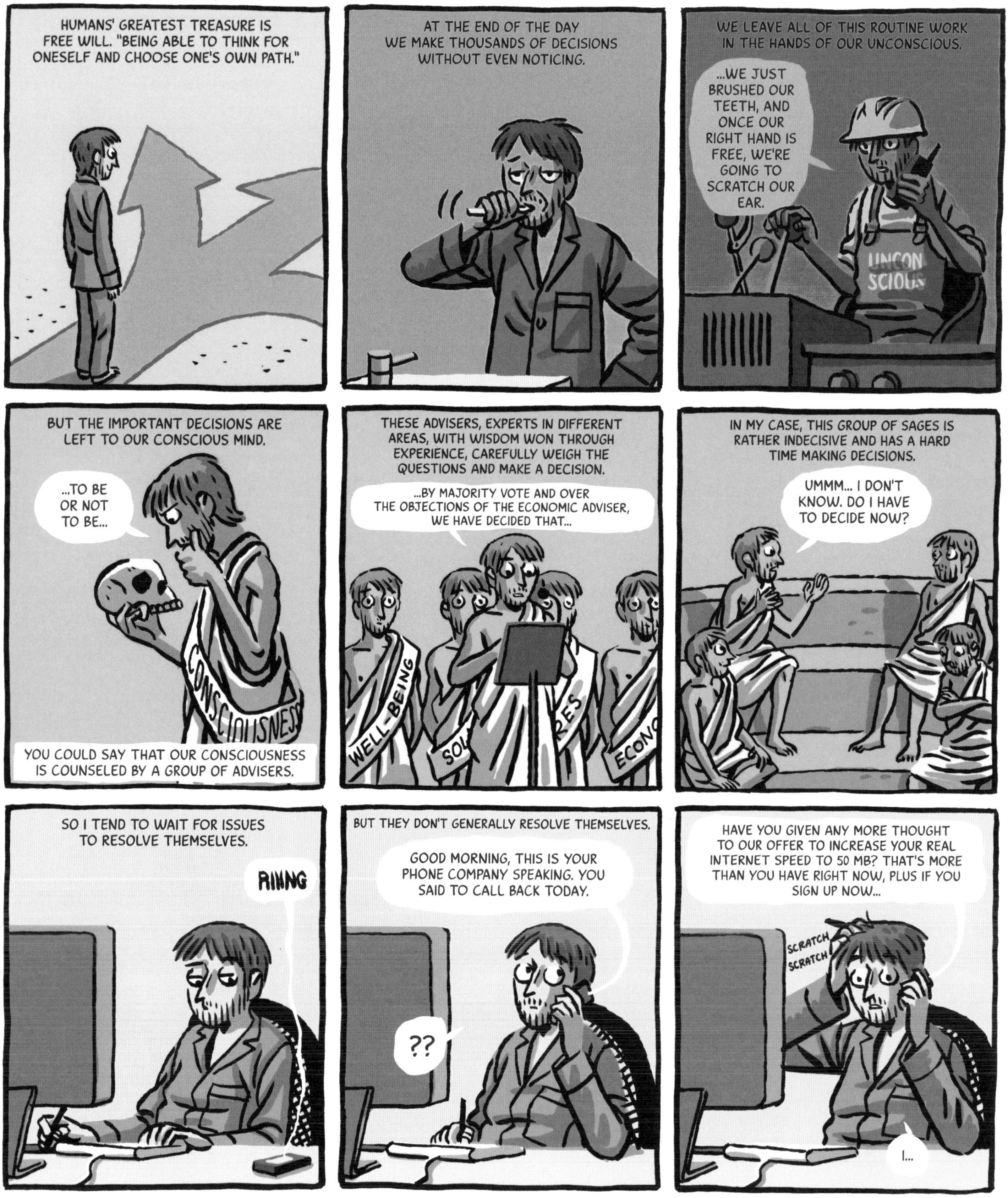
HUMANS' GREATEST TREASURE IS FREE WILL. "BEING ABLE TO THINK FOR ONESELF AND CHOOSE ONE'S OWN PATH."
AT THE END OF THE DAY WE MAKE THOUSANDS OF DECISIONS WITHOUT EVEN NOTICING.
WE LEAVE ALL OF THIS ROUTINE WORK IN THE HANDS OF OUR UNCONSCIOUS.
...WE JUST BRUSHED OUR TEETH, AND ONCE OUR RIGHT HAND IS FREE, WE'RE GOING TO SCRATCH OUR EAR.
UNCON SCIOUS
BUT THE IMPORTANT DECISIONS ARE LEFT TO OUR CONSCIOUS MIND.
...TO BE OR NOT TO BE...
CONSCIOUSNESS
YOU COULD SAY THAT OUR CONSCIOUSNESS IS COUNSELED BY A GROUP OF ADVISERS.
THESE ADVISERS, EXPERTS IN DIFFERENT AREAS, WITH WISDOM WON THROUGH EXPERIENCE, CAREFULLY WEIGH THE QUESTIONS AND MAKE A DECISION.
...BY MAJORITY VOTE AND OVER THE OBJECTIONS OF THE ECONOMIC ADVISER, WE HAVE DECIDED THAT...
WELL-BEING
IN MY CASE, THIS GROUP OF SAGES IS RATHER INDECISIVE AND HAS A HARD TIME MAKING DECISIONS.
UMMM... I DON'T KNOW. DO I HAVE TO DECIDE NOW?
SO I TEND TO WAIT FOR ISSUES TO RESOLVE THEMSELVES.
RIING
BUT THEY DON'T GENERALLY RESOLVE THEMSELVES.
GOOD MORNING, THIS IS YOUR PHONE COMPANY SPEAKING. YOU SAID TO CALL BACK TODAY.
??
HAVE YOU GIVEN ANY MORE THOUGHT TO OUR OFFER TO INCREASE YOUR REAL INTERNET SPEED TO 50 MB? THAT'S MORE THAN YOU HAVE RIGHT NOW, PLUS IF YOU SIGN UP NOW...
SCRATCH SCRATCH
I...

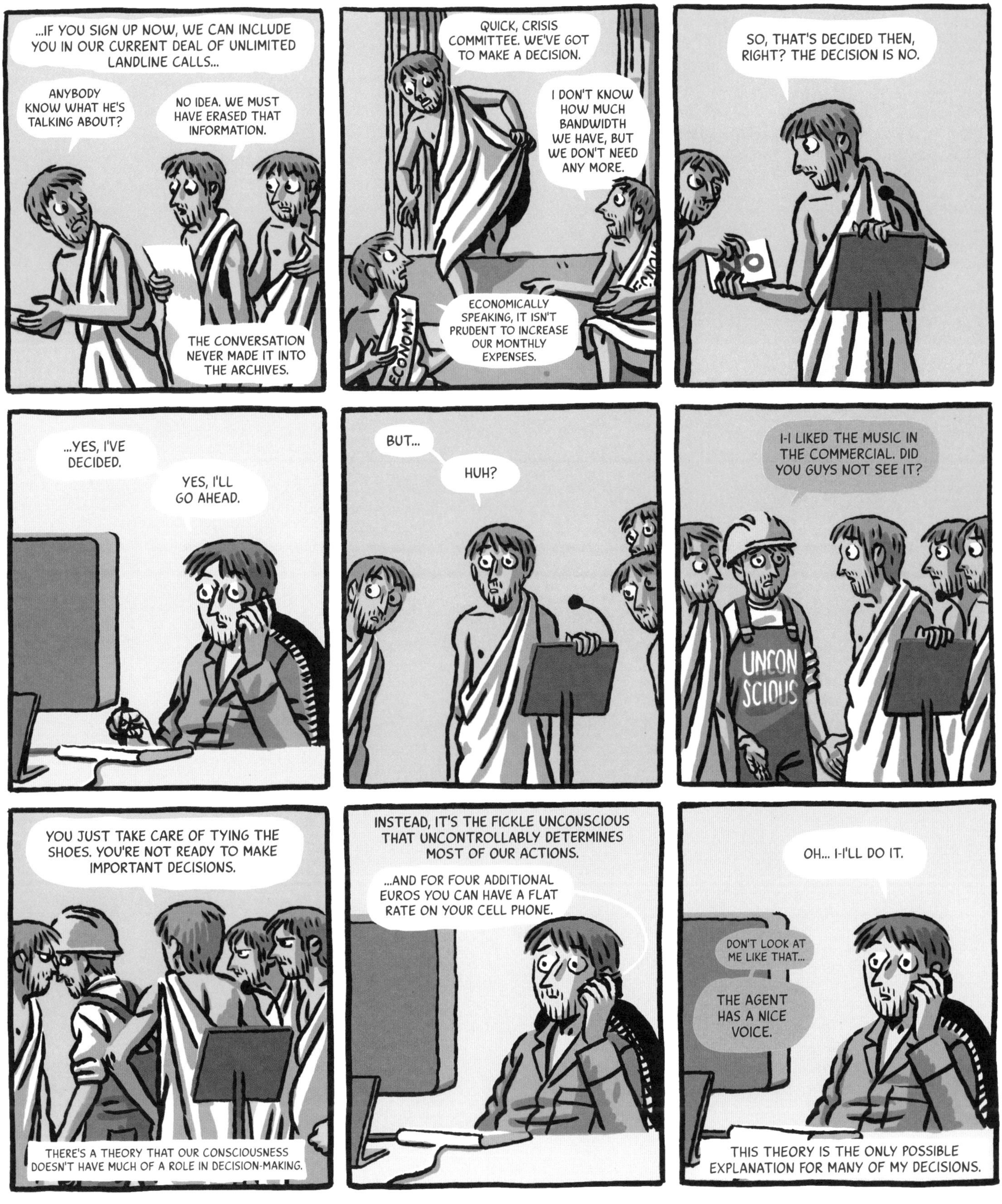
...IF YOU SIGN UP NOW, WE CAN INCLUDE YOU IN OUR CURRENT DEAL OF UNLIMITED LANDLINE CALLS...
ANYBODY KNOW WHAT HE'S TALKING ABOUT?
NO IDEA. WE MUST HAVE ERASED THAT INFORMATION.
THE CONVERSATION NEVER MADE IT INTO THE ARCHIVES.
QUICK, CRISIS COMMITTEE. WE'VE GOT TO MAKE A DECISION.
I DON'T KNOW HOW MUCH BANDWIDTH WE HAVE, BUT WE DON'T NEED ANY MORE.
ECONOMY
ECONOMICALLY SPEAKING, IT ISN'T PRUDENT TO INCREASE OUR MONTHLY EXPENSES.
SO, THAT'S DECIDED THEN, RIGHT? THE DECISION IS NO.
NO
...YES, I'VE DECIDED.
YES, I'LL GO AHEAD.
BUT...
HUH?
I-I LIKED THE MUSIC IN THE COMMERCIAL. DID YOU GUYS NOT SEE IT?
UNCON SCIOUS
YOU JUST TAKE CARE OF TYING THE SHOES. YOU'RE NOT READY TO MAKE IMPORTANT DECISIONS.
THERE'S A THEORY THAT OUR CONSCIOUSNESS DOESN'T HAVE MUCH OF A ROLE IN DECISION-MAKING.
INSTEAD, IT'S THE FICKLE UNCONSCIOUS THAT UNCONTROLLABLY DETERMINES MOST OF OUR ACTIONS.
...AND FOR FOUR ADDITIONAL EUROS YOU CAN HAVE A FLAT RATE ON YOUR CELL PHONE.
OH... I-I'LL DO IT.
DON'T LOOK AT ME LIKE THAT...
THE AGENT HAS A NICE VOICE.
THIS THEORY IS THE ONLY POSSIBLE EXPLANATION FOR MANY OF MY DECISIONS.

THE OTHERS

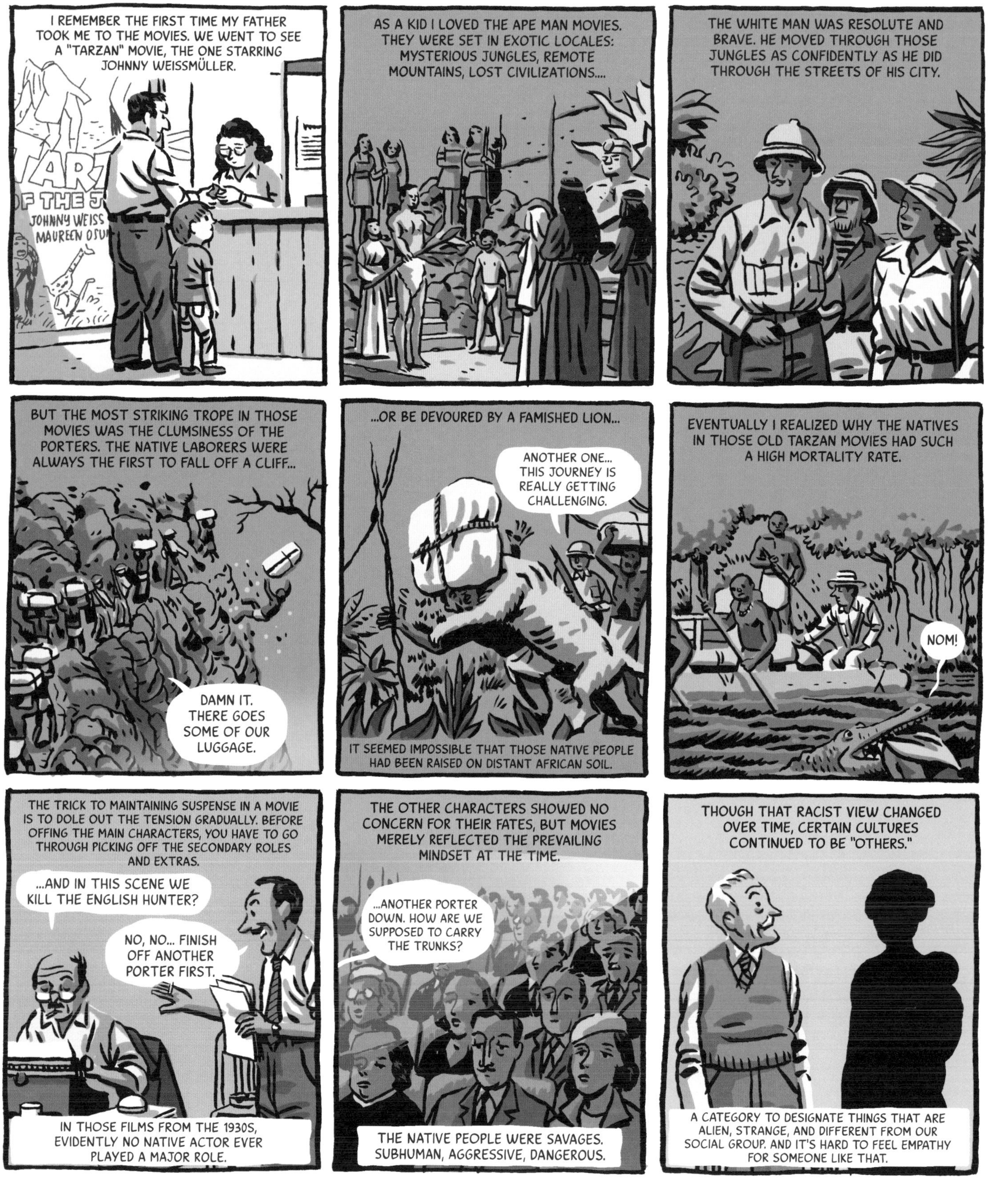
I REMEMBER THE FIRST TIME MY FATHER TOOK ME TO THE MOVIES. WE WENT TO SEE A "TARZAN" MOVIE, THE ONE STARRING JOHNNY WEISSMÜLLER.
AS A KID I LOVED THE APE MAN MOVIES. THEY WERE SET IN EXOTIC LOCALES: MYSTERIOUS JUNGLES, REMOTE MOUNTAINS, LOST CIVILIZATIONS....
THE WHITE MAN WAS RESOLUTE AND BRAVE. HE MOVED THROUGH THOSE JUNGLES AS CONFIDENTLY AS HE DID THROUGH THE STREETS OF HIS CITY.
BUT THE MOST STRIKING TROPE IN THOSE MOVIES WAS THE CLUMSINESS OF THE PORTERS. THE NATIVE LABORERS WERE ALWAYS THE FIRST TO FALL OFF A CLIFF...
DAMN IT. THERE GOES SOME OF OUR LUGGAGE.
...OR BE DEVOURED BY A FAMISHED LION...
ANOTHER ONE... THIS JOURNEY IS REALLY GETTING CHALLENGING.
IT SEEMED IMPOSSIBLE THAT THOSE NATIVE PEOPLE HAD BEEN RAISED ON DISTANT AFRICAN SOIL.
EVENTUALLY I REALIZED WHY THE NATIVES IN THOSE OLD TARZAN MOVIES HAD SUCH A HIGH MORTALITY RATE.
NOM!
THE TRICK TO MAINTAINING SUSPENSE IN A MOVIE IS TO DOLE OUT THE TENSION GRADUALLY. BEFORE OFFING THE MAIN CHARACTERS, YOU HAVE TO GO THROUGH PICKING OFF THE SECONDARY ROLES AND EXTRAS.
...AND IN THIS SCENE WE KILL THE ENGLISH HUNTER?
NO, NO... FINISH OFF ANOTHER PORTER FIRST.
IN THOSE FILMS FROM THE 1930S, EVIDENTLY NO NATIVE ACTOR EVER PLAYED A MAJOR ROLE.
THE OTHER CHARACTERS SHOWED NO CONCERN FOR THEIR FATES, BUT MOVIES MERELY REFLECTED THE PREVAILING MINDSET AT THE TIME.
...ANOTHER PORTER DOWN. HOW ARE WE SUPPOSED TO CARRY THE TRUNKS?
THE NATIVE PEOPLE WERE SAVAGES. SUBHUMAN, AGGRESSIVE, DANGEROUS.
THOUGH THAT RACIST VIEW CHANGED OVER TIME, CERTAIN CULTURES CONTINUED TO BE "OTHERS."
A CATEGORY TO DESIGNATE THINGS THAT ARE ALIEN, STRANGE, AND DIFFERENT FROM OUR SOCIAL GROUP. AND IT'S HARD TO FEEL EMPATHY FOR SOMEONE LIKE THAT.

ONE WOULD EXPECT THAT OVER TIME THE CONCEPTS OF "US" AND "THEM" WOULD DISAPPEAR FROM CONTEMPORARY SOCIETY. WE ARE ALL EQUAL HUMAN BEINGS, REGARDLESS OF OUR PLACES OF BIRTH.

OUR LEADERS ARE DISMANTLING THE FOREIGN AID THAT USED TO PROVIDE MUCH-NEEDED SUPPORT FOR PEOPLE IN DEVELOPING NATIONS.

...WE NEED TO HELP THE PEOPLE HERE AT HOME FIRST.

MAYOR OF VITORIA-GASTEIZ

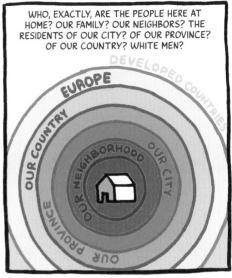

WHO, EXACTLY, ARE THE PEOPLE HERE AT HOME? OUR FAMILY? OUR NEIGHBORS? THE RESIDENTS OF OUR CITY? OF OUR PROVINCE? OF OUR COUNTRY? WHITE MEN?

DEVELOPED COUNTRIES
EUROPE
OUR COUNTRY
OUR PROVINCE
OUR CITY
OUR NEIGHBORHOOD

DO WE REALLY HAVE TO CHOOSE WHICH PEOPLE TO HELP?

JUDGING BY CERTAIN LEADERS' STATEMENTS, THEY SEEM TO DRAW A CLEAR DISTINCTION BETWEEN THE POOR AT "HOME" AND "OTHERS." AGAIN WE PRIORITIZE THE PROXIMATE, THE FAMILIAR, AS OPPOSED TO THE REMOTE AND UNFAMILIAR, FOR WHICH WE HAVE NO EMPATHY.

HUNGRY PLEASE HELP

IT'S AN EFFECTIVE FORM OF MANIPULATION THAT KEEPS US FROM OBJECTING TO THE STEEP CUTS TO FOREIGN AID.

BUT THESE COMMENTS CONTAIN A WHIFF OF RACISM REMINISCENT OF THE COLONIAL-ERA WORLDVIEW.

...THE NEED TO REFOCUS RESOURCES ON VALENCIA ITSELF.

Department of Justice and Social Welfare Government of Valencia

A PARTICULAR POLITICAL CLASS COMES TO SEEM MORE AND MORE ALIEN, REMOTE, DIFFERENT FROM US. AND THEY START TO BECOME THE "OTHERS" IN OUR SOCIETY.

IF I HAD TO MAKE AN UPDATED VERSION OF TARZAN, IT'S OBVIOUS WHO WOULD PLAY THE PART OF THOSE MARGINAL (BUT ESSENTIAL) CHARACTERS IN THE MOVIE WHO FAIL TO WIN THE PUBLIC'S EMPATHY.

...ANOTHER GUY WHO'S EATEN BY A LION.

ARTIST AS JUGGLER

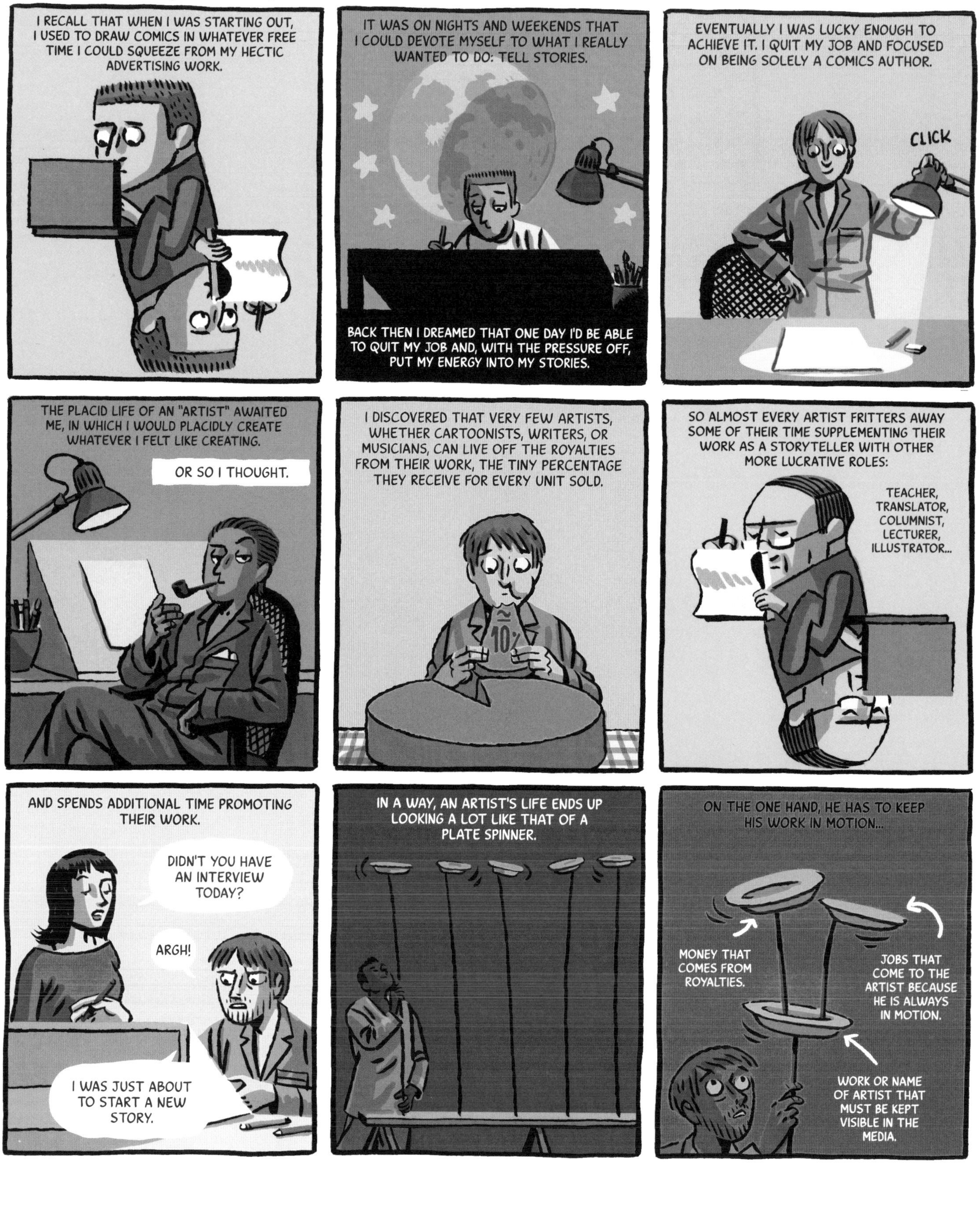
I RECALL THAT WHEN I WAS STARTING OUT, I USED TO DRAW COMICS IN WHATEVER FREE TIME I COULD SQUEEZE FROM MY HECTIC ADVERTISING WORK.
IT WAS ON NIGHTS AND WEEKENDS THAT I COULD DEVOTE MYSELF TO WHAT I REALLY WANTED TO DO: TELL STORIES.
BACK THEN I DREAMED THAT ONE DAY I'D BE ABLE TO QUIT MY JOB AND, WITH THE PRESSURE OFF, PUT MY ENERGY INTO MY STORIES.
EVENTUALLY I WAS LUCKY ENOUGH TO ACHIEVE IT. I QUIT MY JOB AND FOCUSED ON BEING SOLELY A COMICS AUTHOR.
CLICK
THE PLACID LIFE OF AN "ARTIST" AWAITED ME, IN WHICH I WOULD PLACIDLY CREATE WHATEVER I FELT LIKE CREATING.
OR SO I THOUGHT.
I DISCOVERED THAT VERY FEW ARTISTS, WHETHER CARTOONISTS, WRITERS, OR MUSICIANS, CAN LIVE OFF THE ROYALTIES FROM THEIR WORK, THE TINY PERCENTAGE THEY RECEIVE FOR EVERY UNIT SOLD.
≈10%
SO ALMOST EVERY ARTIST FRITTERS AWAY SOME OF THEIR TIME SUPPLEMENTING THEIR WORK AS A STORYTELLER WITH OTHER MORE LUCRATIVE ROLES:
TEACHER, TRANSLATOR, COLUMNIST, LECTURER, ILLUSTRATOR...
AND SPENDS ADDITIONAL TIME PROMOTING THEIR WORK.
DIDN'T YOU HAVE AN INTERVIEW TODAY?
ARGH!
I WAS JUST ABOUT TO START A NEW STORY.
IN A WAY, AN ARTIST'S LIFE ENDS UP LOOKING A LOT LIKE THAT OF A PLATE SPINNER.
ON THE ONE HAND, HE HAS TO KEEP HIS WORK IN MOTION...
MONEY THAT COMES FROM ROYALTIES.
JOBS THAT COME TO THE ARTIST BECAUSE HE IS ALWAYS IN MOTION.
WORK OR NAME OF ARTIST THAT MUST BE KEPT VISIBLE IN THE MEDIA.

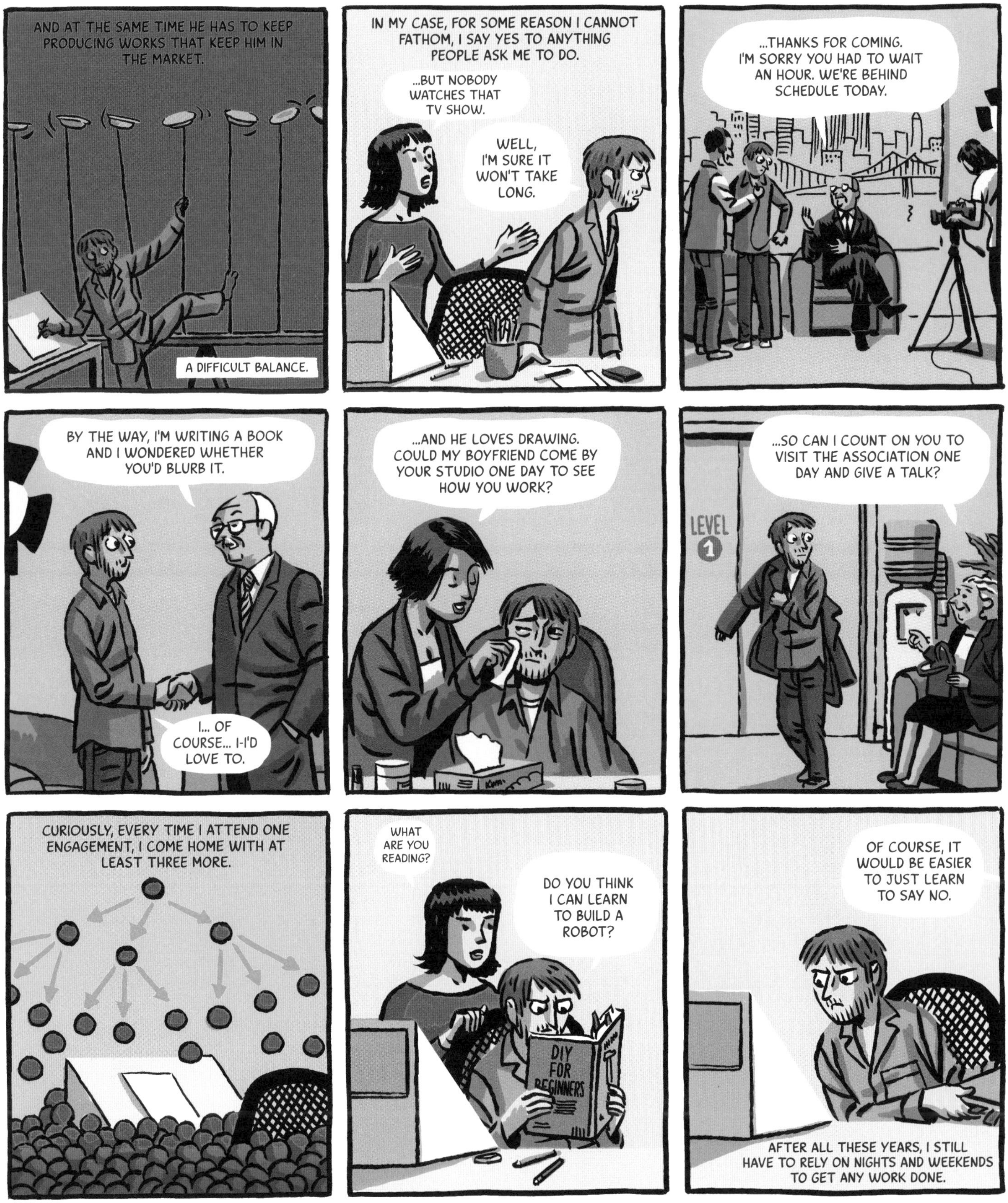
AND AT THE SAME TIME HE HAS TO KEEP PRODUCING WORKS THAT KEEP HIM IN THE MARKET.
A DIFFICULT BALANCE.
IN MY CASE, FOR SOME REASON I CANNOT FATHOM, I SAY YES TO ANYTHING PEOPLE ASK ME TO DO.
...BUT NOBODY WATCHES THAT TV SHOW.
WELL, I'M SURE IT WON'T TAKE LONG.
...THANKS FOR COMING. I'M SORRY YOU HAD TO WAIT AN HOUR. WE'RE BEHIND SCHEDULE TODAY.
BY THE WAY, I'M WRITING A BOOK AND I WONDERED WHETHER YOU'D BLURB IT.
I... OF COURSE... I-I'D LOVE TO.
...AND HE LOVES DRAWING. COULD MY BOYFRIEND COME BY YOUR STUDIO ONE DAY TO SEE HOW YOU WORK?
...SO CAN I COUNT ON YOU TO VISIT THE ASSOCIATION ONE DAY AND GIVE A TALK?
LEVEL 1
CURIOUSLY, EVERY TIME I ATTEND ONE ENGAGEMENT, I COME HOME WITH AT LEAST THREE MORE.
WHAT ARE YOU READING?
DO YOU THINK I CAN LEARN TO BUILD A ROBOT?
DIY FOR BEGINNERS
OF COURSE, IT WOULD BE EASIER TO JUST LEARN TO SAY NO.
AFTER ALL THESE YEARS, I STILL HAVE TO RELY ON NIGHTS AND WEEKENDS TO GET ANY WORK DONE.

TORN CURTAIN

IN MY FINAL HOURS IN GENEVA, I ENTERTAIN MYSELF BY VISITING A NUMBER OF ICONIC SITES FOR SPANISH CORRUPTION AND FRAUD AROUND THE CITY.

BÁRCENAS'S* BANK

BANK

HOTEL WHERE BÁRCENAS STAYED

HOME OF THE INFANTA CRISTINA AND URDANGARIN**

AND, AS USUAL, I MAKE IT TO THE AIRPORT BY THE SKIN OF MY TEETH.

MAKING MY WAY THROUGH BUSINESS CLASS, I CAN'T HELP THINKING IN STEREOTYPES. I PICTURE THE PASSENGERS AS SERVANTS OF THE 1% WHO OWN AS MUCH WEALTH AS 50% OF THE WORLD POPULATION.

GRRR... THIEVES.

GRRR... CROOKS.

AMONG THE PASSENGERS, I THINK I SPOT SEVERAL MEMBERS OF THE NEW SWISS SOCIAL ELITE.

AS A SWISS PROFESSOR OF SPANISH DESCENT TOLD ME:

YOU SEE A LOT OF RUSSIANS AROUND HERE LATELY. THEY HAVE THE MOST EXPENSIVE HOUSES RIGHT ON THE LAKE, THE FANCIEST CARS... AND THEY FLAUNT THEM.

I DIDN'T RUN INTO ANY RUSSIANS, BUT I DID ENCOUNTER THE OTHER SOCIAL EXTREME.

UNE PETITE PIÈCE?

WHAT DO YOU GIVE A HOMELESS PERSON IN A COUNTRY WHERE THE MEDIAN MONTHLY SALARY IS 5,000 SWISS FRANCS?

EVEN AS INEQUALITY AMONG NATIONS HAS FALLEN, THE INEQUALITY WITHIN THEIR CITIZENRIES HAS INCREASED IN RECENT YEARS.

BUT IS INEQUALITY INEVITABLE? OF COURSE THERE ARE SOME PEOPLE WITH LITTLE AMBITION AND OTHERS WHO ARE GO-GETTERS, WHO TAKE ON RISK AND MOVE THE ECONOMY.

SO YOU COULD ARGUE THAT INEQUALITY IS NATURAL, SINCE SOME PEOPLE ARE MORE CAPABLE THAN OTHERS.

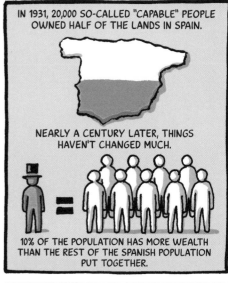

IN 1931, 20,000 SO-CALLED "CAPABLE" PEOPLE OWNED HALF OF THE LANDS IN SPAIN.

NEARLY A CENTURY LATER, THINGS HAVEN'T CHANGED MUCH.

10% OF THE POPULATION HAS MORE WEALTH THAN THE REST OF THE SPANISH POPULATION PUT TOGETHER.

THIS SMALL GROUP OF TYCOONS, MANY OF WHOM GREW RICH THANKS TO LAISSEZ-FAIRE ECONOMICS, HAVE SOMEHOW MANAGED TO INFLUENCE DEMOCRACIES, ALTERING THE LAWS TO THEIR OWN BENEFIT: LOW WAGES AND CHEAP LABOR, LEGAL LOOPHOLES THAT ALLOW FOR FRAUD...

...ULTIMATELY DISMANTLING THE MAXIM THAT SAYS THAT HE WHO HAS MORE PAYS MORE.

LARGE COMPANIES

3.5% OF THEIR PROFITS IN TAXES

SMALL COMPANIES AND WORKERS

BETWEEN 17 AND 35% OF THEIR INCOME TO PUBLIC COFFERS

SPAIN DATA

IN THE END, IT'S NOT THE PEOPLE WHO HAVE MORE WHO ARE KEEPING THE STATE GOING.

THAT'S WHY THE LAW GOES AFTER FRAUD AMONG THE PEOPLE WHO HAVE LESS.

SMALL BUSINESS, FREELANCERS, AND ORDINARY PEOPLE REPRESENT 28% OF FRAUD

GOTCHA!

YOU'RE IN FOR IT NOW.

LARGE FORTUNES AND MULTINATIONAL CORPORATIONS

72% OF FRAUD (43 BILLION EUROS)

*LUIS BÁRCENAS IS THE FORMER TREASURER OF THE PP PARTY AND A FORMER SENATOR. HE BECAME EMBROILED IN CORRUPTION SCANDALS REGARDING ILLEGAL POLITICAL DONATIONS AND WAS SENTENCED TO DECADES IN PRISON AND A HUGE FINE.

**IN SPAIN, THE DAUGHTERS OF KINGS AND QUEENS ARE KNOWN AS "INFANTAS." CRISTINA WAS TRIED FOR FRAUD AND ACQUITTED BUT STRIPPED OF HER TITLE OF DUCHESS OF PALMA DE MALLORCA. SHE WAS MARRIED TO IÑAKI URDANGARIN, WHO IS CURRENTLY IN PRISON FOR EMBEZZLING PUBLIC FUNDS THROUGH HIS NONPROFIT FOUNDATION.

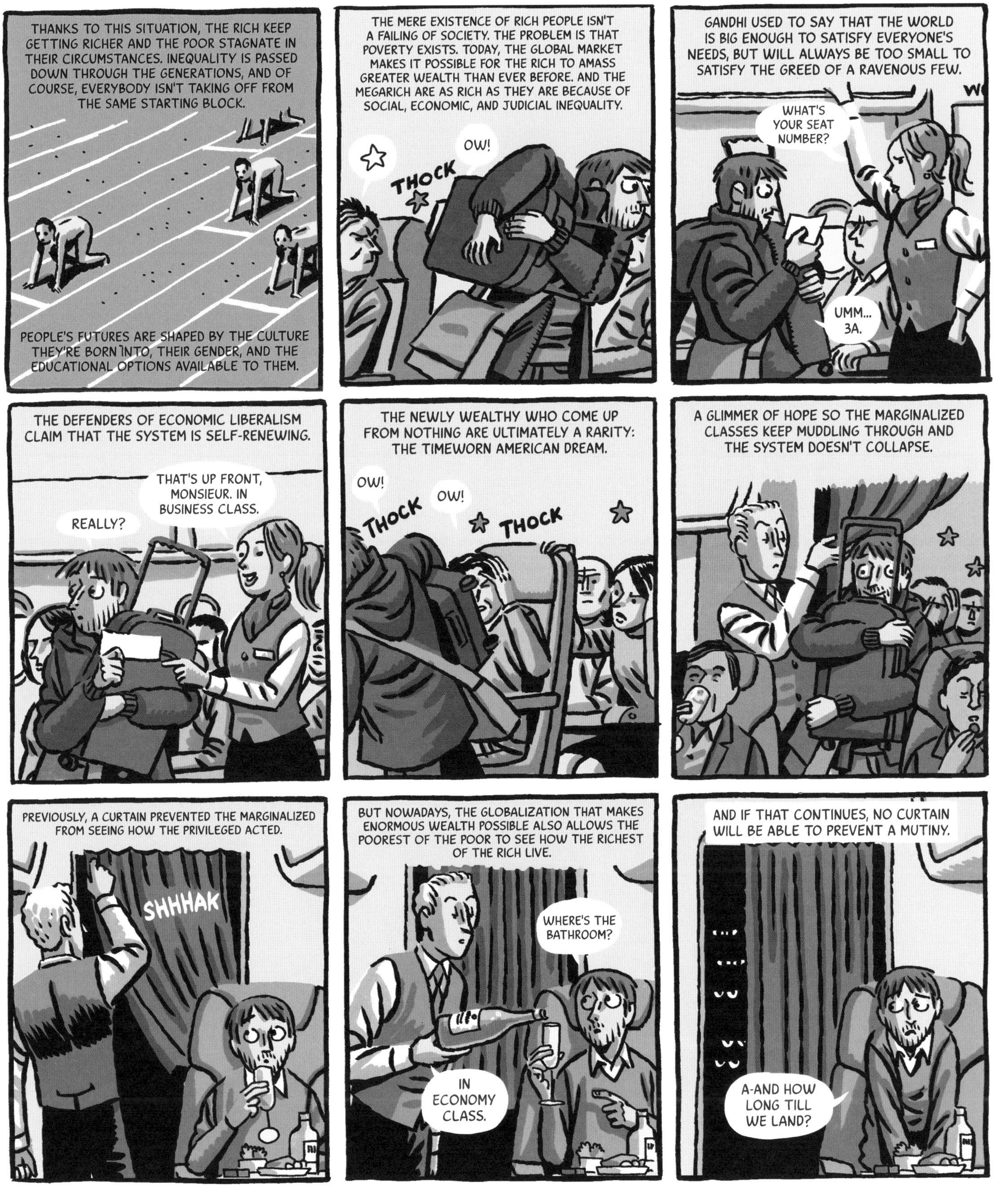
THANKS TO THIS SITUATION, THE RICH KEEP GETTING RICHER AND THE POOR STAGNATE IN THEIR CIRCUMSTANCES. INEQUALITY IS PASSED DOWN THROUGH THE GENERATIONS, AND OF COURSE, EVERYBODY ISN'T TAKING OFF FROM THE SAME STARTING BLOCK.
PEOPLE'S FUTURES ARE SHAPED BY THE CULTURE THEY'RE BORN INTO, THEIR GENDER, AND THE EDUCATIONAL OPTIONS AVAILABLE TO THEM.
THE MERE EXISTENCE OF RICH PEOPLE ISN'T A FAILING OF SOCIETY. THE PROBLEM IS THAT POVERTY EXISTS. TODAY, THE GLOBAL MARKET MAKES IT POSSIBLE FOR THE RICH TO AMASS GREATER WEALTH THAN EVER BEFORE. AND THE MEGARICH ARE AS RICH AS THEY ARE BECAUSE OF SOCIAL, ECONOMIC, AND JUDICIAL INEQUALITY.
OW!
THOCK
GANDHI USED TO SAY THAT THE WORLD IS BIG ENOUGH TO SATISFY EVERYONE'S NEEDS, BUT WILL ALWAYS BE TOO SMALL TO SATISFY THE GREED OF A RAVENOUS FEW.
WHAT'S YOUR SEAT NUMBER?
UMM... 3A.
THE DEFENDERS OF ECONOMIC LIBERALISM CLAIM THAT THE SYSTEM IS SELF-RENEWING.
THAT'S UP FRONT, MONSIEUR. IN BUSINESS CLASS.
REALLY?
THE NEWLY WEALTHY WHO COME UP FROM NOTHING ARE ULTIMATELY A RARITY: THE TIMEWORN AMERICAN DREAM.
OW!
THOCK
OW!
THOCK
A GLIMMER OF HOPE SO THE MARGINALIZED CLASSES KEEP MUDDLING THROUGH AND THE SYSTEM DOESN'T COLLAPSE.
PREVIOUSLY, A CURTAIN PREVENTED THE MARGINALIZED FROM SEEING HOW THE PRIVILEGED ACTED.
SHHHAK
BUT NOWADAYS, THE GLOBALIZATION THAT MAKES ENORMOUS WEALTH POSSIBLE ALSO ALLOWS THE POOREST OF THE POOR TO SEE HOW THE RICHEST OF THE RICH LIVE.
WHERE'S THE BATHROOM?
IN ECONOMY CLASS.
AND IF THAT CONTINUES, NO CURTAIN WILL BE ABLE TO PREVENT A MUTINY.
A-AND HOW LONG TILL WE LAND?

BEING SOMEONE ELSE

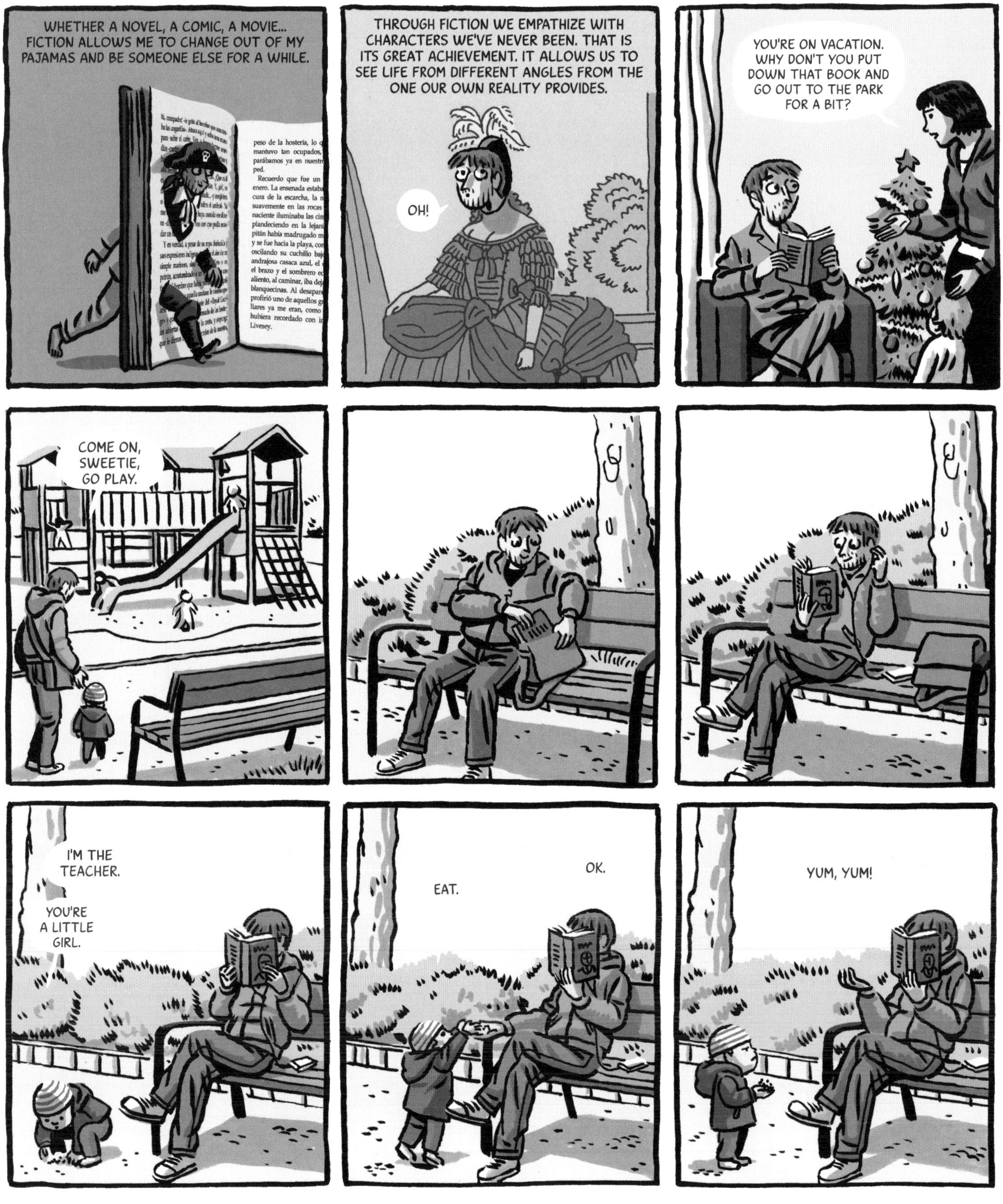

WHETHER A NOVEL, A COMIC, A MOVIE... FICTION ALLOWS ME TO CHANGE OUT OF MY PAJAMAS AND BE SOMEONE ELSE FOR A WHILE.
THROUGH FICTION WE EMPATHIZE WITH CHARACTERS WE'VE NEVER BEEN. THAT IS ITS GREAT ACHIEVEMENT. IT ALLOWS US TO SEE LIFE FROM DIFFERENT ANGLES FROM THE ONE OUR OWN REALITY PROVIDES.
OH!
YOU'RE ON VACATION. WHY DON'T YOU PUT DOWN THAT BOOK AND GO OUT TO THE PARK FOR A BIT?
COME ON, SWEETIE, GO PLAY.
I'M THE TEACHER.
YOU'RE A LITTLE GIRL.
EAT.
OK.
YUM, YUM!

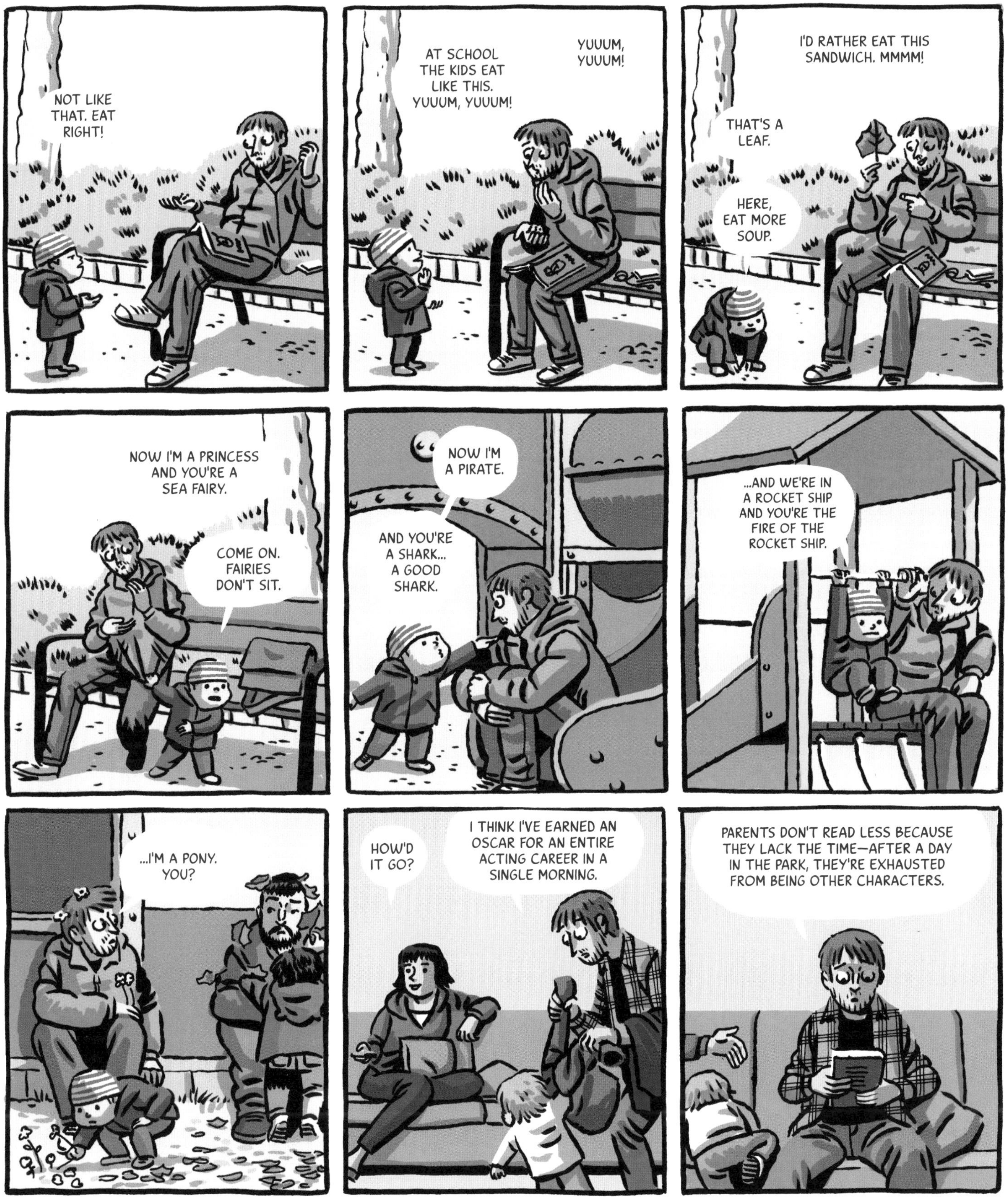
NOT LIKE THAT. EAT RIGHT!
AT SCHOOL THE KIDS EAT LIKE THIS. YUUUM, YUUUM!
YUUUM, YUUUM!
I'D RATHER EAT THIS SANDWICH. MMMM!
THAT'S A LEAF.
HERE, EAT MORE SOUP.
NOW I'M A PRINCESS AND YOU'RE A SEA FAIRY.
COME ON. FAIRIES DON'T SIT.
NOW I'M A PIRATE.
AND YOU'RE A SHARK... A GOOD SHARK.
...AND WE'RE IN A ROCKET SHIP AND YOU'RE THE FIRE OF THE ROCKET SHIP.
...I'M A PONY. YOU?
HOW'D IT GO?
I THINK I'VE EARNED AN OSCAR FOR AN ENTIRE ACTING CAREER IN A SINGLE MORNING.
PARENTS DON'T READ LESS BECAUSE THEY LACK THE TIME—AFTER A DAY IN THE PARK, THEY'RE EXHAUSTED FROM BEING OTHER CHARACTERS.

FEAR OF THE READER

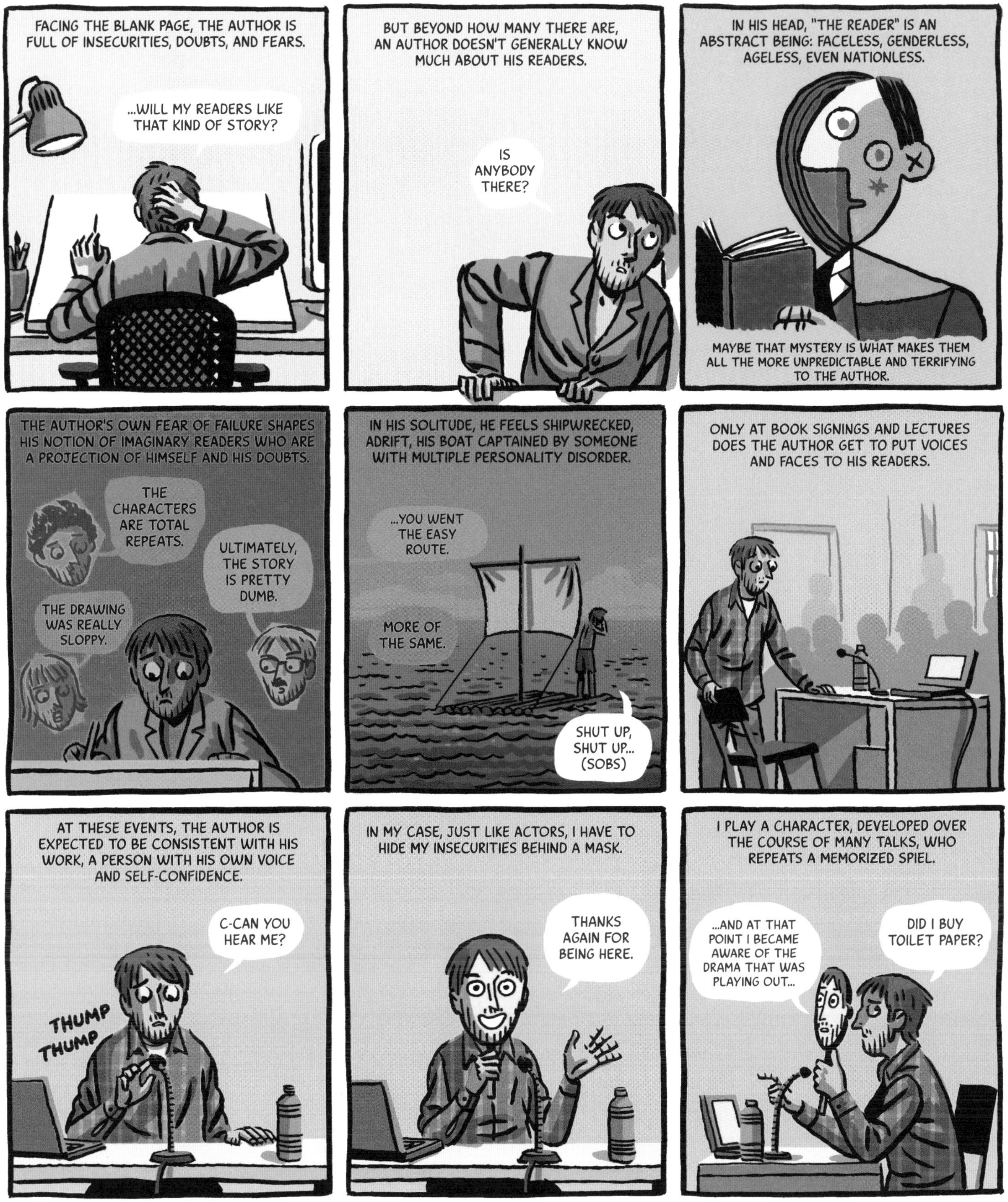

FACING THE BLANK PAGE, THE AUTHOR IS FULL OF INSECURITIES, DOUBTS, AND FEARS.
...WILL MY READERS LIKE THAT KIND OF STORY?
BUT BEYOND HOW MANY THERE ARE, AN AUTHOR DOESN'T GENERALLY KNOW MUCH ABOUT HIS READERS.
IS ANYBODY THERE?
IN HIS HEAD, "THE READER" IS AN ABSTRACT BEING: FACELESS, GENDERLESS, AGELESS, EVEN NATIONLESS.
MAYBE THAT MYSTERY IS WHAT MAKES THEM ALL THE MORE UNPREDICTABLE AND TERRIFYING TO THE AUTHOR.
THE AUTHOR'S OWN FEAR OF FAILURE SHAPES HIS NOTION OF IMAGINARY READERS WHO ARE A PROJECTION OF HIMSELF AND HIS DOUBTS.
THE CHARACTERS ARE TOTAL REPEATS.
ULTIMATELY, THE STORY IS PRETTY DUMB.
THE DRAWING WAS REALLY SLOPPY.
IN HIS SOLITUDE, HE FEELS SHIPWRECKED, ADRIFT, HIS BOAT CAPTAINED BY SOMEONE WITH MULTIPLE PERSONALITY DISORDER.
...YOU WENT THE EASY ROUTE.
MORE OF THE SAME.
SHUT UP, SHUT UP... (SOBS)
ONLY AT BOOK SIGNINGS AND LECTURES DOES THE AUTHOR GET TO PUT VOICES AND FACES TO HIS READERS.
AT THESE EVENTS, THE AUTHOR IS EXPECTED TO BE CONSISTENT WITH HIS WORK, A PERSON WITH HIS OWN VOICE AND SELF-CONFIDENCE.
C-CAN YOU HEAR ME?
THUMP THUMP
IN MY CASE, JUST LIKE ACTORS, I HAVE TO HIDE MY INSECURITIES BEHIND A MASK.
THANKS AGAIN FOR BEING HERE.
I PLAY A CHARACTER, DEVELOPED OVER THE COURSE OF MANY TALKS, WHO REPEATS A MEMORIZED SPIEL.
...AND AT THAT POINT I BECAME AWARE OF THE DRAMA THAT WAS PLAYING OUT...
DID I BUY TOILET PAPER?

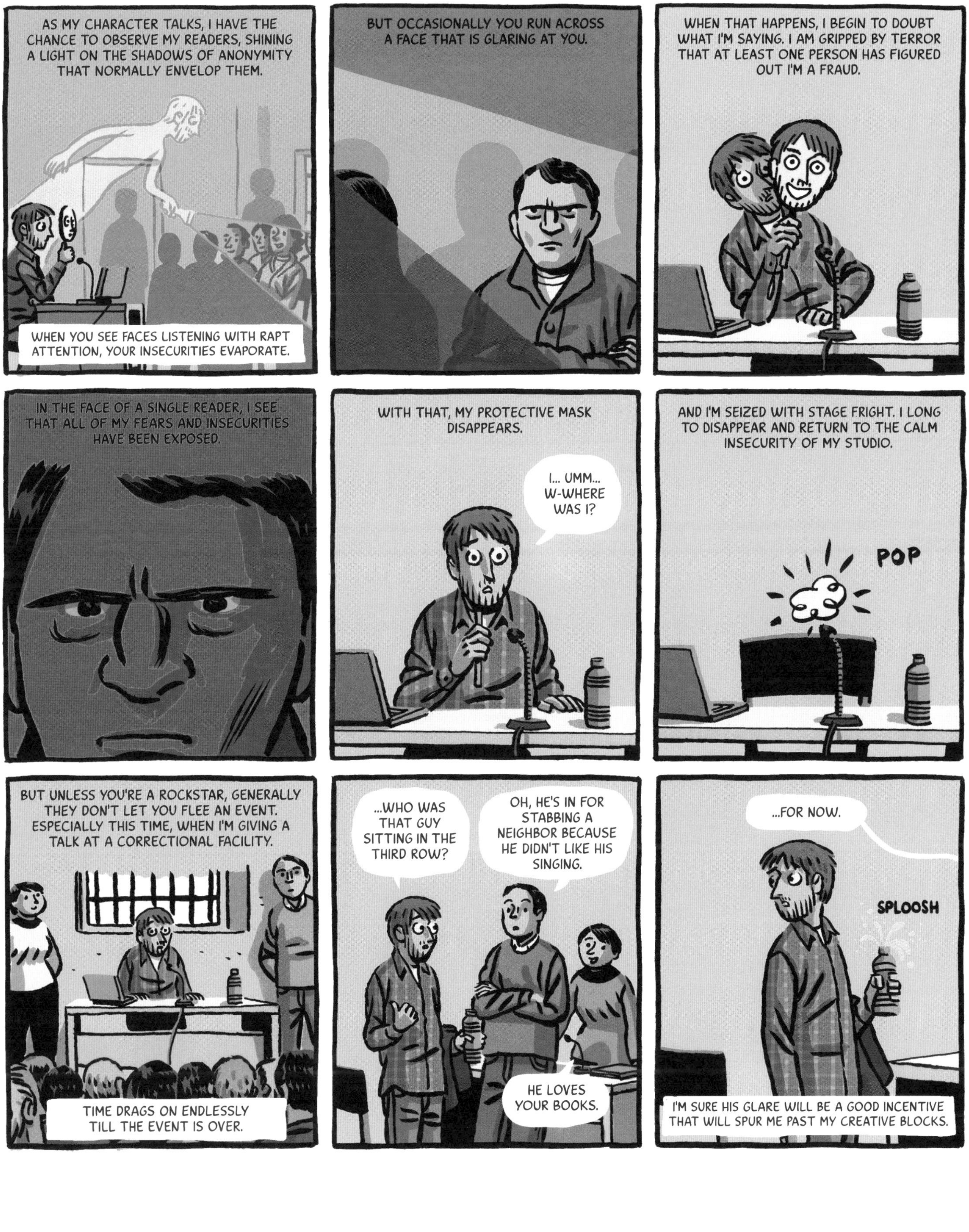
AS MY CHARACTER TALKS, I HAVE THE CHANCE TO OBSERVE MY READERS, SHINING A LIGHT ON THE SHADOWS OF ANONYMITY THAT NORMALLY ENVELOP THEM.
WHEN YOU SEE FACES LISTENING WITH RAPT ATTENTION, YOUR INSECURITIES EVAPORATE.
BUT OCCASIONALLY YOU RUN ACROSS A FACE THAT IS GLARING AT YOU.
WHEN THAT HAPPENS, I BEGIN TO DOUBT WHAT I'M SAYING. I AM GRIPPED BY TERROR THAT AT LEAST ONE PERSON HAS FIGURED OUT I'M A FRAUD.
IN THE FACE OF A SINGLE READER, I SEE THAT ALL OF MY FEARS AND INSECURITIES HAVE BEEN EXPOSED.
WITH THAT, MY PROTECTIVE MASK DISAPPEARS.
I... UMM... W-WHERE WAS I?
AND I'M SEIZED WITH STAGE FRIGHT. I LONG TO DISAPPEAR AND RETURN TO THE CALM INSECURITY OF MY STUDIO.
POP
BUT UNLESS YOU'RE A ROCKSTAR, GENERALLY THEY DON'T LET YOU FLEE AN EVENT. ESPECIALLY THIS TIME, WHEN I'M GIVING A TALK AT A CORRECTIONAL FACILITY.
TIME DRAGS ON ENDLESSLY TILL THE EVENT IS OVER.
...WHO WAS THAT GUY SITTING IN THE THIRD ROW?
OH, HE'S IN FOR STABBING A NEIGHBOR BECAUSE HE DIDN'T LIKE HIS SINGING.
HE LOVES YOUR BOOKS.
...FOR NOW.
SPLOOSH
I'M SURE HIS GLARE WILL BE A GOOD INCENTIVE THAT WILL SPUR ME PAST MY CREATIVE BLOCKS.

TO THE PHARMACEUTICAL COMPANIES' HEALTH

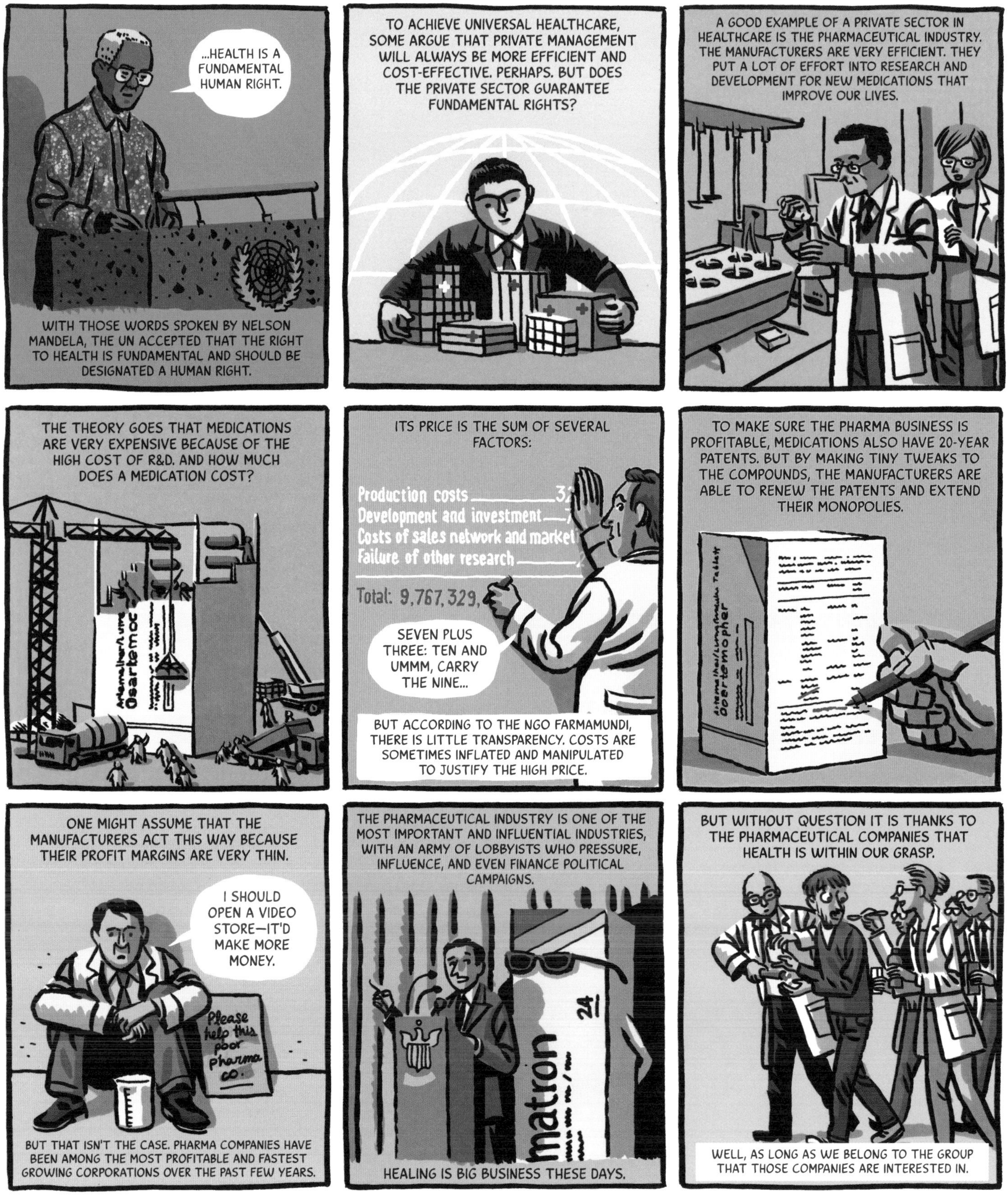

...HEALTH IS A FUNDAMENTAL HUMAN RIGHT.
WITH THOSE WORDS SPOKEN BY NELSON MANDELA, THE UN ACCEPTED THAT THE RIGHT TO HEALTH IS FUNDAMENTAL AND SHOULD BE DESIGNATED A HUMAN RIGHT.
TO ACHIEVE UNIVERSAL HEALTHCARE, SOME ARGUE THAT PRIVATE MANAGEMENT WILL ALWAYS BE MORE EFFICIENT AND COST-EFFECTIVE. PERHAPS. BUT DOES THE PRIVATE SECTOR GUARANTEE FUNDAMENTAL RIGHTS?
A GOOD EXAMPLE OF A PRIVATE SECTOR IN HEALTHCARE IS THE PHARMACEUTICAL INDUSTRY. THE MANUFACTURERS ARE VERY EFFICIENT. THEY PUT A LOT OF EFFORT INTO RESEARCH AND DEVELOPMENT FOR NEW MEDICATIONS THAT IMPROVE OUR LIVES.
THE THEORY GOES THAT MEDICATIONS ARE VERY EXPENSIVE BECAUSE OF THE HIGH COST OF R&D. AND HOW MUCH DOES A MEDICATION COST?
Osartemoc
ITS PRICE IS THE SUM OF SEVERAL FACTORS:
Production costs
Development and investment
Costs of sales network and market
Failure of other research
Total: 9,767,329,
SEVEN PLUS THREE: TEN AND UMMM, CARRY THE NINE...
BUT ACCORDING TO THE NGO FARMAMUNDI, THERE IS LITTLE TRANSPARENCY. COSTS ARE SOMETIMES INFLATED AND MANIPULATED TO JUSTIFY THE HIGH PRICE.
TO MAKE SURE THE PHARMA BUSINESS IS PROFITABLE, MEDICATIONS ALSO HAVE 20-YEAR PATENTS. BUT BY MAKING TINY TWEAKS TO THE COMPOUNDS, THE MANUFACTURERS ARE ABLE TO RENEW THE PATENTS AND EXTEND THEIR MONOPOLIES.
ONE MIGHT ASSUME THAT THE MANUFACTURERS ACT THIS WAY BECAUSE THEIR PROFIT MARGINS ARE VERY THIN.
I SHOULD OPEN A VIDEO STORE—IT'D MAKE MORE MONEY.
Please help this poor Pharma co.
BUT THAT ISN'T THE CASE. PHARMA COMPANIES HAVE BEEN AMONG THE MOST PROFITABLE AND FASTEST GROWING CORPORATIONS OVER THE PAST FEW YEARS.
THE PHARMACEUTICAL INDUSTRY IS ONE OF THE MOST IMPORTANT AND INFLUENTIAL INDUSTRIES, WITH AN ARMY OF LOBBYISTS WHO PRESSURE, INFLUENCE, AND EVEN FINANCE POLITICAL CAMPAIGNS.
matron
24
HEALING IS BIG BUSINESS THESE DAYS.
BUT WITHOUT QUESTION IT IS THANKS TO THE PHARMACEUTICAL COMPANIES THAT HEALTH IS WITHIN OUR GRASP.
WELL, AS LONG AS WE BELONG TO THE GROUP THAT THOSE COMPANIES ARE INTERESTED IN.

THE COMPANIES' BIG PROSPECTS ARE IN DEVELOPING COUNTRIES: IN THEIR GOVERNMENTS, TO WHICH THEY SUPPLY MEDICATIONS, AND IN THEIR CITIZENS, WHOM THEY MEDICALIZE IF NEEDED.

...AND GIVE ME SOMETHING FOR POST-VACATION DEPRESSION TOO. AND SOMETHING FOR TIRED LEG SYNDROME. AND...

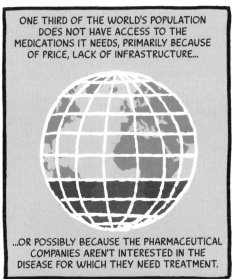

ONE THIRD OF THE WORLD'S POPULATION DOES NOT HAVE ACCESS TO THE MEDICATIONS IT NEEDS, PRIMARILY BECAUSE OF PRICE, LACK OF INFRASTRUCTURE...

...OR POSSIBLY BECAUSE THE PHARMACEUTICAL COMPANIES AREN'T INTERESTED IN THE DISEASE FOR WHICH THEY NEED TREATMENT.

EBOLA IS A GOOD EXAMPLE. AS LONG AS IT WAS A LOCALIZED DISEASE LIMITED TO AFRICA, THE LABS WEREN'T INTERESTED. IT WAS ONLY WHEN IT "JUMPED" TO SPAIN AND THE UNITED STATES THAT THEY ACTED.

THERE'S MONEY HERE.

MALARIA IS ANOTHER EXAMPLE. THERE'S NO PATENT ON THE MALARIA VACCINE, BUT ITS CREATOR, THE BIOLOGIST PATARROYO, AMONG OTHERS, HASN'T FOUND A PHARMACEUTICAL COMPANY WILLING TO TAKE ON THE PRODUCTION COSTS BECAUSE IT ISN'T PROFITABLE.

MMMM... I DON'T SEE IT.

DON'T YOU HAVE ANYTHING FOR HYPERACTIVITY IN CHILDREN?

IT'S CLEAR THAT THE PRIVATE COMPANIES PRIORITIZE PROFITS ABOVE ALL.

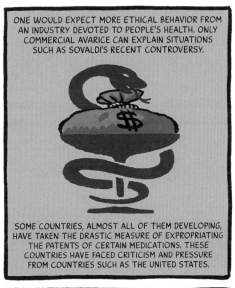

ONE WOULD EXPECT MORE ETHICAL BEHAVIOR FROM AN INDUSTRY DEVOTED TO PEOPLE'S HEALTH. ONLY COMMERCIAL AVARICE CAN EXPLAIN SITUATIONS SUCH AS SOVALDI'S RECENT CONTROVERSY.

SOME COUNTRIES, ALMOST ALL OF THEM DEVELOPING, HAVE TAKEN THE DRASTIC MEASURE OF EXPROPRIATING THE PATENTS OF CERTAIN MEDICATIONS. THESE COUNTRIES HAVE FACED CRITICISM AND PRESSURE FROM COUNTRIES SUCH AS THE UNITED STATES.

THOUGH THE UNITED STATES ITSELF, AFTER THE ANTHRAX ATTACKS (WHICH CAUSED ONLY THREE DEATHS), THREATENED TO OVERRIDE THE PATENT FOR THE ANTIDOTE IF THE COMPANY THAT MANUFACTURED IT DIDN'T LOWER ITS PRICE CONSIDERABLY.

THIS IS FROM UNCLE SAM.

WHEN MY FATHER DIED FROM HEPATITIS C, THERE WASN'T A CURE YET. IF HE'D HELD ON JUST A YEAR LONGER, HE WOULD NOW BE YET ANOTHER PERSON WAITING ON THE MIRACLE OF A SIGNED AGREEMENT BETWEEN AN INEFFECTIVE GOVERNMENT AND THE USURIOUS PHARMACEUTICAL INDUSTRY.

...WELL, I'D BE REALLY PISSED.

I IMAGINE SO.

BUT YOU'VE HEARD OF DIVINE JUSTICE? ONE OUT OF EVERY THREE SOULS UP THERE IS WAITING FOR THE PHARMA PEOPLE TO ARRIVE. WE HAVE ALL OF ETERNITY TO SETTLE SCORES.

ALTHOUGH... WEIRD THING IS, WE HAVEN'T SEEN ANY OF THEM UP THERE YET.

THAT'S BECAUSE THEY'VE DISCOVERED A SECRET MEDICATION THAT MAKES THEM IMMORTAL.

THAT'S WHY THEY NEED TO RAKE IN SO MUCH MONEY.

NARRATOR VERSUS LISTENER

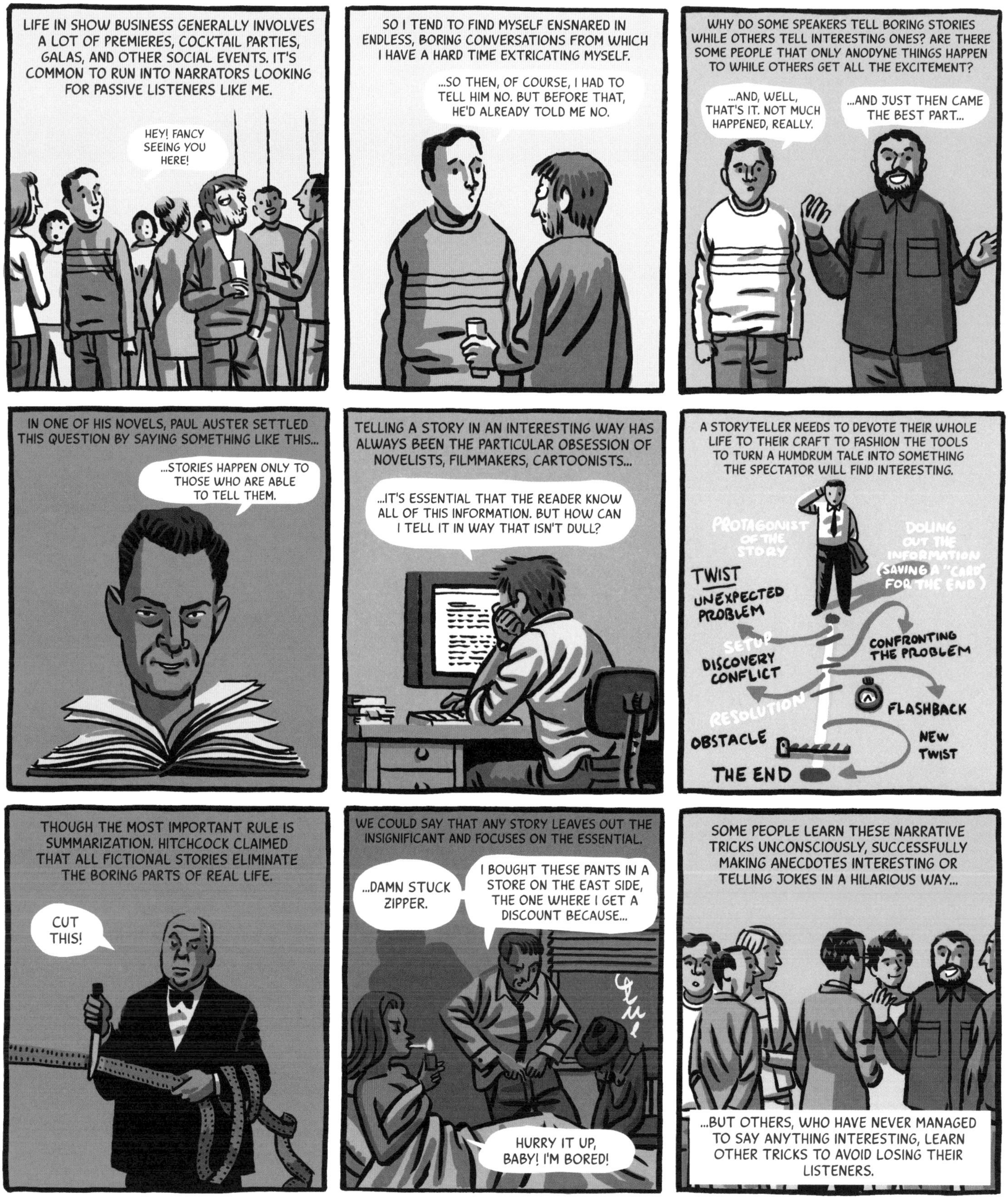
LIFE IN SHOW BUSINESS GENERALLY INVOLVES A LOT OF PREMIERES, COCKTAIL PARTIES, GALAS, AND OTHER SOCIAL EVENTS. IT'S COMMON TO RUN INTO NARRATORS LOOKING FOR PASSIVE LISTENERS LIKE ME.
HEY! FANCY SEEING YOU HERE!
SO I TEND TO FIND MYSELF ENSNARED IN ENDLESS, BORING CONVERSATIONS FROM WHICH I HAVE A HARD TIME EXTRICATING MYSELF.
...SO THEN, OF COURSE, I HAD TO TELL HIM NO. BUT BEFORE THAT, HE'D ALREADY TOLD ME NO.
WHY DO SOME SPEAKERS TELL BORING STORIES WHILE OTHERS TELL INTERESTING ONES? ARE THERE SOME PEOPLE THAT ONLY ANODYNE THINGS HAPPEN TO WHILE OTHERS GET ALL THE EXCITEMENT?
...AND, WELL, THAT'S IT. NOT MUCH HAPPENED, REALLY.
...AND JUST THEN CAME THE BEST PART...
IN ONE OF HIS NOVELS, PAUL AUSTER SETTLED THIS QUESTION BY SAYING SOMETHING LIKE THIS...
...STORIES HAPPEN ONLY TO THOSE WHO ARE ABLE TO TELL THEM.
TELLING A STORY IN AN INTERESTING WAY HAS ALWAYS BEEN THE PARTICULAR OBSESSION OF NOVELISTS, FILMMAKERS, CARTOONISTS...
...IT'S ESSENTIAL THAT THE READER KNOW ALL OF THIS INFORMATION. BUT HOW CAN I TELL IT IN WAY THAT ISN'T DULL?
A STORYTELLER NEEDS TO DEVOTE THEIR WHOLE LIFE TO THEIR CRAFT TO FASHION THE TOOLS TO TURN A HUMDRUM TALE INTO SOMETHING THE SPECTATOR WILL FIND INTERESTING.
PROTAGONIST OF THE STORY
DOLING OUT THE INFORMATION (SAVING A "CARD" FOR THE END)
TWIST
UNEXPECTED PROBLEM
SETUP
CONFRONTING THE PROBLEM
DISCOVERY CONFLICT
RESOLUTION
FLASHBACK
OBSTACLE
NEW TWIST
THE END
THOUGH THE MOST IMPORTANT RULE IS SUMMARIZATION. HITCHCOCK CLAIMED THAT ALL FICTIONAL STORIES ELIMINATE THE BORING PARTS OF REAL LIFE.
CUT THIS!
WE COULD SAY THAT ANY STORY LEAVES OUT THE INSIGNIFICANT AND FOCUSES ON THE ESSENTIAL.
...DAMN STUCK ZIPPER.
I BOUGHT THESE PANTS IN A STORE ON THE EAST SIDE, THE ONE WHERE I GET A DISCOUNT BECAUSE...
HURRY IT UP, BABY! I'M BORED!
SOME PEOPLE LEARN THESE NARRATIVE TRICKS UNCONSCIOUSLY, SUCCESSFULLY MAKING ANECDOTES INTERESTING OR TELLING JOKES IN A HILARIOUS WAY...
...BUT OTHERS, WHO HAVE NEVER MANAGED TO SAY ANYTHING INTERESTING, LEARN OTHER TRICKS TO AVOID LOSING THEIR LISTENERS.

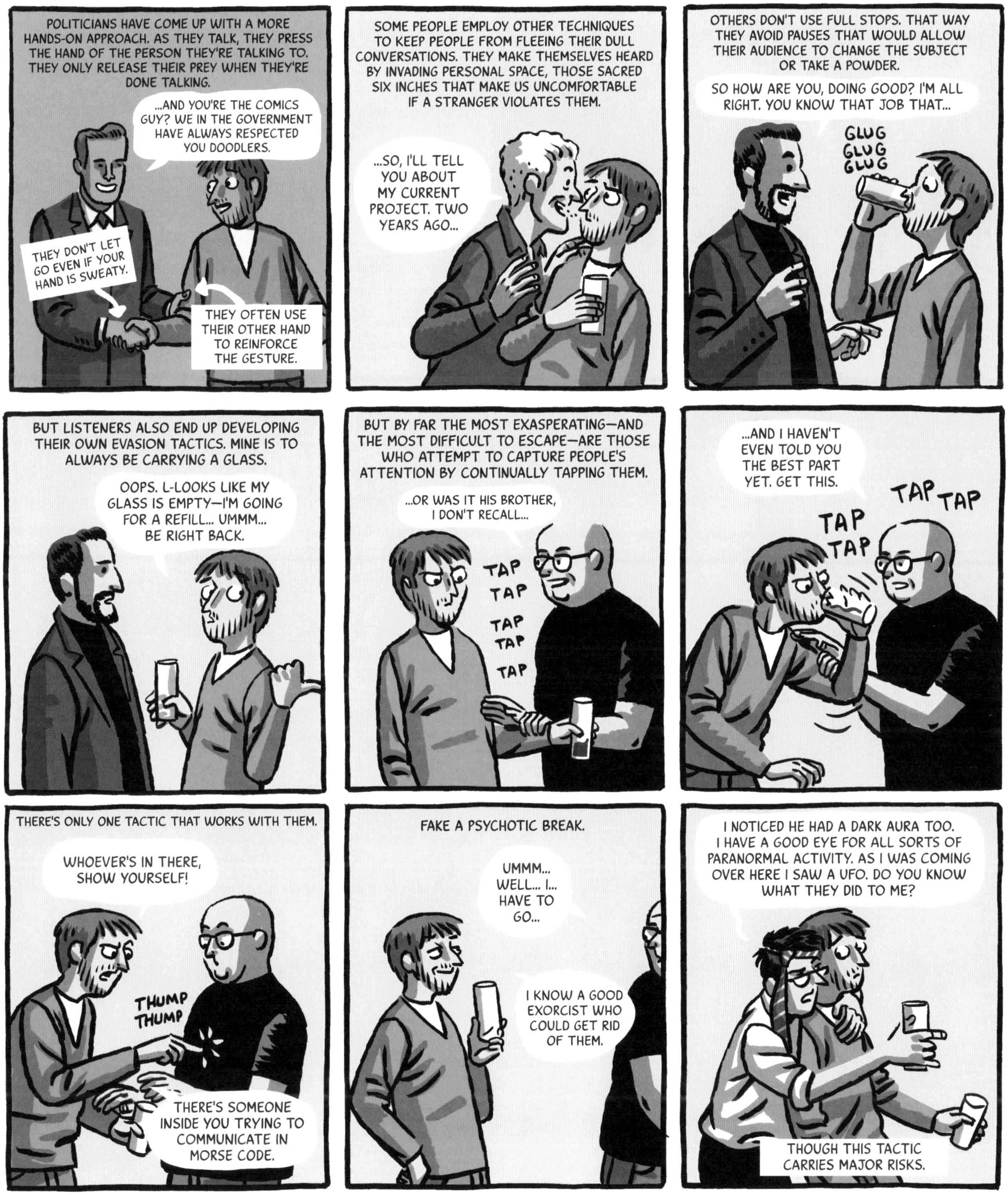
POLITICIANS HAVE COME UP WITH A MORE HANDS-ON APPROACH. AS THEY TALK, THEY PRESS THE HAND OF THE PERSON THEY'RE TALKING TO. THEY ONLY RELEASE THEIR PREY WHEN THEY'RE DONE TALKING.
...AND YOU'RE THE COMICS GUY? WE IN THE GOVERNMENT HAVE ALWAYS RESPECTED YOU DOODLERS.
THEY DON'T LET GO EVEN IF YOUR HAND IS SWEATY.
THEY OFTEN USE THEIR OTHER HAND TO REINFORCE THE GESTURE.
SOME PEOPLE EMPLOY OTHER TECHNIQUES TO KEEP PEOPLE FROM FLEEING THEIR DULL CONVERSATIONS. THEY MAKE THEMSELVES HEARD BY INVADING PERSONAL SPACE, THOSE SACRED SIX INCHES THAT MAKE US UNCOMFORTABLE IF A STRANGER VIOLATES THEM.
...SO, I'LL TELL YOU ABOUT MY CURRENT PROJECT. TWO YEARS AGO...
OTHERS DON'T USE FULL STOPS. THAT WAY THEY AVOID PAUSES THAT WOULD ALLOW THEIR AUDIENCE TO CHANGE THE SUBJECT OR TAKE A POWDER.
SO HOW ARE YOU, DOING GOOD? I'M ALL RIGHT. YOU KNOW THAT JOB THAT...
GLUG GLUG GLUG
BUT LISTENERS ALSO END UP DEVELOPING THEIR OWN EVASION TACTICS. MINE IS TO ALWAYS BE CARRYING A GLASS.
OOPS. L-LOOKS LIKE MY GLASS IS EMPTY—I'M GOING FOR A REFILL... UMMM... BE RIGHT BACK.
BUT BY FAR THE MOST EXASPERATING—AND THE MOST DIFFICULT TO ESCAPE—ARE THOSE WHO ATTEMPT TO CAPTURE PEOPLE'S ATTENTION BY CONTINUALLY TAPPING THEM.
...OR WAS IT HIS BROTHER, I DON'T RECALL...
TAP TAP TAP TAP TAP
...AND I HAVEN'T EVEN TOLD YOU THE BEST PART YET. GET THIS.
TAP TAP TAP TAP
THERE'S ONLY ONE TACTIC THAT WORKS WITH THEM.
WHOEVER'S IN THERE, SHOW YOURSELF!
THUMP THUMP
THERE'S SOMEONE INSIDE YOU TRYING TO COMMUNICATE IN MORSE CODE.
FAKE A PSYCHOTIC BREAK.
UMMM... WELL... I... HAVE TO GO...
I KNOW A GOOD EXORCIST WHO COULD GET RID OF THEM.
I NOTICED HE HAD A DARK AURA TOO. I HAVE A GOOD EYE FOR ALL SORTS OF PARANORMAL ACTIVITY. AS I WAS COMING OVER HERE I SAW A UFO. DO YOU KNOW WHAT THEY DID TO ME?
THOUGH THIS TACTIC CARRIES MAJOR RISKS.

THE UNIFICATION OF THE SELF

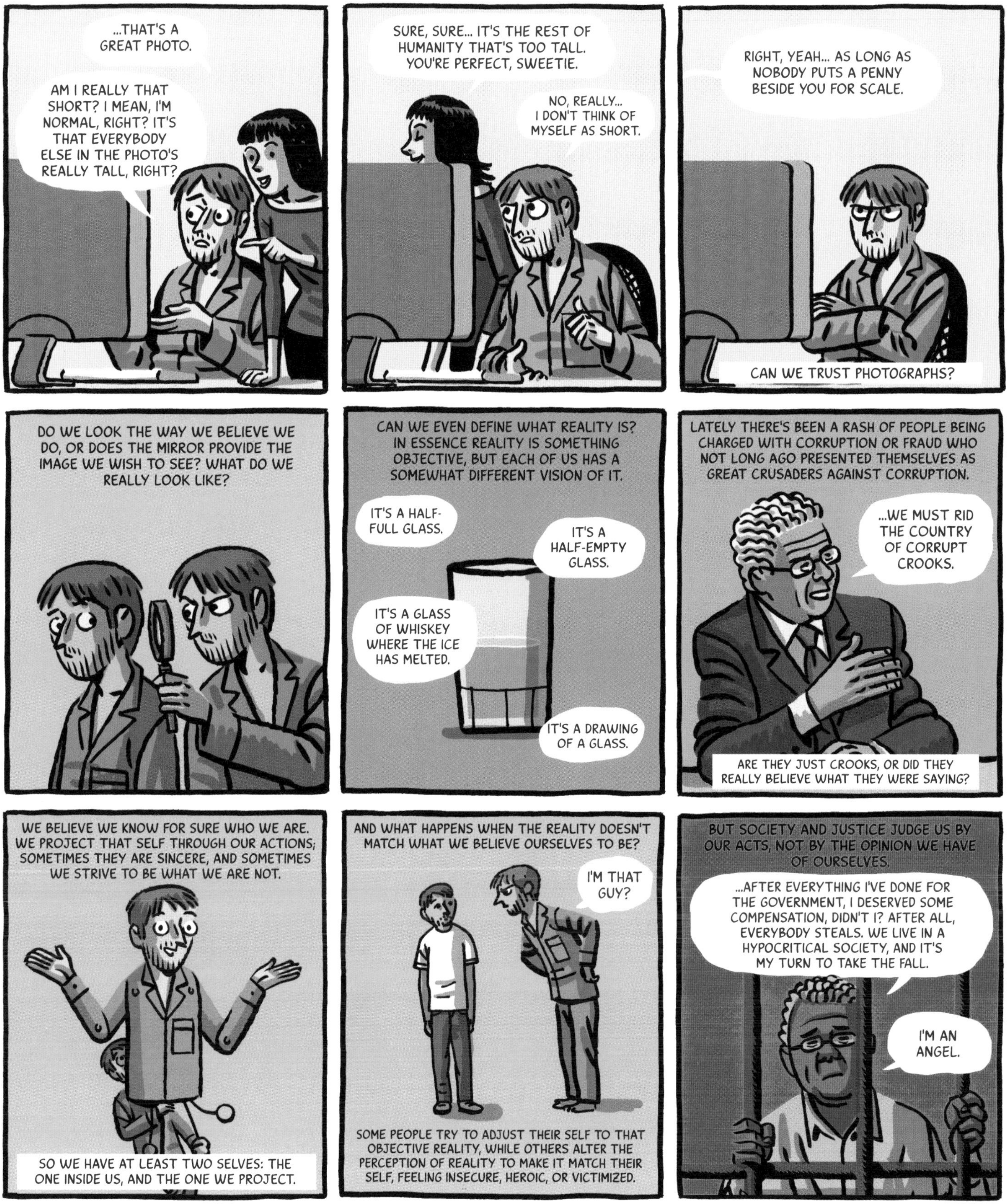
...THAT'S A GREAT PHOTO.
AM I REALLY THAT SHORT? I MEAN, I'M NORMAL, RIGHT? IT'S THAT EVERYBODY ELSE IN THE PHOTO'S REALLY TALL, RIGHT?
SURE, SURE... IT'S THE REST OF HUMANITY THAT'S TOO TALL. YOU'RE PERFECT, SWEETIE.
NO, REALLY... I DON'T THINK OF MYSELF AS SHORT.
RIGHT, YEAH... AS LONG AS NOBODY PUTS A PENNY BESIDE YOU FOR SCALE.
CAN WE TRUST PHOTOGRAPHS?
DO WE LOOK THE WAY WE BELIEVE WE DO, OR DOES THE MIRROR PROVIDE THE IMAGE WE WISH TO SEE? WHAT DO WE REALLY LOOK LIKE?
CAN WE EVEN DEFINE WHAT REALITY IS? IN ESSENCE REALITY IS SOMETHING OBJECTIVE, BUT EACH OF US HAS A SOMEWHAT DIFFERENT VISION OF IT.
IT'S A HALF-FULL GLASS.
IT'S A HALF-EMPTY GLASS.
IT'S A GLASS OF WHISKEY WHERE THE ICE HAS MELTED.
IT'S A DRAWING OF A GLASS.
LATELY THERE'S BEEN A RASH OF PEOPLE BEING CHARGED WITH CORRUPTION OR FRAUD WHO NOT LONG AGO PRESENTED THEMSELVES AS GREAT CRUSADERS AGAINST CORRUPTION.
...WE MUST RID THE COUNTRY OF CORRUPT CROOKS.
ARE THEY JUST CROOKS, OR DID THEY REALLY BELIEVE WHAT THEY WERE SAYING?
WE BELIEVE WE KNOW FOR SURE WHO WE ARE. WE PROJECT THAT SELF THROUGH OUR ACTIONS; SOMETIMES THEY ARE SINCERE, AND SOMETIMES WE STRIVE TO BE WHAT WE ARE NOT.
SO WE HAVE AT LEAST TWO SELVES: THE ONE INSIDE US, AND THE ONE WE PROJECT.
AND WHAT HAPPENS WHEN THE REALITY DOESN'T MATCH WHAT WE BELIEVE OURSELVES TO BE?
I'M THAT GUY?
SOME PEOPLE TRY TO ADJUST THEIR SELF TO THAT OBJECTIVE REALITY, WHILE OTHERS ALTER THE PERCEPTION OF REALITY TO MAKE IT MATCH THEIR SELF, FEELING INSECURE, HEROIC, OR VICTIMIZED.
BUT SOCIETY AND JUSTICE JUDGE US BY OUR ACTS, NOT BY THE OPINION WE HAVE OF OURSELVES.
...AFTER EVERYTHING I'VE DONE FOR THE GOVERNMENT, I DESERVED SOME COMPENSATION, DIDN'T I? AFTER ALL, EVERYBODY STEALS. WE LIVE IN A HYPOCRITICAL SOCIETY, AND IT'S MY TURN TO TAKE THE FALL.
I'M AN ANGEL.

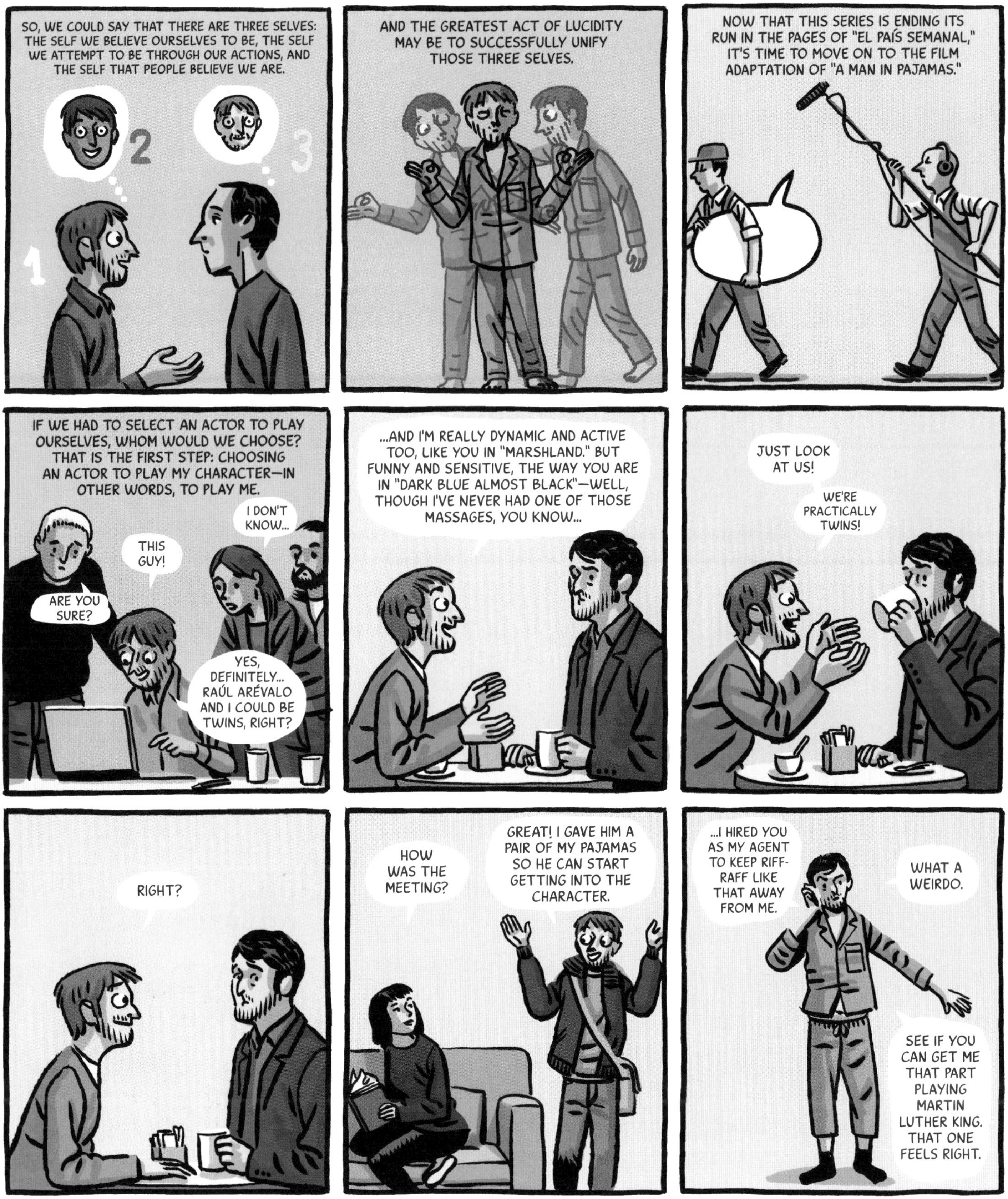
SO, WE COULD SAY THAT THERE ARE THREE SELVES: THE SELF WE BELIEVE OURSELVES TO BE, THE SELF WE ATTEMPT TO BE THROUGH OUR ACTIONS, AND THE SELF THAT PEOPLE BELIEVE WE ARE.
2
3
1
AND THE GREATEST ACT OF LUCIDITY MAY BE TO SUCCESSFULLY UNIFY THOSE THREE SELVES.
NOW THAT THIS SERIES IS ENDING ITS RUN IN THE PAGES OF "EL PAÍS SEMANAL," IT'S TIME TO MOVE ON TO THE FILM ADAPTATION OF "A MAN IN PAJAMAS."
IF WE HAD TO SELECT AN ACTOR TO PLAY OURSELVES, WHOM WOULD WE CHOOSE? THAT IS THE FIRST STEP: CHOOSING AN ACTOR TO PLAY MY CHARACTER—IN OTHER WORDS, TO PLAY ME.
I DON'T KNOW...
THIS GUY!
ARE YOU SURE?
YES, DEFINITELY... RAÚL ARÉVALO AND I COULD BE TWINS, RIGHT?
...AND I'M REALLY DYNAMIC AND ACTIVE TOO, LIKE YOU IN "MARSHLAND." BUT FUNNY AND SENSITIVE, THE WAY YOU ARE IN "DARK BLUE ALMOST BLACK"—WELL, THOUGH I'VE NEVER HAD ONE OF THOSE MASSAGES, YOU KNOW...
JUST LOOK AT US!
WE'RE PRACTICALLY TWINS!
RIGHT?
HOW WAS THE MEETING?
GREAT! I GAVE HIM A PAIR OF MY PAJAMAS SO HE CAN START GETTING INTO THE CHARACTER.
...I HIRED YOU AS MY AGENT TO KEEP RIFF-RAFF LIKE THAT AWAY FROM ME.
WHAT A WEIRDO.
SEE IF YOU CAN GET ME THAT PART PLAYING MARTIN LUTHER KING. THAT ONE FEELS RIGHT.

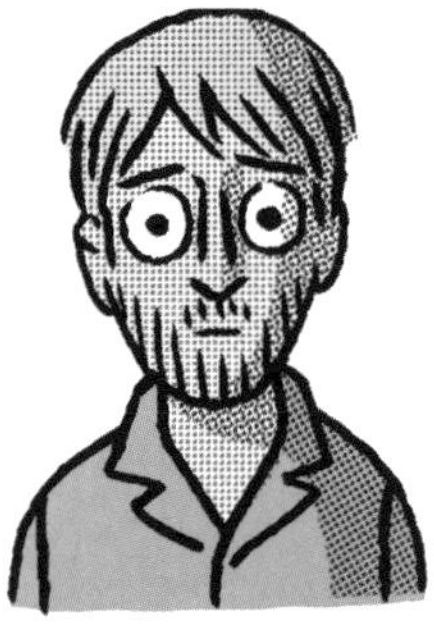

PACO ROCA'S INCREDIBLE INVENTIONS

CARTOONISTS DON'T DRIVE. THIS IS THE CONCLUSION REACHED BY A RECENT STUDY PRESENTED BY DR. COPENHAGUE OF THE FÉDÉRATION NATIONALE D'ACHATS DES CADRES. THE STUDY EXPLORES THE WIDESPREAD LACK OF DRIVING ABILITY AMONG CARTOONISTS. REASONS INCLUDE SCATTERBRAINEDNESS, PETER PAN SYNDROME... INDISPUTABLY, THE CARTOONIST FEARS THE CAR.

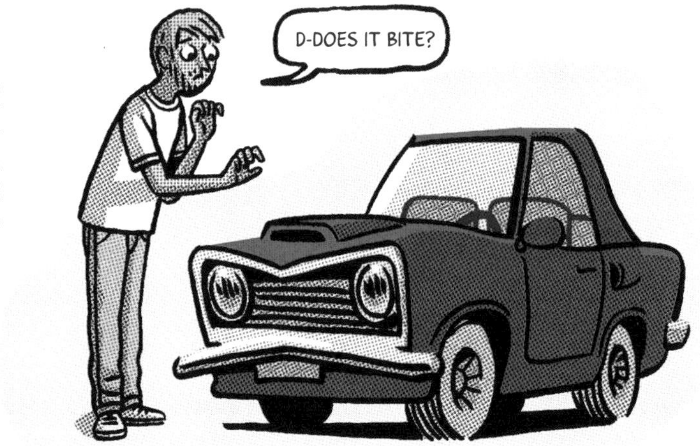
D-DOES IT BITE?

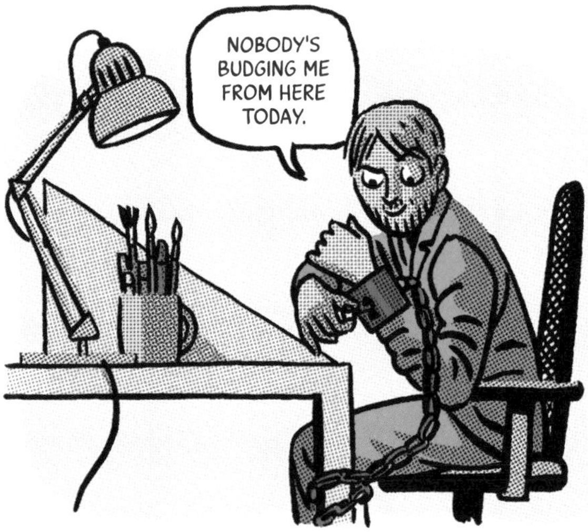
NOBODY'S BUDGING ME FROM HERE TODAY.

THE REPORT ALSO INDICATES THAT CARTOONISTS FEEL AT EASE ONLY IN THEIR NATURAL HABITAT: THEIR STUDIO. DUE TO THE ABSORBING NATURE OF THEIR WORK, CARTOONISTS SPEND MUCH OF THE DAY AT THE DRAWING TABLE, OFTEN IN PAJAMAS. AS A RESULT, THEY FEEL UNCOMFORTABLE OUTSIDE OF THAT ENVIRONMENT, AND WHEN FORCED TO TRAVEL BY CAR, THEY DO SO WITH THE UTMOST DISPLEASURE.

FOR ALL CARTOONISTS WHO HATE DRIVING BECAUSE IT TAKES THEM AWAY FROM THEIR STUDIO AND DISRUPTS THEIR CREATIVE FLOW, THIS VEHICLE WILL SOLVE ALL OF THEIR MOBILITY PROBLEMS.

THE STUDIO CAR

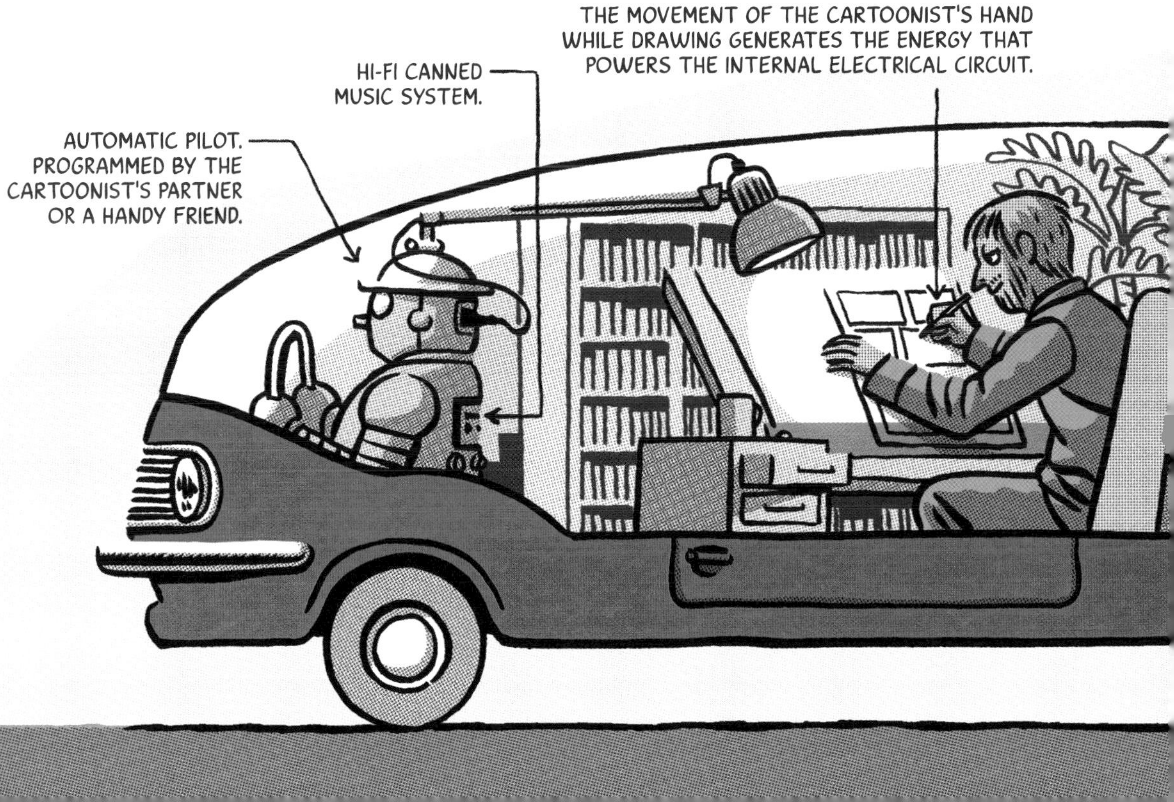
THE MOVEMENT OF THE CARTOONIST'S HAND WHILE DRAWING GENERATES THE ENERGY THAT POWERS THE INTERNAL ELECTRICAL CIRCUIT.
HI-FI CANNED MUSIC SYSTEM.
AUTOMATIC PILOT. PROGRAMMED BY THE CARTOONIST'S PARTNER OR A HANDY FRIEND.

THE STUDIO CAR COMES IN A WIDE VARIETY OF PANTONE COLORS, ALL WITH A MATTE FINISH. THE CARTOONIST CAN ALSO CHOOSE BETWEEN THREE TYPES OF SUSPENSION, DEPENDING ON THEIR GRAPHIC STYLE:

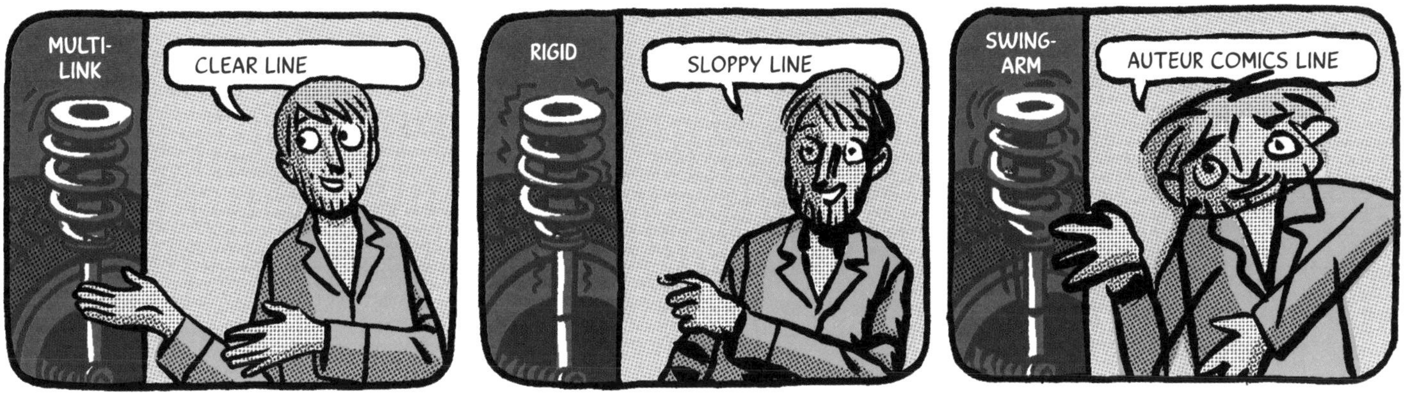
MULTI-LINK
CLEAR LINE
RIGID
SLOPPY LINE
SWING-ARM
AUTEUR COMICS LINE

THANKS TO THIS REVOLUTIONARY CAR, EVEN THE MOST INSIGNIFICANT OF CARTOONISTS WILL FEEL LIKE AN OLD HAND AT THE WHEEL, ABLE EVEN TO DRAW WITH ONE ARM RESTING ON THE WINDOW LIKE A PROFESSIONAL ROAD MASTER.

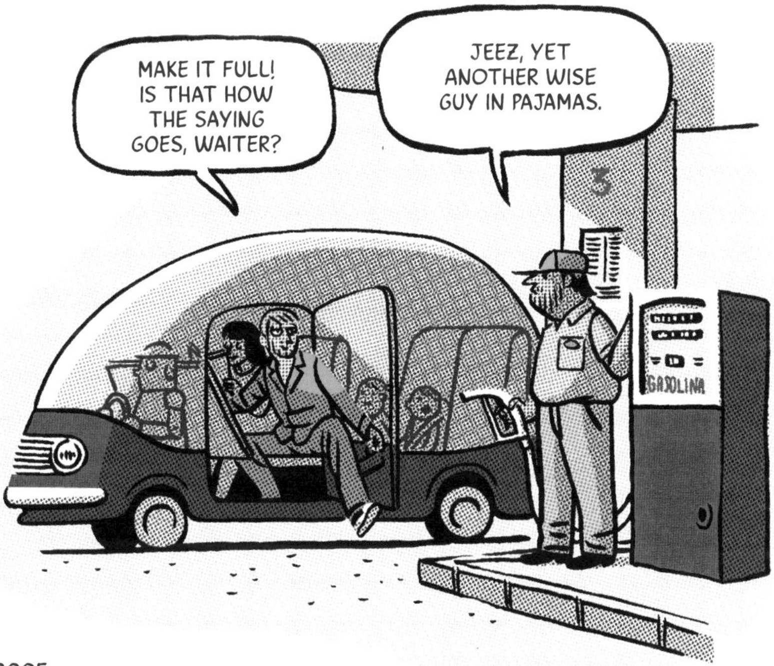
MAKE IT FULL! IS THAT HOW THE SAYING GOES, WAITER?
JEEZ, YET ANOTHER WISE GUY IN PAJAMAS.
GASOLINA

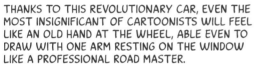

OWNERS MANUAL AVAILABLE IN COMIC FORMAT!

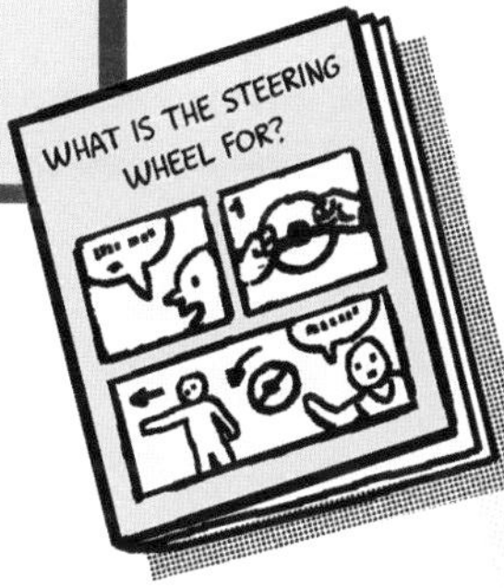
WHAT IS THE STEERING WHEEL FOR?

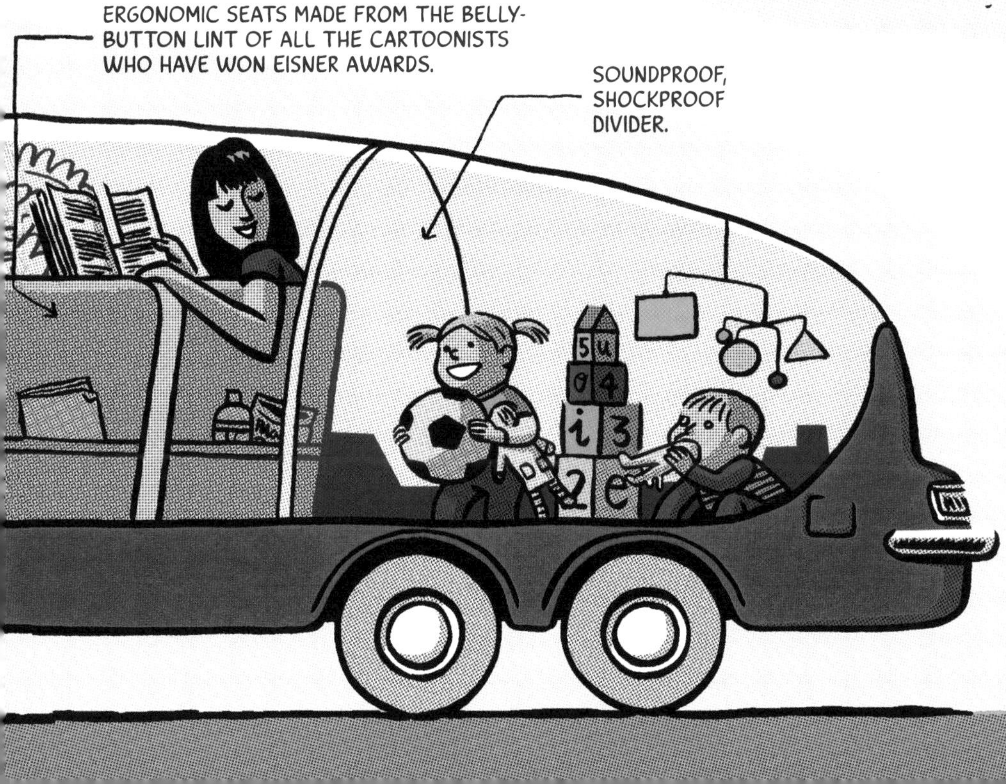
ERGONOMIC SEATS MADE FROM THE BELLY-BUTTON LINT OF ALL THE CARTOONISTS WHO HAVE WON EISNER AWARDS.
SOUNDPROOF, SHOCKPROOF DIVIDER.

IN THE STUDIO CAR, YOU CAN GO THE DISTANCE, CARTOONIST, WITHOUT EVER PUTTING DOWN YOUR PENCIL!

THE UNCOMFORTABLE CHAIR

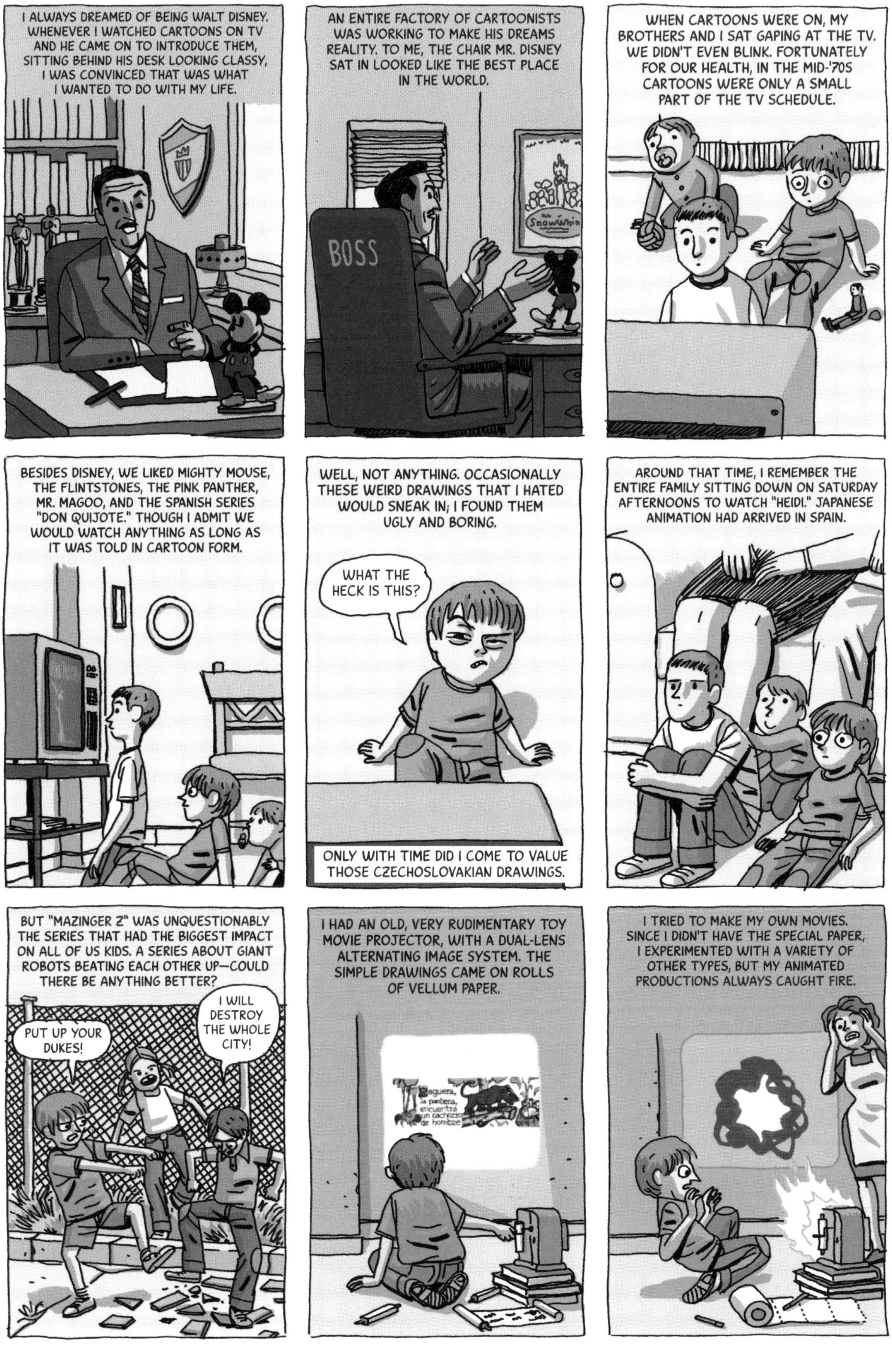
I ALWAYS DREAMED OF BEING WALT DISNEY. WHENEVER I WATCHED CARTOONS ON TV AND HE CAME ON TO INTRODUCE THEM, SITTING BEHIND HIS DESK LOOKING CLASSY, I WAS CONVINCED THAT WAS WHAT I WANTED TO DO WITH MY LIFE.
AN ENTIRE FACTORY OF CARTOONISTS WAS WORKING TO MAKE HIS DREAMS REALITY. TO ME, THE CHAIR MR. DISNEY SAT IN LOOKED LIKE THE BEST PLACE IN THE WORLD.
BOSS
WHEN CARTOONS WERE ON, MY BROTHERS AND I SAT GAPING AT THE TV. WE DIDN'T EVEN BLINK. FORTUNATELY FOR OUR HEALTH, IN THE MID-'70S CARTOONS WERE ONLY A SMALL PART OF THE TV SCHEDULE.
BESIDES DISNEY, WE LIKED MIGHTY MOUSE, THE FLINTSTONES, THE PINK PANTHER, MR. MAGOO, AND THE SPANISH SERIES "DON QUIJOTE." THOUGH I ADMIT WE WOULD WATCH ANYTHING AS LONG AS IT WAS TOLD IN CARTOON FORM.
WELL, NOT ANYTHING. OCCASIONALLY THESE WEIRD DRAWINGS THAT I HATED WOULD SNEAK IN; I FOUND THEM UGLY AND BORING.
WHAT THE HECK IS THIS?
ONLY WITH TIME DID I COME TO VALUE THOSE CZECHOSLOVAKIAN DRAWINGS.
AROUND THAT TIME, I REMEMBER THE ENTIRE FAMILY SITTING DOWN ON SATURDAY AFTERNOONS TO WATCH "HEIDI." JAPANESE ANIMATION HAD ARRIVED IN SPAIN.
BUT "MAZINGER Z" WAS UNQUESTIONABLY THE SERIES THAT HAD THE BIGGEST IMPACT ON ALL OF US KIDS. A SERIES ABOUT GIANT ROBOTS BEATING EACH OTHER UP—COULD THERE BE ANYTHING BETTER?
PUT UP YOUR DUKES!
I WILL DESTROY THE WHOLE CITY!
I HAD AN OLD, VERY RUDIMENTARY TOY MOVIE PROJECTOR, WITH A DUAL-LENS ALTERNATING IMAGE SYSTEM. THE SIMPLE DRAWINGS CAME ON ROLLS OF VELLUM PAPER.
I TRIED TO MAKE MY OWN MOVIES. SINCE I DIDN'T HAVE THE SPECIAL PAPER, I EXPERIMENTED WITH A VARIETY OF OTHER TYPES, BUT MY ANIMATED PRODUCTIONS ALWAYS CAUGHT FIRE.

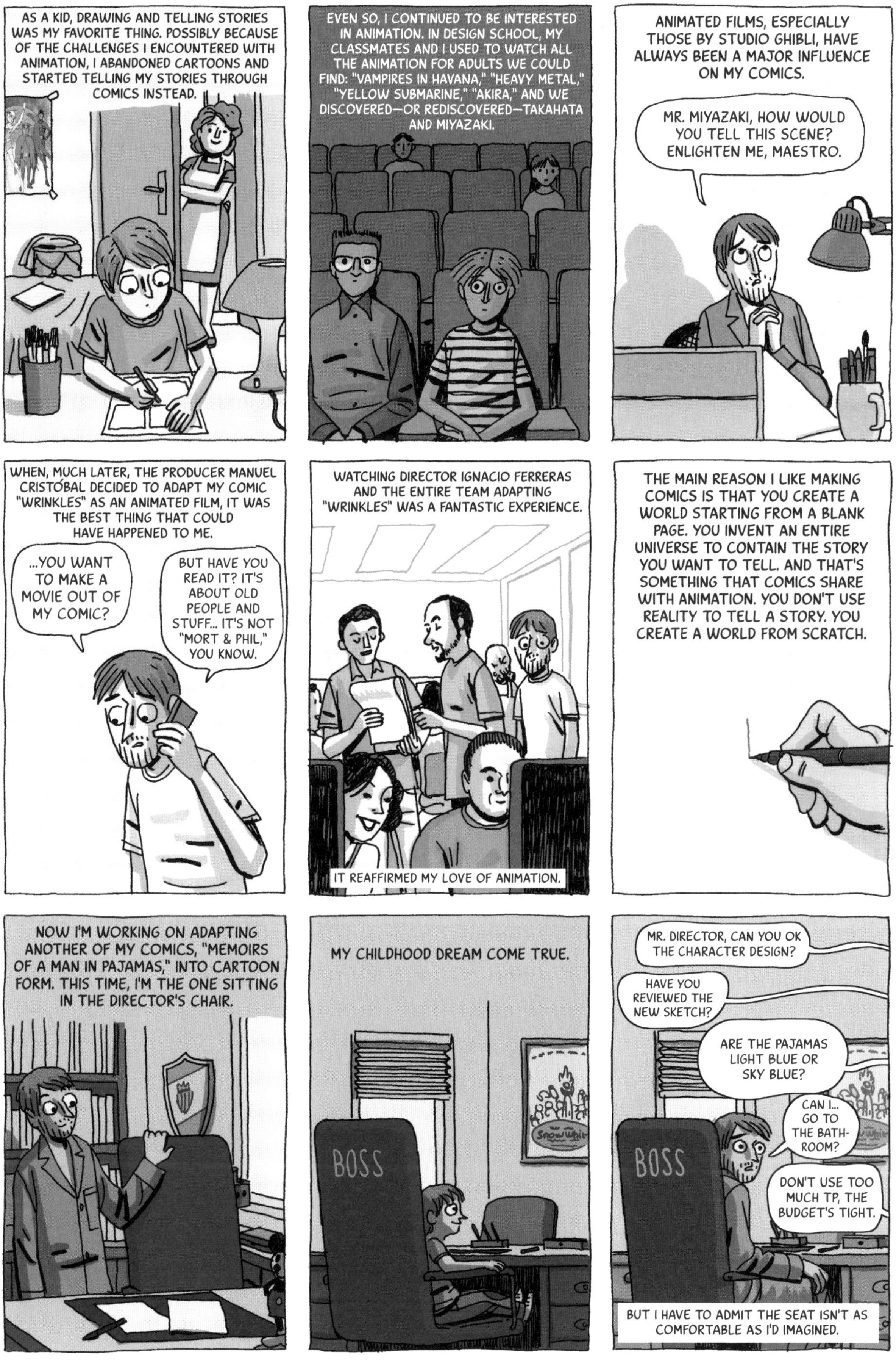
AS A KID, DRAWING AND TELLING STORIES WAS MY FAVORITE THING. POSSIBLY BECAUSE OF THE CHALLENGES I ENCOUNTERED WITH ANIMATION, I ABANDONED CARTOONS AND STARTED TELLING MY STORIES THROUGH COMICS INSTEAD.
EVEN SO, I CONTINUED TO BE INTERESTED IN ANIMATION. IN DESIGN SCHOOL, MY CLASSMATES AND I USED TO WATCH ALL THE ANIMATION FOR ADULTS WE COULD FIND: "VAMPIRES IN HAVANA," "HEAVY METAL," "YELLOW SUBMARINE," "AKIRA," AND WE DISCOVERED—OR REDISCOVERED—TAKAHATA AND MIYAZAKI.
ANIMATED FILMS, ESPECIALLY THOSE BY STUDIO GHIBLI, HAVE ALWAYS BEEN A MAJOR INFLUENCE ON MY COMICS.
MR. MIYAZAKI, HOW WOULD YOU TELL THIS SCENE? ENLIGHTEN ME, MAESTRO.
WHEN, MUCH LATER, THE PRODUCER MANUEL CRISTÓBAL DECIDED TO ADAPT MY COMIC "WRINKLES" AS AN ANIMATED FILM, IT WAS THE BEST THING THAT COULD HAVE HAPPENED TO ME.
...YOU WANT TO MAKE A MOVIE OUT OF MY COMIC?
BUT HAVE YOU READ IT? IT'S ABOUT OLD PEOPLE AND STUFF... IT'S NOT "MORT & PHIL," YOU KNOW.
WATCHING DIRECTOR IGNACIO FERRERAS AND THE ENTIRE TEAM ADAPTING "WRINKLES" WAS A FANTASTIC EXPERIENCE.
IT REAFFIRMED MY LOVE OF ANIMATION.
THE MAIN REASON I LIKE MAKING COMICS IS THAT YOU CREATE A WORLD STARTING FROM A BLANK PAGE. YOU INVENT AN ENTIRE UNIVERSE TO CONTAIN THE STORY YOU WANT TO TELL. AND THAT'S SOMETHING THAT COMICS SHARE WITH ANIMATION. YOU DON'T USE REALITY TO TELL A STORY. YOU CREATE A WORLD FROM SCRATCH.
NOW I'M WORKING ON ADAPTING ANOTHER OF MY COMICS, "MEMOIRS OF A MAN IN PAJAMAS," INTO CARTOON FORM. THIS TIME, I'M THE ONE SITTING IN THE DIRECTOR'S CHAIR.
MY CHILDHOOD DREAM COME TRUE.
BOSS
MR. DIRECTOR, CAN YOU OK THE CHARACTER DESIGN?
HAVE YOU REVIEWED THE NEW SKETCH?
ARE THE PAJAMAS LIGHT BLUE OR SKY BLUE?
CAN I... GO TO THE BATH-ROOM?
DON'T USE TOO MUCH TP, THE BUDGET'S TIGHT.
BOSS
BUT I HAVE TO ADMIT THE SEAT ISN'T AS COMFORTABLE AS I'D IMAGINED.

LIKE OUT-OF-PHASE WAVES

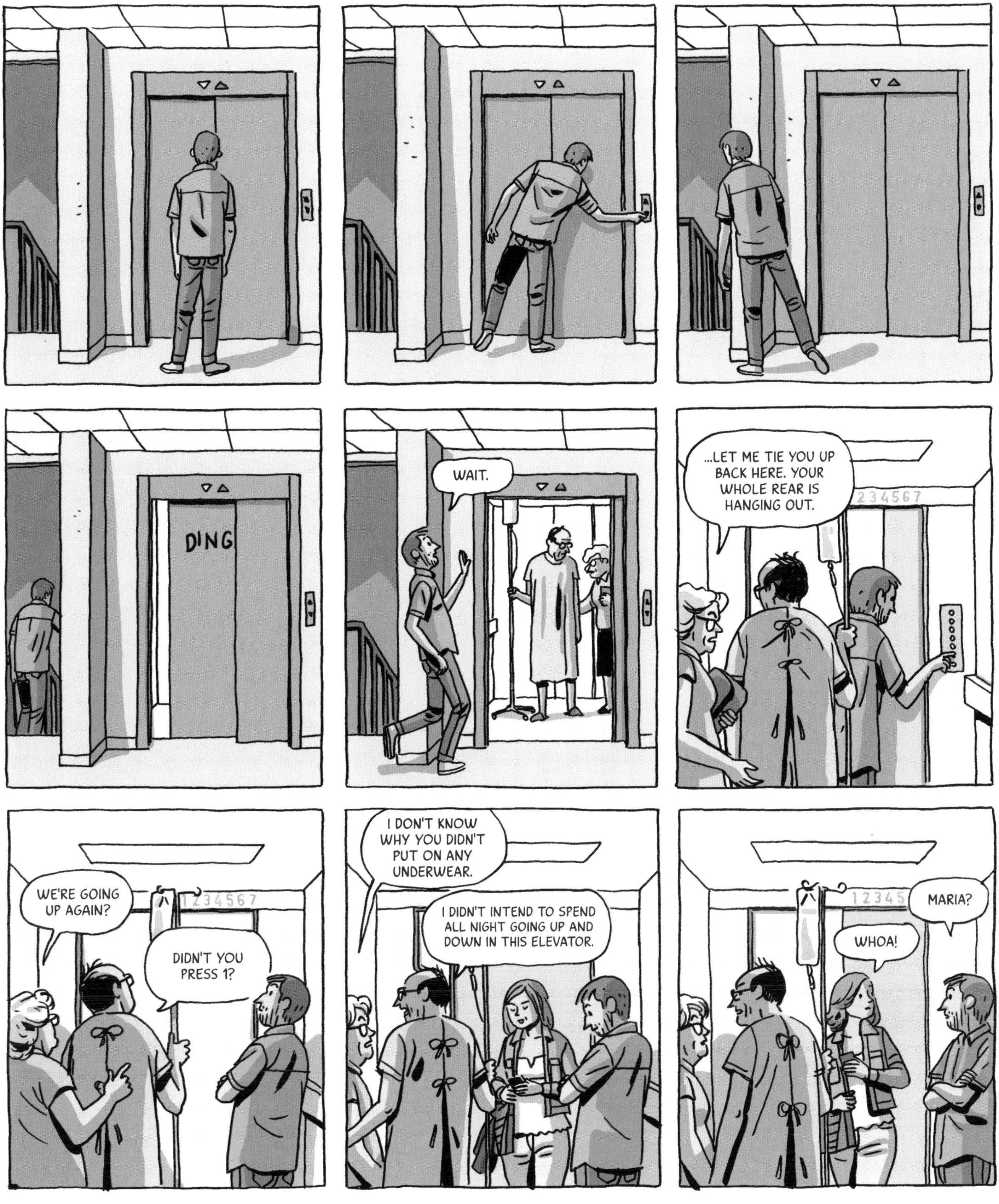

DING
WAIT.
...LET ME TIE YOU UP BACK HERE. YOUR WHOLE REAR IS HANGING OUT.
234567
1234567
WE'RE GOING UP AGAIN?
DIDN'T YOU PRESS 1?
I DON'T KNOW WHY YOU DIDN'T PUT ON ANY UNDERWEAR.
I DIDN'T INTEND TO SPEND ALL NIGHT GOING UP AND DOWN IN THIS ELEVATOR.
12345
MARIA?
WHOA!

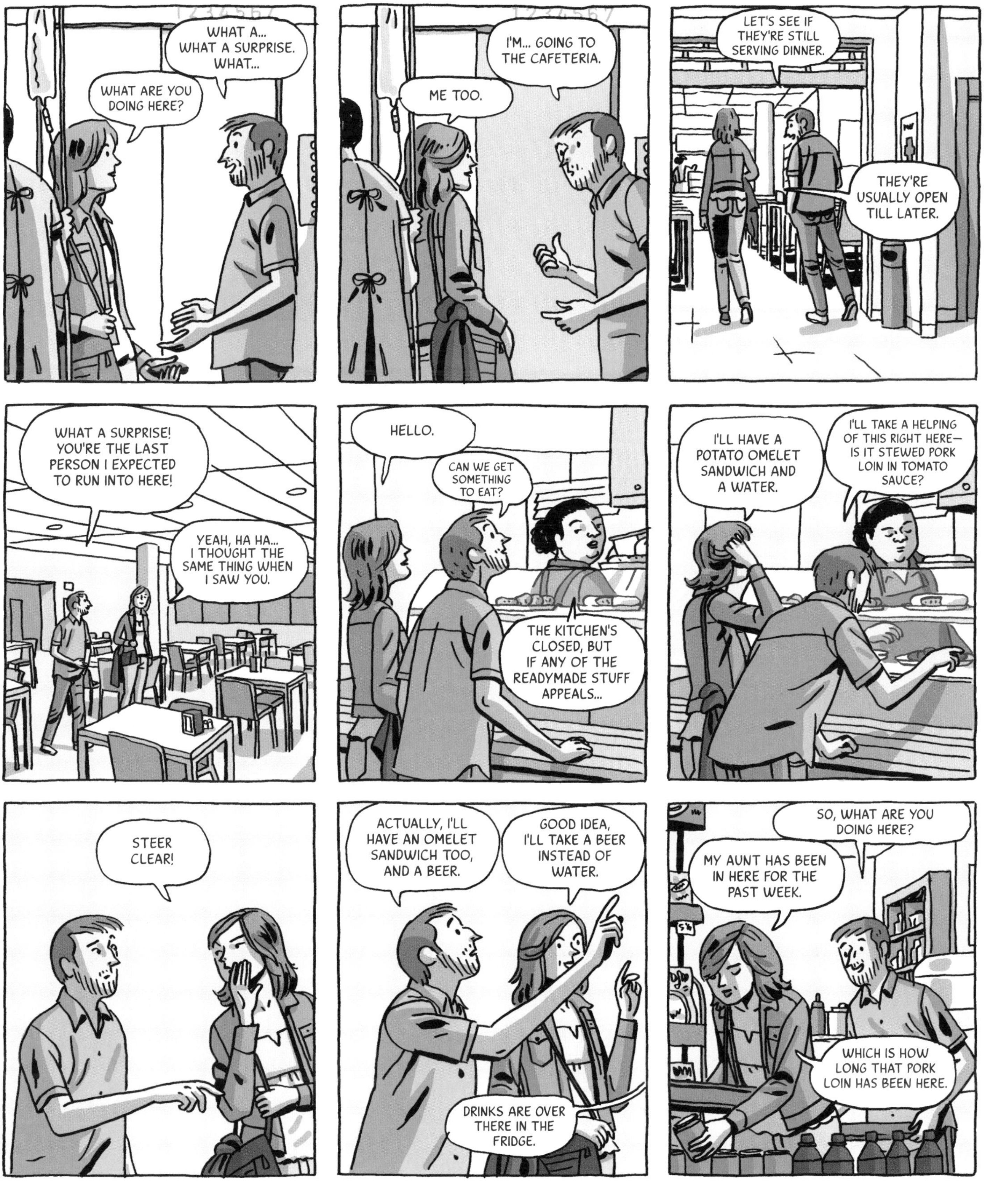

WHAT ARE YOU DOING HERE?
WHAT A... WHAT A SURPRISE. WHAT...
ME TOO.
I'M... GOING TO THE CAFETERIA.
LET'S SEE IF THEY'RE STILL SERVING DINNER.
THEY'RE USUALLY OPEN TILL LATER.
WHAT A SURPRISE! YOU'RE THE LAST PERSON I EXPECTED TO RUN INTO HERE!
YEAH, HA HA... I THOUGHT THE SAME THING WHEN I SAW YOU.
HELLO.
CAN WE GET SOMETHING TO EAT?
THE KITCHEN'S CLOSED, BUT IF ANY OF THE READYMADE STUFF APPEALS...
I'LL HAVE A POTATO OMELET SANDWICH AND A WATER.
I'LL TAKE A HELPING OF THIS RIGHT HERE— IS IT STEWED PORK LOIN IN TOMATO SAUCE?
STEER CLEAR!
ACTUALLY, I'LL HAVE AN OMELET SANDWICH TOO, AND A BEER.
GOOD IDEA, I'LL TAKE A BEER INSTEAD OF WATER.
DRINKS ARE OVER THERE IN THE FRIDGE.
SO, WHAT ARE YOU DOING HERE?
MY AUNT HAS BEEN IN HERE FOR THE PAST WEEK.
WHICH IS HOW LONG THAT PORK LOIN HAS BEEN HERE.

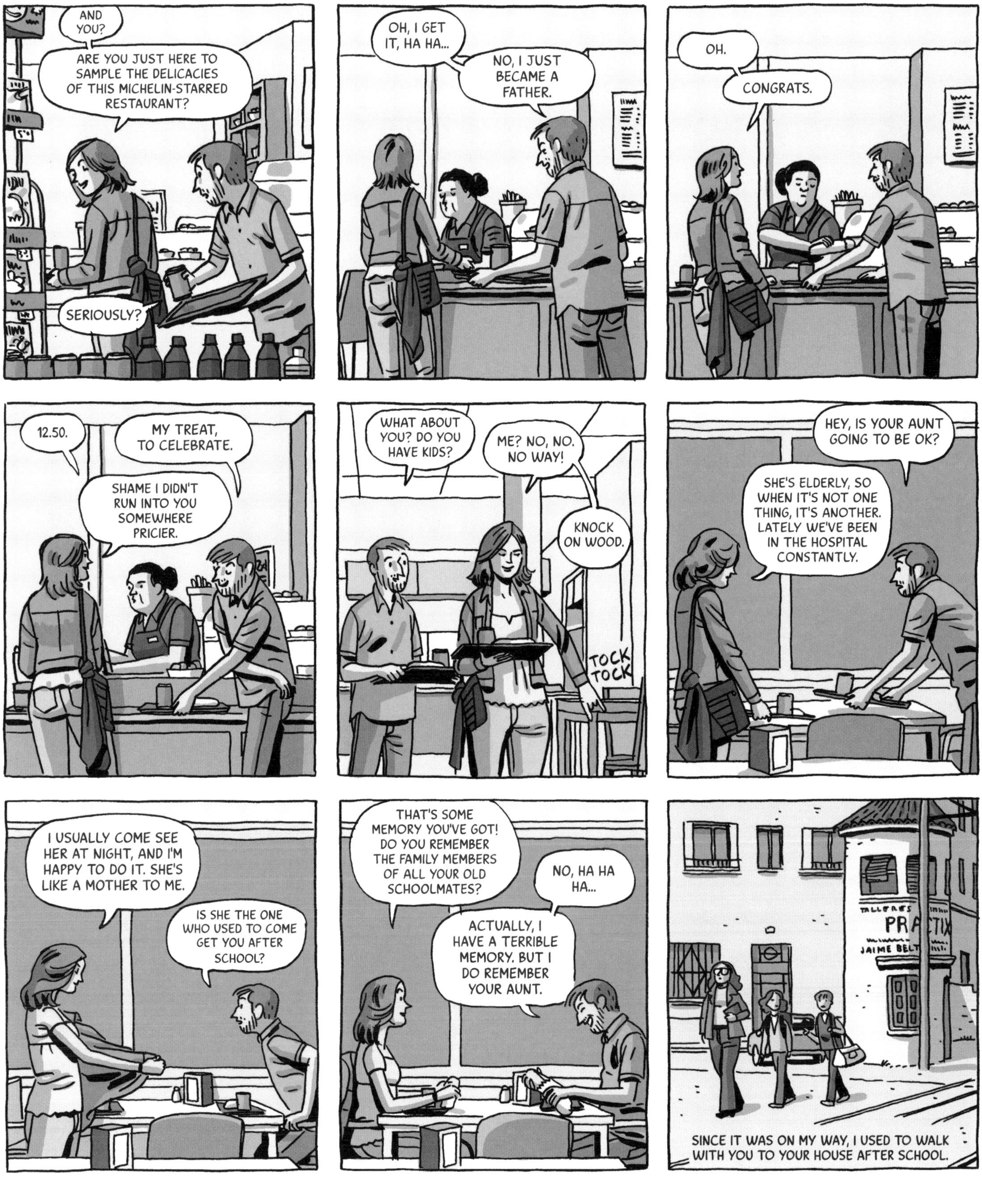
AND YOU?
ARE YOU JUST HERE TO SAMPLE THE DELICACIES OF THIS MICHELIN-STARRED RESTAURANT?
SERIOUSLY?
OH, I GET IT, HA HA...
NO, I JUST BECAME A FATHER.
OH.
CONGRATS.
12.50.
MY TREAT, TO CELEBRATE.
SHAME I DIDN'T RUN INTO YOU SOMEWHERE PRICIER.
WHAT ABOUT YOU? DO YOU HAVE KIDS?
ME? NO, NO. NO WAY!
KNOCK ON WOOD.
TOCK TOCK
HEY, IS YOUR AUNT GOING TO BE OK?
SHE'S ELDERLY, SO WHEN IT'S NOT ONE THING, IT'S ANOTHER. LATELY WE'VE BEEN IN THE HOSPITAL CONSTANTLY.
I USUALLY COME SEE HER AT NIGHT, AND I'M HAPPY TO DO IT. SHE'S LIKE A MOTHER TO ME.
IS SHE THE ONE WHO USED TO COME GET YOU AFTER SCHOOL?
THAT'S SOME MEMORY YOU'VE GOT! DO YOU REMEMBER THE FAMILY MEMBERS OF ALL YOUR OLD SCHOOLMATES?
NO, HA HA HA...
ACTUALLY, I HAVE A TERRIBLE MEMORY. BUT I DO REMEMBER YOUR AUNT.
TALLERES
PRACTIX
JAIME BELT
SINCE IT WAS ON MY WAY, I USED TO WALK WITH YOU TO YOUR HOUSE AFTER SCHOOL.

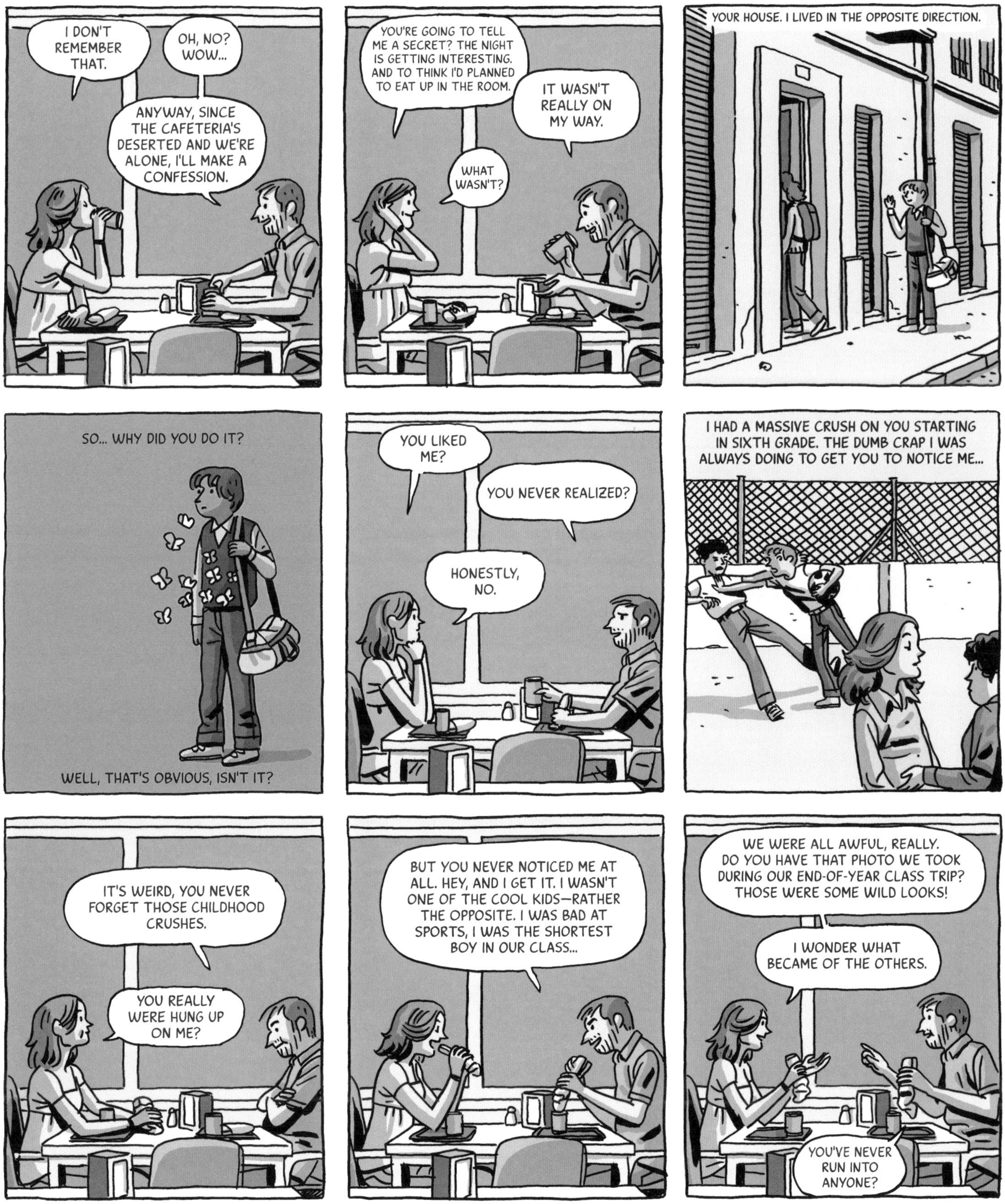
I DON'T REMEMBER THAT.
OH, NO? WOW...
ANYWAY, SINCE THE CAFETERIA'S DESERTED AND WE'RE ALONE, I'LL MAKE A CONFESSION.
YOU'RE GOING TO TELL ME A SECRET? THE NIGHT IS GETTING INTERESTING. AND TO THINK I'D PLANNED TO EAT UP IN THE ROOM.
IT WASN'T REALLY ON MY WAY.
WHAT WASN'T?
YOUR HOUSE. I LIVED IN THE OPPOSITE DIRECTION.
SO... WHY DID YOU DO IT?
WELL, THAT'S OBVIOUS, ISN'T IT?
YOU LIKED ME?
YOU NEVER REALIZED?
HONESTLY, NO.
I HAD A MASSIVE CRUSH ON YOU STARTING IN SIXTH GRADE. THE DUMB CRAP I WAS ALWAYS DOING TO GET YOU TO NOTICE ME...
IT'S WEIRD, YOU NEVER FORGET THOSE CHILDHOOD CRUSHES.
YOU REALLY WERE HUNG UP ON ME?
BUT YOU NEVER NOTICED ME AT ALL. HEY, AND I GET IT. I WASN'T ONE OF THE COOL KIDS—RATHER THE OPPOSITE. I WAS BAD AT SPORTS, I WAS THE SHORTEST BOY IN OUR CLASS...
WE WERE ALL AWFUL, REALLY. DO YOU HAVE THAT PHOTO WE TOOK DURING OUR END-OF-YEAR CLASS TRIP? THOSE WERE SOME WILD LOOKS!
I WONDER WHAT BECAME OF THE OTHERS.
YOU'VE NEVER RUN INTO ANYONE?

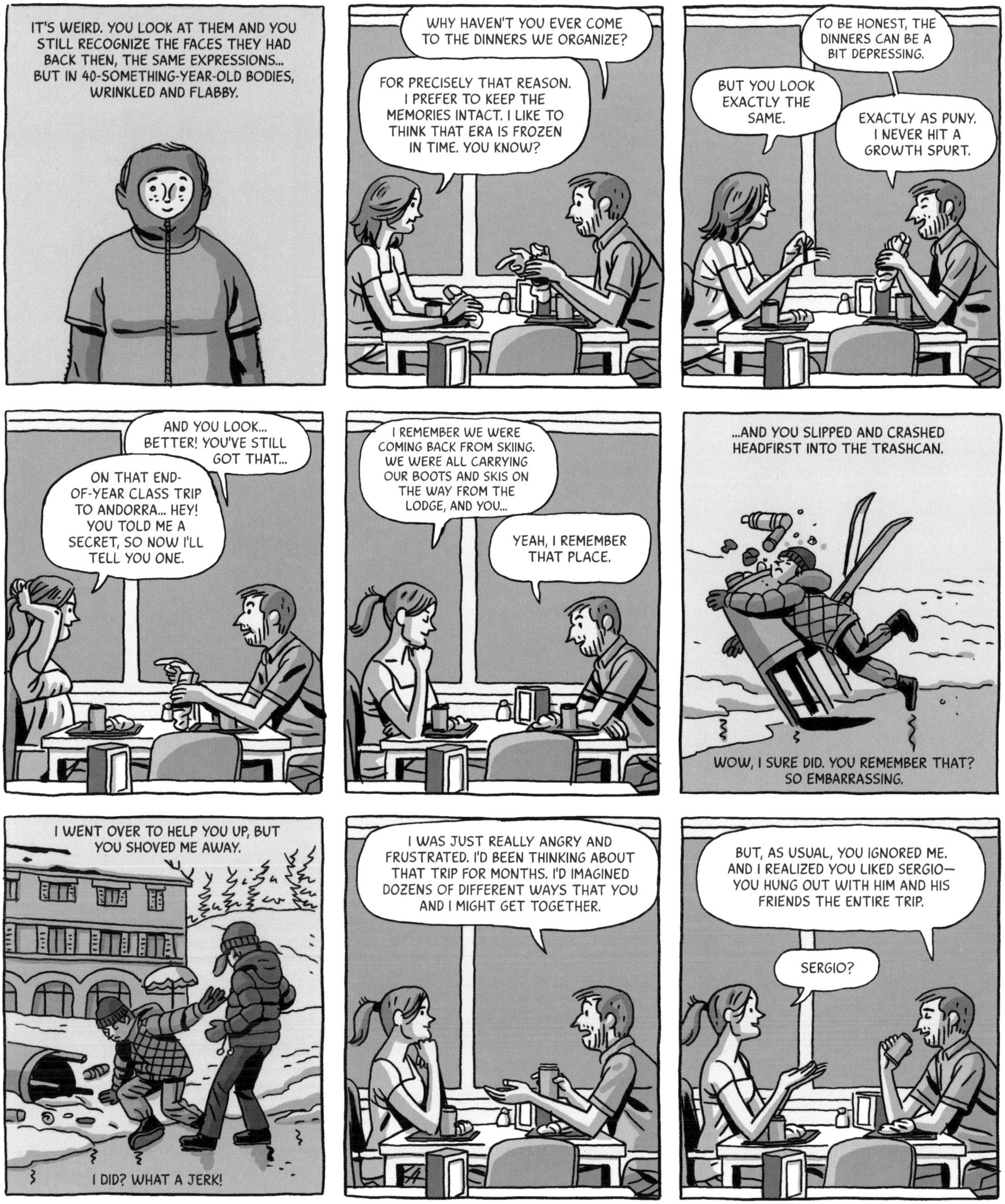
IT'S WEIRD. YOU LOOK AT THEM AND YOU STILL RECOGNIZE THE FACES THEY HAD BACK THEN, THE SAME EXPRESSIONS... BUT IN 40-SOMETHING-YEAR-OLD BODIES, WRINKLED AND FLABBY.
WHY HAVEN'T YOU EVER COME TO THE DINNERS WE ORGANIZE?
FOR PRECISELY THAT REASON. I PREFER TO KEEP THE MEMORIES INTACT. I LIKE TO THINK THAT ERA IS FROZEN IN TIME. YOU KNOW?
TO BE HONEST, THE DINNERS CAN BE A BIT DEPRESSING.
BUT YOU LOOK EXACTLY THE SAME.
EXACTLY AS PUNY. I NEVER HIT A GROWTH SPURT.
AND YOU LOOK... BETTER! YOU'VE STILL GOT THAT...
ON THAT END-OF-YEAR CLASS TRIP TO ANDORRA... HEY! YOU TOLD ME A SECRET, SO NOW I'LL TELL YOU ONE.
I REMEMBER WE WERE COMING BACK FROM SKIING. WE WERE ALL CARRYING OUR BOOTS AND SKIS ON THE WAY FROM THE LODGE, AND YOU...
YEAH, I REMEMBER THAT PLACE.
...AND YOU SLIPPED AND CRASHED HEADFIRST INTO THE TRASHCAN.
WOW, I SURE DID. YOU REMEMBER THAT? SO EMBARRASSING.
I WENT OVER TO HELP YOU UP, BUT YOU SHOVED ME AWAY.
I DID? WHAT A JERK!
I WAS JUST REALLY ANGRY AND FRUSTRATED. I'D BEEN THINKING ABOUT THAT TRIP FOR MONTHS. I'D IMAGINED DOZENS OF DIFFERENT WAYS THAT YOU AND I MIGHT GET TOGETHER.
BUT, AS USUAL, YOU IGNORED ME. AND I REALIZED YOU LIKED SERGIO— YOU HUNG OUT WITH HIM AND HIS FRIENDS THE ENTIRE TRIP.
SERGIO?

NO WAY.

OH, REALLY?

I LIKED DAVID, AND THEY WERE ALWAYS TOGETHER.

MAN. I SPEND MY WHOLE LIFE HATING SERGIO, AND NOW YOU TELL ME. I WAS ALWAYS SO MEAN TO HIM.

HA HA HA.

POOR SERGIO.

BUT THAT'S NOT THE SECRET I WAS GOING TO TELL YOU.

WHEN I SAW YOU LYING THERE ON THE WET GROUND, I FELT SOMETHING FOR YOU.

WHAT? PITY? EMBARRASS-MENT?

I CAN'T DESCRIBE IT.

BUT AFTER THAT TRIP, I PAID A LOT MORE ATTENTION TO YOU.

BUT THE YEAR ENDED SOON AFTER AND WE WENT OUR SEPARATE WAYS.

WOW... I DIDN'T EXPECT THIS. I'M ALL...

I WENT TO HIGH SCHOOL AT THE ONE NEAR MY HOUSE, AND WE NEVER SAW EACH OTHER AGAIN.

UNTIL A FEW YEARS AGO, REMEMBER?

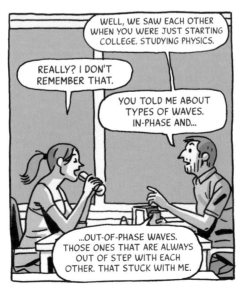

WELL, WE SAW EACH OTHER WHEN YOU WERE JUST STARTING COLLEGE. STUDYING PHYSICS.

REALLY? I DON'T REMEMBER THAT.

YOU TOLD ME ABOUT TYPES OF WAVES. IN-PHASE AND...

...OUT-OF-PHASE WAVES. THOSE ONES THAT ARE ALWAYS OUT OF STEP WITH EACH OTHER. THAT STUCK WITH ME.

APART FROM THAT, I DIDN'T HEAR MUCH ELSE. YOU WERE WITH A GUY YOU WERE DATING. I WAS TRYING TO ACT LIKE IT DIDN'T BOTHER ME, BUT I WAS REALLY AWKWARD AND NERVOUS. I MUST HAVE LOOKED LIKE AN IDIOT. AND I LEFT HATING MYSELF.

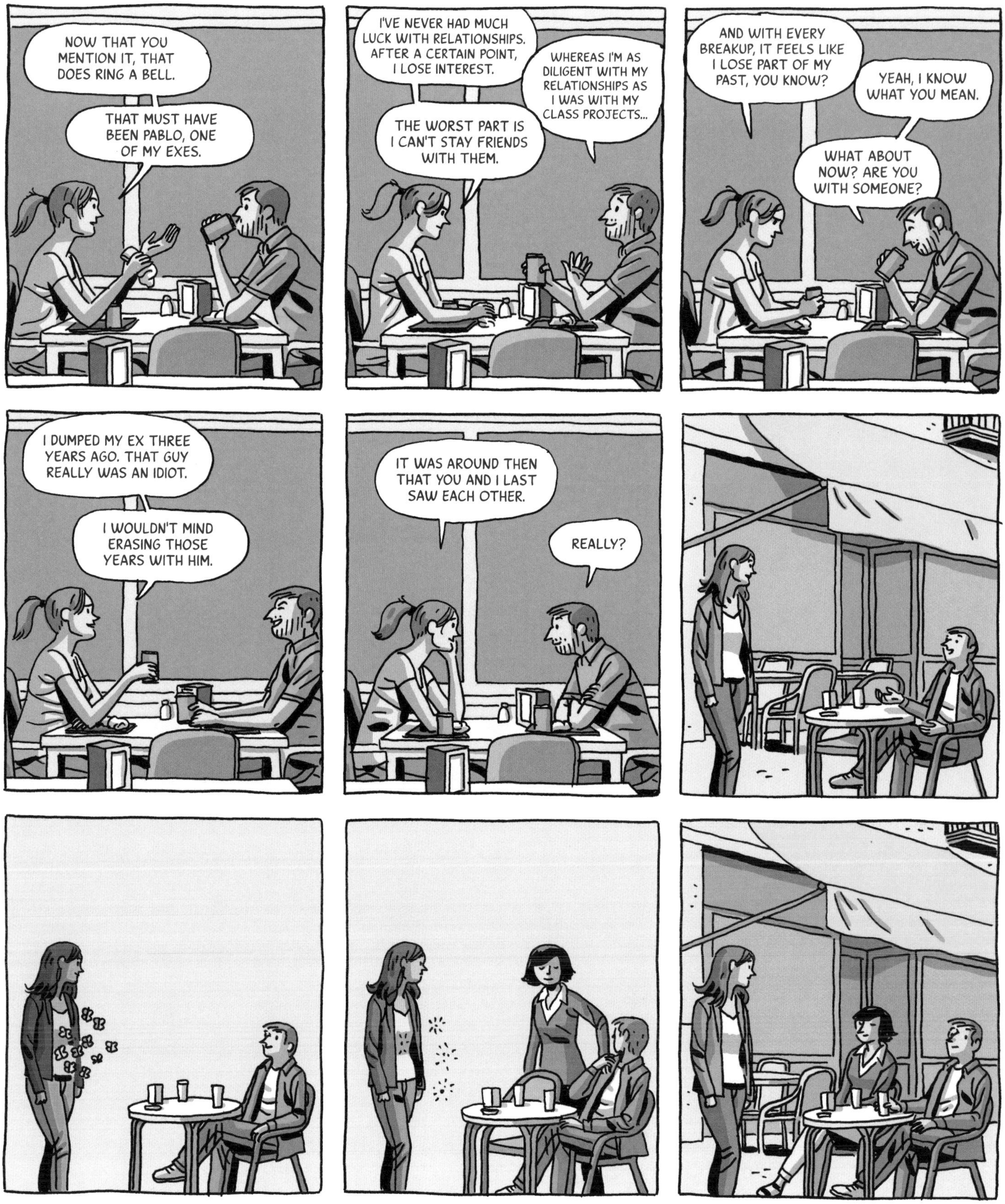
NOW THAT YOU MENTION IT, THAT DOES RING A BELL.
THAT MUST HAVE BEEN PABLO, ONE OF MY EXES.
I'VE NEVER HAD MUCH LUCK WITH RELATIONSHIPS. AFTER A CERTAIN POINT, I LOSE INTEREST.
THE WORST PART IS I CAN'T STAY FRIENDS WITH THEM.
WHEREAS I'M AS DILIGENT WITH MY RELATIONSHIPS AS I WAS WITH MY CLASS PROJECTS...
AND WITH EVERY BREAKUP, IT FEELS LIKE I LOSE PART OF MY PAST, YOU KNOW?
YEAH, I KNOW WHAT YOU MEAN.
WHAT ABOUT NOW? ARE YOU WITH SOMEONE?
I DUMPED MY EX THREE YEARS AGO. THAT GUY REALLY WAS AN IDIOT.
I WOULDN'T MIND ERASING THOSE YEARS WITH HIM.
IT WAS AROUND THEN THAT YOU AND I LAST SAW EACH OTHER.
REALLY?

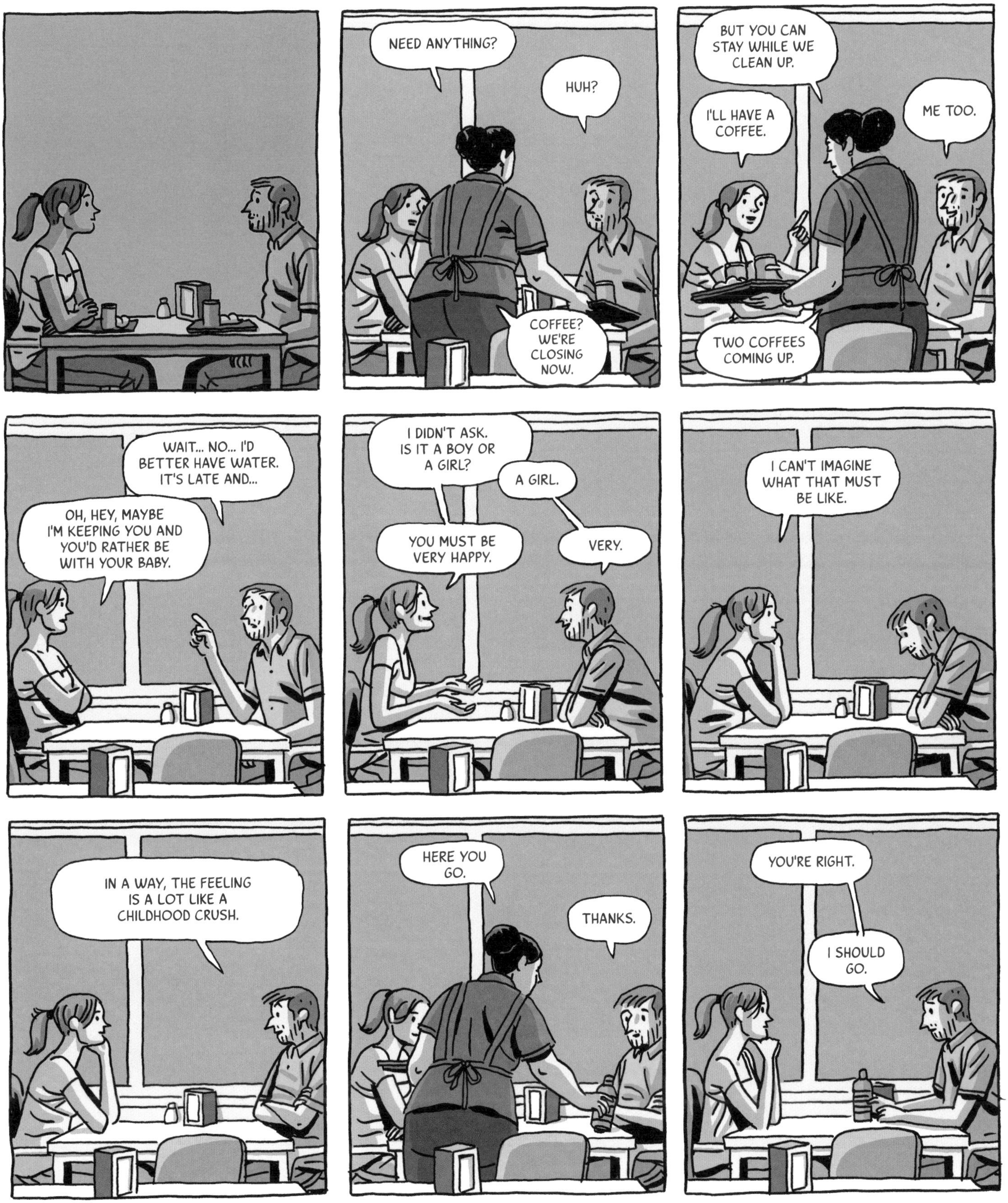
NEED ANYTHING?
HUH?
COFFEE? WE'RE CLOSING NOW.
BUT YOU CAN STAY WHILE WE CLEAN UP.
I'LL HAVE A COFFEE.
ME TOO.
TWO COFFEES COMING UP.
WAIT... NO... I'D BETTER HAVE WATER. IT'S LATE AND...
OH, HEY, MAYBE I'M KEEPING YOU AND YOU'D RATHER BE WITH YOUR BABY.
I DIDN'T ASK. IS IT A BOY OR A GIRL?
A GIRL.
YOU MUST BE VERY HAPPY.
VERY.
I CAN'T IMAGINE WHAT THAT MUST BE LIKE.
IN A WAY, THE FEELING IS A LOT LIKE A CHILDHOOD CRUSH.
HERE YOU GO.
THANKS.
YOU'RE RIGHT.
I SHOULD GO.

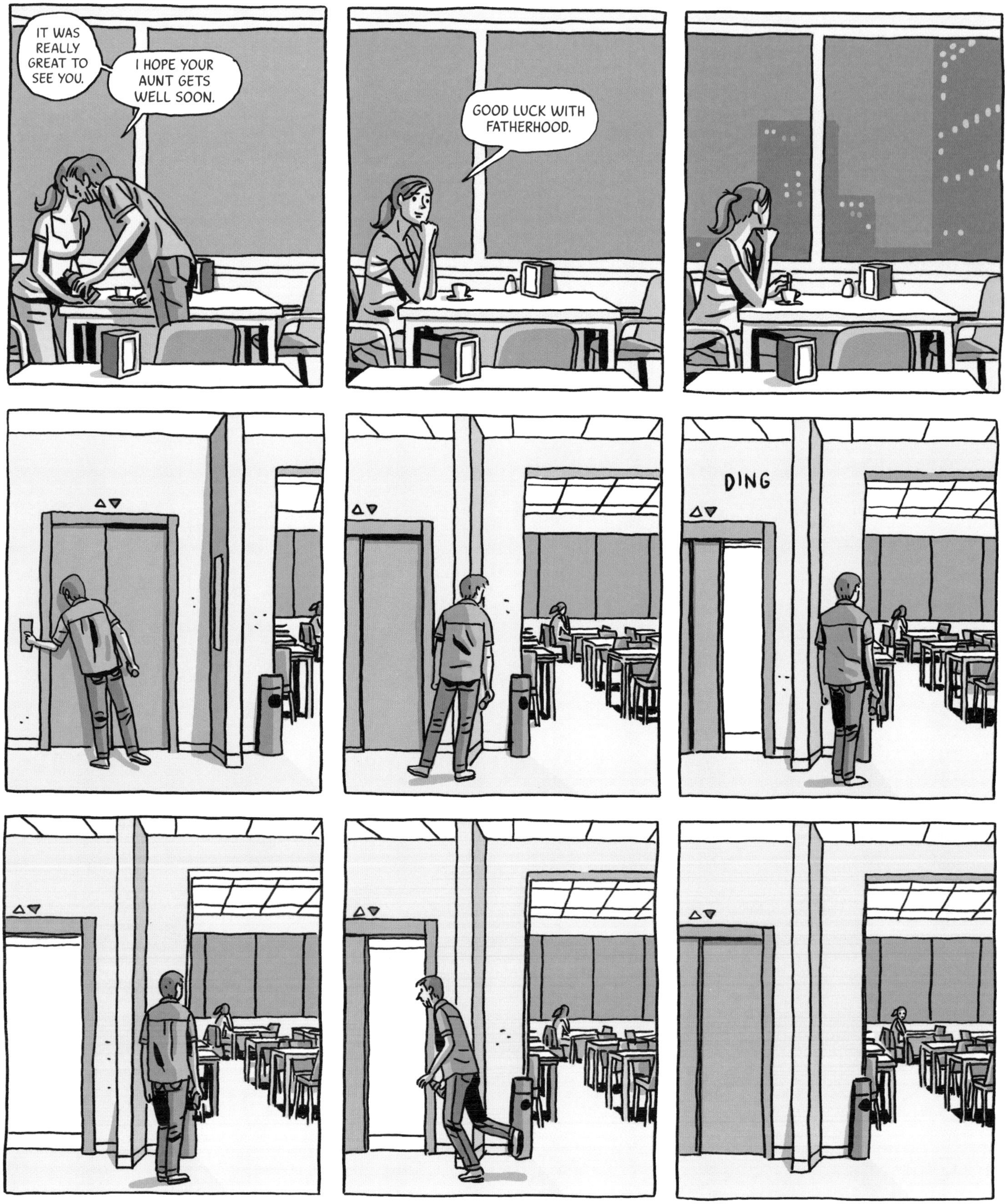
IT WAS REALLY GREAT TO SEE YOU.
I HOPE YOUR AUNT GETS WELL SOON.
GOOD LUCK WITH FATHERHOOD.
DING

MY FAVORITE VILLAIN

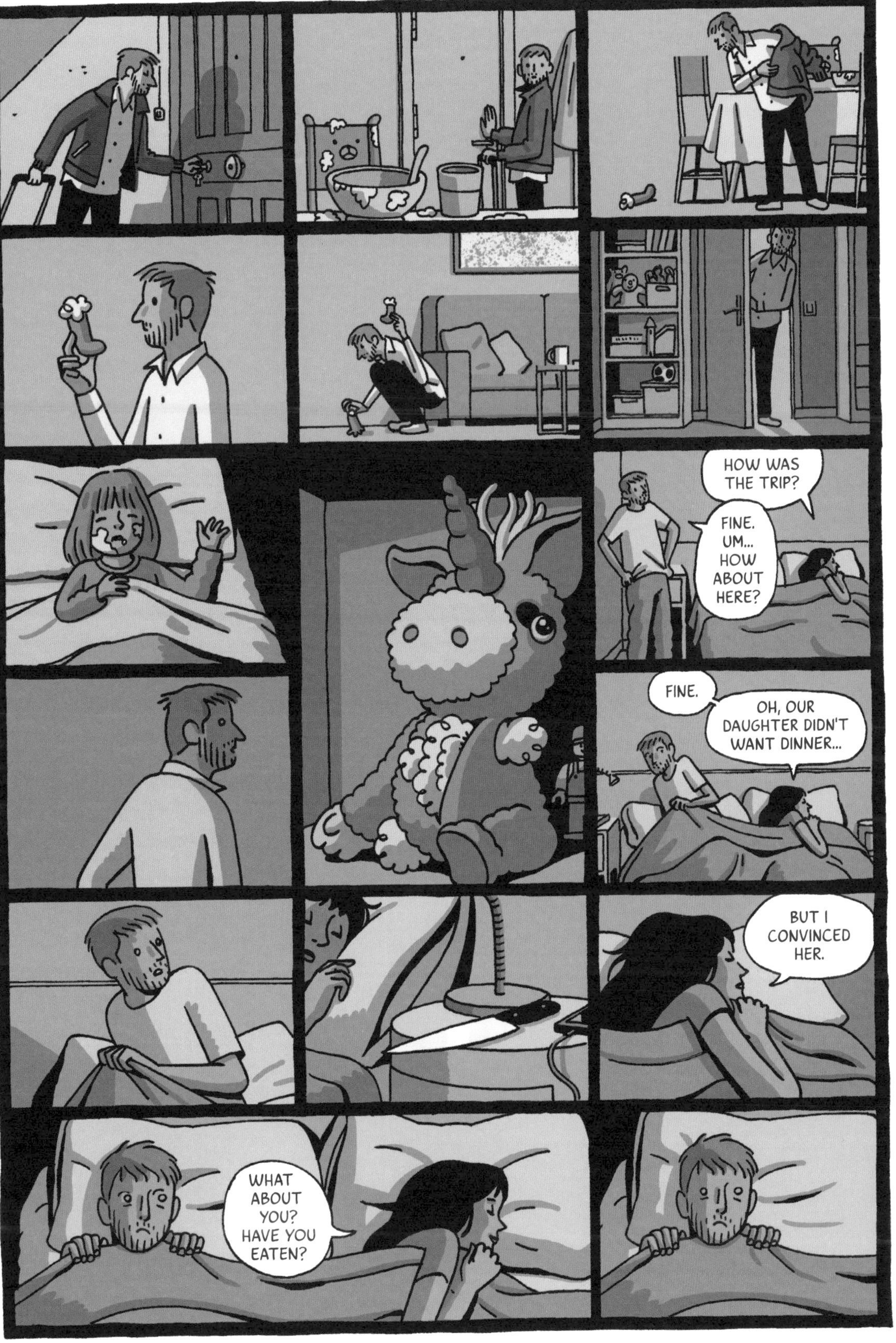

HOW WAS THE TRIP?
FINE. UM... HOW ABOUT HERE?
FINE.
OH, OUR DAUGHTER DIDN'T WANT DINNER...
BUT I CONVINCED HER.
WHAT ABOUT YOU? HAVE YOU EATEN?

LITERARY UNDRESS

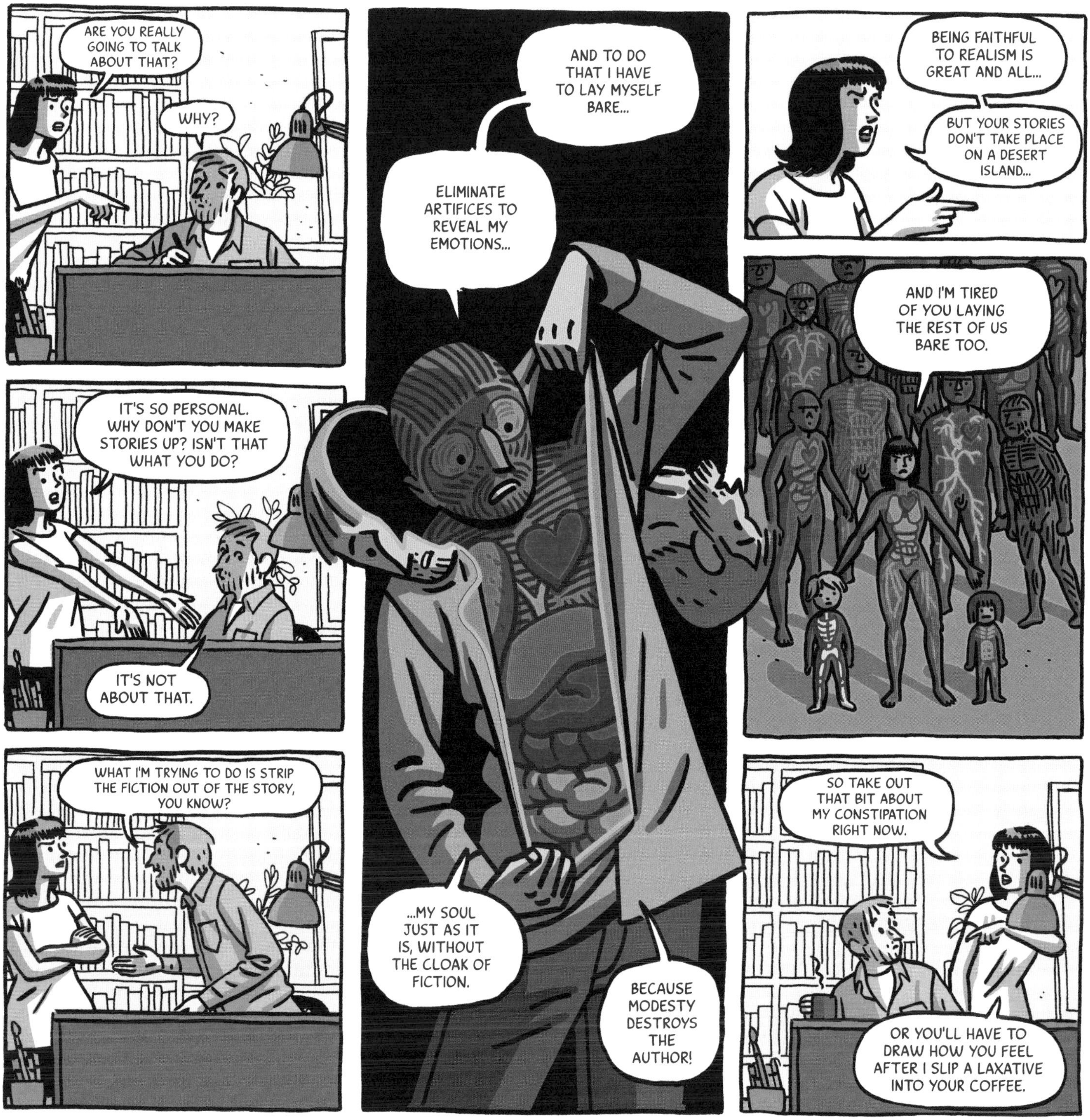
ARE YOU REALLY GOING TO TALK ABOUT THAT?
WHY?
IT'S SO PERSONAL. WHY DON'T YOU MAKE STORIES UP? ISN'T THAT WHAT YOU DO?
IT'S NOT ABOUT THAT.
WHAT I'M TRYING TO DO IS STRIP THE FICTION OUT OF THE STORY, YOU KNOW?
AND TO DO THAT I HAVE TO LAY MYSELF BARE...
ELIMINATE ARTIFICES TO REVEAL MY EMOTIONS...
...MY SOUL JUST AS IT IS, WITHOUT THE CLOAK OF FICTION.
BECAUSE MODESTY DESTROYS THE AUTHOR!
BEING FAITHFUL TO REALISM IS GREAT AND ALL...
BUT YOUR STORIES DON'T TAKE PLACE ON A DESERT ISLAND...
AND I'M TIRED OF YOU LAYING THE REST OF US BARE TOO.
SO TAKE OUT THAT BIT ABOUT MY CONSTIPATION RIGHT NOW.
OR YOU'LL HAVE TO DRAW HOW YOU FEEL AFTER I SLIP A LAXATIVE INTO YOUR COFFEE.

PACO ROCA IN QUARANTINE

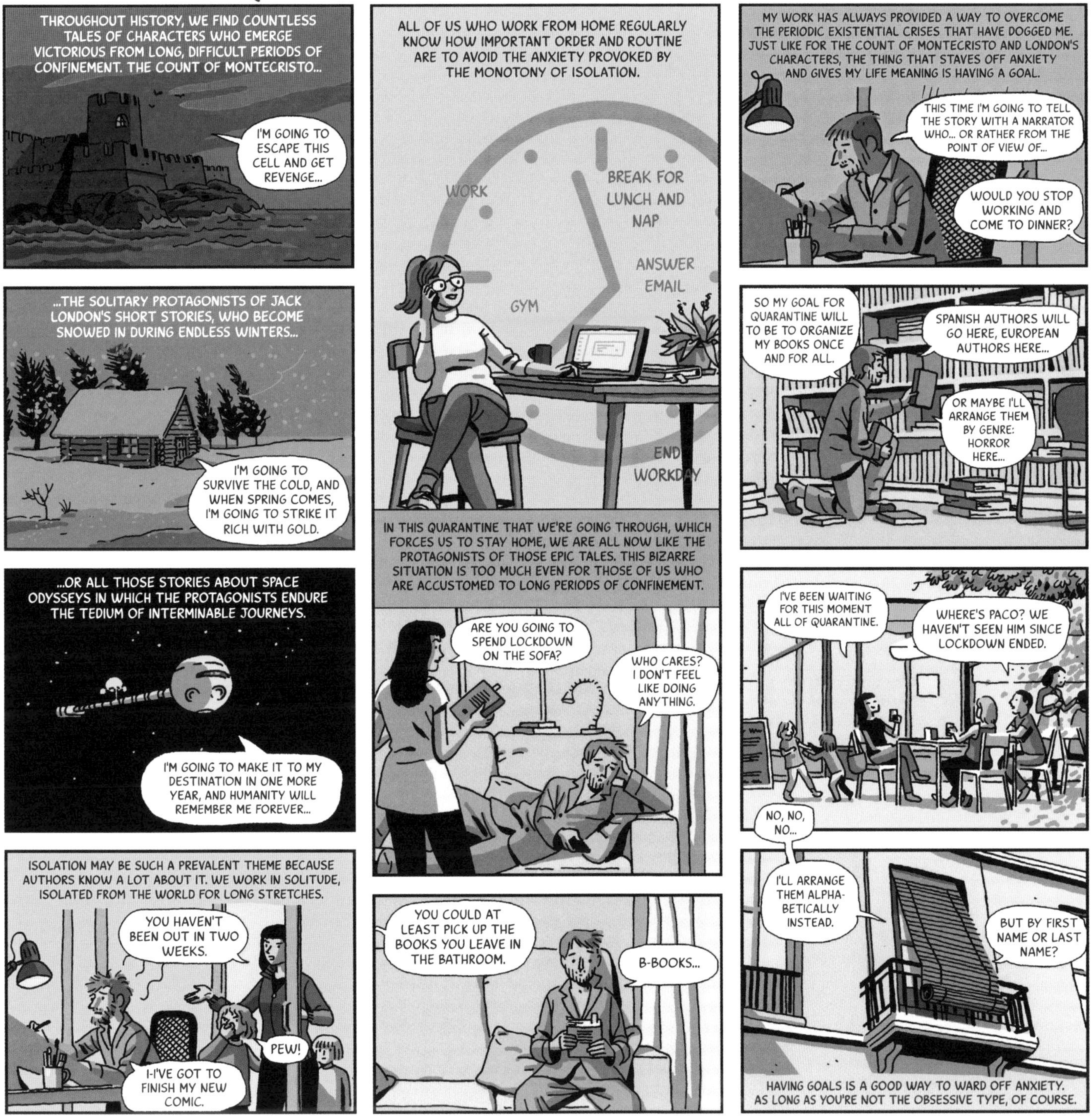

THROUGHOUT HISTORY, WE FIND COUNTLESS TALES OF CHARACTERS WHO EMERGE VICTORIOUS FROM LONG, DIFFICULT PERIODS OF CONFINEMENT. THE COUNT OF MONTECRISTO...
I'M GOING TO ESCAPE THIS CELL AND GET REVENGE...
...THE SOLITARY PROTAGONISTS OF JACK LONDON'S SHORT STORIES, WHO BECOME SNOWED IN DURING ENDLESS WINTERS...
I'M GOING TO SURVIVE THE COLD, AND WHEN SPRING COMES, I'M GOING TO STRIKE IT RICH WITH GOLD.
...OR ALL THOSE STORIES ABOUT SPACE ODYSSEYS IN WHICH THE PROTAGONISTS ENDURE THE TEDIUM OF INTERMINABLE JOURNEYS.
I'M GOING TO MAKE IT TO MY DESTINATION IN ONE MORE YEAR, AND HUMANITY WILL REMEMBER ME FOREVER...
ISOLATION MAY BE SUCH A PREVALENT THEME BECAUSE AUTHORS KNOW A LOT ABOUT IT. WE WORK IN SOLITUDE, ISOLATED FROM THE WORLD FOR LONG STRETCHES.
YOU HAVEN'T BEEN OUT IN TWO WEEKS.
PEW!
I-I'VE GOT TO FINISH MY NEW COMIC.
ALL OF US WHO WORK FROM HOME REGULARLY KNOW HOW IMPORTANT ORDER AND ROUTINE ARE TO AVOID THE ANXIETY PROVOKED BY THE MONOTONY OF ISOLATION.
WORK
BREAK FOR LUNCH AND NAP
ANSWER EMAIL
GYM
END WORKDAY
IN THIS QUARANTINE THAT WE'RE GOING THROUGH, WHICH FORCES US TO STAY HOME, WE ARE ALL NOW LIKE THE PROTAGONISTS OF THOSE EPIC TALES. THIS BIZARRE SITUATION IS TOO MUCH EVEN FOR THOSE OF US WHO ARE ACCUSTOMED TO LONG PERIODS OF CONFINEMENT.
ARE YOU GOING TO SPEND LOCKDOWN ON THE SOFA?
WHO CARES? I DON'T FEEL LIKE DOING ANYTHING.
YOU COULD AT LEAST PICK UP THE BOOKS YOU LEAVE IN THE BATHROOM.
B-BOOKS...
MY WORK HAS ALWAYS PROVIDED A WAY TO OVERCOME THE PERIODIC EXISTENTIAL CRISES THAT HAVE DOGGED ME. JUST LIKE FOR THE COUNT OF MONTECRISTO AND LONDON'S CHARACTERS, THE THING THAT STAVES OFF ANXIETY AND GIVES MY LIFE MEANING IS HAVING A GOAL.
THIS TIME I'M GOING TO TELL THE STORY WITH A NARRATOR WHO... OR RATHER FROM THE POINT OF VIEW OF...
WOULD YOU STOP WORKING AND COME TO DINNER?
SO MY GOAL FOR QUARANTINE WILL TO BE TO ORGANIZE MY BOOKS ONCE AND FOR ALL.
SPANISH AUTHORS WILL GO HERE, EUROPEAN AUTHORS HERE...
OR MAYBE I'LL ARRANGE THEM BY GENRE: HORROR HERE...
I'VE BEEN WAITING FOR THIS MOMENT ALL OF QUARANTINE.
WHERE'S PACO? WE HAVEN'T SEEN HIM SINCE LOCKDOWN ENDED.
NO, NO, NO...
I'LL ARRANGE THEM ALPHA-BETICALLY INSTEAD.
BUT BY FIRST NAME OR LAST NAME?
HAVING GOALS IS A GOOD WAY TO WARD OFF ANXIETY. AS LONG AS YOU'RE NOT THE OBSESSIVE TYPE, OF COURSE.

OTHER BOOKS BY PACO ROCA

Wrinkles
PACO ROCA

WRINKLES
(2016)

TWISTS OF FATE
PACO ROCA

TWISTS OF FATE
(2018)

The House
Paco Roca

THE HOUSE
(2019)

CINZANO
The WINTER of the CARTOONIST
PACO ROCA

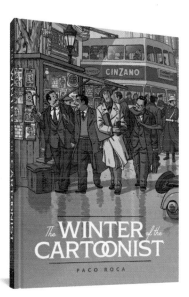

THE WINTER OF THE CARTOONIST
(2020)

Paco Roca & Guillermo Corral
the Treasure of the Black Swan

THE TREASURE OF THE BLACK SWAN
(2022)